PENGUIN BOOKS

CRUSADERS

Dan Jones is the *New York Times* bestselling author of *The Plantagenets, The Wars of the Roses, Magna Carta, Summer of Blood, The Templars, Powers and Thrones*, as well as the novel *Essex Dogs*. He is the host of the podcast *This is History: A Dynasty to Die For* and has produced, written, and presented dozens of TV shows, including the popular Netflix series *Secrets of Great British Castles*.

ALSO BY DAN JONES

Powers and Thrones: A New History of the Middle Ages

The Templars:

The Rise and Spectacular Fall of God's Holy Warriors

Summer of Blood: England's First Revolution

Magna Carta: The Birth of Liberty

The Wars of the Roses:

The Fall of the Plantagenets and the Rise of the Tudors

The Plantagenets:

The Warrior Kings and Queens Who Made England

The Essex Dog Trilogy

Essex Dogs: A Novel

Praise for *Crusaders*

"Jones's writing aims at a you-are-there effect. . . . The immediacy of [his] book is enhanced by physical and psychological descriptions of the heroes and villains of the story. . . . Some of Jones's primary sources are little known, and even enthusiasts for the subject may never have heard of the Russian Daniel the Abbot, Saint Neophytos the Recluse, or *La Chronique de Morigny*."

—*The New York Review of Books*

"Every page of [Dan Jones's] extraordinary book provides vivid evidence of the Crusades' continuing ability to mesmerize. . . . Amid the juicy anecdotes, the great strength of this book is the way in which it illuminates the human networks that underpinned the Crusades." —*The Times* (London)

"Dan Jones writes about history with relish and wonderment. . . . His tale is steeped in scholarly research and lively writing. Were it not for the violence inherent to his subject matter, you might call it divine."

—*The Christian Science Monitor*

"A bloodcurdling examination of the Crusades. Jones's greatest skill as a historian is to bring his subject alive by combining small, often comic detail with the grand cinematic sweep of an epic. At times, you could be reading a great page-turning novel rather than a serious work of nonfiction. A considerable achievement."

—*The Observer*

"Voyages, battles, sieges, and slaughter: Dan Jones's tumultuous and thrilling history of the Crusades is one of the best. . . . Jones is exceptionally good at giving evocative snapshots of medieval life, sometimes poignant, sometimes pure Monty Python." —*Sunday Times* (London)

"Dan Jones brings to life a tremendous cast of characters from every arena of the crusading world, from the eastern Mediterranean to southern Spain, and from Byzantium to the Baltic. Coupling vivid storytelling with a researcher's eye for the telling anecdote, Jones offers a fresh and vibrant—but meticulously constructed—account of a conflict that raged across the medieval centuries, and whose echoes continue to resonate to the present day."

—Jonathan Phillips, author of *The Life and the Legend of the Sultan Saladin* and *Holy Warriors*

"A powerful story brilliantly told. Dan Jones writes with pace, wit and insight, a panoramic gaze and unfailing humanity. The result is utterly compelling."

—Helen Castor, author of *She-Wolves* and *Joan of Arc*

"Jones's sweeping coverage of a conflict of three centuries' duration hews to the highest standards of popular history. It is literate, thoroughly engaging, and serious, without condescension towards either its matter or its readers."

—*Booklist* (starred review)

"Jones paints a vivid and accurate picture of the culture, politics, and personalities of the crusading period, covering vast swaths of history and many personalities with aplomb."

—*Publishers Weekly*

"Dan Jones, author of *The Templars*, returns to dazzle readers with a fascinating look at the Crusades. And lest you hesitate because events that took place a thousand years ago appear irrelevant, rest assured: This is no dry, boring tome. . . . Like *Game of Thrones*, this epic tale is peopled with a large cast. . . . In a thought-provoking epilogue, Jones brings his narrative into the present day."

—*BookPage*

"The centuries of campaigning to reclaim the Holy Land retain their fascination, as demonstrated by this expert mixture of cutthroat politics, battlefield fireworks, and mass murder. . . . As usual, the author has done his homework, laboring mightily to recount century after century of gruesome warfare between profoundly religious cultures with apparently no inhibition against lying and profound cruelty. . . . [Readers] will keep the pages turning."

—*Kirkus Reviews*

"The author's choice to make the people doing the action rather than the act as the focus is insightful. . . . An entertaining and informative look at a potent historical phenomenon whose echoes are still being felt today."

—*Library Journal* (starred review)

CRUSADERS

The EPIC HISTORY *of the* WARS
for the HOLY LANDS

DAN JONES

PENGUIN BOOKS

PENGUIN BOOKS
An imprint of Penguin Random House LLC
penguinrandomhouse.com

First published in Great Britain
by Head of Zeus, Ltd London, in 2019
First published in the United States of America by Viking,
an imprint of Penguin Random House LLC, 2019
Published in Penguin Books 2020

Page 409 constitutes an extension to this copyright page.

ISBN 9780143108979 (paperback)

THE LIBRARY OF CONGRESS HAS CATALOGED THE
HARDCOVER EDITION AS FOLLOWS:
Names: Jones, Dan, 1981– author.
Title: Crusaders : the epic history of the wars for the holy lands /
Dan Jones.
Identifiers: LCCN 2019017922 (print) | LCCN 2019980552 (ebook) |
ISBN 9780525428312 (hardcover) | ISBN 9780698186446 (ebook)
Subjects: LCSH: Crusades.
Classification: LCC D157 .J64 2019 (print) | LCC D157 (ebook) |
DDC 909.07—dc23
LC record available at https://lccn.loc.gov/2019017922
LC ebook record available at https://lccn.loc.gov/2019980552

Printed in the United States of America
3rd Printing

Designed by Amanda Dewey
Maps by Jamie Whyte

For Walter

χαλεπὰ τὰ καλά

In those days men cared as much for furs
as they did for their immortal souls.

—ADAM OF BREMEN
(CA.1076)

CONTENTS

Part III: THE HARVEST OF THE EARTH

LIST OF MAPS

MAJOR CHARACTERS

PART I

Roger I of Sicily (d. 1101)	First Norman count of Sicily, brother of Roger Guiscard and father of the first Sicilian king, Roger II. Credited with first suggesting Christian conquest of Jerusalem in a colorful (if muddled) anecdote related by Ibn al-Athir.
Robert Guiscard (d. 1085)	Norman adventurer, conquered parts of southern Italy and attacked Byzantine territory in the Balkans. Father of the First Crusade leader Bohemond I, Prince of Antioch.
Ibn al-Athir (1160–1233)	Iraqi scholar and historian, and author of one of the most famous and detailed Islamic chronicles of the crusades, *The Perfect Work of History* (*Al-Kamil fi'l Ta'rikh*).
Ibn Hamdis (d. 1133)	Arab Sicilian poet. Fled Sicily following the Norman conquest and took up a position at the court of the Sevillan *taifa* king al-Mu'tamid. Fled Seville following the Almoravid invasion and died in Majorca.
Al-Mu'tamid (d. 1095)	Third and last *taifa* king of Seville. Wrote poetry and embraced sensory pleasures at his court. Defeated by Alfonso VI of Castile and León, he invited the Almoravids of Morocco into his kingdom, who deposed him.
Alfonso VI "El Bravo" (d. 1109)	Christian king of León, Castile and Galicia; waged war on Muslim *taifa* kingdoms early in the Reconquista and claimed the title of "Emperor of the Two Religions."

Anna Komnene (1083–1153)	Author of the great Byzantine history the *Alexiad*, an exculpatory account of her father's, Alexios I Komnenos's, reign as emperor. Fierce critic of the Franks and particularly of Bohemond of Taranto.
Alexios I Komnenos (1048–1118)	Byzantine emperor whose long reign saw assaults on the empire by Seljuq Turks in Asia Minor and Normans, including Robert Guiscard, in the Balkans. His appeal to Western rulers for military assistance was a major factor in the launch of the First Crusade.
Pope Urban II (d. 1099)	Born Odo of Lagery, a monk at the Abbey of Cluny and follower of the reforming Pope Gregory VII. Launched the First Crusade at Clermont in November 1095, but died before the fall of Jerusalem was known in the West.
Adhémar, bishop of Le Puy (d.1098)	One of the first men to take the cross at Clermont. Represented Urban II as papal legate during the First Crusade.
Raymond IV, Count of Toulouse (d. 1105)	Southern French lord also known as Raymond of Saint-Gilles. Took the cross at Clermont. Prominent leader of the First Crusade and subsequently the first Count of Tripoli.
Peter the Hermit (d. 1115)	Charismatic preacher from Amiens in northern France. Raised the doomed, early populist contingent of the First Crusade (the "People's Crusade") and remained a member of the leadership group thereafter.
Bohemond of Taranto (d. 1111)	Norman leader of the First Crusade who became the first Latin Prince of Antioch and pursued a lifelong feud with the Byzantine emperor Alexios Komnenos.
Robert, Duke of Normandy (d. 1134)	One of the princely leaders of the First Crusade. Son of the Norman king of England William the Conqueror. His absence on crusade meant he missed his chance to claim his father's throne. Nicknamed "Robert Curthose."
Tancred of Hauteville (d. 1112)	Bohemond of Taranto's nephew and fellow princely leader of the First Crusade. Regent of the principality of Antioch during Bohemond's absence/imprisonment. Ralph of Caen's *Gesta Tancredi* describes his crusading deeds.

Godfrey of Bouillon (1060–1100)	Duke of Lower Lorraine and prominent leader of the First Crusade. Elected first ruler of the Latin kingdom of Jerusalem but refused the title of king. Succeeded by his brother Baldwin.
Baldwin of Boulogne (d. 1118)	Princely leader of the First Crusade, along with his brother Godfrey. Established the county of Edessa in 1098. Subsequently became first crowned king of Jerusalem, as Baldwin I.
Stephen, Count of Blois (d. 1102)	Prominent leader of the First Crusade. Wrote vivid letters from Syria to his wife, Adela. Scorned for abandoning the crusade at Antioch; returned to the East on further campaigns before his death.
Robert II, Count of Flanders (d. 1111)	Princely leader of the First Crusade. His father, Robert I, had been on pilgrimage to Jerusalem, met Alexios Komnenos and gave military aid to the Byzantine Empire. Prominent at most major campaigns of the First Crusade.
Yaghi-Siyan (d. 1098)	Seljuq emir in command of Antioch at the time of the First Crusade. Abandoned city to the crusaders in 1098 and was murdered during his flight.
Malik-Shah I (1055–1092)	Sultan of the Great Seljuq empire and sometime collaborator with Byzantine Empire. His death precipitated a crisis in Byzantium: this encouraged the appeal to the West that became the First Crusade.
Qilij I Arslan (1079–1107)	Sultan of the lesser Seljuq sultanate of Rum (Asia Minor) at the time of the First Crusade.
Ibn al-Qalanisi (d. 1160)	Muslim chronicler, poet and public servant based in Damascus. Lived through the First Crusade and was an eyewitness to many subsequent events. Author of *Mudhayyal Ta'rikh Dimashq: The Continuation of the Damascus Chronicle.*
Ilghazi (d. 1122)	Turkish general, politician and notorious drunkard. Seljuq governor of Jerusalem before its fall to the Fatimids in 1098. Won a famous victory over crusader forces at the battle of Ager Sanguinis in 1119.
Daimbert, archbishop of Pisa (d. 1105)	Churchman from Mainz involved in crusader wars in Spain and the East. Briefly appointed patriarch of Jerusalem in the aftermath of the First Crusade.

PART II

Sigurd I of Norway (1090–1130)	Viking king of Norway, visited the kingdom of Jerusalem in ca. 1107–1111 and helped Baldwin I take the city of Sidon. Later nicknamed Sigurd Jerusalemfarer.
Roger II of Sicily (1095–1154)	First crowned king of Sicily. Ambivalent toward crusaders of the kingdom of Jerusalem after his mother, Adelaide del Vasto, was rejected as the wife of Baldwin I of Jerusalem.
Adelaide del Vasto, regent of Sicily (d. 1118)	Wife of Roger I of Sicily, regent for Roger II and briefly queen consort of Jerusalem after her marriage to King Baldwin I.
Ismah Khatun (d. 1142)	Patron of scholars in Isfahan and wife of the Abbasid caliph al-Mustazhir. Renowned as highly intelligent and resolute.
Tughtakin (d. 1128)	Atabeg of Damascus and important military leader in the wars between the first generation of crusaders and the emirs of the great cities of Syria.
Baldwin II, king of Jerusalem (d. 1131)	Also known as Baldwin of Bourcq; became Count of Edessa and subsequently king of Jerusalem. Twice captured in battle. Left throne to his daughter Melisende and her husband, Fulk, Count of Anjou.
Joscelin I, Count of Edessa (d. 1131)	Also known as Joscelin of Courtenay. Lord of Turbessel and subsequently Count of Edessa. Took part in wars against Ilghazi and other Turkish emirs during the 1110s and 1120s.
Domenico Michiel (d. 1129)	Doge of Venice between 1118 and his death. Led the Venetian expedition that helped conquer Tyre in 1124, establishing a strong Venetian presence in the crusader states.
Hugh of Payns (d. 1136)	First master of the Knights Templar. Established the order around 1119 and appealed successfully for recognition from the papacy and Christian monarchs. Helped recruit for the unsuccessful 1129 crusade against Damascus.
Fulk of Anjou (1092–1143)	Powerful lord of central France who traveled east to become king of Jerusalem by marriage to Baldwin II's daughter Melisende.

Bernard of Clairvaux (1090–1153)	Cistercian abbot and inveterate lobbyist of popes and kings who played a critical role in crusade-preaching before the Second Crusade. Helped compose rule for the Knights Templar in 1129. Canonized as St. Bernard in 1174.
Melisende, queen of Jerusalem (1105–1161)	Daughter and heir of King Baldwin II of Jerusalem who oversaw a magnificent building program in and around Jerusalem. Ruled jointly with her husband, Fulk, and then with her son, Baldwin III. Relations were difficult with both.
Imad al-Din Zengi (d. 1146)	Fierce Turkish warrior who became atabeg of Mosul and Aleppo. Conquered Edessa in 1144, provoking the Second Crusade. His successors, including his son Nur al-Din, are referred to as the Zengids.
William of Tyre (d. 1186)	Scholar and historian born in Jerusalem. Educated in the West, but returned to the crusader states, becoming archbishop of Tyre. His chronicle, the *History of Deeds Done Beyond the Sea,* is a major source for events in the Latin East in the twelfth century.
Raymond of Poitiers (d. 1149)	Prince of Antioch from 1136 until his death at the battle of Inab fighting forces loyal to Nur al-Din. Rumored to have seduced his niece, Eleanor of Aquitaine, during her visit to the crusader states on the Second Crusade.
Joscelin II, Count of Edessa (d. 1159)	Fourth and last Frankish count of Edessa, expelled from his city when it fell to Zengi. Later captured, blinded and imprisoned by Nur al-Din.
Pope Eugene III (d. 1153)	Cistercian monk and protégé of Bernard of Clairvaux. Became pope in 1145 and was responsible for calling the Second Crusade with the bull *Quantum Praedecessores*.
Eleanor of Aquitaine (1122/24–1204)	Queen of France by her first marriage to Louis VII. Traveled east on the Second Crusade, during which her marriage to Louis broke down. Rumored to have slept with her uncle, Raymond of Poitiers, Prince of Antioch. Subsequently divorced Louis and married Henry II, king of England.
Louis VII, king of France (1120–1180)	Monklike king of France who led one of the major contingents of the Second Crusade. An enthusiastic crusader, his poor generalship was exposed during the march from Constantinople across Asia Minor.

Conrad III, king of Germany (1093–1152)	First Hohenstaufen king of Germany (but never crowned Holy Roman Emperor). Took a large army on the Second Crusade, establishing a major crusading tradition in the Hohenstaufen line.
Otto of Freising (1114–1158)	Bishop, chronicler and half brother of Conrad III. Traveled on the Second Crusade and kept a vivid record of events from a German perspective.
George of Antioch (d. 1151/2)	Admiral and adviser to King Roger II of Sicily. Syrian-born Greek orthodox Christian who terrorized the Greek islands and North Africa in the 1140s, at the time of the Second Crusade.
Afonso Henriques, king of Portugal (d. 1185)	First king of Portugal, assisted in his conquest of Lisbon in 1147 by crusaders traveling to join the Second Crusade.
Manuel I Komnenos (1118–1180)	Byzantine emperor and grandson of Alexios I Komnenos. Allowed armies of the Second Crusade to pass through his territories.
Odo of Deuil (1110–1162)	Chaplain to Louis VII on the Second Crusade, his chronicle, written for the benefit of Louis's chief minister, Abbot Suger, is a major source for the French contribution to the expedition.
Nur al-Din (1118–1174)	Son of Zengi and one of the most formidable Islamic leaders of the crusading era. United major Syrian cities under his leadership. Framed opposition to the Franks of the Holy Land as an expression of jihad, a theme adopted later by Saladin.
Baldwin III, king of Jerusalem (1130–1163)	Bloody-minded ruler of the kingdom of Jerusalem—the son of Fulk of Anjou and Queen Melisende. Struggled against his mother for independent rule in the early 1150s. Led the campaign that captured Ascalon in 1153.
Al-Zafir (1133–1154)	Fatimid caliph murdered by his male lover in a palace coup: an act that destabilized Egypt and helped prepare the way for Ayyubid conquest.
Amalric I, king of Jerusalem (1136–1174)	Podgy, gruff, highly effective king of Jerusalem after the death of his brother Baldwin III in 1163. Attempted to invade and subjugate Fatimid Egypt, but failed, leaving crown of Jerusalem to his leper son, Baldwin IV.
Ibn Ruzzik (d. 1161)	Vizier of Fatimid Cairo following the assassination of caliph al-Zafir in 1154. Assassinated.

Al-Adid (1151–1171)	Fourteenth and last Fatimid caliph, appointed aged nine in 1160, and deposed after Shirkuh and Saladin took control of Cairo.
Shawar (d. 1169)	Egyptian vizier from 1162 until his death. Attempted, unsuccessfully, to play off the crusader kingdom of Jerusalem against Nur al-Din and his Kurdish generals, Shirkuh and Saladin, who eventually murdered him.
Shirkuh (d. 1169)	Also known as Asad al-Din. Gluttonous, hard-bitten Kurdish general in the service of Nur al-Din. Masterminded annexation of Fatimid Egypt. Uncle of Saladin.
Saladin (1137/8–1193)	Also known as Salah al-Din Yusuf ibn Ayyub. Kurdish soldier who rose to become sultan of Syria and Egypt. Destroyed a Frankish army at the battle of Hattin (1187) and returned Jerusalem to Islamic control. Provoked the Third Crusade and earned a legendary reputation among Muslims and Christians alike.
Al-Adil (1145–1218)	Also known as Sayf al-Din or Saphadin. Leading emir during the Third Crusade, his marriage to Joanna of Sicily was briefly mooted. Succeeded his brother Saladin as sultan and continued the Kurdish Ayyubid dynasty's hold over Egypt and Syria.
Baldwin IV (1161–1185)	King of Jerusalem who succeeded his father, Amalric I. Afflicted with severe and progressive leprosy that crippled and eventually killed him.
Sibylla, queen of Jerusalem (d. 1190)	Daughter of Amalric I. Her husband, Guy of Lusignan, became king of Jerusalem through marriage and oversaw defeat to Saladin at the battle of Hattin.
Guy of Lusignan (d. 1194)	Married to Sibylla, daughter of Amalric, king of Jerusalem. Led the Franks to military catastrophe at Hattin. After Sibylla's death took over kingdom of Cyprus, purchased from the Templars.
Reynald of Châtillon (d. 1187)	Pugnacious French knight who joined the Second Crusade and became Prince of Antioch, but was imprisoned by Nur al-Din for sixteen years. Later raided Red Sea ports and robbed Muslim caravan trains, provoking Saladin into punitive raids on the kingdom of Jerusalem.

Henry II, king of England (1133–1189)	Plantagenet king of England. Married the crusader queen Eleanor of Aquitaine. Father of Richard the Lionheart. Declined the crown of Jerusalem shortly before the disaster of Hattin. Took the cross but died before fulfilling his vow.

PART III

Margaret of Beverley (d. ca. 1215)	English pilgrim who fought in Saladin's siege of Jerusalem and was subsequently sold into slavery, freed and left Holy Land with returning warriors of the Third Crusade. Her crusade memoir is a vivid if idealized rendering of her adventures.
Richard the Lionheart (1157–1199)	King of England from 1189 until his death. Most prominent leader of the Third Crusade, during which he clashed repeatedly with Philip II Augustus and established a (much-mythologized) rivalry with Saladin.
Joanna, queen of Sicily (1165–1199)	Younger sister of Richard the Lionheart, rescued from Sicily during the early stages of the Third Crusade. Suggested briefly as potential wife of al-Adil to create a crusader-Ayyubid dynastic union.
Tancred, king of Sicily (1138–1194)	Illegitimate grandson of King Roger II of Sicily who seized the Sicilian throne after the death of his cousin William II. Mistreated William's widow, Joanna, queen of Sicily, and was severely punished by Richard the Lionheart. Nicknamed the "Monkey King."
Philip II Augustus (1165–1223)	King of France from 1180 until his death. Took part in the Third Crusade, helping recapture Acre from Saladin. Left in disgust after spats with Richard the Lionheart.
Isaac Komnenos (1155–1195)	Rogue member of the broader Byzantine Komnenoi dynasty who seized independent power in Cyprus in the 1180s but was deposed and imprisoned by Richard the Lionheart.
Enrico Dandolo (d. 1205)	Blind and elderly Doge of Venice and leader of the Fourth Crusade. Largely responsible for the conquest of the Christian cities of Zara and Constantinople.
Pope Innocent III (1161–1216)	Vastly powerful and influential medieval pope, responsible for preaching the Fourth and Fifth Crusades, and extending crusading far beyond its traditional areas.

Baldwin, Count of Flanders (1172–1205)	Aristocratic leader of the Fourth Crusade who was elected as the first Latin Emperor of Constantinople after the city fell to Frankish and Venetian attacks in 1204.
Alexios IV Angelos (d. 1204)	Byzantine emperor who sought aid of the Fourth Crusade to depose his uncle Alexios III and install himself and his father, Isaac II Angelos, as co-emperors. Murdered during the conquest of Constantinople.
Albert, bishop of Riga (d. 1229)	Pioneering churchman in the early stages of the Baltic crusades. The unruly military order known as the Livonian Swordbrothers formed among the knights of his household.
Simon of Montfort (d. 1218)	French lord who took part in the Fourth Crusade, but abandoned the Venetian fleet at Zara. Later led Albigensian Crusade against Cathars in southern France. Father of Simon of Montfort the younger, English nobleman and rebel against Henry III.
Raymond VI, Count of Toulouse (1156–1222)	Descendent of the First Crusade leader Raymond IV. Married Joanna, queen of Sicily, following her return from the Third Crusade. Later attacked by Simon of Montfort and the Albigensian crusaders.
Oliver of Cologne (1170–1227)	Also known as Oliver, bishop of Paderborn, a high-ranking preacher and leader of the Fifth Crusade, responsible for recruiting volunteers and designing military equipment. Kept a detailed chronicle of the crusade.
John of Brienne (d. 1237)	French knight who became king of Jerusalem (1212–1225) on behalf of his daughter, Queen Isabella II. Leader of the Fifth Crusade and Latin emperor of Constantinople (alongside co-emperor Baldwin II).
Cardinal Pelagius (d. 1230)	Bishop of Albano and papal legate during the Fifth Crusade who clashed with the aristocratic leaders and favored the disastrous decision to march up the Nile in 1221.
Pope Honorius III (1150–1227)	Succeeded Innocent III in 1216 and saw through plans for the Fifth Crusade. Attempts to encourage his protégé Frederick II Hohenstaufen to take command proved futile.

Al-Kamil (d. 1238)	Ayyubid sultan of Egypt. Succeeded his father, al-Adil, in 1218, at the beginning of the Fifth Crusade. Friendly with Frederick II Hohenstaufen, with whom he brokered a deal to return Jerusalem to Christian rule in 1229.
Francis of Assisi (d. 1226)	Italian friar who founded the Franciscan Order and was widely admired for his simple piety and embrace of Christ-like poverty. Appeared in Egypt during the Fifth Crusade attempting to convert al-Kamil to Christianity.
Frederick II Hohenstaufen (1194–1250)	Holy Roman Emperor who combined rule in Germany, northern Italy and Sicily. Led crusaders to the Holy Land in 1220s but was excommunicated four times and had numerous crusades preached against him during his wars with the papacy.
Hermann von Salza (d. 1239)	Master of the Teutonic Order and skilled diplomat. Among the leaders of the Fifth Crusade. Accompanied Frederick II Hohenstaufen in the Holy Land in 1228 and 1229. Masterminded the Teutonic Order's move into the Baltic region.
Pope Gregory IX (d. 1241)	Elected pope in 1227 and pursued a long feud with Frederick II Hohenstaufen, excommunicating him before his arrival in the Holy Land. Established the Inquisition to deal with heresy.
Genghis Khan (d. 1227)	Born Temüjin, founder of the Mongol Empire, which expanded to encompass vast expanses of the Far East, central Asia and the Middle East, and threatened eastern Europe. Succeeded by his son Ögödei.
Al-Salih Ayyub (1205–1249)	Son of al-Kamil. Ayyubid sultan of Egypt at the outset of Louis IX's crusade to Damietta. Allied with Khwarizmian Turks to destroy the crusader army at the battle of La Forbie in 1244.
Al-Salih Isma'il (d. 1245)	Brother of al-Kamil and Ayyubid emir of Damascus. Allied with the crusaders at the battle of La Forbie.
Turan-Shah (d. 1250)	Son of al-Salih Ayyub and short-lived final Ayyubid sultan of Egypt. Murdered in a palace coup by Bahriyya Mamluks.

Louis IX, king of France (1214–1270)	Pious French king who collected relics, sponsored Gothic building projects including Sainte-Chapelle and led an ill-fated crusade to Damietta and Palestine from 1248. Attempted to pursue an alliance with Mongol leaders. Died near Tunis on another crusade in 1270. Canonized as St. Louis.
Qutuz (d. 1260)	Mamluk sultan of Egypt who commanded an army to victory over the Mongols at the battle of 'Ayn Jalut. Murdered by Baybars.
Hülagü Khan (d. 1265)	Grandson of Genghis Khan and founding ruler of the Ilkhanate of Persia. Conquered Baghdad in 1258 and explored the possibility of diplomatic alliance with crusaders via letters to Louis IX of France.
Baybars (d. 1277)	Also known as Rukd al-Din. Fearsome Mamluk sultan who fought at 'Ayn Jalut, murdered his predecessor, Qutuz, and masterminded campaigns against the crusader states.
The Lord Edward (1239–1307)	Future Edward I of England. Traveled to Acre in 1271–72. Frustrated by the truce with the Mamluks, he narrowly escaped murder by an Assassin.
Bohemond VI of Antioch-Tripoli (1237–1275)	Prince of Antioch and Count of Tripoli from 1251. Allied with the Mongols and was punished with loss of Antioch to the Mamluks.
Al-Ashraf Khalil (d. 1293)	Mamluk sultan who completed the destruction of the crusader states of the Near East by successfully besieging Acre in 1291.
Henry Bolingbroke (1367–1413)	Future Henry IV of England. Son of John of Gaunt, whose Spanish wars were dubiously classified as crusades. As a young man, fought alongside Teutonic Knights in Prussia and went on pilgrimage to Jerusalem.
"Boucicaut" (1366–1421)	Also known as Jean II Le Meingre. Famous knight and Marshal of France. Fought in numerous late medieval crusades.
Ferdinand II of Aragon (1452–1516) and Isabella I of Castile (1451–1504)	The "Catholic Monarchs," whose marriage effectively united Christian Spain. War against the last emir of Granada effectively ended the Reconquista. Sponsored Christopher Columbus on his 1492 expedition to the New World.

EUROPE AND THE HOLY LAND
AFTER THE FIRST CRUSADE
c.1099
0
200
400
600
800
Miles
NORWAY
SWEDEN
Oslo
DENMARK
Lund
Baltic Sea
North Sea
SCOTLAND
ENGLAND
York
Dublin
Severn
Oxford
London
Thames
Winchester
English Channel
Hamburg
Bremen
WENDS
POMERANIANS
SAXONY
POL
FLANDERS
Cologne
Aachen
Mainz
Main
Rhine
Reims
Bouillon
Worms
BOHEMIA
Rouen
NORMANDY
Seine
Paris
CHAMPAGNE
LORRAINE
GERMAN EMPIRE
Danube
Le Mans
BRITTANY
Nantes
Blois
Loire
BURGUNDY
SWABIA
BAVARIA
POITOU
Poitiers
FRANCE
Rhône
ATLANTIC OCEAN
Bay of Biscay
Clermont-Ferrand
Lyon
Milan
Venice
HUN
Bordeaux
Garonne
Po
Genoa
Bologna
PROVENCE
Pisa
Florence
Adriatic Sea
GASCONY
Toulouse
Marseille
Oviedo
Compostela
NAVARRE
Ebro
PAPAL STATES
CASTILE
LEÓN
Zaragoza
Rome
Bari
Duraz
Tortosa
Naples
APULIA
Tagus
BALEARIC ISLANDS
MENORCA
Salerno
Tarant
AL-ANDALUS
Valencia
MAJORCA
IBIZA
Lisbon
Córdoba
Alicante
Mediterranean
Palermo
Messina
SICILY
Granada
Seville
Almería
Syracuse
Algiers
Tunis
Kairouan
Mahdia
Sfax
Gabes
Tripoli
ALMORAVIDS
ZIRIDS
Marrakesh

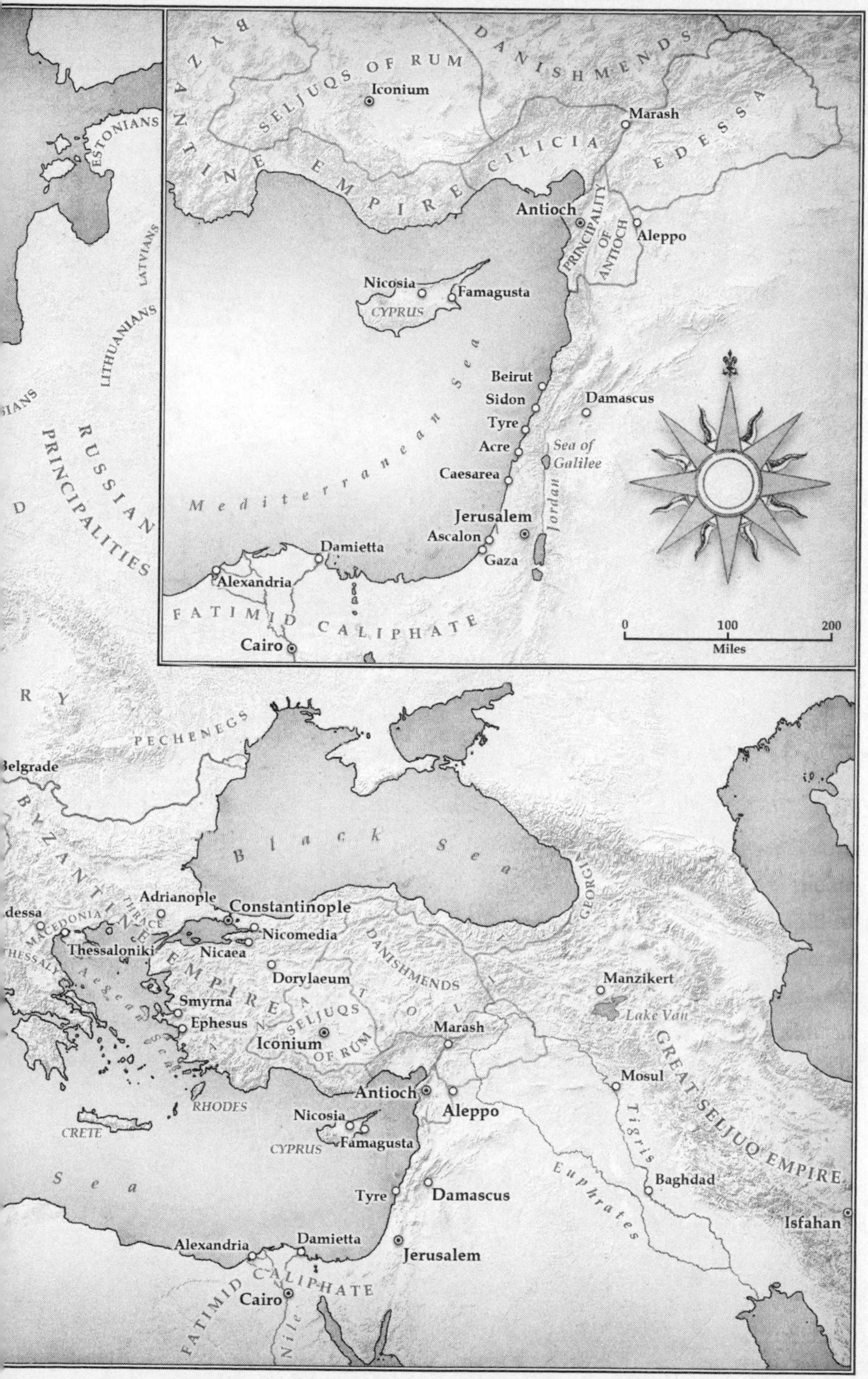
BYZANTINE EMPIRE
SELJUQS OF RUM
DANISHMENDS
Iconium
Marash
CILICIA
EDESSA
Antioch
PRINCIPALITY OF ANTIOCH
Aleppo
Nicosia
Famagusta
CYPRUS
Mediterranean Sea
Beirut
Sidon
Tyre
Acre
Caesarea
Damascus
Sea of Galilee
Jordan
Jerusalem
Ascalon
Gaza
Damietta
Alexandria
FATIMID CALIPHATE
Cairo
0
100
200
Miles
ESTONIANS
LATVIANS
LITHUANIANS
RUSSIAN PRINCIPALITIES
PECHENEGS
Belgrade
BYZANTINE EMPIRE
Black Sea
Adrianople
Constantinople
THRACE
MACEDONIA
THESSALY
Nicomedia
Thessaloniki
Nicaea
Dorylaeum
DANISHMENDS
ANATOLIA
GEORGIA
Manzikert
Lake Van
Smyrna
Ephesus
Aegean Sea
SELJUQS OF RUM
Iconium
Marash
Antioch
Aleppo
RHODES
CRETE
Nicosia
CYPRUS
Famagusta
Mosul
GREAT SELJUQ EMPIRE
Tigris
Euphrates
Baghdad
Isfahan
Tyre
Damascus
Alexandria
Damietta
Jerusalem
FATIMID CALIPHATE
Cairo
Nile

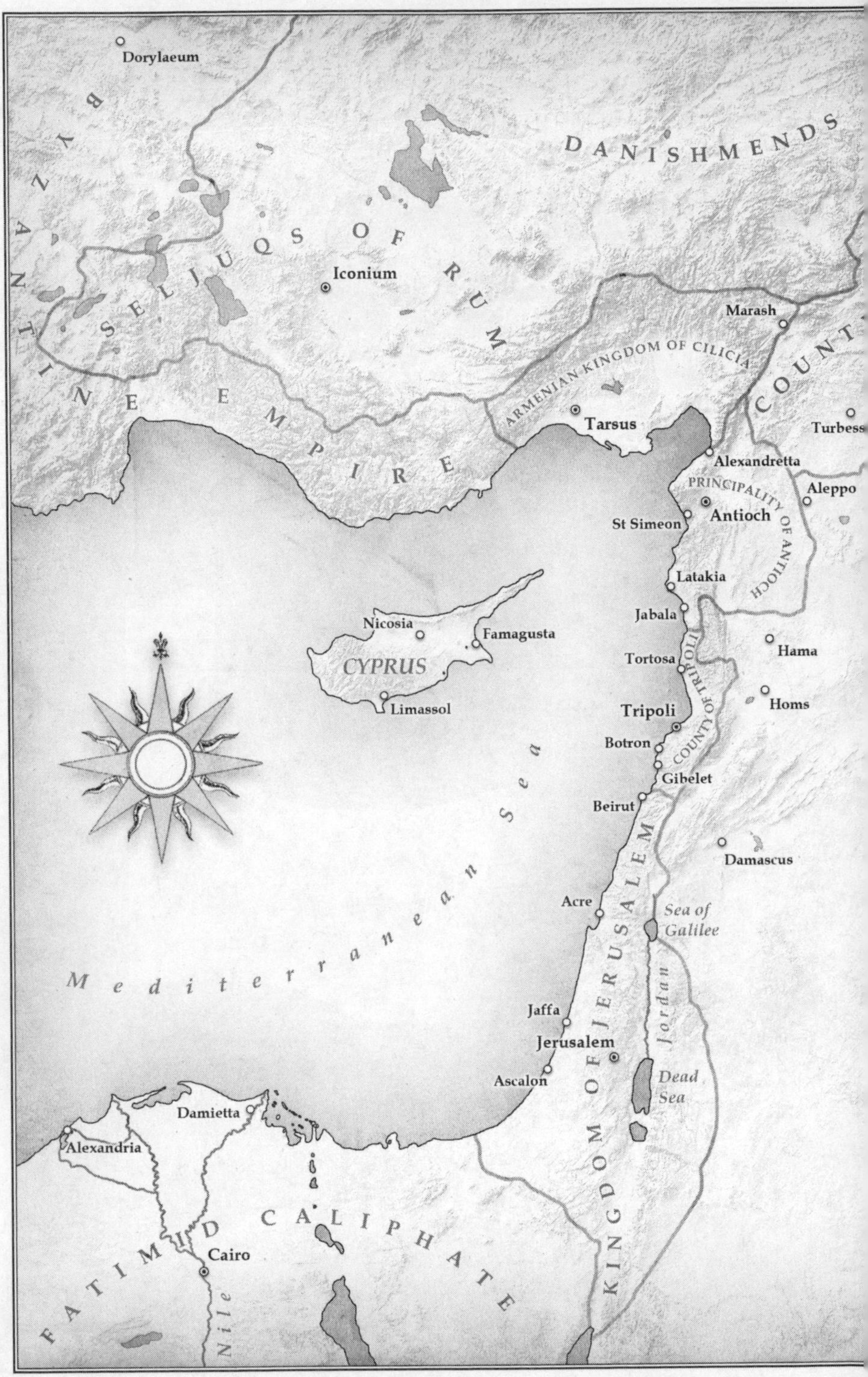
Dorylaeum
BYZANTINE EMPIRE
SELJUQS OF RUM
DANISHMENDS
Iconium
ARMENIAN KINGDOM OF CILICIA
Marash
Tarsus
Turbessel
Alexandretta
PRINCIPALITY OF ANTIOCH
Aleppo
Antioch
St Simeon
Latakia
Jabala
Nicosia
Famagusta
CYPRUS
Limassol
Hama
Tortosa
COUNTY OF TRIPOLI
Homs
Tripoli
Botron
Gibelet
Beirut
Damascus
Mediterranean Sea
Acre
Sea of Galilee
Jordan
Jaffa
Jerusalem
Ascalon
Dead Sea
KINGDOM OF JERUSALEM
Damietta
Alexandria
FATIMID CALIPHATE
Cairo
Nile

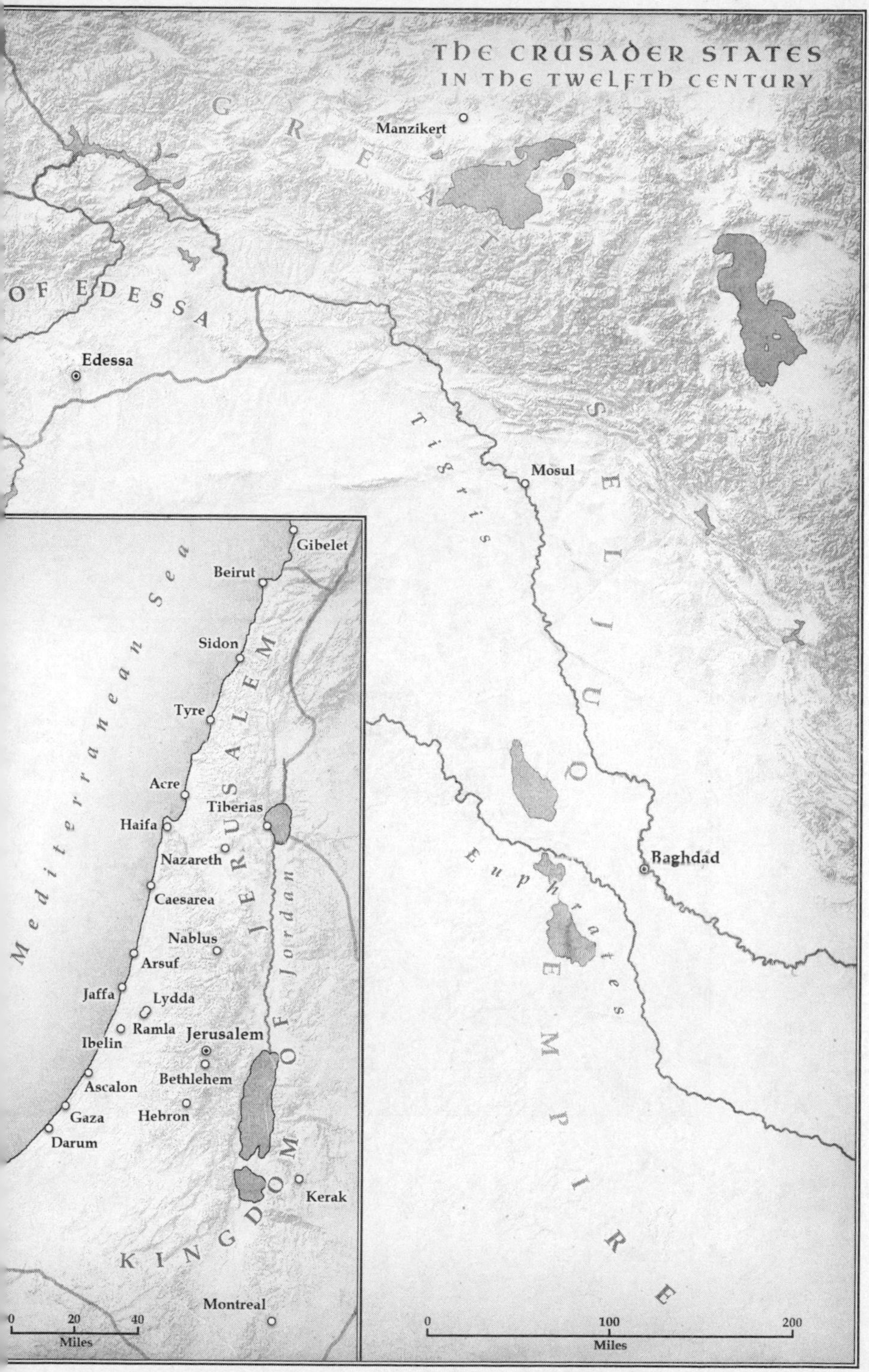
The Crusader States
in the Twelfth Century
Manzikert
Edessa
Mosul
Baghdad
Tigris
Euphrates
GREAT SELJUQ EMPIRE
OF EDESSA
Mediterranean Sea
Gibelet
Beirut
Sidon
Tyre
Acre
Haifa
Tiberias
Nazareth
Caesarea
Nablus
Arsuf
Jaffa
Lydda
Ramla
Ibelin
Jerusalem
Bethlehem
Ascalon
Gaza
Hebron
Darum
Kerak
Montreal
Jordan
KINGDOM OF JERUSALEM
0
20
40
Miles
0
100
200
Miles

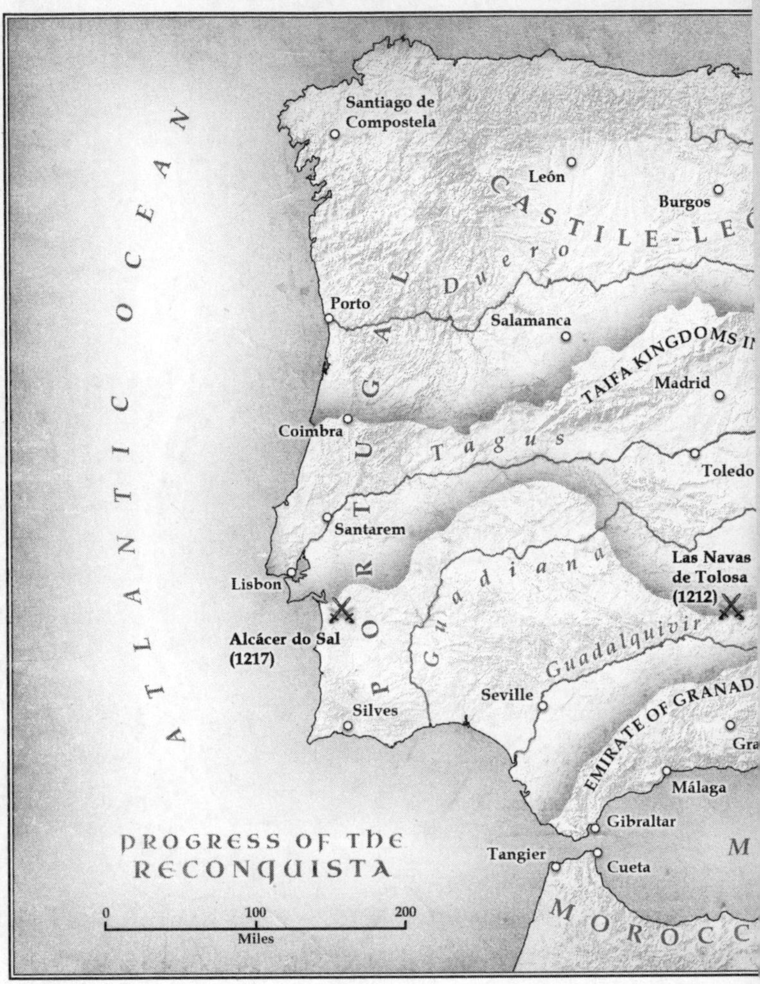
ATLANTIC OCEAN
Santiago de Compostela
León
Burgos
CASTILE-LEO
Duero
PORTUGAL
Porto
Salamanca
TAIFA KINGDOMS IN
Madrid
Coimbra
Tagus
Toledo
Santarem
Guadiana
Las Navas de Tolosa (1212)
Lisbon
Alcácer do Sal (1217)
Guadalquivir
Seville
EMIRATE OF GRANAD
Silves
Gra
Málaga
Gibraltar
Tangier
Cueta
M
MOROCC
PROGRESS OF THE RECONQUISTA
0
100
200
Miles

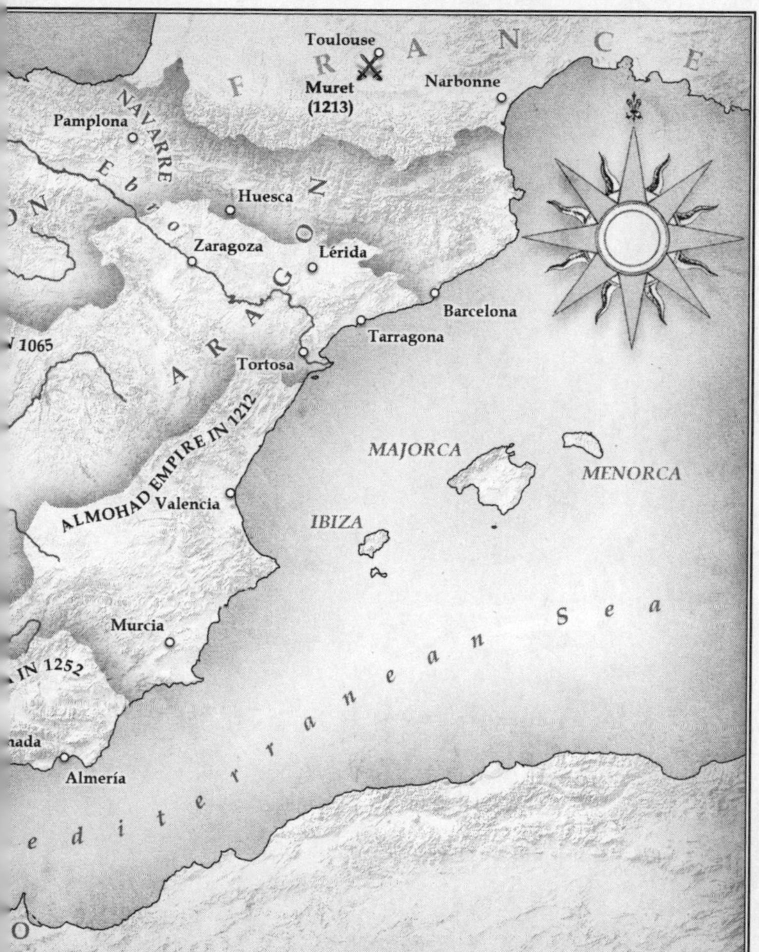

Toulouse
FRANCE
Muret
(1213)
Narbonne
NAVARRE
Pamplona
Ebro
Huesca
ARAGON
Zaragoza
Lérida
Barcelona
Tarragona
Tortosa
ALMOHAD EMPIRE IN 1212
Valencia
MAJORCA
MENORCA
IBIZA
Murcia
Almería
Sea

INTRODUCTION

An epic written in blood . . .

Shortly before Easter in the year 1188 CE, an English archbishop of Canterbury went to Wales on a recruitment drive. Thousands of miles away, war had broken out in the eastern Mediterranean and the archbishop, whose name was Baldwin of Forde, had been tasked with recruiting several thousand able-bodied fighting men to join an army that was being deployed there.

It was on the face of it not an easy assignment. For those who decided to join up, the journey by land and sea to the East and back would take at least eighteen months. It would cost a lot of money. There was a high chance of shipwreck, robbery, ambush or death from disease long before the destination—the Christian kingdom of Jerusalem, in Palestine—was ever reached. The chances of coming home with much in the way of plunder were negligible. Indeed, the prospect of coming home at all was dauntingly slim.

The enemy commander—the Kurdish sultan of Egypt and Syria, Salah al-Din Yusuf ibn Ayyub, colloquially called Saladin—was highly capable and had already inflicted a series of devastating defeats on armies of the Western Christians generically known as the Franks. The previous summer he had crushed a huge army in the field, imprisoned the king of Jerusalem, seized the holy relic of Christ's Cross and evicted a Christian government from the city of Jerusalem. The only sure reward for participants in the war to take revenge on Saladin would be redeemed in the afterlife, where it was assumed that God would look favorably on participants, granting them a smoother, swifter entry into paradise.

Although in a religious age obsessed with tallying and remitting sin this was a more enticing offer than it might seem today, Baldwin nevertheless had his work cut out, as he and his entourage slogged through Wales from town to town: preaching, persuading and whipping up enthusiasm for a war against an enemy none of his audience had ever seen, in a land vanishingly few had ever experienced outside their imaginations.

In a small town called Aberteifi, in West Wales, a young married couple reacted to Baldwin's arrival by having a fight. The husband had decided he wanted to sign up for the crusade. His wife was adamant he was going nowhere. According to the writer Gerald of Wales, who traveled with Archbishop Baldwin and kept a vivid record of the journey (although he sadly omitted the couple's names), the wife "held her husband fast by his cloak and belt, and publicly . . . prevented him from going to the archbishop."[1] They struggled and she won. But, wrote Gerald, her victory proved horribly short-lived: "Three nights afterward, she heard a terrible voice saying, 'You have taken my servant away from me, therefore what you must love shall be taken away from you.'"

That evening, lying in bed, she accidentally rolled over in her sleep and smothered to death her infant son, who was sharing her bed. It was a tragedy. It was also, she realized, an omen. Although by now Archbishop Baldwin had moved on, the distraught couple went to see their diocesan bishop to report the dreadful accident and beg forgiveness.

Only one solution presented itself. They all knew what it was. Those Christians who had agreed to leave to fight Saladin advertised their status as sworn, holy warriors in the army of Christ by stitching a cross made of cloth onto the arm of their clothes.

The wife sewed on her husband's cross herself.

This is a book about the crusades: the wars fought by Christian-led, papal-sanctioned armies against the perceived enemies of Christ and the Church of Rome during the Middle Ages. Its title, *Crusaders*, reflects both its theme and its approach. For a long time during the Middle Ages there was no single word to describe "the crusades" as we have today come to think of them since: a series of eight or nine major expeditions from Western Europe to the Holy Land, supplemented by a series of other, tangentially connected wars fought from the sunbaked cities of the North African coast to the frozen forests of the Baltic region. Yet from the earliest days of the phenomenon there certainly *was* a word for those who participated. The men and women who took part in these penitential wars in the hope of spiritual salvation were known in Latin as *crucesignati*—those signed with the cross. In that sense, then, the idea of the crusader preceded the idea of the crusades, and that is one reason why I have preferred it here.

More important, however, the title *Crusaders* reflects the approach to storytelling that I have taken in this book. It is composed of a series of episodes featuring people who were involved in the crusades, arranged sequentially and chronologically to tell a tableau history that spans the period at large. The individuals whom I have charged with taking us on our journey are the "crusaders" of the book's title, and they are an ensemble cast who I hope, together, can tell us the story of crusading from the front line.

In choosing these crusaders I have deliberately cast my net wide. I have selected women and men, Christians of the Eastern and Western churches, Sunni and Shi'a Muslims, Arabs, Jews, Turks, Kurds, Syrians, Egyptians, Berbers and Mongols. There are people here from England, Wales, France, Scandinavia, Germany, Italy, Sicily, Spain, Portugal, the Balkans, North Africa. There is even a band of Vikings. Some have central parts to play, others mere cameos. But this is their story.

The result, taken as a whole, is an avowedly pluralist history of crusading. Historiographically, that is to say that it does not focus exclusively on the establishment, survival and collapse of the crusader states of Palestine and Syria and wars against Muslims in those regions. Rather, it places that central strand of the story in the context of the concurrent histories of official crusades fought on the Iberian Peninsula, the Baltic, eastern Europe, southern France, Sicily and Anatolia, and unofficial, populist movements raised elsewhere. Narratively, it means that our story is carried along by a multitude of people, a collective who will together provide a kaleidoscope of intriguing and colorful perspectives on their shared age.

That, at any rate, is the aim. Of course, as I submit this book I am acutely aware of—and profoundly grateful for—the many excellent surveys of the crusades that have been written in recent years. Perhaps the greatest, despite its age, remains Sir Steven Runciman's glorious three-volume chronicle, *A History of the Crusades* (1951–1954); but more recently English-language readers have been also blessed by the publication of Christopher Tyerman's *God's War: A New History of the Crusades* (2006); Thomas Asbridge's *The Crusades: The War for the Holy Land* (2010); Jonathan Phillips's *Holy Warriors: A Modern History of the Crusades* (2010); the third edition of the late, great Jonathan Riley-Smith's *The Crusades: a History* (2014); and Paul M. Cobb's *The Race for Paradise: An Islamic History of the Crusades* (2014). All of these books are superb guides to the period, and although throughout the narrative here I have confined myself to quotations exclusively from primary sources, I have been deeply reassured to have them on my shelves—alongside hundreds of other books and articles, both general and specialist, by other crusades scholars. Without the work of generations of crusades historians past and present, this book would simply not have been possible.

Crusaders is presented in three sections. The first covers the period in which the many strands of thought, activity and warfare that influenced the crusading movement developed, from the 1060s onward. It builds toward the astonishing story of the First Crusade and culminates with the fall of Jerusalem in July 1099.

The second part of the book picks up the story a few years later, at the start of the twelfth century. It traces the growth and development of the crusader states in Syria and Palestine, keeps an eye on the wars between Christian rulers and the Islamic powers in Spain (known as the Reconquista) and explores the spread of crusading beyond those two theaters into a new realm around the shore of the Baltic Sea. The narrative of this section of the book is anchored by two major crises: the loss of Edessa in 1144, which triggered the Second Crusade, and the fall of Jerusalem to Saladin in 1187, which provoked the Third.

The final part of the book charts the desperate efforts of Western Christendom to win back Jerusalem in the first half of the thirteenth century, followed by the decline of the crusader states in the East after the rise of the Mongol and Mamluk empires. It also describes the dramatic expansion and politicization of crusading ideology and institutions during and after the papacy of Innocent III, and the process by which crusading was turned upon new enemies: inside and outside the Church, real and imaginary. In keeping with its commitment to telling a story long and broad, *Crusaders* does not conclude in 1291 with the final collapse of the kingdom of Jerusalem, but in 1492, with the completion of the Reconquista and the transmission of crusading's urges and energies west, to the New World. Lastly, a brief epilogue then sketches the survival and mutation of crusading memory up to the present day.

Each chapter of this book could be, and in most cases has been, a full-length study in itself. I hope the general reader will be inspired by what follows to delve deeper into the history of crusading, and those who have read more in this period will appreciate the approach I have taken to the material. As with all my books, I hope most of all that this is a story that will entertain as well as inform. For, as Sir Steven Runciman once wrote, "the romantic story of the Crusades was an epic written in blood."[2]

So it was. And so it is. Let us begin.

DAN JONES
Staines-upon-Thames
Spring 2019

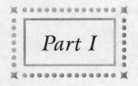

Part I

TRIAL BY ORDEAL

◆ 1 ◆

The Count and the Imam

He perceived two means by which he would profit, one for his soul and the other for his material benefit.

Count Roger of Sicily lifted his leg and farted. "By the truth of my religion," he exclaimed, "there is more use in that than in what you have to say!"[1]

His advisers stood chastened—and a little perplexed. The count before them was in his late forties and salted to his bones with the experience of military campaigning in southern Italy and the islands of the central Mediterranean. As a young warrior he had been described by one flatterer as "tall and well-made, a most fluent speaker, shrewd in counsel, far-sighted in the planning of things to be done, cheerful and pleasant to everyone."[2] In middle age, he had hardened somewhat and was not one to waste his words on fools.

The plan the advisers had recommended had seemed like a good one, as courtiers' plans very often do, before they are shredded by the critiques of short-tempered potentates. Not far across the sea from Sicily—roughly seventy-five miles at the closest point—lay the remains of what had in ancient times been called Carthage, afterward the Roman province of Africa, and now, in the late eleventh century, Ifriqiya.* Its cities—including the capital Mahdia (al-Mahdiyya) on the coast and Kairouan (Qayrawan) inland, where a vast mosque and school had for many generations been frequented by the greatest philosophers and natural scientists in North Africa—were under

*Today this is the eastern Maghreb: that portion of North Africa's coastal littoral roughly covered by northeastern Algeria, Tunisia and northwest Libya.

the shaky command of a crumbling dynasty of Berber Muslims known as the Zirids. The countryside was controlled by various Arab Bedouin tribes sent from Egypt to drive the Zirids out. Political stability was collapsing. Here lay warm and fertile farmlands. There sat prosperous port towns. All ripe for the taking? Roger's counselors thought so, and they had therefore recommended to their testy overlord the proposal of a cousin whom one source names only as "Baldwin."[3]

This Baldwin had come into possession of a great army of Christian soldiers and was casting around for somewhere godless to conquer. He had asked Roger's blessing to come to Sicily and use it as a launchpad for an invasion of Ifriqiya. "I shall be a neighbor of yours," he had exclaimed, as though this were good news. But Roger of Sicily was not feeling neighborly. Ifriqiya was undoubtedly ruled by various followers of Islam, he said, but those infidels happened to be sworn partners of the Sicilians in agreements that kept the peace and allowed for a rich exchange of goods in the island's markets and ports. The last thing he wanted, he ranted to his gathered minions, was a cousin imposing on his hospitality, waging a reckless war that would disrupt Sicilian trade if it was successful and cost him a lot of money in military support if it failed.

Ifriqiya may indeed have been vulnerable, but if anyone was going to exploit that, it was going to be Roger himself. He had spent the last two and a half decades—almost his entire adult life—carving out his rule in the region, and it would have been a limp end indeed if he were now to put it at risk in pursuit of some harebrained scheme cooked up by a kinsman who had never troubled the soil of the island with his sweat.

If this Baldwin wanted to fight Muslims, said Roger, he would have to find a different part of the Mediterranean in which to go about his business. There were plenty of places he could name that would be preferable to Sicily's backyard. He summoned Baldwin's personal envoy to his presence and informed him of his decision. If his master was really serious, he said, then "the best way [to proceed] is to conquer Jerusalem."[4]

And that is how it all began.

Roger, Count of Sicily, was eleventh-century Europe's ultimate self-made man. He was born around the year 1040 as the youngest of twelve sons sired by a minor nobleman from Normandy called Tancred of Hauteville. Given the protocols of inheritance, being born even as a second son implied a lifelong burden of fortune hunting rather than easy inheritance: to have eleven brothers ahead of you was a disaster. But by the end of the century the Normans had begun to conquer their way around Western Europe. They took command of Saxon England in 1066. At the same time, southern Italy fell under their gaze. Opportunities may have been limited for younger sons within Normandy itself—but for anyone prepared to travel, opportunity abounded. As a young man, therefore, Roger had left his homeland in what is now northwest France and set out for territory that had already called many of his kinsmen and countrymen: the rich but unstable southern Italian regions of Calabria and Apulia.

Toe and heel of the Italian boot, Calabria and Apulia were lands where resources were plentiful, authority was contested and an ambitious young man with a yen for politics and warfare might make his name. Other Normans of the Hauteville clan had already found success here, fighting against the rival superpowers in the region: principally the Byzantine Greeks and Roman popes—both of whom regarded the Normans with suspicion bordering on alarm. The most successful of them included Roger's brothers William Iron Arm, Drogo and the exceptionally gifted Robert Guiscard. (In Old French *guischart* means "cunning" or "sly.") By the time Roger arrived the first two were dead and Robert Guiscard had laid claim to the title of "Count of Apulia and Calabria." But there were plenty of adventures to be found. The family had earned the submission of the people of southern Italy by chopping off their noses, hands and feet and gouging out their eyes.[5] The Normans' tribal history told of their descent from a Scandinavian warlord named Rollo who had converted to Christianity mainly as a means of ensuring that men of all manner of kingdoms would bend their knee to his command.[6] Neither Roger nor Robert ever lost the Viking touch for persuasion at the end of a sword.

Thanks in large part to this reputation for extravagant violence, not everyone approved of the Norman invasion of southern Italy. In the opinion of one eminent churchman of the age, the Normans were "the most foul-smelling rubbish in the world . . . sons of filth, tyrants who have risen from the rabble."[7] But from the middle of the century onward, the papacy took a different view, as successive popes softened their hostility to the Normans and began to view them as rough edged but practically useful potential allies who could be employed to advance the agenda of Rome. In part the papacy reached this conclusion under duress: in 1053 the Normans had destroyed a papal army on the battlefield and taken Nicholas's predecessor, Pope Leo IX, prisoner. Be that as it may, in 1059 Pope Nicholas II nevertheless granted the Hauteville family sway over Calabria and Apulia, and permitted them to fly a papal banner* before their armies on the battlefield: an honor he bestowed upon Robert Guiscard in exchange for a gift of four camels. And this was not just an acceptance of the status quo. The pope speculated that one day, one of the Norman clan might "with the help of God and Saint Peter" also conquer and rule Sicily: the large triangular island across the straits of Messina had been under Arab rule since the ninth century.[8] This would represent a major advance in papal ambitions to bring the whole of southern Italy firmly under the sway of the Roman church.[9] If the Normans could do that, ran the reasoning, then all the disruption caused on the mainland in the many decades since the arrival of these roughneck northerners might just have been worth it.

The conquest of Sicily appealed strongly to Roger and his brother Robert Guiscard, although not quite for the same reasons as it appealed to the pope. Pleasing God could quite satisfactorily be done locally by founding and maintaining communities of monks and nuns, praising Christ and observing the saints' feast days. Fighting an expeditionary war to seize and subjugate an island almost ten thousand square miles in size, with a coastal length of nearly nine hundred miles and a large region of volcanic mountains in its center was an act of piety that required more substantial, earthly justification.

Fortunately, on Sicily there were plenty of reasons to be found. Wet in the winter and hot in the summer, the island contained some of the finest farmland in the Mediterranean, producing prodigious quantities of grain by agricultural methods much improved under the rule of its Islamic emirs. Rice, lemons, dates and sugarcane thrived. Sicilian workshops produced cotton and papyrus. Calm waters kept fishermen busy; pilgrim tourists from Muslim-ruled southern Spain stopped for refreshment as they headed to Mecca to perform hajj. Coastal towns including Palermo, Syracuse, Catania, Messina and Agrigento were hub marketplaces in the central Mediterranean, where

*A few years later a papal banner was sent to another Norman lord: William the Bastard, Duke of Normandy, flew it before his armies when he invaded England in 1066.

merchants from the Middle East and northeast Africa could do business with those working trade routes through central and Western Europe. The local population, comprised of Arab and Berber Muslims, Greek Orthodox Christians and Jews, represented a lucrative tax base, as the emirs had demonstrated by following the Islamic practice of imposing an infidel tax known as *jizya* on those non-Muslims who did not wish to convert.

All this being so, the papal hymn of Sicilian conquest sung to Roger and Robert Guiscard in 1059 made a lot of sense. As a Sicilian monastic chronicler called Geoffrey Malaterra told the story, when "that most distinguished young man Roger . . . heard that Sicily was in the hands of the unbelievers . . . he was seized by the desire to capture it. . . . He perceived two means by which he would profit, one for his soul and the other for his material benefit, if he could bring over to Divine worship a country given over to idolatry."[10]

Money and immortality: these two, timeless temptations proved more than enough to coax Roger and Robert Guiscard across the Strait of Messina in a series of invasions beginning in the early 1060s. Taking Sicily from the Arabs was neither easy nor quick, but when the Norman brothers focused their full attention, bringing naval blockades and warriors who were small in number but expert in the Norman style of fighting—with light armor and heavy cavalry, large wooden shields and siege towers—they proved very difficult to resist. They exploited the rivalries of Islamic factions on the island, who had at times in the past hired Christian mercenaries from mainland Italy and were more than willing to collaborate with the Norman armies to further their own ambitions for political supremacy.[11] They indulged in base but effective psychological warfare: raping their enemies' wives or sending carrier pigeons soaked in blood to announce their victories. As a result, Palermo fell in 1072, following a five-month siege. By the mid-1080s most of the island was under Norman command. The inveterate adventurer Robert Guiscard left to seek further excitement fighting in the Byzantine Empire, pushing Norman rule into Dalmatia, Macedonia and Thessaly, and leaving his younger brother Roger to rule more or less as he pleased as Count of Sicily.

By 1091 the conquest of Sicily was complete and Roger was reveling in his role as one of Europe's most admired Christian overlords: entertaining marriage proposals for his daughters from the kings of France, Germany and Hungary, establishing bishoprics across the island that were obedient to the papacy (rather than the Eastern patriarchs of the Orthodox Church) and overseeing a population that remained as richly variegated between faiths and cultures as it had ever been. Roger built and patronized churches and monasteries on Sicily—an act of conventional piety for any ruler of the age, particularly one who had an awkward amount of human blood on his hands. The mosque in Palermo, originally built as a Byzantine basilica, was converted once again, this time into a church observant of the Latin rite. On occasion he seems to have forced defeated Muslim rivals to convert to Christianity.[12] The *jizya* system was effectively reversed, so that Muslims rather than Christians now paid a tax (the *censum* or *tributum*) for the right to their unbelief.[13] Jews also paid a tallage. But Roger was in no sense creating a theocracy. Indeed, visiting churchmen from further north in Europe tut-tutted at the fact that Roger not only allowed Muslims to serve in his armies but (so they said) sometimes actively refused to allow them to convert to the cause of Christ.[14] And the count himself was pragmatic more often than he was dogmatic when he presented himself to his subjects. Copper coins known as *trifollari*, minted for use by his Christian subjects, showed Roger as a glorious Christian knight on horseback carrying a holy lance and were inscribed in Latin with his name, Count Roger (ROQERIVS COMES).[15] Yet each gold *tari*—a coin minted for use by his Muslim subjects—carried an Arabic inscription: "There is no God but Allah, Muhammad is the prophet of Allah." Other of Roger's Arabic coins and his charters in the same language referred to him variously as *imam*, *malik* and *sultan*: Lord, sovereign and king.[16]

What, though, are we to make of the perplexing story of Roger's refusal to extend his success in Sicily by sponsoring an invasion of Ifriqiya? The tale comes down to us via a scholar named Ibn al-Athir, who lived and died in Mosul (today in Iraq) from 1160 to 1233, and whose masterpiece was a magisterial chronicle confidently entitled *Al-Kamil fi'l Ta'rikh: The Perfect Work of History*.

Ibn al-Athir was a serious historian who devoted hundreds of thousands of words to a story of the world, beginning with creation and continuing up to the political and military struggles of and between the wider Islamic world in his own lifetime, upon which he cast a panoptic and often highly insightful gaze. Given the age through which he lived, crusaders and their motives were naturally high among his interests, and he gave serious thought to the origins of the holy wars that flared up spectacularly and often around the Mediterranean basin during his lifetime. His decision to place the responsibility at the door of Roger of Sicily (whom he characterizes as coarse, smelly and cynical—the very archetype of the crusader lord) is important, even if it should not be taken wholly at face value.* The character of "Baldwin" is probably meant to signal Baldwin I, future king of Jerusalem—but there is no corroborating evidence that this exchange happened.

Possibly Ibn al-Athir in his account was conflating what he knew with hindsight of the origins of the crusades in the Holy Land with a particular story of more local origin and flavor. In 1087, according to the chronicler Malaterra, Ifriqiya had come under amphibious attack from an army raised by merchants from Pisa, "who had set out to do business in Africa only to suffer certain injuries."[17] In a much less grotesque and colorful telling than Ibn al-Athir's, Malaterra simply says that the Pisans offered to award Roger the crown of Ifriqiya if he would help them take the city of Mahdia. Roger demurred on the ground that he had only relatively recently agreed to a peace treaty with the authorities there. He made no mention of Jerusalem. According to Malaterra, the Pisans made their own deal with the Zirid ruler and accepted a cash payment to leave Mahdia alone.

Yet there is more to it than that, still. When Ibn al-Athir introduces his story about Count Roger and the state of Ifriqiya, he does so by setting it in a broad Mediterranean context. At around the same time that the Normans were conquering Sicily and menacing the coast of Ifriqiya, he wrote, they also "took the city of Toledo and other cities of Spain. . . . Later they took other parts, as you shall see."[18] And indeed, so "they" did. In Spain, North Africa, the islands of the Mediterranean and elsewhere, clashes between rival rulers obedient to different faiths were commonplace during the decades before the First Crusade began.

These were not wars of religion—indeed, religion was often very plainly secondary to commercial and geopolitical considerations.[19] But they *were* wars between religious men, and they had consequences that lasted for genera-

---

*Interestingly, Roger's demonstrative flatulence was one detail not unique to Ibn al-Athir. Geoffrey Malaterra records an instance of a Norman army besieging Palermo in 1064, during which campaign the army was plagued by tarantulas. "Anyone who was stung by them found himself filled with gas and suffered so much that he was unable to keep the same gas from coming out his anus with a disgusting rattle." Kenneth Baxter Wolf, trans., *The Deeds of Count Roger of Calabria and Sicily and of his Brother Duke Robert Guiscard by Geoffrey Malaterra* (Ann Arbor: University of Michigan Press, 2005), 114.

tions thereafter, so that they could still be seen to be playing out in Ibn al-Athir's day. The collapsing together of wars fought for territory and wars that were waged on the basis of faith and dogma, with the goal of spiritual supremacy, was to play a key part in launching two hundred years and more of conflict that would come to be expressed primarily in terms of a battle for the one true faith.

◆ 2 ◆

Poets and Party Kings

Now that they are strong and capable, the Christians desire to recover what they have lost by force.

As Sicily began its fall to the Normans in the 1070s, the island crumbling city by city before the assaults of Count Roger's barbarian soldiers bearing shields shaped like giant teardrops, a young Muslim poet scooped up his family and fled. His name was Ibn Hamdis ('Abd al-Jabbar Ibn Hamdis) and he was twenty-four years old. Born in Syracuse around 1054, he had grown up in genteel comfort as the son of a well-to-do household, enjoying and absorbing a literary education that left him with a lifelong facility for the popular Arabic verse that was a hallmark of high culture at the time. This talent enabled him to make sense of the destruction, pain and loss he would see during his long and eventful life. It would also make his name and grant him access to the many learned courts of the Islamic Mediterranean.

Leaving Sicily was a wrench to his soul, and his departure left him forever in mourning for the turbulent island of his birth. "I have been banished from Paradise," he once wrote; nostalgia and homesickness permeated the poetry he continued to compose until well beyond his eightieth birthday.[1] But if exile was painful, it was also profitable. After leaving Sicily, Ibn Hamdis headed west and became a salaried companion to one of the greatest artistic patrons of his day, Muhammad al-Mu'tamid ibn Abbad, king of the *taifa* of Seville. Al-Mu'tamid, approaching his fortieth birthday when Ibn Hamdis arrived, was himself a gifted poet who inherited his wordsmithery from a brutish but eloquent father, al-Mu'tadid—whose relentless military campaigning made Seville one of the most powerful states in the region and whose methods of dealing with his enemies were positively treacherous, including on one occasion suffocating a group of visiting diplomats to death in his palace bathhouse.[2]

Al-Mu'tamid was a somewhat less devious ruler than his father and a more talented composer of verse.[3] He adopted Ibn Hamdis as one of a number of lyrical sparring partners and placed him on his payroll. Thus did the Sicilian exile take up residence in one of the most intellectual and sensual courts of the West, where the illicit pleasures of wine and casual sex were freely available and life was, he wrote, "excusable only when we walk along the shores of pleasure and abandon all restraint."[4] Ibn Hamdis yearned eternally for his homeland, but things were, at least momentarily, good.

Seville's preeminence was relatively new. Had a young Muslim man of letters sought refuge in the region a century previously, he would have raced without hesitation to Córdoba, the regional capital of the Umayyed caliphate: a megacity of half a million inhabitants and one of the most sophisticated, awe-inspiring metropolises in the entire world, where scientists, astrologers, philosophers and mathematicians explored the mysteries of the universe while artisans and architects tested the boundaries of artistic perfection. But in 1031 the Umayyad caliphate had collapsed and Córdoba had sunk into intellectual torpor, its libraries looted, books burned and its famous workshops fallen idle.

Out of this vacuum had emerged several dozen small, nominally independent kingdoms—*taifas*—of which Seville ranked the foremost. (The others included Malaga and Granada, Toledo, Valencia, Denia, the Balearic Islands, Zaragoza and Lerida.) The *taifa*—the word means independent princely state, and is sometimes translated as "party kingdom"—of Seville comprised a large swathe of Islamic southern Spain, or al-Andalus. The city of Seville that lent its name lay some hundred and twenty-five miles north of the Strait of Gibraltar, organized around an *alcazar* (castle or palace) on the banks of the Guadalquivir River. Its dominions stretched at their furthest points from Silves and the Algarve on the Atlantic coast of modern Portugal, to Murcia in the east. Under the rule of al-Mu'tamid's dynasty, known as the Abbadids, Seville had swallowed up many of the petty kingdoms that surrounded it, and incorporated fine farmland, busy ports and strategic trading routes linking North Africa to the European mainland. It was famous for the quality of its musical instruments, crimson cloth-dye, sugarcane and olive oils. The prevailing attitude of its governing class was explained in verse by al-Mu'tamid's father. "I divide my time between hard work and leisure, / Mornings for affairs of state, evenings for pleasure!"[5]

Al-Mu'tamid's rule marked the apogee of Seville's power, and had he been a luckier ruler, or faced with somewhat different challenges, it is possible that he would have steadily continued to expand Seville's frontiers until he had reunited all the *taifas* into something that once again resembled the Umayyad caliphate, which collapsed shortly before he was born. As it turned out, he presided over its miserable disintegration, heralded in the first place by a king from the other end of Hispania: Alfonso VI of Castile and León.

Around two hundred fifty miles north-northeast of Seville lay the soaring, turreted stone walls of Toledo, once the mighty capital of the Visigothic empire, and now replete under Islamic rule with fine bridges and public baths, marketplaces and mosques. Toledo bestrode the wide, swift river Tagus—the longest waterway in Iberia, originating in the Montes Universales and emptying six hundred miles later into the Atlantic at Lisbon. Its valley and basin was frontier land, a contested liminal zone beyond which lay territory controlled by the Christian kings of northern Spain. There, as in the south, the country was divided between rival rulers who shared a religion but quarreled and jostled constantly for supremacy. Galicia, León, Castile, Aragon, Navarre and Barcelona were the most prominent of these northern states. and just as in the south, one state and one ruler superseded the others in power and influence.

From 1072 until his death in 1109 on the cusp of his seventieth birthday, King Alfonso VI was that ruler. His nickname was El Bravo, and he determined to live up to it. He held the crowns of Castile and León and ruled over Galicia and parts of Navarre. By territory and by reputation he was the foremost Christian monarch below the Pyrenees. He was described by one admiring chronicler as "a Catholic in all respects" and "so terrifying to evil doers that they never dared to show themselves in his sight."[6] Another wrote that he was "of great strength in both judgment and arms to a degree rarely found among mortal men."[7]

This was conventional praise, undoubtedly (and Alfonso has left far fainter and less romantic an impression on the Spanish popular imagination than his sometime retainer Rodrigo Díaz de Vivar, better known to history as *El Cid*), but these encomia were nonetheless reflective of the fact that, in roughly the same way al-Mu'tamid dominated the *taifas* of southern Spain, so Alfonso held sway in the north. His rise to power came after he overthrew his younger brother, Garcia, to seize Galicia, and subsequently profited from the violent demise of his elder brother, Sancho, who was murdered by trickery during a siege. During the course of his long life he took five wives and two concubines, fought numerous battles against Christian and Muslim foes and collected an impressive number of grandiose titles, including, from 1077, the sobriquet "*Imperator Totius Hispaniae*" (Emperor of All Spain). This was ambitious rather than strictly accurate: his imperium stretched from the Atlantic coast of Galicia in the west to Barcelona in the east, and was never fully secure below the Tagus, where al-Mu'tamid and several other *taifa* kings paid massive financial tributes known as *parias* to Alfonso to be left in peace. But if the title did not quite reflect political reality, it certainly indicated Alfonso's direction of travel. He was determined to expand his kingdom's frontiers, and it was a bold ruler indeed who dared to stand in his way.

During the second half of the eleventh century the ambitions of Alfonso and Christian princes like him were strongly encouraged by the papal court in Rome. There were, of course, ancient historical links between Rome and Spain—the conquest of *Hispania* had been a major theme of expansion for the Roman Republic from the third century BCE until its submission to Augustus in 19 BCE; the province thereafter remained part of the Roman Empire for nearly half a millennium. By the eleventh century CE popes sat where consuls and tyrants had once ruled supreme, and they had a similar form of conquest in mind. From the 1060s successive pontiffs took up the idea of bringing Christian parts of Spain under formal spiritual obedience to Rome: pushing to eliminate the "Mozarabic" liturgy followed by many Arabized Christians throughout the region in favor of the Latin one, and asserting their right to direct religious affairs and take financial tribute from the Christian peoples there.

In this they were partly following the crowd, for there was a growing interest in affairs below the Pyrenees on the part of knights, holy men and ordinary pilgrims from all over Western Europe. Warriors saw the opportunity to earn their fortune fighting in the frequent petty battles between the many rulers of the kingdoms and *taifas*. Monks following the reformed Cluniac rule (named for its origin at Cluny in Burgundy during the tenth century) were increasingly eager to introduce their observance into monasteries. Pious laymen who wished to cleanse their souls of sin followed the penitential road to Galicia known as the Way of Saint James, which led to the shrine of the apostle, known as Santiago de Compostela: one of the holiest sites in the Christian world. This could be a dangerous journey: one French guidebook of the early twelfth century issued grave warnings of the deadly impurity of the river water beside the road, and the loose morals of the people who dwelled there, such as Navarrese farmers who "practice unclean fornication" with their mules and mares.[8] But the journey was worth the discomfort. Miracles were frequently reported along the Way: soldiers' lances planted in a field near Sahagún had grown leaves; Saint James had revived a traveler wrongly hanged for theft; he had healed a young man who cut off his own penis in atonement for the sin of fornication.[9] And in the distant past—it was rumored to have been in the year 834 or 844—Saint James had supposedly appeared in armor at a battle against Spanish Muslims, helping Christian forces to victory—which earned him the nickname Santiago Matamoros—Saint James the Moor-slayer.

It would have been remiss for any occupant of Saint Peter's throne to ignore these trends, and from the 1060s papal proclamations were issued giving the explicit backing of Rome to efforts to expand the reach of Christian princes in Spain. In 1063 Pope Alexander II offered to absolve some of the sins of French or Italian knights who "determined to set out for Spain"—the implication from other letters of around the same time is that in "setting out for Spain" such knights were going to fight Muslims.[10] The ultimate destination of these fighting men would be the town of Barbastro, which was loyal to the Muslim ruler of Zaragoza. The chronicler known as Ibn Hayyan related a siege of forty days conducted by knights whom he generically called "the Christians," who in fact hailed from as near as Catalonia and as far away as Normandy and southern Italy. The siege initially seemed to have been concluded in a peaceful fashion, when the Christians cut off Barbastro's water supply by blocking an aqueduct, and the desperately thirsty citizens offered slaves and bribes for peace. But soon after, a massacre began, in which orders were given for a general looting and slaughter. "Upward of six thousand Muslims fell by the swords of the Christians," wrote Ibn Hayyan, detailing a panicked stampede of Barbastro's inhabitants toward the city's walls and gates, which led to many suffocating to death in a crush. Atrocities including the rape of daughters before their fathers and women before their husbands followed, and a merciless butchering of civilians was claimed by the chronicler to be an "invariable custom with the Christians whenever they took a town by force of arms . . . such were the crimes and excesses committed by the Christians on this occasion that there is no pen eloquent enough to describe them."[11]

With its cosmopolitan knightly presence, papal sanction, spectacularly bloodthirsty methods and explicit invocation of a religious agenda, the attack on Barbastro in 1063 plainly foreshadowed many of what would later come to be seen as the essential elements of Christian "crusading." In the context of Spain in the late eleventh century, however, it was significant because it heralded a shift toward a more aggressive policy of expansion—(later to be referred to as the *Reconquista* or "reconquest") by the Christian states of the north. Inevitably this expansion was directed toward their Muslim neighbors in the *taifas*. And it continued to be heartily encouraged by Rome. Gregory VII was elected pope following Alexander II's death in 1073, and wasted no time in issuing his own views on Spanish conquest.

"We believe . . . that the kingdom of Spain belonged from ancient times to Saint Peter in full sovereignty," wrote Gregory at the beginning of his papacy. Notwithstanding Alfonso VI's own claims to be the emperor of all Spain, this was all the encouragement required. When Alfonso sent one of his lords south into Granada to collect the *paria* tribute due from that *taifa*'s prince, 'Abd Allah, the latter made it clear that he understood exactly which way the wind was now blowing. In a passage recorded in his brilliant chronicle, known as *The Tibyan,* 'Abd Allah summed up the new position. "Al-Andalus originally belonged to the Christians. Then they were defeated by the Arabs. . . . Now that they are strong and capable, the Christians desire to recover what they have lost by force."[12]

'Abd Allah wrote these lines in the 1090s but hindsight did not exactly cloud his judgment. The massacre at Barbastro was followed by a series of concerted campaigns directed by the ubiquitous Alfonso VI. In either 1082 or 1083 following a series of increasingly extortionate demands for tribute payments, al-Mu'tamid of Seville decided to stop paying *parias* to Alfonso. To underline his point, and evoking his father's worst excesses, he executed the ambassador Alfonso had sent to make the demand.[13] In response, Alfonso launched a series of attacks on Seville in the summer of 1083. His troops sliced directly through the middle of the al-Mu'tamid's lands, and Alfonso himself rode all the way to Tarifa, trotting his horse into the waves breaking on the beach, beyond which the rugged coastline of North Africa was clearly visible. "This is the very end of Spain, and I have set foot upon it!" he declared.

A year later he set his sights on a prize closer to home: the city of Toledo, where the ineffectual Muslim ruler al-Qadir had been deposed by his disgruntled people. Affecting to do right by a dispossessed fellow monarch, Alfonso besieged Toledo. The city was overrun by May 6, 1085. But al-Qadir was not returned to power; instead he was shipped off to Toledo's onetime colony of Valencia to serve as a puppet ruler there. In Toledo, Alfonso took direct control of what had until very recently been one of the mightiest cities in Muslim Spain. The conquest was therefore a watershed, both politically and symbolically. It shocked the Islamic world.[14] "We are caught up with an enemy who will not leave us alone: How can one live in a basket together with snakes?" wailed one observer.[15] Alfonso now controlled a huge stretch of the Tagus valley, and a very large number of Muslims both within and outside the walls of Toledo now found themselves living not in a *taifa* but under the protection of a Christian king.

Alfonso avoided the lamentable butchery that had been a feature of Barbastro two decades earlier and he guaranteed freedom of Islamic worship in return for an annual tax and allowed the central mosque in Toledo to remain in Muslim hands. Yet he was not entirely a paragon of tolerance: in 1086 he justified his conquest of Toledo to a clerical audience on the grounds that he had known "it would be pleasing in the sight of the Lord if I, Alfonso the emperor, under the leadership of Christ, were able to restore to the devotees of his faith the city which wicked people under the evil guidance of their leader Muhammad had taken from the Christians."[16] And he augmented his self-aggrandizing title "Emperor of All Spain" with another: the equally vainglorious "Emperor of the Two Religions." The battle to make good on Alfonso's bold claims would occupy Christian rulers of Spain for the next four centuries.

The poet-king al-Mu'tamid had been roundly humiliated by Alfonso, who with the fall of the *taifa* of Toledo now became his direct neighbor. To protect himself, therefore, al-Mu'tamid looked south, across the Gibraltar Strait, to Morocco and western Algeria, where power lay in the hands of a notoriously vicious and puritanical sect of Berbers known as the Almoravids (al-Murabitan). The Almoravids followed a punitively strict interpretation of Qur'anic law, covered their faces with veils, based themselves in fortified monasteries known as *ribats* and had precious little time for the sensual indulgences of al-Mu'tamid's court, where, in the king's own words, "I walk amid squadrons of beautiful women who add luster to high rank. And through the weapons of my warriors scatter darkness / the wine handed round by young women fills us with light."[17] Their leader, Yusuf ibn Tashfin, called himself emir of the Muslims (*amir al-muslimin*)—and possessed a similar level of self-belief as the accursed Alfonso. The Almoravids' conquests in North Africa left no room for doubt about their martial ability. Asking for their assistance in al-Andalus was by definition asking for trouble. But al-Mu'tamid had little choice. On the fall of Toledo he invited Yusuf ibn Tashfin to invade, justifying it with the bleakest humor: he would rather herd camels for the men from the south, he said, than guard a pigsty for the infidels.

He was, in effect, giving up his kingdom. In the early summer of 1086 the Almoravids poured across the strait and, having been sweetened by generous gifts from the supine prince of Seville, marched on Alfonso's armies, heavily defeating them at the battle of Sagrajas (Zallaqa) on October 23. Alfonso was seriously injured, stabbed through the thigh in hand-to-hand combat by a black African soldier whose dagger penetrated so deep that it pinned Alfonso's leg to the padding of his saddle.[18] He lost three hundred knights and about half of his twenty-five-hundred-strong army, but the wound to his prestige was even greater. A later Moroccan chronicler called it "one of the most celebrated victories in al-Andalus . . . by which God . . . cut off Alfonso's ambitions."[19] Yusuf sent the severed heads of the vanquished Christians to the cities of al-Andalus, loaded in great grisly piles on wooden carts.[20] He then went home, leaving Alfonso in possession of Toledo. Both of them had a great deal to think about.

When al-Mu'tamid had sent for the Almoravids he had known that he was making a pact with the devil. In 1090 the awful consequences of his strategy became plain. Yusuf was undoubtedly committed to preserving the Islamic sanctity and unity of al-Andalus—but after consulting legal experts in Morocco he concluded that this did not oblige him to preserve the thrones of the weak and helpless party kings of the *taifas*. The willingness of the latter to pay tribute to the infidel monarchs of the north left them fatally compromised, and—Yusuf reasoned—ripe for deposition by someone better suited to defending Islam.

When in September the Almoravids attacked and deposed al-Mu'tamid's neighbor kings in Malaga and Granada, it became horrifyingly plain what was coming next. In the summer of 1091 Yusuf turned on al-Mu'tamid and besieged Seville. In a hideous irony, al-Mu'tamid sent a plea for assistance to King Alfonso, who was far away fighting against another *taifa* lord in Zaragoza. He answered the call, but too late. In November Seville fell. Al-Mu'tamid's sons were forced to hand over the keys to the *alcazar,* and the poet-king was taken away by ship to prison in Morocco. He had sealed the fate not only of his kingdom but of all the other *taifa* states, which by the end of the century had almost all submitted to the Almoravids, to become part of a North African empire that owed religious obedience (at least in theory) to the Abbasid caliph, far away in Baghdad. Little territory had been won back from the Christian states of the north, although the *parias* were no longer collected. Otherwise al-Mu'tamid's policy had been a total failure.

The sight of al-Mu'tamid leaving his kingdom was evidently a pitiful one. The poet Ibn al-Labbana, a contemporary and friend of Ibn Hamdis in the now disbanded circle of literati who had once frolicked at the court of Seville, wrote:

> I will forget everything
> except that morning
> beside the Guadalquivir
> when they were taken onto the ships
> like the dead to their graves . . . [21]

The lamenting was evidently justified, for al-Mu'tamid also wrote bitterly of his downfall while in prison in Aghmat.

> I say to my chains,
> don't you understand?

I have surrendered to you.
Why, then, have you no pity,
no tenderness?[22]

He was murdered in 1095. His rival Alfonso VI lived on until 1109, when he died while still defending Toledo from an Almoravid attack. In an attempt to curry favor with the Muslims living under his rule, he had taken as a concubine a woman called Zaida, one of al-Mu'tamid's daughters-in-law. But this was as far as his accommodation with Islam went.

Ibn Hamdis, meanwhile, was outcast once again. Thirteen years after arriving in Seville from Sicily, he had seen his adopted homeland go the same way as his birthplace: ripped apart by warfare and seized by a foreign invader—albeit on this occasion an Islamic rather than a Christian one. Ibn Hamdis fled when al-Mu'tamid was captured in 1091 and subsequently wandered for the rest of his life between the courts of Ifriqiya, Algeria and Morocco, where he lived by his pen before ending his days in Majorca. He died blind, alone and full of regret, nearly eighty years old, in 1133. In his verse he advised others to avoid at all costs his own experience.

"Chain yourself to the country which is your beloved homeland," he wrote, "and die in your own abode."[23]

3

Empire Under Siege

The most sacred empire of the Greek Christians is being sorely distressed.

On December 2, 1083, the Byzantine princess Anna Komnene was born—quite literally—to the purple, in the Porphyry Chamber at her father's Great Palace of Constantinople. Her birth was slow and difficult, but later in her life she would repeat with pride the story her mother liked to tell to explain a labor that lasted more than forty-eight hours. As the date of Anna's birth approached, her father, the Byzantine emperor, was absent. The court nervously awaited his return from war against the Normans of southern Italy. Her fifteen-year-old mother, making the sign of the cross over her own hugely swollen belly, vowed not to be delivered of a child until her husband was safely home. This caused some concern in the palace, since the emperor's return was feared to be still a month distant. But fortunately he arrived in time for his firstborn to be healthily delivered. To Anna this "very clearly signified even in [the] womb the love I was destined to have for my parents in the future. For thereafter, when I grew to womanhood and reached years of reason, I had beyond doubt a great affection for both of them alike." [1]

To be born a princess of Byzantium was a privilege; to emerge into the world in the Porphyry Chamber more glorious still. The room looked out over Bosphorus Strait, with a view of the harbor and the sparkling blue Sea of Marmara beyond. Square sided, with its walls tapering to a pyramid roof, the chamber was paved and clad with marble "generally of a purple color . . .

but with white spots like sand sprinkled over it."[2] Porphyry was an imperial stone—originally mined from quarries in the eastern deserts of Egypt. Elsewhere in Constantinople it had been used to construct the Column of Constantine, which commemorated the city's establishment as a new capital for the Roman Empire in the fourth century CE. Purple was the imperial color, reserved for the use of the imperial family alone. Emperors wore purple clothes dyed with a foul-smelling extract made from sea snails. They hung their palaces with purple decorations. They even signed documents using purple ink. And only the children of reigning emperors could be born in this purple-walled room: those who were became known as *porphyrogennetoi*. Anna was one of this exclusive royal group, and she was eternally grateful for it.

Anna's imperial parents were Alexios I Komnenos and his wife, Irene Doukaina. Irene was the daughter of a high-ranking military officer and a Bulgarian aristocrat. Alexios was a hardnosed general who had swept into power as Byzantine emperor in a coup during the summer of 1081, two years before his daughter was born. Anna Komnene described both her parents in glowing terms: Alexios "reminded one of a fiery whirlwind . . . his dark eyebrows were curved and beneath them the gaze of his eyes was both terrible and kind . . . his broad shoulders, muscular arms and deep chest, all on a heroic scale, invariably commanded the wonder and delight of people." Irene, meanwhile, "stood upright like some young, proud, always-blossoming shoot, each limb and her whole body in perfect symmetry and complete harmony . . . her face shone with the soft light of the moon . . . there were rose blossoms on her cheeks, visible a long way off."[3] As for Anna herself, born and raised in palatial splendor on the banks of the Bosphorus, she showed an early and lifelong hunger for learning, letters, rhetoric and philosophy. She surrounded herself with scholars, whom she patronized richly and loved to debate. She was known to one of them as "wise Anna, absolute intellect, home of the Graces."[4]

Anna Komnene's gift to both her beloved parents and to scholarship was to compose, late in life, a long history of her father's reign: the first major Western history by a woman. Written in Greek and with a heavily exculpatory skew, her book, known as the *Alexiad,* narrated, justified and excused the events between Alexios's rise to power in 1081 and his death in 1118. It provided an extraordinary insight into the fraught politics of the Byzantine Empire at the turn of the twelfth century. The *Alexiad* was alive with gossip, insider knowledge, portraits of Byzantines, their friends and their foes, battle stories, tangled tales of political intrigue and effortless scholarly allusions to historians of past times. Despite Anna's bias toward her father, a man she described as being of "supreme virtue"—her book still revealed in its colorful prose the pressures that mounted upon the empire and its emperor during the 1080s and 1090s.[5] Above all, it explained Alexios's fateful decision in 1095 to ask Western Christian rulers to help him stabilize his realm, which eventually opened up the East to crusader armies, who poured forth with extraordinary and epoch-shifting results.

The Byzantine Empire into which Anna Komnene was born was, although linguistically and culturally Greek, in fact the lineal descendent of the Roman Empire. The name, a historians' term coined in the later Middle Ages, derives from its capital city: Constantinople, which had once been called Byzantion or Byzantium. (Today it is Istanbul.) But in Anna and her father's day, people described both city and empire in quite different terms. In 330 CE the city was consecrated by Constantine the Great as a "New Rome" (*Nova Roma*)—a strategically placed metropolis on the intersection of several trade routes and military superhighways from where Roman emperors could govern Roman interests in the eastern Mediterranean—regions such as Egypt, Thessaly, Thrace, Asia Minor, Syria and upper Mesopotamia. It was every inch a Roman city, packed with elegant buildings and great civic spaces, including a forum and hippodrome. After the Roman Empire was partitioned in 395 CE, Constantinople became the capital of the Eastern Empire and it stood defiant when the "old" Rome was sacked fifteen years later and the Western Empire collapsed. Seven centuries on from these upheavals, Anna, her family and everyone else still referred to Byzantium in classical terms. Alexios was the "Roman emperor." His people were the Romans. They lived in the Roman Empire or "Romania." Even Arabic speakers concurred: this was the "Bilad al-Rum" (Land of the Romans).[6]

In the mid-eleventh century Byzantium still commanded a vast swath of territory besides Constantinople and its immediate environs. In the West the empire extended to Apulia and Calabria in Italy and Dalmatia at the northern end of the Adriatic Sea. In the Balkans, virtually everywhere between the Danube and the Peloponnese theoretically answered the emperor's call, and his authority also reached to the northern shores of the Black Sea and the Crimean Peninsula. The islands of Crete, Rhodes and Cyprus in the eastern Mediterranean all fell under imperial rule. And overland, stretching off toward the Middle East, Byzantine dominions included Asia Minor, Cilicia, the coastline of Greater Syria including the city of Antioch, the upper reaches of the Tigris and Euphrates rivers, and the salty waters of Lake Van, formed by the volcanic mountains that today mark the borderlands between Turkey, Azerbaijan and Iran. All of this, in theory, was ruled from Constantinople, where Alexios could most often be found in his favorite residence: the redeveloped and heavily fortified Palace of Blachernae in the north of Constantinople, just inside the vast walls that protected the city's landward approach.

Or perhaps not quite *all*. For when, in 1081, Alexios seized the throne from the hapless Nikephoros III, he found that the imperial crown came with a long list of problems. For a start, aristocratic rebellions of the sort he himself had led against Nikephoros continued to be fomented, and these were now exacerbated by the fact that, as a usurper, the twenty-five-year-old Alexios's right to rule Byzantium was inherently open to question. Just as serious were the external threats that loomed in the further reaches of the empire. In Italy (as we have seen) the Norman adventurers Robert Guiscard and Roger I of Sicily had taken Calabria and Apulia, and were consolidating their gains in that part of the world by subjugating Sicily—itself once a Byzantine colony, before the days of the Arabs. The Normans were also pushing into the Balkans: after a thumping battlefield victory in 1081 over imperial troops at Dyrrhachium (Dyrrakhion, or Durrës in modern Albania), Robert Guiscard had set his sights on snatching the imperial territories of Macedonia and Thessaly.

Meanwhile, in the north, imperial possessions were being continually harassed from the direction of the Danube by the Pechenegs (Patzinak), a semi-nomadic tribal people with an aptitude for bracing, relentless violence, which they deployed at various times against all their neighbors, including the Byzantines. Anna Komnene often called the Pechenegs "Scythians"—a catch-all term for the innumerable peoples who lived north of the Black and Caspian seas.

Finally, in the east loomed Turkic people known as the Seljuqs, who presented a menace every bit as persistent as the Normans and as dangerous as the Pechenegs. Much like the Pechenegs, the Seljuqs were a loose federation of Turkic tribesmen originally from the Oghuz-speaking regions of the central

Asian steppe. By Anna Komnene's day they had already conquered much of Persia, converting to Sunni Islam along the way. A bureaucrat called Ibn Hassul, who worked for the Seljuqs, wrote that "God has created them in the shape of lions, with broad faces and flat noses. Their muscles are strong, their fists are enormous. . . . They ascend high mountains, ride in the face of danger, climb distant peaks, raid narrow abysses and go deep into unknown lands."[7] Expert horsemen and fierce warriors, the Seljuqs had swept into Anatolia during the 1070s. In August 1071 imperial forces had suffered a humiliating defeat at Manzikert in eastern Anatolia, where they were routed by troops under Alp Arslan, the Great Seljuq sultan.* Since then the Seljuqs had been busy carving out their own empire in Asia Minor, which would come to be known as the Sultanate of Rum.

Understandably hostile to these pillagers of the empire, Anna characterized the Turks (*Τούρκοι*—she did not use the term Seljuq) as treacherous barbarians.[8] Another near contemporary called them "winged serpents . . . bloodthirsty beasts . . . the savage nation of infidels."[9] They were certainly as effective as their reputation suggested. By 1085 the Seljuqs had either taken or were on the verge of taking cities throughout the empire, as far west as Smyrna, barely two hundred miles from Constantinople. By 1091 the empire was beset on all sides. Word had spread as far as the courts of Western Europe that Byzantium was teetering on the brink of collapse. Not for the first time, the barbarians were at the gates of Rome. And so, like his contemporary al-Mu'tamid, the king of the *taifa* kingdom of Seville, Emperor Alexios calculated that his best hope of saving his throne was to encourage others to do his fighting for him.

Alexios's decision to counter the threats against the Byzantine Empire by appealing outside the realm for support was not especially novel. In fact, military alliances were the way of the world in Byzantium, where the sheer size of the empire often demanded forms of political and military realpolitik, not stiff-necked dogmatism, let alone faith-based policymaking. As his prob-

*Rather embarrassingly, at Manzikert (August 26, 1071) Alp Arslan took the then emperor Romanos IV Diogenes prisoner, then patronized him by setting him free on payment of a large ransom. On his return to Constantinople, Romanos faced a string of rebellions, following which he was deposed and horribly blinded. He died of infection consequent to his wounds in 1072.

lems mounted, therefore, the emperor began to look for allies wherever he could find them.

On April 29, 1091, Alexios dealt decisively with the Pechenegs by drawing their forces into battle and annihilating them on a plain beside of Mount Lebounion, near the mouth of the Hebros (Marica) River in Thrace. It was a stunning rout—perhaps his greatest military victory. And the key to his success was the fact that the Byzantine army was bolstered that day by another group of tribal warriors, called the Cumans. There was little love lost between the Byzantines and the Cumans: Anna described them as "longing to gorge on human blood and human flesh and . . . more than ready to amass booty from our territories."[10] But, bribed sufficiently, they helped Alexios win a thundering victory. Describing the battle, Anna naturally gave her father a starring role: "charging into the midst of the enemy . . . hacking at his immediate adversaries and with loud cries striking fear into those far off . . . a whole people, numbered not in their tens of thousands, but in countless multitudes, with their women and children, was utterly wiped out on that day."[11]

If the Pechenegs were relatively simply despatched, however, the threat from the Seljuq Turks in the east was of a different order. In part this stemmed from Alexios's ambiguous dealings with the Seljuqs in the first decade of his reign. Despite their frequent incursions into Byzantine territory, the emperor had at times extended the hand of friendship to the Turks. Before the battle of Dyrrhachium in the first year of his reign, he had asked them for military assistance against the Normans, and during the 1080s had cultivated a working relationship with the Great Seljuq sultan Malik-Shah in Baghdad as well as several high-ranking Turkish chieftains on the ground in Asia Minor. Alexios's aim was appeasement by way of striking up collaborative rule in those towns of Asia Minor that the Turks coveted, and which he felt could be entrusted to Turkish lords happy to cooperate with imperial policy on the condition that they defend them against rebellious imperial vassals or other enemies from further abroad.[12] At one point the emperor even considered a proposal from Malik-Shah suggesting a marriage between Anna and the sultan's eldest son, a deal that only fell through because Anna had been betrothed at birth to a Byzantine princeling of her mother's family.* In trying to manage the Seljuqs like this, Alexios was playing with fire, but he had few better options.

*Anna's intended was Constantine Doukas, son of the deposed former emperor Michael VII Doukas (r. 1071–78), *porphyrogennetos* and, from 1081 to 1087, the official "junior emperor" to Alexios.

As it turned out, by 1091 the policy of cautious cooperation with the Seljuqs had spectacularly failed. In that year Malik-Shah died, to be replaced as sultan by a son who quickly proved to be much less accommodating. Soon enough, friendly Turkish governors of Byzantine strongholds were replaced by hostile ones. And four years later, in 1095, the whole fragile system had comprehensively fallen apart. The Turks were in control of cities from Antioch in the east to Nicaea, Nikomedia and Smyrna in the west, and controlled the entire Aegean coast of Asia Minor. In the Balkans, tribesman from Serbia were raiding south into imperial territory, requiring military expeditions to see them off. Alexios's resources were stretched perilously thin and the burden of constant campaigning, together with the cost of bribing allies, was draining the treasury. Debasements of the gold coinage had seriously undermined its worth and credibility. Mutinous rumblings could be heard everywhere in Constantinople, supported by the aristocracy, military, court and church alike. Alexios had come to power by means of a coup, his subjects began to mutter; why should he not be removed the same way?[13] The emperor was facing a grave crisis. And in those circumstances, Alexios chose a course of action that would prove fateful, if entirely in character: he decided to appeal to the West for assistance.

Considering the difficulties the Normans had caused Byzantium over the years, it might be thought odd that in the 1090s Alexios chose to look for help in the very direction from which tormentors like Robert Guiscard had come. For Anna Komnene, writing with hindsight, the people of Western or "Latin" Europe could be described generically as "Kelts" and they were as a rule the last groups she would ever recommend trusting. Yet in the mid-1090s her father's need was great, and his experience suggested that from time to time one did come across a Kelt who was not totally unreliable. At the beginning of his reign Alexios had paid the German emperor Henry IV a massive tribute of 360,000 gold marks to attack Robert Guiscard in Italy: a valuable piece of business that distracted the Norman from his assaults on Byzantine

Before his betrothal to Anna Komnene, Constantine had been betrothed to Olympias, a daughter of Robert Guiscard. The annulment of this betrothal served as a pretext for Robert's invasion of imperial territories. Not for nothing has the word Byzantine become in modern times a byword for "bewilderingly complex."

possessions.[14] A decade later Alexios's greatest military victory—the obliteration of the Pechenegs at Lebounion in 1091—had been aided by five hundred knights from Flanders, sent by their overlord, Robert, Count of Flanders,* who had met Alexios on his way back from a pilgrimage to Jerusalem in 1089.[15] Not all Kelts were bad. And just as Alexios was prepared to turn to the Turks or Cumans as allies when he felt it expedient, so he was more than happy to appeal to the Christians of the West if it seemed to be in the Empire's best interests.

In 1091, around the same time as the great battle of Lebounion, a letter was sent from Constantinople to "Robert, lord and glorious count of Flanders, and to all the princes in the entire realm, lovers of the Christian faith, laymen as well as clerics." It complained that "the most sacred empire of the Greek Christians is being sorely distressed by the Pechenegs and the Turks, who daily ravage it." The author of the letter also told horror stories of atrocities being committed elsewhere in the empire by the Turks: holy places destroyed, decapitations rife, bishops sodomized, boys forcibly circumcised and forced to urinate over their own blood in baptismal fonts, rapists deflowering "virgins in front of their own mothers and forc[ing] them to sing wicked and obscene songs until they have finished having their way with them." The author cried that "almost nothing now remains [of the empire] except Constantinople, which they are threatening to snatch away from us very soon," and he begged the Count of Flanders to send Christian warriors for the love of God and for the salvation of the "faithful Greek Christians."[16]

Who wrote the letter is not at all certain. It has been claimed as the work of Alexios himself. It has been dismissed as a total forgery. But what is not disputed is that other similar appeals *were* made on Alexios's behalf all across the West. From 1091 a campaign of urgent pleas for help went out to noble and royal courts all over Europe, wailing of atrocities and grotesque offenses against Christian propriety. Ambassadors were sent far and wide, tugging on heartstrings and purse strings alike. In Venice lucrative trading privileges were dangled before the *doge*, including tax exemptions, legal immunity for Venetian merchants and exclusive access to the best parts of ports throughout the empire—all in return for financial support for the empire's depleted treasury. In France and Germany, Byzantine diplomats brought gifts of relics

*Robert, Count of Flanders, had a Norman connection: his sister Matilda married William the Conqueror, the first Norman king of England (r. 1066–87).

for churches, coupled with dire warnings of the imperiled state of Christendom and Christians throughout the East, whose fate, they claimed, depended on the whole Christian community throughout the world pulling together against the depravity of "pagans." Tacked on to the tales of woe in the empire were drastic tales of pilgrims being abused and holy places defiled in Syria and Palestine—including in Jerusalem, the city of Christ's ministry and Passion. The intention behind these horror stories was clear and deliberate: to stir up Christians in the West against the enemies of Byzantium in the hope that they would come to the emperor's assistance against the supposed perpetrators.

Alexios, although much put upon, was not stupid. Throughout his reign, whenever he sent for help from faraway powers, he did so in the knowledge that the policy might backfire. In appealing to the West for help against the Turks bearing down on Asia Minor he was well aware of the reputation of the warriors he was calling in to join the fight. They were not quite the veiled Islamic puritans who had crossed from Morocco to southern Spain at the beckoning of al-Mu'tamid of Seville. But the Franks were nevertheless notorious for their "uncontrollable passion, erratic character and their unpredictability, not to mention . . . their greed for money . . . which always led them to break their own agreements without a scruple."[17] Alexios knew this, wrote his daughter, but he called for them anyway. What he was not expecting was that "the whole of the west and the entire people living between the Adriatic and the Straits of Gibraltar migrated in a body to Asia, marching from one end of Europe to another with their whole households in tow."[18]

Yet that is what happened. Alexios's wheedling call from the East was more effective than he, Anna, or indeed anyone around them—including their Turkish tormentors—could have imagined. For it was refracted, modified and delivered to a willing audience by a dangerously brilliant orator, Pope Urban II. The response he incited among his flock would warp the course of history in the Mediterranean and beyond for centuries.

4

Deus Vult!

You must hasten to carry aid to your brethren dwelling in the East.

Pope Urban II was elected by a partial conclave of cardinals in the Italian coastal town of Terracina on March 12, 1088. It was not a very auspicious start to a papacy. Terracina lay about fifty-five miles south of Rome, but the traditional seat of the papacy was barred to Urban and his friends. Instead, the throne of Saint Peter was occupied by an antipope known as Clement III: a puppet and factotum of the Holy Roman Emperor, the headstrong thirty-eight-year-old Henry IV. Henry's imperial troops blocked the gates, and the capricious populace were given to rioting at the arrival of would-be pontiffs who did not meet their approval. The previous year, in his capacity as cardinal-bishop of Ostia, Urban had presided over the consecration of the short-lived Pope Victor III in the Eternal City. But now *his* turn had arrived, and he found himself being installed at a minor cathedral in a second-string seaside resort.

Urban was used to grander things. He was born Odo of Lagery in the 1030s to a noble family of Châtillon-sur-Marne in the northeastern French province of Champagne. The German chronicler Bernold of St. Blasien described him as "distinguished for his piety and learning."[1] The cardinal-bishopric of Ostia, which he held for a decade from 1078, was prestigious, and had earned him work as a papal legate and diplomat to the imperial court in Germany. There Odo had endured some unpleasant hardships, including being briefly imprisoned at the emperor's behest. He had thus learned a great deal about the poisonous political rivalry between the Holy Roman Empire and the Holy

See. The Holy Roman Emperor, who was usually also king of the Germans and the overlord of a swath of central Europe, was conventionally crowned by the pope, in a tradition reaching back to Charlemagne. But in the latter half of the eleventh century cordial relations between emperors and popes broke down completely. Although this meant Urban's coronation was an anticlimax, it also left him constantly alert to projects that could help bring the community of Christendom back together—a wish that was eventually and spectacularly realized in the crusades.

Although Urban had ascended, in a fashion, to office of pope, the formative years of his life had come with a tonsure and not a miter on his head, for he had spent much of his life as a monk at the magnificent and vastly influential Abbey of Cluny in Burgundy. Cluny was the command center for a large and vigorous network of religious houses that had sprung up and spread across Western Europe during the tenth and eleventh centuries. The abbey was founded by Duke William I "the Pious" of Aquitaine in 910 CE, who dedicated it to Saint Peter and granted the brothers who lived there freedom from oversight by any authority save that of the papacy. The monks spent their lives in never-ending, very solemn cycles of worship known as perpetual prayer, which they offered amid a complex of soaring buildings including a majestic abbey church, the second rebuilding of which began in the year of Urban's election to the papacy.* Cluniacs did not reinvent monasticism wholesale, but they popularized a much stricter form of the Benedictine Rule that had been in use since the sixth century. They disdained physical labor, which they considered distracting from contemplative life, and instead embraced a more rigorous approach, conducted in magnificent surroundings but with a puritanical attention to the principles of silence, prayer and solitude.

Just as significantly as remodeling the daily routine of monasticism, Cluny pioneered a new way of organizing monks and their houses. Members comprised the Cluniac Order—a body of churchmen whose shared identity emphasized an overarching, international unity as well as deep seriousness of purpose, dignity, opulence and a bombastic approach to church-building.

Whereas traditional Benedictine monasteries were stand-alone communi-

*Historians call this second rebuilding of Cluny's abbey church "Cluny III"; when complete it would be the largest church building in the world.

ties following the same rule under independent abbots, Cluniac houses were part of a tightly controlled collective in which Cluny was the leader. "Daughter" houses, no matter in which realm they were situated, were classed as priories, and each was answerable to the abbot of Cluny.[2] By the end of the eleventh century there were more than a thousand of these daughter houses: some original foundations and others monasteries that had been transferred by their benefactors to the Cluniac system.

When he was a young man Odo of Lagery had traveled to Cluny and joined the prestigious motherhouse. He arrived—and flourished—under the tenure of the great statesman and future saint Abbot Hugh (Hugh of Semur; later Saint Hugh of Cluny). Hugh's extraordinary physical energy, force of personality and close connections with the leading kings and noblemen of his day provided a model for a career in high politics from within the cloister, and the abbot proved a patron of Odo's throughout his life: promoting him to the lofty position of prior of Cluny, thrusting him toward high diplomatic circles and remaining a close counselor all his life. Odo loved the place—saying later in life that Cluny "shines like another sun over the earth."[3] It fueled his passion for centralization and Church reform. It informed his opinions on relations between Christians and Muslims around the Mediterranean, and the transformative power of mass popular pilgrimage. So although Odo departed Cluny in 1078 for Rome to join a new master-mentor—the equally formidable Pope Gregory VII—much of what he learned in Cluny stuck with him until his dying day. The issues in which Cluny had been entangled and the structures through which it worked shaped his papacy—and consequently influenced the whole development of the crusades.[4]

Nestled away in the Maconnais in southern Burgundy, more than five hundred miles from Muslim Spain, seven hundred from Sicily and twelve hundred from Constantinople, Cluny appeared to be far removed from the front line of tensions between Muslims and Christians in the eleventh century. Yet its recent history told a different story. Only one hundred years earlier, the abbot of Cluny had been a shy and bookish disciplinarian by the name of Majolus (954/956–994 CE), so pious that he had a habit of bursting into tears of rapture on a near daily basis.[5] Majolus had seen conflict between Muslims and Christians at close quarter. In 972, the abbot was traveling through the Alps when he and his companions were set upon by émigré Arabs from al-Andalus who had set up a fortified enclave at Fraxinet (Jabal al-Qilal—today La Garde-Freinet, near Saint-Tropez). These Arabs kidnapped Majolus, offered him the chance to convert to Islam, and, when he refused, clapped him in irons and threw him in a cave, sending word to Cluny that the monks could have him back for one thousand pounds of silver.[6] Fortunately for Majolus, Cluny was flush with coin. Thus the good abbot arrived back in Cluny in one piece and lived another twenty years, displaying a miraculous ability to heal dog bites and cure ailments like blindness, paralysis and fever. The Arabs of Fraxinet, however, were less fortunate. The following year, 973, Count William I of Provence avenged Cluny's honor by raising an army and routing Majolus's kidnappers on a plain beside Fraxinet known as Tourtour. Every one of them was put to flight, enslaved or killed. Although all this had occurred before Odo's time, it was a famous story with two powerful lessons. First, the enemies of Cluny and Christ could be easily conflated. Second, punitive military action was often the only language such people understood.

The gripping yarn of Majolus's adventure with the Arabs was not the only way in which Cluny influenced Odo's worldview—for the abbey was also intimately invested in the Reconquista—the war between the Christian kingdoms of northern Spain and the Muslim *taifa* kingdoms of the south. Cluniac houses could be found all along the roads from France and northern Italy into Spain, for prestigious monasteries were placed deliberately as stopping points where pilgrims to Santiago de Compostela or volunteers heading to join the Spanish wars could sleep, eat, pray and marvel at holy relics as they traveled down through the Pyrenees.[7] Moreover, as the Christian kingdoms of Spain expanded, Cluniac monks set up new houses in their wake, providing hubs for the indoctrination of Mozarabic Christians and Muslim converts and impressing lords and peasants alike with their reputation for *celebritas*, *probitas* and *sanctitas* (fame, probity and holiness).[8]

During Odo's time at Cluny, connections between Spain and the abbey had been strong and personal. Abbot Hugh was a confidant, adviser and uncle to the great Reconquista warrior king Alfonso VI of Castile and León, and the monks of Cluny therefore took care to pray for Alfonso's well-being and salvation. (Considering Alfonso had locked up one of his brothers and may have had a hand in killing the other, there was plenty to pray for.) In recognition of Cluny's role in laundering his soul and enriching his kingdom's spiritual well-being and tourist industry, Alfonso made sure the order was lucratively rewarded. From 1077, he sent two thousand gold pieces (*aurei*) every year to Cluny, with larger one-off payments on request. This lavish commitment, which allowed Abbot Hugh to build on such an enormous scale, was funded by Alfonso's punitive tribute taking from *taifa* kings such as al-Mu'tamid of Seville, al-Muqtadir of Zaragoza and al-Mutawwakil of Badajoz.[9] The chain of appropriation was clear: Alfonso took from his unbelieving neighbors and invested, via Cluny, in the glory of the Church.

Here, then, was a model for Urban's vision of the Church at large: centralized, expansionist, alive to the possibilities of popular devotion, particularly when they involved long-distance travel, integrated with the priorities and even the families of secular kings, and thoroughly approving of attacks on the forces of Islam in the Mediterranean theater. It is telling indeed that one of the former Cluniac Urban's most eye-catching actions in the first year of his papacy was to issue a bull granting the Spanish city of Toledo (snatched by Alfonso from Muslim rule in 1085) primacy in all spiritual matters below the Pyrenees. He later appointed Bernard of Sédirac, a one-time Cluniac monk, as the first archbishop of Toledo. In his confirmation of this appointment, Urban noted approvingly that "through the efforts of the most glorious king Alfonso and with the hard work of the Christian people, after the Muslims were expelled, the city of Toledo was restored to the rite of the Christians . . . [We] offer great thanks to God, as is fitting, for the fact that he granted to the Christian people in our time so magnificent a victory."[10] It was a neat and alluring calculus: what the warrior had plundered, the pope sanctified.

Cluny, then, left its mark. Yet this was only part of the story, for as Pope Urban II, Odo was just as deeply swayed in his pontifical thinking by the agenda of his most belligerent predecessor: the great "reform pope" Gregory VII. Born around 1015 in Tuscany, and given the peasant name Hildebrand by parents of far humbler stock than Urban's, Gregory was an abrasive, relentless pontiff: small and feeble voiced, but propelled through life by a combination of almost unbelievable high-handedness, pugnacity and self-belief. His friend, the intellectual Peter Damian, famously described Gregory as a "holy Satan." His enemies called him far worse.

Between his consecration as pope in 1073 and his death in 1085, Gregory made it his mission to transform the standing of the papacy throughout Christendom, following—and extending—a tradition reaching back to the papacy of Nicholas II (1059–1061). Causes that received the enthusiastic attention of reformers included simony (the buying or selling of church offices) and clerical marriage. But at the heart of the "Gregorian" reform program was an insistence that all secular rulers—be they emperors, kings or anything besides—should acknowledge the supremacy of Christ's vicar on earth. In 1075 Gregory published his *Dictatus Papae,* which laid out in strident terms the political spine of his papacy: twenty-seven axioms asserting doctrines of absolute papal supremacy and infallibility, declaring that all popes were by definition saints, and assigning to them the sole right to call synods, pick bishops, judge the most important cases in the Church courts and depose kings and emperors who displeased them.[11]

This blisteringly forthright view of what it meant to be a pope was more than just a matter of egotism or tyranny on Gregory's part. It was also the cause for a bitter and lengthy feud with the Holy Roman Emperor Henry IV, during the course of which Gregory excommunicated Henry three times and the emperor in turn declared Gregory deposed, sponsored his own antipopes and used military force to install them in Rome. In retaliation, Gregory struck up his own military alliance with the distinctly ungodly Robert Guiscard and the Normans of southern Italy. (This alliance was a mixed success: in 1084, while defending Gregory against his enemies, the Normans sacked and burned half of Rome.)

The dispute between Gregory and Henry IV is generally known as the Investiture Contest, in reference to the polarizing question of whether emperors or popes were best qualified to "invest" (i.e., appoint) bishops. But it mutated into a struggle that outlived both men and poisoned Western Christendom, pitting churchmen and kings against one another, with occasionally murderous consequences.* And it had a marked effect on Urban's papacy from the very beginning. Odo's very choice of the name "Urban" spoke to his desire to rebuild bridges that Gregory had burned. (Urban I, who died in 230 CE, had been noted for his skillful dealings with schismatics.) He sought a common cause behind which he could rally the faithful of Western Christendom. It was just such a cause he perceived in 1095, the seventh year of his papacy, when ambassadors of the beleaguered Byzantine emperor Alexios I Komnenos

*The slaughter of the archbishop of Canterbury Thomas Becket by knights loyal to Henry II of England was directly linked to the same long-running dispute.

appeared below the Alps. They came to ask Urban for his help rallying Christian troops to come to the aid of their poor brothers in the East, who were being butchered, so they said, by the rampaging Turks.

In the first week of March 1095 Alexios's ambassadors found Urban at Piacenza in Lombardy, a way station for pilgrims on their way to Rome, beside the banks of the river Po. Technically this was territory subject to the Holy Roman Emperor, but in reality the people had rejected Henry IV's authority—riled, perhaps, by the fact that five years earlier Henry's partisans had gouged the local bishop's eyes out.[12] Urban was in Piacenza holding a synod—a Church council, whose goals were to debate and pronounce upon issues ranging from royal scandal to run-of-the-mill ecclesiastical reform. The pope was very fond of holding synods—he would convene ten in his eleven years as pope. And according to the official record, the one at Piacenza was particularly well attended, with four thousand clergy and thirty thousand laymen present. There were so many delegates that several sessions were held outdoors in the open fields.

There was plenty for the attendees at Piacenza to hear. Representations were made by diplomats from the king of France, Philip I, whom Urban had excommunicated as punishment for illegally divorcing his wife on the grounds that she was insufficiently fertile and too fat, and instead taking up with his mistress, who was, inconveniently, married to the count of Anjou, a querulous individual known as Fulk the Repulsive. Complaints were heard from the Holy Roman Empress, Praxedis, that her husband Henry IV was an abusive spouse. Less salacious business included detailed injunctions against simony and schismatics and aberrations in the Church calendar. These were important elements of Urban's reform program, but none would carry the lasting impact of the Byzantine delegates bearing bad news.

Who the ambassadors were, when exactly they arrived (the synod sat from March 1–7) and exactly what they said is lost to history.[13] But an account written by Bernold of St. Blasien preserved the substance of what was said. The ambassadors, wrote Bernold, "humbly implored the lord pope and all Christ's faithful people to give him some help against the pagans in defense of the holy Church, which the pagans had already almost destroyed in that region, having seized that territory up to the walls of the City of Constantinople. The lord pope therefore encouraged many men to give this help, so that they even promised on an oath that, with God's help they would go there and with all their might give their most faithful help against the pagans to that emperor."[14] Go East, said Urban, to the thousands of laymen and clerics assembled. Astonishingly, they took him at his word.

Urban's decision to lend his backing to Alexios Komnenos was not impulsive, nor even new. From early in his papacy he had encouraged Christian kings such as Alfonso VI and Roger, Count of Sicily, who were engaged in wars against Islamic rulers. With respect to the Byzantine Empire, he had already opened tentative negotiations to improve relations between the estranged Roman and Greek churches: at one point he had traveled to Sicily (where Latin and Greek rites were both used) to take Count Roger's advice on precisely this matter.[15] The two halves of the Church had been in formal schism since 1054, torn over fundamental theological arguments about the nature of the Holy Spirit, a vicious disagreement about whether leavened or unleavened bread was appropriate for the Eucharist and, especially, an inability to come to terms over the order of precedence of the pope in Rome and the patriarch of Constantinople. Just as he wished to heal the imperial-papal schism in the Western Church, so Urban was also eager to find ways to bridge the much larger division between East and West.

Urban would also have known very well that two decades previously, following the Byzantines' disastrous defeat to the Turks at the battle of Manzikert in 1071, Pope Gregory had sent letters to the great and good of Western Christendom, filled with bold but ultimately futile declarations that he intended to "bring aid to Christians who are grievously afflicted by the most frequent ravagings of the Saracens."[16] In the 1070s these calls had aroused mild interest and little action. In the 1090s, however, there was a much greater and entirely genuine threat to Constantinople. Meanwhile, Alexios's propaganda had sought to combine cries for help in Asia Minor with lurid tales of outrages committed against pilgrims and shrines in the Holy Land at large, with hair-raising (and often entirely fabricated) accounts of Jerusalem steeped in blood and the whole Christian world in jeopardy. "Lest you should lose the kingdom of the Christians and, what is greater, the Lord's Sepulchre, act while you still have time," read the anonymous letter addressed from Constantinople to Robert, Count of Flanders. "And then you will have not doom, but a reward in heaven."[17]

As we have already seen, the authorship of that letter to Robert of Flanders is a matter of some debate. Yet the argument it crystallized—eliding the fate of Constantinople with that of "the Lord's Sepulchre" (i.e., Jerusalem)—was exactly that which Urban developed after he received the imperial envoys in Piacenza. Having concluded his business there, the pope turned not for Rome, but set off over the Alps to begin a summer tour of persuasion, preaching and exhortation in southern France. He met with leading noblemen and princes of the Church—regional strongmen such as Raymond, Count of Toulouse (also known as Raymond of Saint-Gilles); Odo, Duke of Burgundy; and Adhémar, bishop of Le Puy, whose voices carried immense weight with their countrymen. Through them and others he gave voice to appalling tales of Eastern cruelty, later recounted in gory detail by salacious chroniclers: stories of Turks running riot over the Christian territories of Byzantium and Jerusalem, raping, killing, circumcising and torturing God's faithful with abandon.

As Urban laid out this seemingly dire situation in the East, which had stirred his heart to pity, he talked up his mission for his papacy—a policy that would drag Christendom back toward unity. He was looking for the support of large numbers of fighting men for a military expedition to the East, he said: men who would answer the plaintive call of Byzantium, but who could also be sent onward to attack the enemies of Christ defiling the Lord's sacred spaces. The first goal would be Constantinople. The final destination would be Jerusalem.

Urban's tour drew to an end with two great flourishes. In October 1095 he returned to the Abbey of Cluny, where his path to the papacy had begun a quarter of a century earlier. His old mentor Hugh was still the abbot, and although he was facing financial difficulties thanks to the Almoravids' conquests in Spain, which had cut off his lucrative supply of tribute money from *taifa* kings such as al-Mu'tamid, he had not given up on his central passion for building. The new abbey church was well under way, a holy building site spiraling toward the sky. In a grand ceremony Urban stood next to Hugh and officially blessed the high altar. He stayed at the abbey for a week, during which he announced that on November 18 he would convene another great synod, ninety miles away at Clermont, which was to last ten days. The most powerful men in the region were encouraged to attend, and did so in huge number.

Twelve archbishops, eighty bishops and ninety abbots answered the pope's call. The message that they would receive was hardly a secret, for Urban had been spreading it relentlessly about the countryside for the entire summer. Nonetheless, it was the ceremonial finale of his tour, and not to be missed.

The exact text of Urban's sermon at the Council of Clermont has been lost, but a number of near contemporary and partly reliable accounts tell us of its content. It was given on November 27, in a rally held outdoors on a day when winter was rushing in. According to a chronicle written several years after the fact by a priest called Fulcher of Chartres, Urban rehearsed some of his familiar bugbears, inveighing against simony, heresy, peace breaking and abuse of bishops. Then, however, he launched into a rallying cry that would echo down the centuries, speaking of "an urgent task which belongs to both you and God."

He continued:

> You must hasten to carry aid to your brethren dwelling in the East, who need your help for which they have often entreated.
>
> For the Turks, a Persian people, have attacked them . . . and have advanced as far into Roman territory as that part of the Mediterranean which is called the Arm of St. George [i.e., Constantinople]. They have seized more and more lands of the Christians, have already defeated them in seven times as many battles, killed or captured many people, have destroyed churches, and have devastated the kingdom of God.
>
> Wherefore with earnest prayer . . . God exhorts you as heralds of Christ to repeatedly urge men of all ranks whatsoever, knights as well as footsoldiers, rich and poor, to hasten to exterminate this vile race from our lands and to aid the Christian inhabitants in time . . .
>
> For all those going thither there will be remission of sins if they come to the end of this fettered life while either marching by land or crossing by sea, or in fighting the pagans. This I grant to all who go, through the power vested in me by God.[18]

Fulcher's account of Urban's speech made no mention of Jerusalem, but a later writer known as Robert the Monk reported that Urban called on his audience to "set out on the road to the Holy Sepulchre, deliver that land from a wicked race and take it yourselves. . . . This royal city at the center of the world [i.e., Jerusalem] . . . begs and craves to be free, and prays endlessly for you to come to her aid. Indeed, it is your help she particularly seeks because God has granted you outstanding glory in war above all other nations. . . . So seize on this road to obtain the remission of your sins, sure in the indestructible glory of the Holy Kingdom."

After this, wrote Robert, the crowd began to yell as one: *"Deus vult! Deus vult!"* (God wills it! God wills it!)[19]

At the conclusion of the pope's rousing monologue, Adhémar, bishop of Le Puy, rose in a neatly choreographed move and begged on his knees to be allowed to travel on this glorious expedition. So too came declarations of support on behalf of Raymond of Toulouse. The crowd, enraptured by the sight of these great men vowing to undertake such a bold and ambitious errand, duly broke into a mass frenzy of penitence, beating their chests and pushing forward to the pope to beg absolution for their sins before they returned to their homes to prepare for their new task.

Urban told all who wished to join his great pilgrimage to the East to mark themselves out from their neighbors with "the sign of the Cross on [their] forehead or chest."[20] Once again, they took him at his word. From that point on, the practice of literally "taking the cross" would become an essential piece of the visual grammar of crusading. The theater at Clermont had been a roaring, fearsome triumph, which—although it could not have been known at the time—would be imitated for generations afterward. The "great stirring"—later to be known as the First Crusade—had begun.

In the nine months that followed, a veritable battalion of pious clerics went forth to the towns and the countryside of France and beyond, calling on people to join the new movement. The exemplar was the pope himself, who held huge rallies in places like Limoges and Le Mans, Toulouse and Tours, Montpellier, Nîmes and Rouen. As he toured he celebrated Masses, blessed church altars, glad-handed nobles, donated and translated relics (including numerous small fragments of the Holy Cross, which had been brought up from the papal collection), wore his white-and-gold papal tiara in ceremonial splendor, gave sermons in the open air and exhorted fellow Christians to take up arms, roam far from their homes and kill other human beings. Those who heard him obeyed his call. At Clermont, Urban had tried to temper his rabble-rousing with instructions that only those men who were fit, rich and able to fight should join his army, and warned of the disgrace that would descend on those who took the cross but did not travel. Yet as it transpired, his problem would not be backsliders, but unsuitable enthusiasts for the new mission who could neither be stopped nor controlled.

In a sense, this was understandable. A pope riding beyond the Alps, leading a huge entourage packed with cardinals, archbishops, bishops and other dignitaries across hundreds of miles of the French landscape was a once-in-a-lifetime sight, and it had gladdened—and maddened—the hearts of the Christians who saw it. It had been a hard time of late. A succession of droughts, famines and plagues had ravaged Western Europe since 1092, leaving the populace weak and fragile; some of the poorest had been reduced the previous summer to scrabbling in the earth for weed roots to eat.[21] By 1095 and 1096 these troubles had eased, but in their place had arrived spectacular heavenly portents, including meteor showers, eclipses and peculiar aurorae, which painted the skies vivid and wondrous hues and encouraged apocalyptic thinking.[22] Against this backdrop, Urban was offering a chance to atone for the sins that goaded God into inflicting discomforts on his people. The message was all the more potent when Urban talked of Jerusalem as well as Byzantium—with its obvious significance as the city at the center of the world, and the location of Christ's Passion and his empty tomb.

Soon, therefore, Urban's armed pilgrimage was alive with volunteers. "Many people of varied calling, when they discovered that there would be remission of sins, vowed to go with purified soul where they had been ordered to go," wrote Fulcher of Chartres. "How fitting, and how pleasing it was to us all to see those crosses made of silk, cloth-of-gold or other beautiful material which these pilgrims, whether knights, other laymen or clerics sewed on the shoulders of their cloaks."[23]

When Urban gave his sermon at Clermont, he had hoped to set the Church militant on the march. He had succeeded beyond his wildest dreams.

◆ 5 ◆

The Preacher's Tale

Take the helmet of salvation and the sword of the spirit,
which is the word of God.

The tens of thousands of Christians in Western Europe who felt themselves awakened by Pope Urban's call to arms, and by his agents' intensive preaching tour in 1096, included people of all ranks. They ranged from great counts and archbishops who could raise large sums of money for the crusade and lean on their substantial followings of knights and servants to join it, down to ordinary villagers who lacked any sort of means except for faith. Some came from towns and cities, and others from the countryside. There were those who volunteered because they sought adventure and others who genuinely felt the need to defend Christendom against heathen attack—the "barbarians in their frenzy," as Urban put it.[1] Many, like a knight called Nivelo of Fréteval, from the county of Blois in northern France, were strongly attracted by the promise of remission of sins. Nivelo had made a living out of menacing poor villagers in Blois with a gang of other violent men, and he now saw an opportunity to offset his guilt by fighting in a pilgrim army: "to obtain the pardon for my crimes which God can give me."[2] Few, however, made such an impression on writers of the time as the peculiar figure of Peter the Hermit: an aging, wizened religious recluse from Picardy who became the first and in many ways the least likely crusade leader, gaining both honor and notoriety as he took the first of the Christian armies out of the West and along the Danube toward Constantinople.

Charismatic and widely traveled, Peter was a character who fascinated, excited and appalled his contemporaries in roughly equal measure. He came from the city of Amiens, but by his own account had roamed far and wide during his life, and been to the Holy Land and Constantinople long before Urban began preaching war in the East. Certainly he was full of energy and was a highly persuasive speaker: a populist demagogue who knew how to light up both the dreams and the prejudices of his fellow countrymen and whip them into a state of godly animation that matched his own. The chronicler Guibert of Nogent, who clapped eyes on Peter during the height of his popularity (and did not entirely approve), described him sniffily as wearing "a woolen tunic, which reached to his ankles, and above it a hood; he wore a cloak to cover his upper body, and a bit of his arms, but his feet were bare." But Guibert had to admit Peter was "very generous to the poor with the gifts he was given . . . restoring peace and treaties where there had been discord before. Whatever he did or said seemed almost divine."[3] Another writer described Peter as having extraordinary powers of persuasion, which attracted "bishops, abbots, clerics, monks . . . then the most noble laymen, princes of different domains . . . all the common people, as many sinful as pious men, adulterers, murderers, thieves, perjurers, robbers; that is to say every sort of people of Christian faith, indeed, even the female sex."[4] He was so revered that poor folk would pluck hairs from the tail of his donkey to keep as relics.

Part of Peter's success was that he told a good story about his own life. As it was later recounted, he had been to Jerusalem on a pilgrimage as a young man, and while he was there Christ had petitioned him in a dream, giving him a letter that asked him to stir up his fellow believers for a mission to liberate Jerusalem from Muslim rule. Peter said that once he awoke, the patriarch of Jerusalem had approached him with the same request, and this subsequently inspired him to pitch the concept directly to Alexios Komnenos and Pope Urban.[5] In other words, Peter the Hermit claimed to be the first mover and spiritual architect of the mission that the pope had preached at Clermont.

For all his undoubted talents, Peter was a congenital braggart. So while it is plausible that he may indeed have been advocating a millenarian, penitential invasion of Jerusalem by the faithful before the cause was officially adopted as Church policy at Clermont, he may equally have simply latched on to the popular mood of early 1096 and, with or without seeking the formal backing of the papacy, gone out and preached for all he was worth. But whether we now believe his story is irrelevant. What mattered in 1096 was that he was stunningly effective at spreading the word. As Urban and his bishops rumbled grandly around southern, western and central French lands, negotiating with experienced military and religious leaders the best way to raise an army with a realistic chance of success, recruiting the best soldiers, administering oaths, appointing competent commanders and advising those who wished to join the army on financing and provisioning, Peter the Hermit beat his own path about northern France, the Rhineland and western Germany, in areas that were largely neglected by papal preachers. As he bounced along in his bare feet, he encouraged a more spontaneous, populist approach to the task at hand, inviting anyone and everyone who felt the spirit to come along and have a go. As a result, those who answered his call ranged from minor nobles and knights with experience on the battlefield to people who could most generously be described as noncombatants, and whom Urban had explicitly warned not to think of joining the action: clergymen, the elderly, women, children and those so poor or destitute that they had very little else to do.*

Pope Urban stated that the departure date for his crusade should be August 15, 1096: the Feast of the Assumption, the holiest day of the summer. But five months before the official launch date, at Easter, Peter the Hermit's motley band of followers—later called the People's Crusade—was already on the move. They did not travel as one, but in staggered waves and individual bands, ranging from companies of experienced military campaigners like the eight knights and dozens of foot soldiers who followed the French lord Walter of Sans Avoir (the 'Penniless') in one of the earliest departures, to a band of thousands of peasants who walked east behind a miraculous goose and a nanny goat whom they believed to have been possessed by the Holy Spirit.[6] Peter himself marched brandishing a letter of divine authority he claimed had literally fallen from the skies. They were a varied and idiosyncratic bunch. But by the early summer of 1096 the first factions of this bumptious populist movement had already started to appear in Byzantium.

By the time they got to Constantinople, many already had blood on their hands.

---

*Papal agents firmly discouraged those who would be a drain on resources from joining the mission. In one memorable case, the bishop of Toulouse had a tough time convincing one well-off woman, Emerias of Altejas, that she was not fit to fight the infidel and should instead concentrate her philanthropy on founding a paupers' hospice closer to home. See record in "Crusaders to the Holy Land 1095–1149," Digital Humanities Institute, University of Sheffield, www.dhi.ac.uk.

For all the enthusiasm for holy war that swept through Western Europe in the 1090s—whether spread by Urban and his official preachers or the freelance efforts of Peter the Hermit and other demagogues—an awkward paradox lay at its heart. How could the followers of Jesus Christ contemplate going to war in the name of a man whose whole ministry was ostensibly founded on forgiveness? In the Sermon on the Mount, Christ said: "Blessed are the peacemakers, for they will be called the children of God."[7] Yet here were God's would-be children mustering a war band on a scale unheard of in the history of the Church. The fact that they did so with so little disturbance to their collective conscience tells us much about the astonishing plasticity of thinking that had become a hallmark of Christianity in its first millennium.

Jesus of Nazareth was a man of peace. Worldly when he needed to be, and even prone to fits of anger, the Christ described in the Gospels repeatedly stated his preference for meekness over aggression and suffering over revenge. Yet as Urban understood well, Christ's personal interest in turning the other cheek did not entirely override the vast Judeo-Christian literature produced over thousands of years that advocated precisely the opposite.

For all Christ's soothing words, the Old Testament, which was still a profoundly important text to medieval Christians, depicted a jealous God, forever smiting oppressors and demanding spectacular punishments for the iniquitous: eyes for eyes, teeth for teeth and stoning to death for gluttons, drunkards, Sabbath breakers and sodomites.[8] A popular book like Maccabees, which narrated the adventures of a dynasty of Israelite freedom fighters, presented a world in which guerrilla warfare, forcible circumcision and mass slaughter were go-to tactics for God's warriors.* Stories like these seemed to demonstrate that while a servant of God *could* look like Christ, he might equally well resemble Judas Maccabeus: "In his armor, he was like a giant. He took up his weapons and went to war; with his own sword he defended his camp. He was like a ferocious lion roaring as it attacks."[9]

---

*According to Guibert of Nogent's account of Urban's sermon at Clermont, the pope gave the example of the Maccabees to explain why "it is also justly granted you, Christian soldiers, to defend the liberty of your country by armed endeavor." This passage of Guibert's is pungent with justification after the fact, but the example was clearly one he assumed would appeal to his readers. Robert Levine, trans., *The Deeds of God Through the Franks: A Translation of Guibert de Nogent's Gesta Dei per Francos* (Woodbridge, UK: Boydell Press, 1997), 43.

Nor was militarism confined to the Old Testament. Saint Paul, reformed sinner, apostle and letter writer extraordinaire, was deeply fond of martial analogies. His epistle to the Ephesians encouraged them to be Christlike in all their doings by taking up "the helmet of salvation and the sword of the spirit."[10] Paul's message, pacifist as it was, nonetheless adopted a violent analogy that was easily misconstrued. And Paul was no outlier. John of Patmos's book of Revelation was positively gleeful about the bloodbath he thought would accompany the end times (which at the beginning of the second millennium seemed to lie just around the corner). In one lurid passage predicting the fate of two prophets, John wrote: "The beast that comes up from the Abyss will attack them, and overpower and kill them . . . for three and a half days some from every people, tribe, language and nation will gaze on their bodies and refuse them burial. The inhabitants of the earth will gloat over them and will celebrate by sending each other gifts, because these two prophets had tormented those who live on the earth."[11] The two prophets were eventually resurrected. But once more the tone was set. Christ may have abhorred violence, but warfare, killing, bloodshed and even genocide nevertheless remained familiar parts of Christian exegesis.

Several hundred years after Paul and John's deaths, the problem of marrying Christian faith with worldly violence had not gone away. Rather, it had been crystallized by the fact that Christianity was taken up in 380 CE as the official religion of the Roman Empire. Now urgent triangulation was required between the amiable character of Christ's teachings and the realities of statecraft in an empire that existed by virtue of military conquest, subjugation and war. Plenty of serious minds applied themselves to this task, drawing upon a history of political thought going back at least to Aristotle (d. 322 BCE), from which had emerged the concept of the "just war": violence that was regrettable but legitimate and even moral, so long as it was undertaken to protect the state and would ultimately serve to produce or restore peace.[12]

In the fourth century CE this theme was given a specifically Christian bent, first by Ambrose, bishop of Milan, and then, most powerfully, by Saint Augustine of Hippo. Augustine was by no means a man of war: he was a theologian and philosopher whose portfolio of concerns ranged from the nature of original sin and divine grace to the morality of orchard filching and wet dreams.[13] Yet he understood that once Christianity had swapped the status of renegade cult for that of imperial creed, the tenets of faith would have to be made compatible with the demands of an empire built for war. In *City of God* Augustine put up a robust defense of Christianity's place within the Roman state, arguing that "the wise man will wage just wars . . . it is the injustice of the opposing side that lays on the wise man the necessity of waging just wars."[14] Elsewhere he suggested four clearly identifiable conditions under which a war could be considered just: It was fought for a good cause; its purpose was either to defend or regain property; it was approved by a legitimate authority; and the people doing the fighting were motivated by the right reasons.

Augustine was a pragmatist—and Augustinian pragmatism would remain the order of the day after his death. When the Western Roman Empire crumbled and its former possessions were carved up between tribes from the Germanic north, Latin Christianity quickly adapted to a culture in which fringe wars of imperial expansion or defense gave way to the feuds of petty kings and warlords. Once again, Christian thinkers found ways to mold faith to their surroundings, seeking alternately to circumscribe and sanctify violence. Tenth-century churchmen devised the twin concepts of the Peace and Truce of God, both of which were actively promoted at synods like Urban II's at Piacenza and Clermont. The Peace of God was a sworn promise made by knights and other warriors to abstain from attacking the poor, weak, helpless or pious at any time. The Truce of God was similar: an oath taken by warriors to observe periods of total peace, during which they would not attack one another either. The Church also began actively blessing warrior kings and even welcoming them into the traditions of martyrdom. Thus the saints of the church included Saint Oswald, king of Northumbria (d. 641/2), whose conquests throughout the British Isles were deemed by writers like the Venerable Bede to be offset by his enthusiasm for baptisms and prebattle prayer; and William of Gellone (d. 812/814), a Toulousain duke who slew thousands of Spanish Muslims in the late eighth century before retiring to see out his days as a monk.

When the great conqueror Charlemagne was crowned Holy Roman Emperor by Pope Leo III on Christmas Day 800 CE, the pact between warrior kings and the Latin Church was cemented, and by the eleventh century Christianity—in the West at least—was a religion happy to embrace those who killed and maimed, so long as they did so with respect for the liturgies—

and the property—of the Church. So it was that successive popes from the 1060s had been able to justify handing out papal war banners to men like the rambunctious Norman brothers Robert Guiscard and Roger, Count of Sicily; why papal cheerleading for wars against Muslims and other unbelievers in Spain had been consistent for several decades; and why in 1074 Gregory VII had seen nothing unconscionable in proposing to take an army of God to avenge the Byzantines after their defeat to Alp Arslan's Turks at Manzikert. It was also why the sight of Urban and Peter the Hermit, churchmen high and low, making their way around France and earnestly preaching a doctrine of a holy war based on personal penitence and collective justice, was while certainly unusual, not entirely new.[15]

In the late spring of 1096, having been deliberately provoked to a crescendo of Christian chauvinism by the preachers, it was unsurprising that the early crusaders who left the Rhineland on Peter the Hermit's inspiration were on the lookout for anyone who might be perceived as an enemy of Christ. They did not have to travel very far from home. The first targets and victims of the crusading vanguard were not the dread infidel at the gates of Constantinople, but communities of Jews living in cities of Western and central Europe, such as Cologne, Worms, Speyer and Mainz.

One of the small-time leaders who came to the fore in the first half of 1096, influenced strongly by Peter and the populist strand of crusade preaching, was Emicho of Flonheim: a wealthy nobleman judged by one chronicler to be "of very ill repute on account of his tyrannical mode of life."[16] In 1096 Emicho's band was part of a contingent of twelve thousand Rhineland crusaders who assembled in Mainz. There they launched a grotesque attack on the city's Jewish population. "As they were led through the cities of the Rhine and the Main and also the Danube, they either utterly destroyed the execrable race of the Jews wherever they found them (being even in this matter zealously devoted to the Christian religion) or forced them into the bosom of the Church," wrote the same chronicler, revealing the anti-Semitic bigotry he shared with Emicho, even as he disapproved of the count's character.[17]

The Jewish people of Mainz had already heard of the terror that was barreling along the highway before it arrived in their city: there had been house and synagogue burnings in many nearby cities, along with beatings, mass murders and the theft of large amounts of money from Jews involved in the moneylending business that was forbidden to Christians by canon law. When the attacks began many Jews sought protection from Rothard, archbishop of Mainz, who offered about seven hundred people shelter "in the very spacious hall of his own house, away from the sight of Count Emicho and his followers, that they might remain safe and sound in a very secure and strong place." But the hall was neither secure nor strong enough to resist the depravity of the crusaders, who besieged the archbishop's residence at dawn, smashed down the doors and began a massacre in which, according to the chronicler Albert of Aachen, "they killed the women . . . and with their swords pierced tender children of whatever age and sex. The Jews, seeing that their Christian enemies were attacking them and their children, and that they were sparing no age, likewise fell upon one another, brother, children, wives, and sisters, and thus they perished at each other's hands. Horrible to say, mothers cut the throats of nursing children with knives and stabbed others, preferring them to perish thus by their own hands rather than to be killed by the weapons of the uncircumcised."[18]

This was by no means a sight unique to Mainz. In Worms, Isaac, son of Daniel, was hauled through the muddy streets by a rope tied around his neck, his tormentors challenging him to convert or die. Eventually, as his tongue was popping out of his head, Isaac drew his finger across his own throat. The crusaders and townspeople of Worms around him needed no further invitation. They cut off his head.[19] In Wevelinghofen, north of Cologne, mass suicides took place as young men and women threw themselves into the Rhine and fathers killed their children rather than see them fall into the hands of the enemy.[20] Whether this orgy of anti-Semitic violence was inspired by the crusaders' widely shared agenda of revenging Christ's betrayal at the time of his Crucifixion, or whether it simply represented the bloodlust of a frenzied mob who could not wait to exercise their righteous fury, is probably unanswerable.[21] But the sad effect on the Jews of Mainz was clear. "From this cruel slaughter of the Jews a few escaped," wrote Albert of Aachen, noting that of those few, several were forcibly baptized into Christianity. "With very great spoils taken from these people, Count Emicho . . . and all that intolerable company of men and women then continued on their way to Jerusalem, directing their course toward the Kingdom of Hungary."[22]

The road that the first vanguard of the crusaders had chosen was a well-trodden one, along which many generations of pilgrims and merchants traveling to and from the East had walked before, stretching back at least until the fourth century CE. Emerging from southern Germany, the route initially tracked the course of the Danube, taking those who followed it out of the Alps and down through forests, fields and marshland, on a long dogleg toward Belgrade. From here, an ancient Roman route known as the Via Diagonalis (or Via Militaris) could be picked up, which ran all the way through the Balkans to Constantinople. In total, the journey was about twelve hundred miles: a massive distance to travel by foot, and one on which regular reprovisioning and friendly relations with local rulers were vital. As the various bands of the People's Crusade inspired by Peter the Hermit discovered, this was far from straightforward.

The first problems arose in Hungary. Although this was nominally friendly territory, ruled by a Christian king, Coloman I, anyone who knew the history of that realm would be aware that Hungarian rulers had only converted to the way of Christ in the early eleventh century, and the most recent bloody anti-Christian uprisings were well within living memory.[23] Hungary was not organized as a Western-style feudal aristocracy but rather as a semitribal kingdom potentially very dangerous to Westerners unfamiliar with such a different world. It was alien territory, where wise heads would have counseled caution. Instead, far from home and fired up, many of the early crusaders behaved atrociously and were rewarded in kind.

The first members of the People's Crusade who entered Hungarian territory were the small party led by Peter's ally, the well-to-do minor French lord Walter of Sans Avoir. Reasonably unthreatening and too small to be a serious burden on the foreign countryside, Walter and his followers were granted safe conduct through Hungary, which included the right to buy food and other supplies at local markets. They made it safely through the kingdom and were picked up at Belgrade by Byzantine guides who saw them on their way to Constantinople.

Two weeks behind them came Peter the Hermit, with his heavenly letter in his hand and between fifteen and twenty thousand people at his back—some of them armed and even trained for war, but an equal number of pilgrims with little or nothing to their name. Having vented some of their spite on the Jews of the Rhineland, these brigades also crossed Hungary in June with relatively little trouble. But the next wave, following in their wake, fared very differently. In July, two separate bands of German crusaders aroused the extreme ire of King Coloman, by pillaging and abusing local populations, with one serious skirmish beginning after a gang of crusaders "stabbed a certain young Hungarian in the market street with a stake through his private parts."[24] Unwilling to tolerate this abuse of his people or his hospitality, Coloman sent in his troops, first to disarm and then to kill troublemakers. And when the violent Count Emicho of Flonheim's larger and virulently bellicose forces arrived at the beginning of August, Coloman simply closed his borders. This prompted Emicho to lay siege to a border fortress at Wieselburg for three weeks. This ended with the Hungarians scattering Emicho's army to the wind.[25] The door to further populist crusading bands was, at least temporarily, closed.

Ahead, in Byzantine territory beyond Belgrade, trouble was also mounting. Although Alexios's imperial authorities had taken care of the first small bands of crusaders, and even organized markets were policed by officers who could speak Western languages, as the numbers of Westerners congregating in Byzantine territory swelled from hundreds to tens of thousands, tensions and outbreaks of fighting became the norm, with running battles breaking out against local Greek militias in Nish (Niš) and along the road to Sofia. By now the crusaders' mere presence was becoming a serious cause for concern. The imperial princess Anna Komnene remembered the trepidation felt in Constantinople when the populace learned that the first of the long anticipated "Frankish armies" were these unruly hordes. Anna heard people snigger that the leader was called "Koukoupetros"—literally, Peter the Cuckoo—and she noted that a plague of vine-stripping locusts heralded his arrival. This cuckoo's armies, she said, contained a few warriors surrounded by "a host of civilians, outnumbering the sand of the seashore or the stars of heaven, carrying palms and bearing crosses on their shoulders."[26]

Predictably, their arrival in the capital on August 1 occasioned further uproar, as "these men, lacking as they did a wise prince to lead them" were soon "destroying churches and palaces in the city, carrying off their contents, stripping the lead from the roofs and selling it to the Greeks."[27] It took no time at all for Alexios to weary of seeing his city torn to pieces, so he encouraged the united forces of Peter the Hermit and Walter of Sans Avoir to cross the Bosphorus and set up camp in Kibotos to await reinforcement. But here, once again, patience proved beyond them. Anna recorded that once in Asia Minor the crusaders acted "with horrible cruelty to the whole population; babies were hacked to pieces, impaled on wooden spits and roasted over a fire; old people were subjected to every kind of torture."

Now it became apparent that, no matter how impressive Peter's recruitment drive had been, and how astonishing his achievement in merely raising and marching a huge volunteer army across twelve hunded miles of mostly foreign terrain, the armies of the People's Crusade were seriously out of their depth. They were reliant for survival on supplies Alexios sent across the Bosphorus, and beyond that, on whatever they could find to pillage from among the Greeks and Turks of the immediate area. They were also now highly vulnerable to attack, for once east of Constantinople they were in territory contested by the Byzantines and the Seljuqs of Rum. After a group of German and Italian knights seized an abandoned castle near Nicaea called Xerigordo, they were besieged by a force of Turks summoned by the warlord Qilij Arslan I, who ruled Nicaea and controlled enough of Turkish Asia Minor to call himself a sultan.

Laid under siege in the castle during a broiling Anatolian midsummer, the crusaders at Xerigordo suffered appalling thirst: reduced to drinking horse blood and human urine to survive. Weakened, they were eventually annihilated by an army composed of "men of war who were very experienced with the horn-and-bone bow and were very mobile archers." Eventually agile Turkish horsemen swarmed the castle, kidnapped a few of the prettiest and most youthful crusaders, slaughtered the rest by various inventive means (including tying them to posts and shooting arrows at them), then made a hillock from the corpses, which they left to rot as a warning to subsequent Latin armies who approached Nicaea from the West.[28] The main body of the army camped at Kibotos demanded that their leaders take revenge with a march on Nicaea. But this only prompted further assaults by Turkish troops. By the time autumn arrived, the pilgrims and warriors of the People's Crusade had been sunburned, starved and harried into submission. On October 21 Qilij Arslan launched a major attack on Kibotos itself, killing Walter of Sans Avoir and several others, and breaking up the sorry remains of the surviving crusader army.

Peter the Hermit escaped this horrible fate and scuttled back across the Bosphorus to Constantinople. He would preach another day, and remained a constant if now largely peripheral figure on the crusade as it unfolded. But many of his followers had been killed, while those knights who made it out of Kibotos alive now found themselves at large without commanders. It was plain that they—and everyone else—urgently needed generals with gravitas and experience. Alexios Komnenos had sent to the West to summon God's armies. In the spring of 1096 it seemed entirely possible that he had instead opened the back door of the empire to a pack of devils.

◆ 6 ◆

March of the Princes

Stand fast all together, trusting in Christ and in the victory of the Holy Cross. Today, please God, you will all gain much booty.

Fate decreed that Robert Guiscard's son Bohemond would grow up to be a prince. Even as a baby his parents knew he had an outsize destiny. His baptismal name was Mark, but his father took one look at the size of the child and awarded him his peculiar-sounding nickname in reference to a mythical giant, *Buamundus Gigas*, whose entertaining deeds Robert had heard recounted at a dinner party.[1] It would turn out to be an apt moniker. In adulthood Bohemond traveled the world, involved himself in many hair-raising adventures and impressed, even if he did not delight, everyone he met. He made "a fine figure even among the greatest," wrote one admiring chronicler.[2] Another saw "a hero of great stature."[3] A third described a "great warrior" and "very distinguished man."[4] The author of the epic crusading poem known as the *Chanson d'Antioche* lauded Bohemond as "noble and brave."[5] Anna Komnene thought him spiteful, malevolent, deceitful, treacherous, inconstant, greedy, bitter, a congenital liar and a "supreme mischief-maker" who surpassed "in his villainy and sheer gall" all the other Latins who made their way through Byzantium.[6] But even she had to admit that he was magnetically beautiful: tall, broad-chested and handsome, with large hands and a solid stance, captivating light blue eyes and a fair complexion, his hair cut short around his ears and his chin shaved quite smooth, both provocatively out of keeping with a world in which tresses and beards were the usual symbols of machismo.[7]

Despite being out of step with mainstream fashions, Bohemond was ambitious, cunning and a natural warrior highly adept at siegecraft. Like his father, Robert, and his uncle Roger, Count of Sicily, he discovered that the most reliable way to get ahead in the world was with a sword in one's hand, and he had been blessed with the physicality and family connections to do just that. Anna Komnene's scorn was earned at length: Bohemond joined his father's military attacks on Byzantium in the early 1080s, as the Normans of southern Italy attempted to expand their territories into the Balkans. In 1088 he claimed the Italian title of Prince of Taranto, a grand rank awarded to allow for the fact that he was deprived of any substantial territory to rule when his father died in 1085. (The prestigious duchy of Apulia was settled on Bohemond's insipid half brother, Roger Borsa.) But what Bohemond lacked in patrimonial lands he made up for with long experience on the battlefield—his résumé included command of a division of the Norman army at the famous battle of Dyrrhachium. Bohemond was in the prime of his martial life when the Latin world began to mobilize behind Pope Urban's preaching in 1095. He surmised that the new crusade would be the making of him—and he was right.

Much of what is known about Bohemond's crusade was recorded by an anonymous and energetically sycophantic follower whose chronicle, known today as the *Gesta Francorum* (*Deeds of the Franks*) narrates the Prince of Taranto's crusading career from 1096 onward. Describing Bohemond's decision to join the movement, the author gives the impression of a lord seized spontaneously by the spirit of the Almighty:

> He was besieging Amalfi [between July and August 1096] when he heard that an immense army of Frankish crusaders had arrived, going to the Holy Sepulchre and ready to fight the pagans. So he began to make careful enquiries as to the arms they carried, the badge which they wore in Christ's pilgrimage and the war-cry which they shouted in battle. He was told, "they are well-armed, they wear the badge of Christ's cross on their right arm or between their shoulders, and as a war-cry they shout all together 'Deus vult! Deus vult! Deus vult!' " Then Bohemond, inspired by the Holy Ghost, ordered the most valuable cloak which he had to be cut up forthwith and made into crosses,

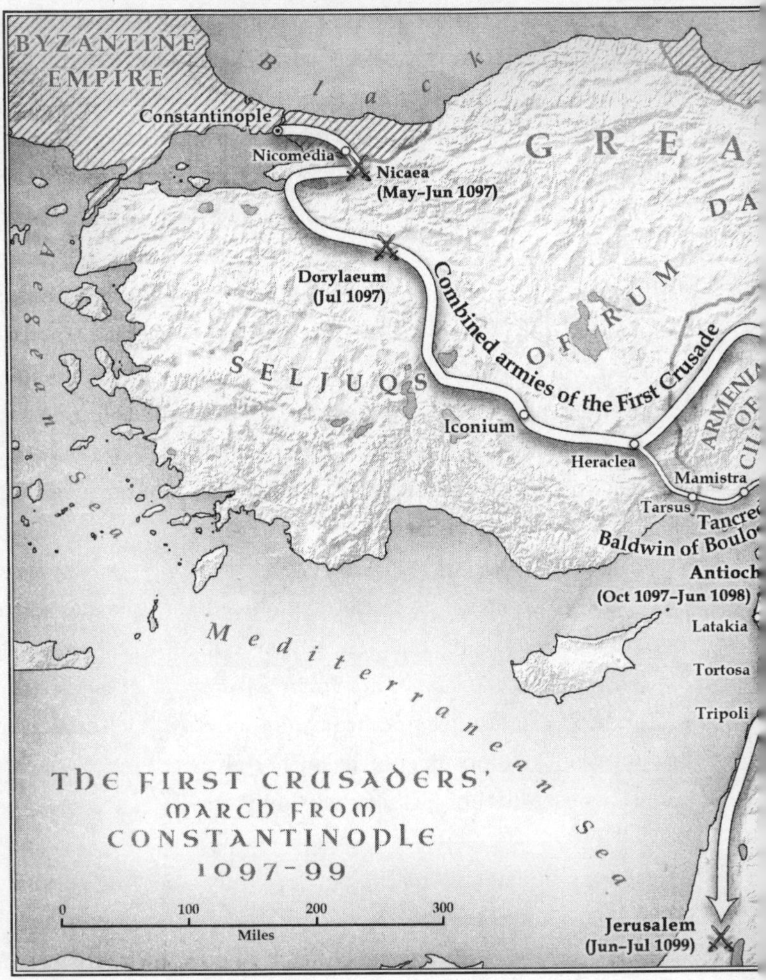

BYZANTINE EMPIRE
Black
Constantinople
Nicomedia
Nicaea
(May–Jun 1097)
GREA
DA
Dorylaeum
(Jul 1097)
Aegean Sea
Combined armies of the First Crusade
OF RUM
SELJUQS
Iconium
Heraclea
Mamistra
Tarsus
Tancre
Baldwin of Boulo
Antioch
(Oct 1097–Jun 1098)
Latakia
Tortosa
Tripoli
Mediterranean Sea
THE FIRST CRUSADERS' MARCH FROM CONSTANTINOPLE 1097–99
0
100
200
300
Miles
Jerusalem
(Jun–Jul 1099)

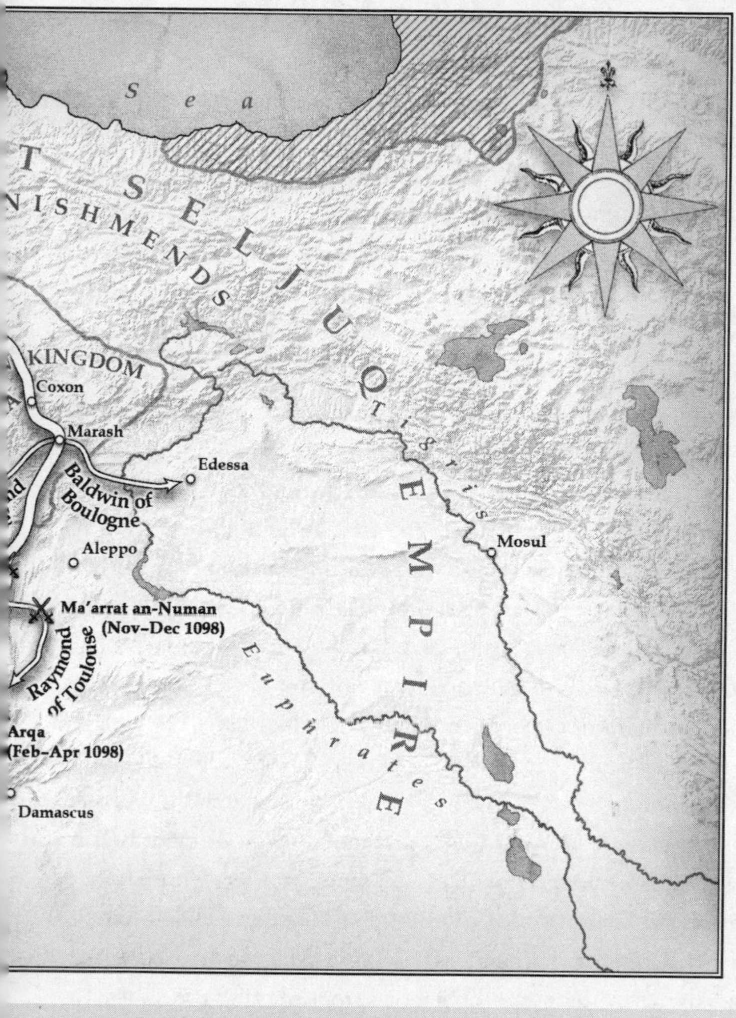
Sea
NISHMENDS
SELJUQ
EMPIRE
KINGDOM
Coxon
Marash
Edessa
Baldwin of Boulogne
Aleppo
Ma'arrat an-Numan
(Nov–Dec 1098)
Raymond of Toulouse
Arqa
(Feb–Apr 1098)
Damascus
Mosul
Tigris
Euphrates

and most of the knights who were at the siege began to join him at once.[8]

This is a good story, but it rather stretches the imagination to believe that the worldly and well-connected Bohemond—a member of the Norman clan who had provided armies to protect Gregory VII and Urban from their enemies in the Holy See—heard of Urban's great project only when he saw the armies of Christ march past his field tent. That the crusade required the attention and involvement of men of status had been made plain from the start and proven by counterexample during the People's Crusade.[9] Thus Bohemond—who spoke Greek and perhaps some Arabic too, knew the Komnenoi well and had experience fighting around the fringes of Anatolia—was almost certainly taken into Urban's confidence early on. His sudden conversion to crusading during the siege of Amalfi in the summer of 1096 was a pantomime; all that was surprising was that he had hidden his intentions for so long.

There was a strongly Norman flavor to much of the leadership of the First Crusade. True, Raymond, Count of Toulouse, and Bishop Adhémar of Le Puy, the great baron and bishop who had been the first to join the crusade at Clermont, were men of the French south, while Philip I of France's brother Hugh, Count of Vermandois—another high-profile recruit—was signed up to ensure the involvement of the Capetian royal dynasty.* But most of the other prominent "princes" (as they were generically, if not completely accurately, known) were either Normans or closely connected to the Normans. One major contingent was raised by Robert "Curthose," Duke of Normandy, and Stephen, Count of Blois: son and son-in-law respectively of the late William the Conqueror, king of England.† Another was commanded by Godfrey of Bouillon, Duke of Lower Lorraine, and Baldwin of Boulogne: brothers whose father had fought alongside the Conqueror at the Battle of Hastings. They brought with them Robert II, Count of Flanders, whose aunt Matilda had been the Conqueror's wife. And then there was Bohemond, representing the southern branch of the Norman diaspora. With him rode his twenty-year-old nephew Tancred of Hauteville, his cousin from Salerno known as Richard of the Principate, and so many other knights of their family circle that Bohemond's un-

*The king of France was still excommunicated in 1095 and therefore persona non grata.

†William the Conqueror died in 1087 and was succeeded in England by the second of his three sons, William II Rufus (d. 1100).

cle, Roger, Count of Sicily, who notoriously scorned the notion of crusading with a great guff of disgust, "was left almost alone."[10]

What possessed all these men—some of the mightiest, richest and most feared lords in the West—to leave their homes and join the crusade was a matter on which contemporaries gave various opinions.[11] The need of the Eastern Church was certainly taken seriously.[12] The promise of remission of sins was another huge attraction, particularly to those who sinned for a living: knights and other warriors of the sort who dominated the Norman courts. (The *Gesta Francorum* laid special emphasis on remission of sins, implying that the prospect of soul-laundering really mattered to Bohemond and his circle.[13]) Reviving the glories of a half-remembered golden age of Church-approved militarism also had its appeal: one chronicler suggested that the princes were encouraged to "not fall short of, but be inspired by, the courage of your forefathers."[14] Finally, there was the promise of plunder. Geoffrey Malaterra, who knew the southern Normans well, claimed that Bohemond went crusading for the sake of conquest first and his soul a distant second. This was slightly unfair: faith, glory and gold could not easily be disentangled. (One of Bohemond's army would return from the East delighted to have acquired something he considered far more precious than coin or a lordship: a lock of hair of the Virgin Mary.[15]) In truth, there were myriad reasons why noblemen and knights went crusading in 1095 and 1096; what mattered in the end was that they went.

Working to the pope's suggested deadline of August 15, and setting off in staggered waves by divergent routes so as to ease the logistical demands on the territories they crossed, Bohemond and the other princes departed for Byzantium during the late summer and autumn of 1096, just as the People's Crusade was petering out. Their followers numbered perhaps eighty thousand: knights, squires, servants, clerics, cooks, navigators, grooms, engineers, translators, unarmed pilgrims, children, women and many more besides. Chroniclers described vividly the scenes in towns and households across Europe, as husbands filled with godly wanderlust bade their wives good-bye—or else packed up their whole families for the trip of a lifetime, while knights mortgaged their homes to raise the capital they needed for an expedition expected to last a year or more. Some, like Ralph the Red of Pont-Echanfray and Hugh the Berserk, who came from Montescaglioso in southern Italy, were experienced soldiers used to fighting in the Normans' wars. (Ralph had served both Bohemond and his father before taking the cross.) Others were leaving home for the first time. Bohemond's military chaplain, Ralph of Caen, who wrote a crusading biography of Tancred of Hauteville, described the latter's mood as the crusade began: "It was as if the vitality of the previously sleeping man was revived, his powers were roused, his eyes were opened and his boldness set in motion. . . . His soul was at a crossroads. Which of the two paths should he follow? The Gospels or the world? His experience in arms [now] recalled him to the service of Christ. This twofold opportunity for struggle energized the man."[16]

That energy would serve the princes well on the journey that awaited. Bohemond and Tancred crossed the Adriatic in October 1096, landing in the Balkans and setting off eastward along the pilgrim road through Macedonia and Thrace that had been known since Roman times as the Via Egnatia. (Others like Godfrey of Bouillon went overland through Hungary, along the route followed by the People's Crusade.) Bohemond's three to four thousand troops were probably the smallest of the princely armies, and at first he did not seem to be in any sort of hurry. His men fairly traipsed, their pace averaging a paltry three miles a day. They celebrated Christmas at Kastoria and did not see Constantinople until Easter. Yet the sluggish pace was not a sign of apathy. Bohemond realized that he was by some stretch Alexios Komnenos's least favorite Latin warrior; he slowed his army's pace to a crawl in order to avoid appearing overintent on pouring troops into the Byzantine capital. He also insisted that his men refrain from robbing and antagonizing Byzantine subjects. In return, Alexios made sure that Bohemond's army was escorted watchfully and respectfully by two of his high-ranking household advisers, known as *kyriopalatios*, who kept strife with suspicious locals to a minimum.[17]

On April 1, 1097, Bohemond halted his army at Rusa (Keshan), about one hundred and twenty miles from Constantinople, and traveled on to the capital with only a personal retinue, to be received by the emperor in the north of the city at Blachernae, his fabulous palace newly restored at prodigious expense. Even for a man long acquainted with Byzantium, Constantinople was a fabulous sight, described in rapt terms by Robert the Monk as "equal to Rome in the height of its walls and the noble structure of its buildings." Behind soaring defenses a constellation of beautiful churches held the greatest collection of Christian relics in the world—including a vial of the Holy Blood, chunks of the Holy Cross, the Crown of Thorns, body parts of all the apostles and seven saints' heads, including two belonging to John the Baptist.*

Whether Constantinople was pleased to see Bohemond was another matter. Rival accounts of Bohemond's first appearance in Byzantium were shot through with hostile intent. To Anna Komnene, Bohemond personified the perfidious Latin, "a born perjurer" who hoped "to seize the imperial capital itself."[18] Pro-Norman writers called Alexios "the wretched emperor" and "the tyrant" who was "wily and smooth-talking, a prolific and ingenious deceiver."[19] However, when Bohemond arrived in Constantinople bygones were momentarily bygones.[20] Norman-Byzantine rivalry may have dated back nearly twenty years, but enmity gave way to cautious familiarity now that Bohemond arrived as a friend and not a nuisance. Crucially, Bohemond knew how to handle the emperor, which was generally a matter of extreme flattery, no matter how insincere. The same realization took time to dawn on the other princes. When Hugh of Vermandois wrote to announce his journey to the imperial court—where the inheritors of Augustus and Constantine were accustomed to sit enthroned in purple, guarded by giant mechanical lions and attended by dozens of eunuchs—he introduced himself as "king of kings, the greatest of all beneath the heavens" and demanded that "I should be met on my arrival and received with the pomp and ceremony appropriate to my noble birth."[21] Anna Komnene scoffed: "absurd."

Bohemond knew better. Although always wary (there was a minor diplomatic incident when he accused the emperor of poisoning his food), he nevertheless devoted himself to a gratuitous show of charm, accepting the emperor's smothering hospitality and his lavish gifts of jewels and trinkets with good grace. Just as importantly, he ensured that his men refrained from wreaking any avoidable damage on Byzantium.

Most significantly for the course of future crusades, during Bohemond's stay in Constantinople he took a vow of allegiance to the emperor that resembled very closely a feudal oath of homage. Then he cajoled, bullied and browbeat many of the other princes who had been arriving at the city's gates since the previous December into doing the same. In some cases this aroused

---

*A third head of John the Baptist could be found in Damascus.

considerable antipathy. Nevertheless, oaths were taken on relics including the Holy Cross and Crown of Thorns by Godfrey of Bouillon, Hugh of Vermandois, Robert of Flanders, Stephen of Blois, Tancrede of Hauteville and many of the lesser lords, all of whom vowed to restore to the empire any Turkish-held towns and strongholds that they might capture along the road to Jerusalem.[22] Even Raymond of Toulouse, who detested the emperor, grudgingly committed not to damage his property. In turn Alexios swore he "would not cause or permit anyone to trouble or vex our pilgrims on the way to the Holy Sepulchre." He also awarded the crusading princes eye-poppingly large gifts of treasure and expensive religious vestments and dangled the prospect of land grants far to the east of Asia Minor—assuming the crusaders got there.[23]

Bohemond's sudden display of subservience toward Alexios confused the author of the *Gesta Francorum:* "Why did such brave and determined knights do a thing like this? It must have been because they were driven by desperate need."[24] Another chronicler marveled that the mighty Latins had been prepared to bend their knees to "the puny Greeks, laziest of all people."[25] In fact self-interest loomed large on both sides. Alexios had invited the armies into his territories and fully intended to see them deployed clearing the Turks from Asia Minor before they disappeared off toward Jerusalem. The crusaders, for their part, could not hope to proceed without the emperor's goodwill and financial support. Bohemond himself had arrived with the smallest army and lowliest standing among all the princes; he realized there was much to be gained in prestige and power if he could become the man who held the Eastern and Western leaders together. To that end Bohemond even petitioned the emperor to appoint him as his *domestikos*—a title that would connote supreme command in Asia Minor. (Alexios demurred—Bohemond could not "out-Cretan the Cretan," said Anna.*) Their exchange of oaths, brokered by Bohemond, effectively cemented a relationship that would—for a time—yield spectacular results for both sides.

With Easter celebrated, homage sworn, and tens of thousands of troops—including seventy-five hundred heavy cavalry and perhaps six times as many light infantry—waiting across the Bosphorus on the western tip of

*Cretans had a reputation for slyness. The modern idiom is: "Don't bullshit a bullshitter."

Asia Minor, there was little point in wasting time. At the beginning of May Bohemond and the other princes marched their armies southeast toward the first target agreed with the emperor: Nicaea, the Seljuq sultan of Rum, Qilij Arslan's capital. They arrived and set up camp on May 6. A week later they laid the city under siege.

Bohemond had attacked plenty of cities in his life, but at Nicaea he encountered formidable defenses. Huge walls, punctuated with towers topped with catapults, protected three sides of the city.[26] A large lake called Askania (Ascanius or *Iznik*) rendered the fourth side inaccessible to the besiegers while allowing resupply of food, firewood, armor and other provisions to the citizens within. Robert the Monk reckoned it "the chief place to which no other is equal in Anatolia."[27] The princes camped in orderly fashion around the walls (Bohemond's men took up their position before Nicaea's main gates) to effect a land blockade while their engineers built siege engines. One eyewitness saw battering rams; mobile sheds to protect sappers known as "sows," "cats" and "foxes"; wooden towers and *petrariae,* or stone-throwing catapults.[28] When these were constructed an exchange of missiles to and from the battlements began, with occasional skirmishing between besiegers and besieged. "The supporters of Christ deployed their forces around the city and attacked valiantly," wrote Robert the Monk. "The Turks, fighting for their lives, put up strong resistance. They fired poisoned arrows so that even those lightly wounded met a horrible death."[29]

Soon, amid the sawing and hewing of half-built war machines, the crash of stone pelting stone and catcalls from the ramparts, came more ominous shrieks. On May 16 the woods behind the crusaders suddenly sprung to life. A relieving army sent by Qilij Arslan came forth, "exulting in their certainty of victory, bringing with them ropes with which to lead us bound into Khorasan [i.e., as slaves to be taken to Persia]."[30] They charged the besiegers and a major engagement began outside the city walls.

The relievers may have assumed that one crusading army was much like another, and that the princes' armies would be as easily dispatched as Peter the Hermit's followers had been the previous year. They were soon disabused of the notion, beaten backward by a cavalry charge commanded by Raymond of Toulouse and Bishop Adhémar. Large numbers were killed on both sides, and grisly retribution followed. The crusaders decapitated corpses and flung the severed heads over Nicaea's walls. The citizens let down grappling hooks from the ramparts, fishing for Latin soldiers, whose bodies they hanged in mockery from the towers.

On June 1 sappers tunneled beneath one of Nicaea's towers. That night they set fire to the wooden struts supporting their mine, collapsing it and bringing down a section of the wall above. Now a breach existed in the walls, where efforts to storm the city could be focused. A daily contest began, in which crusading troops attempted repeatedly to rush the breach, while the defenders inside the city piled up rubble to barricade it. For those involved it was almost impossibly exciting. "I do not think that anyone has ever seen, or will ever again see, so many valiant knights," exclaimed a Latin eyewitness.[31]

However, after several inconclusive days of this, the siege was slipping into stalemate. As long as the city could be supplied via the lake, it could tolerate any amount of bombardment. What broke the deadlock was action undertaken not by Bohemond and his Latin allies, but by the emperor they had taken such care to woo. Alexios had held back from the action at Nicaea, having no desire to take part in a fight he had hired foreigners to pick on his behalf. But he had crossed the Bosphorus and hung back a day's ride away, monitoring events from the safety of a magnificent marquee shaped like a city, with a turreted atrium, which took twenty camels to transport it.[32] To represent him among the princes he sent one of his most trusted military advisers, a grizzled, jocular Arab-Greek eunuch by the name of Tatikios, who had fought against Bohemond's father, Robert, in the 1080s, and who was distinguished both by his exemplary military record and his missing nose, in place of which he wore a golden prosthesis. Even more valuably, Alexios sent a small flotilla of ships, dragged twenty-five miles overland from the shores of the Bosphorus by oxen and men wearing leather straps on their shoulders. These were launched quietly into Lake Askania, in readiness for a major combined assault.

At daybreak on June 18 the flotilla set sail across Askania toward Nicaea's waterfront. Crewed with heavily armed turcopoles (imperial mercenaries recruited from the same ethnic group as the enemy), the vessels floated slowly and ominously into view of Nicaea's defenders. On the landward side, a heavy assault by siege towers and catapults was taking place. "[When] those in the city saw the ships, they were terrified out of their wits and, losing the will to resist, fell to the ground as if already dead. All howled, daughters with mothers, young men with young girls, the old with the young. Grief and misery were everywhere because there was no hope of escape," wrote Robert the Monk.[33]

Having held out for more than seven weeks, the Nicaeans' spirits were broken. They sued for a truce, and the garrison (along with Qilij Arslan's wife and children) surrendered, to be taken off to prison in Constantinople. As the city fell, there was plunder aplenty: some of the Frankish knights now treasured curved Turkish scimitars, taken from the dead hands of the enemy. The fall of Nicaea had proceeded from a model of cooperation between Latins and Byzantines. "It was Gaul that assured it, Greece that helped and God who brought it about," remarked Ralph of Caen with satisfaction.[34]

In line with the oaths sworn, Nicaea was handed over to Alexios, who showered the Latin princes, including Bohemond, with gifts and handed out alms to the rank and file of the crusader army. Ten days later, having refreshed and revived themselves, and taken counsel from the emperor about the best way to fight the Turks in the field (as well as his gracious permission to leave*), the princes packed up their camp and struck out eastward into the Anatolian interior. They divided their army into two divisions, who were to follow parallel roads toward an abandoned Roman military encampment at Dorylaeum (Dorylaion), about four days' march away. The first division was led by Raymond of Toulouse, Bishop Adhémar, Godfrey of Bouillon and Hugh of Vermandois. The second was headed by Bohemond, Tancred and Robert Curthose, Duke of Normandy. A long and difficult summer march across Asia Minor awaited them. Qilij Arslan would assuredly be rallying his own troops for another attack.

It did not take long for Qilij Arslan's next strike to come. As Bohemond's army approached Dorylaeum, which lay at the confluence of two valleys, in the early morning of July 1, "an innumerable, terrible and nearly overwhelming mass of Turks suddenly rushed upon [them]."[35] The author of the *Gesta Francorum* recalled hearing cries of "some devilish word I do not understand"—surely the Islamic battle cry of *Allahu Akbar* (God is great).[36] Chroniclers suggested (with poetic license) that more than a quarter of a million Turks, reinforced with Arab soldiers, descended on Bohemond's army, forcing them to scramble a defense in which knights repelled the first waves

*Alexios had little interest in joining the Franks on their journey further east: he was not secure enough in his political position in Constantinople and feared attack in the western territories if he were to depart for the east.

while lighter-armed foot soldiers pitched a defensive camp in which the non-combatants could be protected. This formation held for a while but it was clear that, separated from Raymond, Godfrey and Adhémar's army, the Latins were badly outnumbered. As the Turks closed in on the camp, every able person was deployed: women shuttling water to refresh men near the front line and cheering encouragement. Despite being outnumbered and occasionally panicked, with leaders including Bohemond contemplating a disorderly retreat, the crusader ranks did not break up. According to the *Gesta Francorum*, a motivational motto was passed down the line. "Stand fast all together, trusting in Christ and in the victory of the Holy Cross. Today, please God, you will all gain much booty."[37]

In later years the battle of Dorylaeum would gain legendary status as the moment the First Crusade truly sprang to life. The writer Raymond of Aguilers, who traveled in the retinue of Raymond, Count of Toulouse, reported on sightings within the Latin lines of miraculous, ghostly protectors: "two handsome knights in flashing armor, riding before our soldiers and seemingly invulnerable to the thrusts of Turkish lances."[38] (That these sounded remarkably like the heavenly warriors who were said to have protected Judas Maccabeus in ancient times was probably no coincidence.[39]) It was certainly the first time that a full-scale battle had been fought against Turkish mounted archers, whose tactics of lightning raids and feigned retreat under a hail of arrows were designed to cause chaos in enemy ranks and drag them apart, inviting cavalry to attempt pursuit rather than holding a disciplined formation. Alexios had sent the golden-nosed eunuch Tatikios out with the princes in order to advise them on resisting this stratagem (and the motto of "Stand fast" suggests that his words were heeded). Nevertheless, it was everything that Bohemond and Robert Curthose could do to keep their warriors from abandoning camp and fleeing in confusion, as they sent desperate word to the other princes to hurry across country and reinforce them.

A brutal contest of devastating arrow-shot against butchery at close quarters lasted from around 9:00 A.M. until midday. For one perilous moment a rout looked possible when the Turks broke through into the middle of the Latin encampment. Raymond of Toulouse charged into the valley with several thousand of his own knights, fresh to the battlefield; the Turks turned tail and fled, hoping to fight another day. The Franks, overwhelmed with relief and puffed up with pride at having survived, celebrated by chanting belligerent verses from the Old Testament ("Thy right hand, O Lord, hath dashed in pieces the enemy"), buried as martyrs all the dead who wore a crusader's cross, plundered and desecrated the corpses of those who did not, and prepared to continue their march eastward.

So under the leadership of Bohemond and the other princes, the debacle of the People's Crusade was gradually forgotten. Robert the Monk later imagined a furious Qilij Arlsan berating Turkish troops he encountered running away from Dorylaeum: "You are totally insane. You have never come up against Frankish valor or experienced their courage. Their strength is not human: It comes from heaven—or the devil."[40] Fanciful this may have been, but Qilij Arslan did not attempt to engage the crusader army on the battlefield again. In a way, he did not need to. Buoyed by victory, the princes decided to head for the vast city of Antioch that lay at the gates between Anatolia and Syria. A three-month summer trek through bitterly hostile countryside awaited them. They would have enough problems as it was.

• 7 •

The Longest Winter

The earth was covered with blood . . .

The men and women who had joined the march of the princes overland from Constantinople to the Holy Land had set off knowing that it would be brutally and even fatally hard work. Tested by force of arms at Dorylaeum, they subsequently endured three months of discomfort, want and danger as the columns of armed and unarmed pilgrims, tens of thousands strong, headed southeast in the direction of Iconium (Konya), and beyond it, Antioch. Ahead of them Qilij Arslan's Turks operated a scorched-earth policy, abandoning cities and withdrawing garrisons, and removing stores of livestock and foodstuffs, gold, silver, church ornaments and anything else useful to the Frankish armies.

These wasting tactics were not subtle, but they were well judged to exacerbate the Latins' difficulties as they marched. The princes, acting on the advice of Alexios and his deputy Tatikios, had deliberately plotted a circuitous route east through Asia Minor, including a nearly two-hundred-mile digression through the Taurus Mountains. The aim was to win back Alexios's lost territory—and they succeeded. With little serious opposition they recovered several important Byzantine cities from Turkish rule: Antioch-in-Pisidia, Iconium, Heraclia, Caesarea-in-Cappadocia, Coxon and Marash. Liberating Jerusalem may have been the crusaders' ultimate ambition, but the princes had not forgotten their duty to Byzantium and their oaths to its emperor.

This was all very helpful to Alexios, back in Constantinople: a worthy return on the many gifts and feasts he had lavished on the Frankish leaders during their visit to his capital. But for the crusaders it made for a long expedition through terrain every bit as menacing as the Turkish mounted archers who occasionally appeared to harass them. Long stretches of the arid Anatolian plateau consisted of steep, uneven, uninhabitable country; negotiating it provided the penitential misery so many crusaders had sought when they took the cross.[1] The writer Peter Tudebode, a priest from Civray, near Poitou, recorded that "hunger and thirst beset us at every turn. Our only food consisted of spiny plants picked at random and rubbed off [peeled] by hand. . . . many of our knights took to foot because most of the horses died."[2] As their mounts collapsed, fighting men were forced to ride oxen, using goats, sheep and even dogs to carry their packs. The crusaders were "overwhelmed by the anguish of thirst." One writer described the agonies of pregnant mothers miscarrying their children on the roadside through severe dehydration: "Their throats dried up, their wombs withered, and all the veins of the body drained by the indescribable heat of the sun and that parched region."[3]

From time to time the armies passed through fertile and well-watered terrain such as in Pisidia, where drought and heat gave way to bounty: "delightful meadowlands" where the rank and file of the crusaders could refill their waterskins and forage or bargain for supplies, while the princely leaders enjoyed surroundings "most fruitful for the hunts in which the nobility enjoyed amusing themselves and taking exercise."[4] Even this, however, was not quite safe. When the army stopped to camp near one wooded region, Godfrey of Bouillon was attacked by a gigantic bear, which ripped him from his horse with its claws, tried to maul his throat and "roused all the forest and mountains with its dreadful roaring." In panic, Godfrey got his sword tangled up in his legs and cut one of his own calf muscles to the sinew. Only the quick thinking and bravery of a peasant called Husechin saved Godfrey's life: he leaped on the bear and stabbed it through the liver. The count survived and was treated by army doctors; the bear was portioned up for its fur and meat. But "the whole army was thrown into confusion by the wicked news."[5]

Another source of confusion lay with Godfrey's brother Baldwin of Boulogne. As the crusade army passed Heraclia and prepared to branch off onto its loop into the Taurus Mountains, the headstrong Baldwin decided to peel away from the main body of troops and take his men south in the direction of Tarsus (Tarsos), in Cilicia. This was a vividly storied city: site of the first meeting between Mark Antony and the Egyptian empress Cleopatra, and the birthplace of Saint Paul the Apostle. It also lay close by the Mediterranean coast, in prime position to help maintain a supply chain between Byzantium and the coastal littoral of Syria and Palestine—should the crusaders ever get that far.

Ralph of Caen described Tarsus as marvelous for "the heights of its towers, the length of the walls, the prideful stature of the homes."[6] It was so rich that it attracted not only Baldwin of Boulogne but another of the princes: Bohemond's young nephew, Tancred of Hauteville. They took Tarsus easily, as the Armenian and largely Christian citizens threw open the gates without meaningful resistance. But serious violence did occur after an argument *between* the princes over whose banner should be flown above the captured citadel. Tempers frayed, then snapped, and swords and lances were readied, with the lords' knights attacking one another in a bloody melee. "It seemed insane that those who had set out together against an enemy should turn on each other," sniffed Ralph of Caen. But turn on each other they did, engaging in running hostilities as they pushed on through Cilicia. By the time they rejoined the main crusade armies at the Armenian town of Marash around the middle of October, they had captured towns including Adana and Mamistra. But the first cracks in control had been exposed.

They came down from the mountains into Antioch in mid-October 1097. The city was a fine sight to behold. Founded by the Seleucids in the early fourth century BCE at a ford in the valley of the river Orontes and mightily fortified during the sixth century CE by the Eastern Roman emperor Justinian the Great, it had grown to become a magnificent outpost at the frontier between empires of the West and East. The Amanus (Nur) Mountains to the north of the city contained passes connecting Syria with Asia Minor. To the northeast, the Orontes valley opened into a stagnant marsh, beyond which lay the broad plains of the Aleppo plateau, and further on still, Mesopotamia. To the west Antioch was served by a new Mediterranean port, Saint Simeon,* which was small but adequate to the city's needs and destined to boom during the twelfth century. And its natural defenses were awe inspiring. "The rivers and mountains ran along its flanks. The city was even joined up to the flank of the mountain [Mount Silpius or Habib-I Neccar] with walls reaching up to its summit and a citadel built there as well," wrote a gobsmacked Ralph of

*Antioch's ancient seaport, Seleucia Peria, had silted up and fallen into disrepair by the fifth century CE.

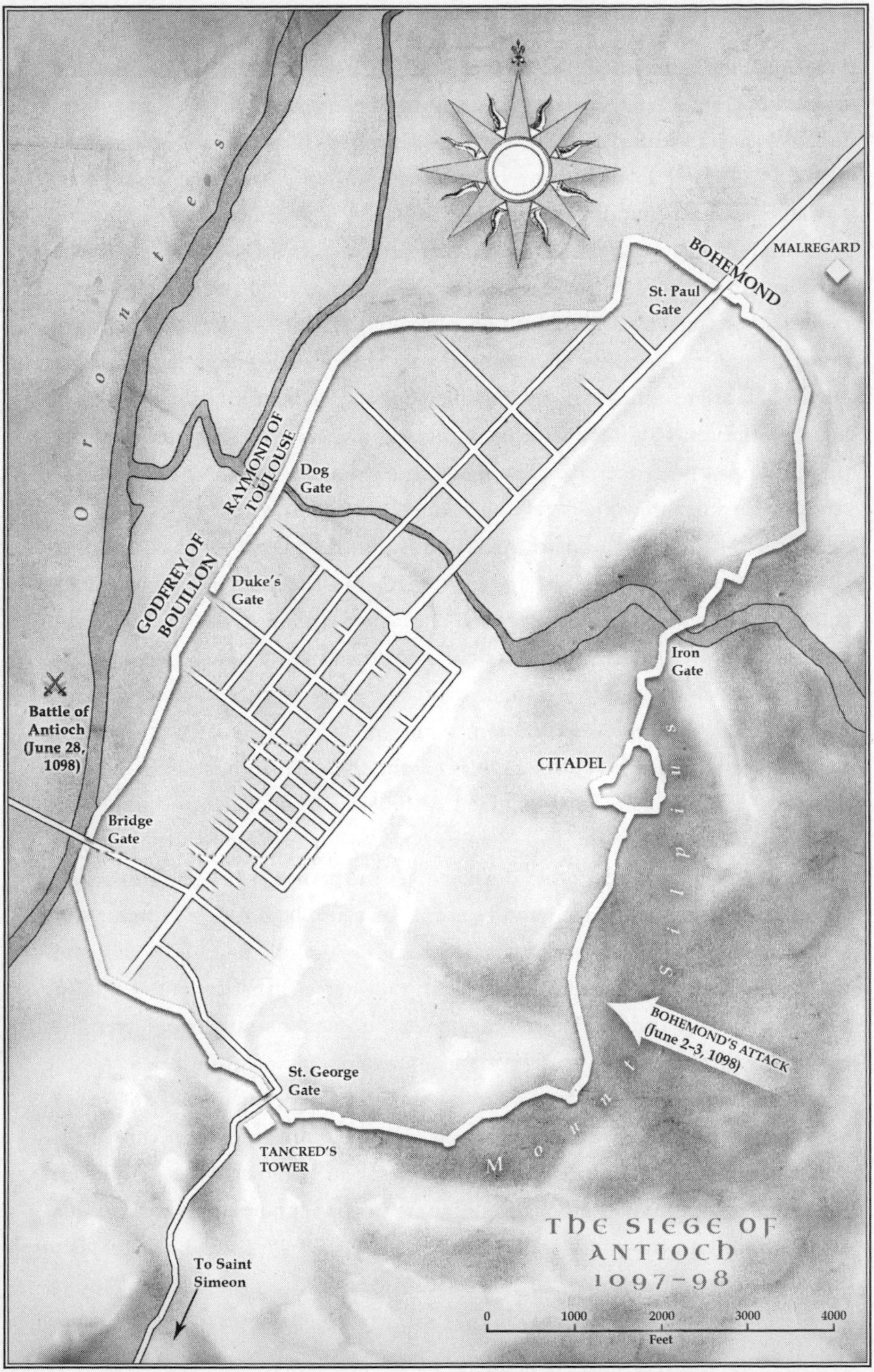
Orontes
BOHEMOND
MALREGARD
St. Paul Gate
RAYMOND OF TOULOUSE
Dog Gate
GODFREY OF BOUILLON
Duke's Gate
Iron Gate
Battle of Antioch (June 28, 1098)
CITADEL
Bridge Gate
Mount Silpius
BOHEMOND'S ATTACK (June 2–3, 1098)
St. George Gate
TANCRED'S TOWER
To Saint Simeon
The Siege of Antioch 1097–98
0
1000
2000
3000
4000
Feet

Caen.[7] Stephen, Count of Blois, wrote to his beloved wife, Adela, reporting that Antioch was "bigger than one can imagine, extremely strong and unassailable," and reckoned that inside its walls were "five thousand courageous Turks . . . as well as an infinite number of Saracens . . . Arabs, Turcopoles, Syrians, Armenians and other peoples."[8]

Yet for all this apparent natural security, Antioch was also deeply unstable. Far beneath the city in the earth itself, a complex junction of three tectonic faults caused frequent and calamitous earthquakes. One major tremor in 115 CE brought buildings toppling down and nearly killed the Roman emperors Trajan and Hadrian; another in 526 CE killed about a quarter of a million people and caused fires that burned the city almost to the ground. Appropriately, the politics of Antioch were also turbulent and even murderous: the long view of Antioch's history was one of rebellion, upheaval and invasion.

Antioch had served Roman, Arab and Byzantine masters, but at the time the crusaders appeared before its walls, it was in the care of a Seljuq emir called Yaghi-Siyan. He had been governor of Antioch since that proud city had been pried away from Byzantium's grasp by the Great Seljuq sultan Malik-Shah in 1084. He was an aged man, wrote one chronicler, with an enormous head, "wide and hairy" ears and long white hair and a beard that flowed all the way down to his navel.[9] But as ruler of Antioch, he had much to cause him to stroke that lush beard in alarm. Under Malik-Shah the Seljuq sultanate was briefly stable, unified—and vast. The sultan's authority covered—in theory at least—territory from Merv and Transoxiana in the northeast to the Persian Gulf in the southeast, and the shores of the Aegean, Black and Mediterranean seas in the west.* Rivals were at bay: advances in Anatolia by Qilij Arslan and the so-called Seljuqs of Rum kept the Byzantines at arm's length; while in southern Syria and Palestine the Seljuqs maintained a stranglehold over the crumbling Shi'ite dynasty of Egyptian caliphs known as the Fatimids.

Yet when Malik-Shah died in 1092, however, Yaghi-Siyan and the other Seljuq emirs like him, who held cities such as Aleppo, Damascus, Mosul and Homs, were suddenly plunged into a state of self-inflicted crisis and civil war. A power struggle for control of the sultanate broke out between Malik-Shah's brother and sons, the effects of which rippled out swiftly through the empire.

*The Seljuqs therefore dominated the major overland trade routes, which bottlenecked through the Middle East as they connected the markets of Europe with the workshops of central Asia and China.

Each emir looked to himself, his own city and his own private ambitions rather than the well-being of the empire itself. Petty rivalries and shifting allegiances abounded. Yaghi-Siyan, who supported Malik-Shah's brother Tutush in his bid for the sultanate, was left uncomfortably insecure when Tutush was killed in battle in 1095 by armies loyal to Malik-Shah's fifteen-year-old son, Barkiyaruq.

Yaghi-Siyan was not removed from his post in Antioch, but he could no longer automatically assume the support or confidence of the young sultan Barkiyaruq in the various Seljuq capitals of Isfahan, Baghdad and Rayy. He also had to deal with the fact that his near neighbors and fellow emirs in Syria were divided by the factional lines that had emerged during the succession period, and that not all of them could be relied upon to ride to his aid should Antioch come under attack. So in 1098 when the crusader princes came down into the Orontes valley, he was far from perfectly prepared to defend either his city or the honor of the Seljuqs.

Word had been spreading throughout Syria at least since December 1096 that "the armies of the Franks had appeared from the direction of the sea of Constantinople with forces not to be reckoned for multitude." Ibn al-Qalanisi, a chronicler based in Damascus, remembered that "as these reports followed one upon the other, and spread from mouth to mouth, far and wide, the people grew anxious and disturbed in mind."[10] News of the Latins' victory at Dorylaeum preceded them: "A shameful calamity to the cause of Islam," harrumphed Ibn al-Qalanisi. What was not clear was the moment at which the crusaders could be expected—which is why in October 1097 Yaghi-Siyan was not to be found readying Antioch for its imminent assault, but was instead on campaign with a fragile coalition of other emirs in central Syria.[11]

When the news arrived that Bohemond and the other princes had crossed the Orontes at a fortified river crossing known as the Iron Bridge, bickering broke out among the emirs as to the best response. Yaghi-Siyan scrambled back to Antioch, but he was not immediately joined by his comrades. It was a mark of the lack of confidence that the Antiochene governor felt toward the fate of his city that his first action was to expel all the Christian men who lived there, to guard against an uprising from within. Messengers were then dispatched to Damascus, Mosul and every other city within the Seljuq empire imploring the lords there to send troops to prevent the Franks from overturning his rule and establishing a foothold in Syria from where they could begin to raid south toward Jerusalem. This delay in organizing resistance was of enormous assistance to the princes. "Our enemies the Turks, who were inside the city, were so much afraid of us that none of them tried to attack our men for nearly a fortnight," recalled the author of the *Gesta Francorum*. "Meanwhile we grew familiar with the surroundings of Antioch and found there plenty of provisions, fruitful vineyards and pits full of stored corn, apple trees laden with fruit and all sorts of other good things to eat."[12] The Muslim chroniclers recalled events in rather less bucolic terms: the Franks ravaging, slaughtering indiscriminately and inciting the inhabitants of castles and forts in the region to rise up and murder their garrisons.[13] (This occurred most helpfully—or unhelpfully—in Artah, known as "the shield of Antioch," which guarded the city's eastern approach.[14]) People noted that a strange comet had been seen passing through the heavens for twenty days in midsummer; increasingly this looked like an omen.[15]

The first crusaders, led by "the gallant Bohemond," arrived before the gates of Antioch on the evening of Tuesday October 20, and barred the main road into the city "so that no one could go out or come in secretly by night."[16] The following day the main army drew up behind them on the banks of the Orontes and set about mounting as full a blockade as they could muster at key points on the city's gargantuan perimeter. They allowed the expelled Christians to camp with them, although there was some suspicion that this was inviting espionage, since the men's wives and children were being held under Yaghi-Siyan's protection—and therefore also at his mercy—inside the city walls. To protect the army from mounted sallies from within the city, the princes dug a large ditch in front of their main camp. Patrols were set to prevent essential goods and supplies from being brought into the city—Ibn al-Qalanisi reported the price of essential commodities like olive oil and salt in Antioch fluctuating wildly according to the success or failure of smugglers who braved the Frankish guard.[17] The main challenge to the crusaders was the sheer size of the city—its sprawl across the valley made a full blockade extremely difficult to maintain and its massive walls negated the possibility of blasting in by battering ram and catapult. Yet Yaghi-Siyan, for his part, could not be in the least confident of a coordinated effort of sufficient strength to drive the Franks away. Both sides dug in for a long and unhappy winter.

As the crusaders camped outside Antioch, and the various emirs of northern Syria debated the best way to come to the aid of Yaghi-Siyan in his hilltop citadel, one of the Frankish princes was notable by his absence. Baldwin of Boulogne, having diverted from the main army twice during the march through Asia Minor, did so a third time before the descent toward Antioch, taking a route of his own across the Orontes and on to the Euphrates, where he found his way to the city of Edessa. The governor of Edessa, an Armenian Christian called Thoros, who ruled as a puppet of the Seljuqs—had sent word to Baldwin asking him to free him from subservience. Baldwin reached the city in mid-February 1098, invested it with his troops, persuaded Thoros to undertake a public ritual in which he hugged Baldwin to his bare chest and thereby adopted him as his son, then set about leading a combined crusader-Edessan army around nearby cities and forcing the Turks there into obedience or death. But very soon after his arrival Baldwin incited—or at least declined to prevent—a popular coup in which his newly acquired father was murdered. On March 10 Baldwin was officially proclaimed as *doux* (a Byzantine style for ruler) of Edessa. He translated the title to a more familiar, Western style, becoming "count" of the county of Edessa, but otherwise made a deliberate effort to adapt his appearance to the Armenian manner, growing his dark-brown hair and beard long and dressing in a toga. He married an Armenian nobleman's daughter, whom tradition has come to call Arda, although in private his lifelong preference was for the company of men.[18] That was neither here nor there. Baldwin had established the first Latin "crusader" state in greater Syria. It would not be the last.

As Baldwin overran Edessa, back in Antioch, Yaghi-Siyan could still look out from his mountain citadel and see the rest of the crusader armies arrayed before his gates and up and down the sides of the valley. It was not an encouraging sight. The Latins had been resupplied at the beginning and end of the winter by Western ships arriving at Saint Simeon by way of Cyprus—Genoese shipping appeared in November, followed by twenty-two English and Italian vessels in March 1098, whose crews formally secured the port, as well as nearby Latakia, for the crusading army.[19] North of the city walls, on a hill known as Malregard, engineers who had arrived on one of these boats constructed a small fort. The princes had also made significant gains in the local area, as Bohemond, Tancred, Godfrey of Bouillon, Robert of Flanders and Robert of Normandy spread out and raided towns subject to the rule of either Antioch or neighboring Aleppo. Moreover (and very significantly) envoys from the Ismaili Shi'ite Fatimids in Cairo had been received, and a nonaggression pact agreed.

Yet these successes could not hide the fact that the crusaders were suffering. They had endured for more than six months the dreadful privations of a winter siege—exposure, malnutrition and disease—as well as fighting off major attacks on foraging parties led by the rulers of Aleppo and Damascus, who had belatedly raised themselves for the task of assisting Yaghi-Siyan. Stephen of Blois wrote to his wife expressing his horror that the searing summer heat of Anatolia had given way to a winter of "extremely cold temperatures and an endless downpour of rain" that was little different from those of northwest Europe.[20] Ralph of Caen complained of winds so strong that "neither tent nor hut could stand." Horses died and people starved. "Rust seized hold of all the iron and steel weapons. Shields lost their nails and leather coverings. . . . Bows lacked their sinews and arrows were bereft of their shafts." The princes, Ralph wrote, endured the same miserable conditions as the poor—although he noted that "it was much harsher for nobles inasmuch as the peasant is tougher than the noble."[21] Spirits were dropping everywhere. Tatikios left the siege in February 1098, apparently with the intention of returning to Constantinople to request more troops. Peter the Hermit, who had traveled overland with the princes' crusade but kept a much lower profile than on his own misadventure in 1095 and 1096, also tried to abandon the city and had to be dragged back and berated by Bohemond for his disloyalty.

Spring brought relief from the elements, but stalemate continued until the start of June, when the deadlock was broken, perhaps inevitably, by Bohemond. He was the most experienced and wily of the princes; during the winter months when there had been regular danger of relief expeditions from Aleppo and Damascus, the other princes had voted him their overall commander. (This was a significant shift in the military organization of the crusade—until this point it had been under the nominal authority of Alexios Komnenos and the spiritual guidance of Bishop Adhémar of Le Puy.) At the end of May, Bohemond demonstrated why his colleagues had invested their faith in him. As told by the Mosuli chronicler Ibn al-Athir, "after the siege of Antioch had lasted long, the Franks made contact with one of the men garrisoning the towers, who was a Greek-speaking armorer."[22] This armorer was Bohemond's key to unlocking Antioch. Ibn al-Athir gave his name as Ruzbah, while according to Ibn al-Qalanisi he was an Armenian called either Nayruz or Fayruz. On the Christian side, Fulcher of Chartres recorded an exciting but perhaps fanciful story that Christ had appeared to the armorer in a dream three times and convinced him to sell out the city.[23] Whatever his name and his backstory, he changed the course of the siege—and Bohemond's career. Via secret messages exchanged with Ruzbah/Fayruz, Bohemond promised him a rich reward if he would turn traitor.

On June 2, 1098, Bohemond's gambit was launched. During the afternoon a large contingent of the crusading army began a phony march off into the Syrian interior to convince the defenders the siege was being lightened or withdrawn. That night, however, they returned to find a ladder made from bullhide let down from one of the three towers under Ruzbah/Fayruz's watch. At a signal from their mole, a party of crack troops shimmied up the ladder, overpowered the guards at the top of the tower and began to bellow *"Deus vult!"* to their comrades below. Shortly after, a gate was unlocked and men bearing Bohemond's blood-red banner poured through. "They all came running as fast as they could and entered the city gates, killing all the Turks and Saracens whom they found there," wrote the author of the *Gesta Francorum*, who took part in the assault.[24] Dawn was breaking over Antioch.

The trumpet blasts that announced the presence of Bohemond's men on top of the ramparts roused Yaghi-Siyan from his bed; he found his men panicking. Their panic was infectious. Incorrectly assuming the citadel had fallen to the Franks, the emir "was seized with fear, opened the city gate and left in headlong flight with thirty retainers," wrote Ibn al-Athir. "That was a boon for the Franks. Had he held firm for a while, they would have perished."[25] Instead, his small party rode helter-skelter in the direction of Aleppo, hoping to save their necks if not their city.

In the end, Yaghi-Siyan saved neither. After several hours on the road "he started to lament and bewail having abandoned his wife, his children and the Muslim population." Then, overcome either by heartbreak or heatstroke, he fell from his horse insensible. "An Armenian, who was cutting firewood and came across him at his last gasp, killed him, cut off his head and took it to the Franks at Antioch," reported Ibn al-Athir.[26] The huge, big-eared, bearded trophy was presented to the Latin princes in a bag. And it was far from the only head to be taken as the city fell to a massacre, led by the crusaders and supported by insurgent Christians from among the population. Ibn al-Qalanisi reckoned "the number of men, women and children killed, taken prisoner and enslaved from its population is beyond computation."[27] Since it began in the half-light of the early morning, the killing was indiscriminate; the German chronicler Albert of Aachen wrote that "the earth was covered with blood and the corpses of the slaughtered . . . the bodies of Christians, Gauls as well as Greeks, Syrians and Armenians mixed together." Several hundred fled to the citadel at the pinnacle of the city: the only place Bohemond's forces could not overrun. But in the scramble up a steep path to reach it, many fell over the edge and "perished with broken necks, legs and arms and all their limbs in an incredible and amazing fall."[28]

The fall of Antioch could not have come at a more propitious moment for the crusaders, for as their scouts had been telling them with increasing urgency for several weeks, a huge relieving army was gathering, assembled under the leadership of the new sultan's military commander, Qiwam al-Dawla Karbugha, atabeg of Mosul. ("Atabeg" was a term denoting a regent or military governor ruling on behalf of a young or absent emir.) Karbugha gathered troops from Damascus, Sindjar, Homs, Jerusalem, Asia Minor and elsewhere to form an army that one fevered writer improbably numbered at 800,000 cavalry and 300,000 infantry.[29] During May, Karbugha's purple war banner and the many and varied others of his allies had been raised near Edessa, where for three weeks they besieged the new ruler, Baldwin. Once news of Antioch's fall reached them, however, they left Baldwin and marched west, arriving in the Orontes valley just four days after Yaghi-Siyan had abandoned his post.

The tables were turned. The crusaders occupied the city (although not the citadel), while outside the walls there gathered a huge army intent on bringing them out. But there was one key difference. Whereas Yaghi-Siyan had sufficient supplies to see the population of Antioch through nine months of blockade, now the stores were almost dry. The effectiveness of the crusaders' own embargo had ensured there was no food left.

Realizing what was about to happen, thousands fled the city before Karbugha's army sealed it off. They included Stephen of Blois, who claimed (or feigned) illness and took as many as four thousand pilgrims and warriors with him to seek refuge in the friendly city of Alexandretta. This reduced the pressure on resources in Antioch, but shattered morale. Bohemond did all he could to berate and shame those who tried to desert, but rumors whipped around the city that the princes wished to sue for peace. It was said that back in Constantinople, Alexios Komnenos declined a request to send reinforcements. Bishop Adhémar did his best to rally the spirits of the dejected pilgrims, but the best spin he could put on the situation was martyrdom: "Let us stand firm and die in the Lord's name as is the purpose of our journey."[30]

By the third week of June Karbugha had sealed off Antioch, and conditions inside the city were already appalling. "Our men ate the flesh of horses and asses, and sold it to one another," remembered the author of the *Gesta Francorum*. "So terrible was the famine that men boiled and ate the leaves of figs, vines, thistles and all kinds of tree. Others stewed the dried skins of horses, camels, asses, oxen or buffaloes."[31] Ralph of Caen recorded people boiling soup with the leather from the soles of old shoes.[32]

Driven to the brink by heat, hunger and the intensity of the conflict, people inside and outside Antioch began to experience signs and visions. A meteor fell into the besiegers' camp on the night of June 13–14. The *Gesta Francorum* tells the vividly embellished tale of Karbugha's mother, a soothsayer, who warned her son against attacking the crusaders. Having "studied the planets and the twelve signs of the Zodiac and all kinds of omens," she had "found prognostications that the Christian people is fated to defeat us utterly," and that Karbugha himself would eventually be killed in the course of a great war.[33]

Meanwhile, inside Antioch a poor pilgrim from Provence called Peter Bartholomew began to dream of Saint Andrew the Apostle, who told him that buried in the Church of Saint Peter was a relic of the Holy Lance that had been used to pierce Christ's side on the Cross. On the morning of June 14, amid much fanfare, a hole was dug in the church, into which Peter jumped, "clad only in a shirt and barefooted." He duly retrieved the head of the Holy Lance, and was rewarded with much jubilation from his weary comrades and a final visit from Saint Andrew, who brought Jesus Christ along with him and commanded Peter to kiss the Lord's bloodied foot.[34] Not everyone believed Peter's miraculous discovery, and some months later he was subjected to an ordeal by fire to test the veracity of his claims, which resulted in him dying in agony from severe burns.[35] But in mid-June it was a thread on which the starving and dejected crusaders—whose fighting ability was diminishing with every horse they ate—could hang their slender hopes of survival.

The moment of truth came on the morning of June 28. The crusaders—commanded by Bohemond, captained by the princes, fortified by the Holy Lance, and rendered desperate by the fact that they faced certain death by starvation if they waited any longer—sallied out of Antioch looking for a fight that would decide their campaign. Karbugha had sworn they would be shown neither mercy nor terms, sending a message to the holders of Antioch that "my sword alone will eject you."[36] The atabeg was playing chess with one of his officers when the gates of the city swung open and the six divisions of the bedraggled Frankish armies marched out, white-frocked priests and monks chanting at the head of their lines, and other churchmen calling for God's protection from the walls of the city above. He rose from his board and ordered his troops to form up.[37]

A light rain was falling. The Franks were almost entirely on foot, with no more than two hundred horses fit for battle in the entire army. Their ragtag appearance was exacerbated by the presence of a regiment of Tafurs—pauper warriors who carried large wooden shields and whose reputation for ferocity was bolstered by stories that they enjoyed eating their enemies: "They carved them into joints in full view of the pagans and boiled or barbecued them . . . then they gobbled them eagerly without bread or any seasoning, saying to each other: 'this is absolutely delicious, much better than pork or roast gammon.' "[38] But if the crusaders were weak and rough around the edges, they were also disciplined and fighting for their survival. Karbugha, meanwhile, commanded an ambivalent army that when pressed into battle split into its component factions. The leaders bickered about the best tactics for resisting the Frankish sortie, and the hesitancy spread to the troops.

Bohemond and the princes urged their men forward into a battle on the banks of the Orontes in which they swiftly overwhelmed the portion of Karbugha's forces posted there, then fought off an attack from the rear. Panic spread throughout the rest of the Muslim army. Instead of standing to fight, they simply melted away. Karbugha also ran, along with the last of his officers, leaving behind the noncombatants and a company of volunteers who had sworn to fight as *mujahidin*, seeking martyrdom. "The Franks slew thousands of [Karbugha's troops] and seized as booty the provisions, money, furnishings, horses and weapons that were in the camp," wrote Ibn al-Athir. There, many atrocities were committed: children were trampled beneath horses' hooves; women were speared through the bellies with lances. One great prize of war was Karbugha's large pavilion, designed "in the style of a town with turrets and walls of various colors and silks."[39] The participants could scarcely believe their victory. Raymond of Aguilers, who fought among the crusading ranks that day, later gave thanks to Saint Peter and Saint Paul for delivering them, "because through those saintly intercessors the Lord Jesus Christ brought this triumph to the pilgrim church of the Franks."[40] Inside Antioch, the garrison holding the citadel surrendered. Against all odds, the crusaders had taken one of the great cities in Syria. Ahead of them, Jerusalem now beckoned.

8
Jerusalem

The rulers were all at variance . . .
and so the Franks conquered the lands.

When Najm al-Din Ilghazi ibn Artuq, co-ruler of Jerusalem, was sober he was a force to be reckoned with: an audacious general and politician and one of the most competent of all the petty emirs within the troubled Seljuq empire. But he was also an incorrigible drunkard, and when tempted by the wineskin or the fermented mare's milk that was a staple intoxicant in Turkic nomadic culture, he was prone to disappear on enormous benders. The inevitable debilitating hangovers often rendered him incapable even of movement for days on end.[1] These dipsomaniacal urges made him unpredictable. He was capable of sadistic violence, frequently ordering that his prisoners be tortured to death: buried alive or strung up by their feet and riddled with arrows. A penchant for cruelty was hardly unusual for the age: Ilghazi's ally and contemporary Tughtakin, ruler of Damascus,* enjoyed beheading his enemies and having their skulls fashioned into bejeweled ceremonial drinking cups; among the crusaders, torture and mutilation were practiced without compunction upon enemies and suspected spies.[2] But even in a ferocious age Ilghazi left an impression on his contemporaries as a practitioner of inventive atrocity.

Ilghazi and his brother Sokmen had inherited the governorship of Jerusalem in 1091, following the death of their father, Artuq, who had been in the

*During the crusaders' assaults on Antioch and Jerusalem, Tughtakin was atabeg of Damascus, serving Alp Arslan's grandson Duqaq. In 1104 he became ruler in his own right.

post since 1079. Like Artuq, Ilghazi and Sokmen were appointed under the authority of the Great Seljuq sultan Malik-Shah. But like all Seljuq governors during the fractious 1090s, Ilghazi and Sokmen had found their positions increasingly tenuous after Malik-Shah's death. Their problems came to a head in August 1098, directly after the fall of Antioch, when siege engines including more than forty huge trebuchets appeared before Jerusalem's famous walls and started bombarding them with stones, causing large portions to collapse. The siege lasted "somewhat more than forty days," recorded Ibn al-Athir.[3] It was a sudden and violent attack conducted with acquisitive purpose and religious zeal. It caused Seljuq rule in Jerusalem to collapse. And it paved the way directly for epochal change in the politics of the Holy Land. But it was not the work of the crusaders.

The stone-throwing monsters that appeared outside Jerusalem in 1098 were in fact sent by an enemy of much longer standing: the Fatimids of Egypt. The Fatimids were a dynasty of Ismaili Shi'ite Muslims—adherents of a branch of Islam whom the Seljuqs, loyal to the Sunni Abbasid caliph in Baghdad, considered heretical. Doctrinally the differences between Sunni and Shi'a reached back to the seventh century CE: the product of poisonous divisions among the Prophet Muhammad's immediate relatives and descendants. The Fatimids of the eleventh century claimed descent and legitimacy from Muhammad's daughter Fatimah, and her husband, Ali. From their origins among Berber tribes in Algeria in 909 CE, the Fatimids had risen swiftly to commanded an empire that at its largest stretched from the Mahgreb to the Red Sea littoral in Arabia, and a long way north into Syria. By 1098 the empire had collapsed considerably in extent and authority from its peak, and was riven by schism and factionalism.* But it was still a force to be reckoned with around the eastern Mediterranean. Fatimid caliphs embodied what they considered to be supreme spiritual authority from their seat in Cairo, while their viziers dispensed political and military power on their behalf. Fatimid naval galleys prowled the seas between the Nile Delta and Asia Minor and their generals were capable of projecting force overland as far north as Damascus. There was absolutely no love lost between the Seljuqs and the Fatimids, since they vied

*The principal cause of schism in the Fatimid empire in the 1090s was a succession dispute that followed the death of the caliph al-Mustansir in 1094. Followers of his eldest son, Nizar, who was disinherited and murdered, rejected the authority of the new caliph, al-Musta'li. This split both dissolved Fatimid unity in Egypt and led indirectly to the formation of a Shi'ite, Persian-origin "Nizari" splinter state in Syria, most commonly (if inaccurately) known as the Hashishiyya or Assassins.

for influence over the same ports, the same trade routes, the same tribute-paying towns and the same holy sites. Indeed, such was their enmity that Islamic chroniclers of the time suspected the Fatimids of actively welcoming the crusaders into Syria, hoping they would weaken the Turks' hold on the Fatimid sphere of influence by creating a Christian buffer zone between their lands and those of the Seljuqs.[4] Whether this was true or not, it was very clear that the Seljuqs' woes at the siege of Antioch were far from a cause for solidarity among all Muslims. Rather, they were a chance for opportunist gain between entrenched and implacable enemies who had been at each others' throats long before the Latins showed their faces.[5]

The leader of the Fatimid forces who attacked Jerusalem in 1098 was a vizier who went by the immodest name of al-Malik al-Afdal ("the Excellent Prince"). The thirteenth-century scholar and biographer Ibn Khallikan praised al-Afdal as "an able ruler" who "possessed a superior judgment" and an unlimited appetite for conspicuous displays of consumption.[6] Al-Afdal owned at least one hundred gold-embroidered turbans, wrote Ibn Khallikan, which hung on individual gold hooks in the ten sitting rooms of his palace apartments. He had more livestock and treasure than could be counted, used a jewel-encrusted golden inkhorn and supplied his female slaves with golden knitting needles. When he arrived before Jerusalem he brought what Ibn al-Qalanisi called "a strong *askar* [army]" and an unwavering desire to seize the city from the two brothers who held it.

The ferocity of the bombardment al-Afdal unleashed on Jerusalem was more than Ilghazi and Sokmen were able to resist. After the walls were breached, al-Afdal's men fought their way in to the citadel and offered the brothers their lives in exchange for a businesslike transfer of the city to Fatimid control. "He showed kindness and generosity to the two emirs," wrote Ibn al-Qalanisi, "and set both them and their supporters free."[7] Al-Afdal could afford to be generous, and Ilghazi and Sokmen knew the game was up. They headed north toward Damascus, to fight another day. The vizier went home to Egypt, leaving a man called Iftikhar al-Dawla in charge of the Holy City. By mid-September 1098 all was quiet once more in Jerusalem. But it would not remain that way for long.

Five hundred miles to the north, the crusaders were starting for the first time to wobble in their purpose. The fall of Antioch had been an enormous coup, but it also exposed divisions in their leadership, centered around the role

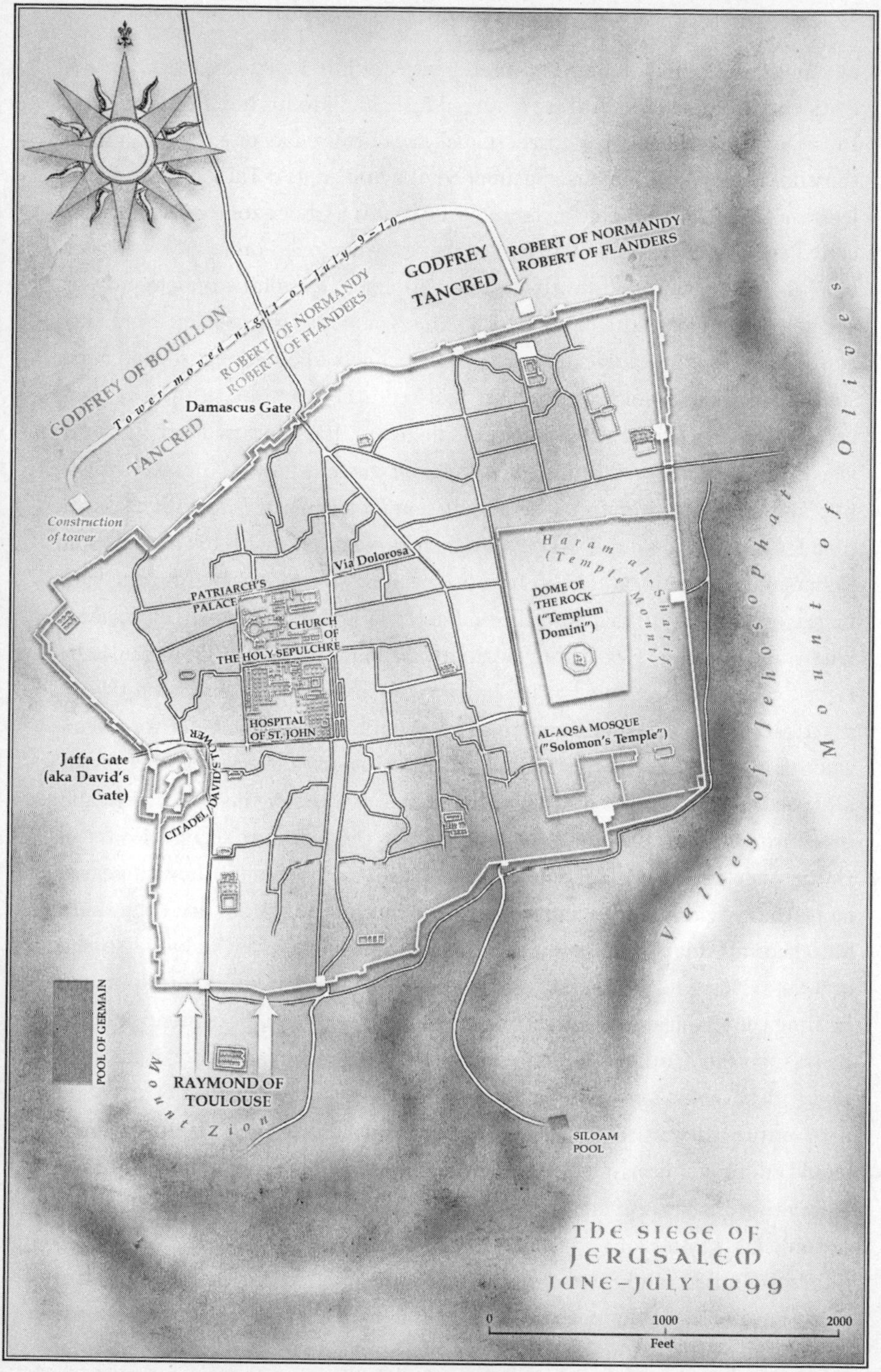

GODFREY OF BOUILLON
Tower moved night of July 9–10
ROBERT OF NORMANDY
ROBERT OF FLANDERS
TANCRED
GODFREY
TANCRED
ROBERT OF NORMANDY
ROBERT OF FLANDERS
Damascus Gate
Construction of tower
Via Dolorosa
PATRIARCH'S PALACE
CHURCH OF THE HOLY SEPULCHRE
HOSPITAL OF ST. JOHN
Haram al-Sharif (Temple Mount)
DOME OF THE ROCK ("Templum Domini")
AL-AQSA MOSQUE ("Solomon's Temple")
Jaffa Gate (aka David's Gate)
CITADEL/DAVID'S TOWER
TOWER
Valley of Jehosophat
Mount of Olives
POOL OF GERMAIN
RAYMOND OF TOULOUSE
Mount Zion
SILOAM POOL
THE SIEGE OF JERUSALEM JUNE–JULY 1099
0
1000
2000
Feet

and ambitions of Bohemond. In the first week of July 1098 the garrison inside Antioch's hilltop citadel had surrendered formally into his hands, rather than to the princes en masse or to the papal legate Adhémar of Le Puy as their spiritual chief. (Adhémar, as it happened, died on August 1, 1098, passing his legatine authority to Flemish clergyman Arnulf of Chocques.) Bohemond received the city gladly and moved in as its new ruler.

This power grab was immediately controversial. The oaths Bohemond and the rest of the princes had sworn to Alexios Komnenos the previous year suggested that whoever took command of Antioch would only be a stopgap ruler subject to the emperor's approval, as had been the case in cities the crusaders had overrun across Anatolia. Yet Bohemond, having raised his flag over the citadel, now showed precious little desire to see it lowered in favor of the imperial banner. In the face of fierce dissent, voiced most forcefully by Raymond, Count of Toulouse, who invested parts of the city with his own troops, Bohemond asserted that as the first princely entrant to Antioch he ought to be the one to keep it. He cited the emperor's failure to support the crusaders with an army from Byzantium during their darkest hours. "How can it be right for us to renounce what we have won by our own sweat and toil?" he asked, according to Anna Komnene.[8] For Anna, Bohemond's behavior at Antioch epitomized his double-dealing and fecklessness and informed her generally scathing portrait of him. For Raymond and others, this was the height of selfish irresponsibility. Having emerged as the foremost secular leader of the crusade during the march across Asia Minor, Bohemond now appeared to be bailing before Jerusalem was in sight. But nothing—not even the fierce objections of Raymond—would change his mind. After all the blood spilled and the misery endured at Antioch someone needed to take responsibility for holding the city against insurrection or Seljuq reconquest. Bohemond decided he was that man, and in doing so he established a second crusader state to sit alongside Baldwin's fledgling county of Edessa. The principality of Antioch, a powerful gateway state between Byzantium, Cilicia and northern Syria, would endure for nearly two centuries. As Bohemond went about securing the frontiers of his new appanage, it was clear that his attention was no longer on Jerusalem.[9]

With Tatikios and Stephen of Blois having both headed back west toward Constantinople, Baldwin absent in Edessa and Adhémar in his grave—the bishop was buried in the very same hole from which the Holy Lance had been retrieved—it was a depleted crusader army that finally moved off south from Antioch in November 1098. Squabbling among Bohemond, Raymond and the other princes had made for a demoralizing four-month hiatus in their march, and divisions continued between the leaders even as they departed for the next stage of their adventure. According to the chaplain Raymond of Aguilers, ordinary pilgrims and soldiers had begun to mutter of cowardice among the princes and to talk of either mutiny or desertion, saying to one another: "My goodness! a year in the land of the pagans and the loss of two hundred thousand soldiers; isn't this enough?"[10] When at last they were on the road again, they went in bloodthirsty mood.

Four or five days from Antioch the small town of Ma'arrat an-Nu'man (Marra) fell within their sights. Fifty years previously the Persian scholar and poet Nasir Khusraw had traveled through Ma'arrat and noticed flourishing markets selling figs, olives, pistachios and almonds to townsfolk whose homes were protected by stone walls and a cylindrical column inscribed with a charm to keep away scorpions.[11] When the crusaders arrived on November 28, the citizens rushed to the tops of the walls and began to bombard the army beneath with a hail of "stones . . . darts, fire, beehives and lime" to inhibit attempts to scale and sap the defenses.[12] It worked, but only for a time. During the next fortnight Raymond of Toulouse's Provençal engineers built a large, four-wheeled mobile siege tower and worked to fill in a ditch alongside one of the city walls, while Bohemond's soldiers attacked from the opposite side. On December 11, Raymond's tower, along with other ladders and engines, was pushed up against the fortifications. As the sun set, the city fell to storm. All night a disorganized mob of ordinary infantry ran amok through the streets, looting houses and lighting fires to smoke out citizens who had taken refuge in their cellars. "When the plunder [underground] proved disappointing, they tortured to death the hapless Muslims in their reach," remembered Raymond of Aguilers.[13] Women and children were massacred, and slaves were taken to be sold back in Antioch. The author of the *Gesta Francorum* witnessed the carnage: "No corner of the city was clear of Saracen corpses, and one could scarcely go about the city streets except by treading on the dead bodies of the Saracens." With midwinter approaching, there was little more food to be found either inside or outside the town than there had been at Antioch and once again the dolorous specter of cannibalism awoke. "[Our men] ripped up the bodies of the dead, because they used to find bezants [i.e., gold coins] hidden in their entrails," wrote the author of the *Gesta Francorum*. "Others cut the dead flesh into slices and cooked it to eat."[14] Then, with their bellies full and their appetites for butchery whetted, they set off for their next target.

As the crusaders ground through Syria toward the Lebanese coast, with crosses before them and human fat congealing in their beards, a poet called Mu'izzi composed verses for the Seljuq sultan Berkyaruq in Isfahan. He implored the king to be revenged in the name of "the Arab religion" on the Latins who defiled Muslim lands. "You should kill those accursed dogs and wretched creatures, the wolves who have sharpened their teeth and claws," he wrote. "You should take the Franks prisoner and cut their throats, with jeweled, life-devouring, blood-spurting daggers. You should make polo balls of the Franks' heads in the street, and polo-sticks from their hands and feet."[15] Yet the more that the accursed Franks stormed, slaughtered, tortured, massacred, enslaved and ate their way through the dar al-Islam, the further receded any realistic chances of playing ball games with their skulls. Across Syria, and especially along the route to Jerusalem that ran by the coastal road through the regions of Lebanon and Palestine, Seljuq emirs and semi-independent rulers of cities caught between Seljuq and Fatimid influence sent tribute to the crusader princes, negotiating to be left alone. (For any crusaders who had experience of warfare in against the *taifa* kingdoms of Spain, this was a familiar course of events.) Meanwhile, the princes continued to bicker among themselves: Bohemond left the crusade on March 1 to return to Antioch for good, while others, like his nephew Tancred, split into ever-shifting political factions. Mutual suspicion festered between the Provençal crusaders who followed Raymond of Toulouse and the Normans and other Franks. The unity of the previous year was evaporating. Yet they were closing in on their target. They had covered about two thousand miles since leaving Europe; now just two hundred more remained between them and Fatimid-held Jerusalem.

The last bastion of significant resistance to the crusaders' march was a fortress at Arqa (Akkar), which held out against a brutal three-month siege between February and May 1099, during which the crusader rank and file gorged themselves on "little honey-flavored reeds"—sugarcane—and knights sallied far and wide seeking battle and plunder.[16] The ruler of Tripoli, who was lord of Arqa, eventually wearied of seeing his men die and gave a peace offering of fifteen thousand gold pieces, along with horses, mules and rich fabrics. Elsewhere the ruler of Jubayl (Jableh) gave five thousand gold pieces and "an abundant supply of wine."[17] By Easter rumors were arriving from Constantinople suggesting that Alexios Komnenos had finally decided to set sail with a fleet in support of the crusade, bringing massive reinforcements of troops, gold and supplies. He would never appear, but even without the emperor behind them the crusaders were relentless. It was not clear who, if anyone, would be able to command an effective resistance.

In Cairo, the gold-turbaned Fatimid vizier al-Afdal was monitoring events with interest, if not yet alarm. Unlike Qilij Arslan, Yaghi-Siyan, Karbugha and the rest, he had not personally encountered the resilience and peculiar good fortune of the Franks, who were increasingly convinced that they were protected by martial saints like George and Andrew. But he was about to. During the siege of Antioch he had agreed to a nonaggression pact with the princes; now, as they swept toward his territories, that fell apart. Dipping his pen into his golden inkwell, al-Afdal wrote rallying letters that were transmitted via carrier pigeon to the rulers and faithful Muslims of Acre, Caesarea and elsewhere. The vizier exhorted the emirs to resist with all their might "a generation of dogs, a foolish, headstrong, disorderly race."[18]

This was easier said than done. During the second half of May, Tyre, Acre, Haifa and Caesarea all allowed the crusaders to march past with the barest minimum of resistance. "People fled in panic from their abodes before them," recorded Ibn al-Qalanisi.[19] The army was troubled less by Seljuq or Fatimid troops than by "fiery snakes" they encountered near Sidon. The snakes' bites could be fatal; one of the only known remedies was immediately to have sex with someone in order to "be released from the swelling and the heat of the poison."[20] By June 2 the crusaders had turned inland at Arsuf and were headed for Ramla on the road across the Judean hills to Jerusalem. All they found as they marched were the signs of abandoned strongholds. The Fatimids had burned the port of Jaffa (Tel-Aviv or Jafo) and left Ramla standing empty. They had effectively cleared the path. And so, on Tuesday June 7 the unbelievable finally happened: guards posted on the walls of Jerusalem reported to the governor Iftikhar al-Dawla that they had spied an army of Franks approaching: "rejoicing and exultant," weeping with joy and singing hymns. Many were thirsty or starving, others riddled with disease or suffering from malnutrition. The army, reduced to no more than fifteen thousand fighting men, of whom only about fifteen hundred were knights, was only a third the size of that which had set out from Constantinople. It had lost several of its most prominent leaders and those who remained were frequently at odds. Nevertheless, the crusaders had arrived at their destination, and the fate of the city was about to be decided.

Jerusalem was a modestly sized but well-protected city. Nestled in the Judean hills, on its eastern side it enjoyed the natural defensive lie of the steep-sided Jehoshaphat valley; on this and every other side the city was also guarded by thick walls punctuated by gatehouses, watchtowers and a citadel known as David's Tower (the *mihrab dawud*), which overlooked the gate adjoining the road from Jaffa. A series of moats provided further protection on the northern side. The defenses had been improved since al-Afdal's men had punched holes in the walls the previous summer, and Iftikhar al-Dawla had a garrison of about one thousand troops at his disposal to protect a population of no more than thirty thousand. Besides regular militias raised from the citizenry, these soldiers included four hundred elite horsemen sent from Cairo by al-Afdal, which included, as Fulcher of Chartres put it, "Arabs as well as Ethiopians" (by which he meant black Africans).[21] The city had its own water supply, and Iftikhar al-Dawla had taken care to block the wells outside the city, ensuring that the crusaders, if they did not wish to die of thirst, would have to bring their own water from miles away, carried in large canteens stitched together from oxhides, or else risk drawing it from the Pool of Siloam, which was well within arrow shot of the battlements.* Although at several points the city walls were overlooked by high ground from which missiles could easily be launched into the streets, and while it had already been conquered twice in the previous thirty years by exactly the sort of siegecraft in which the Franks had proven themselves deadly proficient, the governor was assured by messengers from the vizier that he would not have to hold out for very long before an army would come thundering up from Egypt to his rescue "to engage in

*Numerous Latin chroniclers related stories of the foulness and scarcity of the water available at the siege of Jerusalem, which caused widespread disease and much ill feeling, as those collecting water charged extortionate rates to their fellow crusaders for the privilege of drinking even a mouthful of polluted, worm-riddled slurry.

the Holy War against [the crusaders], and to destroy them, and to succor and protect the city against them."[22] All he had to do was wait it out.

Set against this, Iftikhar al-Dawla had two troubling considerations. The first was a point of military practicality: the crusaders knew as well as he did that al-Afdal was preparing a relief expedition, because captured messengers had told them that it could be expected by the end of July. They were making their plans accordingly. The second was a point of motivation. Sun-weathered, parched, diseased and weary the Franks may have been, but they were now arrayed before a place they considered the object of their pilgrimage and, cosmologically, the center of the earth. It was the place of Christ's ministry, Passion, Resurrection and Ascension; the burial place of the head of the first man, Adam, and the starting point of the journeys of the apostles. "What other city has ever experienced such a wonderful mystery, from which stemmed the salvation of all the faithful?" asked the chronicler Robert the Monk.[23] For Jews the city was also of profound importance as the place where the Ark of the Covenant had once resided. To Muslims it was the location of al-Aqsa Mosque and the Dome of the Rock, where Muhammad had prayed and ascended to the heavens to confer with God and the patriarchs during his Night Journey. But in July 1099 it was the Christians of the Latin West who had made the most incredible journey to stand in the shadow of Jerusalem's ramparts. That would count for much.

For the first month of the siege the defenders sat tight. All Christian visitors and residents were expelled from the city as soon as the Franks arrived. The crusaders were occupied with the difficult tasks of provisioning in the near waterless hills and reassembling—or building from scratch—the towers, battering rams and catapults they required to reduce the walls. They were aided in that effort on June 17 when a small fleet of six Genoese ships put into the remains of the razed port of Jaffa with building supplies. The ships were attacked by Egyptian galleys while at anchor, and the crews were forced to burn their vessels and flee, but not before they had unloaded valuable supplies of wood and carpentry equipment.

By the beginning of July Frankish armies could be seen at two key points around the city. In the south, outside the Zion Gate, camped the Provençal army of Raymond, Count of Toulouse. Almost all the rest of the princes—the Roberts of Normandy and Flanders, Godfrey of Bouillon and Tancred of Hauteville—were lined up to the north, where they were filling in moats and hammering at the walls between the far northeast corner of the city at the top of the valley and the so-called Quadrangular Tower fifteen hundred yards away to the extreme northwest. Ambushes were set along the paths running away over the Mount of Olives, where messengers regularly scrambled out of the least heavily defended side of the city to take information to the vizier in Cairo. When the Franks captured one unfortunate errand boy, they tortured him for his intelligence, bound him hand and foot and flung him in the direction of the city from the leather bucket of a trebuchet. (He did not make it, crashing well short of the walls onto a rocky outcrop, where he "broke his neck, his nerves and his bones," and died instantly.[24])

Despite these unpleasant spectacles, the defenders held out for a month, watching the crusaders below them toil in the heat. But on Friday, July 8, they were greeted by a new sight, as, from the direction of the valley of Jehoshaphat appeared a religious parade of penitents. Inspired by a visitation from the ghost of the late Bishop Adhémar and the advice of a local hermit, a stylite who lived in "an ancient and tall tower," the crusaders had all been fasting for three days.[25] Now they processed barefoot and solemn from the Mount of Olives to Mount Sion, close to Raymond of Toulouse's camp. As they walked, unarmed and carrying holy relics, Iftikhar al-Dawla's men enjoyed a field day. On the battlements Muslim troops gleefully brought out crosses from within the city, spitting and urinating on them, hanging them from miniature gallows and dashing them to pieces against the walls. Then they took aim with their bows and killed or wounded many of the clerics and laymen. It was, it seemed, all too easy.

The following week, however, everything changed. It had taken several weeks for the crusaders to assemble their heaviest artillery, but once built it was lethal. Over the weekend following the religious procession, the armies in the north transported all their siege machinery to concentrate on a seven-hundred-yard stretch of double walls running east from St. Stephen's Gate. The following Thursday, July 14, an almighty battery began. Three mangonels started the assault, forcing the defenders to retreat from the walls. Shields of large straw-packed cushions had been hung from the walls to deaden the impact of trebuchet shot, but Godfrey of Bouillon deployed a hail of burning arrows to clear them. Then came the sickening, percussive thud of a vast, iron-headed battering ram of "horrendous weight and craftsmanship."[26] This crunched through the outer of the two walls, opening a breach that was eventually large enough* to push through one of the crusaders' larger siege towers. The tower was a wooden structure a spear's length taller than the wall itself, topped with a gleaming gold cross, and covered with flame-retardant horse and camel skins stretched over a wicker cage, which protected the occupants against an inflammable concoction of sulfur, pitch and molten wax known as Greek fire, which Jerusalem's guards hurled in pots that "vomited" flames.[27]

It was now obvious that help would not arrive from Egypt in time to defend the city. Iftikhar al-Dawla had fourteen of his own mangonels inside Jerusalem, and he divided these between the two vulnerable points in the defenses, which held up the crusaders' progress for a time, preventing them from moving their towers close enough to the wall to allow an attempt on the ramparts. But as night fell on Thursday, July 14, after a long day of utterly ferocious battle, it was clear that he could not hold on much longer. At dawn the following day the great golden-crossed tower was finally edged into position against the inner wall in the northeast, with Godfrey on top of it, shooting from his crossbow. (To the south, Raymond of Toulouse's men also made contact with the stonework, but their siege engine was burned with Greek fire.) The top of Godfrey's tower was a perilous place to be: with a steady and increasingly desperate rain of missiles, the Jerusalem garrison almost brought it to the ground. They watched it lurch and nearly topple, threatening to throw everyone aboard to their deaths.[28] A stone launched from inside the city narrowly missed Godfrey and hit the soldier standing next to him: "His skull was broken and his neck shattered," wrote Albert of Aachen.[29]

Had the tower or the prince fallen, the city might have survived. But neither did. Inside the city a stone from a Frankish mangonel crushed to death two women who were said to have been attempting to cast a spell over the enemy artillery, along with three little girls standing by them.[30] High above a sudden burst of arrows tipped with flaming cotton pads cleared the ramparts just long enough for a drawbridge to be let down out of the siege tower.[31] The

*To make room for the siege engine to attack the breach, the crusaders had first to set on fire the battering ram, which had become jammed in the walls after doing its job; they managed to do this despite the defenders pouring water over the walls to douse the fire.

first Frankish troops, commanded by Godfrey, poured over the top. Soon they had fought their way down from the towers to the city streets. White-frocked priests chanting the *Kyrie Eleison* ran with long ladders to help the armies below the tower surge up and over the abandoned wall. Then, the ladders were no longer required: bolts were pulled back on the gates, and the whole might of the crusader army poured in. Many had waited nearly four years for this moment. As they swarmed elated into the city where Christ had died in agony for the salvation of their sins, they made it their mission to be revenged on every unbeliever they encountered. The vizier al-Afdal was nowhere to be seen. His people, abandoned, were about to be destroyed.

The slaughter of Jerusalem in the days following its fall to the crusaders on Friday, July 15, 1099, was one of the atrocities of its age, an extreme example of the rights of a victorious party to withhold mercy from the vanquished, and a biblical wasting in keeping with other Norman-inspired massacres like William the Conqueror's "Harrying" of northern England in 1069 and 1070. As the crusaders swooped, Iftikhar al-Dawla cut a deal to save his own skin and those of the Egyptian forces who had survived the defense of the ramparts. Under Raymond of Toulouse's protection they were rushed out of the city and escorted to the nearest Fatimid stronghold at Ascalon. Behind them, in Ibn al-Athir's words, "the inhabitants became prey for the sword."[32] Since the Christians had been expelled at the beginning of the siege, every inhabitant was now considered legitimate quarry for the thousands of zealous warrior pilgrims who ran from house to house murdering and looting for a full week. Raymond of Aguilers was among them, and later wrote that "some of the pagans were mercifully beheaded, others, pierced by arrows, plunged from towers, and yet others, tortured for a long time, were burned to death in searing flames. Piles of heads, hands and feet lay in the houses and streets, and indeed there was a running to and fro of men and knights over the corpses."[33]

In scenes reminiscent of the disgraceful riots that had taken place in the Rhineland at the outset of the People's Crusade, a large number of Jews were murdered: they "assembled in the synagogue and the Franks burned it over their heads."[34] Thousands of Muslim citizens fled to the large raised platform of the Temple Mount, where they took shelter in, around and even on top of al-Aqsa Mosque. Tancred of Hauteville and another lord, Gaston of Béarn, offered them their banners as a sign of protection, but the princes had long ago lost control of the orgy of violence. Thousands upon thousands were killed, either by the hands of the mob or by their own design, as they leaped from the Temple Mount in despair to escape being tortured to death. Some were drowned in cisterns. Babies ripped from their mothers were smashed headfirst into walls and door frames. Many Christian chroniclers saw in this mass extermination on the site of Solomon's Temple the realization of a prophecy from the Revelation of Saint John. They wrote, echoing John's words, of crusaders riding in blood up to their knees or the bridles of their horses.[35] Naturally, alongside the killing came a frenzy of rapine, as princes and poor pilgrims alike filled their arms with treasure: "gold and silver, horses and mules and houses full of all sorts of goods." Tancred, notwithstanding his futile concern for the well-being of the Muslim citizenry, greedily pillaged the shrine around the Dome of the Rock (which the crusaders called the Temple of the Lord). His personal bodyguard spent two days ripping down "an incomparable quantity of gold and silver from the walls," an act of naked freebooting for which Tancred was later censured.[36] Across the city in the Church of the Holy Sepulchre, some pilgrims had decided to pray, clapping and singing and chanting the Office of the Resurrection, which was normally reserved for Easter.[37] All the while their fellows enjoyed themselves putting whole families to death, "so that not a suckling little male child or female, not even an infant of one year would escape alive the hand of the murderer."[38] The violence only abated when the streets were so full of bodies that they had begun to stink. At this point, priests gave the order for corpses to be dragged outside the walls and incinerated. "They were burned on pyres like pyramids and no one save God alone knows how many there were," wrote the author of the *Gesta Francorum*.[39]

When survivors who had managed to flee Jerusalem reached the court of the Sunni Abbasid caliph in Baghdad, they told a story that "brought tears to the eye and pained the heart." At Friday prayers the news was broadcast to the faithful in the mosque: a tale of "the killing of men, the enslavement of women and children and the plundering of property that had fallen upon the Muslims in that revered august place."[40] To Ibn al-Athir and other scholars writing after the event, it was clear what had brought about the calamity: "The rulers were all at variance . . . and so the Franks conquered the lands."[41]

Back in Jerusalem, the victorious crusaders took a higher view of their conquest. "Omnipotent God, what deep emotion, what joy, what grief they felt, after unheard-of sufferings, never experienced by any army, like the tortures of child-birth, when, like new-born children, they saw that they had attained the fresh joys of the long-desired vision," rhapsodized Guibert of Nogent.[42] Whether they had succeeded through political failing among their enemies, their own heroic feats of endurance or the will of the Almighty no one could say for sure. Whatever the case, Jerusalem had fallen. Urban II's mission had been accomplished. The Franks had come to the Holy Land, and now they were there to stay.

◆ 9 ◆

Dividing the Spoils

So much for the barbarians . . .

Shortly before Christmas in 1099 Bohemond of Antioch and Baldwin of Edessa came down to Jerusalem to complete their pilgrimages with a first visit to the Holy City. It was another foul winter, and the journey of almost two hundred and fifty miles from northern Syria to Palestine brought the familiar evil weather and perpetual lack of supplies. Fulcher of Chartres traveled with Bohemond and Baldwin and recorded the dismal conditions: hunger alleviated only by eating donkey and camel meat or chewing sugarcane; Muslim bandits "lurking around the narrow paths along the way" to rob or kill foragers; "excessive cold and frequent rainstorms" after which "the heat of the sun was not sufficient to dry our sodden clothes when another rain would harass us for four or five days."[1] It was so wet and cold that troops died from exposure in their tents.

Along the way they met no one who would sell them food or supplies, save the Fatimid-aligned emirs of Caesarea and Tripoli, who traded grain and bread at extortionate prices. And when they reached Jerusalem on December 21 their outpourings of pious joy and relief were tempered by the lingering sights and smells of their fellow crusaders' victory five months earlier. "What a stench there was around the walls of the city . . . from the rotting bodies of the Saracens slain by our comrades, lying wherever they had been hunted down," wrote Fulcher.[2] Passing through the city gates the pilgrim party were forced to cover their mouths and hold their noses against the nauseating miasma.

In Jerusalem they found Baldwin's elder brother, Godfrey of Bouillon, ruling supreme. Godfrey had been elected to preeminence eight days after the city fell, on July 22. He declined to take the title of king, instead choosing to be called "Advocate [or Defender] of the Holy Sepulchre." Alongside him, Arnulf of Chocques was confirmed as the first Latin patriarch of Jerusalem on August 1. As soon as Godfrey was appointed, he was forced to march an army out of Jerusalem to the Fatimid coastal redoubt of Ascalon, forty miles away, where the Fatimid vizier al-Afdal was belatedly assembling an army to storm Jerusalem and evict the impertinent unbelievers.

Somehow, yet again, the crusaders had triumphed, defeating a large Fatimid army in a terrible battle fought outside Ascalon's walls on August 12. Al-Afdal was put to flight and his sword was captured. (Naturally, this was found to be a glorious weapon valued at sixty bezants.[3]) "The battle was terrible, but the power of God was with us," wrote the author of the *Gesta Francorum*.[4] And indeed, the crusaders' run of successes on the battlefield was starting to seem miraculous. It was true that they had grown wily through long experience and were hardened to extreme misery, but now they also had in their possession a remarkable new divine prophylactic: a shard of the True Cross. Encased in a golden reliquary, it had been discovered by torturing the Orthodox priests at the Holy Sepulchre who guarded it. When carried into battle by the patriarch, this relic—which explicitly and obviously rivaled another portion of the Cross held in Constantinople by Alexios Komnenos—was thought to make the crusaders invincible to the assaults of the infidel. It did not, however, make them impervious to the machinations of each other, as Bohemond and Baldwin's visit at Christmas 1099 was to show.

The two princes of the northern crusader states did not arrive in Jerusalem alone. At the start of their journey they had collected another formidable character by the name of Daimbert (or Dagobert), archbishop of Pisa, a high-ranking churchman originally from the German lands around Mainz, whom Urban II had most likely appointed as a papal legate.[5] Daimbert had been at Clermont in 1095 and had preached the First Crusade in his Italian archdiocese. Yet he never joined the armies of the princes. Instead, the pope had sent him in 1098 to Alfonso VI of Castile and León to help organize new lands conquered from the Muslim rulers in Spain on behalf of the Roman Church. According to Albert of Aachen, who regarded Daimbert with unmasked contempt, this had been a profitable enterprise. The archbishop, said Albert, siphoned off large amounts of treasure presented to him by Alfonso, most notably "a golden ram of marvelous and beautiful workmanship," which was intended as a present for the pope.[6] Instead of sending this glittering trinket to Rome, Albert alleged, Daimbert kept it for himself and was still carrying the ram and a cache of his Spanish treasure when he arrived in the Holy Land aboard a large fleet of Pisan ships in the autumn of 1099. Along the way he had looted various Greek islands and fought running battles against Byzantine vessels equipped with bronze lion heads that sprayed Greek fire from their mouths. Daimbert made contact with Bohemond at the Byzantine city of Latakia, which the new prince of Antioch was enthusiastically besieging, sent his ships on to Jaffa and went south with the delegation that appeared in Jerusalem on December 21.

To judge by the account given by Fulcher of Chartres, Bohemond, Baldwin and Daimbert's visit to Jerusalem was a peaceful, celebratory affair, in which the princes visited the Church of the Holy Sepulchre "and the other holy places," then traveled eight miles south of the city to Bethlehem. On Christmas Eve, in the large, cruciform Church of the Nativity they joined prayers on the spot where the infant Christ had been placed in a manger.[7] Christmas Day was spent back in Jerusalem, and at New Year the group went out of the city once again to bathe in the river Jordan. During the first week of January 1100, they cut palm leaves from the famous trees of Jericho* before Bohemond and Baldwin set off back north to return to their new homes via Tiberias and the Sea of Galilee. It was, or appeared to be, a happy Christmas.

Yet beneath the celebrations, matters were not quite so peaceful. In the course of his festive narrative, Fulcher noted that while Bohemond and Baldwin were in Jerusalem, Godfrey "and the other chief men" appointed "Lord Daimbert to be Patriarch in the Church of the Holy Sepulchre." This meant that after just six months, Arnulf of Chocques was elbowed aside. Fulcher did not explain this abrupt change in Jerusalem's nascent Latin leadership. Had he done so, he would have been forced to concede that it was in fact a coup, orchestrated in favor of Bohemond. Seemingly from nowhere, an outsider who

---

*These palm leaves were highly valued by crusaders, who took them as trophies of their victory, often carrying them back to the West to be laid upon the altars of local religious institutions as a mark of their mission accomplished. On this, see Jonathan Riley-Smith, *The First Crusaders: 1095–1131* (Cambridge: Cambridge University Press, 1997), 144–45.

had played no part in the long march to the East had been gifted the most prestigious new office in the Christian world. The patriarch had of course brought treasure, Pisan warships and the backing of Rome—but more important than any of that was his usefulness to the artful prince of Antioch.

When Anna Komnene reflected in her chronicle on Bohemond's behavior around this time, she wrote that he was "not changed a jot, a man who had never learned what it was to keep the peace . . . a thorough rogue."[8] Certainly, he always had an eye for his own advantage. During the Christmas visit of 1099, Daimbert used his new patriarchal powers to bless Bohemond in his title as Prince of Antioch. He thereby officially sanctioned on behalf of the Latin Church the blatant oath-breaking that Bohemond had undertaken when he refused to turn the city over to Byzantium the previous year. To reinforce the point he also confirmed a raft of new ecclesiastical appointments in Antioch, overriding the right of the Greek patriarch there.[9] Byzantine claims to Bohemond's city and the state he intended to build around it were being systematically stripped away. Furthermore, Daimbert's introduction as patriarch in Jerusalem came at a direct cost to the Latins, as he demanded control over a large swath of the city (which became the "patriarch's quarter" and included the Holy Sepulchre itself) as well as extensive rights in the port of Jaffa. It was little wonder that, writing her chronicle many years later, Anna Komnene gnashed her teeth at Bohemond's selfishness and impudence, and deplored the depravity of his Pisan allies. "So much for the barbarians," she wrote.[10] Bohemond would get his comeuppance: in August 1100 he was captured while campaigning in Melitene (Malatya), north of Edessa on the banks of the upper Euphrates, and taken off in chains as a prisoner of Danishmend Ghazi, the ruler of northeastern Asia Minor who was a sometime ally of the Seljuq petty sultan Qilij Arslan. He was only released in May 1103, on payment of a vast ransom of 100,000 bezants. Yet this was not the end of his career, and his troubled relations with the Emperor Alexios were destined to continue for the rest of the decade, giving plenty more cause for Anna Komnene's displeasure. If all the iniquity and duplicity of the Franks—or Kelts, as she called them—could have been given a single human form it would have been that of Bohemond.

As a new century dawned, the map of the Holy Land and the eastern Mediterranean was changing rapidly. In Jerusalem, a Latin kingdom became a reality late in 1100, when Godfrey of Bouillon died and his brother, Baldwin of

Edessa, was summoned south to celebrate a second Christmas in Bethlehem. There, on December 25, he was crowned Baldwin I, king of Jerusalem. He was destined for a far longer reign than his brother, who had been weakened terribly by his arduous crusade, and perhaps had never fully recovered from the severe injuries he sustained fighting the bear in Asia Minor. Baldwin would rule until 1118 (his cousin, Baldwin of Bourcq, succeeded him as count of Edessa) and during that time waged a steady war against the Fatimids. This war necessitated not only defensive actions against armies marching out of Egypt but also campaigns to secure further cities for Frankish rule. It was a matter of existential importance that the crusader kingdom expanded beyond the city of Jerusalem the narrow, perilous corridor of land running off to Jaffa and the sea. So during the first decade of his reign Baldwin targeted, with varying degrees of success, Arsuf and Caesarea, Acre and Tyre, Beirut, Sidon and Tripoli. Little by little, over the course of Baldwin's reign, a genuine crusader kingdom would start to emerge.

In these campaigns Baldwin was aided by comrades old and new. Of the princes who had set out after Clermont, some—like Godfrey, Baldwin and Tancred of Hauteville—settled in the East. Others went back to the West—Robert of Flanders and Robert of Normandy decided to return to their homelands, which were suffering considerably for lack of stable lordship. A few—Bohemond among them—would attempt to straddle the two sides of the Mediterranean, traveling back and forth between France, the Balkans, Byzantium and the new crusader states. And others still tried to keep the momentum of the First Crusade alive. Stephen of Blois had abandoned the crusade at Antioch in 1098, for which he was lambasted as "a scoundrel and a wretch" by the author of the *Gesta Francorum*, and he was determined to atone for his failure.[11] Both he and Hugh of Vermandois—along with the irrepressible Raymond of Toulouse—joined an army of Western lords and peasants that set out to reinforce the crusaders by marching overland from Constantinople through Asia Minor in the summer of 1101. Their ill-starred mission was scattered by the united armies of Qilij Arslan; Radwan, emir of Aleppo; and Danishmend Ghazi. Both Stephen and Hugh died in the course of this campaign. Raymond, however, stayed on in the East and worked until his own death in 1105 to establish a fourth crusader state between Jerusalem and Antioch, which (in 1109) would become the County of Tripoli.

In Western Europe, meanwhile, hundreds of crusade survivors were staggering back to their homes—some ill, some wounded, very few having earned more than they had spent—carrying palm leaves and telling jaw-dropping stories of suffering and derring-do. Some carried relics, and scores of churches and monasteries in France, Flanders, England, Italy and elsewhere were endowed with fragments of stone chipped from the tomb of Christ at the Holy Sepulchre, shavings of metal from the tip of the Holy Lance of Antioch, splinters of the True Cross and assorted portions of saints' bodies, including the arm, shoulder and rib bones of Saint George, which were pilfered from a marble chest in a monastery somewhere in Cilicia and ended up in the abbey of Anchin in Flanders.[12] But many more crusaders brought back only mental and physical scars. Raimbold of Caron, who fought at Antioch and claimed to have been the first man over the walls of Jerusalem on July 15, 1099, came back with one of his hands missing, and fell into a life of decidedly unholy violence, which eventually earned him fourteen years of penance imposed by the Church as punishment for ordering the beating and castration of a monk from Bonneval.

Few of these survivors wished to go back to the East, but there were others who did. Then there were the newcomers. Although the fall of Jerusalem had been a seemingly miraculous triumph, it had not brought an end to the impulses that lay behind crusading. There were plenty of knights still traveling from the West in search of a penitential fight against the infidel: Albert, Count of Biandrate, and his brother Guy came East with the bishop of Milan and a group of other Lombards in 1101 and was killed fighting the Turks. An English sea captain called Godric of Finchale joined two separate missions to the East in the decade after Jerusalem's fall, after which he retired back in the West to become a hermit.

For certain families, such as the intermarried Montlhéry and Le Puiset dynasties of central France, armed pilgrimage to crusader states would become a tradition and a duty passed down through the generations.[13] For other groups, such as the acquisitive and adventurous seafaring merchants of Italian city-states like Pisa, Genoa and Venice, assisting with the survival and growth of the crusader states became a matter not only of piety but of hard-nosed business opportunity. The Pisan ships that had brought Patriarch Daimbert to the East did not linger long, but in June 1100 the Doge of Venice's son, Vitale Giovanni, arrived via Rhodes with two hundred ships and proceeded to lend Venetian sea power to crusader attacks on the Levantine coast. The Genoese sent more than one hundred and fifty galleys between 1100 and 1109, joining campaigns from Caesarea in the south to Mamistra, inland in Cilicia to the north, and keeping detailed accounts of the politics of Jerusalem and the Holy Land in their city annals.[14]

These essential contributions to stabilizing the crusader states were undertaken with pious intent and a sensitivity to both the wish of individual citizens to make penitential armed pilgrimages and the wider desire of the civic community to gain a reputation for religious deeds. Yet at the same time, the galleys went into battle only on the condition that their occupants were awarded lucrative trading rights and revenues in every city that was taken. Faith and business were two sides of the same coin.[15]

This was no radical departure. Pisan and Genoese vessels had been engaged in warfare against Muslim enemies since at least 1087, when amphibious attacks on Mahdia in Ifriqiya, undertaken primarily for commercial advantage, had been justified as the pursuit of righteous war against the infidel and the manifestation of "our Redeemer's most mighty hand, by which the Pisan race vanquished a most impious people."[16] They had been granted special trading rights for assisting crusaders since Bohemond issued a charter privileging Genoese merchants on July 14, 1098, just one month after the fall of Antioch.[17] The opportunity to buy permanent outposts in the newly Latinized cities of the eastern Mediterranean was too good to pass up, combining as it did a chance to demonstrate civic piety and attachment to the crusading movement with economic expansion. Italians who took their crusading vows and set out to help win, defend and man trading stations on the Syrian and Palestinian coast would be a common sight in the crusader East for generations to come.

In Sicily, Bohemond's uncle Count Roger I, who had steadfastly refused to be taken in by the lure of holy warfare either in Ifriqiya or in Palestine, was coming to the end of his reign by 1099. History was destined to recall only dimly his wars against Muslim powers of the Mediterranean, which paled in drama and renown next to the business of the Jerusalem crusade. Yet in his own way, he had achieved just as astonishing a feat.

By the turn of the century, Sicily had been wrenched firmly and permanently from Arab rule. Malta, too, was conquered in 1090. Roger overrode longstanding Byzantine claims to oversee the Church in his new territories by creating a Latin ecclesiastical hierarchy that the count himself oversaw. In 1098 Pope Urban II had taken the unprecedented step of awarding Roger legatine status. This meant he was permitted to appoint his own bishops—an astounding privilege considering that investiture had been at the heart of wars between popes and kings across the West for decades. Having come to southern Italy as a younger son seeking a fortune, Roger ended up the most powerful man in that region. His son Roger II, born at Christmastime in 1099, grew up to become Sicily's first Norman king and a towering presence in Mediterranean history during the twelfth century. In winning a crown, he fulfilled the royal ambitions of his father. The elder Roger died in June 1101 and was buried in a fine tomb at the abbey of Mileto in Calabria, where above his Romanesque marble sarcophagus was erected a canopy made from porphyry—the purple-flecked stone that was supposedly reserved only for use by Byzantine emperors.[18] His widow, Adelaide del Vasto, who oversaw the construction of that fine tomb, later went on to become, albeit for a short and unhappy period, the queen consort of King Baldwin I of Jerusalem. Whatever Roger's reticence about crusading, he had proven himself an important figure in the development of the movement and the wider story of his times.

Then there was Spain, where, just as in Sicily, papal-sanctioned warfare against an Islamic foe had long preceded Urban II's crusade preaching. Here the new shape of war that had been set in the 1080s was between rulers such as Alfonso VI of Castile and León—the "Emperor of the Two Religions"—and the Almoravids of northwest Africa. The 1090s were dominated by a long-running series of battles over Valencia, ruled by El Cid. The struggle for Valencia was won by the Almoravids: El Cid died in July 1099, and three years later in 1102 his widow, Jimena Díaz, was counseled by Alfonso to abandon her attempts to defend the city and its appurtenances, burn it and retreat to fight another day. Other than Valencia, the Almoravids won back no more significant territories from the Christian princes of the north, but their dramatic arrival on the European mainland, riding roughshod over the fractured *taifa* states and taking aim at the Christian kings, had done much to advance the idea that the perpetual boundary squabbles of the peninsula were giving way to a cosmic, existential struggle between two faith-defined blocs in which there could only be a single winner. Alfonso, for his part, lived on until

1109, when he died while organizing the defense of Toledo, the greatest prize of his career, from attack by the Almoravids. He was buried at the monastery at Sahagún on the Way of Saint James, which had been converted to Cluniac obedience under his direction and had therefore played its own role in the spread of ideas of Christian holy warfare and Roman expansion into Muslim-held areas. It was an appropriate place for Alfonso to take his rest, and the twelfth-century Tunisian legal writer and historian Ibn al-Kardabus wrote that his death came as a great relief to all Muslims.[19]

Thanks to Alfonso and others like him, by the dawn of the twelfth century Spain had unquestionably came to be seen as a major frontier of holy war between Latin Christian and Muslim rulers. If there was any doubt that clashes in the region were explicitly linked to the conflicts of the East, it had been swept away in 1096 when Urban wrote to several noblemen on either side of the Pyrenees to urge them *not* to travel to the Holy Land, but rather to stay and fight the Almoravids. "If any one of you . . . plans to go to Asia, let him try to fulfill the desire of his devotion here," wrote Urban. "For there is no virtue in delivering Christians from Saracens there while exposing Christians here to the tyranny and oppression of the Saracens."[20] Besides the appeal to simple geographical convenience, Urban added the assurance that the same remission of sins and "participation in life eternal" promised to the Eastern crusaders would greet those who fell as martyrs while fighting in Spain. Crusading, it seemed, was not exclusively about Jerusalem. The chronicler Guibert of Nogent and patriarch of Jerusalem Daimbert of Pisa—both of whom had experience of the wars against the Almoravids before their adventures in the East—referred to Muslim-held territories in Syria and Palestine by the generic term "Hispania." Apparently they recognized no especial difference between the struggle against the masked Berber zealots of west Africa and *taifa* kings whom they displaced in southern Iberia, the Sunni-aligned Seljuqs of Asia Minor and Syria or the Shi'ite Fatimids of Egypt.[21]

Whether this was all as Urban had intended at Clermont would never be known. Nor is it recorded how the pope responded to the news in 1099 that Jerusalem had been conquered. A letter addressed to him in September 1099 by Daimbert, Godfrey of Bouillon and Raymond of Toulouse triumphantly narrated the crusaders' escapades in "fulfilling through us what [God] had promised in ancient times." The authors continued: "We call on you, all the bishops, devout clerics, monks and all the laity, to glory in the marvelous bravery and devotion of our brothers, in the glorious and very desirable reward of the Almighty, in the remission of sins which we hope for through the grace of God, and in the exultation of the Catholic Church of Christ and the whole Latin race, so that God who lives and reigns for ever and ever will sit you down at His right hand." And they requested that the pope and all the faithful should look after veterans coming back from the campaign, helping them to settle their debts.[22]

Yet Urban never received the letter, and he never learned of Jerusalem's fall, for by the time news came back to the West he was dead. He breathed his last on July 29, 1099, to be succeeded by another Cluniac, who took the name Paschal II. Paschal continued to back wars against the "Moabites and Moors" in Spain, and took considerable interest in assisting with efforts to ensure the survival of the Christian states in the East that would come to be known collectively as Outremer. He bickered long and hard with Holy Roman Emperors and he tried without success to improve relations with the Komnenoi in Byzantium. He did not attempt to repeat Urban's rallying cry at Clermont—indeed, it would be many years before another pope dared call for another mission on the epic scale of the First Crusade. But there would be, in the meantime, no shortage of willing crusaders.

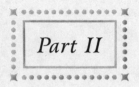

Part II

KINGDOM OF HEAVEN

◆ 10 ◆

Sigurd Jerusalemfarer

Sixty ships sailed . . . by holy heaven's decree.

Tall with red-brown hair, "not handsome, but well proportioned" and never inclined to speak unless he had something important to say, Sigurd I of Norway became a king at about the age of thirteen.[1] That was 1103, the year his father, Magnús Barelegs, was struck in the neck with an ax by an Irishman and fell down dead, leaving the crown jointly to the teenage Sigurd and two of his half brothers: Eystein, a few months older, and Olaf, who was little more than a toddler.

Magnús—the "Barelegs" sobriquet referred to his fondness for clothing cropped short above the knee in the British fashion—had been a stern and warlike ruler of Christian faith but classic Viking inclination, possessed by a seafaring wanderlust that led him to conquests around the North Sea and beyond. When Sigurd was a child, his father had taken him on one of his habitual long expeditions, and they had sailed together to Orkney and the Hebrides, the Isle of Man and north Wales. Sigurd watched as his father battled Gaels, Manxmen and Normans, wearing a crimson silken tunic decorated with gold lions and swinging a sword with a hilt of walrus ivory, which he had given the pet name Legbiter.[2]

Sigurd had seen his father burn countryside, butcher men and demand tribute from conquered islands. He had also seen him undertake small acts of mercy, and even of piety, as when Magnús stopped on the holy isle of Iona, in the Hebrides, proclaimed peace to all who lived there and ostentatiously refused, out of reverence, to plunder the ancient cell of Saint Columba. In general, however, Magnús preferred the battlefield to the cloister, telling his friends that "one should have a king for glorious deeds, not for a long life."[3] It was abrupt but not surprising when he was cut down in his prime while making war somewhere near Downpatrick, Ireland, at the age of twenty-nine.

Now, all of a sudden, Sigurd and his brothers were joint kings. The two older boys parceled up Norway between them and agreed to rule in tandem as they waited for Olaf to grow up and claim his part of the patrimony. This was an unconventional arrangement, and as soon as Sigurd was on the threshold of manhood he began to plot his own travels away from the congested kingdom. For him the North and Irish Seas were not enough. In the first years of the twelfth century travelers had begun to trickle back to Norway from much further afield. Some had been to Palestine, others to a place they called Miklagarth—the Great Stronghold—where they had "acquired great fame and could tell of many events."[4] This was Constantinople, and it is likely that some spoke of lucrative mercenary service in the Varangian Guard, the foreign legion that made up the Byzantine emperor's elite personal bodyguard, and recruited its members from England, the Germanic states and Scandinavia. (During the 1030s, Sigurd's great-grandfather Harald Hardrada had been a commander, traveling and fighting in Sicily, Asia Minor and Mesopotamia.) Others must have seen action in the First Crusade and the nascent crusader states. Certainly one near neighbor, Sven of Denmark, had marched fifteen hundred men across Asia Minor toward Antioch in 1097, achieving his martyrdom rather too early when he was set upon by Qilij Arslan's forces; his men were routed and Sven and his wife, Florina of Burgundy, were riddled with arrows.[5]

So the notion of Scandinavians found far from home, fighting with and against peoples of the eastern Mediterranean, was not entirely strange.[6] But in the first decade of the twelfth century, talk of events taking place on the other side of Christendom filled the Norwegians with unprecedented excitement, and men across the kingdom began to talk of traveling to the Holy Land. When he was seventeen, Sigurd—possessed by a young man's instinct for adventure and, perhaps, the generations-old Viking sense that great riches were usually to be found across the seas—agreed to lead them. He made a pact with his elder brother, by which Eystein agreed to rule the whole kingdom while Sigurd took an expeditionary army to the Mediterranean. In the autumn of 1107, Sigurd fitted out a fleet and went to sea with, it was later reckoned, ten thousand men under his command. "Sixty ships sailed, gaily planked, hence by holy heaven's decree," wrote an Icelandic *skald* (bard poet) called Thórarin Stuttfield.[7] The armada of five dozen longships—typically thirty yards in length, with dragons snarling from the prow, billowing square sails and a crew of up to sixty oarsmen in each—was a mighty and daunting sight.[8]

Sigurd made the first stop of his journey in England, where Harald Hardrada had contended for the throne during the upheavals of 1066. Five decades on the Normans were fully in command there and one later chronicler claimed that "peace remained undisturbed."[9] This was not entirely true. William the Conqueror's son Robert, Duke of Normandy, one of the princes of the First Crusade who had helped take Jerusalem, had returned from the Holy Land in 1100 to find his youngest brother occupying the English throne as King Henry I. Robert had missed his chance to wear a crown, and in 1105 and 1106 things got much worse. Henry invaded Robert's duchy of Normandy, defeated him in battle near Tinchebray and took him back to England as a prisoner. When Sigurd arrived to overwinter, the crusading hero was locked away in Devizes Castle. He would see out the rest of his life in jail, dying in Cardiff Castle in 1134, by which time he was in his eighties.

Sigurd, since he came in peace, was treated much better than Robert. The chronicler William of Malmesbury said he was "comparable to the bravest heroes," and he was shown the full protection of the Norman Crown.[10] To show his gratitude, and in keeping with his status as a pilgrim on his way to the Holy Land, Sigurd donated vast sums to various English churches. Then, when the wind picked up in the spring of 1108, he left England, sailed across the Channel and headed south. His fleet made stately progress along France's Atlantic coastline before rounding the Bay of Biscay. Toward the end of summer they put into port in Galicia, which the Norwegians knew as *Jákobsland*—the land of Saint James, or Santiago de Compostela.

Here again they overwintered, although it was a less peaceful stay than they had enjoyed in England. Galicia's ruler, Alfonso VI of Castile and León, had less than a year to live and was preoccupied elsewhere in his sprawling territories. His male heir, Sancho, had been killed in battle by the Almoravids that summer, and the authority of Alfonso's newly designated successor, his daughter Urraca, was highly uncertain until the king could decide upon the magnate to whom he wished to marry her. Galician hospitality, therefore, relied on the goodwill of the local nobility.[11] An agreement with an unnamed earl (*jarl*) to provide the Norwegians with a permanent winter market fell through, and after Christmas the northerners were obliged to forage the countryside for sustenance, with predictable results. There was a confrontation between the earl and Sigurd's men, "whereupon the earl fled as he had but a small force."[12] Sigurd plundered the earl's castle, resupplied his army, then set sail, heading south once again. His men now had a taste for battle, and when they encountered their first Muslims—a pirate fleet who attacked them at sea—they responded ferociously, seizing eight of the pirate galleys and scattering the rest.

On they went. To their left as they sailed was the county of Portugal. This was frontier country: under Muslim rule, but firmly in the sights of Alfonso VI's son-in-law Henry of Burgundy, who was trying to extend his own Christian dominion in the region. The Norwegians did not pass peacefully. According to the thirteenth century Icelandic poet and chronicler Snorri Sturluson, the king set upon the Muslim-held castle at Sintra, where "the heathens had established themselves and harried the Christians. He conquered the stronghold and killed all the people in it, because they refused to be baptized." Although writing far after the events, Snorri entertained no doubts about Sigurd's status as a soldier of Christ, even if he had not taken any formal crusading vow. He also noted that his hero "made much booty there."[13]

There was booty, too, a little further on in Lisbon (al-Ushbuna), which had a mixed population of Christians and Muslims. Sigurd was not the first Scandinavian warrior to have disembarked at Lisbon with a sword in his hand: In 844 a Viking army led by a Dane named Halstein and the Swedish king Bjorn Ironside held the city for thirteen days on their way to an audacious attack on Seville. The contemporary Arabic-speaking historian Ibn Idhari imagined how they "filled the ocean with dark red birds, in the same way as they had filled the hearts of men with fear and trembling."[14] Of course, there was one important difference: the visitors of 844 had been pagan pirates, whereas in 1109 Sigurd came as an explicitly Christian plunderer, lauded by his contemporary, the *skald* Halldór Skvaldri, for vanquishing the "hapless heathens."[15]

After further raiding at a castle south of Lisbon and a battle against Muslim corsairs around Norvasund—or Gibraltar—Sigurd next hit land at the tiny arid outpost of Formentera in the Balearic Islands. The islands, which also included Majorca, Menorca and Ibiza, were still an independent *taifa* kingdom, for the Almoravids had yet to cross the Balearic Sea and subjugate them. Formentera—barren, sandy, and only about thirty square miles in its entirety—was occupied by black African freebooters who "harried far and wide on the island" and had created a makeshift fortress by adding stone walls to a cave system in the cliffs, located perhaps near the present-day Far de la Mola in the island's extreme east. They were not in the slightest bit intimidated by the arrival of a band of pale northerners at the foot of the cliffs. According to Snorri Sturluson they "brought out costly stuffs and other precious things out on the wall, shook them at the Norwegians, shouted at them, egged them to come on, and taunted them."[16]

Come on at them they did. Obeying his father's maxim about glorious deeds trumping a long life, Sigurd commanded his troops to find a path by which they could drag two small boats to the clifftop. Once they had done so, men piled on board, and the launches were lowered on strong ropes down to the cave mouths. From this position the Norwegians unleashed a hail of stones and arrows, forcing the defenders to retreat from their outermost wall. Meanwhile, Sigurd led a hair-raising climb up the cliff face. When he and his fellow climbers reached the top, they pulled the defensive wall to pieces and lit fires that filled the caves with choking smoke. "Some of the heathens lost their lives [in the fire], others hurled themselves against the weapons of the Norwegians; but all were either killed or burned," wrote Snorri Sturluson. "The Norwegians took the greatest amount of booty they had gotten on this expedition."[17] Already, it seemed, fighting in the name of the Lord was proving a profitable business.

After Formentera, Sigurd and his men spent a little time terrorizing Ibiza. Then, in the words of Halldór Skvaldri, they "crimsoned" their spears "on green Menorca," before heading on across the sea to friendlier terrain in Sicily, arriving in the spring of 1110.[18] Here Sigurd was greeted by a ruler with whom he had youth in common, for count Roger II was just 14 years old. Unlike Sigurd, however, Roger was not yet exercising power by himself. Instead, Sicily was controlled by his mother, Adelaide, who around the time of Sigurd's arrival described herself as "the great female ruler, the *malikah* of Sicily and Calabria, the protector of Christian faith."[19]

Snorri Sturluson claimed that Sigurd and Roger banqueted together for a full week, with the Norwegian king being personally served at table by the young count. This may or may not have been correct—certainly Snorri was mistaken when he wrote that Sigurd conferred full kingship on Roger; the Sicilian count was not elevated to a crown of his own until 1130. Nevertheless, Sicily was a natural stopping point for anyone traveling east by sea, and a period of feasting and mutual celebration would have been an understandable way for these two young rulers to pass the time while Sigurd's men repaired and reprovisioned their ships. They were both members of a new generation of warrior rulers who would have to find their place in a world where warfare between Christian and Muslim forces would inevitably be framed within the context of crusading, and perhaps they discussed that fact. Or perhaps they simply made merry amid the exotic splendor of Roger's court. Whatever took place between them, for Sigurd and his band of Vikings, the Palestinian coast was now tantalizingly close.

The sea-lanes around Palestine were busy—and a little perilous—during the summer of 1110. The first decade of the twelfth century saw an influx of pilgrims from all across the Christian world, and their vessels swelled the usual traffic of merchants, Fatimid military patrols and pirates. One pilgrim diary written after 1102–3 recorded the scenes in southern Italy as pilgrims took ship to the Holy Land from Bari, Brindisi, Barletta, Siponto, Trani, Otranto and Monopoli: every major port on Apulia's Adriatic coast.[20] And this was only Apulia. Sigurd would have passed dozens more such hectic ports as he traversed the "Greek Sea"—that is, the Aegean—a route that involved sticking close to shore and island-hopping from the Peloponnese through the Cyclades and Dodecanese islands, then following the coast of southern Anatolia before crossing to Palestine via Cyprus.[21] Here went a huge volume of human traffic, with visitors descending on the eastern Mediterranean from everywhere between the British Isles and the Ukrainian steppe. In the days in 1110 when Sigurd and his men sailed into view of the coast there were also three ships carrying pilgrims from Flanders and Antwerp and another from Byzantium loaded with "merchandise and provisions," being pursued by a Fatimid naval fleet.[22] The crusade and its dramatic recasting of the balance of power in Syria and Palestine had opened up tempting possibilities for those who wished to pray, to fight, to make money—or to do a little of all three. These were busy waters.

The first fight the Norwegians tried to pick on arriving in Palestinian waters was with the townsfolk of Ascalon. Despite the battle of August 1099 Ascalon remained in Fatimid hands and it provided a haven for Egyptian ships, which could come to the aid of Muslim cities further up the coastline that were under assault by the crusader states. Sigurd approached Ascalon and "anchored in the harbor of the town . . . for whole hours of the day and night in order to see if any men from the town would meet him by land or sea, with whom he might contrive some battle by accident or design," wrote Albert of Aachen. "But . . . the Ascalonites kept quiet and did not dare to come out."[23] Fighting would have to wait. With no battle on offer, Sigurd ordered his fleet to move off north, dropping him at Jaffa before continuing on to Acre. In Jaffa, Sigurd met King Baldwin I and the two monarchs showered each other with kisses of mutual respect before heading east to the Holy City.

Sigurd had the honor of being the first Western king to visit the crusader states, and he was given appropriately royal treatment. He and Baldwin marched in splendor to Jerusalem, accompanied by "all the clergy, clothed in albs and in all the splendid dress of divine religion, singing hymns and songs."[24] A tour of the holy sites in and around Jerusalem followed, after which the two kings bathed together in the Jordan. The great *skald* Einar Skúlason later composed a verse to commemorate the moment:

> Peaceful pilgrimage made
> the prince—under wide heaven
> nobler lord was never
> known—through Land the Holy.[25]

Baldwin gifted Sigurd a splinter of the Holy Cross and the younger man promised to take it home and display it at the tomb of Saint Olaf: a former Norwegian king famous for promoting Christianity in the then-pagan realm, who was canonized some decades later despite having led a colorfully violent life that ended when he was murdered by his own subjects in 1030.[26] Having nevertheless agreed that this Olaf was a man who deserved veneration with a piece of the holiest relic in the known world, the two Christian kings agreed that their next duty was to travel north and lay siege to Sidon.

By the time of Sigurd's arrival in the East, the crusader states had expanded considerably. The kingdom of Jerusalem had swollen to command more or less the entire coastline between Jaffa and Acre, the handsome and well defended port city that had fallen in 1104. To the north, the newly established county of Tripoli and, beyond it, the principality of Antioch, held virtually every major settlement between Beirut and Alexandretta. However, between these two areas the Lebanese cities of Tyre and Sidon were obstinately holding out. With a fleet of warships and thousands of men under his command, Sigurd was perfectly positioned to help bring one or more of them under Latin rule.

According to Ibn al-Qalanisi, writing in Damascus, the siege of Sidon lasted for forty-seven days, beginning on October 19, 1110. Sigurd's sixty ships, "laden with men-at-arms," enforced a blockade and their numbers ensured that the Egyptian fleet, stationed twenty-two miles away in the secure port at Tyre, did not dare to venture north to try and interrupt it.[27] Meanwhile, from the landward side, Baldwin made preparations for a storm of the walls. The citizens tried to drive away the besiegers with rocks thrown by hand and from a catapult. The Latin army's engineers set to work on a siege tower with pulley wheels on its base and a webbing of "branches of vines, mats and damp oxhides as a protection against missiles and Greek fire."[28]

When this was ready, it was wheeled up to Sidon's walls, allowing soldiers standing on its upper deck to shoot crossbow bolts into the city streets below. According to Ibn al-Qalanisi these fighters were equipped with buckets of water and vinegar to douse themselves if they were set on fire. Albert of Aachen heard that the citizens of Sidon tried to burrow mines underneath the tower, but that their plan was leaked and foiled. Eventually the besieged decided they had had enough. On December 4 Sidon surrendered to King Baldwin. The garrison marched out under guarantee of safe conduct and all those Muslims who wished to leave were permitted to go down to Damascus. Those who stayed behind were subjected to a collective tribute of twenty thousand dinars, which Ibn al-Qalanisi said "reduced them to poverty."[29] Snorri Sturluson, as always, mentioned that Sigurd's troops took much booty.[30] They had extracted so much plunder on their journey that when they cruised the seas, the very sails of their ship gleamed with costly trinkets that they had attached to advertise their prestige.

Having helped take Sidon and made his pilgrimage to Jerusalem, Sigurd considered his mission accomplished. He departed the crusader kingdom via Acre, stayed awhile on Byzantine Cyprus and then, in 1111, followed the shore of Asia Minor west, all the way to Constantinople. As they approached "Micklagarth," wrote Snorri, their ships sailed in such tight formation that they looked "like an unbroken wall."[31]

Alexios Komnenos, as was his wont, greeted the visitors with open arms. Other men might have had their fill of crusaders, for in 1107 and 1108, while Sigurd had been tormenting Galicia, the emperor's old adversary Bohemond had marched an army against Illyria—imperial territory in the Balkans—in an assault Bohemond claimed as a crusade. (Bohemond's army, raised in France, England, Italy, Germany and elsewhere, contained at least one Norwegian, by the name of Hamundr of Vatnsfjord.) Yet for once this clash had ended in victory for Alexios. After a heavy defeat at Dyrrhachium, Bohemond was forced to agree a treaty by which he acknowledged himself as the emperor's feudal vassal and agreed that he would respect Byzantine rights in Antioch. Anna Komnene gleefully recorded the terms of Bohemond's humiliation. "Like a fisherman caught unawares by a storm, [I] have learned my lesson," she had him say. "I have regained my senses, helped not least by [Your Majesty's] spear-point. . . . I undertake to arm my right hand against all who oppose your power, whether the rebel be a Christian or a stranger to our faith, one of those whom we call the pagans." It was a resounding calamity from which Bohemond never recovered. Six months after agreeing to the Treaty of Devol, the wily old Norman died in Lombardy.

Sigurd, much to the emperor's delight, was not another Bohemond, and Alexios could afford to treat him magnanimously. Snorri Sturluson wrote that Sigurd was feted in Constantinople with a massively extravagant series of municipal games, on which Alexios expended the equivalent of six hundred pounds of gold. He was lavished with gifts and flattery. Then, finally, it was time to go home. Sigurd traded his ships with Alexios for horses, and in a mark of respect, donated the great gilded dragons from the front of the king's flagship to be installed in one of the emperor's churches. Many of the ships' crews also chose to linger in Byzantium and join the emperor's service. Those who did not joined Sigurd as he traveled overland through Bulgaria, Hungary and the German states. He arrived home to find his realm thriving and his people glad to see him back. "It was thought that no more honorable expedition had ever sailed from Norway," wrote Snorri.[32] Sigurd was still only twenty years old.

In his later years, Sigurd of Norway went mad. He imagined he saw fish swimming in his bathtub and was forever after prone to descend into bouts of manic cackling, which rendered him helpless. Despite this, he managed to share kingship with his brothers peacefully enough, and outlived both. It has been conjectured that he suffered some form of post-traumatic stress disorder, but that is unknowable. He did not deposit his fragment of the True Cross at the revered Olaf's tomb, but instead donated it to a church of his own foundation in Kungahälla, along with an altarpiece he had commissioned in Byzantium: "bronze and silver, beautifully gilded and set with enamel and jewels."[33] In 1135 the city, located near what is now Gothenburg, Sweden, was sacked and burned by a pagan people known as the Wends. By that time, Sigurd was dead, at the age of forty, having ruled as a king for twenty-seven years.

Sigurd's tour through almost every corner of Christendom between 1107 and 1111 was a journey that not only gives us a snapshot of the Mediterranean world as it had been altered by the armies of the First Crusade and other Christianizing invasions in Iberia and Sicily, but also hinted at the ways in which that world—and crusading—was about to develop during the decades to come. The Norwegian attack on Lisbon foreshadowed a much greater crusader assault that left the city half ruined in 1147. On the other side of the Spanish peninsula, Sigurd's men had also shown another path for enterprising Christian warriors in the Balearic Islands. Following the Norwegian attacks a joint Christian army of Pisans and Catalans, with volunteers from across the Italian city-republics and southern France, began to plot a more concerted effort to conquer the islands and sweep away the *taifa* state. Between 1113 and 1115 a series of assaults, blessed with official papal recognition under a bull issued by Pascal II, captured all the major cities on the islands, including Palma on Majorca. This turned out to be futile, for in 1116 the Almoravids finally crossed the Balearic Sea and evicted the Christian conquerors in a move that would ensure that the islands remained in Muslim hands for another century and more. Yet Sigurd with his earlier softening up of Ibiza, Menorca and Formentera, had shown what might be done.

In Sicily, meanwhile, Sigurd had associated himself with the growing prestige of the Norman Hauteville regime established and secured by Robert Guiscard and Roger I. He appears, if Snorri Sturluson can be believed, to have found favor with the regime of Countess Adelaide and the young Roger II, and at the same time marked out a path that would be followed by many others after him, most notably at the end of the twelfth century, during the crusade of Richard the Lionheart.

When he reached the Latin states, Sigurd had demonstrated precisely what sort of working relationship might be established between Western monarchs visiting on a militarized pilgrimage and the kings of Jerusalem who would always be needful of assistance from the wider Latin world. Sigurd's men do not seem to have shown the same interest in locking down permanent trading rights in the East in the manner of the naval adventurers from Pisa, Genoa and Venice; their economic interests lay far away in the North Sea and the Baltic. Nevertheless, they had shown that the prospect of valuable plunder in the Holy Land was achievable for those who dared to be bold. And in their dealings with the emperor Alexios, they had suggested that whatever rancor had been caused by the division of spoils after Antioch in 1098, it was still possible for outsiders to be on friendly terms with both the Latins and the Greeks of the eastern Mediterranean. Many others would fall short of this bipartisan ideal.

Whether Sigurd's journey can be truly classed as a crusade is a matter of some conjecture. By 1110 the ultimate goal of the First Crusade had long been achieved. Jerusalem was in Latin hands. Urban II was dead. So far as we know, Sigurd did not take an official crusading vow. He was not answering the call of Rome or even Byzantium—but of his own Norwegian subjects, who rather liked the prospect of a long-range raiding expedition in search of the "booty" and fights with "heathens" that are mentioned relentlessly by the sources recounting the adventure. The nickname he earned for his deeds—Sigurd Jerusalemfarer (*Jórsalafari*)—makes clear that reaching Jerusalem was his objective and his most notable achievement. But did that make him a crusader or merely an armed pilgrim?[34] Or would that distinction, perhaps, not have meant very much to him?

Whether Sigurd definitively thought of himself as a pilgrim, a pious plunderer who happened to do rather a lot of killing, or as the leader of a mission directly analogous to that undertaken by the first crusaders is impossible to judge and probably inconsequential. More important is that this king of the north felt a strong enough bond to the wars of the southern and eastern Mediterranean to spend three years away from home risking his life to be part of the them. Sigurd's journey—be it pilgrimage or crusade—showed that the events of 1095 to 1099 had begun a process by which expanding and defending Christian lands from Palestine to Lisbon was becoming a corporate enterprise attractive to the whole of Western Christendom: a cause to which volunteers of all stripes would flock, hoping to achieve bountiful reward, whether in this world or the next.

◆ 11 ◆

Fields of Blood

Not only poor and weak people have dangers to face.

The caliph's wedding party in Baghdad, held during Ramadan in March 1111, was supposed to be a time of grand public celebration. Al-Mustazhir bi-Allah was the spiritual leader of the Sunni world and head of the Abbasid dynasty that had occupied that office for more than three hundred and fifty years. As the *Amir al-Mum'minin*—Commander of the Faithful—his name had been read aloud at Friday prayers in all obedient realms since his accession in 1092, and the elegant gold dinar coins struck in Baghdad's mint bore his inscriptions. It was true that for many generations the authority of the Abbasids had been crumbling, as the practical power of sultans, emirs and warlords rose. But al-Mustazhir bi-Allah was still the caliph, just as the Prophet's father-in-law Abu Bakr had been, all those years ago. He expected his recent marriage to be lauded in style.

His bride was Ismah Khatun, a granddaughter of the Great Seljuq sultan Alp Arslan, daughter of Malik-Shah and sister of the current sultan, Muhammad I. Her name, Ismah, meant "modesty." Her lineage was also impressive, in its way, and her character even more so. One thirteenth-century Baghdadi scholar praised her as "a highly intelligent woman, an aristocrat and a virago [whose] resolve was unswerving."[1] During the course of her life she would found one of the world's foremost law schools. In March 1111 she was coming from Isfahan, where the couple had already been married, to take her place in the caliph's palace. In preparation for her arrival Baghdad's streets had been shut to traffic and lavish decorations hung all around.[2]

After a journey of over six hundred miles Ismah Khatun swept in to the city on March 22. According to Ibn al-Qalanisi, she entered "in such magnificence and with such quantities of jewelry, moneys, utensils, carriages and riding beasts of all kinds, furniture, varieties of gorgeous raiment, attendants, guards, slave-girls, and followers, as exceeds all reckoning."[3] Yet at the moment that this opulent parade arrived, all Baghdad's carefully choreographed public happiness dissolved. The disturbance, as was coming quite regularly to be the case, stemmed from the deeds of the accursed Franks.

A month before the princess's arrival another delegation had arrived in Baghdad. This one came from Aleppo, and in place of camels, slave girls and expensive baubles it was composed of Sufis, disgruntled merchants and lawyers. They were in Baghdad to complain about the lack of effective support shown by the caliphs and sultan for the Muslims of Syria, who for more than a decade had been striving, without any meaningful success, to stop the European unbelievers from taking their cities, storming their fortresses, robbing their caravans, killing their neighbors and kidnapping their wives and children. Despite dozens of attempts to contain and repel the crusaders, by means that included siege, battle and truce, the Franks remained, obstinate and greedy, a menace to the faithful and a drain on the land. Most recently King Baldwin and another of the infidel kings—who brought with him sixty ships—had taken and subjugated Sidon. It was not hard to imagine that great Muslim-governed cities like Tyre, Aleppo or Damascus might be next.

Thus animated by fear and frustration, on Friday, February 17, the Aleppan protestors had presented themselves for the first time at the sultan's mosque in Baghdad. According to Ibn al-Qalanisi, they "drove the preacher from the pulpit and broke it in pieces, clamoring and weeping for the misfortunes that had befallen Islam at the hands of the Franks. . . . They prevented the people from carrying out the service, while the attendants and leaders, to quieten them, promised on behalf of the Sultan to dispatch armies."[4] But armies were not raised at the snap of the fingers, so the following Friday, February 24, the protestors did it all again. This time the target was the palace, where the caliph's own mosque was vandalized: another pulpit was demolished, another set of prayers broken up, and the railings to the *maqsura*—the caliph's private prayer sanctum—were damaged.[5]

It was common knowledge in Baghdad that Alexios Komnenos's envoys had made enquiries about forming an audacious alliance between Seljuqs and Byzantines against the Latins of northern Syria, and this fact was hurled in the face of the authorities. "Are you not ashamed before God Almighty that the Byzantine emperor shows greater zeal for Islam than you?" came the question from the angry Aleppan mob.[6] No answer was forthcoming. So the protestors lingered in Baghdad awhile longer. And, understandably, when Ismah Khatun's bridal procession arrived in the city a few weeks later, fragrant with wealth and finery, they lost their self-control once again. "The tranquillity of the city and joy at her coming were disturbed," wrote Ibn al-Qalanisi, tartly. The caliph was indignant and demanded that the protestors be arrested and punished. Sultan Muhammad, perhaps advised by his intelligent virago of a sister, demurred. Instead he sent word around Baghdad that all the emirs and commanders there present should return to their cities "and make preparations for setting out to the Holy War against the infidels, the enemies of God."[7]

In Jerusalem, Tripoli, Antioch and Edessa the enemies of God—or as they saw themselves, the people protected by the grace of God and the power of his relics, including the True Cross—had their own concerns. Although they had made steady gains along the coastline, and were beginning to strengthen their hold on the countryside inland, there was a significant cost to expanding and defending the crusader states, and they were heavily dependent on support from the western end of the Mediterranean for manpower and supply. It was true, as the distressed citizens of Aleppo had complained, that the Franks had seen off the assaults of various Syrian emirs, including a major expedition led against Edessa by Tughtakin, atabeg of Damascus, in 1110. Yet there was always a sense, expressed by King Baldwin's chaplain Fulcher of Chartres, that if the Islamic world ever saw fit to unite and attack as one, then the Franks would be doomed. "It was a wonderful miracle that we lived among so many thousands of thousands and, as their conquerors, made some of them our tributaries and ruined others by plundering them and making them captives," he wrote.[8]

Pilgrims who traveled to the Latin states almost always noted the parlous state of security in the Christian east. Daniel the Abbot, a Russian clergyman who came to Jerusalem shortly after the First Crusade on a sixteen-month pilgrimage from somewhere north of Kiev (possibly Chernigov), wrote in awe of the holy sites he saw and adored, and the wide banks of the river Jordan, which reminded him of the river Snov in his native land. But he also warned others of dangerous Palestinian roads where "pagans come forth in great numbers and attack," and the mountainous areas around Bethlehem that could only be explored with a Muslim guide, "because of the pagans, for Saracens abound and carry on brigandage in those mountains."[9] A British pilgrim named Saewulf undertook a similar voyage at around the same time. He suffered shipwreck on several occasions, was attacked by Fatimid pirates and recorded seeing the corpses of other travelers littering the roadside through the Judean hills between Jaffa and Jerusalem, left unburied with their throats cut by robbers. "Not only poor and weak people have dangers to face, but also the rich and strong," he wrote.[10]

Unfortunately for Saewulf, Daniel and their ilk, there was only so much that Baldwin of Jerusalem and the other lords of the crusader states* could do to protect them. After the Aleppan protests in Baghdad of 1111 had stirred the caliph and sultan into action, they faced not only run-of-the-mill brigandage and piracy, but a renewed waves of attacks from the Seljuq empire. In the summer of 1111 a coalition including emirs from Mesopotamia and Turkish-ruled Armenia and led by Mawdud, atabeg of Mosul, launched a successful attack on Turbessel (Tell Bashir), close to Edessa, which forced the ruler of the city, Joscelin of Courtenay, to pay tribute in order to relieve his walls. The following year a Frankish siege of Tyre, led by King Baldwin, was defeated when the citizens burned the siege engines and Tughtakin threatened with a relieving army. In May 1113 another army, composed of troops led by Tughtakin and Mawdud, raided northern Palestine and, in a battle fought near Tiberias on the banks of the Sea of Galilee, briefly captured Baldwin I himself, stripping him of his weapons before the king managed to escape. Baldwin survived but sufficient of his men were killed that, according to Ibn al-Qalanisi, "the water was so mixed with blood that the troops abstained from drinking it."[11]

Yet if the Seljuqs briefly held the advantage, they could not press their advantage home. On October 2, 1113, Mawdud was murdered, cut down on

*In 1111 the other rulers of the crusader states were: Bohemond II of Antioch (Bohemond of Taranto's young son, who was served as regent by Tancred of Hauteville and then Roger of Salerno); Bertrand, Count of Tripoli (the son of Raymond of Toulouse); and Baldwin of Bourcq, Count of Edessa (the future King Baldwin II of Jerusalem).

his way to the mosque in Damascus by a single assailant, probably a member of the Nizari Ismaili sect known to history as the Assassins. The Assassins* based themselves in mountain fortresses in eastern Syria and Persia and were loathed in equal measure by Sunni and Shi'a alike, not least because their elite warriors trained in the art of suicide attacks, killing prominent politicians in public, knowing that they would themselves be torn to pieces by bodyguards or the common mob in retaliation. This is precisely what happened to Mawdud in Damascus. An Assassin stabbed him once in the lower belly and once in the upper leg, so that he bled to death within an hour, despite the best efforts of doctors to stitch him up. (The Assassin was immediately seized and beheaded.) Mawdud's death took all the sting out of the defeat he and his allies had inflicted on Baldwin at Tiberias; it also heightened tensions between the Seljuq emirs. Their infighting ultimately prevented the sultan in Baghdad from organizing any more meaningful centrally directed attacks on the Franks for several years. But it did not stem the rising tide of Seljuq resistance completely. The man who eventually inflicted the most serious damage on the Franks was not Sultan Muhammad, but Ilghazi ibn Artuq, the hard-drinking career soldier who had been seen riding out of Jerusalem when it fell to the Fatimids in 1098, the year before the armies of the First Crusade arrived.

Since leaving Palestine Ilghazi had enjoyed a varied and lively career in Seljuq circles, working for the sultan in Baghdad, then taking control of the fortress town of Mardin, roughly halfway between Aleppo and Mosul, from where he commanded an army of Turcoman warriors recruited from around the nearby banks of the river Tigris. This brought him naturally into the orbit of the Latin rulers of Edessa and Antioch. Relations were at first relatively cordial, but as the decade drew to a close they would clash in spectacular fashion. The focus of most of these clashes was the city of Aleppo.

By 1119 the Aleppans who had complained so bitterly to the caliph at the time of his wedding had received very little by way of satisfaction. One of their chief antagonists was Roger of Salerno, regent of Antioch on behalf of the un-

*The Assassins were also referred to as the Batani and the Hashishiyun, from which their colloquial modern name derives. "Hashishiyun" has been construed as a reference to the sect's supposed fondness for smoking hashish, although this is likely to be historical slander.

derage and absent Bohemond II, still only eleven years old. Roger was a man cut from the same abrasive cloth as his late kinsmen Bohemond and Tancred. He advertised his martial prowess by minting coins bearing Saint George slaying a dragon, and he had been making steady progress toward Aleppo for some time, hoping to take advantage of the deaths, in quick succession, of the long-standing Aleppan ruler Radwan (d. 1113) and the atabeg Lulu (d. 1117). Roger was particularly free to act because in August 1118 Alexios Komnenos had also died, sparking a succession battle in Constantinople between his son John and daughter Anna, which momentarily relieved Byzantine pressure on Antioch from the West.* As a result, Roger had taken control of Aleppo's satellite castles on its northern and western approaches—most notably Azaz, the gateway to the city. The citizens had written to every neighboring prince of the Muslim faith begging for assistance; according to a later Aleppan chronicler, Ibn al-Adim, the letters that reached Ilghazi warned of "incessant attacks" by the Franks and a "desperate situation."[12] Although more of a self-serving pragmatist than a zealot of the faith, Ilghazi was not content to sit by and allow Latin armies to encroach ever further toward his own borderlands. In alliance with his father-in-law, Tughtakin of Damascus, he began to assemble a massive army—one estimate put it at forty thousand strong—with the intention of destroying "the factions of infidelity and error . . . for the succor of the Faith and the rooting out of the stiff-necked misbelievers."[13]

As news of a large troop buildup began to spread, Roger of Salerno sensed trouble. He began to raise his own army to defend his new possessions from recapture and Antioch from any retaliatory attack. His force included almost the entire military strength of the principality—save for the soldiers needed to garrison castles—along with a contingent of several hundred Armenian mercenaries and turcopoles, or light cavalry recruited from northern Syria and Asia Minor. Roger's columns mustered at Balat, near Sarmada, on the road between Antioch and Aleppo, to await Ilghazi's arrival. They did not have long to wait. On June 28, the lord of Mardin swooped.

A ferocious battle was fought that day, which would later become known as Ager Sanguinis: the Field of Blood. It was a thundering triumph for Ilghazi. Thousands of Latins and Armenians were slaughtered, including Roger of

*The power struggle was won by John, who became the new emperor, and is known as John II Komnenos. He ruled until his own death on April 8, 1143.

Salerno himself, who died when a sword was plunged "through the middle of his nose right into his brain."[14] According to Ibn al-Qalanisi, the whole affair took only an hour, after which "the Franks were on the ground, one prostrate mass, horsemen and footmen alike, with their horses and their weapons, so that not one man of them escaped to tell the tale." The battlefield was strewn with dead horses "stretched out . . . like hedgehogs because of the quantity of arrows sticking into them."[15] According to the Antiochene writer known as Walter the Chancellor, who was captured and imprisoned after the Field of Blood, the unlucky Christian survivors were either flayed and beheaded on the spot, or bound with their hands behind their backs and their legs in chains, "in the manner of dogs tied together two by two by the neck."[16] The day after the battle the bound prisoners were marched naked beneath a blistering sun into a nearby vineyard, where a large number were tortured before being run through with swords. Others were taken back to Aleppo for ransom, death or sale into slavery. It was a grim fate. And the strategic reversal was just as bad. In the space of a morning's work, Ilghazi had transformed the balance of power in northern Syria.[17] He celebrated with a drinking spree that lasted several weeks.[18] Aleppo was saved. Antioch had lost its regent, its army and its regional dominance.

The blow to the Franks was made doubly serious by the fact that the crusaders had also lost their first king. Less than three months before the catastrophe at the Field of Blood, the old warrior Baldwin I had died, having suffered on and off for many years with bouts of infection from a wound he sustained defending the kingdom of Jerusalem in the early years after the first crusade. On April 2, 1118, during an expeditionary campaign against the Fatimids in northeastern Egypt, the king ate a breakfast of freshly caught fish, fell ill and died. In accordance with his deathbed wishes, his body was disemboweled, "salted inside and out, in the eyes, mouth, nostrils and ears, also embalmed with spices and balsam, then it was sewn into a hide and wrapped in carpets," before being tied onto the back of a horse and rushed back to Jerusalem.[19] This crude mummification, while appropriate to his place of death, was intended to preserve Baldwin's body long enough for it to be buried next to his brother Godfrey's in the porch of the Holy Sepulchre. It did its job. His corpse was marched through the valley of Jehoshaphat on Palm Sunday with a phalanx of soldiers behind it, and laid to rest inside the great church at the point that was thought to mark the foot of Calvary.

Baldwin's succession was not a straightforward matter. Having preferred to share his bed with his favorite male servants rather than any of his three wives, Baldwin left no direct heir of the body. He also left several unhappy former spouses, including the Armenian princess Arda, his second wife, whom he discarded and sent to a convent, from which she later ran away to Constantinople; and Adelaide, regent of Sicily, whose brief tenure as Baldwin's queen was annulled in 1118 on political grounds, leaving the lady so indignant that when she died soon after, she bequeathed to her son Roger II of Sicily a contempt for the affairs of Jerusalem so fierce that he never lifted a finger during his life to come to the crusader kingdom's aid.[20] The candidates to succeed Baldwin were his brother, Count Eustace of Boulogne, an elderly veteran of the First Crusade who had gone home to his western lands, and Baldwin of Bourcq, who had been Count of Edessa for nearly two decades. The latter, who was one thousand miles closer to Jerusalem than his distant cousin Eustace, easily won the race. He was anointed shortly after the old king's funeral, and eventually crowned in a separate ceremony held at Bethlehem on Christmas Day 1119, alongside his wife and consort, the Armenian princess Morphia.

Baldwin II was approaching sixty at the time of his accession, and William of Tyre, although not old enough to have seen him in person, heard that he was "of striking appearance and agreeable features. His beard, though thin, reached to his breast; his complexion was vivid and ruddy for his time of life. . . . He had had much experience in the art of war and was wise in governing his men and successful in his campaigns."[21] This experience and wisdom would be sorely tested from the beginning, as he attempted to shore up Frankish power between Antioch and Aleppo, where Ilghazi's victory in the Field of Blood had changed the balance of power so abruptly.[22]

The Field of Blood had not merely damaged the fighting capability of Antioch and caused a major reshuffle among the princes of the Latin East. It also struck a fierce blow to the powerful self-assurance that had grown among the Franks ever since their long march from Constantinople to the walls of

Jerusalem the previous century. Whereas every success during and after the time of the First Crusade had been interpreted as a sign of God's manifest support for the Latins and their exploits, now a tone of self-doubt crept in to letters sent from crusaders to their comrades on the other side of the Mediterranean. They began to question their own moral conduct. Was it gluttony, drunkenness, rampant fornication or the fondness of the crusader settlers for roistering in brothels that had vexed God? It was hard to tell. Warmund of Picquiny, who was appointed as the patriarch of Jerusalem following Baldwin II's accession to the crown, wrote shortly after the Field of Blood to his colleague in Galicia, Diego Gelmirez, archbishop of Santiago de Compostela. A canon of the Holy Sepulchre whom he referred to only as "R." had been on a recent diplomatic mission to Spain, and Warmund was keen to encourage a culture of mutual prayer between the two great shrines of Western Christendom. He also wished to let off steam. After complaining about plague, drought, locusts and "innumerable grasshoppers" who laid waste the crops in the ground, Warmund bemoaned the fact that "we are surrounded by Saracens on all sides. Babylon [i.e., Baghdad] is to the east. Ascalon to the west. [Tyre] on the coast. Damascus to the north. . . . Every day we are invaded, every day captured or slaughtered. We are decapitated and our bodies thrown to the birds and the beasts. We are sold like sheep. What more can I say?"[23]

As it turned out, the patriarch could say a good deal more. While he and Gerard, prior of the Holy Sepulchre, who cosigned the letter, claimed they were ready to die in defense of Jerusalem and the Holy Sepulchre, they argued that it would be much better if the people of Galicia would "strive to come into the army of Christ and quickly come to our aid. If you are not able to come yourself, send those forces you can . . . with the help of God we will undo the chains of the sins of anyone who comes to our aid as long as he undertakes to do penance."[24] Although this underscored the continuing spiritual calculus that lay beneath the crusading movement—military service in return for remission of sins—it also ignored the fact that papal fiat expressly commanded those in Spain to stay there rather than traveling to fight the crusade in the East. But it was far from the last such message that crusader grandees would send to the West during the decades that followed. The well-being and survival of the crusader states depended in large part on the extent to which these calls to faraway allies were heeded.

In 1122 Ilghazi died of apoplexy. This came as some relief to Baldwin and his supporters. The veteran commander may have been a sadistic dipsomaniac, but he had masterminded the defense of Aleppo, inserting himself into the city as its ruler in the process and putting down rebellions as they occurred (insurgents could expect to be blinded or lamed, to have their tongues ripped out or their eyes burned in their heads).[25] Despite having to contend with attacks on his lands in northern Syria by Georgian warriors marauding south from the shores of the Black Sea, Ilghazi had managed still to be a bane to the Latins in Syria for three consecutive years. "Like a gnawing worm he was ever seeking whom he might injure," complained William of Tyre.[26] His death meant aspirations of Frankish conquest in Aleppo could be revived once again.

However, Ilghazi's successes outlived him, and twice in the months following his death the Latins flirted with outright disaster. On September 13, 1122, Joscelin, Count of Edessa (the lord of Turbussel who had succeeded Baldwin II to the northern county) was captured by one of Ilghazi's nephews and erstwhile lieutenants, Balak: "a magnificent and powerful prince" who had stepped up to fill the vacuum created by his uncle's death.[27] Ambushed inside his own lands Joscelin suffered the undignified experience of being transported off to jail in the fortress of Kharput sewn inside a camel skin. Soon even worse followed. A little over six months later, in April 1123, Baldwin—who was acting regent of Antioch following Roger of Salerno's death at the Field of Blood—was also taken prisoner. He was thrown into the same prison as Joscelin. Balak marched to Aleppo and stepped into his late uncle's position as master of the city.

Baldwin was imprisoned for more than a year. He was only released after Balak died in May 1124—shot in the shoulder with an arrow while organizing a siege against one of his own rebellious emirs—and rule in Aleppo passed to Ilghazi's son, Timurtash, "a man who loved the calm and easy life," according to Ibn al-Athir. Timurtash preferred to govern as an absentee lord from his patrimonial city of Mardin.[28] He granted Baldwin his freedom on the promise of paying a ransom of eighty thousand dinars. Baldwin walked free, welched on the deal and began planning to attack on the very man who had freed him. A final chance to seize Aleppo beckoned, and Baldwin tried to make the most of it.

On his release from prison, Baldwin was buoyed by the news that Tyre, the last major coastal stronghold north of Ascalon that remained unconquered by the crusaders, had finally fallen to Christian rule, following an assault jointly led by the royal constable Eustace Grenier and the Doge of Venice, Domenico Michiel. Encouraged by Pope Calixtus II to aid the Latins of the East (and rewarded with papal banners), the doge had equipped seventy-two ships, packed them with warriors who had taken the cross, and sailed them via Corfu and Cyprus to the Levantine coast, arriving in 1123.[29] The naval power of the Venetians was renowned across the Mediterranean and the republic was historically adept at spotting an opportunity to use it both to advance the city's pious reputation and to make a lot of money. According to stories heard by William of Tyre, when they engaged a Fatimid naval patrol near Ascalon, their sailors fought so ferociously that they ended up "completely covered with the blood of the fallen," leaving "the shores . . . so thickly covered with corpses thrown up by the sea that the air was tainted and the surrounding region contracted a plague from the putrefying bodies of the dead."[30]

In exchange for Venetian help in reducing Tyre, the doge was promised vastly lucrative trading privileges: a third of Tyre's revenues once it fell, freedom for Venetians who settled in the city to regulate their own weights and measures, to establish their own churches, courts, bathhouses and mills, to enjoy immunity from virtually every tax and custom and to be assured that any Venetian residing in Tyre would be "as free as in Venice itself."[31] The doge made such sweeping demands because he calculated that his ships were the key to taking Tyre. He was right. When the Franks and Venetians attacked, neither the Fatimids nor Tughtakin of Damascus was willing or able to come to Tyre's aid. On July 8, 1124, its governor, Saif al-Dawla Mas'ud, formally handed the city over to the Franks and all able-bodied Muslims left. "Its conquest greatly weakened the Muslims," lamented Ibn al-Athir. "For it was one of the strongest and most impregnable of cities."[32]

Fresh from jail and encouraged by this news, in October 1124 Baldwin II arrived at the walls of Aleppo with his barons and men in such high spirits that they had grown "convinced they could take the whole of Syria."[33] Just as his constable had done, Baldwin brought not only his own troops, but those of a useful ally: the Shi'ite Arab lord Dubays ibn Sadaqa, lord of al-Hilla in Iraq, who had promised Baldwin that if the king installed him as lord of Aleppo in place of Timurtash, he would be "an obedient deputy" to the Christian king.[34] In preparation for a winter siege, Baldwin's engineers erected semipermanent buildings outside the city walls and the blockade began. A failed harvest had left Aleppo poorly prepared to resist. The chronicler Kemal al-Din wrote that people were forced to eat dogs and human cadavers to survive, which caused rampant disease.[35]

Outside the walls, the Franks raided Muslim funeral chapels, took coffins to repurpose as storage chests for their camp, then goaded the citizens with the sight of their dead relatives' corpses being grotesquely desecrated. "They tied ropes to the feet of the bodies that had not yet fallen into decay, and dragged them in front of the Muslims, shouting at them 'Look! It's your prophet Muhammad! Look! It's Ali!'" wrote Ibn al-Adim, whose grandfather had been one of the besieged. He also reported that one Frankish soldier outside Aleppo took a copy of the Qur'an and tied it to his horse's tail so that it was regularly fouled with manure, bringing whoops of laughter from his comrades. Whenever the Franks captured an Aleppan Muslim, they cut off his hands and testicles.[36]

Despite these elaborate rituals of depravity, which had come to pass for routine psychological warfare, Baldwin and his Arab allies did not manage to seize Aleppo that winter, and in January the king was forced to abandon his efforts when the Mosuli lord Aqsunqur al-Bursuqi (who had succeeded the murdered Mawdud in 1113) launched a series of raids into Antiochene lands. Unconvinced that he could win Aleppo without losing Antioch in the process, Baldwin withdrew, returned to Jerusalem for the first time since before his captivity, then came north again to shore up Antioch. There was one more clash with Aqsunqur in May 1125, but from that point onward Frankish attempts to take Aleppo and definitively secure their dominance in northern Syria faded. Attentions turned instead to targets further south, like Damascus and Ascalon.

The struggle over Aleppo, which had taken shape in the years before the Baghdad protests of 1111, had taken nearly fifteen years and a horrendous amount of bloodshed, torture and slaughter to resolve in favor of little more than the status quo ante. By 1124 and 1125 the Franks had confirmed what was becoming apparent even in the months after the First Crusade: that they were resourceful enough and possessed sufficient third-party naval power to take control of the Levantine coastal cities from Byzantium to the Egyptian border, but that in the absence of the sorts of armies that had swept into the Holy Land in 1098, they were incapable of breaking major new ground in the Syrian interior. The Fatimids, meanwhile, had been shown to be in a decline that looked as though it would soon be proven terminal, while the Seljuqs to the east were strong but ruinously disunited and reliant on the efforts of charismatic leaders like Ilghazi to make any significant incursions into the lands of the infidel. To alter this unstable balance of power would take either a massive influx of warriors from the West on a new crusade, or the emergence of a leader in either Cairo or Baghdad who could unite the house of Islam in the Near East and send the perfidious Franks back the way they came. As it happened, the century that followed would provide both.

◆ 12 ◆

A New Knighthood

More people went . . . than ever before,
since the time of the first crusade.

On May 2, 1125, King Baldwin II visited Acre. The fortified seaside city, which sat on a small, rocky peninsula at the north of the bay of Haifa, was fast becoming the most important commercial hub in the Latin East. It was well connected by water and land to the rest of the Latin states, while pilgrims and merchants alike appreciated its harbor, sheltered from the waves by artificial walls sunk into the seabed during the rule of the ninth-century Abbasid governor Ibn Tulun, and protected from enemy shipping by a large chain that could be drawn across the entrance at night.[1] Acre was a regular stopping point for kings of Jerusalem, who claimed direct rule over the city and its environs—unlike most of the rest of the kingdom, which was granted out as feudal holdings to barons and vassals of the crown. Along with Jaffa, Acre was the most important entrepôt to the crusader states in the twelfth century.[2]

During his visit to Acre, Baldwin confirmed a charter that rewarded Domenico Michiel, doge of Venice, and his crusader sailors for their part in conquering Tyre the previous year.[3] The sweeping privileges that had been promised to the Venetians in return for their crusade—permission to set up a profitable, self-governing Venetian colony in Tyre and to live according to their own rules and customs everywhere else in the Latin East—had originally been granted by Warmund, patriarch of Jerusalem, because Baldwin was in jail. Now the king put his own seal to the agreement. In doing so he ensured that the affairs of the Holy Land would be of interest to the doges and citizens of Venice for generations to come. He acknowledged the need to be on amicable terms, not least because after their assault on Tyre the Venetians had sacked Byzantine towns throughout the Aegean and Ionean seas, launching a major attack on Rhodes and stealing the relics of Saint Isidore from Chios.* He confirmed his commitment to building a network of overseas supporters upon whom the kings of Jerusalem might call for military support, and furthered a policy of managing conquered towns by carving them up between various colonizing powers from afar. Baldwin's treaty with Venice would prove to be extremely important in the history of crusading and the crusader states—although the full consequences would not become clear for nearly eighty years. And tucked away at the end of the charter was another detail that would prove similarly significant both in the 1120s and beyond. The witnesses included a man called Hugh of Payns, the first and founding master of the Order of the Poor Knights of the Temple of Solomon—or, for short, the Templars.

Hugh of Payns originally came from the Champagne region of France. He arrived in Jerusalem at some point after the First Crusade, although whether he initially set out east to fight Seljuq Turks like Ilghazi and Tughtakin or simply to worship and atone more peacefully for his sins is not quite clear. Either way, by 1119 Hugh had settled in the Holy City and spent most of his days in and around the precincts of the Church of the Holy Sepulchre. The courtyards near the rotunda that enclosed Christ's empty tomb had been earmarked for a massive program of extension and rebuilding—eventually completed in 1149. But in 1119 they were best known as a meeting spot for people like Hugh: pilgrim soldiers searching for a role within the nascent crusader states.[4]

A group of Augustinian canons who lived at the Holy Sepulchre were responsible for ministering to the thousands of pilgrims who visited each year,

---

*These attacks were an unsubtle attempt to force the new Byzantine emperor John II Komnenos to renew a favorable trading treaty that he had canceled following his father's death. They succeeded: the treaty was renewed in 1126.

and after observing these black-habited priest-brothers at work, Hugh and several others decided that they too ought to devote their lives to a stricter, rule-bound, communal way of life. Given their occupations as knights—trained killers rather than learned servants of the Lord—this was an unusual ambition. It was not, however, beyond the realm of imagination. Close by the Holy Sepulchre stood a Benedictine monastery known as Saint Mary of the Latins, which had been established by Christians living under Fatimid rule in the mid-eleventh century. Volunteers associated with the monastery, living under religious vows, staffed an auxiliary pilgrim hospital dedicated to John the Baptist. In 1113 Pope Paschal II granted papal protection to the brothers of this hospital, along with freedom to elect their own leaders and considerable immunity from Church taxation.[5] The Hospitallers—as they became known—would in time take on duties well beyond their medical responsibilities. And through their voluntary service, undertaken with pious intent for the aid of fellow pilgrims, they presented another model of living in the East that Hugh and his companions decided they could emulate: one that would be true to the spirit of the first crusaders themselves.

In 1119 this model became reality. Like the canons of the Holy Sepulchre, Hugh and his men—there were somewhere between nine and thirty of them—formally agreed to devote themselves to a regimen of quasi-monastic poverty, chastity and obedience to the instruction of the patriarch of Jerusalem, relying on charitable handouts for food and clothing. Like the brothers of the hospital they went out to seek a calling among the world, helping pilgrims. Like the first crusaders, they did their duty to God with a sword in their hands. Many years after the event, William of Tyre wrote that the Templars' main duty "was that as far as their strength permitted, they should keep the roads and highways safe from the menace of robbers and highwaymen, with especial regard for the protection of pilgrims."[6] This meant providing military escorts between Jaffa and Jerusalem and around holy sites like Bethlehem and Nazareth, manning patrols and skirmishing with bandits. It also meant recruiting other like-minded men to sign up as brothers. As the Welsh writer and courtier Walter Map put it, Hugh decided to plead with every fighting man he encountered in Jerusalem to "surrender themselves for life to the service of the Lord."[7] He may not have realized it straightaway, but Hugh had struck upon a clever, novel idea that would prove hugely attractive across Latin Christendom.

So it was that in May 1125 Hugh appeared in Acre in the presence and service of Baldwin II, as the king sealed his charter to the Venetians. At this point Baldwin and Hugh had known one another for at least six years. In 1119, when Hugh set out on his first round of fund-raising, the king had agreed to lease him a set of apartments in al-Aqsa Mosque on the Temple Mount (the mosque was deconsecrated after the First Crusade but had since been neglected) and granted him revenues drawn from taxes and tolls on several villages close to Jerusalem. It was from their residence in this prestigious spot—associated with the long-lost Temple of Solomon and still extant Temple of the Lord—that Hugh's men earned their name. And Baldwin would remain a keen supporter of the Templars thereafter, recommending the new order to princes both secular and ecclesiastic throughout Christendom. In one letter he described the Templars as having been "raised up by the Lord for the defense of the kingdom."[8] The fact that Hugh was in the king's company in 1125, sufficiently trusted to be called as a charter witness, alongside archbishops, bishops and other senior churchmen, demonstrated Baldwin's high regard for his mission and his talents.

Two years later, Baldwin gave Hugh his first official mission, when he sent the master of the Temple back to Western Europe in the company of William of Bures, Prince of Galilee, and "several other men of religion." According to William of Tyre, their overarching mission was to petition "the princes of the West for the purpose of rousing the people there to come to our assistance."[9] Specifically that meant raising troops for a major assault on Damascus, which had by now superseded Aleppo as the most attractive target for expansion into the Syrian interior.[10] But there were side missions, too. William of Bures had been asked to visit the veteran warrior Fulk of Anjou—one of the most powerful lords in central France—and offer him the hand in marriage of the king's eldest daughter, Melisende. Since Baldwin II had no sons, this effectively meant recruiting Fulk to become heir to the crown and Jerusalem's king-in-waiting. It was a solemn task in which Hugh of Payns would prove useful, since he knew Fulk personally. Meanwhile Hugh himself planned to use the opportunity of a trip to the West to attract funding, political support and recruits to join the Templars.

Having set out some time around the late summer 1127, Hugh was welcomed home with open arms and great generosity. Besides his personal charm, he offered a new way to engage with the crusading movement: either by joining an institution for perpetual crusade or else by sponsoring it, which allowed pious individuals to support the war for the greater good of Christendom without actually traveling to the East themselves. Almost as soon as he arrived, people began giving him things. In October Theobald IV, Count of Blois, awarded the Templars a house and farmland near Provins; shortly afterward William Clito, Count of Flanders, offered tax relief on any property the Templars acquired in his territories. This was significant patronage, which advertised the approval of great men and opened up new revenue streams that would help to fund the Templars' mission. That it was Theobald and William who made the grants was important: both came from crusading families and both men's fathers had been princes of the First Crusade.* Their support for the new wave of crusading was financial rather than personal, but that fact was most likely of little concern to Hugh of Payns. His aim was to raise support for the struggle in the East by any means he could.

By April 1128 Hugh was at Fulk of Anjou's court in Le Mans. In times past this might have been a dangerous place to be seen: the Angevin counts liked to boast that they were descended from the devil. Count Fulk, however, was rather less diabolical than some of his forebears (and indeed his descendants). A little short of his fortieth birthday, Fulk was described by William of Tyre as ruddy faced but "gentle, affable, kind and compassionate." (William thought these "unusual traits in people of that complexion.")[11] Fulk's only real personal flaw was that he was incredibly forgetful and never remembered a face, on occasion even forgetting his own servants' names.

Whether Fulk immediately recognized Hugh of Payns is not recorded, but when the master of the Temple arrived before him in the spring of 1128 they were renewing an old acquaintance. Hugh had hosted Fulk in Jerusalem around the year 1120, shortly after the Templars' establishment, and Fulk had duly proven a grateful early patron, sending the brothers a stipend of thirty

*Theobald's father was Stephen, Count of Blois, scorned for abandoning the crusade at Antioch in 1098. William's father was Robert, Duke of Normandy, who was at this time languishing in prison in England, a captive of his own brother, Henry I.

pounds in Angevin coin every year. Evidently, the renewal of personal relations was successful. On May 31, Hugh and William of Bures were present when Fulk took the cross. Together these envoys from the East had convinced him to set his soul, his career and his county on a new path. Within months Fulk would be handing over control of Anjou to his fifteen-year-old son Geoffrey "Le Bel"* and moving permanently to Jerusalem. There he would marry Melisende, becoming heir presumptive to the holy crown.

Under the arrangements made for Fulk to leave Anjou, his young son Geoffrey was married to an eligible widow named Matilda. By right of her first marriage Matilda claimed the honorary title of empress of Germany; by right of blood she was heir to both the kingdom of England and duchy of Normandy—Anjou's neighbor and fierce rival. Geoffrey and Matilda's wedding took place on June 17, and if Hugh was present then he may have met Matilda's father, Henry I.[12] In any case, soon afterward Hugh appeared in Henry's kingdom soliciting money and assistance, exciting his audiences with talk of a looming new war between the forces of Christianity and the heathen hordes, and a plan to expand the godly kingdom of Jerusalem into new, untapped territory.

According to *The Anglo-Saxon Chronicle*, the English king devoured this news and presented Hugh with "great treasures of gold and silver" from his Norman treasury. When Hugh arrived in England, he was "welcomed by all good men. He was given treasures by all, and in Scotland too." It was a fabulously successful journey. "Much wealth, entirely in gold and silver, was sent to Jerusalem," wrote the chronicler, and many people also dedicated themselves to travel back to the East to fight in the coming war. This was not the first time that the English and Scots had committed to crusading: a number of minor lords and knights had traveled in Robert, Duke of Normandy's entourage in 1196, as had an unusual character called Lagmadr, king of the Isle of Man and the Hebrides, who went to Jerusalem and died there doing penance for blinding his brother Harald. But it was still a period of unusual enthusiasm. "More people went [to the east], either with [Hugh] or after him, than ever before since the time of the first crusade," wrote the chronicler.[13] And the energy Hugh sparked was not limited to the British Isles. From Flanders to Avignon, wherever Hugh went he managed to whip up volunteers and finance.[14] He was, in effect, preaching a mini-crusade.

---

*Aka Geoffrey "Plantagenet": father of Henry II of England and founder of the dynasty that ruled England from 1154 until 1485.

If recruiting a new heir to the crown of Jerusalem was the most striking public achievement of Hugh's tour of Europe, there was, however, one more showpiece occasion left. In 1126 King Baldwin had written ahead of Hugh to vouch for the Templars as an organization that enjoyed the royal favor, and to encourage powerful figures to lobby Rome so that the Templars should be granted the approval of the pope. In January 1129 the campaign was rewarded. A church council opened at Troyes, on the borders of France and Burgundy, during which the Templars were granted papal recognition, a quasi-monastic code by which to live, a uniform and a formal place within the hierarchy of the Church. On January 13 Hugh made a speech to an assembly that included two archbishops, ten bishops and seven abbots. He spelled out the ideas and practices that underpinned the Templar organization and put them up for debate and refinement. Within a matter of a few days the drafting process of a formal rule for the Western Church's first official "military order" had begun. The guiding hand in that process belonged to a figure with a huge future in the crusading movement: Bernard, abbot of Clairvaux.

Bernard of Clairvaux, known today simply as Saint Bernard, was the most valuable patron Hugh of Payns ever found. Born at Fontaines-lès-Dijon in the year 1090, Bernard had at a young age decided to join an new, reforming monastic movement known, after their motherhouse at Citeaux, as the Cistercians. Rejecting the worldliness of the Benedictines and the grandeur and pomp of the Cluniacs, Cistercian monks devoted themselves to lives of abject, grinding poverty and hard work, usually performed in abbeys founded in out-of-the-way locations. They wore white robes to symbolize their purity and allowed themselves virtually nothing in the way of bodily comfort. Bernard, who founded Clairvaux Abbey with twelve other monks in 1115, was frequently ill from the exertions of his spare diet and uncomfortable living conditions. His main pleasure came from composing sermons and letters telling other people how to improve their lives—a skill at which he was unmatched.[15] Bernard's talent as an advocate, diplomat and political counselor was sought by popes and kings, although he was no snob, and never above giving his advice to fallen young women or runaway monks. To whomever he was writing, his opinions were highly regarded, and when he appeared at the Council of Troyes to support Hugh of Payns—to whom he had been introduced by Baldwin II—it was a great coup.

The Rule of the Templars—or rather, that part of it that came to be known as the Latin or Primitive Rule*—bore Bernard's unmistakable imprimatur. In Hugh's Templars, Bernard saw a militarized version of the Cistercians, who could do battle with steel and mail as well as through prayer and contemplation. The prologue to the rule described the Order of the Temple as a redemptive home for knights "who up until now have embraced a secular knighthood in favor of humans only, and in which Christ was not the cause." Within its fold these reformed knights would live a life of monastic obedience and seriousness, in which diet was strictly regulated and leisure time heavily circumscribed. Uniforms were prescribed, in white or black according to the member's status as a knight-brother or sergeant-brother; some years papal permission was granted for these to be emblazoned with a red cross. Templars were to live only for prayer, patrolling and fighting the infidel; frivolity was to be rejected and the company of women, "through which men are accustomed often to be endangered" was to be shunned.[16] In a different text, which became known as *De Laude,* Bernard called the order "a new kind of knighthood" through which Christ would rid the Holy Land of "the children of disbelief." The Templars, as he saw it, were instituted for the purpose of seeking martyrdom and killing infidels. "Surely," he wrote of the idealized Templar knight, "if he kills an evil doer, he is not a man-killer, but an evil-killer. . . . Should he be killed himself, we know he has not perished, but has come safely home."[17] When the Council of Troyes concluded its business, Hugh was no longer the leader of a small volunteer corps on the edge of Latin Christendom, but the master of an international military order that embodied the very essence of Christian holy war, backed by the papacy and in large part designed by the foremost churchman of the age.

If Hugh's mission to the West had been a resounding success, his return to the East in 1129, following the Council of Troyes, was not quite so glorious.

*Over the course of Templar history the rule would be significantly expanded and revised, to encompass a military handbook and a large body of case studies concerning contraventions of the rule and the penances due to rule breakers.

Hugh had proven himself adept at rallying men and soliciting valuable support for his order. But what he could not control was the outcome of the crusade for which he had been chief recruiting officer. Many volunteers had signed up—plenty of them attracted through connections to the wider Montlhéry family that counted Baldwin among its members.[18] And many traveled to the kingdom of Jerusalem (as Hugh most likely did) in the company of Fulk of Anjou. But as the author of *The Anglo-Saxon Chronicle* put it, "when those multitudes got there, they were pitiably duped."[19] Hugh had promised a great war. What followed was a single, ill-starred and ultimately humiliating campaign.

Having given up on attacking Aleppo after the debacle of the Field of Blood, in 1125 and 1126 Baldwin II had made probing raids on Damascus and its environs, on both occasions deploying relatively small contingents of men drawn from the kingdom of Jerusalem. Although during the second of these campaigns he had drawn Tughtakin into a confused and inconclusive battle, he had never come close to seizing the city. The king had come to believe that the key to doing so was to deploy an army on the scale of those that had captured Antioch and Jerusalem a quarter of a century previously, when he had been a young man. This, of course, was the reason why Hugh of Payns and others had been dispatched to the West, and Baldwin decided to wait for their arrival before attacking Damascus again. Indeed, he was so intent on biding his time that he passed up the chance to attack Damascus even when Tughtakin died on February 12, 1128, ill and worn out by a long career in the field.[20] Baldwin's decision not to exploit the transition of power to the new atabeg, Tughtakin's son Taj al-Muluk Buri, would look feeble in hindsight. But at the time he was waiting until he could put in the field what Ibn al-Qalanisi called "a vast host."[21] That time arrived after the arrival of Hugh and the fresh crusaders in the late autumn of 1129.

Damascus had been described by the explorer al-Muqaddasi as "the metropolis of Syria," packed with palaces and monuments dating to the age of the Ummayads, the jewel among them being the city's stunning eighth-century mosque, a vast and dazzlingly beautiful building lacquered in gold décor, which was considered to be the fourth-holiest site in the Islamic world. The city that spread out around it was also famously pleasant: "crisscrossed by streams and surrounded by trees," wrote al-Muqaddasi, who praised the magnificent quality of Damascene bathhouses and fountains, and the probity of the citizens. (Their only serious flaw, he thought, was a disappointing liking for tough meat and dry bread.[22]) To the Franks, who cared little for mosques but a lot for holy relics and strategic trading posts, it was a highly alluring prize. Damascene markets served the silk roads that connected the workshops of China with Byzantium and the Latin West. The head of John the Baptist was said to have been buried under one of the pillars in the great mosque.

In late November, Baldwin rode out with an army that Ibn al-Athir reckoned to contain two thousand knights and "infantry beyond counting."[23] Alongside him was an impressive contingent of new crusading leaders: his new son-in-law, Fulk of Anjou; the young Bohemond II of Antioch, who had finally arrived in 1128 to take possession of his late father's principality; the veteran Joscelin of Edessa; and Pons, Count of Tripoli. Inside Damascus, they knew, the new atabeg Buri had problems. A major rebellion of Nizaris (the sect of the Assassins) living in Damascus led to popular riots and lynchings in the streets. Crucified Nizari corpses decorated the battlements of the city walls, while the charred remains of the former vizier Abu Ali, who had been beheaded for allegedly conniving with Nizaris, lay on an ash heap near the citadel. Stray dogs had been feasting on human carrion for days.[24] Those Nizaris who had managed to flee the city had sought sanctuary with the Latins and signed over the nearby town of Banyas as a mark of their good faith. It was from Banyas that the Frankish army had advanced, setting up camp six miles south of Damascus at a place called the Wooden Bridge, near Darayya; supposedly the point on the road to Damascus where Saul the Pharisee had seen the blinding light that occasioned his conversion to the Christian apostle Saint Paul.[25]

Thirty years previously, during the winter siege outside the walls of Antioch, a large Frankish army had needed to give constant thought to provisioning—which was in large part done by foraging the nearby land. Now the Franks before Damascus did the same. William of Bures detached a very large contingent of knights—half the cavalry, according to William of Tyre's chronicle—who then splintered into smaller raiding parties and went off to roam the countryside for supplies. This turned out to be a grave error. Buri was by no means as fierce a ruler as his late father, Tughtakin, but he was alert enough to see an opportunity. He tasked a group of "the doughtiest Turks of Damascus," along with several other contingents of allies who had come to the city to aid in its defense, and sent them out to engage the Frankish foragers.[26] They surprised the bulk of the raiders near the village of al-Buraq and "made great slaughter among them," put William of Bures to flight and "surrounded the remainder with blows of swords and thrusts of lances and showers of arrows" until "they were prostrate on the ground and befouled with dust beneath the horses' feet."[27]

This was a serious setback, and as it transpired, one from which the crusaders could not recover. As they prepared to mount a counterattack, a storm of fog, torrential rain, thunder and lightning blew up that churned the roads into impassable mud. "The tempest had been sent upon them because of their sins," sniffed William of Tyre.[28] With half the army scattered to the winds, Baldwin had no option but a disorderly retreat. As soon as the disaster at al-Buraq was reported, the Frankish army burned what they could not carry and fled. Ibn al-Qalanisi, like William of Tyre, saw the hand of the Almighty at work. "The people [of Damascus] felt secure and went out to their farms . . . freed from sorrow and anxiety, and visited by unlooked-for and undreamt of mercy and goodness from God—to Him be praise," he wrote. "After this disaster it was scarcely possible for the infidels to assemble in full force, so many of their knights had perished, such numbers of their men were destroyed and so much of their baggage was lost."[29]

No wonder, then, that the author of *The Anglo-Saxon Chronicle* passed a scathing judgment on the 1129 crusade, summing it up as nothing but deceit and failure. The Franks had pressed hard at both Aleppo and Damascus during the 1120s, but even with the might of an army that stood comparison with the great levies of the First Crusade, they had come up short. The dream of conquering another of the great cities under Islamic rule had not died: further expeditions against Aleppo, Damascus and Cairo, to the south, would continue—and the need to pick off Ascalon, the last coastal stronghold between Egypt and Byzantium, would not be forgotten, either. But from the 1130s, expansion in the East slowly gave way to retrenchment, and in the 1140s, as we shall see, retrenchment gave way to panicked defense.

In this regard the most important development of the 1129 Damascus crusade was less the outcome of the battle itself than the campaign of recruitment that had preceded it. With the establishment of the Templars under Hugh of Payns, a formal crusading institution had been created, which gave lasting expression to the urges of young warriors to fight penitential holy war, and perpetual connections between the lands of the Latins in the East and West. From the 1130s the Templars' mission was imitated by the Hospitallers, who added a military branch to their medical and palliative duties. During the following decades, Templar and Hospitaller castles, watchtowers and commanderies (also known as preceptories, meaning monastic-style military barracks) would spring up throughout the crusader states, inhabited by permanent garrisons of religious warriors whose duties encompassed not only protecting pilgrims but defending the Christian Holy Land itself. Templar and Hospitaller knights and sergeants came to be regarded as the elite units in Frankish armies, customarily forming the vanguard and rear guard in the field, and earning a reputation among their enemies as "the fiercest fighters of all the Franks." Meanwhile, in Europe the military orders also flourished: offered institutional support and sweeping tax relief by successive popes, they took an active role in the crusader wars of the Spanish peninsula, while expanding and staffing their profit-making property networks in more peaceful lands through the efforts of individuals who donated either their property or their persons to the Templars or Hospitallers in the hope of eternal reward.

While these new crusading institutions began to expand and flourish, however, it was not entirely clear where the future of crusading lay. After 1129 there was scant appetite for another major expedition from West to East—for there was, it seemed, no cause that demanded one. The resurgence of crusading, to the East at least, would come to depend on obvious and existential danger to the Latin states: it would be a defensive and not an offensive tool. It was more than a decade before such a danger reared its head—but when it did, it was a fearsome sight, driven by a leader as imposing as Tughtakin and Ilghazi combined.

◆ 13 ◆

Melisende the Magnificent

You must set your hand to great things,
and although a woman, you must act as a man.

In the high summer of 1131 Melisende, the eldest of Baldwin II's four daughters, was summoned to her father's deathbed. She found the old king languishing in the patriarch's palace in the compound of the Holy Sepulchre, dressed as a monk. A few days earlier, when he realized he was mortally ill, Baldwin had set aside the trappings of his royal state and asked his servants to carry him to comfortable lodgings as close as possible to Christ's tomb. He took religious vows and assumed the cowl, in the hope of improving his chances in the afterlife. "He had full hope that the One who had overcome death . . . would make him a sharer in his own resurrection," wrote William of Tyre.[1] But Baldwin had not entirely abandoned all thoughts of the earthly realm: he had important plans for the future of his crown and his family—as the twenty-six-year-old Melisende was about to find out.

Melisende and her three sisters—Alice, Hodierna and Yvette—would all in their ways become prominent in the dynastic politics of the Latin states. Alice had married Bohemond II of Antioch—but was now a young widow since Bohemond had died the previous year, aged twenty-three, while fighting the Danishmend Turks of Anatolia: his head was lopped off in the fighting and sent as a gift to the caliph in Baghdad. Hodierna was unmarried. But within a few years she would become one of the preeminent women of the region. The youngest sister, Yvette (also known as Joveta), had been marked for a career in the convent, but her life was nevertheless dramatic from its earliest years.

As a five-year-old Yvette was caught up in negotiations for her father's release from imprisonment at the hands of Ilghazi's son, Timurtash. Traumatically, she was taken from her home to be kept in honorable confinement pending payment of Baldwin's ransom. The girls were born to testing times and necessity made them tough. Half Frankish and, through their late mother Morphia, half Armenian, all four were determined and notable women of the second generation of Frankish settlers in the Holy Land. Their interwoven stories would illustrate the emerging tensions and rivalries that gripped the Latin East as the deeds of the first crusaders slipped from living memory into the realm of history and legend.

Melisende arrived at her father's bedside in the company of her husband, Fulk, and their infant son. She had married Fulk promptly on his arrival in the Holy Land in 1129, fulfilling the deal struck with the Angevin lord before the Damascus crusade. The couple had promptly done their dynastic duty and produced an heir, whom they unsurprisingly named Baldwin. That could have been the moment that Melisende disappeared from politics: as a vessel for kingship to be transmitted first by marriage and then by childbirth, her duty to the kingdom was in its narrowest sense done. But Melisende was not one for going quietly. Moreover, in the early twelfth century queens were enjoying a moment of brief acceptability: in England Henry I died in 1135 leaving his crown to his daughter (and Fulk's daughter-in-law) Matilda; in Castile and León Alfonso VI had transmitted his crown through his daughter Urraca; in Sicily the minority of Roger II had been adroitly managed by his mother, Adelaide. Queenship did not stir quite the same instinctive antipathy as it would later in the Middle Ages, and in Baldwin's mind there was much to recommend it. So it was that as Melisende, Fulk and the infant Baldwin assembled to learn that the dying king was about to stand his kingdom on its head.

The deal that brought Fulk to the Holy Land was made on the understanding that the Count of Anjou was arriving with a view to taking over the crown. Yet in his last moments Baldwin equivocated about what that meant. Rather than Fulk alone becoming king, he said, Jerusalem was to be ruled by the family together: Fulk, Melisende and, when the time came, the infant prince.[2] This was not quite the bargain struck back in the West, but the old king was entitled to do as he saw fit. Thus he changed his mind and promptly died, departing the world on August 21, 1131. A little over three weeks later, on September 14—the day of the Exaltation of the Holy Cross—Fulk and Melisende were anointed and crowned together in the Church of the Holy Sepulchre by the patriarch of Jerusalem, William of Messines. The young Baldwin, being a minor, was not yet included, and the tradition of crowning monarchs at Bethlehem on Christmas Day was broken. So everything was unusual: the venue, the date and the arrangement. Quite how this double- and, it was envisaged, triple-headed rule of the Latin kingdom and its dependent states was going to work was unclear. As Ibn al-Qalanisi wrote from Damascus, "by the loss of Baldwin, [the Franks] were thrown into discord and confusion."[3]

Fulk acceded to the crown of Jerusalem with a clear idea of how he intended to exercise authority. This amounted, more or less, to a clean sweep. Writing far away in Normandy (many hundreds of miles distant but in a territory well acquainted with Fulk's methods and means of government) the chronicler Orderic Vitalis recorded the abrupt changes brought about by Fulk's rise. "As a new ruler he banished from his counsels the leading magnates who from the first had fought resolutely against the Turks and helped Godfrey and the two Baldwins to bring towns and fortresses under their rule," wrote Orderic. "[He] replaced them with Angevin strangers and other raw newcomers. . . . Consequently, great disaffection spread, and the stubbornness of the magnates was damnably roused against the man who changed officials so gauchely. For a long time . . . they turned their warlike skills, which they should have united to exercise the heathen, to rend themselves."[4]

Fulk brought his own administrators, his own castellans and his own churchmen to the East and—understandably if not wisely—created from them an Angevin circle around the crown that seemed to exclude older hands. He exhibited a particular prejudice against men associated with the Normans—be they of Normandy proper or of the Hauteville clan of Apulia, Calabria and Sicily, which had produced Bohemond I, Tancred and other famous crusaders. From the start of the reign, Angevins were promoted, while Normans and those connected to Baldwin's Montlhéry family were let down. Most egregiously, Fulk tried to swat aside the deathbed wishes of his father-in-law and sideline Queen Melisende in Jerusalem and her sister Alice in Antioch.

In 1130 Alice, newly widowed, had earned the wrath of her father Baldwin II by asserting her right to rule the northern principality on behalf of Constance, her two-year-old daughter by Bohemond II. Attempting to show that she could secure Antioch's borders by diplomacy even if she could not ride at the head of an army, Alice had made overtures to the most energetic of the Seljuq leaders in the region: Imad al-din Zengi, atabeg of Mosul and Aleppo, a swarthy, gray-haired soldier in his fifties who was regarded with awe and a healthy dose of fear by enemies and followers alike.[5] William of Tyre heard many years later that these overtures included a gift of a snow-white palfrey with a silver bridle and silk saddlecloth.[6] While this ghostly steed may have pleased Zengi, it only served to enrage Alice's father. He marched on Antioch, taking Fulk with him. The city gates were thrown open by the citizens and Alice was forced to fling herself at her father's feet and beg mercy. Baldwin sent her off in disgrace to live in Laodicea and Jabala—two of Antioch's port cities. He took the regency of Antioch into his own hands.

As soon as Baldwin was dead and Fulk was king, however, Alice tried her luck again. "An extremely malicious and wily woman," tutted William of Tyre, patronizingly; but he also acknowledged the strength of opinion that suddenly swung behind Alice and the concerns that other nobles harbored about Fulk at the start of his reign. The "Princess of Antioch," as she styled herself, was backed in her bid for power by both Pons of Tripoli and a new count of Edessa, Joscelin II—both of whom were anxious to maintain a measure of independence over the affairs of their counties.* To bring all three into obedience, Fulk was obliged to deploy armed force, fighting a battle against Pons to secure the count's submission in Tripoli, and imposing a royal regime in Antioch, under the constable Rainald Mazoir. This sort of discord was highly irregular among the Latins. In Damascus, Ibn al-Qalanisi noted with surprise that "fighting had taken place between [the Franks], in which a number of them were killed."[7] Yet this was far from the end of Fulk's problems. Scarcely had he brought Antioch and Tripoli to heel than he returned to Jerusalem to find more rebellion brewing, orchestrated in favor of Alice's elder sister: his wife, Melisende.

It is hard to examine the events of the early 1130s without concluding that Fulk brought many of his troubles upon himself. Confident that Baldwin II's final wishes could not be pressed upon him once that venerable old king lay cold in a vault beneath Golgotha, he scorned propriety and from the start of his reign tried to freeze Melisende out of the processes of government.

*Joscelin I of Edessa died within a few weeks of Baldwin II of Jerusalem, in the autumn of 1131. Joscelin II was his son.

But Melisende was no doormat and she did not lack for supporters. Fulk was rewarded for his bullish approach with a full-blown rebellion, led by two of the leading nobles of the Latin kingdom: the blue-blooded Hugh of Le Puiset, Count of Jaffa, and Romanus of Le Puy, former Lord of the Transjordan (or *Oultrejordain*), lands that lay east of Jerusalem across the river Jordan.

According to a scurrilous tale repeated several decades later by William of Tyre, trouble began because Hugh of Le Puiset—young, tall, handsome and an excellent swordsman—was said to be conducting an affair with his second cousin Melisende. "The count . . . was rumored of being on too-familiar terms with the queen, and of this there seemed to be many proofs," wrote William, without mentioning what any of those proofs might have been. "Hence, spurred on by a husband's jealousy, the king is said to have conceived an inexorable hatred against the man."[8] This was a romantic yarn, and little more than tittle-tattle. The root cause of Hugh's dissatisfaction was not sexual longing for his cousin but a deep concern at the way the new king was trampling roughshod over the interests of their extended families and marginalizing the queen.

Matters came to a head at a gathering of the *Haute Cour* (the high court of Jerusalem's leading nobles) in 1134, when a loyalist lord, Walter of Caesarea, accused Hugh in open court of making treasonous plots against Fulk's life. Hugh demanded to defend his honor in hand-to-hand combat, then failed to appear at the designated time, most likely under pressure from his wife, Emolata, since Walter was her son from an earlier marriage. Hugh was declared guilty in his absence and responded in the stupidest way imaginable. He sailed to the Fatimid city of Ascalon and agreed to a treaty that provided for Muslim assistance in taking up arms against the king of Jerusalem. In short order Fatimid raiding parties "invaded our territories with unwonted boldness and presumption," wrote William of Tyre.[9]

Just as Princess Alice had overreached in trying to curry favor with Zengi, so now Hugh of Le Puiset found himself at the mercy of his own rash mistakes and his overlord's anger. Fulk drove off the Ascalonites, then besieged Hugh in Jaffa—quickly bringing him to surrender as the people of that city declined to fight against their king. Hugh was deprived of his county and sentenced to three years' exile from the kingdom. He could count himself lucky to have escaped with his life—but only briefly. Hugh was in Jerusalem settling his affairs before taking ship back to the West when, as he sat playing dice one night on a street known for its furrier shops, he was set upon by a knight from Brittany, who stabbed him half to death. Hugh recovered from his wounds sufficiently to leave the kingdom but died not long afterward in Apulia, where the king Roger II of Sicily had granted him sanctuary and a lordship.

Now, once more, Fulk was under pressure. Denying any part in the attack, he had the knight who wielded the blade mutilated—although he instructed the torturers not to cut their victim's tongue, lest it should be said that he wished to silence the truth. But Fulk could not forestall public opinion, which—fairly or otherwise—blamed him for a disgraceful attack upon a man of noble blood. Neither could he look past the fact that his attempts to oust Melisende from an active political role had caused trouble he could have done without. There were enough dangers looming without starting a civil war: the Fatimids had demonstrated that their appetite to attack the south of the kingdom remained undimmed; Antioch and Edessa in the north were under growing pressure both from Zengi in Mosul and Aleppo and the Byzantine emperor John II Komnenos in Anatolia and Cilicia. Belatedly Fulk realized that wrestling with his wife and her faction was a pointless distraction from the real business of rule. In 1135 he backed down and agreed to rule in tandem with her, as Baldwin II had requested. This was quite a turnaround. "The king became so uxorious that, whereas he had formerly aroused her wrath, he now calmed it," continued William, "and not even in unimportant cases did he take any measures without her knowledge and assistance."[10]

With Melisende belatedly raised to her rightful place beside her husband—witnessing charters, engaging in policy and in 1136 bearing a second son, named Amalric—Jerusalem took new shape. The young kingdom, in which a second generation of colonizing Franks rubbed shoulders with new arrivals from the East, ruling a mixed population of Christians of all stripes alongside Jews, Arabs, Syrians and Turks, was overhauled—in many places being literally rebuilt from the ground up. Year by year, a new kingdom began to emerge. Reflecting an environment in which merchants, artisans, artists and pilgrims from Persia, Byzantium, Egypt and all over the Mediterranean mingled, the architecture and art produced for Melisende and Fulk was frequently dazzling.

One of the finest examples of crusader art in the age of Melisende was a small but stunningly formed book known as the Melisende Psalter: a devotional manual containing a liturgical calendar and texts of the psalms. It was the product of a workshop in the Church of the Holy Sepulchre—commissioned perhaps as a gift from Fulk to Melisende to soothe their marital strife—and its astonishingly lavish production values epitomized the cross-cultural genius at work in the crusader kingdom. The psalter, which survives today, is a riot of color and craftsmanship: pages of elegant Latin text with illuminated lettering, images from the zodiac, bright illustrations depicting the life of Christ and gold leaf inscribed with Greek phases. The folios were bound between delicately carved ivory covers featuring scenes from the life of King David, tableaux of animals tearing each other apart and soldierly figures representing the virtues violently slaughtering others standing for the vices. The whole thing was fastened with embroidered silk ribbon.[11] Between four and six highly accomplished artists worked on the psalter, under the guidance of a Greek-trained master called Basil, whose work blended Frankish, Italian, Byzantine, Anglo-Saxon and Islamic influences, and in whose workshop the highest standards of calligraphy, bookbinding, metalwork, penmanship and needlework were maintained.[12]

Book production was only a small part of Jerusalem's cultural effusion during Melisende's time as queen. Religious artifacts were brought from the Near East to the Latin West by wealthy or well-connected pilgrims: around the start of Melisende and Fulk's reign a German monastery in Denkendorf, which was dedicated to the Holy Sepulchre, sent a mission to obtain splinters of the True Cross from Jerusalem. The fragments, gifted on the authority of the patriarch, came back to Bavaria encased in a stunning, silver-gilt reliquary in the shape of a double-armed cross (known as a *crux gemina*), mounted with pearls, amethysts and chippings of the precious rock of Golgotha.[13] Other items to find their way back from the crusaders states included Islamic-style printed textiles and drinking jugs cast in the shape of fierce or fantastical beasts. After these were imported from the Holy Land they were often copied in Latin workshops catering to a new appetite for exotic items from the East.[14]

Alongside the production of magnificent trinkets and luxury goods began several massive building projects. Some of these were undertaken independently of crown policy, such as the massive expansion of the Hospital of Saint John that took place between 1140 and ca. 1155. Much work, however, was directly sponsored by the king and queen. Some of Jerusalem's covered markets were constructed under Melisende's direction: one close by the Hospital of Saint John and the Holy Sepulchre contained three parallel streets of cramped shops beneath vaulted passages: these were the Street of Herbs, the Street of Bad Cooking and the Covered Street.[15] On the Temple Mount the Dome of the Rock (or as the crusaders knew it, the Temple of the Lord) was renovated and redecorated ahead of its reconsecration as a Christian church with a chapter of Augustinian canons in 1141. The Dome of the Rock had been badly depleted during the First Crusade: Ibn al-Athir heard of gold and silver candlesticks and candelabra being looted en masse in 1099 in a plunder of booty that was "beyond counting."[16] Now that the mosque had been converted into a church—a project that had been started more than fifteen years previously—Melisende ensured that its splendor was not neglected. She paid special attention to new mosaics inside the shrine and ordered an ornate wrought-iron grille to be erected around the huge rock itself, which had been covered in marble. A small octagonal baptistery (today the *Qubbat al-Mi'raj*) was also built nearby, topped with a little dome and decorated with thirty-two short columns with intricately carved capitals.

Meanwhile, to the east of the Temple platform, in Bethany, which lay a mile and a half outside the city walls on the slopes of the Mount of Olives, Melisende founded a nunnery. For centuries this had been a pilgrimage site associated with Lazarus, whose supposed tomb was served by an attractive pilgrim church.[17] Now a grand new convent with a second church was raised on the site, both for the glory of the Almighty and the comfort of Melisende's youngest sister, Yvette, who had professed as a nun at the Monastery of Saint Anne and who eventually became abbess at Saint Lazarus in 1144. Melisende endowed the nuns under her sister with sufficient revenue to make theirs the richest monastic house in the entire kingdom. According to William of Tyre the queen kept up a steady supply of vestments, treasure, "chalices, books and other ornaments pertaining to the service of the church." William, who saw the Convent of Saint Lazarus fully built, noted that it was protected by a strong tower "of hewn and polished stone," which made it "an impregnable fortress against the enemy."[18]

It must have seemed during the 1130s and 1140s that all Jerusalem was a building site.[19] And no work was more spectacular or important than the reconstruction of the Holy Sepulchre. Planning must have begun in the 1130s, so vast and complex were the proposals to reconfigure the church at the center of the Christian world. Although repairs to the church after its razing by the "mad caliph" al-Hakim in 1009 had resulted in a respectable site, ambitions had expanded considerably in the first decades of Frankish occupation. Now plans were drawn up to join the Rotunda containing the holy tomb with the shrine built over Calvary and the chapel that marked Christ's prison. A new choir, apse and nave were designed, along with a series of chapels. A new dome would rise above the new choir. The tombs of Godfrey and the two Baldwins would be visible immediately on entering the new building from its southern courtyard. The outer doors opening out into this courtyard would be topped with Romanesque arches typical of the old Latin world; above the portals were to be placed elaborate decorative stone lintels carved with images from Christ's Passion amid branches and leaves. The broad effect would feel familiar to all Frankish pilgrims who had previously trodden the path to Santiago de Compostela and seen the numerous Romanesque cathedral complexes built along the way.[20] But the decorative detail of columns and lintels, doorways and windows, mosaics and icons were enthusiastically hybrid: Byzantine, Latin, Arab and Syrian motifs and influences all muddled together to create an exciting and unique "crusader" style. It was perhaps not as daring as the soaring Gothic school of architecture about to burst into life back in France during the mid-twelfth century. But it was striking enough. Work began on the huge new church during the early 1130s and the scaffolding may still have been in place on July 15, 1149, when a parade through the city marked fifty years to the day since it had fallen to armies of God.

While designs were drawn up for this great religious rebuilding project, Fulk and Melisende also oversaw a castle construction program, with fortresses commissioned across the kingdom of Jerusalem and beyond. A ring of fortifications went up: some, like Ibelin, Blanchegard and Gaza were designed to hem in the Fatimids at Ascalon; others guarded the borderlands of crusader influence on the east side of the river Jordan, others still were placed on the approaches toward Damascus. Castles ranged from small watchtowers supplied with water by underground cisterns, to walled compounds large enough to house patrols and raiding parties; by the 1160s they had evolved into huge concentric coastal or hilltop fortresses that amounted to full military barracks. One of the first castles built under Fulk and Melisende was erected at Bayt Jibrin (Beth Gibelin or Bet Govrin), an ancient village between Jerusalem and Hebron. William of Tyre knew Bayt Jibrin as "a strong fortress surrounded by an impregnable wall with towers, ramparts and a moat."[21] The ruins, still visible today, bear out the description.

To solve the problem of garrisoning this military outpost far outside Jerusalem itself, in 1136 Fulk granted Bayt Jibrin to the brothers of the Hospital of Saint John, who took over its maintenance and in turn started to encourage Frankish farming families who had come on crusade or pilgrimage and never returned home to settle and work the land nearby.[22] Its transfer to Hospitaller management marked the beginning of the order's transformation into a military auxiliary force to rival the Templars.[23] This tactic was by no means limited to the kingdom of Jerusalem alone. In the county of Tripoli during the early 1140s the Hospitallers were granted five important border castles—chief among them Crac des Chevaliers, which, after its own extensive redevelopment, came to be one of the most imposing and iconic fortresses in the Latin East. The Templars, for their part, took over a chain of fortresses in Antioch—Baghras, Darbsak, La Roche Guillaume and La Roche de Roussel—which guarded the passes into Syria that came down from the Amanus Mountains. By the end of the twelfth century the two orders would bear the primary responsibility for castle-guard throughout the Latin states.

This was just as well, because guarding was what the Latin states increasingly required. Fulk had managed to make peace with his wife, but as his reign progressed the pressure mounted from other quarters. High among his concerns was the fierce Turkish atabeg Zengi, steadily increasing his power in the Seljuq empire and turning his attentions to the possessions of the infidels by the coast. Having expanded his authority first from Mosul to Aleppo, Zengi pressed hard in the 1130s to take control of Damascus, a conquest that would unite the three greatest Muslim cities in Syria under one ruler, thereby presenting a severe and possibly existential danger to the Latin states.

That danger was evident from the mid-1130s. In Tripoli, Count Pons was killed in battle against the Turks of Damascus in 1137; during the same campaign Fulk himself was besieged by Zengi in the city of Montferrand and was lucky to escape alive. This brought to power a new count of Tripoli,

Raymond II, who had married Melisende's sister Hodierna. Raymond was young and vigorous, but his grip on Tripoli was shaky, and he was heavily reliant on the burgeoning military orders in taking on large swaths of his territory, which would be exposed to any potential conquest of Damascus by Zengi.

Things were no easier in Antioch. There, Alice's campaign to impose herself as regent ended in a third and final failure in 1135 and 1136. Amid a temporary power vacuum in Antioch caused by the death of the elderly patriarch Bernard of Valence—one of the last of the generation of first crusaders—Alice once more seized power on behalf of Constance, by now eight years old. Yet again she was outmaneuvered, this time by the new patriarch, Ralph, former archbishop of Mamistra. Instead of handing power to Alice, Ralph summoned from Europe a new prince entirely: Raymond of Poitiers, the charming and erudite second son of the larger-than-life troubadour duke of Aquitaine, William IX. The old duke was one of the few survivors of the disastrous crusade of 1101 that had been annihilated in Asia Minor by Qilij Arslan; his son Raymond enthusiastically took up the invitation to do better. Raymond arrived in Antioch in 1136 and took command of government, to be faced by two daunting problems. From the east loomed Zengi. From the west the Byzantine emperor John II Komnenos was taking a long-overdue military interest in Antioch and neighboring Cilicia, seeking to enforce the rights of imperial overlordship that his father Alexios had claimed in 1098 but never realized.

Raymond had a reputation as an inveterate gambler with a great fondness for shooting dice. As prince of Antioch he would spend the next seven years playing a desperate, high-stakes game: trying to muster Byzantine military support against Zengi's encroaching armies without having his principality gobbled up by Byzantium in the process. There was some relief—albeit temporary—when in early April 1143 John Komnenos went out hunting for wild boar, tussled with a particularly massive specimen and grazed his hand on his own quiver of poisoned arrows. His hand swelled alarmingly; John refused amputation despite his doctors' pleadings, and on the eighth day of the month he was dead, having chosen his son Manuel to succeed him.[24] But the respite was fleeting. Manuel Komnenos would prove an outstanding emperor in the mold of his grandfather Alexios; Raymond soon found his problems mounting dizzyingly around him.

Back in Jerusalem, meanwhile, Melisende's problems were also multiplying. On November 10, 1143, she went out riding with Fulk near Acre; as they rode, their servants' horses disturbed a hare in a ditch. Like all respectable aristocrats, Fulk was addicted to slaying lower creatures, so he spurred his horse and charged, brandishing his lance. As he galloped, his horse stumbled, threw him off and rolled on top of him, crushing his skull.[25] Fulk's brains spurted out of his nostrils and ears. And as he departed both the kingdom of Jerusalem and the earth, Melisende found herself finally in possession of the regal authority to which she had clung so tenaciously at the start of their marriage. She wailed for her dead husband—but not for long.

Bernard of Clairvaux, never one to refrain from offering his opinion for fear of presumption, wrote several times to Melisende when he heard that she was widowed. (The news came to him via his uncle Andrew of Montbard, a high-ranking officer in the Templars.) Since the old king was dead and the elder of her two boys, Baldwin, was still a child, wrote Bernard, "the eyes of all will be upon you, and on you alone the whole burden of the kingdom will rest. You must set your hand to great things and, although a woman, you must act as a man.

"You must arrange all things prudently and discreetly," he continued, "so that all may judge you from your actions to be a king rather than a queen and so that the Gentiles may have no occasion for saying 'Where is the king of Jerusalem?' "[26]

On Christmas Day 1143 Melisende was crowned for the second time, amid the building site of the Holy Sepulchre in Jerusalem. This time her thirteen-year-old son, now officially recognized as Baldwin III, was beside her. Melisende's relationship with her son would be even more complicated than it had been with his father, and the next decade would bring to Jerusalem not only a new crusade but a full-blown civil war. But in the context of 1143 Melisende might have been forgiven a moment of quiet, personal triumph. "She had risen so far above the normal status of women," wrote William of Tyre, "that she dared to undertake important measures. It was her ambition to emulate the magnificence of the greatest and noblest princes and to show herself in no wise inferior to them."[27]

◆ 14 ◆

The Swords of Our Fathers

With loud outcry people on every side began to demand crosses.

In the late spring of 1145 messengers appeared in the West from the Holy Land bearing bad news.[1] They came from Jerusalem and Antioch, but the sorry tale they told concerned the county of Edessa. The first of the crusader states to have been established and the supplier of the first two Latin kings of the East, Edessa had been under pressure for years, its borderlands a target for the Turkish emirs and atabegs of the Seljuq empire. For nearly half a century it had resisted, guarded by competent Latin lords and fortified by holy relics, including the remains of Christ's disciples, Saints Thaddeus and Thomas. Legend held that in the city of Edessa "no heretic, no Jew, no pagan can live, no tyrant can do harm," for as soon as the unrighteous attacked, Saint Thomas would intercede so that "the enemy either goes away or makes peace."[2] Now, it seemed, the blessed Thomas was sleeping.

During the autumn of 1144 Edessa had come under sustained attack by Imad al-din Zengi, the fierce master of Mosul and of Aleppo. At the end of November 1144, when Count Joscelin II of Edessa was in his castle at Turbessel on the far bank of the river Euphrates, Zengi had besieged his capital. For four weeks Zengi battered the city with stones from his mangonels. For four weeks his sappers dug tunnels to weaken Edessa's towers and fortifications. On Christmas Eve the city fell, its curtain wall mined and breached. The messengers told grave stories of the violence that had befallen the Frankish Christians there, which was later characterized by William of Tyre: "Legions rushed in together from all directions, entered the city and put to the sword all whom they encountered."[3] Women and children were crushed as they fled for safety in the citadel. Hugh, bishop of Edessa, who had been leading the siege defenses, was trampled to death.

Although Zengi did not allow a massacre or a razing—"When he had seen the city he was impressed with it and thought that no sensible policy would permit the demolition of such a place," wrote the Iraqi chronicler Ibn al-Athir—his seizure of Edessa had nonetheless struck a severe blow against the Franks.[4] The whole people of Jerusalem, said the messengers, had felt terrible pain and the anguish of loss to the depths of their souls.[5] They came to the old kingdoms of the West to beg their rulers for a response.

The envoy who brought news of Edessa's fall to the papal court was Hugh, bishop of Jabala. Having been held up by the winter weather, which shut the sea-lanes, Hugh only arrived in the West around May 1145. He found the papacy in an unsettled state. Revolution on the streets of Rome had momentarily produced a commune with its own populist government, inspired by the radical preaching of a canon from Lombardy called Arnold of Brescia, who denounced Church wealth and property ownership in general. The papal court had therefore repaired sixty miles north to Viterbo. The pontiff who sat there on Saint Peter's temporary throne had only been elected in February. His name was Bernardo Paganelli, and he was a former bishop of Pisa and Cistercian monk who had taken the name Eugene (Eugenius) III. He already had plenty on his mind.

The existence of a Roman commune stemmed largely from the fact that for most of the 1130s the Roman Church was in schism, with an aristocratic antipope known as Anacletus II sitting in opposition to the more widely supported Innocent II. The antipope's backers were a small but belligerent party: they included Roger II of Sicily, who traded his support of Anacletus for official blessing of his right to call himself a king. Most of the schismatics were brought back into obedience in 1139 at the Second Lateran Council (which excommunicated Roger for his impertinence). But in the mid-1140s the wounds that had been opened in the Western Church remained raw and bloody. Eugene's immediate predecessor, Lucius III, had died of injuries sustained fighting in a street battle against the schismatic communards in Rome. It was popularly said that Eugene owed his election as Lucius's successor to the fact that no one else could be found who was brave or naïve enough to aspire to the tiara at such a daunting time. It was incumbent on him when he had taken on the job to find a grand project—such as a new crusade—behind which all of Western Christendom could reunite.

The unity of the Western Church and Rome's occupation by violent communards was not the only issue that gnawed at Eugene. From France came news of rogue preachers filling good Christians' heads with dangerous heresies. Most prominent and incorrigible among them was the long-bearded, elegantly spoken demagogue Henry of Lausanne, a runaway monk who had been wandering France in his bare feet for more than thirty years, urging people to reject such familiar pillars of Christian faith as marriage, infant baptism and the Eucharist. Henry was an associate of the notorious Peter of Bruys, who made a name for himself in the 1130s by chopping down crucifixes and setting fire to them in great piles outside church doors, a practice that earned him commensurate reward when he was burned to death by an angry mob.[6] His errors lived on through Henry, and it fell to Eugene as pope to stamp them out.

Disquiet in the West, however, did not blind Eugene to the woes of the East. Even before Hugh of Jabala arrived from Antioch in the spring of 1145, Eugene had been providing for the defense of Latin Christendom and exploring alliances that might help strengthen Frankish hands, both in the crusader states and in Spain, where the war against the Almoravids continued. One of the first bulls he issued after his coronation was *Militia Dei* (the Army of God), sealed in April, which confirmed and extended papal protection for the Templars, by granting the military order financial privileges and tax relief to help them fund their mission. Next Eugene turned his attention to struggles against the Almoravids in Spain, issuing letters calling for the reconquest of Tarragona and offering relief from penance for any Christian warriors who assisted in the mission by donating to the military orders. At the same time, he was entertaining overtures from the Church of Armenia for closer official links with the West.

In all of this, Eugene was supported by a circle of gifted and well-educated churchmen. They included the Cluniac abbot Peter the Venerable—a critical but highly engaged student of Islamic text and practice who oversaw the first Latin translation of the Qur'an and had observed at first hand the course of the wars in Spain—and Otto, bishop of Freising, a former Cistercian monk with impeccable political connections, which sprang from the fact that his half brother Conrad III was the king of the Germans.[7] None of these, however, was so closely associated with Eugene's papacy as his mentor and counselor Bernard of Clairvaux.

Eugene had first met the great abbot Bernard around 1135 in Pisa, and the spindly, charismatic ascetic from Clairvaux made such an impression that Eugene had shortly afterward taken holy orders as a Cistercian, becoming first a brother of Bernard's own house and later the head of the Abbey of Saints Vincent and Anastasius, known also as Tre Fontane—the Abbey of the Three Fountains, located among malarial marshes on the outskirts of Rome. His elevation to the papacy was a surprise but also triumph for Bernard and the Cistercians. Eugene was the first member of the order to have achieved such high office, and the first monk-pope since Urban II's successor, the Cluniac Paschal II.* When Bernard wrote to congratulate Eugene, he said that "when I heard this my spirit came to life within me and I cast myself prostrate on the ground in thanks to God."[8]

Eugene's response to the news of Edessa's fall therefore bore the stamp of Cistercianism in general and Saint Bernard in particular.[9] On December 1, 1146, the pope issued a bull known as *Quantum Praedecessores*, which set out his official reaction to the troubles in the East. *Quantum Praedecessores* was a strident call to the faithful to rise once again and rescue their beleaguered brothers in the Holy Land by joining the armies of a new crusade. Eugene drew heavily on nostalgia for the deeds of the first crusaders: "The most strong and vigorous warriors of the kingdom of the French, and also those from Italy, fired with the ardor of love," who assembled a great army and "not without much shedding of their own blood but attended by divine aid, freed from the filth of the pagans that city in which it was Our Savior's will to suffer for us."[10] Having thus invoked Jerusalem, Eugene then recounted the fall of Edessa: explaining that the archbishop had been killed and "the relics of the saints trampled under the infidels' feet and dispersed." He argued that it was the righteous duty of a new generation of Franks to "vigorously gird themselves to oppose the multitude of the infidels who are now rejoicing in the victory they have gained over us . . . so that the dignity of the name of Christ may be enhanced in our time and your reputation for strength, which is praised throughout the world, may be kept impaired and unsullied."

*Only one other Cistercian would wear the tiara: Benedict XII (r. 1334–42).

This was masterly rhetoric: an appeal to both the piety and the vanity of the knightly classes, and a challenge to prove that the world was not going soft. To fail, wrote Eugene, would prove that "the bravery of the fathers will have proved to be diminished in the sons." Across Europe knights would have heard the tales of the first crusaders and seen the trophies they had brought back from the East. Churches across the continent heaved with relics and trinkets that had traveled west with veterans: a typical example was a reliquary held at a church in Ardres that contained the hairs of Christ's beard, shavings from his cross, a piece of the Holy Lance discovered in Antioch and relics of Saint George.[11] Few across the West could have failed to have seen relics like these, and Eugene knew it. He also understood that crusading in his time was best sold as a family tradition—a deed that burnished lineage and gave glorious form to the Fifth Commandment: Honor thy father and mother.

Yet *Quantum Praedecessores* did more than simply tug on heartstrings and jog memories. Just as Pope Urban II had done in 1095, Eugene offered the faithful who heeded his call a handsome package of spiritual benefits: Church protection for "wives and children, goods and possessions," immunity from legal suit and relief from interest payments on debts. Most precious of all, Eugene promised that "whosoever devoutly begins and completes [a journey to the East] or dies on it will obtain absolution from all his sins of which he has made confession with a contrite and humble heart." Ever the good Cistercian, he spelled out to his audience exactly the sins from which they might need to be relieved. Echoing closely Bernard of Clairvaux's words from the Rule of the Templars, Eugene drew attention to the worldly excesses of secular knights who "care for precious clothes or elegant appearance or dogs or hawks or other things that are signs of lasciviousness . . . multicolored clothes or minivers or gilded or silvered arms." Rise up, he exhorted them—and "receive the fruit of everlasting recompense." The bull was published on December 1, 1145, and plans were laid for a preaching tour the following spring. By that time, however, the first and most illustrious crusaders were already committing themselves to the cause.

Eleanor, Duchess of Aquitaine, was once said to have described her husband King Louis VII of France as "a monk and not a monarch."[12] She was the tenacious, bewitchingly beautiful and politically astute daughter of a louche and lively southern court that sprawled inland above the Pyrenees from the bay of Biscay. He was a handsome young man, long haired and pleasant of countenance. But priesthood and not kingship had been Louis's ambition, and as a boy he was sent to school in Paris to prepare for high office in the Church. Only when his elder brother Philip's horse tripped over a pig in the road and threw the prince to his death was Louis taken out of his classes and installed as heir to the Capetian crown, to which he acceded after his father Louis VI's death in the summer of 1137. And while the crown had descended upon his head, it never quite suited him as well as a miter or a tonsure might have done. He was said to have loved Eleanor with childlike jealousy. Their marriage was destined to be difficult, and would not end well.

In December 1145, however, Eleanor was the queen and Louis the king, and the royal couple were presiding over a large and lavish Christmas court in Bourges. The scene was recorded by Odo of Deuil, one of Louis's chaplains, who wrote a detailed chronicle of the king's deeds in the late 1140s. According to Odo, Louis had invited "bishops and magnates of the realm . . . in great numbers" and planned to reveal to them "the secret in his heart."[13] And so he did. As Louis and Eleanor presided over festive celebrations, the king dropped some very broad hints about his interest in eastern affairs. The way ahead was marked clearly when the former Cistercian prior Godfrey de la Roche, bishop of Langres, gave a bombastic sermon denouncing the devastation of Edessa and "the arrogance of the heathen" and called upon all the great men present to show their loyalty to the king by preparing to fight on his behalf for the succor of all Christians.[14] There was much sympathetic lamentation, recorded Odo. Something big was brewing.

It is not clear whether Pope Eugene's crusading bull had reached the French court at Christmastide 1145, or whether in turning his attentions eastward Louis was fulfilling a vow made by his late brother, Philip. Whatever the case, both the pope and the French king saw clearly the need for a collective response to Edessa's fall. By the spring that response had been properly coordinated. On March 1, 1146, *Quantum Praedecessores* was reissued, this time addressed specifically to Louis and his subjects. As it circulated throughout the French kingdom preparations were made for a meeting that would closely resemble the Council of Clermont in 1095. Two weeks before Easter Sunday a grand assembly descended on Vézelay in northern Burgundy. A wooden platform was erected in the fields outside the town. On March 31, Louis VII himself stood upon this platform wearing a crusader's cross. Beside him was the slender but unmistakable figure of Bernard of Clairvaux, preparing to make the sermon of his life.

Nothing about Vézelay was mysterious or unplanned. Just as had been the case at Clermont fifty-one years previously, what took place was a carefully choreographed piece of public theater in which Bernard made a rousing address on the themes already popularly promulgated by papal bull, and the people responded with adulation. The crowds had assembled ready—eager, even—to be uplifted, and Bernard gave them the performance they wanted, rousing them to a righteous frenzy and then handing out crosses to everyone who agreed to join King Louis on a new crusade. This ecstatic bout of planned spontaneity was then reported by recruiting officers and preachers far and wide throughout the realm. "When heaven's instrument [i.e., Bernard] poured forth the dew of the divine word . . . with loud outcry people on every side began to demand crosses," wrote Odo. "And when he had sowed, rather than distributed, the parcel of crosses which had been prepared beforehand, he was forced to tear his own garments into crosses and sow them abroad."[15] Here indeed was a tableau with which to inspire a new adventure: the famous abbot—"who bore a hardy spirit in his frail and almost lifeless body"—literally rending apart his clothes like Jacob.[16] It began a period of intensive preparation for a crusade led not by princes, but by kings and queens. A popular song in old French captured the spirit of the moment. "Anyone who now goes with Louis need have no fear of Hell, for his soul will be in Paradise with the angels of our Lord," went the chorus, while a verse insisted that "God has organized a tournament between Heaven and Hell."[17]

After rousing the French at Vézelay, St. Bernard went off to Flanders and the Rhineland to spread the word of the new crusade and perform miracles. These included having a short conversation with a statue of the Virgin Mary and healing several hundred people who were lame, blind or deaf: a little girl had her withered hand healed; one man was actually raised from the dead.[18] As Bernard went he kept up his usual flood of correspondence, so that he could persuade even where he could not preach. An epistle to the people of England alternated between flattery and rebuke: "What are you doing, you mighty men of valor?" he asked, warning the English of an impending threat to Jerusalem. "Will you cast holy things to dogs, pearls before swine? How great a number of sinners have here confessed with tears and obtained pardon for their sins since the time when these holy precincts were cleansed of pagan filth by the swords of our fathers? . . . What think you my brethren? Is the hand of the Lord shortened . . . so that he must call on us, petty worms of the earth, to save and restore him to his heritage?"[19] In another missive he urged Duke Wladislaus and the people of Bohemia to believe that a crusade was an "opportunity which will not come again. I ask and advise you to put this business of Christ before everything else."[20] The crusade, he explained, was due to set off from the West at Easter 1147—there was not much time to lose.

Even as Bernard preached, however, it became clear that for some would-be crusaders, Easter 1147 could not come quickly enough. In the months before the First Crusade, unauthorized popular preaching and run-of-the-mill bigotry had combined to inflame and incite large mobs who went out to harm any non-Christians they could lay their hands on. Then, the vigilante violence had been worst in the Rhineland. And so it proved again half a century later. Traveling separately from Bernard was another French Cistercian preacher by the name of Raoul, who went on his own demagogic perambulation up and down the Rhine valley, whipping up enthusiasm for crusading and folding it into old hatreds of Jews. Bernard regarded Raoul with bridling contempt, and wrote in fury to the archbishop of Mainz to complain that Raoul was "a fellow without sense and void of all modesty! A fellow whose foolishness has been set up on a candlestick for all the world to see!"[21] But during the high summer of 1146 Raoul's powerful charisma and lamentably populist message momentarily drowned out the abbot's complaints. And so, once again, the Jews of the Rhineland felt the naked fury of the crusader hordes.

A Jewish writer, Ephraim of Bonn, kept a record of the atrocities committed at Raoul's urging and recounted the rogue preacher calling on Christians to "avenge the crucified one upon his enemies who stand before you; then go to war against the Ishmaelites."[22] As a result, deaths, mutilations, blindings, beatings, home invasions and robberies occured in towns including Mainz, Cologne, Speyer and Worms. Simon of Trier was decapitated by having his head crushed in a winepress. Mistress Mina of Speyer had her ears and thumbs cut off.[23] Bernard of Clairvaux gnashed his teeth in fury at Raoul's rabble-rousing. "I find three things most reprehensible in him," he wrote. "Unauthorized preaching, contempt for episcopal authority, and incitation to murder."[24] Jews were for converting, not killing, thought Bernard. This would have been cold comfort indeed to the victims, particularly those tragic casualties who chose suicide over forced baptism at the hands of a crusader gang—as did a young woman called Gutalda of Aschenburg, who drowned herself rather than apostasizing her faith.[25] But by the late autumn Bernard had at least managed to track down Raoul in person, in Mainz. He censured him very severely and "prevailed upon him to the point where he promised to obey and to return to his monastery."[26] Losing their firebrand did not go down well with Raoul's followers, who were only dissuaded from insurrection by a grudging respect for Bernard's saintliness. It did, however, stall an even worse orgy of anti-Semitic violence and stood testament if nothing else to Bernard's ability to command the respect of the crusading masses as well as the great secular lords the pope had tasked him with recruiting.

The greatest of those lords fell under Bernard's spell at Christmas 1146 in Speyer. Conrad III had been elected king of the Germans (also known as king of the Romans) in 1138, and although he was never crowned as Holy Roman Emperor, he was nevertheless the mightiest monarch in the West, with his sphere of influence and command stretching from Denmark in the north to Lombardy in the south, and from the borders of France all the way east to Hungary. His support for the new crusade would amount to a significant coup. As usual Bernard of Clairvaux proved equal to the task. According to Conrad's brother Otto of Freising, Bernard charmed the Christmas court and "persuaded the king with Frederick [his nephew] and many other princes and illustrious men to accept the cross, performing many miracles both publicly and privately."[27]

This was an extraordinary achievement, which spoke not only to Bernard's capacity for personally inspiring the great and good, but to his skills as a diplomat operating at the highest level. The factionalism of German politics ran deep and sour, and in order to free Conrad to leave his kingdom on a long and dangerous journey from which there was at best only an even chance of returning, he had to convince many others that they should either join the king or stand aside and let him go in peace. Most critically this included persuading Welf VI of Bavaria—Conrad's most dangerous political opponent—that he too should agree to travel to the East on crusade. Not only did Bernard do so, wrote Otto of Freising, he also managed to attract a penitent group of criminal ne'er-do-wells. "So great a throng of highwaymen and robbers (strange to say) came hurrying forward [to take the cross] that no man in his senses could fail to comprehend that this so sudden and so unusual a transformation came from the hand of the Most High," he wrote.[28]

And so the stage was set. By the spring of 1147, when Bernard began to wind down his preaching tour, he had effectively made peace in Germany, induced two of the most powerful monarchs in Europe to be the first royals since King Sigurd of Norway to go crusading, charmed knights and ordinary pilgrims seeking salvation into doing the same, performed literally hundreds of miracles, written as many letters and earned such fame that he was sometimes physically endangered by the adoring and marveling multitudes who turned out to see him on his travels. The only thing he had not done was to undertake to travel to the crusader states himself. Bernard always maintained that Jerusalem to him lay in Clairvaux—and of course, with his slight and deliberately weakened body he would likely not have survived the journey east. Despite devoting so much of his life and career to fulminating for crusade, he would never go to glimpse the infidel at close quarters.

Others, however, would. At Easter in 1147, by ship, on horseback and on foot, armies of a size not raised in more than half a century said their prayers and their farewells, entrusted their possessions to the Church and their souls to the Almighty and began to move off to come to the rescue of the kingdom of Jerusalem. Not all of them would arrive there—and many of those who did took very circuitous paths, beset with danger from enemies old and new. When they did arrive in the East, they did not find it quite as they had imagined. All the same, after half a century a Second Crusade had materialized to follow in the footsteps of the first. It had been two and a half years since Edessa had fallen. What adventures and agonies lay ahead of these new crusaders, God only knew.

◆ 15 ◆

Converted or Deleted

This is an occasion for you to save your souls and, if you wish it, acquire the best land in which to live.

In the middle of June 1146, as northern Europe began to stir itself for crusade, George of Antioch, the grizzled vizier of Sicily, sailed a fleet of ships to the shores of Muslim-ruled Ifriqiya and prepared to attack the city of western Tripoli (Tarabalus).* Somewhere close to his sixtieth birthday, distinguished by his long white hair and full, straight, neatly manicured beard, George had been the preeminent minister at the court of King Roger II for nearly half his life.[1] He was a financial expert and an adept administrator, but he was nowhere more effective than in command of a fleet of galleys. George's honorific title—*ammiratus ammiratorum*—could be translated from its Latin form as "emir of emirs," although an alternative rendering was "admiral of admirals."[2] During the summer of 1146 he confronted the walls of Tripoli and considered the best way to bring the inhabitants quickly into obedience.

George had been in these waters many times before. Born to a Syrian Christian family, he had trained in public accountancy in pre-crusader Antioch and subsequently at the Zirid court in Mahdia, the largest port in Ifriqiya, which lay almost four hundred miles along the coast from Tripoli. Some time shortly after 1108 he absconded and arrived in Sicilian service, working in the cities

*Western Tripoli (Tarabalus al-Gharb) is the city found on the coast of modern-day Libya, and is not to be confused with the Syrian/Lebanese Tripoli (Tarabalus al-Sham) that was the capital of the crusader state of the East.

of Messina and Palermo, and occasionally visiting the Fatimid court in Cairo as an envoy. From the 1120s he led raids on the coastal towns of his former employers; in 1142, he returned to Mahdia, sailed right into the harbor and confiscated ships at anchor, as punishment for the Zirids' defaults on their debts to King Roger for shipments of Sicilian grain. Since then he had overseen yearly attacks, plundering and conquering strongholds including Djidjelli (Jijil), Brask (Sidi Brahim) and the Kerkennah Islands.[3]

The reason for the sudden wave of Sicilian aggression was that Zirid Ifriqiya was starving and vulnerable. North African harvests had been failing, and unrest had ripped through the coastal cities and countryside alike. "Because of starvation the nomads sought out the towns and the townspeople closed their gates against them," wrote Ibn al-Athir. "Plague and great mortality followed. The countryside was emptied and from whole families not a single person survived."[4] The effects soon touched Sicily. Piracy was rife in Ifriqiyan ports and the gold caravans that traveled to the coast from Sudan were disrupted by general unrest. Refugees came flooding across the Mediterranean to Sicily in the hope of finding food and safety. Their desperate state persuaded the king and his vizier that conquering Ifriqiya, a deed that Roger's father had eyed with skepticism and caution, was now tantalizingly possible.[5]

Tripoli was no small target, for it was defended by both seaward and landward walls. But according to the account given by Ibn al-Athir, the citizens made George of Antioch's job easy. When the Sicilian ships arrived on June 15 Tripoli was already facing a serious crisis of internal order. The governor, a member of the Arab clan known as the Banu Matruh, had been overthrown in favor of a visiting dignitary from the Almoravids, the veil-wearing, intolerant puritans who had overrun Morocco and Muslim Spain. Having stopped in Tripoli on his way to perform hajj at Mecca, the Almoravid suddenly found himself defending the city from a Sicilian fleet off the coast while trying to quell rebellion in the streets. Seeing the disarray and scenting an easy victory, George of Antioch sent his men to erect ladders and scale the defenses. "After fierce fighting the Franks took the city by the sword," wrote Ibn al-Athir. The battle was followed by "a bloodbath and seizure of women and property."[6]

From this point, conquest of Ifriqiya proceeded apace. Town governors abandoned their allegiance to the Zirids of Mahdia in favor of the Franks across the water. George of Antioch forced the hand of those who resisted.

In short order Gabès, Susa and Sfax became formal Sicilian protectorates. In 1148, when Mahdia itself fell, the Zirid palaces would be looted and their riches shipped back to Palermo.

At a time when the Second Crusade had just been called and preachers all over Western Europe were summoning Christians to take up arms against Islamic enemies, a campaign of conquest and tribute taking by a Christian king against Muslim neighbors was bound to attract notice, even if it occurred many hundreds of miles away from the Holy Land. When Ibn al-Athir wrote about the Sicilian campaigns against Ifriqiya many years later, he placed them squarely in his broader narrative of Frankish reaction to the fall of Edessa. This was a natural enough conclusion. That Roger and George of Antioch's assaults amounted at least superficially to a campaign of Christian expansion seemed to be confirmed in 1148, when Pope Eugene formally appointed an archbishop of Africa. Unsurprisingly many Muslims in Ifriqiya burned with the humiliation of being subjugated by unbelievers: after the governor of Gabès sent an envoy to negotiate peaceful submission to Roger, he was kidnapped by his disgusted rivals and tortured to death, ending his days choking on his own severed penis. (The governor's envoy, meanwhile, was dressed in a pointed hat covered in bells, paraded about Mahdia strapped to a camel and then stoned to death by a mob.)[7]

Despite this, however, Roger of Sicily's attacks on Ifriqiya did not fit neatly into Bernard of Clairvaux and Pope Eugene's rhetoric and theory of crusading. For one thing, Roger himself made no serious effort to place his African ambitions in the context of crusade preaching and did not personally take the cross. He no doubt remembered that at the height of the Roman Church's schism in the 1130s, Pope Innocent II had preached holy war against Sicily and the other supporters of Anacletus, stating that participants would earn crusade privileges. Nor did George of Antioch's fleet set sail under crusader crosses, baying for blood. They were primarily agents of a pragmatic, self-serving policy focused on economic gain and a desire to expand Sicilian kingship far beyond the shores of the island itself.

Nowhere was this more obvious than in Tripoli itself. After the city fell there was the customary period of plunder. But soon enough George of Antioch declared an amnesty, promised to protect citizens' property and invited those who had fled in fear of their lives to return to the city. A Sicilian garrison was installed, the walls strengthened and a moat dug. Yet Tripoli was neither occupied nor forcibly Christianized. Six months later the Banu Matruh recognized Roger's lordship and were returned to power, having agreed that Muslims in Tripoli now owed to the king of Sicily the same taxes as Muslims on the island: the *jizya* and a land tax.[8] The Arab governor (*wali*) would henceforth wear a robe of office sent directly from Palermo, but a balance of power sensitive to the ethnic makeup of the population was achieved by the appointment of a Berber chief magistrate (*qadi*).[9] An active policy of resettlement began, with Sicilians and others under Roger's rule being encouraged to cross to Ifriqiya. So while Tripoli had been taken by a Christian fleet that inflicted considerable bloodshed, soon enough it was back under Islamic government and its economy was booming. "It quickly flourished and its affairs prospered," wrote Ibn al-Athir.[10]

Here, then, was a form of Christian expansion that defied easy categorization, even against the background noise of Second Crusade preaching. It reflected, perhaps, Roger's complex cultural inheritance and that of Norman Sicily at large. Although certainly a Christian, and related by blood to many illustrious crusaders, Roger was also strongly influenced by Arabic and Greek culture. His royal mantle, made in Palermo's leading workshop to celebrate his coronation, gave this mixed inheritance striking visual form. A beautiful red silk garment decorated with garnets, pearls, rubies and sapphires, it was embroidered in gold thread with lions attacking camels—a metaphor for the Norman victory over the Arab world.[11] Yet this handsome cloak was also proudly inscribed with Kufic Arab script, which gave the date of its creation in Islamic form (528 rather than 1133–34). When Roger occasionally issued charters in Latin (he preferred Greek and Arabic), he was king "by the grace of God." But coins minted during his reign declared him "powerful through the grace of Allah." In a contemporary mosaic (commissioned by none other than George of Antioch) in the Church of Santa Maria dell'Ammiraglio in Palermo, Roger is depicted receiving his crown from Christ while dressed like a Christian emperor. Yet he generally preferred to comport himself like an Egyptian caliph: wearing Arab dress, only showing his face on feast days, parading with horses decked in gold and silver before him and having a parasol borne above his head—a distinctive symbol of specifically Fatimid preeminence.[12]

Roger's genius, aided and abetted by George of Antioch, was his ability to combine, into a singular Sicilian whole, elements of all the cultures that coexisted under his leadership. Ibn al-Athir, writing after the events, looked at

Roger and merely saw an acquisitive, piratical "Frank" to be cursed with the rest of them; but Roger was actually a very long way from the stereotype of the zealot crusader. It was telling indeed that he and George of Antioch limited their assaults on the Islamic world during the 1140s to the North African trading stations that could serve Sicily's economy. When the armies of the Second Crusade began to move in mid-1147 Roger thought less of supporting their adventure in the Holy Land than of exploiting the disruption caused by Louis and Conrad's march on Constantinople to plunder Byzantine islands in the Adriatic.

As Roger focused his efforts on expanding Sicilian rule into North Africa, the real crusaders beyond the Alps were driving toward departure for the East. In a grand council held in Châlons-sur-Marne in early February 1147 the French and German crusade leaders decided that they would not travel via Sicily. (Conrad in particular had no wish to deal with Roger II, whom he regarded as a deadly enemy.) Pope Eugene had called on the faithful to emulate the deeds of their forefathers, so it was in their forefathers' footsteps they would go: following the Danube through Hungary and then traversing the Balkans to Constantinople, crossing Asia Minor with the support of the eastern emperor Manuel I Komnenos before descending into the crusader states via Antioch. Planning and provisioning for this notoriously difficult journey, along with the political preparations for regencies in both the French and German kingdoms, occupied the weeks leading up to Easter, the symbolic date on which the two armies had agreed to set out.

As they plotted their route, however, a new strand to crusading emerged. In Saxony a faction of crusaders had come together whose motivation was no less self-interested than Roger of Sicily's. They too saw their opportunities much closer to home: not among the Judean hills or on the Aleppan plateau, but in the riverlands that fed the Baltic Sea. Here—in what is now northern Poland and northeast Germany—lived Slavic tribes referred to collectively (if imprecisely) as the Wends (*Wenden*). The Wends were pagans. Their deities were to be found not in heaven but in the features of the natural earth, such as oak trees, brooks and rocks. They worshipped in timber-built temples rather than stone churches. They sacrificed cattle and revered inhuman idols such as the four-headed Svantovit (*Svetovid*), and they did not take kindly to

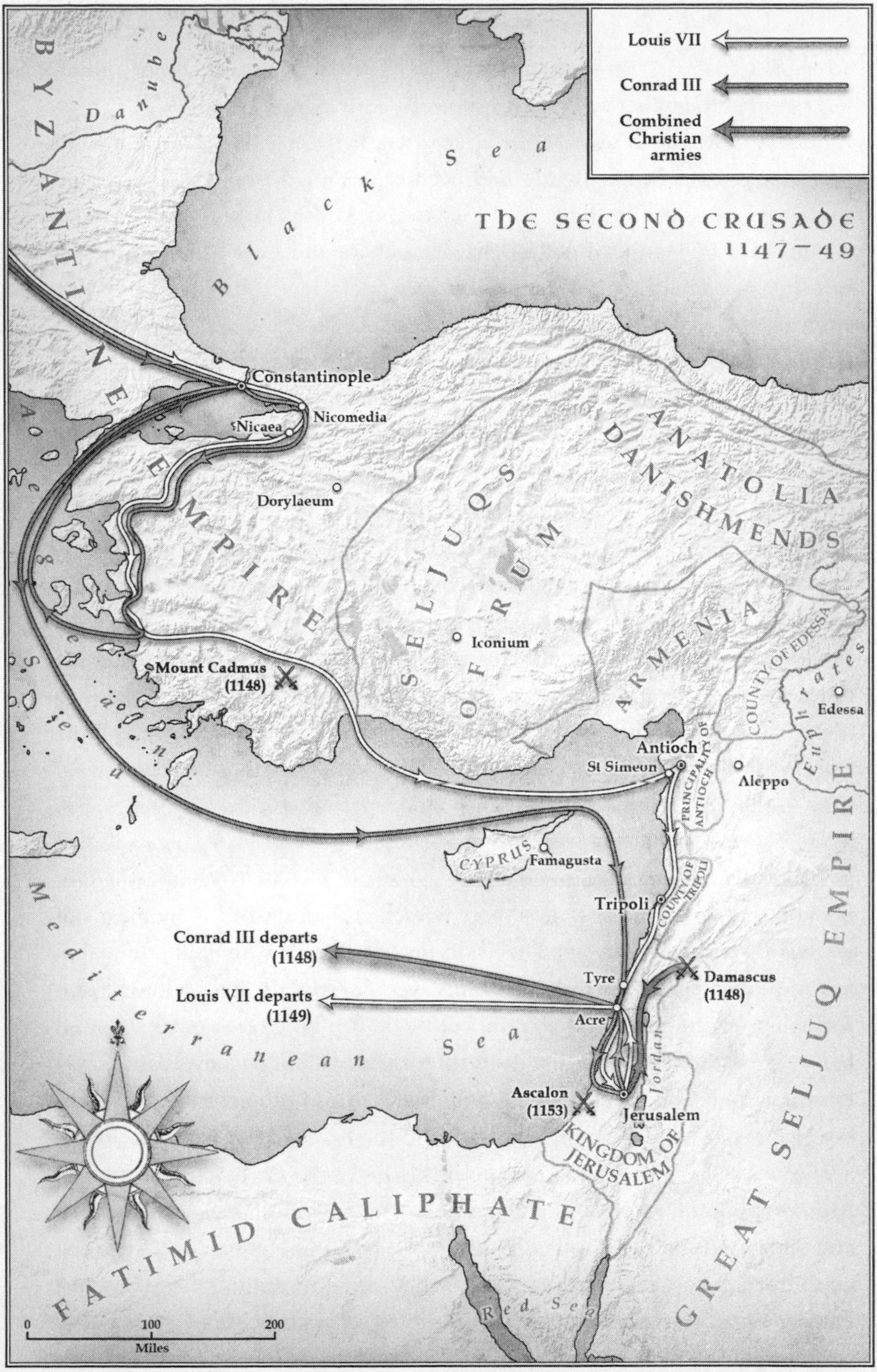

THE SECOND CRUSADE
1147–49
Louis VII
Conrad III
Combined Christian armies
BYZANTINE EMPIRE
Danube
Black Sea
Constantinople
Nicomedia
Nicaea
Dorylaeum
Aegean Sea
Mount Cadmus (1148)
SELJUQS OF RUM
Iconium
ANATOLIA
DANISHMENDS
ARMENIA
COUNTY OF EDESSA
Euphrates
Edessa
Antioch
St Simeon
PRINCIPALITY OF ANTIOCH
Aleppo
CYPRUS
Famagusta
COUNTY OF TRIPOLI
Tripoli
Conrad III departs (1148)
Louis VII departs (1149)
Tyre
Acre
Damascus (1148)
Mediterranean Sea
Jordan
Ascalon (1153)
Jerusalem
KINGDOM OF JERUSALEM
GREAT SELJUQ EMPIRE
FATIMID CALIPHATE
Red Sea
0
100
200
Miles

attempts to baptize them into subservience. They were, in the view of a small but significant number of Conrad's subjects, entirely fair game.

Just as was the case in Ifriqiya, sparring between Christians and non-Christians in the Baltic regions had been under way for many years before the genesis of crusading. Since Carolingian times in the ninth century armies commanded by God-fearing lords had fought wars of expansion into pagan territory and left their cultural stamp by appointing bishops and building churches. (This had been done most successfully in Denmark, where Christianity had been embraced in the 960s.) By the eleventh century the eastern boundary of Christian dominion coincided more or less with the course of the river Elbe. Then, for a time, missionaries rather than soldiers crossed the line into Wendish country. But by the early twelfth century a desire to colonize and Christianize by force was rising once again.

Around the year 1108 a Flemish clerk in the service of Adalgod, archbishop of Magdeburg, composed a document known as the Magdeburg Letter. It made an impassioned case for external military assistance against the Wends who, the letter claimed, were committing many atrocities against good Christian folk. "We have been weighed down for a very long time by the many kinds of oppressions and disaster which we have suffered at the hands of the pagans," it stated. "They have profaned the churches of Christ with idolatry . . . they invade our region very frequently and, sparing no one, they lay waste, kill, overthrow and afflict with carefully chosen torments. They behead some and offer the heads to their demons . . . they allow some to endure the gibbet and to drag out a life that is more wretched than death . . . by means of gradual dismemberment. . . . They skin many while they are still living and, after scalping them, they disguise themselves with their scalps and burst into Christian territories." Lurid accounts of blood-drinking ceremonies followed before the author called on his "dearest brothers in all of Saxony, France, Lorraine and Flanders" to "prepare for holy war . . . this is an occasion for you to save your souls and, if you wish it, acquire the best land in which to live."[13] The country, he wrote, with a faint but distinct echo of the famous biblical description of the Promised Land (Exodus 3:8), was rich in meat, honey, corn and birds "and if it were well cultivated none could be compared to it for the wealth of its produce."[14] In 1108 all this had come to nothing because Pope Paschal II had declined to authorize crusading against the Wends. But nearly four decades on things had changed.

During the early 1140s a dozen or so Christian noble families from Saxony had begun a unilateral military push into Wendish country to enrich themselves on colonized land. They cut a swath through the borderlands known as the Saxon Limes, ousting Slavic Wagrian and Polabian people and building fortresses to mark the extent of their land grab. In their wake came families of Christian settler-farmers and teams of missionary priests. Wendish serfs were driven from their lands. Wendish chiefs were forced to accept the lordship of Christian lords like Albert the Bear, margrave of Brandeburg.[15] This was in itself bad news for the Wends. With the outbreak of crusading fervor in 1146 and 1147, things got a lot worse.

In March 1147 Bernard of Clairvaux attended a meeting in Frankfurt, convened to thrash out arrangements for Conrad III's march on the Holy Land. But far from agreeing to join their king, however, the Saxon nobles put their case for staying home and fighting the Wends. "They had as neighbors certain tribes that were given over to the filthiness of idolatry," recalled Otto of Freising, "and in like manner took the cross in order to assail these races in war."[16] Recognizing that this was a considerable deviation from the crusading mission Eugene envisioned when he heard that Zengi had stormed the walls of Edessa, the Saxons had come up with a new style of crusader cross: "not sewn simply to their clothes, but brandished aloft, surmounted on a wheel."[17]

This was plainly unorthodox, but Bernard of Clairvaux was never one to recoil from radical ideas. He liked what he saw, and straightaway dipped his pen to support the Saxons' right to make holy war not on Muslims but on the Wends. In a letter packed tightly with biblical allusion and apocalyptic bombast, he declared that the Baltic pagans, through little more than their existence in places that the Saxons wanted to colonize, represented perfectly well the enemies of God, "whom, if I may say so, the might of Christendom has endured too long."[18] No truce or peace was to be made with these people, he thundered. They were to be battled until such time as they were either "converted or deleted."[19] On April 13, Pope Eugene formally agreed. He issued a bull, *Divina Dispensatione,* permitting the same remission of sins and spiritual benefits for fighting in the Baltic region as accrued to those joining Conrad and Louis. Thus, from July 1147 armies of Danes and Saxons roared into Wendish territory and spent several months burning temples and forcibly baptizing prisoners. They were only partially successful: captured Slavs tended to accept baptism with a shrug before returning to pagan ritual and thinking no more about it; and eventually the Wendish chief Prince Nyklot agreed to pay tribute for peace, in the sort of deal Bernard of Clairvaux had specifically abominated. Nevertheless, in 1147 a new front of crusading had been opened. For the next four decades the Wends would be steadily pursued to the conversion or deletion that Bernard of Clairvaux had commanded, and their lands divided greedily between the various Christian powers who connived at their destruction. By the 1180s, they had effectively been wiped out. But the appetite for Christian expansion in the Baltic, under the guise of crusading, was not. Three hundred years of warfare between Germanic armies and pagan tribes and kingdoms had begun.

The final target of the Second Crusade was far from the lands of the Zirids and the Wends, and further still from Edessa and Jerusalem. Indeed, it was about as far west as one could go in mainland Europe before being swallowed up by the uncharted maw of the Atlantic Ocean. It was the kingdom of Portugal. Here, once again, long-standing warfare between Christian warriors and infidels advanced significantly. The focus was the conquest of Lisbon—a monumental feat attempted by crusader armies who arrived before that unfortunate city in July 1147.

Since the time of Sigurd of Norway's visit to Galicia in the first decade of the twelfth century, crusaders from the north and northwest of Christendom had been seen regularly on the fringes of the Spanish peninsula. The region was a natural stopping point for any seaborne travelers journeying from northwest Europe to the eastern Mediterranean, by the simple fact of geography and the need of thirsty sailors to resupply before heading toward the hostile coastline of Almoravid al-Andalus. In 1112 a fleet of English pirate-pilgrims stopped in Galicia on their way to Jerusalem and were co-opted into a civil war between Urraca, daughter of the late king Alfonso VI of Castile and León, and her husband, Alfonso I "the Battler" of Aragon.

During the 1140s, however, the arrival of holy warriors from the chillier parts of Latin Christendom had become a matter of military planning rather than simple happenstance. Their arrival was chiefly encouraged by Afonso Henriques, the vigorous ruler of the county of Portugal, whose sobriquets included "the Great," "the Founder" and "the Conqueror." Afonso was a grandson of the famous Alfonso VI through one of the old warrior's illegitimate daughters, Theresa. The county of Portugal, where he took sole command in 1129 when he was about twenty years old, consisted of a large parcel of territory fanning out around the coastal city of Porto (Oporto). This was frontier country of the most precarious sort—sandwiched between the Christian kingdom of Galicia above and the realm of the Almoravids below. Afonso had high ambitions both to expand and secure his county and to raise its status to that of a kingdom. Both of these objectives required outside help.

Through dogged determination and constant warring against Muslim and Christian neighbors alike, Afonso had managed by 1143 to have his right to a crown recognized. His soldiers hailed him as a monarch after he destroyed an Almoravid army on July 25, 1139; by the Treaty of Zamora of October 5, 1143, his cousin, King Alfonso VII of Castile and León, and a papal delegate accepted this as political reality.* Yet building Portugal from a parchment monarchy into a stable realm was a more difficult matter, and it relied heavily on forcing the Muslim-ruled cities and strongholds south of Porto into submission.

In such a campaign Lisbon, the prosperous port nearly two hundred miles south of Porto, sheltered from the Atlantic eight miles inside the mouth of the river Tagus, was the largest, most lucrative and most strategically important target of all. It was a highly defensible port with mercantile connections to west Africa and excellent links inland through the Tagus valley. An excitable Anglo-Norman cleric who has been identified as a priest named Raol wrote a detailed account of the battle for Lisbon in 1147, and recorded a tale that the city had been founded in classical times by Odysseus. Raol noted that in his day it produced a lush banquet of natural produce: fish and shellfish, birds in abundance, citrus fruits and olives, salt and honey, grapes and pomegranates, more figs than could be eaten by the sixty thousand families who lived there. The Tagus spat out nuggets of gold onto its banks in the early spring, while merchants brought plenty more from Africa throughout the year. Lisbon was, reckoned Raol, "the richest [city] in trade of all of Africa and a great part of Europe."[20]

When the call to crusade went out in 1146, it was clear that there would be some element to it that concerned Spain as well as Edessa and Jerusalem. Papal confirmation of spiritual benefits for Spanish crusaders had been issued ever since Pope Urban's time. The First Lateran Council, convened by

*This being said, it should be recognized that it was not until 1179 that Afonso Henriques's kingly status was officially endorsed by the pope.

Calixtus II in 1123, stated baldly that crusading in Spain and the East were of equivalent merit. Pope Eugene was consistent: in April 1147 he approved a plan by Alfonso VII of Castile and León and the Genoese to attack Almería, in the far southeast of the peninsula, voicing his enthusiasm for fighting the infidel anywhere and everywhere.[21] (This attack duly took place during the summer of the same year.) To a certain constituency of crusaders both inside Portugal and far beyond, conquering Lisbon would be a perfectly acceptable answer to this call, and an *amuse-bouche* before the main task of restoring Christian dominion in Edessa. In 1142 Afonso Henriques had tried and failed to take the city despite the aid of seventy ships "from the parts of the Gauls," ultimately bound for Jerusalem.[22] By 1147, however, circumstances were ripe. News from Morocco said the Almoravid state was in grave trouble, with their armies being crushed by those of another Berber sect, known as the Almohads. Crusade fervor was lighting up Europe. Now, calculated Afonso, was his moment to strike.

With this in mind, the previous year thousands of would-be pilgrim warriors had been stirred to action in England, Scotland, the Rhineland, Flanders and Normandy on the understanding that they would take a different but potentially more lucrative path to the Holy Land than Conrad and Louis's overland route. Effectively they would mirror Sigurd's 1107 to 1109 expedition: plundering their way to the Holy Land by ship on a journey through the western Mediterranean. Many of these new crusaders, particularly those from England, were not of high lordly status, but middling folk with a yearning to leave a country that had been torn by the civil war known as the Anarchy for more than ten years. Only a few English leaders, such as Saher of Archel and Henry de Glanvill, were of noble status; other captains such as Simon of Dover and the Viel brothers of Southampton were of lowlier stock. These men had little to mortgage to their local monastic houses in order to finance a crusade: looting along the way was a much more attractive—indeed, their only—option.[23]

So it was that as many as ten thousand pilgrim soldiers from the British Isles and the Low Countries set sail from Dartmouth on the south coast of England on May 23, 1147, in a huge fleet of 164 ships. Before they left they agreed on rules among themselves, designed to keep the peace among an army speaking many languages and drawn from many realms. "They sanctioned very strict laws, such as, for example, a life for a life and a tooth for a tooth," wrote Raol. "They forbade all display of costly garments. . . . They ordained that women should not go out in public . . . that each ship should have its own priest . . . that everyone make weekly confession and take communion on a Sunday."[24] After a hair-raising journey, during which many inexperienced sailors thought they could hear Sirens calling them to their doom, on June 16 they arrived at Porto to be met by the bishop of that city, since Afonso himself was already marching to Lisbon with an army that included a contingent of Portuguese Templars. The bishop gave the crusaders a rousing sermon. He drew on the themes of *Quantum Praedecessores* and praised them for leaving behind "the alluring affection of wives [and] the tender kisses of sucking infants at the breast" to carry with them only the "torturing memory of their native land."[25] Their mission, he said, was worth every pang and heartache, for they would "raise up the fallen and prostrate church of Spain; re-clothe her soiled and disfigured form with the garments of joy and gladness."[26]

After several weeks at sea, this was just the spiritual nourishment the crusaders needed. Refreshed and reprovisioned, they set sail south to join Afonso at Lisbon. They arrived at their destination amid a show of portentous weather in which black-and-white clouds seemed to do battle in the sky above them. Great cheers went up aboard the ships: "Behold, God is with us! the power of our enemies is destroyed!"[27]

The siege of Lisbon began at the very end of June with running battles between Muslims defending the suburbs beyond the city walls and crusaders beaching and disembarking their ships on the banks of an inlet in the Tagus. It continued for three and a half months, during which they felt the privations familiar to every generation of crusaders before them. Ahead of serious military operations the crusade leaders agreed with Afonso a contract that assured them of their rights to loot the city for all its worth and take hostages for ransom before handing it over to the king. Then they went to work. On July, infantry stormed Lisbon's suburbs, armed with slingshots and bows. Houses burned. Civilians fled. In the crusader camps siege engineers—including one expert drafted from Pisa—began constructing towers, protective shelters known as cats and sows, and giant mangonels that, when complete, could hammer the walls with five hundred stones per hour.[28] Miners struck ground on a tunnel to destroy the foundations of the city walls. Serious thought was given to building a floating fortress of towers mounted on interconnected boats, which could attack the battlements from the river. A nightly watch rota was established so that the gates could be blockaded around the clock. Messengers who snuck out were captured and their letters confiscated, while those demoralized citizens who came out begging for mercy and baptism were sent back to the city with their hands cut off.

Inside the city, conditions were terrible. The collapse of the Almoravid state and the rise of the Almohads in Morocco meant that there was precious little hope of rescue by a relieving army, and King Afonso had ensured that all nearby towns had been rendered neutral, either by sending troops there to menace them or by negotiating truces.[29] The defenders sent repeated sorties out of Lisbon's three main gates to disrupt the blockade but were driven back each time with heavy losses. Burning siege engines was always a reliable method of defense, but even this proved difficult, for the engineers had built their towers to withstand flame—covering them in oxhides and other fire-retardant material. The only effective weapon in the citizens' armory seemed to be strong language. From the walls, wrote Raol, "they derided us and hurled many a taunt at us, adjudging us worthy of a thousand deaths." The crusaders were goaded in lurid terms: "They taunted us with numerous children about to be born at home in our absence, and said that on this account our wives would not be concerned about our deaths, since they would have bastard progeny enough." The Virgin Mary was robustly slandered, and Christ's divine nature was made the subject of unkind theological speculation. "Besides, they displayed the symbol of the cross before us with mockery," Raol continued. "And spitting upon it and wiping the filth from their posteriors with it, and finally making water upon it as something vile, they threw it at us."[30]

Sadly for the people of Lisbon, siege machines and stones proved far more hurtful than words. Most decisive, however, was the fact that very early in the siege the crusaders seized the main warehouses containing Lisbon's food supplies. The besiegers were therefore blessed with "a rich abundance of bread and wine and fruits," while inside Lisbon the only food available was "the refuse which was thrown out from [crusader] ships and borne up by the waves beneath their walls."[31] As autumn set in, hunger and hopelessness broke Lisbon's spirit. The final assault took place in the second half of October, when a mine brought down two hundred feet of one section of the city walls, while a siege tower's operators succeeded in lowering their drawbridge onto another. The game was up. On October 23 the defenders sued for peace. A short period of squabbling over rights of plunder broke out between the English, Flemings and Portuguese, but this was settled soon enough. An enthusiastic sack took place, during which several murders were committed, including that of the Mozarabic bishop of Lisbon, who had his throat cut. Then Afonso Henriques raised his flag over the garrison, the central mosque was consecrated as a church and within two days a stream of refugees was to be seen hurrying out of the city to seek solace and a new life elsewhere in Islamic Iberia. "The city was captured, the Saracens were killed, sold and expelled and the whole city was cleansed, a [Latin] bishop was established in the city, churches were constructed and clergy were ordained," wrote a later chronicler.[32] It was a formidable start to a crusade whose main target was still about twenty-five hundred miles away.

With the onset of winter no more travel was possible, so the English and Flemish crusaders settled down in Lisbon and awaited the fresh winds and friendly seas of spring, which would bear them to the Holy Land. The portents for their journey seemed good. On the other side of the Spanish peninsula, Almería had fallen nearly simultaneously, after a siege directed by Alfonso VII of Castile and León and his Genoese allies. In the Baltic, the Wends were feeling the first righteous blows of a new Germanic crusading movement. In North Africa, Sicilian fleets were subjugating the Muslim people of Ifriqiya. Raol, the Lisbon chronicler, reflected on the miserable fate that had descended on the enemies of Christ. "As we see the city in ruins and the castle overthrown . . . and as we behold their mourning and lamentations, we are inclined to feel pity for them in their vicissitudes . . . and feel sorry that the lashings of divine justice are not yet at an end," he wrote.[33] But Raol's was a voice crying in the wilderness and his pity was in short supply. Elsewhere the second crusaders went proudly forward toward Edessa, with only the vengeance of the Almighty on their minds.

16

History Repeating

Thence arose a cry that pierced to heaven.

On December 1, 1147, Anna Komnene turned sixty-four. She passed her birthday at the convent of the Mother of God *Kecharitomene* ("full of grace") in the Deuteron neighborhood of Constantinople. This well-endowed nunnery had been founded by Anna's mother as a dignified and palatial retirement home suitable for female members of the Byzantine royal family, and Anna had lived in it for more than twenty-five years, having being sent there by her brother John II Komnenos for plotting against him following their father's death in 1118. Although effectively under house arrest, Anna used her time in the veil well, establishing around her a court of distinguished scholars who worked on Christian Scripture and the writings of the ancient philosophers. She was the equal of any of them: a highly accomplished historian with a deep interest in grammar and rhetoric, metaphysics and medicine, who had read Plato and Aristotle and committed to memory large portions of the Bible and the works of Homer.

It was in this convent, during the mid-1140s, that Anna began to compose her life's great work, the *Alexiad,* celebrating her father's achievements in a grand style reminiscent of the Greek historians of old. To assemble it Anna drew on her own memories as a child and teenager during Alexios's reign, interviews with veteran soldiers, and documents from the imperial archive.[1] She wrote of Alexios and of her mother, Irene, of Robert Guiscard and Bohemond of Taranto, of Pechenegs from the north, Turks from the East and marauding, barbarian crusaders from the West. In doing so, she summoned back to life all the ghosts of a world from which she was one of the few living relics.

There could have been no better time to compose such a history than the late 1140s when, as another Greek writer put it: "Normans and French and the nation of Gauls and whoever lived around old Rome and British and Bretons and simply the whole western array had been set in motion, on the handy excuse that they were going to cross from Europe to Asia to fight the Turks . . . and recover the church in Palestine and seek the holy places, but truly to gain possession of the Romans' land by assault and trample down everything in front of them."[2] It was as if all the events of the 1090s were repeating.[3]

Anna's nephew, the twenty-nine-year-old Byzantine emperor Manuel I Komnenos, prepared very carefully for the arrival of the new crusaders. Although Conrad's and Louis's armies were treading the same roads that their ancestors had trodden, aiming to descend upon Constantinople before crossing Asia Minor to Antioch, there was one crucial difference between their journey and the First Crusade they sought to recreate. The original armies of what Anna called the "Kelts" had traveled east in large part because Alexios had called for them. In 1147 Manuel Komnenos had made no such request. The crusaders were coming on their own account, and experience both past and present suggested they were not to be trusted. For evidence, one needed look no further than the western fringes of the empire, where in the autumn of 1147 George of Antioch was cheerfully terrorizing Greek islands with a Sicilian fleet: capturing Corfu, kidnapping aristocratic women from the Peloponnese for sale into slavery, and filling his ships with treasure and stolen relics.

It was not surprising, therefore, that Manuel responded cautiously to Conrad's and Louis's plans. He massively renovated the city's ancient defenses: the double ring of walls, which dated back to the time of Theodosius II in the fifth century CE, was strengthened, and the moats deepened. Banners fluttered from the battlements, advertising the military might and unsurpassed prestige of the empire.[4] Envoys were dispatched to the frontiers of the imperial territories to await the crusaders' arrival and escort them with as little disturbance as possible through the Balkans. To Louis, Manuel wrote that "when I heard you were coming to my kingdom, I gave thanks and was pleased to hear it."[5] But behind the flattery he was preparing for the worst.

The first crusader army to arrive was Conrad's. The German king set out ahead of Louis, traveled down the Danube, and had entered Byzantine territory by the late summer of 1147. He brought a very large force of perhaps fifty thousand fighting men, along with thousands more nonfighting pilgrims, commanded by a group of elite German nobles including his nephew Frederick, Duke of Swabia—later to be known as Frederick Barbarossa.[6] One Byzantine poet, Manganeios Prodomos, demonstrating the usual combination of moral disdain and physical revulsion reserved by Easterners for Westerners, described the Germans as "Gadarene swine":* filthy, demonic and wild with destructive intent.[7]

The poetic reference to the pigs of the Gadarene soon proved horribly apposite. By September 7, 1147, the German crusaders had been herded across the western empire by Manuel's envoys, with only sporadic disorder along the way. But when they arrived within two days' march of Constantinople, they pitched camp at the plain of Choirobacchoi (Bahsayis), watered by two rivers and lush with fodder for their horses and pack animals. There, disaster struck. Violent storms in the night caused the rivers at Choirobacchoi to burst their banks, and in the flood the crusaders suffered terrible losses of men, animals and baggage. Conrad's half brother Otto, bishop of Freising, described the panic in the camp. "You might have seen some swimming, some clinging to horses, some ignominiously hauled along by ropes to escape the danger," he wrote. "A great many . . . were swept away by the rush of the river, injured by the rocks, and, swallowed up by the force of the eddies."[8] The Greek chronicler John Kinnamos, a good deal less sympathetic, concluded that "one might reasonably guess that the Divinity was angry at them."[9]

Manuel Komnenos had no interest in seeing Conrad's crusade fail on his doorstep. He had a family tie to the German king: Conrad's wife, Gertrude of Sulzbach, was the empress Irene's elder sister.† Equally, however, he had no great wish to see Western crusaders camped en masse at the gates of Constantinople. So once Conrad's army dried itself off he hurried them across the Bosphorus and into Asia Minor. This suited Conrad, who planned, ambitiously, to march quickly and be in Antioch by the following spring.[10] The

*In the story of the Gadarene Swine (Matthew 8:28–34; Mark 5:1–20; Luke 8:26–39) Jesus encountered a man possessed by a legion of demons. He exorcised them and cast them into a herd of around two thousand pigs, who promptly ran into the Sea of Galilee and drowned themselves.

†The empress Irene was born Bertha of Sulzbach and married Manuel in 1146, changing her name to something more classically Greek.

German king divided his forces, sending his brother, Bishop Otto, to lead the pilgrims along the meandering coast road through Ephesus, while he followed the first crusaders' route directly southeast along the ancient Roman road past Nicaea toward Dorylaeum, site of the great victory over Qilij Arslan in 1097. From there he would brave the sultan's capital of Iconium (Konya) before heading through the mountains into northern Syria. They set out on about October 15.

In the time that had elapsed since the First Crusade, Asia Minor had grown no less physically inhospitable nor had the Turks become any fonder of adventurous Westerners. The sultan of Rum by this time was Qilij Arslan's son Mas'ud I. In the course of his long reign (which began in 1116), he had considerably strengthened the authority of the sultanate over areas previously under the control of tribal chiefs.[11] The Turkish tactics of deploying light mounted archers on shoot-and-run raids, feigning retreats to exhaust heavy cavalry and then descending with their swords on men riding tired horses were as devastating as ever. And as the Germans marched and rode, increasingly uncomfortably, through the country around Dorylaeum, Mas'ud was amply revenged for his father's defeat half a century earlier. Before the crusaders had even entered Turkish territory, the raids began. After ten days the Germans had suffered losses that threatened the survival of their crusade. They were also running out of food. "Death and slaughter commingled with the Franks until a vast number of them perished," wrote Ibn al-Qalanisi.[12] Conrad himself wrote of the Turks who "were unceasingly attacking and slaughtering the common foot-soldiers."[13] The king was badly injured in one attack; by the end of the month his barons convinced him that he had little choice but to turn his army around and head back to Byzantine territory, where he might throw himself on the mercy of Manuel Komnenos and join what remained of his army with that of Louis of France. By Christmas, the German king was back in Constantinople.

Louis, his queen, Eleanor of Aquitaine, and the mass of French crusaders left Europe some weeks behind the Germans, their departure delayed until Louis had completed a series of extravagant rituals to mark his exit from the kingdom. During Easter Pope Eugene and Bernard of Clairvaux joined Louis for a series of public pageants including one on Easter Day 1147, when king and pope worshipped together at the Abbey of Saint-Denis and Eugene blessed an ornate new gold and jewel-encrusted cross that had taken goldsmiths several years to construct. On June 11, the king visited a leper colony outside Paris's gates to undertake the traditional task of washing the sufferers' feet. Later that same day, back at Saint-Denis, Louis formally requested the sacred *oriflamme*—the scarlet war banner that symbolized Frankish kingship stretching back to Charlemagne. This extended piece of political-religious theater took so long that Eleanor nearly fainted in the summer heat. But after a fashion the king was satisfied. He had "aroused great lamentation and received the blessing of everyone's deepest affection."[14] He committed his kingdom to the safe hands of his most trusted minister, Suger, abbot of Saint-Denis. Then, with Eleanor at his side, he struck out for the East.

There may have been some French subjects who inwardly sighed with relief when Louis finally disappeared into the European interior, for his expedition had already cost a fortune. France was in the grip of a long famine that had left many of its people destitute, yet royal agents thought only of raising money for the kingdom of Jerusalem. Exorbitant demands had been placed on the king's wealthier subjects—particularly those who held high office in the church—with requests for hundreds and even thousands of silver marks in contributions.[15] Those pious individuals and families who wished to join the crusade could be found selling their family heirlooms or mortgaging their homes, farms and estates to Jewish financiers or Christian monasteries to raise enough money to go crusading. Despite this, the French had barely made it as far as Hungary before Louis was writing home to Abbot Suger and asking him to send more money. It was becoming apparent that the crusaders had set out poorly prepared for a journey whose hardships they had underestimated.

They first clapped eyes on the so-called Queen of Cities on October 4. Successful diplomacy—which included correspondence between Eleanor and Empress Irene—ensured Louis was granted "a very great reception from the emperor."[16] Constantinople's gates were barred to the rank and file of Louis's army, but the king was welcomed to the Palace of Blachernae, where the astonishing sight of so much marble and gold sent Odo of Deuil into raptures. ("Its exterior is of almost matchless beauty but its interior surpasses anything I can say about it."[17]) The monarchs spoke publically through interpreters, then Louis was banqueted and given a tour of Constantinople's holy shrines by

Manuel himself. Beneath the bonhomie, however, tensions lingered. Odo of Deuil described the Greeks as degenerate and womanly, "despicable in their excessive debasement," and prepared to say "whatever they thought would please us, but they neither kept faith with us nor maintained respect for themselves."[18] Behind the crusaders' backs Manuel had agreed to a ten-year truce with Sultan Mas'ud: a prime example, thought many, of the Byzantines' innate treachery. But mutual suspicions and cultural misunderstandings could not be indulged too long. News from Asia Minor soon revealed that the crusaders had far more serious problems.

Having shuttled his own troops across the Bosphorus and persuaded his barons to swear an oath of fealty to the emperor, by which they agreed not to conquer any towns belonging to Byzantium, Louis could now contemplate his route across Asia Minor. The sight of bedraggled Germans returning malnourished and bloodied from their misadventures at Dorylaeum was enough to dissuade him from attempting to take the direct road to Antioch via Iconium. As Conrad limped back to Constantinople to recover from his injuries he poured out his heart to Louis in person, bemoaning his arrogance in thinking he could breeze past the Turks. Louis agreed to take what remained of the German forces east under his own command and decided to take both armies along the winding coastal road through Smyrna and Ephesus. This route was treacherous, and the unarmed German pilgrims who had attempted it under Otto of Freising had been forced back, with much bloodshed. But there was little other choice.

It took until after Christmas for Louis's army to pick their way around the coast and pass out of Byzantine territory. As soon as they did so, they came under attack. On December 28 and 29 Turkish light cavalry began to harass them in the Maeander valley. The French knights drove their tormentors away, fortified by the appearance among their ranks of a ghostly "white-clad knight" who "struck the first blows in the battle."[19] This would become a reliable motif of crusader victories against non-Christians in the crusader era, and the French celebrated their victory with glee. But it was the last piece of divine fortune that they enjoyed.

Eleanor's famous barb that her husband was more monk than king was given substance after the French columns passed through Laodicea on January 3,

1148. Weeks earlier Conrad's brother Otto had drawn up short at this point, and the blood of recently butchered pilgrims could still be seen, dried where it was spilled on the rocks and roadside.[20] Laodicea was the limit of Byzantine authority, and even if Manuel had wished to give the Franks his full backing he could no longer do so. Worse, the people who lived along the coastal roads had gone into hiding, refusing to sell any provisions to the armies. Syria was still weeks away, and suddenly Louis realized that it was going to be impossible to reach it on foot. Instead he decided to head for the coastal city of Adalia. This was an isolated Byzantine stronghold surrounded by Turkish territory, where markets might be found and ships chartered to transport some of the crusaders by sea to the principality of Antioch.

The march to Adalia took fifteen days, and Turkish attacks continued throughout. The most serious occurred on or around January 6 as Louis's army attempted to cross the huge swell of Mount Cadmus (Homaz), a mountain "steep and rocky," traversed at its highest point by "a ridge so lofty that its summit seemed to touch heaven and the stream in the hollow valley below to descend into hell."[21] The plan was to cross slowly and carefully over the course of a day; to move faster was to send horses and men tumbling to their deaths as they slipped from the narrow paths. All the French had to do was stand firm against Turkish sniping, and stay together.

Unfortunately they did neither. At the head of the troops was Louis's standard bearer: Geoffrey de Rancon, Lord of Taillebourg, and one of Queen Eleanor's most senior vassals. He was tasked with leading the vanguard who would go over the mountain first. The queen traveled in the middle column with the baggage train, while Louis rode with the rear guard. But communication was difficult on the mountain, and Geoffrey was overeager. Under his command the vanguard pushed too far ahead, and the French columns quickly became separated. The Turks lying in wait saw their moment and swooped. Odo of Deuil was in the midst of the pilgrims' column and recorded the panic as raiders pounced and the mountainside rang with screams of terror. "They thrust and slashed, and the defenseless crowd fled or fell like sheep," he wrote. "Thence arose a cry that pierced to heaven."[22] The cries lasted all day, until eventually the Turks retreated and left the Franks to count their dead, who included at least half a dozen of the king's senior noblemen. Louis himself only escaped capture by scrambling to safety on top of a large rock. Discipline, such as it was, had disintegrated, and the king was forced to sign over military command to a company of about 130 Templar knights who had been traveling with the army since it left Paris. Only with their expert military guidance, marshaled by a senior Templar officer named Gilbert, did the crusaders crawl into Adalia on about January 20. They were a sorry sight.

The crusaders camped outside Adalia for two miserable months, enduring storms, blizzards and irregular Turkish attacks. The Greeks of the city showed them precious little sympathy. They charged the king extortionate prices for food and bargained hard for shipping, which was in any case inadequate to the task of carrying the whole army to the crusader states. After a while, the army simply broke up. In early March the king and queen took the core of the army to Antioch by ship. Some of the crusaders who remained behind tried to continue the march overland toward Antioch and were killed. Several thousand accepted safe conduct back through Turkish lands toward Constantinople. Many more died of malnutrition or disease. "The flowers of France withered before they could bear fruit," sighed Odo of Deuil.[23] Eventually, on March 19, 1148, Louis arrived in Antioch. The Second Crusade had at last limped to its destination, almost two and a half years after Edessa had fallen. What exactly it could now achieve was unclear.

By the time the crusaders arrived, Zengi was dead. Indeed, he had been dead for some time. The wily old atabeg was besieging the fortress of Qal'at Jabar, near Raqqa, on September 14, 1146, when one of his servants—named by Ibn al-Qalanisi as "a man of Frankish origin called Yaranqash"—crept into his tent and stabbed his master to death.[24] The grievance Yaranqash nursed is not known, but Zengi had made plenty of enemies during his career, and his mamluks—slave soldiers who attended on the atabeg's person—simply looked the other way as he was murdered. Zengi—who was almost as fond of alcohol as Ilghazi had been—was even drunker than usual so could not fight back.[25] Yaranqash "slaughtered him upon his bed" and ran away. He left Zengi's armies leaderless and his supporters in Mosul and Aleppo all in confusion. The Franks of the crusader states cheered Zengi's demise. William of Tyre recorded a joke made among the Latins, who remarked on the fact that "a guilty murderer with the bloody name *Sanguinus*, has become ensanguined with his own blood."[26] But there was not very much time for joyful punning, for no sooner was Zengi in his grave than up sprang an even more dangerous new leader of the Islamic Near East.

Zengi's second son was known as Nur al-Din. Tall, swarthy and almost beardless, with a broad forehead and dancing eyes, his name meant Light of the Faith. Ibn al-Athir wrote paeans to Nur al-Din's modest bearing, intelligence and bravery "of the highest order," noting that he would ride into battle armed with two bows and two quivers of arrows.[27] William of Tyre agreed: Nur al-Din was "a just prince, valiant and wise and, according to the traditions of his race, a religious man." But he was also, said William grimly, "a mighty persecutor of the Christian name and faith."[28]

When Zengi's possessions were divided between his sons, Nur al-Din received Aleppo. (Another brother, Saif al-Din, took command of Mosul, and a third son, Qutb al-Din Mawdud, became emir of Homs.) As a matter of political geography Nur al-Din took a close interest in Edessa. Straightaway his terrifying approach to rule was laid bare. On Zengi's death the displaced Edessan count Joscelin II tried to rally an army to retake the city, and encouraged an uprising of the Armenian Christians who still lived there. Nur al-Din responded with a severity equal to anything his father had imposed. He marched troops from Aleppo to Edessa, sent Joscelin packing, then sacked the city, destroying its defenses, killing Armenians en masse and sending captive young women as slaves and sexual playthings to his brothers and friends.[29] The chronicler Michael the Syrian wrote in overblown but telling terms of Edessa's fate, bewailing a city "enveloped in a black cloud, drunk with blood."[30] There was no prospect of recovering Edessa without Western help.

One northern lord in particular had reason to hope that the French crusaders would be useful allies. Raymond of Poitiers had been Prince of Antioch since 1136, when he arrived to put an end to the long series of regencies there by marrying Bohemond II's daughter Constance. Like most princes of Antioch, Raymond found himself in perpetual conflict with the Byzantine Empire on his western frontiers; the fall of Edessa had sharply raised the dangers on his eastern borders, too. His overarching goal, therefore, was to secure this front by repelling the advances of Zengi and Nur al-Din, then conquering Aleppo and nearby cities including Shaizar, Hama and Homs. A crusading army could, Raymond thought, be most useful in pursuing this goal—and a

French one even more so, for the queen of France, Eleanor of Aquitaine, happened to be Raymond's niece.

The relationship between Eleanor and Raymond would turn out to be one of the most scandalous and highly scrutinized aspects of the Second Crusade. Raymond had "counted greatly on the interest of the queen" with her husband, wrote William of Tyre.[31] When the couple arrived the prince went out of his way to fete them, with lavish receptions in which everything was "handled with the greatest magnificence."[32] For Eleanor, it was likely a source of comfort to visit such a close kinsman and see the exotic court he kept, which presented all the perfumed joys of an Eastern capital but was populated by Occitan-speaking men and women from her native lands in the French southwest.[33] Eleanor and Louis spent ten days as Raymond's guests; it was a welcome contrast to the miseries that they had endured since leaving Constantinople, and Eleanor enjoyed herself. Very quickly, however, everything soured.

Notwithstanding Raymond's generosity, Louis announced shortly after arriving in Antioch that he had no intention whatever of deploying his troops to help enlarge the northern principality. Despite the heavy financial exactions he had taken from his French subjects before departing, the journey to the East had virtually bankrupted him, and he was reduced to borrowing huge sums from the Templars in order to keep his crusade afloat. Meanwhile, word had arrived from further south that Conrad was finally on his way by ship to Acre. So far from charging off on a campaign of conquest in northern Syria, he told Raymond, he would be leaving for Jerusalem to fulfill his vows as a pilgrim. He would meet Conrad in the Holy City, take the counsel of Queen Melisende and her son Baldwin III and make a plan of action.

Raymond was furious. "Frustrated in his ambitious designs he began to hate the king's ways; he openly plotted against him and took means to do him injury," wrote William of Tyre.[34] To do so he used his relationship with Eleanor. As the queen's later career would bear out, she was highly independent minded—far from a royal doormat to be trampled by her husband. Raymond now lobbied her assiduously to back him over Louis—and she did. As the king left for Jerusalem, Eleanor remained in the north, where her relationship with her uncle rapidly became the subject of salacious gossip. "Contrary to her royal dignity, she disregarded her marriage vows and was unfaithful to her husband," wrote William of Tyre—a phrase that would thereafter be used to suggest that Eleanor and Raymond began an incestuous affair. In fact, William was almost certainly referring to the domestic treachery of disobedience, which he and stiff-necked churchmen like him considered a sin of equal magnitude to sexual infidelity. Either way, Raymond's gambit failed, Eleanor's reputation was blackened, and for Louis the scandal in Antioch proved to be the beginning of the end—of both his marriage and his crusade.

The main military action of the Second Crusade turned out to be as poorly conceived and badly executed as the march that preceded it. Shortly before Easter 1148, Conrad sailed into Acre's splendid harbor in a fleet of triremes captained by first-rank Byzantine naval officers, provided by the open-handed Manuel Komnenos.[35] It soon became obvious that he had no more interest in going to war in northern Syria than Louis. Conrad had been generously treated in Constantinople, with civic games at the Hippodrome to entertain him and the best doctors laid on to help with his recuperation. He was accordingly wary of any policy that would interfere directly in the Byzantine interests—which of course included Antioch. A choice between helping Raymond and antagonizing Manuel was no choice at all. So the German king went nowhere near either Antioch or Edessa, instead heading to Jerusalem to inspect the Church of the Holy Sepulchre and take up residence in the former al-Aqsa Mosque, now the headquarters of the Templars. There, in consultation with the Templars' master Everard des Barres, he concocted a plan for the Second Crusade that bore no relation whatever to its original purpose. Rather than restoring Edessa or attacking Nur al-Din, the crusaders would take aim at a different target entirely. In late June a formal assembly met in Palmarea to confirm the crusade's purpose. It was attended by all the interested parties: Baldwin; Louis; Conrad; the patriarch of Jerusalem, Fulcher of Angoulême; Everard of the Temple and more or less every major baron and bishop from among the crusaders and the kingdom of Jerusalem. "It was agreed by all that it would be best to besiege Damascus, a city of great menace to us," wrote William of Tyre. And so the die was cast.

The consequent siege of Damascus, which began on July 24, 1148, was nothing short of a fiasco. Since the campaigns of the late 1120s Damascus had more often been allied with the Latin states against Zengi than a hostile power—and although Nur al-Din was feeling his way diplomatically toward asserting his power, the difficulty of capturing such a large and proud city had been illustrated—and appreciated—for many years. Nevertheless, on the first day the crusader armies hacked their way through large orchards on the western outskirts of the city, fighting running battles with the citizens and troops deployed from inside Damascus by its governor, Mu'in al-Din Unur. Conrad performed bravely: fighting on foot in the German style, rather than on horseback, he was "said to have slain in the most remarkable way a Turkish knight who was making a strenuous and courageous resistance. With one blow of his sword he severed from the body of his enemy the head and neck, the left shoulder with the arm attached and also a part of the side."[36] Sadly for the crusaders, this was as good as it got. They made it through the orchards to start investing the western walls of the city with siege engines. But on July 27, either through poor generalship or treachery (both were later alleged), the leaders decided abruptly to abandon their positions and move to the opposite side of the city, where defenses were said to be lighter. Straightaway, momentum was lost. The defenders were able to reorganize themselves and "the position which had been won with great toil and loss of men was abandoned."[37] Having withdrawn from the orchards, which they had been plundering to feed the army, the crusaders' supply lines began to fail. Inside the city, Mu'in ad-Din Unur had appealed to Nur al-Din and Saif al-Din to help him drive away the unbelievers. He sent word out to the crusader camp that these dangerous brothers were fast approaching with their *askars*. They would arrive within a fortnight, he said, and if the crusaders did not depart he would hand over the city to them for good.

The folly both of the crusaders' goal and strategy was now exposed. Ibn al-Qalanisi wrote that they were shaken by news of "the rapid advance of the Islamic armies to engage in the Holy War against them . . . and they became convinced of their own destruction and of the imminence of disaster. Having taken counsel of one another, they found no way of escape from the net into which they had fallen and the abyss into which they had cast themselves."[38] The only option was disorderly retreat. At dawn on July 29 the crusaders broke camp and ran away. Their war, for which men and women had tramped thousands of miles in appalling conditions, spending their lives' fortunes and trusting their souls to God, had lasted all of five days. All they had to show for it were the corpses of the fallen, which emitted such a stench, wrote Ibn al-Qalanisi with satisfaction, "that [they] almost overcame the birds in the air."[39]

Neither Louis nor Conrad was eager to stay for another attempt at conquest. Baldwin III and the barons at the royal court of Jerusalem had switched their attention away from Nur al-Din and Syria to consider the merits of attacking Ascalon, the last coastal city held by the Fatimids of Egypt. If it fell, it was reasoned, expansion into Egypt might one day be possible. But neither Conrad nor Louis wanted any part in this. Conrad tarried only a short while in Jerusalem before departing from Acre in early September. He had barely been in the crusader kingdom for six months and he had achieved virtually nothing, other than the fulfillment of his pilgrimage vows. Louis remained a while longer, indulging his true interests: not attacking dusty cities about which he knew almost nothing and understood less, but visiting shrines and praising Christ. At Easter 1149 he and Eleanor, delicately reconciled after the queen's betrayal in Antioch, also left for home, albeit on different ships. After a perilous crossing, during which their vessels were separated and Louis was caught up in a battle between the fleets of Roger II and Manuel Komnenos, both arrived in Sicily. Eleanor had fallen seriously ill on her voyage, and her humor was unlikely to have been improved when word arrived from Antioch that her uncle Raymond had been captured while fighting Nur al-Din's forces at the battle of Inab. His ambitions in Aleppo had failed in the most singular fashion possible. Nur al-Din ordered that his head be cut off and sent in a silver box as a gift to the caliph in Baghdad.

From Sicily, Louis and Eleanor went on, still traveling apart, until they were eventually reunited—in person if not in spirit—at Pope Eugene's villa in Tusculum (Frascati), about twelve miles southeast of Rome. Eugene made some futile attempts to bring them together, offering a marital bed draped with his finest fabrics. It did no good. Within eighteen months of their return to France that November, their marriage had been annulled, and Eleanor had married into another family of crusaders: taking as her second husband Henry Fitzempress—Fulk of Jerusalem's grandson and the future Henry II of England. Their children would include one of the most famous crusader kings of all time. "A foolish woman," was William of Tyre's typically misogynist judgment.[40] But whatever William thought, the truth was that Eleanor had been surrounded by even more foolish men. The Second Crusade, far from repeating the achievements of the first, had succeeded only in demonstrating how extraordinary, and perhaps unrepeatable, the events of 1096 to 1099 had been. Far from stalling the resurgence of the enemies of Christ, the generation of 1147 to 1149 had in fact hastened the collapse of the kingdom they professed to adore. "Such was the extreme arrogance in which the barbarian exulted," wrote Anna Komnene, who completed her *Alexiad* not long before her own death in 1153.[41] She was writing of events that had taken place half a century earlier, but her judgment could have applied very well to the time at hand.

17

The Race for Egypt

O blind cupidity of men, worse than all other crimes!

The twelfth Fatimid caliph of Egypt, al-Zafir, was murdered by his lover in a house near the sword-makers' market in Cairo when he was twenty-five years old. The lover was an extremely handsome and unscrupulous man of the caliph's own age named Nasr ibn 'Abbas, and the two men enjoyed carousing in Cairo's streets by night, wearing disguises so that al-Zafir, the supreme spiritual leader of the Ismaili Shi'ite world, would not be recognized. They were so close that it was said they seldom spent an hour apart, and al-Zafir had showered Nasr with extravagant gifts: thousands of silver dinars, whole herds of camels and mules, and luxurious, flamboyant outfits of clothing. Sadly for the caliph, he was repaid only with ingratitude and savagery: lured from his palace on the evening of April 15, 1154, on the promise of a night's feasting, he was cut to ribbons in his companion's sitting room before his body was thrown down a well, along with that of his black African manservant.[1]

The morning after killing al-Zafir, Nasr went to the palace with his father, the Fatimid vizier 'Abbas, and the two men conducted a violent coup. Backed by armed retainers they pronounced al-Zafir's brothers guilty of his murder and set up his five-year-old son, al-Faiz, as a puppet caliph, whose youth meant he would present no challenge to 'Abbas's authority. Uproar ensued. "There were a thousand swords unsheathed in the palace," wrote the scholar and soldier Usama ibn Munqidh, who was an eyewitness to the grisly events.[2] Heads were severed, bellies slit, and intestines pulled out. The caliph's brothers were summarily executed. Many others among the palace staff and its guard of eunuchs and African guards were also slain, and as their blood spritzed the fine carpets, marble floors and opulent curtains of the palace, 'Abbas paraded around the golden throne in triumph, carrying little al-Faiz upon his shoulders. Then he, Nasr and their henchmen helped themselves to "money, jewels and precious objects," leaving "only what had no value."[3] They were—briefly—unchallenged in command of an empire. Yet their crimes had ensured that empire's final collapse.

By the 1150s the Fatimid caliphate had been declining for decades. During its heyday in the late tenth century, Fatimid power stretched from the Atlantic coast of North Africa to Baghdad.[4] Fatimid caliphs were the guardians of Mecca, Medina and Jerusalem, Fatimid navies dominated both the Red Sea and the eastern Mediterranean, and Fatimid workshops produced cloth, crystal, jewelry and ceramics traded far and wide across the Western world. Cairo (al-Qahira al-Mu'izziyya), established as the empire's capital in June 973, was endowed with the magnificent al-Azhar university-mosque, dazzling royal palaces, some of the greatest libraries in the world and buzzing marketplaces that entertained trade between merchants of the Mediterranean, the Red Sea, the trans-Saharan caravan routes and the fertile Nile floodplains of Upper Egypt. A writer who passed through Egypt at the height of Fatimid power called the region one of "the wings of the world," and Cairo "the glory of Islam . . . the marketplace for all mankind . . . the storehouse of the Occident, the entrepôt of the Orient." Yet if there was glory, there was also danger. The same writer warned that "calamities visit the people constantly."[5]

By the 1150s the empire had shrunk in every direction. In northwest Africa the Almohads now held sway. Ifriqiya, where the Fatimid dynasty was born, had been overrun: first by Zirids, then by Sicilians; by 1160 it too would be in Almohad hands. Seljuq sultans and emirs acting in the name of Sunni Islam and the Abbasid caliph had pushed the Fatimids out of the Syrian interior. The crusaders had ejected them from Jerusalem and the coastal cities of Palestine and the Lebanon. In 1153 the final Fatimid naval base on the Palestinian littoral was lost, as Baldwin III led a Frankish assault on Ascalon: a siege successfully conducted by the combined forces of the kingdom of Jerusalem, Templars, Hospitallers and several hundred pilgrims who arrived with that year's spring sailing. For the crusaders, the fall of Ascalon completed a long-held ambition to close off their ports to Egyptian shipping and secure a possible bridgehead for raids on northeast Egypt and the Nile Delta. For the Fatimids it was yet another defeat in a series stretching back nearly a century, a loss received with much "grief and distress" throughout the Muslim world.[6]

Loss of territory was not the only trouble that had befallen the Fatimids, for the caliphate had also long been in a state of spiritual dissolution, splintering into factions that rolled together political succession disputes with theological debates about where and to whom lay the true loyalty of the Ismaili Shi'ite community. Since the 1130s the Fatimid empire had been divided between three mutually hostile groups: the Hafizis of Egypt (so named for al-Zafir's father, al-Hafiz); the Nizari Assassins of Persia; and a group known as the Tayyibis, who held sway in Yemen. Inevitably, this extended schism had chipped away at the caliphs' dignity and authority, and even before al-Zafir's murder they had been reduced to the status of trophy rulers, perfumed and pampered in their throne rooms while the real business of government and military command rested with their viziers. That these same viziers by 1154 saw fit to kill caliphs on a whim was shocking—but not surprising.

Nor, then, was it so very strange that in 1154 one revolution was immediately followed by another, as 'Abbas and Nasr were chased out of Cairo little more than six weeks after they had seized control. Within days of al-Zafir's murder an alliance formed between his sisters and a faction of palace eunuchs outraged at the death of their former master. The women cut off locks from their hair and sent them with letters summoning to Cairo a high-ranking officer in the Fatimid army known as Tala'i Ibn Ruzzik: a grizzled Shi'ite of Armenian descent who was stationed at that time in Upper Egypt. Ibn Ruzzik gathered his troops and marched downriver toward the capital, upon which a general revolt began among the common soldiers of Cairo, and public order broke down. Supporters of 'Abbas and Nasr could barely step outside their homes without scornful women pelting them with stones from the windows of buildings. By the end of May 'Abbas had concluded that he could not safely remain, and he set out with his son for Syria. On his way he was killed by a raiding party of Franks, and Nasr was captured by the Templars—eventually to be ransomed back to Cairo and executed for his treachery by the women of the palace, who beat him to death with their shoes and hung his body above one of the city gates. Meanwhile, Ibn Ruzzik marched into Cairo. He and his troops came dressed head to toe in black and flying black banners above their lines. Ostensibly they did so in mourning for the murdered caliph. But it did not pass unnoticed that black was the color of the rival Abbasid caliphs of Baghdad. And so began the death spiral of the Fatimid caliphate, which had once been one of the mightiest powers in the Mediterranean world. Sixteen years after al-Zafir was hurled into a well, the last of his line would be dead and Egypt would be in foreign hands. The only question was—whose?

In 1163 Amalric, Count of Jaffa and Ascalon, the second son of Fulk of Anjou and Queen Melisende, was crowned king of Jerusalem. His elder brother Baldwin III had died on February 10. According to William of Tyre, who knew Amalric well, the new king was a gruff, serious and resilient character with a sharp memory, who was not especially well educated, but "listened eagerly to history and preferred it to all other kinds of reading."[7] Blonde with a receding hairline, and prone to blubbery fatness despite his modest intake of food and drink, Amalric had no gift for courtly small talk and was a poor public speaker with a slight speech impediment. Yet the strength of his political instincts, his curiosity about the worlds both physical and divine and his manner of laughing—on those occasions when he was amused—so hard that his entire body shook, made him a strangely attractive character. His only real vices, wrote William of Tyre, were that he seduced married women and was immoderately interested in money.[8]

Amalric was crowned at the age of twenty-seven and he turned his attention almost immediately to Egypt. It looked plump and ripe for conquest—or as one writer put it: "a beautiful bride, led out by her attendants," just waiting to be carried away.[9] In the seven years since Ibn Ruzzik had marched on Cairo, the brittleness of Fatimid power had become horribly obvious. As vizier, Ibn Ruzzik had calmed the immediate crises of 1154 and expended much energy conducting raids on shipping around Frankish cities including Tyre and Beirut. But eventually he succumbed to the same violent forces that had first brought him to the palace. When young al-Faiz died after an illness in 1160, he orchestrated the accession of another child caliph, the nine-year-old al-Adid, to whom he married his daughter. This all-too-familiar bid to arrange politics for a vizier's personal gain resulted in an all-too-familiar response. In September 1161 Ibn Ruzzik was attacked in the palace by troops of the Fatimid army's black African corps, known as the Sudan, who had been put up to the job by one of the caliph's aunts. Ibn Ruzzik was mortally wounded, and as he was carried off to safety a major skirmish broke out between his personal guard and the Sudan. Fifty men were killed, and the princess who had connived at Ibn Ruzzik's death was strangled with her own veil. Al-Adid remained caliph, but during the next two years the post of vizier passed through the hands of three men: Ibn Ruzzik's son, then a Kurdish officer called Shawar ibn Mujir al Sa'di (or, simply, Shawar) and finally a courtier and chamberlain of the palace known as Dirgham. At each turn of the wheel, the man who became vizier carried out a deadly purge of perceived opponents in the Fatimid army "to clear the land of rivals to himself."[10] And with each of these purges the governing class was further weakened. This was a state in crisis.

Amalric of Jerusalem knew exactly what stresses abrupt reorderings of political order could levy on a realm. Ten years previously he had seen his mother and brother reduce the kingdom of Jerusalem to civil war as Baldwin, having reached his majority, demanded to be allowed to rule as sole king, while Melisende, splendid in her regality, refused to hand over the reins of power. Their argument, which at one point saw Baldwin besieging his own mother in the citadel of Jerusalem, had only been settled after a tortuous period of civil strife and a brief partition of the kingdom. Melisende, like her son, was now dead.* But Amalric had absorbed the lesson of their quarrel and as a result he recognized his moment to launch an assault on the fractured and fractious caliphate in Egypt. In the first year of Amalric's reign the vizier Dirgham decided to withhold financial tribute owed to Jerusalem under the peace treaty agreed after the fall of Ascalon. The king prepared for a full-blown invasion.

Amalric was not the only ruler with a greedy eye on Egyptian affairs. In Syria, Nur al-Din had spent the 1150s rebuilding and then expanding the coalition of Seljuq emirates that his father Zengi had assembled, a task he undertook with astonishing alacrity. By 1151 he had stamped out forever the embers of crusader resistance in Edessa—whose last count, Joscelin II, died, blinded and helpless in an Aleppan prison in 1159. Meanwhile in Antioch, Nur

*Melisende died in 1161 and was buried outside the walls of Jerusalem within the church built over the tomb of the Virgin Mary.

al-Din had killed Prince Raymond of Poitiers at Inab in 1149, and subsequently seized approximately half of the northern and eastern territory belonging to the principality, reducing it to a strip of land between the Orontes River and the Mediterranean coast.[11] (Following Inab, Nur al-Din demonstrated his apparent invincibility in the region by going down to bathe at his leisure in the Mediterranean.) Within the Seljuq empire itself, Nur al-Din had joined together Aleppo—his inheritance from Zengi—with his younger brother's emirate of Mosul, over which he asserted his rights as overlord in the 1150s and which he would finally annex outright in 1170. Then, at last, in 1154 he added the jewel in the crown: Damascus, which he entered on Sunday, April 25, deposing the city's insipid ruler, Mujir al-Din, after an economic blockade followed by a short military siege. The Damascene citizens welcomed him in. Ibn al-Qalanisi, weary of "sufferings from famine, the high cost of food, and fear of being besieged by the Frankish infidels," recorded Nur al-Din's arrival with approval, praising the new ruler's "justice and good reputation" and remarking favorably on his decision to abolish taxes on melons and vegetables.[12]

Nor was this the end of Nur al-Din's triumphs. In the late 1150s he secured a peace treaty with Manuel Komnenos to prevent the Byzantine emperor from helping the crusaders defend the Antiochene frontiers, and in 1160 he captured Raymond of Poitiers's successor as prince, the pugnacious, larger-than-life adventurer Reynald of Châtillon, whom he imprisoned for what turned out to be sixteen years. By 1160 Nur al-Din controlled more of Syria than any ruler in living memory, and had done so at the perfect moment, for in 1157 the long-reigning—and last—Great Seljuq sultan Ahmad Sanjar died and the empire fractured into its component pieces. Nur al-Din was therefore preeminent in its western frontiers, with no sultan above him. He had completed the annihilation of crusader Edessa and threatened to do the same to Antioch. His presence in Damascus put him in striking distance of both Jerusalem and the county of Tripoli, and his reputation as a masterly strategist and pious warrior was second to none. Apparently miraculous recovery from two bouts of serious illness in the 1150s increased his personal commitment to jihad, convincing him that it was God's will that he should reclaim crusader lands everywhere in the name of Islam. For the rest of his political life Nur al-Din would promote this idea of a united Islamic jihad against the unbelievers to justify his policies of accruing as much territory and power as possible in Syria and beyond—and to use it as a distraction when that meant making war on fellow Sunni Muslims. A minbar or ritual pulpit built on his orders in the 1160s bore an inscription describing him as "the fighter of jihad in His [i.e., God's] path, the one who defends against the enemies of His religion, the just king . . . the pillar of Islam and the Muslims, the dispenser of justice to those who are oppressed in the face of oppressors."[13] Nur al-Din correctly calculated that if he were able to extend his power further south into Egypt, he would completely encircle Frankish territories with his own: a situation that would allow him to dream of ejecting the unbelievers from Syria and Palestine once and for all. So just as Amalric trained his sights on the rotten Fatimid caliphate, so too did Nur al-Din. The decade that followed eventually became a race to Cairo. It was a race neither side could afford to lose.

From the beginning the struggle for Egypt was tightly poised. Nur al-Din certainly had the tools for subjugation at his disposal in the form of a faction of ambitious Kurdish emirs among his army, who were straining to be let loose on Cairo and the Nile Valley, where they saw much potential for carving out lucrative fiefdoms. Nur al-Din was also building his personal standing in the wider world of the Islamic Near East: he made his case as the preeminent pious force in the region in 1161 when he traveled to Mecca (across the Red Sea in the region of Arabia known as the Hijaz) to perform hajj. Mecca was theoretically under the guardianship of the Fatimid caliphate, but as so often, real power lay in action and perception, not in legal detail. While in Arabia, Nur al-Din ordered the rebuilding of the walls of Medina; in doing so he made an emphatic statement about his own burgeoning power.[14]

Amalric, for his part, could hardly claim religious guardianship over the Muslims of Egypt, and his intentions toward the Fatimids were generally concerned with material reward rather than righteousness, or "crusading" in anything but the very broadest sense. But with Ascalon in his hands he controlled the Via Maris—the main road out of Greater Syria into Egypt—and thus presented the closest and most obvious military threat. In September 1163, as the fierce heat of the summer was starting to wane, he set out to demonstrate as much. Amalric "descended upon Egypt with a great host," met Dirgham with an army in the desert and forced the vizier back to Bilbays (Bilbeis), a fortress city about forty miles northeast of Cairo, reinforced by Ibn Ruzzik specifically in anticipation of a crusader king marching on the capital. The Egyptians now panicked, fearing Amalric "might decide to lead his armies against the more remote parts of the realm," wrote William of Tyre.[15] They resorted to the last and most elemental means of defense: opening the agricultural irrigation dykes that ran away from the Nile. This flooded the countryside, cutting off the crusaders from Cairo with a massive natural moat. Amalric was compelled to withdraw his army. But he would be back.

In Syria, meanwhile, Nur al-Din was preparing his own foray into Egypt. Shawar, the vizier whom Dirgham had deposed directly before Amalric's invasion, had escaped with his life and fled to Syria during the summer of 1163, where he went to Damascus and begged Nur al-Din to restore him to power. William of Tyre described Shawar as "wise and able . . . particularly farsighted." Certainly he was a master of making lavish promises to anyone he thought could further his cause, usually without much care as to whether he would be able to deliver on them. Thus in 1163 he promised Nur al-Din a third of the revenues of Egypt and a free hand in dictating policy to the caliph if he backed him. Nur al-Din, under no illusion as to the sort of man he had before him, hesitated. But soon enough he decided that the potential gains in Egypt outweighed the near certainty that Shawar would try to welch on the deal. He sent him back to Egypt with the most capable and ruthless of his generals, a Kurdish emir by the name of Asad al-Din Shirkuh. The relationship between Shirkuh and Shawar was to determine the fate of the Fatimid state.

Short, fat and advanced in years, with one eye milky from cataracts, Shirkuh did not much resemble the lion his name (*Asad*) suggested. But in the words of Ibn al-Athir, he was "the greatest and bravest emir of the state . . . he had such courage and determination that he was worried by no fear."[16] Shirkuh also hankered after Egypt's riches, and he would, over the coming years, press Nur al-Din repeatedly to allow him to take personal direction over the struggle for control there, arguing that the Egyptians were "devoted to luxurious living and ignorant of the science of war" and easy meat for his sword.[17] In April 1164 Shirkuh marched out of Syria, skirted Frankish territory and barreled through Egypt, heading straight toward Cairo. When Dirgham brought an army out to meet him, he was killed, struck down by an arrow shot from among his own troops and left lying where he fell for two days. On May 24 Shirkuh presented Shawar with the vizier's robes. In return, Shawar did precisely what Nur al-Din had feared: he reneged on the deal. Instead of submitting the Fatimid state to the governance of Shirkuh and his Syrian masters, Shawar politely but firmly asked them all to go home. When Shirkuh declined, marched to Bilbays and bivouacked his army there, the unscrupulous vizier sent envoys to Amalric of Jerusalem requesting military assistance in return for a large financial payment.

This willingness to turn his coat without the least compunction was to become Shawar's trademark, for he knew what value Egypt held to both the crusaders and the Syrians and he played his hand accordingly. On receiving the call for aid, Amalric—as Shawar knew he would—sent a large force down to besiege the Kurdish general in Bilbays. Shirkuh was renowned even among the crusaders for his "great endurance under hardships" and his ability to bear "hunger and thirst with an equanimity quite unusual for that time of life."[18] He lasted three months under blockade before eventually a truce was agreed. Amalric, his attention required at home, stood down, and Shirkuh marched his army in an orderly fashion back to Syria. As they left, the fat Kurd rode among the rear guard, an iron ax grasped defiantly in his hand. When asked if he was not afraid that the Franks would ambush him during his retreat, he replied: "I wish they would do so, so that you could see what I would do. By God, I would wield my sword and not one of our men would be killed until he had killed several [enemies]. . . . We would take their lands and any survivors would perish."[19]

For a while, however, he had to wait, as other fronts took priority. Nur al-Din had more than Egypt alone to consider—as did Amalric. As the crusader king was occupied at Bilbays, Nur al-Din had struck hard further north, annihilating an undisciplined coalition of Franks, Byzantine troops and Armenians. At the battle of Harim (near Artah, between Antioch and Aleppo), this army was "overwhelmed and shattered by the swords of the enemy," and Bohemond III, Prince of Antioch; Raymond III, Count of Tripoli; Joscelin, son of the last Count of Edessa; the Armenian prince Thoros II; and Constantine Kalamanos, Byzantine ruler of Cilicia, were all taken to Aleppo, "chained like the lowest slaves" and cast into prison, where they became "the sport of the infidels."[20] Shortly afterward Nur al-Din stormed Banyas (Banias), a vital fortification on the frontier between Damascus and the crusader cities of Acre and Tyre. "These great changes and dire disasters so seriously affected the condition of the Christians that they were reduced almost to the last extremity," wrote William of Tyre. "No ray of hope now remained."[21]

The arrival in Jerusalem of the veteran crusader Thierry, Count of Flanders (on an unprecedented fourth expedition to the East, his first having been in 1139), and the military effort needed to shore up Antioch and Tripoli distracted Amalric from Egyptian affairs. Meanwhile, Nur al-Din's focus on matters to the north also meant Shirkuh had to bide his time before petitioning for the resources he needed to head back south. By late 1166 however, Shirkuh's persistence had persuaded Nur al-Din to let him continue the conquest. With his master's blessing, Shirkuh assembled two thousand cavalry and many more foot soldiers and in January 1167 marched once more into Fatimid territory, setting up camp outside the walls of Cairo in the shadow of the Sphinx and the mighty pyramids at Giza. This time he took with him a rising star of his Kurdish entourage: his twenty-nine-year-old nephew, a former police chief from Damascus called Yusuf ibn Ayyub.

Once again, as danger approached, Shawar called upon his enemy's enemy for help. As usual, crusader support came at a price—or at least, a nominal one. Shawar promised Amalric the extraordinary sum of 400,000 gold dinars—almost 2 tons of gold by weight—for his help. To give a patina of plausibility to this ridiculous offer, Shawar invited two Frankish envoys—Hugh of Caesarea and a prominent Templar named Geoffrey Fulcher—to Cairo to meet al-Adid himself. They found the young man—eighteen years old but baby-faced, with only a light down of hair sprouting on his chin—in a palace stocked with exotic animals and strange birds, and thronging with eunuchs and flunkies. Here al-Adid sat on his gold throne, hidden from view by a curtain stitched with pearls and gold thread.[22] Revealed with a flourish on Shawar's command, al-Adid gave his word that the Franks should indeed have their bounty, if only they could save him from the Sunni menace. Accordingly, during the early spring Amalric and a Frankish army piled into Egypt in pursuit of the Kurds, braving storms and whirlwinds that at times forced them to dismount and burrow into the desert sand to survive. Fierce fighting broke out across Egypt, with clashes far south of Cairo in al-Bilbayn (el-Babein) and a grueling siege of Alexandria on the Nile Delta, the defense of which was led by Yusuf ibn Ayyub.

Once more in 1167 the two sides fought each other to a stalemate, although when both withdrew in August it was Amalric who had more obvious reason to be pleased, for he left military advisers and a garrison of Frankish troops in Cairo and secured at least the first payments of tribute from al-Adid's treasury. But the matter was not finished.

In 1161, when Ibn Ruzzik was dying from the wounds inflicted by his assassins, the old vizier lamented that he never used his forward base of Bilbays as a launchpad from which to attack the Franks. In October 1168 his concern was finally borne out, as Amalric, now fixed on conquest, moved on the fortress town with a massive army drawn from all over the crusader kingdom. This was a significant shift in strategy, from irritant neighbor to outright aggressor. The previous year Amalric had contracted a marriage with Maria Komnene, daughter of Manuel I Komnenos, and with a call on Byzantine naval power now theoretically available to him he prepared to throw over his obligations to his ally Shawar and complete the job of turning Fatimid Egypt into a crusader protectorate. Not everyone in his kingdom agreed—the Templars in particular denounced the folly of abandoning treaty obligations without pretext. But their opposition was not enough. On November 4 Amalric's army arrived at Bilbays to find Shawar's son Tayy commanding the garrison. "Do you think Bilbays is cheese for eating?" he asked Amalric scornfully. "Yes," replied Amalric. "And Cairo is butter."[23] His troops swarmed the Egyptian defenses and sacked the town mercilessly. "Most of the citizens were put to the sword without regard for age or sex," wrote William of Tyre. "If by any chance they escaped death, they suffered loss of liberty and fell under the miserable yoke of bondage."[24] Then they marched on Cairo.

Shawar, falling back and trying to create a brake on Amalric's marauding forces, now took desperate action. He set fire to the old part of Cairo outside the main walls, known as al-Fustat. According to Ibn al-Athir, the blaze burned continuously for fifty-four days. But this futile and self-destructive gesture did nothing to deter Amalric. He promptly laid siege to Cairo proper, giving Shawar a taste of his own medicine when he told him he would only lift the siege on payment of 1 million gold dinars (nearly 5 tons of gold). Shawar—

with little other option, although as always, no intent of compliance, not least since many of the taxpayers from whom he might have raised such a sum had just seen their homes in al-Fustat burned to the ground—agreed. Blinded by the promise of vast riches, no matter how improbable, Amalric retreated from Cairo and made camp while he waited for his money.

The pause proved fatal. Shawar, a double-dealer to the last, now played his final trick. He wrote to Nur al-Din and begged him to send Shirkuh to drive away the infidel from his gates. Audacious as this was, he did not need to ask twice. Nur al-Din also saw the end approaching. He equipped Shirkuh with two thousand cavalry from his standing army, a huge force of infantry and 200,000 dinars to hire mercenaries. Once more Yusuf ibn Ayyub traveled south with his uncle, although this time unwillingly, for he was by now enjoying high office in Aleppo, where he was had become Nur al-Din's favorite polo partner.

In December 1168 Shirkuh, Yusuf ibn Ayyub and their huge force entered Egyptian territory, outflanked Amalric and bore down on Cairo. Initially the crusader king favored meeting Shirkuh and Yusuf ibn Ayyub in battle. But on Christmas Day, his scouts told him of the monstrous size of their army. Amalric had come as a conqueror, but had been bought off with hollow promises of wealth instead of pushing for a decisive military strike. He could now entertain no hope of support from Shawar, while the people of Cairo themselves were hardly likely to rise in support of an army of unbelievers over one composed chiefly of Muslims, Sunnis or no. The king suddenly saw that his million dinars would not be forthcoming; and that "the Turks were at hand and we must depart."[25] By January 2 his army was marching home to Jerusalem.

Shirkuh, having come so far into Egypt, and not for the first time, now began the endgame. After the Franks left, he set up camp outside Cairo and spent the first two weeks of January holding a series of friendly meetings with Shawar to negotiate a plan for stabilizing Egypt. The tone of their conversations was unfailingly gracious and cordial: Shirkuh remained patient while Shawar wriggled and prevaricated over his promise to assign to Nur al-Din a third of Egyptian revenues. But on January 18, Shawar appeared at Shirkuh's camp to continue their conference, and was met on horseback by Yusuf ibn-Ayyub and an emir called Izz al-Din Jurdik. They invited him for a short parlay, wrestled him from his mount and took him prisoner. Shawar's luck, which he had ridden so hard for so many years, had finally expired. His head was cut off the same day, and on Shirkuh's orders it was taken to the caliph's sumptuous palace, where, behind the pearl-and-gold curtain, it was presented as a gift to young al-Adid himself. The caliph sent back by way of thanks a set of vizier's robes for Shirkuh. Outside a mob tore Shawar's house to pieces. Back in Jerusalem Amalric was left to count the cost of his failures. "O blind cupidity of men, worse than all other crimes!" wailed William of Tyre. "O wicked madness of an insatiable and greedy heart!"[26] The race for Egypt was over and the great strategic game had fallen the way of Nur al-Din and his Kurdish proxies. The crusader states had been founded and thrived because of sectarian and political division in the Islamic Near East between Sunni and Shi'a, Syria and Egypt. Now the road was open for one leader to draw Syria and Egypt together under Sunni rule, and to do so under the banner of jihad: a holy war ideology as powerful and perhaps even more enduring than that of the Latin Christian crusade.

Shirkuh did not live to enjoy for very long the fruits of his victory. In fact, his reign as vizier of Fatimid Egypt was even shorter than that of any of the motley group—Ibn Ruzzik, Shawar, Dirgham—who had preceded him. On March 22, 1169—just two months and five days after he had taken Cairo—Shirkuh embarked on one of his periodic eating binges, gorging himself on rich meats. More often than not this gave him chronic indigestion; on this occasion it irritated a quinsy—or infected abscess behind the tonsils—the effects of which killed him. God did not smile, it seemed, upon gloaters or gluttons. "When they had rejoiced in what they had been given, we seized them suddenly," wrote ibn al-Athir, quoting the Qur'an.[27] It was an abrupt but not entirely unexpected way for Shirkuh to depart the earth.

Shirkuh's legacy was an odd one. He had helped to bring one of Islam's most famous empires to its knees, striking a devastating blow to the security of the kingdom of Jerusalem and glorifying the name of Nur al-Din along the way. But most importantly, his adventures also brought to the fore a man whose career and reputation among Muslims and crusaders alike would eclipse his own, Nur al-Din's and Zengi's combined. That man was Shirkuh's nephew, the Kurdish emir Yusuf ibn Ayyub: soon to be sultan of Egypt and Syria, destroyer of the Fatimids, nemesis of the Zengids, scourge of the Franks and almost single-handedly the target of many thousands of individual crusades. He would cast a long shadow over his age and his nickname would be remembered for generations—indeed, centuries—after his deeds had faded. Yusuf ibn Ayyub was better known as Salah al-Din—a sobriquet which meant "the righteousness of the faith," but which history and legend have contracted and mythologized as Saladin.

◆ 18 ◆

Because of Our Sins

All the kingdoms adjacent to us
have been brought under the power of one man.

Al-Adid, last of the Fatimid caliphs, died twice in the space of ten days. His first death occurred in a mosque in Cairo during Friday prayers on September 3, 1171. On every Friday, in accordance with proper Islamic practice, a preacher would ascend the ritual pulpit and deliver a sermon known as a *khutbah* in which he offered praise to God, blessings upon the Prophet, a spiritual message and an invocation in the name of the ruler of the day. But in Cairo on September 3 this ritual was rudely interrupted. Before the preacher could begin, a visiting Persian called Muhammad ibn-Muwaffaq—better known as "the Scholar emir"—climbed the stairs on the minbar and offered a bidding prayer of his own, calling down blessings upon the name of the man he considered to be the rightful caliph.[1] That should have been al-Adid. But instead the Scholar emir uttered the name of al-Mustadi, the Abbasid caliph in Baghdad.

This was the first time in nearly two centuries of Egyptian history that the name of a Sunni caliph was invoked in place of an Ismaili Shi'ite, and it should have shaken Egypt to its foundations, for the right to be named at Friday prayers was (like the right to mint coins) the exclusive privilege of a caliph and head of state. To offer the name of another was not just blasphemy—it was treason. Yet on this day the mention of an Abbasid in place of a Fatimid passed the assembled faithful by without a whisper. "No one expressed any disapproval," wrote Ibn al-Athir.[2] So on the following Friday, September 10, the vizier of Egypt, Saladin, commanded that al-Mustadi's name be read in every mosque in Cairo. Once again, wrote Ibn al-Athir, "no two goats butted heads over it."[3] A week later, al-Adid had been replaced in the *khutbah* in every mosque in Egypt. Everywhere, blessings rained upon the name of the Abbasid one thousand miles away in Baghdad. By right al-Adid should have been incandescent with rage and indignation. But he was past caring. On September 13, following a short, severe and—it was muttered—conveniently timed illness, al-Adid died, ten days short of his twenty-first birthday.[4] His physical demise thus coincided neatly with his legal extinction—and with him, Fatimid rule in Egypt came to an end.

After al-Adid's death Saladin and one of his lieutenants, an emir known as Qaraqush, rounded up al-Adid's family in the caliph's palace. They told al-Adid's eldest son, Da'ud, that because his father had died without explicitly designating him as heir, he could not succeed. He and his male relatives were placed under house arrest for the rest of their natural lives, kept well away from women to ensure they could not produce any sons. Their servants and slaves were dismissed or sold. Saladin sifted the caliph's treasure house, marveling at jars filled with gigantic pearls and rubies, a glorious emerald-studded sword hilt, archaelogical curiosities like giant fish ribs from some long-dead behemoth of the deep, and a medicinal drum that cured trapped wind by causing any person who sounded it to fart.[5] He organized a military parade of Kurdish and Syrian troops through the streets of Cairo to offset any public dismay that might accompany al-Adid's funeral. He himself mourned ostentatiously and publicly. Then he continued the task, already two years in the making, of purging Fatimid loyalists from the Egyptian army and bureaucracy and turning Egypt into a base from which Saladin and his supporters could launch an audacious bid for mastery of the Holy Lands and everything around them.

Salah al-Din Yusuf ibn Ayyub was born in a castle in Tikrit, one hundred and ten miles upstream from Baghdad on the banks of the river Tigris, in either 1137 or 1138 CE.[6] His father, Shirkuh's brother Ayyub, was a Kurd from the ancient Armenian city of Dvin, described by Ibn al-Qalanisi as "a man of resolution, intelligence and knowledge of affairs."[7] Ayyub used his talents working for the Seljuq sultan, and later for Zengi and Nur al-Din. He raised his sons—Shahanshah, Turan-Shah, Saladin, al-Adil (also known as Sayf al-Din or Saphadin), Buri and Tughtakin—in Mosul and Baalbek, where he was governor. Through his service Ayyub eventually achieved considerable rank within the Zengid military hierarchy, becoming so esteemed that he was said to be the only man permitted to remain seated in Nur al-Din's presence. He ensured that Saladin and his brothers grew up equipped for a similar career; by early adulthood Saladin was a skilled horseman, adept administrator, smooth courtier and pious Muslim who was assiduous with his prayers and took pleasure in hearing daily readings from the Qur'an and Hadith. While in his twenties Saladin demonstrated his military competence fighting in Egypt alongside Shirkuh and other members of what became known as the Ayyubid clan; these included Ayyub himself and Sayf al-Din. It was a mark of his rising reputation that he was trusted to hold Alexandria against Amalric of Jerusalem in 1167.

Thanks to Saladin's extraordinary achievements and his natural talent for self-promotion, many vivid, highly skewed pen portraits were produced during his lifetime. The most fulsome was by the Mosuli lawyer and scholar known as Baha al-Din Ibn Shaddad, who entered Saladin's service as judge of the army in the late 1180s and penned a soaring, heroic biography of his master at the peak of his powers. Ibn Shaddad's book, entitled *The Rare and Excellent History of Saladin*, was intended for its subject's personal enjoyment, self-consciously burnishing Saladin's reputation as *mujahidin*: the stick God had chosen to flog the wretched Franks. In a long paean introducing his work, Ibn Shaddad praised Saladin's personal virtues: he was impeccably pious, generous, a strict keeper of the Ramadan fast, preternaturally hardworking, kind to children, "gentle and merciful, a supporter of the weak against the strong," and astonishingly brave. "Saladin was one of the great heroes, mighty in spirit, strong in courage and of great firmness, terrified of nothing," wrote Ibn Shaddad. "I have never at all seen him consider the enemy too numerous nor exaggerate their strength."[8] Most of all, he wrote, Saladin was the embodiment of the righteous jihadi. "The Jihad, his love and passion for it, had taken a mighty hold on his heart and all his being, so much so that he talked of nothing else, thought of nothing but the means to pursue it, was concerned only with its manpower and had a fondness only for those who spoke of it and encouraged it."[9]

Teasing out the facts of Saladin's life from the sugary encomia produced by Ibn Shaddad and his ilk (other pro-Ayyubid writers included the Persian scholar Imad al-Din al-Isfahani, Saladin's chancellor, and the later, Damascus-based writer Abu Shama) is not easy. Certainly, when Ibn Shaddad was writing in the 1180s, Saladin appeared indeed to have struck heavier blows against the crusader cause than anyone before him. He seemed by that time, even to Christian observers, the embodiment of a divine fury sent "to rage and exterminate the obstinate people" of the crusader states.[10] Yet clear-eyed analysts of Saladin's career would always be able to discern a more ambiguous reality. Saladin fought other Sunni Muslims at least as often as he fought Christians. He was defeated in battle as often as he triumphed and the empire he assembled had broken up within two decades of his death. The legend was never the same as the man. And certainly during the 1170s, as Saladin and the Ayyubids plotted the destruction of Fatimid Egypt and their own path to preeminence, the picture—and Saladin's reputation as the anticrusader ne plus ultra—was not so clear.

Initially Nur al-Din gave Saladin broad license in Egypt. He did not demur in the summer of 1169 when the vizier moved against factions in Cairo who threatened his rule: assassinating the palace official Mu'tamin al-Khilafa and then purging the fifty-thousand-strong black Sudan corps in a hair-raising two-day battle that left buildings scorched with Greek fire and crows picking over corpses.[11] He supported Saladin with troops in the autumn of 1169 when the Ayyubids defended Damietta against joint assault by a Frankish army and Byzantine naval fleet. In 1171, when news of al-Adid's death reached Baghdad, there was dancing in the streets. The caliph, delighted at the demise of his heretical rival, sent Saladin and Nur al-Din black Abbasid flags to fly in celebration and dictated letters bearing fulsome thanks. Al-Mustadi would no doubt have been delighted to learn that since Saladin had received the viziership two and a half years earlier, he had redoubled his commitment to religious propriety, giving up wine and adopting a conservative style of clothing.

At this point Nur al-Din, who saw himself as the sole guarantor of Saladin's power, boasted patronizingly that "Turkish arrows are the only defense against Frankish lances."[12] But as Saladin consolidated his position in Cairo during the early 1170s—sweeping aside the Fatimid caliph, sending lieutenants like Qaraqush to the Upper Nile, Yemen, Ifriqiya and the Mahgreb to take command of the trans-Saharan slave and gold caravan trails, courting the ordinary folk of Cairo by cutting taxes and buying the loyalty of the reformed Egyptian army with generous grants of farmland (known as *iqta*) made to troops and emirs alike—Nur al-Din's concerns about his upstart Kurd began to grow.[13] Equally, as Saladin increased his own power, so he became ever more concerned that it might be taken away.

This mutual suspicion between Nur al-Din and Saladin broke into the open when, in the months after the Fatimid caliph al-Adid's death, Saladin aborted a joint Syrian-Ayyubid attack on Frankish positions in southern Palestine. He realized that any conquests he made in the kingdom of Jerusalem would effectively bring him closer to a land border with Nur al-Din's territories in Syria. Better, he reasoned, to keep a Frankish buffer zone between Egypt and Syria until he was sufficiently secure that he could obey or ignore Nur al-Din's commands as he pleased.[14] This was certainly not the action of a dyed-in-the-wool anti-Christian jihadi. Neither, for that matter, was it the action of a man who stood to serve Islamic unity over his own political ambition.

On May 15, 1174, Nur al-Din died in Damascus, having developed a fever after a bad-tempered polo match and refused his doctors' requests to bleed him. Nur al-Din's funeral elegy, composed by Imad al-Din, deplored his death as a catastrophe for Islam: "Religion is in darkness because of the absence of his light. . . . Let Islam mourn the defender of its people, and Syria the protector of its kingdom and its borders."[15] Saladin wrote that it was an "earthquake shock"—a particularly poignant phrase since much of Syria had been severely damaged by one of the largest seismic events in its history just four years previously.[16] This was a typical poetic obituary, of course, but it sprang from truth. Nur al-Din's piety was indeed beyond reproach. He had revived almost single-handedly a link between war against the Franks and jihad, and during his twenty-eight years in power he had also done more than anyone else to advance the unity and military reputation of the Muslims of the Holy Land. Yet for all his supreme virtues, Nur al-Din was still human. And when he died, he left as his heir an eleven-year-old son, al-Salih, a situation that left the future of his empire wide open.

To complicate matters, less than two months after Nur al-Din's death, Amalric of Jerusalem also died, following an acute attack of dysentery. He too left an underage heir: a thirteen-year-old who was crowned Baldwin IV. Saladin sent cooler diplomatic courtesies to the crusader kingdom than he had to al-Salih, and in private he gloated at Amalric's demise: "May God curse him and abandon him and lead him to bitter punishment."[17] He had every reason to celebrate. Baldwin—Amalric's son with his first wife, Agnes of Courtenay—was clever, energetic and of "a lovable disposition," and his manners of walking and speaking were eerily reminiscent of his father.[18] But there was one crucial difference. As the new king grew up it became apparent that he was suffering from an incurable and hideously debilitating form of leprosy so severe that William of Tyre mistook it for elephantiasis.[19] Baldwin's youth, his disease and the abject behavior of the adults who jockeyed for power around him would eventually bring the crusader kingdom to its knees.

In 1174, then, Saladin had a choice to make. Both the Zengid and Latin Christian regions of the Near East were suddenly weakened, while in Egypt he was increasingly secure. If he wished to establish himself as the new and rightful defender of Islam he had to decide whether to take aim directly at the infidels in Palestine or to focus his energies on doing what Nur al-Din had not, and bring Syria and Egypt together under his own, uncontested leadership. He chose the latter. For the next decade Saladin devoted his best efforts not to crushing the crusader states but to asserting himself as ruler of the emirates on their borders: Damascus, Aleppo, the Jazira (upper Mesopotamia) and Mosul. He did not entirely neglect war against the Christians: in the summer of 1174 he enjoyed a pulverizing naval victory in the Nile Delta against a fleet sent against Alexandria by the new Sicilian king William II. In 1177 he suffered an almighty reverse after marching an army into the kingdom of Jerusalem and encountering a smaller but more organized and determined force of crusader knights, including a large number of Templars. In 1179 he successfully halted the construction of a Templar castle at Jacob's Ford, on the Via Maris between Acre and Damascus, leaving bodies of construction workers lying crumbled and bloody beside their wheelbarrows. In 1183 he tried and failed to provoke a full muster of the kingdom of Jerusalem's army to a pitched battle. These were all significant clashes. But by and large, during the first half of his career Saladin preferred to make truces with the crusader states that freed him to afflict his coreligionists in Syria. His main focus was not the jihad but the decidedly less morally clear-cut task of sweeping clean the Syrian map of Nur al-Din's Zengid relatives and descendants.

Little by little, Saladin began to piece together an empire. He entered Damascus, initially to act as atabeg on behalf of al-Salih, in 1174. During the course of the next two years he twice defeated the combined armies of Aleppo (where al-Salih had been taken following his father's death) and Mosul (which was ruled by one of Nur al-Din's nephews). In 1175 he took Homs. In 1176 the governor of Aleppo agreed to recognize him as lord in his own right; Saladin formally annexed the city in 1183, two years after al-Salih died, aged just eighteen. Mosul held out until 1186, but after a long siege its ruler had submitted to Saladin's will. By that time the Abbasid caliph had granted him the right to call himself Sultan of Egypt and Syria. It was no empty title.

Yet the sultanate was not Saladin's reward for smiting the enemies of God, but rather the enemies of Saladin. In the twelve years between Nur al-Din's death and Mosul's submission the vizier-sultan expended a combined total of around thirteen months skirmishing with the Franks and nearly thirty-three on active military maneuvers against other Muslims.[20] The most serious threats to his rise to supremacy came from the Nizari Assassins (who twice came close to killing him) and a very serious, possibly malarial, illness during the campaign for Mosul in 1185, which caused his doctors to despair of his life. He only barely survived the fevers and pain, emerging emaciated and frail. Nevertheless, he was alive, and his prestige as the effective military ruler of the Islamic world in the Near East was at its peak. Moreover, recovering from his fever had filled Saladin with a desire to turn to the task he had put off for so long: the destruction of the realms of unbelief in Jerusalem, Tripoli and Antioch.

William of Tyre, writing in the 1180s, recognized the singular danger that Saladin's conquests in Syria presented to the kingdom of Jerusalem. "In former times almost every [Muslim] city had its own ruler," wrote William. "They were not dependent on one another; they were rarely actuated by the same motives but in fact, very often by those directly opposite . . . but now, since God has so willed it, all the kingdoms adjacent to us have been brought under the power of one man."[21] The sultan had created a ring of Islamic territories around the Latin states, from which the only escape was into the sea.

To make things worse, the crusaders states were not only surrounded: they were riven with faction and troubled by the sense that since the debacle of the Second Crusade, the West had lost its appetite for large-scale crusading to the

Lord's Sepulchre. Each spring brought boatloads of pilgrims and warriors, it was true. The military orders were enjoying booming membership and patronage as they took increasing charge of defending the frontiers and fortresses of the Holy Land. And from time to time great lords would also arrive on private minicrusades—such as that led by Philip of Alsace, Count of Flanders, who came to the East in 1177 to atone for the sin of having had the lover of his adulterous wife Elizabeth's beaten to death with a mace and dumped headfirst in a lavatory.[22] But all this was not enough to sustain anything more than survival and periodic retrenchment.

Although there had been numerous papal pronouncements of crusade since the deaths of Eugene III and Saint Bernard of Clairvaux in 1153, the energy of the crusading movement seemed to be drifting in other directions. Crusades were authorized in Spain in 1153, 1157 and 1175, while in the same period at least six military orders were founded and given papal permission to operate in the Spanish peninsula, including the Order of Calatrava (1158), the Order of Santiago (1170) and the Order of Alcántara (around 1175). In 1171 and 1172 Pope Alexander III had authorized further crusading against the pagans of northeast Europe in a bull known as *Non Parum Animus Noster*, which explicitly confirmed that fighting against the heathen in Europe would be considered a cause equally worthy to fighting Muslims in Palestine and Syria.[23]

Amalric, when he was alive, had written on numerous occasions to the aging Louis VII of France, imploring him to return on another crusade to recover the lands then lost to Nur al-Din. "It is obvious that your kingdom is strong enough to wrench it from the hands of the infidel and reclaim it from God," he wrote. Six months later he practically begged the French king to return: "like tassels hanging from your head-dress, we bow to your majesty . . . do not hesitate to come now when Christendom's needs are great and its problems are many."[24] Nor was he the only plaintiff: in the 1180s the patriarch of Jerusalem, Eraclius, wrote to all the archbishops, bishops, abbots, priors, kings, dukes, counts, "indeed all sons of the Holy Church who read this letter" warning of "the adversities and misfortunes which will no doubt force us to flee and abandon Jerusalem."[25] But despite these repeated warnings, it seemed that a revival of the crusading spirit of the 1140s—still less the 1090s—had never been further away. As the Second Crusade had served to demonstrate, it required a disaster of earth-shattering nature to stir the Western powers for the expense, pain and uncertainty of a major joint expedition to the Holy Land.

Indeed, it was symbolic of the drifting engagement with Eastern affairs that Eraclius was roundly rebuffed when he traveled to Europe in 1184 and 1185, bringing with him the keys to the Holy Sepulchre, the city of Jerusalem and the Tower of David, to recruit a great lord to come to Jerusalem as Fulk of Anjou once had, as an elected successor to Baldwin IV. On January 29 the patriarch laid the keys at the feet of Henry II, the Plantagenet king of England, duke of Normandy and Anjou, grandson of King Fulk, nephew of Baldwin III and Amalric, and husband (albeit an estranged one) of a crusader queen, Eleanor of Aquitaine.* Henry agreed to consider Eraclius's offer of his grandfather's old crown, but after consulting with all his barons and bishops, concluded that he was more needed in his own kingdom than far away seeking "the preservation of the easterners."[26] He promised money and men, but nothing more; Eraclius was forced to take his leave, grumbling as he went that Jerusalem would greatly prefer leadership to wealth.[27]

Henry's refusal to take up the offer of Jerusalem's crown left the crusader kingdom shorn of both political direction and military resources. The crusader states did not lack for income—ports like Acre were thriving mercantile hubs, while the populace had been induced, more or less grudgingly in 1183, to pay a tax for the defense of the realm. What was absent was manpower on the scale a full crusade could provide and—more than anything else—undisputed authority. Amalric's reign had left Jerusalem with rival branches of the royal family, each with its own attendant court parties. Ambitious barons clustered around Amalric's first wife, Agnes of Courtenay (whom he had discarded after his coronation on the grounds of consanguinity), her children Baldwin IV and Sibylla and the circle of her new husband, the intelligent, cultured and repulsively ugly lord Reginald of Sidon. Others gravitated toward Amalric's second wife and queen, the Byzantine princess Maria Komnene, who had borne the king a daughter called Isabella and who, after Amalric's death, married the powerful Balian of Ibelin. Woven around these party lines were the petty squabbles of a clutch of high-ranking noblemen: Raymond III,

*Eleanor of Aquitaine's marriage to Henry II was notoriously fractious: although they produced seven adult children (five of whom themselves became a king or queen) Eleanor rebelled against Henry in a civil war in 1173 and 1174 and subsequently spent fifteen years under house arrest as punishment.

1. The Crusader World

A typical thirteenth-century *mappa mundi* shows Jerusalem as the center of the world. As the place of Christ's ministry, death and resurrection, there was nowhere with greater power over the medieval Christian imagination. Freeing Jerusalem from Muslim rule was the ultimate target of the First Crusade.

2. Alexios Komnenos
The Byzantine emperor Alexios I Komnenos is seen here with his son John and wife Irene Doukas. Alexios's decision to summon western military aid against his Turkish enemies was a driving force behind the First Crusade. Missing from this family portrait is Alexios's brilliant daughter, Anna Komnene, author of the *Alexiad.*

3. Pope Urban II
Drawing together spiritual arguments about the possibility of salvation through fighting Christ's enemies with the great political considerations of his day, Urban II launched the First Crusade in 1095. Once a Cluniac monk, Urban is pictured here blessing the altar at Cluny Abbey during his crusade preaching tour.

4. Peter the Hermit
This charismatic preacher was one of the first leaders of a crusading army. His followers caused violent unrest across the Rhineland and, later, in the Byzantine empire. According to Anna Komnene, the residents of Constantinople gave him the scornful nickname "Koukoupetros": Peter the Cuckoo.

5. Crusader pogroms
The militant ideology of the crusades had terrible consequences for Jewish people in Europe. During the the First Crusade there were massacres of Jews in cities including Worms and Mainz. Sickening pogroms also took place in England around a century later, during preparations for the Third Crusade.

6. Dorylaeum
Despite the many privations of the First Crusade, the main armies led by the western "princes" won a series of extraordinary battles. One of their most famous triumphs came at Dorylaeum in Asia Minor on July 1, 1097, when they routed the armies of Qilij I Arslan.

7. Church of the Holy Sepulchre
The Church of the Holy Sepulchre remains one of the great landmarks of Jerusalem. A church has existed in some form on the site since the fourth century, covering both Calvary, where Christ was crucified, and the empty tomb from which he rose. To worship at the Holy Sepulchre was the ultimate goal of countless medieval pilgrimages.

8. Alfonso VI of Castile and León

Crusading was never directed exclusively toward the eastern Mediterranean. Conflict between Christian and Islamic rulers in Iberia provided another arena for penitential Christian warfare. Alfonso VI, known as El Bravo, was one of the early leaders of what became known as the Reconquista.

9. Roger II of Sicily

The first crowned king of Sicily (shown here in a mosaic in Palermo) ruled over a realm in which Arab, Greek and Latin Christian influences all intermingled. Roger's father was credited (dubiously) by one Muslim chronicler as having been the first person to suggest a crusade to Jerusalem.

10. The marriage of Fulk of Anjou and Melisende

Fulk, count of Anjou, was headhunted from western Europe to become king of Jerusalem after the death of Baldwin II. His wedding to Baldwin's daughter Melisende is pictured here in a late medieval illumination. The marriage was uneasy at first, as Melisende refused to be sidelined from politics by her husband.

11. Crac des Chevaliers

Built by the Knights Hospitaller in the county of Tripoli, Crac des Chevaliers guarded the approach to that crusader state from the Syrian city of Homs. Its massive walls and vast size made it a formidable part of the crusaders' defensive network. The castle could garrison several thousand men. It was captured in 1271 by the Mamluks.

12. Nur al-Din's minbar
This ritual pulpit, or minbar, was built in Aleppo on the orders of Nur al-Din and later installed by Saladin in Jerusalem's al-Aqsa mosque. It was considered a masterpiece of medieval Islamic art, inscribed with Arabic calligraphy and complex geometric patterns. The original minbar was destroyed by arson in the 1960s but has since been rebuilt.

13. Eleanor of Aquitaine
This composite image shows (left) Eleanor of Aquitaine marrying Louis VII of France in 1137 and (right) Louis departing on crusade ten years later. Eleanor joined her husband on his treacherous overland journey to the east, which ended in scandal and military failure. Their marriage was annulled not long after their return home.

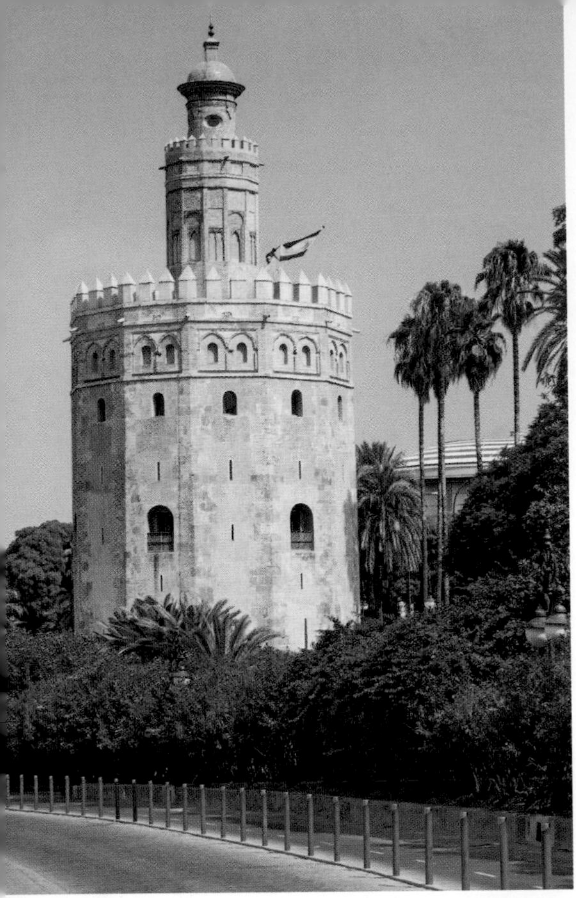

14. Muslim Spain
The Torre del Oro in Seville was begun in the 1220s when the city was ruled by the Almohads. It was a chain-tower, which allowed Seville's governors to block access to the city via the Guadalqivir river. The upper elements of the tower were added after Seville fell to Christian rule in the late Reconquista.

15. The True Cross
This ornate reliquary contains a supposed fragment of the True Cross on which Christ died. Many such relics of the Cross existed during the crusading period; the most famous was that kept in the Church of the Holy Sepulchre. It was seized by Saladin at the Battle of Hattin and disappeared forever.

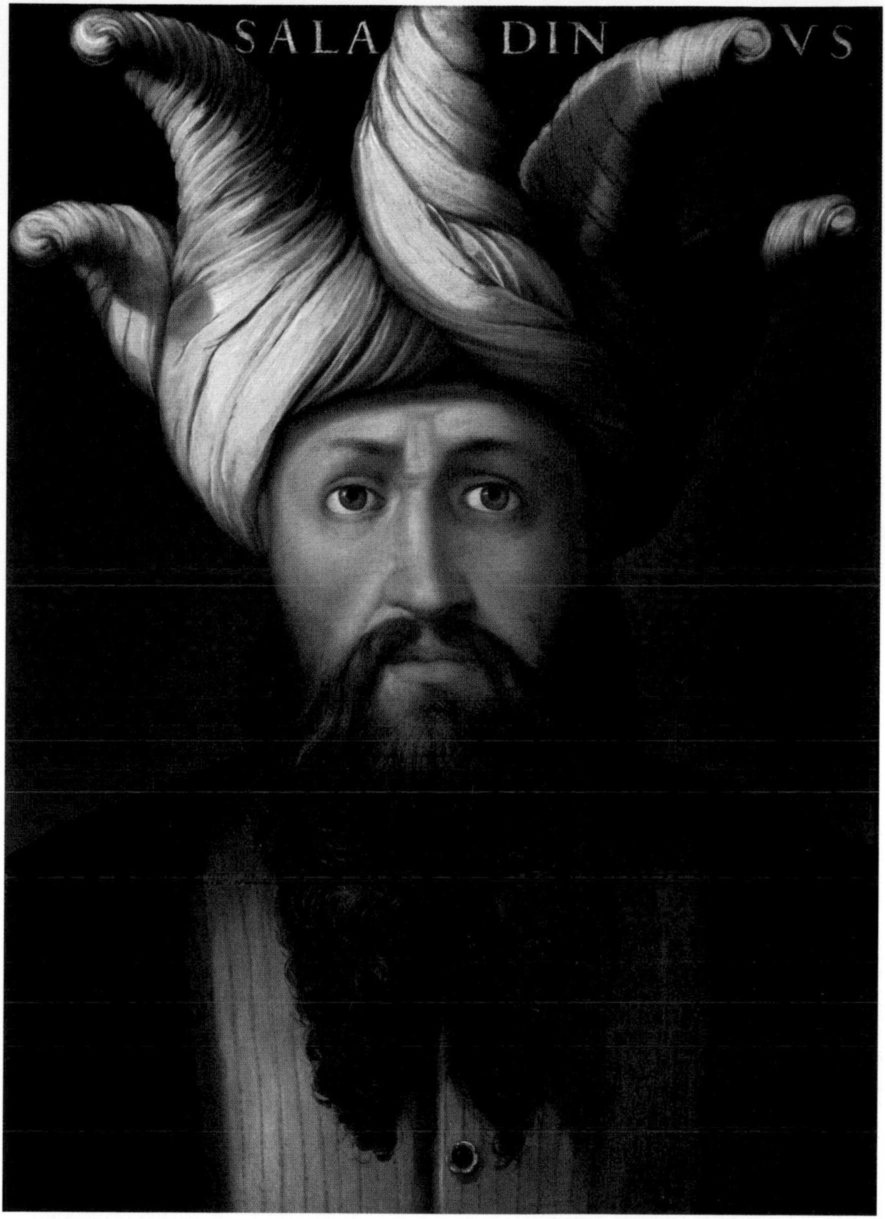

16. Saladin

During his meteoric career Saladin rose from relative obscurity to become sultan of Egypt and Syria. Fervently committed to the cause of jihad, his greatest victory over the crusaders of the Holy Land came in 1187, when he obliterated a Frankish army at the Battle of Hattin and returned Jerusalem to Muslim rule.

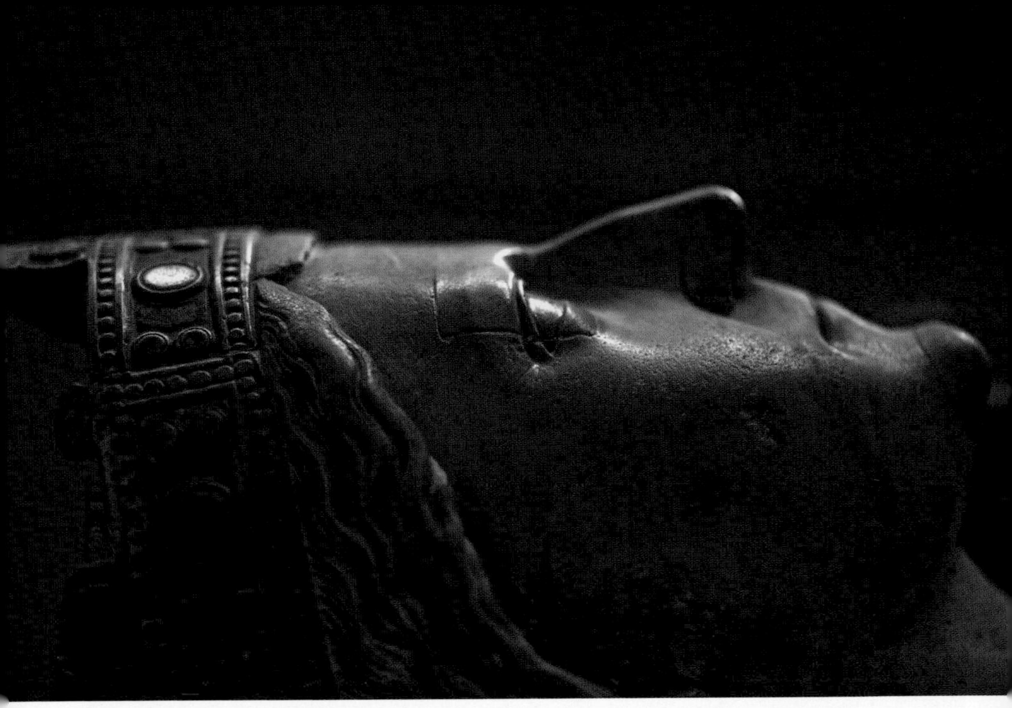

17. Richard the Lionheart
One of the most prominent leaders of the Third Crusade, the warlike Richard I of England arrived in the crusader kingdom in 1191 and reversed many of Saladin's gains. He never recaptured Jerusalem but still left an indelible mark on crusading history and lore.

18. The siege of Acre
After Jerusalem was lost, Acre became the capital of the crusader realm. The siege to liberate it from Saladin in 1189–91 is shown here: the machine outside the city walls is a trebuchet, or giant catapult, capable of hurling huge stones and other missiles over long distances.

19. Hermann von Salza
Along with the Templars and Hospitallers, the Teutonic Knights were an important military order of religious warriors who dedicated their lives to fighting crusades. Hermann von Salza, shown here, was one of their most successful leaders: politically shrewd and a tireless diplomat, on easy terms with popes and Holy Roman Emperors alike.

20. Innocent III
Under Innocent's papacy crusading was turned against perceived enemies of the Roman Church wherever they appeared. Heretics in France, pagans in the Baltic and Greek Christians in the Byzantine empire all became targets. Innocent did more to shape the crusade movement than any pope since Urban II.

21. The conquest of Constantinople
In 1204 Venetian and French crusaders burned and sacked the Byzantine capital, Constantinople. This fiasco was embarrassing to the papacy and did absolutely nothing to advance the crusading cause in the Holy Land. The Byzantine empire never recovered.

22. Enrico Dandolo
The doge of Venice was blind and around ninety years old when he served as a leader of the Fourth Crusade. He was buried in Constantinople at the Hagia Sophia.

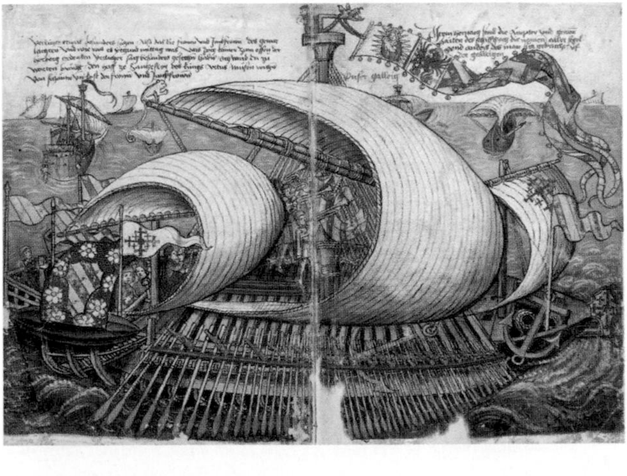

23. Venetian sea power
Venice emerged during the crusading era as a dominant power in the western world, in large part thanks to the galleys built in the city's shipyards. Powered by sail and oar, they could transport goods, cash and troops across the Mediterranean.

24. Damietta
This detail from Matthew Paris's chronicle shows knights in combat at Damietta during the Fifth Crusade. Paris was kept informed of events in the Nile Delta by regular updates sent by leading crusaders to the English royal court.

25. Frederick Hohenstaufen and al-Kamil
The Holy Roman Emperor and sultan of Egypt enjoyed a close diplomatic relationship thanks to Frederick's broadminded interest in Arab culture and scientific research. They negotiated a peace settlement that placed Jerusalem back into Christian hands from 1229 to 1244.

26. Louis IX
The saint-king of France was an enthusiastic, if not very successful crusader. He was evacuated and ransomed after a disastrous crusade up the Nile in 1249 and died while on a second crusade to north Africa in 1270. Louis explored an alliance with the Mongols against the Mamluks, although this too came to nothing.

27. Mongols
Arriving from the east in the middle of the thirteenth century, the Mongols were a formidable addition to the crusader world. Crusades were raised to try and stop them advancing through eastern Europe; they were also courted as potential allies in the Holy Land. Mongol warriors are seen here attacking Baghdad in 1258.

28. Mamluks vs Mongols
The Mamluks were a slave-soldier caste who rose to take control of Egypt in 1250. Their rivalry with the Mongols came to a head at the Battle of Ayn Jalut in 1260. The Mamluks routed the Mongol army, then set about invading and dismantling the crusader states.

29. The walls of Acre

This romanticized painting shows Acre falling to a Mamluk army in 1291, which in hindsight marked the end of the crusader states in Syria and Palestine. Overstretched and overwhelmed, the crusaders evacuated Acre amid much bloodshed and retreated to a ghost kingdom on Cyprus.

30. Crusade revival

During the fourteenth century numerous schemes were hatched to return to the Holy Land and take back the lost crusader states. This map, by Pietro Vesconte, accompanied one such plan by the Venetian statesman and merchant Marino Sanudo the Elder.

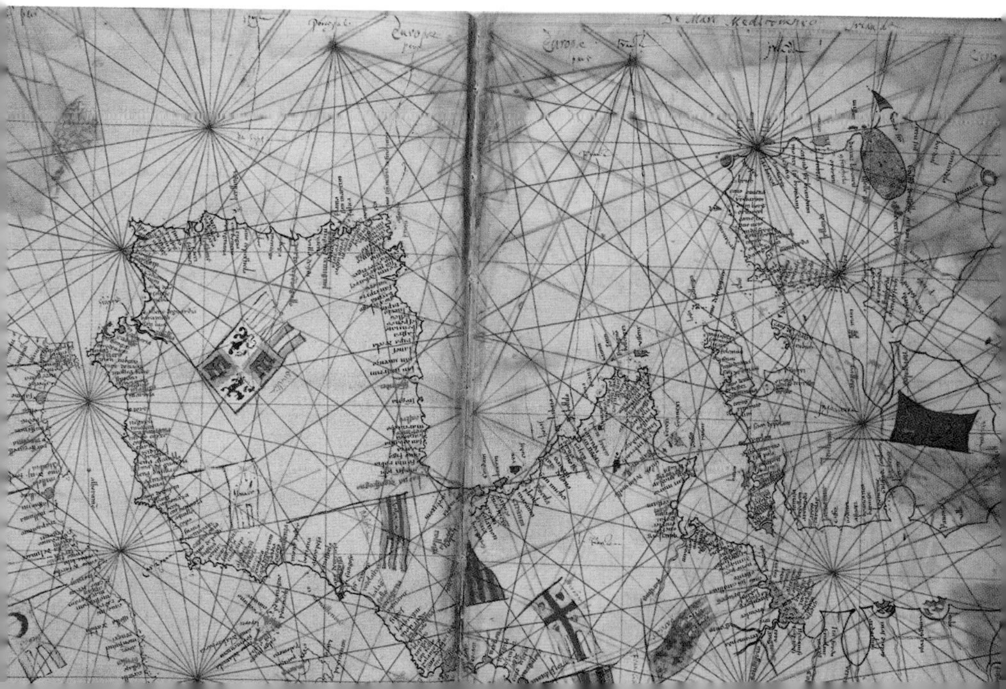

31. Boucicaut

The self-styled greatest knight of his age, Jean II le Meingre, aka Boucicaut, crusaded against pagans with the Teutonic Knights and made a devotional pilgrimage to Jerusalem. By his time crusading had become just one element in the broader culture of aristocratic piety and chivalry.

Count of Tripoli; Joscelin III of Courtenay (Agnes's brother and putative heir to the lost county of Edessa); Reynald of Châtillon, whose sixteen years in an Aleppan jail had left him with a pathological ill will toward Islam and many perceived scores to settle; Princess Sibylla's insipid and luckless husband, Guy of Lusignan; and the overbearing and fanatically zealous master of the Templars, Gerard of Ridefort. So deep ran some of the hatreds between these men and women that in 1186 Raymond of Tripoli actually preferred to make a nonaggression pact with Saladin against the crown of Jerusalem than seek common cause with his rivals among the Franks. The tangled web of these men's ambitions, marriages, prejudices, personalities and blood feuds was not atypical of a medieval Frankish state. But as was found at some point in almost every twelfth-century realm organized on the basis of monarchy and military might, periods of weak kingship eventually prompted the polity to devour itself.

The years that followed Baldwin IV's accession were the very definition of weak kingship. Baldwin reigned just less than eleven years before his leprosy killed him on March 16, 1185. He presented a pitiful sight by the end: blind, terribly disfigured, in near constant pain and reduced to being carried about his realm on a litter. Equally woeful was the accession in 1185 of his sister Sibylla's eight-year-old son Baldwin V.* This Baldwin lived only a year before he, too, died, to be succeeded by his mother and her husband as Queen Sibylla and King Guy, who were jointly crowned after a poisonous elective process late in 1186. The succession of the crown of Jerusalem since the death of Amalric thus ran: a leper, a child and a woman married to a widely scorned booby. The factional divisions that were deepened by Sibylla and Guy's coronation left the crusader states staggering toward a civil war far more serious than that which had erupted between Melisende and Baldwin III in the early 1150s. The only thing that prevented this war from breaking out was the fact that a much greater crisis was looming, in the shape of Saladin.

Saladin's last truce with the kingdom of Jerusalem expired on April 5, 1187. Now, in the words of the urbane Spanish Muslim traveler Ibn Jubayr, the sultan was filled with "zeal in waging holy war against the enemies of God."[28] He had no wish to make another peace, and ample excuse to start a war, the end goal of which was to seize every Frankish castle and city possible. His casus

*Baldwin V was crowned as co-king in 1183 during Baldwin IV's lifetime; he became king in his own right on the leper king's death.

belli presented itself most conveniently in the form of Reynald of Châtillon, former prince of Antioch, who on his release from Nur al-Din's prison in 1176 had been given the lordship of Kerak, across the river Jordan from Jerusalem in the region known as Transjordan or *Oultrejordain*. It was from Kerak, late in 1186, that Reynald carried out the supremely ill-advised robbery of a rich merchant caravan making its way slowly past his walls en route from Egypt to Damascus. Saladin already loathed Reynald, who had in 1182 and 1183 sent five galleys to plunder the coasts of the Red Sea, where they seized or scuttled merchant ships and pilgrim boats and aimed, so it was said, to go to Medina and steal the body of Muhammad.[29] The abominable Reynald's actions in Kerak now provided ample pretext for revenge.

The first major clash of forces in Saladin's invasion of the kingdom of Jerusalem occurred less than a month after the truce expired, at an oasis known as the Springs of Cresson (Ain Gozeh), near Nazareth. On May 1, 1187, a group of about 140 Christian knights, mostly Templars and Hospitallers, charged a division of 7,000 Muslim warriors riding under the leadership of Saladin's son al-Afdal. The result was a massacre from which barely a man on the Christian side escaped, save Gerard of Ridefort and a handful of his companions. "The master of the Hospitallers had his head cut off, and so did all the knights of the Temple," wrote one chronicler.[30] This was only the beginning.

The disaster that shook Christendom to its core occurred at the beginning of July at the Horns of Hattin: a double-peaked extinct volcano in Galilee about four miles from Tiberias. At the height of summer, in relentless heat, Saladin drew into battle a Christian army composed of virtually the entire military population of all three crusader states, along with what remained of the Templars and Hospitallers after Cresson. This army had been mustered under emergency protocol known as the arrière-ban, by which every able-bodied fighting man had been summoned from his town or castle to defend the kingdom against attack. Whether this army—numbering perhaps twenty thousand when hired Syrian Christian mercenaries known as turcopoles were included—would be enough was unclear. Saladin, wrote one correspondent in the immediate aftermath of the battle, had "an army whose numbers could not be counted."[31] His troops were recruited from Egypt and the Upper Nile, Damascus, Aleppo, Mosul, Iraq and the Jazira. The sultan was "eager for the victory of Islam."[32] The crusaders, for their part, were uneasily reconciled behind the leadership of King Guy, who had only with some difficulty managed to persuade the next most powerful Christian lord of the region, Raymond of Tripoli, to abandon his peace pact with Saladin and fight in the name of the Cross. To fortify this troubled army, the Templars had brought out from Jerusalem the relic of the True Cross that was ordinarily kept in the Church of the Holy Sepulchre and which was customarily paraded under heavy guard before every major crusading army. It was the symbol of everything for which the crusaders' forefathers had toiled some ninety years earlier. This, and the inscrutable mystery of God's will, would have to decide the day.

Exploiting divisions among the Franks' leaders and the dithering of King Guy (who had been roundly criticized for failing in the past to be sufficiently stern in dealing with the Ayyubid menace and had therefore responded by becoming much too reckless) on Friday, July 3, Saladin lured the crusader army into pursuing his own out of Saffuriya and into the wilderness, toward the arid peaks of Hattin. Once the march was set, the sultan sent troops behind the crusader rear guard and cut off their water supply. This forced Guy's army to spend a day and night in broiling heat, going increasingly mad through thirst. Then, to redouble the agony, Saladin's men set fire to piles of tinder-dry brushwood and dried grass, filling the air with choking, blinding smoke that was intended not only to be uncomfortable but to give the infidels a taste of the hell that awaited them. Ibn Shaddad described the trap into which the crusader army walked. "They were closely beset as in a noose, while still marching on as through being driven to a death that they could see before them, convinced of their doom and destruction and themselves aware that the following day they would be visiting their graves."[33]

On the morning of Saturday, July 4, full battle was joined, and despite a valiant effort the parched crusader army was surrounded and slowly crushed by Saladin's superior numbers. The fighting, agreed everyone who later wrote of the battle, was very fierce, lasting about eight hours, from daybreak until 3:00 P.M. The Ayyubid army used their superior numbers to gradually hem in Guy's divisions, raining arrows on them through smoke from the brushwood fires and resisting the efforts of the Frankish cavalry to punch their way out of the stranglehold with coordinated charges. Steadily, as the battle went on, the Franks were pressed backward, separated and slaughtered until what remained was a company of knights penned around King Guy's bright red tent on the slopes of the volcano, where the royal banner fluttered above the relic of the True Cross. There the exhausted Frankish knights made their last stand, charging desperately in wave after wave to try to bludgeon their way to freedom.

Saladin's son al-Afdal recalled some years later having watched the final minutes of the battle of Hattin alongside his father, who tugged nervously at his beard with each Frankish surge and urged his men on, crying, "Give the lie to the devil!"[34] The sultan snapped irritably at al-Afdal for predicting victory for the Muslims prematurely. But after a while, the two men saw King Guy's red tent crumple and the king beside it surrender. The True Cross was confiscated. Saladin dismounted his horse and threw himself on the ground, praising God and weeping with joy. Later he wrote to the Abbasid caliph in Baghdad, telling him how, not for the first time, he had crushed the enemies of Syria and the Almighty. For the Franks, defeat was all but total. "Amid the noise of trumpets and the neighing of horses," read a letter sent to Germany reporting the outcome of the battle, "the Lord put his people to the sword."[35]

Slaughter and surrender on the Horns of Hattin left the crusader states wide open for Saladin to sweep through, as castles stood ungarrisoned and towns were defended by priests and women. The rank and file of the crusader army who were not killed had been taken off in chain-gang processions to be auctioned into a life of slavery. The leaders who were captured and were held for ransom included King Guy; his brother Aimery; Gerard of Ridefort; and leading barons including William, Marquis of Montferrat, Humphrey of Toron, Hugh of Jabala and Hugh of Gibelet. Reynald of Châtillon was taken prisoner and presented to Saladin, who struck with his own scimitar the first blow of Reynald's execution. Two hundred knight-brothers of the Templars and Hospitallers were ritually beheaded by members of Saladin's religious and clerical entourage. "Alas, it is impossible . . . to recount the numerous huge calamities that the wrath of God has allowed us to suffer because of our sins," wrote Terricus, one of the few Templar officials who escaped the battlefield, contrary to the rule of his order, which mandated brothers fight to the death.[36]

Terricus went on to describe how in the aftermath of Hattin, Saladin's armies were "like a swarm of ants covering the whole face of the earth from Tyre to Jerusalem, even as far as Gaza."[37] Between July and September Saladin's armies took Gibelet, Beirut, Sidon, Acre, Tiberias, Nazareth, Nablus, Haifa, Caesarea, Arsuf, Jaffa, Ascalon, Lydda, Ibelin, Toron, Bethlehem and Hebron.[38] On September 20 they arrived before the walls of Jerusalem.

The defense of the city was led by Balian of Ibelin, husband of the queen dowager Maria Komnene. Balian was a tenacious and powerful noble, physically distinguished by a covering of body hair so thick that it grew like a bear's fur. In Jerusalem he commanded a garrison of troops that numbered no more than few dozen experienced soldiers. Outside the city's walls massed an army that numbered in the tens of thousands. From September 25 they besieged the Holy City with the heavy machinery of ladders, siege engines, sapping equipment and stone-throwing catapults, concentrating their assaults from the western side in the later afternoon, so that the glare of the setting sun blinded the defenders manning the walls, before moving around to the vulnerable northern side where the first crusaders had entered in 1099.

Inside Jerusalem Christian women shaved their children's heads and monks processed barefoot and penitential as they called in desperation for the Lord to save them. It did no good, said one Latin chronicler, for "the stench of adultery, of disgusting extravagance and of sin against nature would not let their prayers rise to God."[39] After eight days of bombardment Balian of Ibelin realized the situation was beyond saving and asked Saladin for a truce in which the Christian citizens could ransom themselves within fifty days and leave with their lives. On Friday October 2—the anniversary, as the sultan believed, of the Prophet's Night Journey to Jerusalem in 621 CE—the keys to the city were handed over and refugees began to stream out of the gates. Amid cries of *Allahu Akbar*, Saladin entered Jerusalem. The large cross that had been erected over the Dome of the Rock was pulled down, and straightaway men went to work purifying the mosques that had been sullied by Christian rites. A week later, at Friday prayers on October 9, Saladin worshipped at the Dome of the Rock. A learned Damascene preacher called Muhyi al-Din ibn al-Zaki performed the *khutbah,* in which he praised Saladin as the restorer of the world and of religion, and offered prayers for the Abbasid caliph.[40]

Victory was complete.

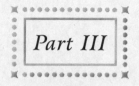

Part III

THE HARVEST OF THE EARTH

◆ 19 ◆

Lionesses and Lionhearts

Some died slowly, others quickly,
but all fell victim to the same fate.

When Saladin laid siege to Jerusalem in late September 1187 an Englishwoman wearing a borrowed coat of armor and a cooking pot for a helmet helped defend the city walls. Margaret of Beverley had been born in the crusader kingdom while her parents were on pilgrimage to the Holy Land in the mid-twelfth century, but she grew up in the north of England, helping to raise a much younger brother, Thomas, who eventually became a Cistercian monk. Later, when she was perhaps in her twenties, Margaret returned to Jerusalem on pilgrimage. It was hardly a settled realm, and through bad luck and worse timing Margaret found herself trapped in the Holy City as the Ayyubids swept in. In years to come she would recall the terror of the siege, during which citizens had to scramble whatever sort of a defense they could in the absence of able-bodied soldiers.

"Although a woman," read Margaret's account, "I looked like a warrior."[1] She launched missiles from a slingshot at Saladin's armies beneath the ramparts, and she ran back and forth between the streets and walls fetching water for her comrades—all the while swallowing down her fear. At one point a rock the size of a millstone, thrown from one of Saladin's catapults, crashed into the city and narrowly missed her. She was cut by shrapnel as it shattered, leaving her with a wound so deep it scarred.[2] Quick medical attention ensured the injury did not prove life threatening, but when the city fell Margaret was taken captive, and forced like the rest of her fellow Christians to buy her freedom. The price set for a woman's liberty under Saladin's truce with Balian of Ibelin was five dinars.

Margaret's experience during the siege of Jerusalem was similar to that of many other women during the crusades—her story was unusual chiefly in the fact that it was written down. Fighting may have been a man's work, but Frankish women were allowed and even expected to get their hands dirty—or bloody.[3] Unfortunately for Margaret, women were also particularly vulnerable during wartime: liable to be taken as bounty, forced into marriage or condemned to sexual slavery. No sooner had Margaret paid her ransom and left Jerusalem than she was captured near Lachis (Lachish, just over a mile from the Jaffa Gate) and taken prisoner again. This time there was no easy escape. She was set to work chopping wood and gathering stones, and she endured beatings, threats and the torment of hard labor throughout two bitter winters. "If I refused I was beaten with sticks," she recalled. "My chains rusted with my tears." After fifteen months of ill-treatment Margaret was sold to a wealthy man from Tyre: one of the few crusader cities that had managed to resist Saladin.[4] Margaret's buyer in Tyre granted her freedom as a pious act to celebrate the birth of one of his sons. But her sufferings were far from over. She was left penniless, dressed in rags that barely covered her, to wander a land in which Christian authority had collapsed. God had forsaken the Franks—and Margaret was suffering as much as any of them.

The fall of Jerusalem stunned Christendom. Even in Byzantium, where sympathy for the Franks was not always guaranteed, the news was received with horror. "Who would not lament from the depths of his heart and soul such a disaster?" asked the Cypriot hermit Saint Neophytos the Recluse. "The holy flock in that Holy Land was ousted and the holy of holies was delivered to the dogs."[5] It was said that Pope Urban III fell down dead after learning of the city's fate.[6] It was left to his short-lived successor Gregory VIII* to break the dreadful news to the princes and the people of the West. On October 29 Gregory issued a papal bull known as *Audita Tremendi*, which called upon all men to do their duty as Christian soldiers and rally to the defense of the East.[7] "[The pope] sent to all the great men of Christendom—emperors,

*Gregory became pope on October 21, 1187, and died on December 20 of the same year. He was succeeded by Clement III.

kings, counts and marquises—and to the knights and sergeants telling them that he would take upon himself and acquit before God all the sins of those who would bear the sign of the cross and go to recover the Promised Land," wrote one chronicler.[8] This time there could be no prevarication. The crusader states were, perhaps for the first time in their history, genuinely and unarguably threatened with annihilation. As Pope Gregory put it, "Anyone of sane mind who does not weep at such a cause for weeping, if not in body at least in his heart, would seem to have forgotten not only his Christian faith . . . but even his very humanity."[9] The reward on offer for individual crusaders was the customary remission of all confessed sins, Church protection for crusaders' families and property and immunity from all legal suit and interest on debts for the duration of the crusade.[10]

From the autumn of 1187 onward, then, preparations began for a Third Crusade. In Germany, the sixty-five-year-old Holy Roman Emperor, Frederick I "Barbarossa" (*Rotbart*)—so called for his golden hair and reddish beard—renewed the vow he had first made four decades previously, when he accompanied his uncle Conrad III on the Second Crusade. Frederick had spent nearly a quarter of a century in conflict with the papacy, but by 1187 he was sufficiently reconciled with Rome to embrace the sacred mission with gusto. Henry, cardinal-bishop of Albano, a Cistercian, was sent into Germany to rouse the people, which he did by asking them to consider why God "would allow the wood of the Cross to be carried away by unbelievers, unless it was for Him to be crucified once again?"[11] The army that answered the call was estimated at anywhere between thirty thousand and (less plausibly) six hundred thousand strong.[12] They set off down the Danube from Regensburg around May 10, 1189, aiming for Hungary, the Balkans and Constantinople. They were led by an impressive contingent of leaders drawn from the nobility of Bavaria, Saxony, Swabia, Austria and beyond. "A glorious desire now burned bright among the most valiant of warriors for battle against those who had invaded the Holy City and the most Holy Sepulchre of the Lord," wrote one chronicler. "That whole vast multitude of men seemed to think of nothing except 'to live is Christ, and to die is gain.' "[13]

As Frederick and his imperial troops mobilized, Henry II of England—who had declined to abdicate his Western crown to assume command of

Jerusalem—was now finally shamed into taking the cross. He did so in January 1188, after making peace with the young king of France, Philip II "Augustus," who had succeeded his father Louis VII in 1180. The two kings—perpetually at war—agreed to cease attacking each other's territories, and to levy on their subjects a 10 percent income tax known as the Saladin tithe, to pay for the relief of Christendom. Henry's energetic and bellicose son Richard, Count of Poitou—soon to be known by his sobriquet "Lionheart"—had already taken the cross, making his vows in November 1187, the day after he heard of the fall of Jerusalem. As it transpired, it was Richard who came to lead the English contingent of the Third Crusade—for on July 6, 1189, Henry died in Chinon Castle.

As befitted both his nickname and his famous parents, Richard was a force of nature. According to a romantic pen portrait recorded after his death by the author of a chronicle known as the *Itinerarium Peregrinorum*, Richard was "tall, of elegant build; the color of his hair was between red and gold; his limbs were supple and straight. He had quite long arms, which were particularly effective for drawing a sword and wielding it." Riding before an army, said the same author, Richard wore a fine red cap in the Flemish style, a tunic of rose samite and a cloak covered with little silver half-moons and shining suns. "The sight of him was a pleasure to the eyes."[14] Less starry-eyed writers noted that in fact Richard was pale-faced, carried too much fat, and suffered with ulcers and fevers.[15] What everyone agreed upon, however, was his extreme love of and talent for warfare, into which he threw himself headlong from his teens until his dying day. Gerald of Wales wrote that he physically trembled with nervous energy, "and his trembling makes the whole world tremble and fear."[16] History called him to the crusade at the right moment and Richard answered the call with all he had.

Richard was crowned on September 3 and immediately began a fire sale of public offices and crown possessions to raise crusading funds. At the same time royal officials frantically stockpiled the necessary goods for the long journey: hundreds and thousands of salted pig carcasses, wheels of cheese, beans, biscuits, wineskins and barrels of ale, fodder for horses, horseshoes and nails, arrowheads and crossbow bolts.[17] Crusade preachers roamed the British Isles targeting the most talented warriors to join the army: the archbishop of Canterbury Baldwin of Forde raised about three thousand men on a circuit of Wales.[18]

Richard's impatience to torment the infidel rapidly infected the English populace and led to months of riots against England's Jews, which started on Richard's coronation day and culminated in York in March 1190, when several hundred Jewish people were burned alive by a mob while supposedly under royal protection in the city's castle. The experience of Benedict of York, who was chased through the street by a mob, beaten up and dragged to a church to be forcibly baptized, was commonplace.[19] "[The people] dispatched their bloodsuckers bloodily to hell," wrote the chronicler Richard of Devizes.[20]

This violent and bigoted response to the crusade was, if horrifying, nonetheless in keeping with the times. Aggression, hatred and orgiastic displays of personal and public cruelty attached every bit as easily as piety to the crusading muster. And in 1190 the crusading instinct, energized by the loss of Christ's city, ran through the Western realms like a fever. Monks were reported to be abandoning their cowls and running away to join the army. Laymen goaded one another into joining up. "A great many men sent each other wool and distaff, hinting that if anyone failed to join this military undertaking they were only fit for woman's work," wrote the author of the *Itinerarium Perigrinorum*. "Brides urged their husbands and mothers incited their sons to go, their only sorrow being that they were not able to set out with them because of the weakness of their sex."[21] This last image—of feeble women waving their doughty menfolk farewell—was exaggeration rather than fact, as Margaret of Beverley's experience showed. But it was a powerful popular trope. A contemporary song described a crusader's heart breaking at the sadness of those who left homes and lovers to join the holy war:

Good lord God, if I for you
Leave the country where she is that I love so,
Grant us in heaven everlasting joy,
My love and me, through your mercy,
And grant her the strength to love me,
So that she will not forget me in my long absence.[22]

In the summer of 1190 the time for such precious farewells arrived, as the first part of the English fleet set sail from Dartmouth. Their king was already on the continent with Philip of France. On July 4—the third anniversary of Hattin—the two kings and their armies departed from Lyon, traveling separately but both heading south. Unlike the German emperor, Richard and Philip had decided to follow a sea route to the Holy Land. The French headed to the port of Genoa, while Richard and his army aimed for Marseille. They agreed to reconvene in Sicily with their navies and travel on from there. As the armies marched, the ground trembled.[23]

On Sicily, Henry II's youngest daughter, Joanna, had not seen her brother Richard for more than ten years. He had been raised to rule in the French and English territories of the Plantagenet family. She was sent away at the age of eleven to marry the Sicilian king, William II, "the Good." He was heir to his father, William I, a physically intimidating man with a massive black beard and such strength in his forearms that he could bend two horseshoes straight. By contrast, William II was neither a strongman nor a fighter—but he was an enthusiastic supporter of the crusading cause.[24] During the 1170s William II sent ships to attack Saladin in Alexandria and Ifriqiya; he fitted out galleys every summer to patrol the seaways for the safety of pilgrim ships; and after the fall of Jerusalem he instructed his grand admiral, Margaritus of Brindisi (the heir in spirit to Roger II's *ammiratus ammiratorum* George of Antioch) to take a fleet to support the Franks holding out in isolated cities like Tyre and Tripoli on the Palestinian coast.[25]

By the time Richard arrived on Sicily in 1190, King William was dead, having passed away in Palermo the previous autumn. He and Joanna had no surviving children, so on William's death power had been seized by his cousin Tancred, an illegitimate grandson of King Roger II. Tancred was praised by one Anglo-Norman observer as "cunning" or "farsighted," but defamed by the Italian polemicist Peter of Eboli, who made great play of his short stature and unattractiveness, calling him an "unhappy embryo and detestable monster," nature's laughing-stock, a monkey-king and "a man that looks like a miscarriage."[26] When Tancred seized Joanna's late husband's crown, he did her the grave dishonor of confiscating the lordship of Monte Sant'Angelo—a rich parcel of territory Joanna had been awarded to provide her with a private income—along with various precious items that had been gifts from her father, including a golden table twelve feet long, a large dining tent, twenty-four golden dining plates and a fleet of warships. Unfortunately for the monkey-king, Joanna's brother Richard did not take theft from his family lightly.

Richard crossed the Strait of Messina on September 23, arriving outside that city with great pomp and military circumstance. "The whole sea was covered by galleys full of competent men, fighters, bold of countenance," flying pennons and banners, wrote the chronicler Ambroise.[27] Those crusaders who had traveled to Sicily by way of the Spanish peninsula already had blood in their nostrils, having stopped on their journey to help the Portuguese king Sancho I fight the Almohads before sacking the Christian city of Lisbon. Using the excuse of rioting by the so-called "Griffons" of Messina—Greek-speaking citizens who took deep exception to the unruly crusaders—Richard let his troops off the leash. On October 4 he raised his war banner—a giant standard bearing the image of a dragon—and marched against the city, reduced the gates to splinters with a battering ram, and swept into the streets. In a matter of hours, Richard's men had "captured all the fortified places up to Tancred's palace," terrifying the French king, Philip, who had arrived on Sicily ahead of Richard and was staying in apartments nearby. Tancred and Philip could only watch, helpless, as English banners were raised on Messina's walls and engineers outside the gates started work on a wooden fortress that they nicknamed "Griffon-Batterer."[28]

Faced with this live military demonstration by a king who "knew nothing better than storming cities and overthrowing castles"—Tancred quickly repented his misdeeds. Joanna was reunited with her brother, who sent her to stay in Calabria while he negotiated the return of her rightful possessions. In the end Tancred paid twenty thousand ounces of gold in compensation for the lands and treasure he had snatched and was allowed to keep his throne. By Christmas Day peace had been restored sufficiently that Richard could hold a celebratory feast in the hall of "Griffon-Batterer." While he overwintered on Sicily an oracle told him he was fated to defeat Saladin and eject the Muslims from the Holy Land. The spring sailing could not come quickly enough.

Richard and Joanna left Messina to continue their journey to "the abused land of God" on April 10, 1191.[29] They sailed amid an armada refreshed by the winter break. "The sun had never risen over such a rich fleet," wrote Ambroise—but not everyone was happy.[30] Ten days earlier Philip Augustus had left Sicily in high dudgeon. He was deeply perturbed by Richard's high-handed actions in Messina, and his ire was fueled all the more when it emerged that the English king had decided to cancel his betrothal to Philip's sister Alix. The couple had been contracted to marry since childhood, but Richard had now changed his mind, arranging instead to wed the Spanish princess Berengaria of Navarre, a descendant of the great Reconquista king Alfonso VI of Castile and León. Berengaria was hand-delivered to Sicily by the elderly and magnificent Eleanor of Aquitaine—who knew full well what it was like to be a young bride on crusade. In repudiating Alix, Richard made the outrageous allegation that the girl had slept with his father, Henry II, while being raised as a ward in the English royal household. Once more, the French king could do little, except acquiesce and fume. But repercussions of these romantic and political insults would become horribly apparent as the crusade unfolded.

After leaving Sicily, storms separated the English fleet at sea, and before long Joanna found herself the cause of another fight. She and Berengaria had traveled east aboard the transporter ships known as busses. After about a fortnight at sea they put into port at Limassol on Cyprus only to find it already overrun with battles between the crews of English ships that had either docked at Limassol to take on supplies or been shipwrecked off the coast. Joanna and Berengaria were deeply wary of disembarking in case they should be taken prisoner by the ruler of Cyprus, Isaac Komnenos.

The women's caution was well founded. Isaac was described by one English chronicler as a "tyrant," "the most wicked of all bad men," who "surpassed Judas in faithlessness" and had supposedly made a pact of friendship with Saladin, sealed when the two rulers drank each other's blood.[31] This was not merely the anti-Greek slander customary to Latin writers. On the death of Manuel Komnenos in 1180 and the accession of his fourteen-year-old son, Alexios II, Byzantium had descended into a catastrophic period of contested rule, coup, countercoup and foreign invasion from the Balkans to Asia Minor. Taking advantage of this chaos, Isaac had taken command of Cyprus and began to rule it like an old-fashioned autocrat, torturing and mutilating his people with abandon. Even Byzantine chroniclers castigated him him for his opportunism and cruelty, describing him as a "hot-tempered wretch," and a "hideous and accursed lecher" who committed "unjustifiable murders by the hour."[32]

When Richard landed at Limassol on May 6 to find his crusaders skirmishing with Isaac's troops, and his sister and bride-to-be cowering on their ship, he wasted no time. He stormed ashore, beginning a lightning fifteen-day campaign in which he seized control of all of the island's major cities and several castles, and captured both Isaac and his favorite daughter. The tyrant of Cyprus was clapped in silver manacles (as befitted his pretended status of emperor) and imprisoned for life.[33] The campaign was so straightforward that Richard had time to pause in the midst of it and marry Berengaria of Navarre. But the wedding celebrations were brisk. Richard had not taken his crusading vows in order to have a party on Cyprus. He made plans to sell the island to the Templars (who in their turn later sold it on to the exiled Guy of Lusignan, the king of Jerusalem defeated at Hattin). Then on June 7, 1191, the English king boarded a galley at Famagusta and cast off for the Holy Land. Joanna and Berengaria had again gone ahead aboard the transport ships. The first target of their crusade lay just three days away. They were heading for the siege of Acre.

By the time Richard set sail from Cyprus, Acre—which had fallen to Saladin after the battle of Hattin—had been under siege by crusader forces for nearly two years. As the most important mercantile city on the coast and hitherto the entrepôt for Italian traders and Frankish pilgrims to the crusader states and caravan trails of the Near East, it was a prize second only to Jerusalem, and it was guarded by a garrison of Ayyubid soldiers more than three thousand strong, led by Saladin's veteran lieutenant Qaraqush. Camped on a hill called Tell al-Ayyadiyya, a few miles to the east, was the sultan himself, with an army that fluctuated in size depending on how many soldiers from his widely recruited army he could keep in the field at any one time. Between them, trying to maintain a landward blockade of Acre in the hope of starving it into submission, were Guy of Lusignan and an army composed of survivors of Hattin, troops mustered from the county of Tripoli and principality of Antioch, first responders to the preaching of the Third Crusade and a Genoan fleet maintaining a beachhead on a strip of coast to the north. Guy—who had been fortunate to be ransomed by Saladin* following his capture at Hattin—had lost his wife when Queen Sibylla died of camp fever in 1190 during the

*Guy was extremely lucky to have his freedom. Saladin's decision to release him after Hattin was an act of low political cunning dressed up as high chivalry. Calculating that the widely disliked Guy would cause more trouble among the Franks as a free man than in an Aleppan jail, Saladin had let him go on the promise that he would not attack any Muslims. Guy broke his promise almost immediately.

siege. He was also at a loss as to the best way to break a siege that had settled very early into a stalemate. He could not drive Saladin's relieving force away from its position, nor could he totally maintain a sea blockade that would starve Acre into submission. Saladin, for his part, was unable to muster sufficient strength to scatter the besiegers, who were reinforced periodically by shiploads of volunteers arriving from all over Europe, including Pisans, Flemings, Germans, Bretons, Danes, Welsh and Cornish. Yet despite the arrival of these reinforcements, which swelled the crusader army to around thirty thousand, the crusaders still lacked sufficient numbers to both defend themselves and break down the thick walls of Acre. Only the coming of the kings could break the deadlock.

The first monarch of Latin Christendom to enter the fray was supposed to be Frederick Barbarossa. His German army, reinforced with several thousand Hungarian troops, had made good progress along the land route through Byzantium, scoring a major victory over the Seljuq sultan of Rum, Qilij Arslan II, when, on May 18, 1190, they stormed and sacked his capital of Iconium.[34] Yet a little over three weeks later, on June 10, disaster struck. While swimming in the Seleph (Göksu) river Frederick drowned—apparently immobilized by a heart attack or stroke, then dragged under shallow water by the weight of his clothing. "Appalling grief and lamentation, not unmerited given the death of such a great prince, lodged in every heart," wrote a German chronicler.[35] Frederick's stunned troops carried on to Antioch under the leadership of his son, Frederick of Swabia. There, however, calamity struck again as "an unparalleled disease and pestilence struck down absolutely everyone. . . . Some died slowly, others quickly, but all fell victim to the same fate." Frederick of Swabia was among those who perished. The army scattered to the winds. After nearly a year on campaign, barely any of the Germans made it to Acre. And so the siege went on.

Philip Augustus reached Acre before Richard, on April 20, 1191, having left Sicily early in the spring, and steered clear of entanglements on Cyprus. He brought six ships and numerous impressive French nobles at his back, including the veteran Philip, Count of Flanders, and Hugh, Duke of Burgundy. Their arrival was most welcome to the weary army outside the city walls;

Philip was received, according to one French writer, as "an angel of the lord."[36] And immediately he galvanized the siege: his engineers erected a great battery of artillery pieces to hurl stones at Acre around the clock; French sappers started tunneling below the walls and ordinary pilgrims set to work filling in Acre's moat with rubble to form a platform for ladders and siege towers. One of the most famous laborers was a Christian woman sadly unnamed in the sources, "who worked without stopping . . . encouraging others as she went." According to the melodramatic author of the *Itinerarium Peregrinorum*, "while this woman was busy depositing the load of earth she had brought, a Turkish sniper shot her with a dart [i.e., a crossbow bolt], and she fell writhing to the ground. As she lay groaning with the violence of her pain, her husband and many others came running to her side, and in a weak voice she tearfully begged [them] for a favor." She demanded that after her impending death her corpse should be thrown with the rest of the ballast into the moat, "so that I can feel I have achieved something."[37]

Richard and the English crusaders reached Acre on June 8, amid even greater rejoicing than had greeted Philip—who briefly put propriety above personal resentment and helped Queen Berengaria ashore. Among the rank and file of the crusader army, trumpets, horns, pipes and cornets blared, wine was poured and songs sung. Huge bonfires blazed in celebration. "All were full of hope," wrote the chronicler known as Ambroise.[38] And with good cause. Richard brought twenty-five galleys, thousands of men and barrel-loads of treasure, which he distributed liberally among the besiegers. Even before landing at Acre his fleet had sunk a massive Ayyubid transporter ship intending to run the sea blockade, destroying in the process nearly one thousand infantry, seven emirs, a huge cache of weapons, one hundred camels and two hundred poisonous snakes to be deployed as biological weapons. "The king was the outstanding man of his time for bravery, cunning, steadfastness and endurance," wrote Ibn al-Athir. "In him the Muslims were tried by an unparalleled disaster."[39] Ibn Shaddad agreed: Richard was "a mighty warrior of great courage and strong in purpose."[40]

Richard's troop surge was only slightly offset by the fact that from the middle of June both he and Philip were laid low by camp fever and a strange, scurvylike condition called arnaldia, which caused hair and fingernails to drop out and teeth to loosen. Saladin, on hearing of this, chivalrously sent ice and daily deliveries of fresh fruit to the crusader camp. But his generosity was not reciprocated. Throughout June an artillery battle raged, with two massive crusader catapults—nicknamed "Bad Neighbor" and "God's Stonethrower"—battling one known as "Bad Cousin," operated by the city garrison. Sappers continued burrowing beneath the walls, targeting a large fortification called the Cursed Tower. Defenders on the walls burned siege engines with Greek fire. All the while, an exchange of the usual insults and small arms continued, in which no victory was too petty to cheer. Ibn Shaddad reported with glee the news that two of Joanna's Sicilian servants—who were like many Sicilian palace eunuchs, secret followers of Islam—deserted and went over to Saladin's camp. He also recorded the sultan's surprise at receiving as a trophy the wooden bow taken from a female crusader known for wearing a striking green cloak. While fighting off a raid by Saladin's troops on the besiegers' camp, she had wounded several of the sultan's men with her arrows before she was overpowered and killed.[41]

Increasingly, however, small victories were all that the Ayyubids had to celebrate, for Philip and Richard's arrival meant the end to the siege was now close at hand. Under tight naval blockade the city was beginning to starve. The besiegers had dug in their camp so deeply, with palisades, trenches, earthworks and armed guards, that there was no hope of Saladin driving them away. On July 3 sappers brought down a massive section of Acre's walls, and the following day the garrison sued for peace. Following eight days of fractious negotiations, conducted against the continuing rumble of flying masonry and the sound of miners tunneling beneath the Cursed Tower (which also collapsed, on July 11), terms were agreed. Acre was to be handed over, the True Cross returned, several thousand prisoners exchanged and 200,000 bezants delivered to Richard and Philip by the sultan. The terms were sent off to Saladin for his ratification. Meanwhile, the keys to the city were produced. The crusader army, with hymns and exultations on their lips, flooded in.

The fall of Acre in July 1191 might have been the end of the Third Crusade—and indeed, for many of Frankish leaders it was. Dividing the spoils of the city and restoring to the many interested parties—Genoans, Pisans, Venetians, Templars, Hospitallers and the rest—their possessions, districts, tax breaks and commercial privileges was a difficult task. Quarrels broke out among the various factions of the army. Leopold, Duke of Austria, took particular offense at his poor recompense for surviving the Germans' crusade to assist at Acre, and after seeing one of his banners trampled in the mud, apparently by one of Richard's followers, he left Acre for his homeland, cursing the English king all the way.

He was followed by Philip Augustus. The French king's stockpile of grievances had grown even higher during the siege of Acre. He deplored Richard's high-handedness, his easy dispensing of patronage, his differing views on strategy and his preference for Guy of Lusignan's claim to be recognized as king of Jerusalem over that of Philip's own ally and candidate, Conrad of Montferrat, ruler of Tyre. Enough was enough: as Acre fell Philip decided he had more than satisfied his crusading vow and took his leave, returning to France, where he planned to attend to domestic affairs and stir up trouble among Richard's dominions in the West. "On leaving he received more curses than blessings," wrote Ambroise. Although many of his men stayed, Philip had had his fill.

Richard did not abandon Acre. Taking a broader view of his crusade obligations, he began to plot a campaign that would exploit the momentum gained at Acre and push on to recover the whole kingdom of Jerusalem. On August 20, having tired of waiting for Saladin to return the relic of the True Cross, pay his bounty and ratify the peace agreed on with Acre's garrison, Richard marched twenty-six hundred unarmed and bound prisoners of war onto the plain before Acre and executed them all—an act of despicable cruelty, excessive even by the standards of the day, which, if technically legal, has been described as a war crime.[42] Yet atrocity was part of the fabric of twelfth-century warfare. Saladin and many before him had sold prisoners into slavery and ordered mass killings of prisoners. There was precious little time for thoughts of human rights on either side.

After the butchery at Acre, Richard and his refreshed army marched out of Acre and aimed south, heading down the coast road to Jaffa, and beyond it, Jerusalem. In the next three weeks they inched their way seventy-five miles down the coast, provisioned and protected by their fleet on their right flank, dodging native wildlife including aggressive tarantulas and knight-eating crocodiles, while fending off repeated raids and attacks from Saladin's army, who tracked them on their left flank. Ahead, Muslim garrisons abandoned castles and cities and razed the defenses to render them militarily obsolete and damagingly expensive to restore. Around the halfway point, at Arsuf (Arsur) on the fiercely hot morning of September 7, the two sides contested a great pitched battle, described by one chronicler as "bitter tribulation," in which Saladin threw all his units, including black Africans and Bedouins, against Richard's lines, hoping to scatter them and force a disorderly retreat.[43] But through Richard's steadfast leadership and a series of perfectly timed heavy cavalry charges, the crusaders won a resounding victory. Three days later they liberated Jaffa and negotiations began for a truce.

Despite the long, hot, tough campaign, not everyone in the crusader ranks favored a negotiated peace—least of all Joanna, who traveled by sea from Acre to Jaffa once the latter city had been conquered. In the early stages of talks, Richard discussed terms in person over a meal with Saladin's brother al-Adil (Saphadin), who impressed him. A few days later, the king suggested a deal in which Jerusalem would remain under Ayyubid control but be opened freely to Christians, who could worship at designated shrines and churches, while the other Palestinian coastal towns would be handed back to the crusaders. It would be sealed by the marriage of al-Adil and Joanna.[44] Whether Richard was entirely serious is hard to say. Joanna was appalled. Al-Adil and Saladin were merely amused. After six weeks of consideration the plan fell by the wayside and peace talks broke up.

Richard subsequently marched a crusader army on Jerusalem twice: coming within sight of the Holy City in December 1191 and again in the spring of 1192, concluding on both occasions that he lacked sufficient manpower to repeat the effort of 1099 and take the city by force. The last stage of this campaign finally proved beyond him. Moreover, politics among the Franks were becoming murderous—literally so. Elections among the Eastern-born Latin nobles to appoint a new king of Jerusalem to replace Guy of Lusignan resulted in the choice of Conrad of Montferrat, who was married to Amalric's sole surviving child, Isabella. Conrad nursed a longstanding rivalry with Guy of Lusignan—Richard's choice for reinstatement to the crown—and there were many who saw the English king's hand at work when, a few days after Conrad's election, the Italian was ambushed by night and murdered by two assailants sent by Rashid al-Din Sinan, the head of the Nizari Ismaili Assassins, nicknamed "the Old Man of the Mountain."

By the summer of 1192, then, Richard's time in the East was coming to an end. He had been away from his kingdom for more than two years, and news from the West suggested that his feckless younger brother John was conniving against him with Philip of France. It was time to go home. After a final victory over Saladin's troops in battle on the beaches at Jaffa, on August 8, a truce was sealed, under which the coastal cities between Jaffa and Acre were returned to Frankish rule and Christian pilgrims were granted access to the Holy City for the purposes of worship. The new capital of the crusader kingdom would be Acre. Economic fact thus trumped religious idealism: a sustainable strategy for survival in the hostile territory of the East, but a decision that would change forever the nature of the crusader kingdom. Richard had not won back all that had been lost, and he had not quite combined the houses of Ayyub and Plantagenet in dynastic union—but his intervention in the Third Crusade had still been decisive. If nothing else, for years to come, Muslim mothers would scare their unruly children with the dire threat that if they did not behave, King Richard would come and get them.

On his way back to England, Richard's missteps in the crusader kingdom finally rebounded on him. Shipwrecked in the Balkans, he tried to travel home incognito overland but was captured by Leopold of Austria, still sulking about his treatment in Acre. Leopold handed Richard over to the new Holy Roman Emperor, Henry VI, and in 1194, after more than a year in prison, the English king was ransomed back to his people for the massive fee of 100,000 pounds of silver. Once released, Richard spent much of the rest of his reign fighting Philip Augustus, their natural rivalry as rulers of neighboring territories heightened by the personal animus that had germinated in Sicily and Acre.

Fortunately for Joanna and Berengaria, Richard sent them West in a separate sailing, and they arrived safely in Brindisi before the end of 1192, only learning of Richard's captivity when they paid a visit to a new pope, Celestine III, in Rome. Following in their footsteps was another veteran of the East: Margaret of Beverley, who had fought Saladin with a saucepan on her head before any of the more illustrious ladies had even dreamed of wars in the East. Richard's intervention in Acre and his restoration of Christian access to the holy sites had allowed Margaret to complete her extended pilgrimage and return with a boatload of English pilgrims from liberated Acre. She continued her pious travels, visiting Rome and Santiago de Compostela before tracking down her younger brother, Thomas, in his monastery at Froidmont, regaling him with her extraordinary adventures and settling down to her own life contemplative, as a nun in the Cistercian convent at Montreuil, later known for its possession of the relic of the holy veil of Saint Veronica.

Berengaria survived Richard, seeing almost nothing of him during the remainder of their marriage, bearing him no children and spending much of her adulthood sponsoring religious building projects in Le Mans. Joanna, meanwhile, having spurned marriage to al-Adil, missed her opportunity to be the wife of a sultan: for al-Adil ultimately succeeded his brother as ruler of Syria and Egypt after Saladin died on March 4, 1193.[45] Perhaps not entirely rueful, Joanna remained in the West and instead married Raymond VI, Count of Toulouse, great-grandson of the famous first crusader of the same name who had founded the county of Tripoli. Their short marriage produced a future count (Raymond VII) and much excitement. Joanna had learned from her time with her brother's crusading armies, and shortly after the birth of her son, in 1197, she commanded a siege of a castle held by rebels against her husband.

Nor was that the end of her adventures. When Richard died besieging the castle of Chalus-Chabrol in the spring of 1199, having sustained blood poisoning after a crossbow bolt struck him in the shoulder, Joanna, pregnant once again, ordered the man who made the fatal shot to be flayed alive. It was a typically Plantagenet way to signify the affection in which she held her brother, and it was Joanna's last major political act. The princess herself died in childbed in September of the same year and her remains were taken for burial next to Richard's, in the family mausoleum at the Abbey of Fontevrault in Anjou.

◆ 20 ◆

Consumed by Fire

There never was so great an enterprise undertaken by any people since the creation of the world.

Enrico Dandolo became Doge of Venice in June 1192, when he was around eighty-seven years old. Dandolo was blind, and had been for many years. Rumor said he lost his sight when he fell foul of the Byzantine emperor Manuel Komnenos during a visit to Constantinople in the 1170s; according to the whispers, the emperor had Dandolo tied up and burned his retinas out with sunlight beamed from polished glass. Although macabre—and given the inventive cruelty that sometimes prevailed at the imperial court in Constantinople, plausible—the story was not true. During his long career in the service of the Venetian Republic Dandolo had certainly spent time around emperors. But it was not Manuel Komnenos who had taken his sight.[1] Rather, as Dandolo told the French knight and chronicler Geoffrey de Villehardouin, he suffered a bang to the back of his head in 1175, which caused his vision to fail over the course of a year.[2] This was inconvenient, and meant he had to be led about on his horse, but it was not a fatal impediment to the old man's career.[3] Despite his disability and his great age, after he was elected doge Dandolo would serve for more than a decade as the leader of the most ambitious maritime state in the Adriatic—a power broker who held in his hands the fate of emperors and kings.

Venice had appeared, as if bubbling up from its lagoon at the northern tip of the Adriatic, around the sixth century CE. By Dandolo's day it was a proud, pious and rich aristocratic republic, ruled by an elected doge and council and cautiously respected by the other major powers in its sphere: Rome, Byzantium and the Holy Roman Empire. The city was home to sixty thousand souls, living on a network of islands clustered around the Rialto, which was bisected by the Grand Canal and identified from afar by the handsome, late-eleventh-century Basilica of Saint Mark, modeled on the Church of the Holy Apostles in Constantinople. Venice's greatest treasure was Mark's body—stolen from the Egyptian city of Alexandria in 828 CE by enterprising merchants who smuggled it past Muslim customs officials, hidden in a barrel of pork.

In its earliest years Venice was built on salt production, agriculture and fishing, but a spectacular boom during the eleventh and twelfth centuries stemmed from mastering the seas. Venetian ships—swift, sleek fighting galleys equipped with vicious battering rams and manned by teams of thickly muscled oarsmen; and fat, high-masted sailing ships that moved commodities and cash from port to port—could be seen everywhere in the Mediterranean. Like the other northern Italian maritime powers, Pisa and Genoa, Venice sold its military capability on the open market, trading seaborne violence for commercial advantage. In the 1080s, Alexios I Komnenos struck a deal in which Venetian galleys targeted Norman shipping, and Byzantine ports and markets were opened up to Venetian merchants tax-free.[4] In the twelfth century Venetian galleys patrolled the Levantine coast on behalf of crusader kings; in 1124 crusaders from Venice helped seize Tyre and earned the right to establish independent mercantile colonies in every city in the Frankish East.[5] The consequent wealth and prestige thrust Venice to the fore of European politics: a status confirmed in July 1177 when the city hosted a spectacular peace conference between Frederick Barbarossa and Pope Alexander III, in which the Holy Roman Emperor publicly bowed to kiss the pontiff's toes in Saint Mark's Basilica. Barbarossa had suggested Venice as a suitable venue for this pageant on the grounds that it was "subject to God alone."[6]

The Dandolo clan had risen in tandem with the republic, and their success was reflected in their luxurious compound in the center of the Rialto, stretching away from the bank of the Grand Canal. By Enrico's day, the family had served the city conspicuously for nearly two centuries. Domenico Dandolo established the family name in the early eleventh century through trade missions to Byzantium, including one visit where he acquired for Venice the relics of Saint Tarasios. Enrico's father, Vitale Dandolo, had been a close adviser and judge to the doges Vitale II Michiel (who held office from 1155 to 1172) and

Sebastiano Ziani (from 1172 to 1178). His uncle, another Enrico, was patriarch of Grado—the preeminent cleric in Venice and an energetic reformer of the Venetian Church. Both Vitale and the elder Enrico were crusaders who took part in the 1124 assault on Tyre.

The younger Enrico, for his part, made his name as a diplomat. He visited Byzantium in 1171 as part of an armed expedition that sought recompense when Manuel Komnenos stripped Venetians of their trading rights and imprisoned about ten thousand merchants. This was a dreadfully ill-fated mission, which ended in disaster, as the Venetian sailors caught the plague, limped home to Venice bringing the disease with them and faced a populace so angry that they stabbed the then-doge to death in the streets. Dandolo, however, emerged unscathed, and in 1174 and 1175 he was in Egypt, first to seek a conference with William II of Sicily and then to explore the possibility of a trade deal with Saladin. In the 1180s he was once again in Constantinople, dealing with the political fallout from the "massacre of the Latins": rioting against wealthy Westerners, in which thousands were murdered and a papal legate's head was cut off and tied to a dog's tail. Enrico may have been sightless and elderly when he was elected doge, but long experience and his calculating, pragmatic demeanor suited the republic's needs well. In his oath of office he promised to "consider and attend to and work for the honor and profit of the Venetians in good faith and without fraud."[7]

The first nine years of Dandolo's reign were busy, for his duties were many and varied: doges were expected to judge legal cases, set economic policy, oversee foreign diplomacy and relations with the Church, and much else besides. But even as he passed his ninetieth birthday Dandolo discharged these duties with vigor and verve. He passed strict laws limiting the immigration of new merchants into the republic. He oversaw improvements to Venice's complex legal code. He fundamentally reformed the Venetian coinage, introducing a new coin known as the *grosso,* struck from 98 percent pure silver.* He conducted a steady stream of diplomatic correspondence with successive

*In an age in which coins minted elsewhere in the Mediterranean world—from the kingdoms of the West to Byzantium and the Ayyubid states—were declining sharply in their precious metal content, the introduction of the *grosso* was a stroke of economic genius, which made Venetian money the most reliable and desirable currency for international trade.

Byzantine emperors in an attempt to restore the working relationship that had existed decades earlier. As the twelfth century drew to a close, Dandolo could regard his term in charge of Venice with some satisfaction. Business was booming, and the republic was thriving. Then, in early 1201, six envoys from France appeared from the passes down from the Alps, presented themselves at the doge's court and offered Dandolo the deal of a lifetime. And suddenly, everything changed.

The envoys who arrived to call upon Dandolo in February 1201 represented three of the most powerful lords in France: Theobald, Count of Champagne, Louis, Count of Blois and Baldwin, Count of Flanders. (One of these envoys was Geoffrey de Villehardouin, who was selected in his capacity as the marshal of Champagne, and kept a vivid account of the negotiations.) Their lords, said the envoys, had been inspired by papal preachers urging a new campaign to complete the work of the Third Crusade by reclaiming the Holy Sepulchre and the city of Jerusalem. All were young men: Theobald was twenty-one; Louis and Baldwin were twenty-eight. In common with most young men of their class, their minds were alive with the ideals of knightly chivalry, which was flourishing in the courts and banqueting halls of Western Europe, celebrated in popular ballads of heroes real and imaginary, ranging from King Arthur to the first crusaders.[8] All came from families of storied adventurers in the East, and all of their territories had long been fertile recruiting grounds. Theobald could even claim a king of Jerusalem among his siblings: his elder brother Henry went crusading, married King Amalric's youngest daughter, Isabella, in 1192 and became the king consort of Jerusalem until 1197—when he fell to his death from a window at the royal palace in Acre.[9]

The preaching that had so excited Theobald, Louis, Baldwin and their contemporaries and peers had been commissioned by another youthful ruler: Pope Innocent III, who was elected pope in 1198 at the tender age of thirty-seven. Born Lotario dei Conti di Segni, Innocent was a high-handed aristocrat with a long-bridged nose and a neat, bushy mustache beneath it. He was a brilliant lawyer and a gifted theologian-philosopher. More than anything he had a gift for persuasion—be it by cajoling or harangue—and in 1198 he used this talent to convince fighting men like Theobald, Louis and Baldwin that they ought to be leading their generation in a new assault on the Holy Land. In a masterly bull published just seven months after his election, known as *Post Miserabile*, Innocent had bemoaned in familiar terms "the wretched fall of

Jerusalem . . . the deplorable invasion of that land on which the feet of Christ had stood . . . the ignominious removal of the life-giving cross."[10] He had spelled out in precise, legalistic detail all the worldly and spiritual benefits of crusading. And most stirringly, he framed the call to crusade in high chivalric terms, casting the loss of Jerusalem as a personal affront to the reputation and honor of all vigorous young Christian warriors. Innocent imagined the intolerable slander that must have been pouring ceaselessly from the mouths of the Ayyubids as they celebrated their preeminence. "They are saying: 'Where is your God, who can neither deliver himself nor you from our hands? Behold! Now we have profaned your sanctuaries. Behold! Now we have extended our hands to the things you most cherish. . . . Already we have weakened and broken asunder the lances of the Gauls, baffled the efforts of the English, crushed the strength of the Germans, and . . . subdued the haughty Spaniards. . . . Where then is your God?' "[11] Fiction this may have been—but it was a pitch-perfect appeal to the knightly classes of Western Europe at the turn of the century; a call that chimed perfectly with the attitudes and obsessions prevalent among early-thirteenth-century warriors.

By the time the envoys of Theobald, Louis and Baldwin arrived in Venice, momentum was gathering behind Innocent's call for a Fourth Crusade. Among the ordinary people it was said that the devil had been born in Babylon—meaning Cairo—and that if nothing was done then very soon the world would come to an end.[12] In France this mood was excited further still by preachers like Fulk of Neuilly, an unusually gluttonous priest well known around Paris with a talent for public speaking and miraculous deeds; or the Cistercian abbot Martin of Pairis, who on May 3, 1200, preached a famous sermon at the Cathedral of Saint Mary in Basel in Alsace in which he railed against the domination of the Lord's Sepulchre "by the barbarism of a heathen people."[13] Others—including Theobald and Louis—had taken their crusader vows while on the field of combat, during a tournament held by Theobald in the fields around his castle of Écry on November 28, 1199.*

*Despite being severely frowned upon by the Church for their endemic violence and celebration of secular vanities, tournaments were a vital expression of knightly culture at the turn of the thirteenth century. Tournaments at this time had romantic elements, and were lively social occasions, but they were also dangerous affairs: full-blooded mock battles fought between huge teams of knights ranging over miles of open countryside in which bones were cracked and lives sometimes lost. See Richard

Sworn crusaders included the counts of Brienne, Amiens, Saint-Pol and Perche and the bishop of Soissons as well as dozens of barons' sons, adventurous knights and hundreds of lesser men. Contingents of barons and churchmen were also beginning to stir in the German empire, despite the fact that a German crusade to assist in recapturing Beirut and Sidon in 1197 and 1198 had ended in confusion, and the Holy Roman Emperor Henry VI died while attempting to impose himself as king of Sicily (which he claimed to rule as a result of his marriage to the old king Roger II's daughter Constance).

However, while crusading enthusiasm was spreading, the crusader lords had serious logistical challenges. No Western monarch deigned to lend his name to the movement—Philip Augustus was loathe to repeat his misadventures of the previous decade; Richard the Lionheart's successor as king of England, his younger brother King John, was far too occupied with defending his lands on the continent from Philip's depredations to concern himself with the plight of the Jerusalemites; and the Germans had lost their previous two rulers on crusade and were now squabbling over who ought to be king. Without the resources of a royal patron, the lords needed to engage another wealthy European power to their cause—ideally one with crusading experience and the wherewithal to move troops and matériel about the Mediterranean. They needed ships and military advisers, which was why they had come to see Dandolo. As Villehardouin put it: "In Venice they might expect to find a greater number of vessels than in any other port."[14]

For Dandolo, the coming of the envoys gave him much to ponder. Their proposal was alluring—and dangerous. Both the Republic of Venice and the Dandolo family stood to gain much in the way of potential plunder, mercantile advantage and pious reputation from a crusade. But when the doge opened talks with the envoys, the numbers they proposed were mind-boggling. Villehardouin and his companions spoke of raising an army of more than thirty thousand fighting men. That would mean chartering hundreds of ships—fifty galleys and three times as many transport ships—most of which would have to be built from scratch in the Venetian shipyards known as the Arsenal. Crewing such a fleet would mean mustering literally half the able-bodied men

---

Barber and Juliet Barker, *Tournaments: Jousts, Chivalry and Pageants in the Middle Ages* (Woodbridge, UK: Boydell Press, 2000), 13–27.

of the republic. It would easily be the biggest military contract in Venetian history. Dandolo told the envoys it was not something that he could simply agree to on a whim. But he was intrigued enough to take the request to the council, and for eight days Venice's power brokers retired to debate the cause. Eventually they came to a decision. They would help—at the level requested—assuming the people of Venice agreed.

At the end of the month ten thousand Venetians gathered in and around the Basilica of Saint Mark and, after hearing Mass, cried their support for the doge and council. Venice, they agreed, should build, supply, crew and provision the gigantic armada, large enough to carry thirty-three and a half thousand crusaders and four and a half thousand horses to the East. They would devote to this cause not only the shipyards at the Arsenal, but virtually the entire city's resources for a year. They would draw lots to select the one man in two from the populace who would be required to serve on board the ships. In return the crusaders committed to pay eighty-five thousand marks—a sum equivalent to twice the annual revenues of the whole kingdom of France—and grant Venice a half share of everything and everywhere they seized on campaign.[15] Secret terms set the first destination of the crusade as Alexandria in the Nile Delta, on the understanding that the wealthy city would be a soft target—Egypt was struggling with famine and dearth brought on by five successive years of failed Nile floods—and a sensible strategic precursor to a push northeast into Palestine.* A date was set for the whole army to assemble in Venice in the spring of 1202.

This was an extraordinary gamble by both sides. The French envoys had employed at a huge cost the finest naval power in the West and sworn on holy relics to raise an army to fill the fleet they had chartered. Dandolo and the Venetians had agreed to divert the entire resources of the republic to a single military enterprise, which would either be the most lucrative expedition since the conquest of Tyre in 1124 or would leave the republic bankrupt. Both sides knew how high the stakes were. When the treaty was ratified, emotions ran high. "For pity many a tear was shed," wrote Villehardouin. "And straightaway

*Grinding a path to Jerusalem via conquests in Egypt was a policy advanced but not realized by Richard the Lionheart. The crusaders had also to consider the fact that the kingdom of Jerusalem had agreed a long-term truce with the Ayyubids that techinically precluded a direct assault on Jerusalem but did not cover crusader attacks on Egypt.

messengers were sent to Rome to Pope Innocent that he might confirm this covenant—which he very willingly did."[16] Meanwhile, the Venetians set to work. The Fourth Crusade was under way.

After a year of frantic hammering, sawing, planing and caulking in the Arsenal, the Venetians produced the "goodliest fleet that was ever yet seen," consisting of about two hundred galleys, warships and transport busses. Mass purchasing of wine, meat, cheese and horse fodder on the markets of Italy had filled the transporters with all the necessary supplies. But the crusader army that began arriving in Venice in the early summer of 1202 and set up camp on the long sandbank known as the Lido was not the one that had been so confidently promised. For a start, Count Theobald of Champagne was dead, having succumbed to a fever in May 1201. In his place, the middle-aged, northern Italian Boniface, Marquis of Montferrat, had been offered, and accepted, overall command, although he would not join the crusade for many months. The army that did arrive represented only a small fraction of the vast one envisaged. Across northern France there had been a surge of activity as men and women took the cross, stockpiled goods and weapons, mortgaged their lands, made gifts to local religious houses to ask for their blessings ahead of the long and uncertain journey.[17] But the sum total of all this activity had not even vaguely matched the bold projections made to Venice. Not only did recruitment fall short of the huge numbers promised; many who did take the cross decided that navigating the Alps to muster in the lagoon was an unnecessary chore when they could travel to Marseille, Genoa or southern Italy and take a berth on the regular spring sailings to Acre. Dandolo had gambled on the crusaders keeping their side of the bargain.[18] They had not, because they could not. Less than one third of the promised crusader army showed up; they were outnumbered two-to-one by the Venetian crews. Worst of all, their leaders could not afford to pay the full eighty-five thousand marks contracted for the Venetians' efforts. They had a little over fifty thousand.

This was nothing short of a crisis. The Venetians had toiled for a year, at huge cost, and were now facing ruin. Dandolo had to act. He was acutely aware of the need to navigate a course of action that would salvage the impending financial disaster faced by his fellow citizens, while also allowing the crusaders to save face by at least leaving port. So he came up with a bold solution: as a first stop on their journey, they would alight fewer than two hundred miles from Venice itself and plunder the port of Zara.

To Dandolo and his fellow Venetians there was every reason to feel justified in this course of action. Zara (Zadar), on the Dalmatian coast, had at one time owed tribute and obedience to the republic, but since rebelling in the 1180s its leaders claimed to be under the lordship of the Christian king Emeric of Hungary. This blatant breach of loyalty, argued Dandolo, deserved to be punished. But for lords of the French contingent, such as Simon of Montfort, diverting so far from the original object of the crusade was unconscionable—not least because Emeric was a Christian king obedient to Rome, who had himself taken his crusader vows. Innocent had suspected that at some point Dandolo might try to use the crusader fleet to punish Zara and had specifically warned him not to attempt to do so. Now the doge was proposing direct insubordination. The summer months—intended for a glorious assault on Alexandria and then, God willing, Jerusalem—passed in debate, dissent and mass boredom among the ordinary troops. Eventually, in the first week of October—the last possible sailing date before the seas turned impossibly rough—the leaders realized they could prevaricate no longer. It was a choice between sailing to Zara or going home. They chose the lesser of the two evils. The doge took his crusading vows in front of a large congregation, having his cross pinned to his hat rather than sewn on his shoulder. Some time later, to the sound of trumpets and drums, his massive fleet, comprising fifty large transport ships, sixty war galleys, one hundred horse transporters and many other light craft towed in their wake, moved out of Venice onto the open sea.[19] Dandolo's galley, decked out in vermilion cloth and silver, was the very last to leave. He was never coming home.

When the fleet arrived from Venice outside the port of Zara on November 10 and 11, 1202, the citizens unfurled banners bearing crosses on the walls to remind the Venetians and French that they, too were crusaders. Dandolo did not care. Ignoring howls of protest from his crusader clients, he ordered an assault. Venetian galleys broke through the chain that secured the city's port. Troops disembarked and launched a catapult bombardment and set sappers to work on the city walls. Inside Zara the citizens panicked, begged peace terms after three days and eventually opened the gates on condition that they would be spared a massacre. Little blood was spilled, but when the Venetians and the French moved in, they plundered what they pleased before occupying half of the city each and settling in for the winter. Dandolo would later justify his actions in Zara as perfectly legal. The writer Gunther of Pairis called it a "detestable business."[20]

Many others agreed. When news of the crusaders' deviation from their mission reached Innocent III, he was enraged. In his fury he reached for the most terrible sentence available to him: he excommunicated everyone involved. There was bitter irony here. Every person who had joined the crusade had done so assuming they would be forgiven their sins; now, should they die on their journey, they would be going straight to hell. The crusade leaders did their best to suppress news of the pope's pronouncement, which would have caused mutiny among the rank and file; envoys rushed back to the papal court to beg Innocent to reconsider, on the grounds that "necessity was an extenuating factor."[21] Innocent eventually and grudgingly agreed, but he sent stern commands that such abominable actions should not be repeated. The crusaders, he wrote, were henceforth "neither [to] invade nor violate the lands of Christians in any manner."[22] But Dandolo and the Venetians could scarcely have cared less. When they left Zara in spring 1203 they pulled down the walls and burned everything but the churches to the ground. Then they set out East. Yet the armada was heading not for Acre or even Alexandria. The target—incredibly—was Constantinople.

Byzantine affairs, tied up with the crusading movement since its earliest inception, had become bloody and fraught during the 1190s. Richard the Lionheart, alighting on Cyprus on his way to Acre in 1191, had witnessed the turmoil spreading across the empire as rule was contested between rival branches of the Komnenoi. Ten years later Byzantium was as troubled as ever. In 1185, Isaac II Angelos—a minor prince, amiable and well meaning but best known for his addiction to lavish building projects, perfumed baths and expensive clothes—had seized the throne of Byzantium. For ten years this "dandy [who] strutted like a peacock and never wore the same garment twice" held on to power, but in March 1195 he was toppled in a coup by his elder brother Alexios III Angelos, who had Isaac blinded and imprisoned for life, on a simple diet of bread and wine.[23]

Alexios III very soon had cause to regret taking the throne, for his reign descended into a string of crises in which the empire was attacked at all points by the Seljuqs of Anatolia, Hungarians, Bulgarians and Balkan peoples known as the Vlachs. As he tried to cope with these assaults, Isaac II's teenage son, also called Alexios, busied himself planning revenge. In 1201 the boy escaped the empire in disguise and fled to the West, lodging at the court of Philip, Duke of Swabia, king of the Germans, who was married to his sister Irene Angelina. Alexios was no more than nineteen years old when he fell into Philip and Irene's orbit, and was judged by almost everyone who met him as hopelessly immature, easily given to frivolity and drunkenness. Nevertheless, in Germany he had a platform from which to engineer his uncle's downfall, and he used it. At Philip of Swabia's court in 1201 he met the crusaders' leader Boniface of Montferrat and planted the seed of a truly terrible idea.

As the Venetian and French crusaders overwintered in Zara in 1202 and 1203 they received ambassadors from Prince Alexios, who offered an incredible deal. If they helped the young man regain his father's imperial throne, said the messengers, then Alexios would place the entire Byzantine Empire under obedience to the pope, pay a fee of 200,000 silver marks, join the crusade in person or send ten thousand troops to join the eventual march on Alexandria and maintain for the rest of his life five hundred knights (a force roughly equal to the entire mounted capability of the Templars in the East) to defend the kingdom of Jerusalem.[24] This astonishing offer would not only solve the crusaders' financial problems at a stroke; it would offer the real possibility of destroying the Ayyubids for a generation. These were, promised young Alexios, "the best terms ever offered to any people."[25]

Like all offers that seem too good to be true, Alexios's deal was a tightly wrapped package of bravado and lies. Bitter quarreling raged throughout the crusading army between those who could see this and those who would not. The more sensible heads among the crusaders—including Simon of Montfort and Renaud of Montmirail—now abandoned the crusade in disgust and made their own way to Syria. "It seemed to them foolish and wrong for a small band of pilgrims . . . to forsake their intended holy pilgrimage and to declare war, with its certain danger, on such a city, so fortified and populous, in order to accommodate a stranger," wrote Gunther of Pairis. "This war could not be concluded without a good deal of carnage on one side and, possibly, on both."[26] But Conrad of Montferrat, Baldwin of Flanders, Louis of Blois and Hugh of Saint-Pol accepted the prince's offer, hoping that they could count on the simple anti-Greek prejudice of ordinary crusaders, who had long been fed a narrative of Byzantine treachery as the source of past crusader failures, and thought of Eastern Christians as effeminate and depraved: "scum of scum."[27] Critically, Dandolo also committed, for little about his predicament had changed. He had invested the fortunes of his republic so deeply into the misadventure that he had no choice but to keep going.

On April 25, 1203—the feast day of Saint Mark—Prince Alexios arrived in Zara to join the crusade. In the early summer he and the fleet had weighed anchor, pillaged Corfu, rounded the Peloponnese and headed toward the Dardanelles. As they closed on Constantinople they passed two ships carrying "pilgrims and knights and sergeants" who had answered Innocent's call, set off from Marseille instead of Venice, completed their vows by fighting for a year in the kingdom of Jerusalem and were going home. "When they saw our fleet so rich and well appointed they conceived such shame that they dared not show themselves," wrote Villehardouin. But his words rang very hollow.[28]

On June 23 the fleet arrived within view of Constantinople, the sight of which was as magnificent as it had always been. An awestruck Villehardouin marveled at the "high walls and strong towers . . . and the rich palaces and mighty churches."[29] The Queen of Cities had been ill-governed under the indolent regimes of the Angelos brothers, but it was still the most enormous and stoutly defended metropolis west of Baghdad, as well as the holiest east of Rome—with the relics of nearly five hundred Christian saints in its many churches.[30] Villehardouin realized the enormity of what the crusaders had agreed to do. "No man there was of such hardihood but that his flesh trembled," he wrote. "And it was no wonder, for there never was so great an enterprise undertaken by any people since the creation of the world."[31]

Having arrived at Constantinople, Dandolo advised the crusaders not to attack immediately but instead to wait awhile and plunder nearby islands for provisions. They took his advice, and the next fortnight passed in a form of phony war. But on July 10 the great enterprise began, with an amphibious landing from the Bosphorus and an assault on the suburb of Galata, where a fortress controlled the great chain that sealed off the Golden Horn, the inlet that provided access to the eastern stretch of Constantinople's seawalls and gave access to the landward defenses running away south from the Blachernae Palace. Armed resistance from Greek troops sent out by Emperor Alexios III quickly melted. At sea the Venetian galleys swept through a squadron of Greek triremes, while on land a large division of foot soldiers and cavalry disembarked and forced their way into Galata, where they let down the chain and allowed the whole fleet to enter the Golden Horn. The young pretender Alexios was paraded before the curious citizens who peered from the top of Constantinople's walls. The overwhelming reaction to his arrival was scorn.

During the next week, the crusaders disembarked their ships, built a camp and erected siege engines. Then on July 17 they began a "horrendous battle . . . fraught with groaning on both sides."[32] The French used battering rams to smash the walls around the towering Blachernae Palace, doing battle with native Greek soldiers, Pisan mercenaries, and members of the Varangian Guard bearing battle-axes. The Venetians attacked the city from the water. As they did so, they provided one of the most famous scenes in the history of crusading. As battle trumpets sounded, the aged, blind Dandolo stood on the prow of his vermilion-covered galley, with the Venetian banner showing a winged lion of Saint Mark fluttering behind him. Then the galleys beached, disgorged their crews and began an attack on the shoreline.

Meanwhile, the larger transport ships, covered with oxhides to make them resistant to Greek Fire, sailed as close as they could to the seaward defenses, latched on to the walls using grappling hooks, then winched scaling ladders across from the ships' masts to the ramparts. These formed high, precarious "flying bridges," along which attackers with a head for heights could run and try to scramble onto the city's towers. Using these, Venetian and French troops "engaged the defenders on the towers and easily routed them."[33] Having secured a section of the wall, they then set fire to the houses below it, starting a blaze that destroyed a swath of the northern quarter of city, from the Blachernae Palace to the monastery of Evergetes nearly two miles away. As night fell, the city was alive with flames, screams and angry yells of the populace, outraged that Alexios III had not been able to defend them. Alexios, however, decided he had seen enough. When darkness fell, he collected one thousand pounds of gold and as much treasure as his servants could carry, and ran away. The very next morning his blind brother, Isaac, was taken out of prison and restored to the throne he had lost eight years previously. Twelve days later, on August 1, the crusaders sent Isaac's son Alexios into the city, where he was crowned co-emperor, assuming the regnal name of Alexios IV.

The fall of Constantinople was cheered by the crusaders as a miracle.

Against all the odds, and despite their dissensions and self-doubt, God had smiled on them. Count Hugh of Saint-Pol, still thinking in the chivalric terms encouraged five years previously by Innocent III, wrote home to boast of his achievements. "If anyone wishes to serve God . . . and wishes to bear the distinguished and shining title of 'knight,'" he wrote, "let him take up the cross and follow the Lord, and let him come to the Lord's tournament, to which he is invited by the Lord himself."[34] But Hugh's high spirits would soon evaporate. The crusade was far from over.

Two immediate problems faced the co-emperors and the crusaders who had restored them to power. First, the citizens of Constantinople were close to mutiny. Second, the imperial treasury did not contain the 200,000 silver marks young Alexios IV had promised. It was not long before trouble was brewing once more. On August 19, 1203, riots broke out against Latin Christians in the city, spurred by the emperors' desperate policy of looting churches for religious icons and ornaments to be melted down to pay the crusaders. In retaliation, a party of Westerners led by Venetians attacked a mosque that served Muslims in Constantinople under imperial protection. Soon rioting turned into running street battles and once again the crusaders chose fire as their best defense. An even bigger conflagration was now lit that tore through the entire city, "from sea to sea," destroying more than four hundred acres of ancient temples and palaces, houses and public monuments, marketplaces and judicial courts, and threatening both the Hagia Sophia and the Hippodrome. It was, wrote the proud Greek Niketas Choniatēs, simply "horrendous."[35]

Equally horrendous was the predicament in which the new emperor Alexios IV still found himself. Unable to pay the crusaders' fee, yet with considerable use remaining for their military assistance as he launched forays into the lands around Constantinople to impose his authority on Thrace and the wider empire, he had contracted them to remain camped across the Bosphorus at his command until April 1204. But the longer the crusaders stayed unrewarded the more agitated they became. By the time winter set in, payments to the French and Venetians had dried up and relations had broken down completely. In a stormy meeting held between Dandolo and Alexios at the harbor in December 1203, the doge warned the emperor that his ingratitude and double-dealing were leading them all into serious trouble. Alexios tried to brush him off and Dandolo flew into a rage. "We have dragged you out of the dunghill, and into the dunghill we will cast you again!" he shouted.[36] He was not joking.

Events now moved quickly. An attempt on New Year's Day in 1204 to burn the Venetian fleet at harbor in the Golden Horn made it plain that war was approaching. Meanwhile, inside the city, opposition to the emperors who had literally brought barbarians to the gates boiled over with regular outrages against public order. Inside the palace an opposition faction, including members of the Varangian Guard, began to gather around the nobleman Alexios Doukas "Mourtzouphlos" (his nickname referring to his oddly overhanging eyebrows). And at the end of January, when the elder Emperor Isaac died, most likely of natural causes, Mourtzouphlos seized his moment. He and his supporters arrested Alexios IV and threw him into the palace dungeons, shackled by his ankles. The crusaders, led by Dandolo, sent increasingly furious messages demanding their wayward ally's release and the honoring of his obligations—ideally in the form of the 100,000 marks still outstanding on their account. In response, on the night of February 8 Mourtzouphlos had Alexios strangled and—according to the rumors that reached Baldwin of Flanders in the crusader camp, personally disemboweled the young man with an iron hook. He took the imperial crown for himself, as Alexios V Doukas, and sent the crusaders a blunt message. If they did not "depart and vacate his land" within a week, he would "slay them all."[37]

As emperor, Mourtzouphlos made urgent provision to repair and improve Constantinople's already considerable defenses, for he realized that war was now looming. Both sides spent much of Lent arming themselves, and both convinced themselves of the inevitability of victory. They could do little else: with Alexios dead, the crusaders could only extract the payments he had promised at Zara by deadly force; Mourtzouphlos could only secure his throne by proving he could defend the imperial capital.

The fighting began on Friday, April 9, 1204. The Venetians immediately tried to repeat the trick of scaling the city's walls and towers with flying bridges. But the task was not so easy as it had been the previous year. The towers had been reinforced, the wind blew against their ships, and from inside the city came a barrage of Greek fire and huge rocks hurled by catapults. It seemed there was no hope of finding a way past. The crusaders were forced to withdraw and regroup. During a weekend spent in camp, preachers assured them of the righteousness of the cause. But on top of the ramparts the Byzantine defenders "began to hoot and to shout right lustily," pulling down their trousers and contemptuously waggling their buttocks.[38]

Unfortunately for the gleeful buttock-barers, on the afternoon of Monday, April 12, the wind changed direction and their hooting abruptly stopped. Now the Venetian crews managed to sail their ships directly up to the city walls. Two ships—the *Paradise* and *Pilgrim*—were lashed together with flying bridges jutting from both their mighty masts. At last, crusaders swarmed across. The first man on the walls, a Venetian, was butchered by Varangian axes. But behind him came too many attackers for the Byzantines to hold off. As French and Venetian flags were raised above the towers, down below a hole was punched in the walls at a bricked-over gate. The die was cast. By the time darkness fell, Constantinople was on the brink of collapse.

Now, not for the first time, a Byzantine emperor fled. In the dead of night Alexios V took a fishing boat across the Bosphorous and abandoned the city to its fate. When dawn broke and the remaining nobles and military commanders realized what had happened, they sent out the most senior clergy in the city to beg for a peaceful surrender. They were whistling in the wind. The crusaders had come to Constantinople in search of riches. They had camped outside its walls for nearly a year on the promise that reward would come. Now they would embrace the chance to plunder the richest city in the West.

Rhapsodizing about the appalling destruction that the Venetians and French alike wrought on Constantinople during the days after its fall on April 13, Gunther of Pairis wrote:

> Break in! Now, honored soldier of Christ, Break in!
> Break into the city that Christ has given to the conqueror.
> Imagine for yourself Christ, seated on a gentle ass,
> The King of Peace, radiant in countenance, leading the way.
> You fight Christ's battles. You execute Christ's vengeance,
> By Christ's judgment. His will precedes your onslaught.[39]

This was stirring for his audience, no doubt. But as another chronicler, Niketas Choniatēs, watched his city fall, he was struck by the awful banality of the sack. There were no divine portents, he wrote. No bloody rain or fiery stones falling from the sky. There was merely a lot of crime. "On the day on which the City fell, the despoilers took up quarters in the houses spread out in all directions, seized everything inside as plunder, and interrogated their owners as to the whereabouts of hidden treasures, beating some, holding gentle conversations with many and using threats against all."[40] Rape, theft, arson and sacrilege were commonplace. Hundreds of holy relics, including a shroud in which Christ had been wrapped, His brother's preserved head and the Virgin Mary's robe were all taken as bounty.[41] (Among the treasures seized by Venetian looters were four beautiful bronze horse statues, created in the second or third century CE, which were stolen from the Hippodrome and sent back to Venice, where they are still proudly displayed at Saint Mark's Basilica.) Choniatēs saw his ruined neighbors standing around "ashen in complexion, their faces corpselike and their eyes bloodshot, shedding more blood than tears."[42] In the Hagia Sophia a prostitute from the crusader camp sat in the patriarch's throne and danced around the altar. The capital of Byzantium had fallen, and with it, the Greek empire itself was no more.

Alexios V did not survive long after fleeing his city: in the autumn of 1204 he was captured, blinded, brought back to Constantinople and hurled to his death as a traitor from the Column of Theodosios in the old Roman forum. By that point a new emperor had been chosen: Baldwin of Flanders was raised up as Baldwin I, the first Latin Emperor of Constantinople. Baldwin was elected after Enrico Dandolo declined the post, and he had the modesty to try to refuse the appointment himself. But on May 16 he was crowned. It was scarcely an outcome he could have predicted when he first took the cross four years earlier. But the Lord worked in mysterious ways.

Dandolo, having turned down an imperial crown to remain a doge, wrote to Innocent III in 1205 to recount his version of events. Innocent, fuming but helpless, had absolved the crusaders of their misdeeds, but Dandolo knew the pope was not pleased that his crusade, billed as a tournament against the infidel, had turned into a persecution of fellow Christians. Innocent refused to let the doge consider his crusading vow complete. In protest, Dandolo told Innocent he had become a crusader to fight for Jesus Christ and the Roman Church, and claimed that everything he had done from building the fleet that transported the fourth crusaders to destroying a Christian empire that had lasted more than eight hundred years had served that aim.[43] He sensibly played down the fact that the Venetians had come out very well from their rampage around the Christian East. When the spoils of Constantinople's plunder were accounted, Venice had finally made its money back.[44]

Reflecting on the terror and the carnage, the flames and the murder that had been inflicted on Constantinople during the events of 1203 and 1204, Niketas Choniatēs heaped much of the blame on Dandolo's shoulders. The ancient Venetian was, he wrote, "a sly cheat who called himself wiser than the wise and, madly thirsting after glory as no other, he preferred death to allowing the Romans to escape the penalty for their insulting treatment of his nation."[45] Choniatēs thought the whole torrid affair was a secret plan concocted by Dandolo and a cabal of villains in the Venetian lagoon as revenge for insults dating back to the 1170s and 1180s—when many of those who took part were still children.[46]

Whether this was fair or not, in the end it was hard to judge the Fourth Crusade—forged and facilitated by Venice and her doge Dandolo—as anything other than a disaster that perverted every principle of the crusading movement: carving out a new Latin state from Christian territory, doing appalling damage to one of the greatest cities in Christendom, dragging the reputation of crusading through the mud and enriching rather than tormenting the Ayyubids. As Constantinople burned, Alexandria had remained untouched, while Damascus, according to the Islamic chronicler Abu Shama, was actively beautified with marble looted from churches in Constantinople and sold to Muslim traders in Syrian and Egyptian markets.[47] True, the crusaders now had a bridgehead from which to launch attacks on the Syrian coastline. But for all the blood shed and money spent, they had singularly failed to even threaten Egypt, let alone Jerusalem.

A year after the fall of Constantinople, Enrico Dandolo was still in the new Latin Empire, which was—perhaps predictably—under attack on all sides. True to character, he was engaged in more schemes: buying the right to conquer the island of Crete along with a handful of bad debts from Boniface of Montferrat, and securing for Venice a handsome share in the carving up of Byzantium that proceeded as the Fourth Crusade dissolved. In the partition Venice claimed valuable properties along the coastal littoral of Byzantium, from Durazzo to the Peloponnese, including the islands of Corfu and

Kefalonia. Dandolo himself received the odd but not inaccurate title of "lord of three-eighths of the Roman Empire."

He was occupied with defending this three-eighths of an empire and assisting Baldwin in his wars to subdue the enraged and exiled Greeks when he died, aged ninety-eight. His death was agonizing: the rigors of the campaign left him with a hernia, in which a part of his intestine dropped and became lodged in his groin, causing a fatal infection. He was buried in Constantinople at the Hagia Sophia—the only person ever to be laid to rest there. The ancient doge had ensured that his and Venice's name would be forever remembered in the history of crusading and of the affairs of the great Christian empire of the East. He had bravely defied his physical disability and his decrepitude, and his pragmatic leadership and dauntless personal valor were beyond question. Yet in the end Dandolo had turned his talents to a wholly disreputable end, playing a leading part in a dreadful episode that, even by the cruel standards of the crusading era, thoroughly deserved the epithet leveled against it by Choniatēs: "Outrageous."[48]

◆ 21 ◆

Enemies Within

Wounds that do not respond to the healing of poultices must be lanced with a blade.

Far away from the fire and fury of Constantinople, in the miserable Baltic winter of 1205 to 1206, Albert, bishop of Riga, put on a mystery play. As a medium for spreading the word of God among the ordinary people of Christendom, mystery plays could be very effective. Actors took on the roles of characters from Bible stories and re-created the miraculous events of divine history, accompanied by commentary or song. Mystery plays were a colorful, dramatic way for the illiterate masses to absorb the events and messages of the Bible and they were popular all over Europe. But Bishop Albert—an ambitious but incorrigibly greedy prelate with a stronger instinct for diplomacy and statecraft than the care of souls—saw a particular use for them in his newly established bishopric of Riga, an ancient trading port in Baltic frontier country: not only to entertain and educate the faithful, but to engage those who had never heard, or cared about, the word of Christ in the first place.

The play Albert staged in 1205 and 1206 was for the benefit of a pagan people known as the Livs. The Livs were part of a large group of Finnic tribes who dwelled in a region of the northeastern Baltic around the Gulf of Riga, known as Livonia (roughly equivalent to modern Latvia). According to one Christian poet-chronicler, the Livs were "haughty pagans" whose great aim in life was to "take the lives and goods of Christians."[1] But another chronicler, Arnold of Lübeck, described Livonia as "abundant in riches" and "never lacking in servants of Christ and planters of the new Church." The unchristianized sweep of lands that lay between the German lordships and the Orthodox Christian realm of Rus'—comprising modern Estonia, Latvia and Lithuania—were fertile and productive, rich in fur, wax, timber, fish and amber, and highly attractive to enterprising merchants and ambitious churchmen looking to expand their dioceses. The only problem was the people who lived there. The Livs and their neighboring tribes—the Letts and Estonians to the north and Selonians, Semgallians and Lithuanians to the south—were lukewarm at best about receiving the word of the Lord and submitting to the taxation and discipline of the Roman Church. Under duress they might convert, if it meant saving their lives or striking a short-term deal with Christian militias to attack a rival tribe. But even under these circumstances the Livs would usually renounce Christ as soon as the opportunity arose, jumping in the closest river to wash away the stain of baptism. Bishop Albert was determined to show them what they were missing.

Unfortunately for Albert, his mystery play went down badly. According to the chronicler Henry of Livonia, a missionary priest who wrote up his version of events in the Baltic a couple of decades later, the story performed by Albert's actors was too close to the bone for its pagan audience's tastes. For years, the Livs had endured annual raids into their territory by Christian warriors from Germany and Scandinavia seeking to convert them at the point of a sword. They knew that those who came to Christianize also came to plunder, massacre, drive away cattle, burn crops and pull down houses—and although they fought back as ferociously as they were attacked, the experience had undoubtedly been traumatic. Recently the raiders had been spearheaded by roughneck members of a new military order called the Brotherhood of the Knighthood of Christ in Livonia—or simply the Swordbrothers. They had been founded by the knights of Albert's household in 1202. The Swordbrothers wore uniforms modeled on those of the Templars—white mantles emblazoned with a red cross and sword—and they lived comparably austere lives, cohabiting in drafty barracks, dining on cabbage and devoting their lives to prayer and killing in roughly equal measure.[2] According to one disapproving writer, the Swordbrothers were criminals "who expected to live on their own without law or king."[3] Their chief purpose was to ensure the conversion or eradication of Livs and other pagan people, and secure under Christian rule the valley of the Dvina (Daugava) River, which emptied into the sea at Riga. The Swordbrothers went about their work with bloody efficiency, grinding their way up the Dvina valley mile by mile, bullying or bribing as they went, building hill forts and watchtowers in anticipation of Christian colonists, Cistercian monks and missionary priests following in their wake.

The Livs who were persuaded to watch Bishop Albert's mystery play were already, therefore, ill-disposed to its message. They especially disliked the play's gory battle scenes, depicting the army of Gideon fighting the Mideanites.[4] This clash of swords was inspired by events from the Old Testament book of Judges, and it was recreated by the bishop's troupe with too much gusto. For the assembled Livs, the sight of three hundred holy warriors smiting indiscriminately in the name of their God was a painful reminder of incidents they had experienced in real life. Only recently rumors had arrived from further south suggesting fifty Lithuanian women had hanged themselves in despair after their husbands were killed by Christians.[5] Panic spread, and before the play could be completed, the audience had run away.

In Rome, Pope Innocent III knew little of the specifics of mystery plays and Livs. But he understood well enough, and approved wholeheartedly of, the fact that on the chilly fringes of northeastern Europe a holy war was taking place against unbelievers. Of course, it was nothing new. Ever since the assaults on the Wends of 1147, would-be crusaders in northern Germany had been allowed to substitute a difficult journey to fight Muslims in Palestine, Egypt or Spain with battling pagans closer to home—so long as they claimed to be defending converted Christians from oppression.

This remained as tenuous a piece of theological gymnastics as it ever had been, but sixty years of military activity had been enough to justify crusading on the basis of tradition. And one of Innocent's first acts as pope had been to ensure that this continued. In the first year of his papacy he confirmed that anyone who underwent a pilgrimage to protect newly converted Livonian Christians could consider themselves a crusader, with all the attendant spiritual benefits. He reconfirmed the grant in 1204 and would do so again in 1215, when he encouraged Christians in the Baltic to sally forth "against the barbarians to fight for the new plantation of the Christian faith."[6] In 1209 he wrote to King Waldemar II of Denmark, urging him to "confound with their idols the filth of the pagans. Fight this battle bravely and strongly like an active knight of Christ."[7] Innocent's enthusiastic support for crusading in the Baltic helped foster a popular local belief that Livonia somehow represented the promised land and was specifically under the patronage and protection of the Virgin Mary.[8] Soon reports of miracles were filtering back from the front line of the campaign to clear, colonize and convert pagan lands. The dead ceased to rot. The lame learned to walk again.

In one sense the Livonian crusade, and subsequent expeditions against the Estonians and other pagans, was simply a small part of a long push by Danish, German and other Scandinavian lords to extend their power over the non-Christian Baltic lands, often at the expense of trading rivals from Rus' and elsewhere in the east. But in the context of Innocent III's papacy, however, repeated grants of crusader status for warriors like Bishop Albert's Livonian Swordbrothers represented something different and more ambitious still. For under Innocent's guidance, crusading became not only a matter of defending the far-flung boundaries between the Latin Christian world and the realms of Islam, but as a political tool to coerce secular rulers everywhere to do the pope's bidding. During his eighteen years as pope, Innocent proclaimed six crusades and inspired a seventh. Not one of them reached Jerusalem.[9] Indeed, the most notorious of Innocent's crusades (after the debacle of the Fourth Crusade to Constantinople) occurred not thousands of miles away from Rome, but in the kingdom of greater France, as Church resources were directed and Christian warriors were stirred up against a sect known as the Albigensians, or Cathars.

The Cathars, unlike the Livs or the Estonians, were not pagans. Rather, they were heretics, who in the eyes of the Church had deviated from the teachings of Christ to adopt a foolish and perverted set of beliefs about the origins of the world and the nature of divinity. Catharism was a Christian dualist belief system, which held that as well as a beneficent God there was another, evil Creator, identified either with Satan or the God of the Old Testament. While the good God was responsible for all things spiritual, the cruel and sinful physical world was Satan's work. Catharism sprang in part from the teachings of the Bogomil Church, which appeared in the Byzantine Balkans from the tenth century and sent missionaries to the Rhineland, southern France and

Italy from the 1140s to the 1160s. But Catharism was not simply Bogomilism in exile. By the time the heresy put down roots in the realms of the Christian West it had become a phenomenon peculiar to itself.

Cathars (the name derived from the Greek *katharos*, meaning "pure" or "clean") believed that fallen angels stolen from Heaven by the evil God had been trapped in corrupt bodies from which they could only be released by strict observance of Cathar doctrine and, ultimately, by partaking in a ceremonial rite known as the *consolamentum* (comforting), a form of adult baptism after which the candidate's soul was considered to have been freed, and he or she became one of the priestly class known as the *perfecti* (or in the case of women, *perfectae*). Ordinary Cathars (*credentes* or believers) were expected to live by the rites and teachings of the Cathar Church, which was as hierarchical as the Roman Church, maintaining bishoplike elders and acolytes (known as elder and younger sons), observing rites such as confessing sins, blessing food, preaching and prayer. Most *credentes* would only take the *consolamentum* when they were close to death because the *perfecti* and *perfectae* lived intensely and impractically ascetic lives, at least as harsh as those of the most rigorous Cistercian monks. What little food they ate was strictly vegetarian; they abstained from all sexual contact and abhorred pregnancy and childbirth. They were in that sense part of a broader movement around the turn of the thirteenth century toward orders of living that concentrated on extreme poverty, preaching and self-denial: other groups on the spectrum included the Waldensians (followers of Peter Waldo of Lyon, who were declared heretical and viciously persecuted), the *humiliati* (a northern Italian order of poor preachers who were eyed with suspicion by the Church authorities but not suppressed) and the Franciscans (wandering friars who followed the example of the pious merchant's son Saint Francis of Assisi and were warmly embraced by the Church after 1209).

At the core of Cathar belief was an institutionalized disgust for the human body. The theological implications of this made it impossible for a Cathar to believe that Jesus Christ could possibly have been the living incarnation of the good God; it also made taking the Eucharist impossible. This was about as heretical as it was possible to be—and the Cathars placed themselves even further outside mainstream Christianity by their unconcealed contempt for the apparent worldliness, avarice and corruption of the Roman Church, and their forbidden penchant for translating religious texts including the Vulgate

Bible out of Latin and into vernacular tongues. Yet this was no secret sect: Cathars pursued their errors in plain sight, with halls of residence for *perfecti*, study and worship groups for *credentes* and graveyards for their dead.[10]

At the Third Lateran Council—a grand parliament of the Church convened in Rome in 1179—Catharism was described as a "loathsome heresy," "wickedness," "error" and "sin."[11] But neither official insults, nor preaching missions undertaken by Cistercian monks had been able to prevent Catharism taking root among ordinary people across Western Europe, particularly in regions where secular power was contested or weak; its heartlands were the Midi and Languedoc regions of southern France, in and around cities such as Toulouse, Carcassone and Albi—from which the name "Albigensian" derived.

One of Innocent's priorities as pope was to beat Catharism and other heresies back and restore the unity and orthodoxy of the Church. For the first five years of his reign he kept up a relentless campaign directed at senior bishops across the West for what he perceived as their slackness in sniffing out heretics who were "entangling innumerable people with their snares and . . . corrupting them with the yeast of falsehood."[12] When this did not yield acceptable results, Innocent decided to engage the blunt instrument of the warrior classes. He wrote in 1207 to Philip II Augustus of France, telling him that "the perverseness of heresy . . . gives birth continually to a monstrous brood . . . and a detestable succession of criminals emerges." He had tried, said Innocent, to reason with the heretics. But "wounds that do not respond to the healing of poultices must be lanced with a blade."[13]

Innocent's anger toward heretics, and his frustration that few around him seemed to share it, could be measured in a letter he sent to the citizens of Viterbo in central Italy when in 1205 they elected several Cathars to the city council. "If the earth should rise up against you, and the stars of heaven should reveal your iniquity and manifest your stains to the whole world . . . so that not only humans but the very elements themselves would join together for your destruction and ruin and wipe you from the face of the earth . . . even that punishment would not be sufficient," he railed. "You have rotted in your sins, like a beast in its dung . . . we believe the Lord himself is moved to nausea."[14] He sent a particularly severe missive to Count Raymond VI of Toulouse—the great-grandson of the famous First Crusade leader who had established the county of Tripoli in the East—in which he lambasted the count for allowing heresy to flourish in his territories: "What pride swells your heart, what madness captures you, oh pestilent man?"[15]

Yet until 1208 it appeared that Innocent's was a lone voice, crying into a heretical wilderness. Although he offered crusade privileges to knights who would help bring to justice Cathars and other heretics in southern France, and passed laws in lands ruled directly by the papacy commanding that heretics' houses be torn down and all their goods confiscated, the intransigence of rulers like Raymond of Toulouse made his task impossible. Raymond was not himself a Cathar—he was a patron of the Knights Hospitaller and a personally orthodox follower of the Roman rite. But many of the lesser baronial families who made up the landed society of the county of Toulouse were indeed either *credentes* or patrons of the Cathar Church, and there was very little Raymond could do to reverse this trend, even after he was excommunicated twice, in 1207 and 1208. Raymond could not have stamped out Catharism in Toulouse even if he had wished to do so—and he did not appreciate the high-handed manner in which missives and messengers from Innocent's court tried to railroad him into doing so.

Then, in the first days of 1208, a single violent act provided the pope with the opening he needed. On January 13 a papal legate, Peter of Castelnau, met Count Raymond at the Abbey of Saint-Gilles to implore the count to heed the papal agenda. Raymond as usual paid no attention, and the two men quarreled bitterly, exchanging insults before parting. Having set out for home that evening, Peter camped overnight by the banks of the river Rhône, around ten miles from Saint-Gilles. The next morning he had scarcely finished hearing Mass when a knight from Raymond's retinue appeared, speared him through the back with his lance and fled, leaving Peter to die on the riverbank. It took about six weeks for the news of this savage deed to reach Innocent in Rome, and mere days for Innocent to declare Peter of Castelnau a martyr in the tradition of the murdered English archbishop Thomas Becket. The pope blamed Raymond—whom he denounced as a servant of the devil, "crafty, slippery and inconstant"—directly for Peter's death.[16] And from this point on Innocent's letters against heresy, sent to the great lords and princes of the West, had real bite. The heretics and their protectors had shown their true intent, he said. They were violent, treacherous murderers, more dangerous even than the Saracens. "The perverters of our souls have also become the destroyers of our flesh," railed the pope. It was incumbent on all Christian soldiers to join him in exterminating them.

In June 1209 a crusading force gathered in Lyon. It had been recruited by Cistercian preachers working the northern parts of France above the river Loire, traditionally fertile crusader country and a region geographically, culturally, linguistically and temperamentally far removed from the Occitan-speaking, sunbaked and sensuous Languedoc. The army—which initially numbered perhaps five thousand cavalry and twice as many others—included veterans of the Third and Fourth Crusades, and lords such as Odo, Duke of Burgundy, and Henry, Count of Nevers, who, despite the fact that they despised one another, were nevertheless two of the most powerful noblemen in France. Both arrived with the blessing of the French king Philip II Augustus who, since returning from his uncomfortable experience on the Third Crusade in 1191, had devoted his efforts to imposing the power of the French Crown on areas of the greater kingdom, where traditionally it had been weak. In 1204 he had evicted the Plantagenet king of England, John, from almost all of the latter's French possessions, thereby restoring to supervision of the Capetian crown the duchies of Normandy and Brittany, counties of Anjou, Maine and Touraine and much of Aquitaine. Languedoc, and the county of Toulouse in particular, had traditionally been another bastion of resistance to French overlordship; in offering his tacit support to Innocent's crusade against Count Raymond, Philip rightly calculated that another troublesome part of his kingdom might be brought into line.

Unmistakable and unmissable among Philip's vassals who joined the crusader ranks was Simon of Montfort, ruler of a small lordship near Paris centered on the forest of Yvelines.[17] This was the same Montfort who had taken the cross at Theobald of Champagne's tournament of Écry in 1199, abandoned the Fourth Crusade in high dudgeon when it was at Zara, and fulfilled his vows by traveling independently to Syria to campaign against the Ayyubids. Montfort was fanatically pious, bloody minded and zealous, a highly capable military leader who could galvanize men behind him. He put the fear of God, quite literally, into his foes. Peter of les Vaux-de-Cernay, a Cistercian monk who knew Montfort well and joined him on his crusading adventures, described him as "tall, with a splendid head of hair and fine features . . . broad-shouldered with muscular arms . . . agile and nimble of hand and foot, quick and active . . . eloquent of speech . . . of impeccable chastity . . . eager to set about a task, tireless in completing it and totally dedicated to the service of God."[18] Less starstruck observers might have added that Montfort was stiff-necked and stubborn, a zealot and an implacable brute, whose severity was exceptional even by the standards of his age. Montfort also nursed an aristocratic inferiority complex: although he was, in Peter of les Vaux-de-Cernay's words "of illustrious birth," the lordship of Montfort was a second-rate patrimony at best, and his claim through his mother to a share in the prestigious English earldom of Leicester had proven impossible to secure, given the fractious politics of England and France during the reign of King John.* His piety therefore bled into a hunger for property and noble title and he would use his part in the Albigensian Crusade to feed this craving.

On June 24 Montfort and the other crusaders, including the papal legate Arnaud Amaury, set off down the Rhône from Lyon into Cathar country, to teach Raymond of Toulouse and the heretics he protected a severe lesson. But they were disconcerted as they traveled to learn that Raymond had preempted their arrival by making peace with the pope. In a ceremony at the Abbey of Saint-Gilles the count had apologized for his errors. A papal legate ceremonially whipped him on his bare back before Raymond was paraded in public before the coffin of the murdered Peter of Castelnau. Temporarily, at least, the count's willingness to humiliate himself stayed the hand of the crusaders. Instead they decided to attack Raymond's twenty-four-year-old nephew and neighbor, Raymond-Roger Trencavel, Viscount of Béziers and Carcassone.

The crusader assaults on those two cities, which began on July 22, demonstrated what violent passions Innocent had aroused. At Béziers the citizens refused to hand over their Cathars, having heard of summary burnings of men and women suspected of heresy as the army approached. So after a short siege the town was taken by storm, and an indiscriminate massacre ensued, in which women, children and clergymen who had fled to the city's churches were pulled out from their hiding places and killed. Arnaud Amaury reported back to Innocent that twenty thousand people had died, the vast majority of

*Montfort was a vassal of Philip Augustus, with whom King John of England was fighting a bitter and protracted war. Although in 1207 Simon briefly inherited many of the lands of the earldom of Leicester, these were almost immediately confiscated from him by John, who took the lands and their revenues for himself. Simon's famous son, Simon of Montfort the younger, made good the claim during the reign of Henry III.

whom were plainly not Cathars. The legate was later credited with the infamous phrase: "Kill them all, God will know his own."

After Béziers was burned to the ground, the crusaders moved on to Carcassone. Here Viscount Raymond-Roger scrambled what defenses he could, pulling down all the mills in the suburbs to prevent the crusaders from making bread to sustain themselves during a siege and ordering that the stalls of churches be dismantled and the wood deployed as a barricade. But this was as much as he could do. The crusaders arrived on August 1 and set up their siegeworks. Seeing that resistance was hopeless, on August 14 Raymond-Roger ordered the citizens to go out and beg for mercy, dressed humbly and penitentially in their undershirts, while he himself surrendered. He was imprisoned and three months later he died, still in prison, either from dysentery or foul play.[19]

With Béziers smoldering and Carcassone laid bare to be ransacked, the crusaders had finally put into action all the furious words Innocent had leveled against heresy and Catharism during the previous decade. But the crusade was far from over. For after the fall of Carcassone, the crusaders elected Simon of Montfort as ruler of Raymond-Roger's confiscated lands and the formal secular leader of the crusade. These two posts were inextricably linked. From this point onward, actions against heretics and their protectors in the Languedoc were driven by Montfort's agenda, which was arranged around two major themes. The first was to inflict as much pain and terror as possible on those who had strayed from correct religion. The second was to subdue under his own rule the viscounty he had snatched from the late Raymond-Roger, and then to start expanding his power into the county of Toulouse.

Between the summers of 1209 and 1211, Montfort single-mindedly pursued both goals. Efficiency and cruelty were his watchwords, and he was assisted in his efforts by an artful siege engineer, William, archdeacon of Paris, a renowned expert at building catapults.[20] At Minerve in the summer of 1210 Montfort bombarded the city walls with a catapult nicknamed "Bad Neighbor"—the same name Philip Augustus had given to his own trebuchet during the siege of Acre in 1191. When the walls crumbled, Montfort's army "burned many heretics, frantic men of an evil nature and crazy women who shrieked among the flames. . . . Afterward their bodies were thrown out and mud shoveled over them so that no stench from these foul things should annoy our foreign forces."[21] The following spring, when Montfort took the castle of Lavaur, one of the two authors of *The Song of the Cathar Wars* wrote that "there was so great a killing that I believe it will be talked of till the end of the world."[22] The lady of the castle, Girauda, a Cathar *perfecta*, was thrown in a well and pelted with stones until she drowned. Her brother, Sir Aimery, was hanged with eighty of his knights. Four hundred of the supposedly heretical townsfolk were burned to death in a meadow.[23] At Castelnaudary in September of the same year the crusaders defeated a combined army of Raymond of Toulouse (who despite his humiliating penance in 1209 had once more been excommunicated by the pope) and the Count of Foix. During the following year, all over the Languedoc, castles and towns surrendered.

Viciousness now characterized the war on both sides: defenders of the Languedoc patrolled the roads in gangs, kidnapping stray crusaders and gouging out their eyes or cutting off their noses. One aristocratic couple, Bernard of Cazenac and his wife, Hélis, who were sympathetic to the Cathar cause, amputated the hands and feet of suspected Montfortian sympathizers, and cut off the nipples and thumbs of their women to render them useless either for nursing or handiwork.[24] But these terror tactics did not dismay Montfort. Under his command the crusaders' numbers ebbed and flowed with the seasons: his force was sometimes reduced to no more than thirty knights, reliant on freebooting for their survival. Nevertheless, he continued to move steadily through the county of Toulouse, hunting heretics and increasing his sphere of command. His troops kept their spirits up by singing godly anthems like "Veni Creator Spiritus" while they besieged and burned and bombarded. Peter of les Vaux-de-Cernay stayed busy by compiling accounts of the miracles that seemed to them to prove God had sanctioned their deeds.

By the end of 1212 Innocent III had begun to weary somewhat of affairs in southern France. Despite Montfort's reign of terror and his promulgation in December of the Statutes of Pamiers—a set of laws that spelled out the rights of the people who now lived under his command while instituting a form of apartheid over the conquered lands in which people were divided into heretics and nonheretics and governed accordingly—Catharism had not been wiped from the earth.[25] But the pope's attention was beginning to turn to other crusading arenas. In the summer the unintended consequences of his ceaseless crusade preaching had become apparent with the appearance of the so-called Children's Crusade—in fact two separate popular movements, both of which included large contingents of young people. In the Rhineland a charismatic shepherd called Nicholas of Cologne whipped up thousands of supporters and encouraged them to follow him south across the Alps to Genoa, where he promised that the sea would part and allow them to cross to Egypt, so that they could convert the Muslims. Meanwhile in France, another young village boy, the twelve-year-old Stephen of Cloyes, raised a mob with miracle working and promised to lead them to Jerusalem. In the end, Stephen merely herded his followers from Paris to Marseille—a long journey, no doubt, but not quite a trip to the Promised Land. Nicholas, meanwhile, led nearly seven thousand people to Genoa, marching behind a T-shaped (*tau*) cross, but he was perplexed to discover that the Mediterranean would not open up before him. He took some of the German "crusaders" to the papal court, where Innocent indulged them with an audience before sending them home.

At the same time as this, Innocent was also occupied with Spain and Portugal, where since early in his papacy he had been trying to encourage the five kings of the Iberian peninsula to band together and fight the Almohads, the austere Berber sect from North Africa who had swept to power in Islamic southern Spain in place of the Almoravids. On July 18, 1195, near Calatrava (roughly halfway between Toledo and Cordoba), the Almohad caliph Abu Yusuf Ya'qub al-Mansur had inflicted a stinging defeat known as the disaster of Alarcos (al-Arak) on a combined army of Castilian knights and members of the Spanish military orders of Santiago and Évora. Almohad gains were now threatening to stall, or even to reverse the progress of the Reconquista: in the words of Ibn al-Athir, "Christendom was weakened at that time and the cause of Islam in Andalusia grew strong."[26] Impressing upon the Christian monarchs the importance of fighting the enemies of Christ rather than one another had proven unexpectedly difficult, even when Innocent proclaimed that crusade privileges were available to all who joined the struggle. But in 1212 there was finally a breakthrough. On July 16, at the battle of Las Navas de Tolosa (al-'Iqab), a combined Castilian-Aragonese-Navarrese-Portuguese army, reinforced with French volunteers and members of various military orders, surprised and routed the new Almohad caliph al-Nasir and a large expeditionary force of Berber warriors. The caliph's tent and battle standard were captured and sent to Innocent as a trophy. Al-Nasir scuttled back to Marrakesh, where he was murdered. Building on this success and using its momentum to rally a fifth great crusade to the East now became the pope's main goal, to which end he was preparing a major new crusade bull, which would become known as *Quia Major.*

Standing awkwardly in the way of this revival of conventional directions of crusading—against Almohad caliphs and Ayyubid princes—was now Montfort, whose advances in southern France had begun to vex potential crusading allies, most notably the Aragonese king, Pedro II. Ever hungry for supposedly heretical lands, Monfortian forces had overrun the lordships of Foix and Commignes, which extended into the Pyrenees and therefore owed their allegiance to Pedro, and not to the king of France. The Aragonese king (who also happened to be Raymond of Toulouse's brother-in-law) complained bitterly to Innocent, and the pope duly tried to bring Montfort into line, telling him and the legate Arnaud Amaury that "you have extended greedy hands into lands which have no ill reputation for heresy . . . it does not seem credible that there are heretics in those places."[27] But Monfort's response, when it came, was as uncompromising as ever. On September 12, 1213, he met Pedro II on the battlefield at Muret, on the outskirts of Toulouse, defeated his army and killed him. "Great was the loss, the sorrow, the disaster," wrote the author of *The Song of the Cathar Wars*. "It dishonored the whole of Christendom, it dishonored all humanity."[28] Montfort did not care. With Pedro dead and the heir of Aragon, James I, a toddler, he carried on gaily where he had left off: persecuting heretics, cannibalizing the territories of the Count of Toulouse and establishing himself as the premier lord of the French south. Innocent, who had by now published *Quia Major* and was focusing on Eastern affairs, had little choice but to acquiesce. Montfort had long since slipped out of his control.

In November 1215 Innocent convened one of the largest synods of the Western Church in history, the Fourth Lateran Council. The principal goals of this gathering were to make arrangements for the Fifth Crusade, reform and raise the general standard of living among Latin churchmen, oppress the Jews and order the ordinary faithful of the Church to take Eucharist and confession at least once a year. The council also took pains to condemn heretics to excommunication. But by this stage the pope's own direct interest in Catharism had cooled from the white heat of the previous decade, and the energy of the Albigensian Crusade had been diverted well and truly behind the Montfortian campaign of self-aggrandizement. Shortly before Lateran IV, Montfort finalized his annexation of the bulk of the county of Toulouse, which Innocent formally approved. In 1216 Montfort paid homage for Toulouse to King Philip of France, thereby bringing the greatest lordship of the French deep south into obedience to the French Crown for the first time in living memory. It was a victory for both men, and one that had been secured explicitly through the radical deployment of the holy war, as Montfort's friend Peter of les Vaux-de-Cernay acknowledged. "All those territories within his domains had been won by the crusaders from the heretics and their supporters."[29]

Simon of Montfort died, appropriately enough, while inspecting the walls of Toulouse during a siege on June 25, 1218. The city had been occupied by Raymond of Toulouse's son and successor—also called Raymond—who was not prepared to accept his father's disinheritance without a fight. As Montfort cast his eye over the defenses, a group of women operating a large catapult inside the city took a lucky shot and succeeded in landing a large rock directly on Montfort's head. He died instantly and was buried in Carcassone, the site of one of his earliest operations against the Cathars.*

Quite what he had achieved on behalf of the Church—as opposed to his property portfolio and reputation—was unclear. His immediate legacy in southern France was one of terror, endemic violence, social upheaval and a civil war that ended with the county of Toulouse deprived of its long-standing independence and yoked to a newly assertive French Crown. The problems of heresy in the Languedoc and beyond, however, had not gone away. Indeed, after Simon's death, a groundswell of resistance led by Raymond the younger of Toulouse and inadequately resisted by Philip Augustus's son and heir Louis "the Lion" (who acceded as Louis VIII of France in 1223), led to many of the lands Montfort had taken being reconquered. A long and bitter civil war in the French south was only settled in 1229, after two full decades of bloody upheaval. And despite this, complaints about Catharism corrupting the French Church echoed around the region for more than a century afterward. The movement was only truly run to ground by the persistent efforts of the Inquisition in the fourteenth century.

In the short term, the most striking beneficiary of Simon of Montfort's involvement in the Albigensian Crusade was his son and namesake, Simon of

*Some years later his body was removed and reburied at Montfort l'Amaury.

Montfort the younger, who enjoyed a career that was in its way as dramatic as his father's. The younger Simon, his reputation gilded by descent from such a famous crusader, successfully laid claim to the earldom of Leicester, married Eleanor, sister of the English king Henry III, and then turned rebel, leading an uprising in England that all-but deposed King Henry in the 1260s. In the course of his political campaign against the English Crown, Simon the younger appropriated the clothes of crusade and had his army sew white crosses onto their uniforms. He ended his days hacked to pieces on a battlefield, with his severed testicles hanging from his nose.

At the time that Simon of Montfort was crushed to death in 1218 his sponsor Innocent III had already passed on. The pope died suddenly in Perugia on July 16, 1216, aged fifty-five. He had done more to influence crusading than any pope since Urban II and his broad, pluralist deployment of holy war had radically reshaped whole regions of the Christian world. In Spain he had galvanized the warring princes to strike back against the Almohads. The battle of Las Navas de Tolosa was a blow from which Islamic Spain did not recover, and the Reconquista began a slow but steady path to completion. In France, Innocent's use of crusading against the Cathars catalyzed a radical reform of the relations between the southern French lords and the Capetian Crown, as well as ensuring that heretic hunting would remain a sport in the south deep into the thirteenth century. In the Baltic, Innocent's wholehearted approval of crusading as a cover for German and Danish conquests in Lithuania, Latvia and Estonia ensured that paganism was persecuted to extinction, although that effort was not completed until the early fifteenth century. Thanks to Innocent's Fourth Crusade Byzantium was fatally weakened, partitioned between the Latin Empire of Constantinople and several splinter Byzantine states whose leaders plotted constantly to restore the empire that had been taken from them in 1204. And in the Holy Land, the Fifth Crusade was brewing; a general mobilization of the West in pursuit of Jerusalem was about to begin under the guidance of Innocent's successor, Honorius III. For better or worse, all this had been achieved in a papacy that lasted just eighteen and a half years, and during which there were many other political crises and calls on Innocent's attention.

Despite all his achievements, however, Innocent did not enjoy an entirely dignified afterlife. In July 1216 the French prelate, preacher and chronicler Jacques de Vitry passed through Perugia seeking an audience with the pope, only to find him dead and lying in repose in the city's cathedral. Through a lapse in security, Innocent's clothes and jewels had been stolen by grave-robbers, and the mightiest prince of the Church lay in his coffin all-but naked and in the early stages of decomposition.[30] The only consolation was that others were treated worse. Raymond VI of Toulouse died in 1222, still under the sentence of excommunication. He could not be buried in consecrated ground, so his body was kept in its coffin under a pall in the house of the Hospitallers in Toulouse. It remained there for more than a century, as successive popes stubbornly refused Raymond posthumous absolution, until eventually his flesh had been entirely eaten by rats and his coffin by woodworm. It was a dismal end for a luckless prince. Between Montfort, Innocent, Raymond and the countless "heretics" and crusaders who were cut to pieces in a war that disturbed southern France for a generation, there was little to advertise crusading had a glorious future, either.

◆ 22 ◆

The River of Paradise

All the word is warring here.

Only the gentlest breath of a summer breeze moved the grass in the meadow outside Bedum in Frisia (modern Netherlands) as a preacher and academic called Oliver of Cologne gathered the townsfolk to tell them about the coming war in the East. Thousands of men and women had assembled, and after listening to Mass sung, they sat on the ground while Oliver addressed them on a theme he borrowed from Saint Paul's letter to the Galatians: "God forbid that I should glory, save in the cross of Our Lord Jesus Christ."[1]

For the faithful Christians of Bedum this was something of a treat. Oliver, aged around forty-four in that summer of 1214, was a charismatic polymath who had served as headmaster of Cologne's cathedral school before going to study at the emerging university of Paris. In time his talents would earn him promotion to the bishopric of Paderborn and eventually a cardinal's hat. In 1214, however, Oliver was a recruiting officer for the Fifth Crusade. He took to his task with aplomb, traveling busily around the towns and cities of northwest Europe, signing up volunteers and soliciting donations* for a mission that would, in the words of Innocent III's crusading bull *Quia Major*, free the Holy Land from the "perfidious Saracens."[2]

---

*One of Innocent's most important contributions to the development of crusading institutions was the provision in *Quia Major* for those who lacked the resources or physical strength to join a crusade army to send a substitute in their place or make a direct financial contribution to the crusading fund, both of which would allow the donor to access the spiritual benefits of actually traveling to the crusading theater.

No good crusade preacher could do his job without the aid of signs, portents and miracles, and one reason Oliver was so successful was that when he preached, the elements seemed to rally behind him. As he embarked on his sermon at Bedum a strange cloud appeared in the sky. Oliver later recounted the event in a letter to the count of Namur. The cloud shone, he said, "and on it was a white cross." Then came "another cross of the same color and shape, thirdly a great cross appeared between and above these . . . which had on it the form of a human body, so it seemed, as tall as a man, naked . . . his head leaning on his shoulders and his arms not stretched out straight but raised up above. There were, clearly visible, nails through the hands and feet."[3]

One of the first people to spot this mysterious cloud formation was an eleven-year-old girl who, encouraged by her mother and grandmother, stirred up those around her into fits of religious ecstasy. Even townsfolk who had been of two minds about crusading were now seized with holy fervor. "One of the local people rushed up to me . . . saying 'Now the Holy Land has been recovered,' " recalled Oliver, "as though treating the event as a sure prophecy for the future."[4] And so the people of Bedum committed themselves to the Fifth Crusade.

Three years later, on May 29, 1217, pilgrims and warriors from the Rhineland and Frisia, including those who had taken the cross after the miracle at Bedum, finally piled onto three hundred transport ships at Vlaardingen, in southern Holland, and prepared to depart for the East. Their crusade had been a long time coming—so long, indeed, that Pope Innocent was now dead. But this extended period of preparation had always been part of the plan: to give ample time for provisioning, recruitment and preparation, and to allow for anticipated trouble recruiting volunteers from France, where the Albigensian Crusade was diverting attention, and England, where a civil war between supporters of King John and a coalition of baronial rebels had produced years of political stagnation and crisis. But even an unusually long delay in departing had not dimmed the enthusiasm of the participants, whom the English chronicler Roger of Wendover called "a great movement of brave and warlike men."[5] In keeping with generations of Flemish and other northern pilgrims before them, they set sail down the English Channel, stopping at Dartmouth to collect English volunteers eager to escape the death throes of the civil war,

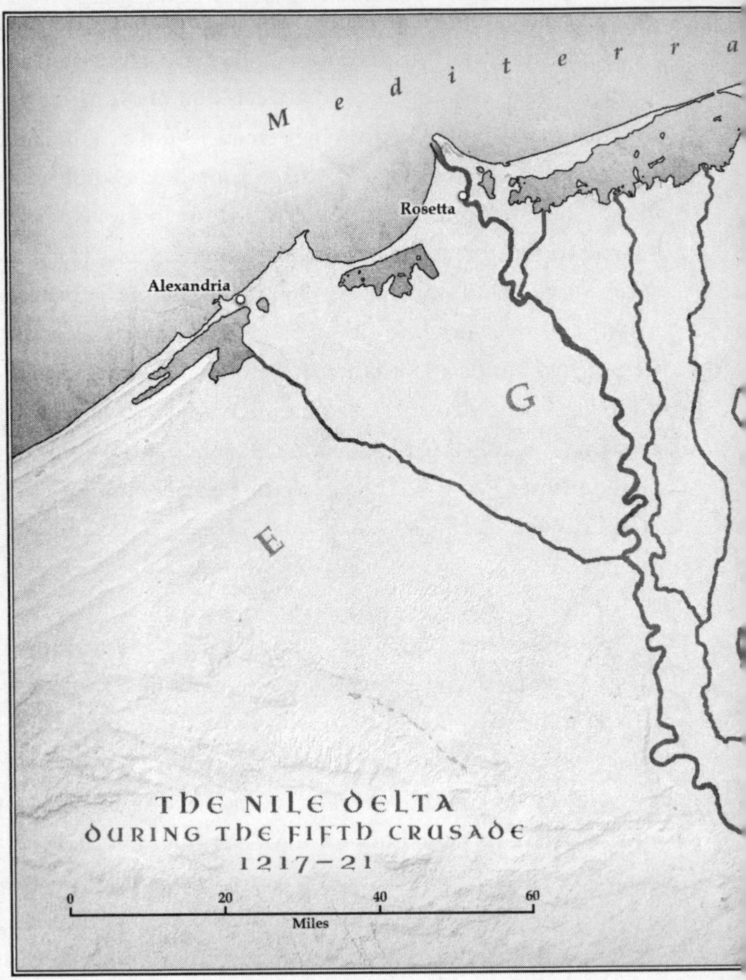
M e d i t e r r a
Rosetta
Alexandria
G
E
THE NILE DELTA
DURING THE FIFTH CRUSADE
1217–21
0
20
40
60
Miles

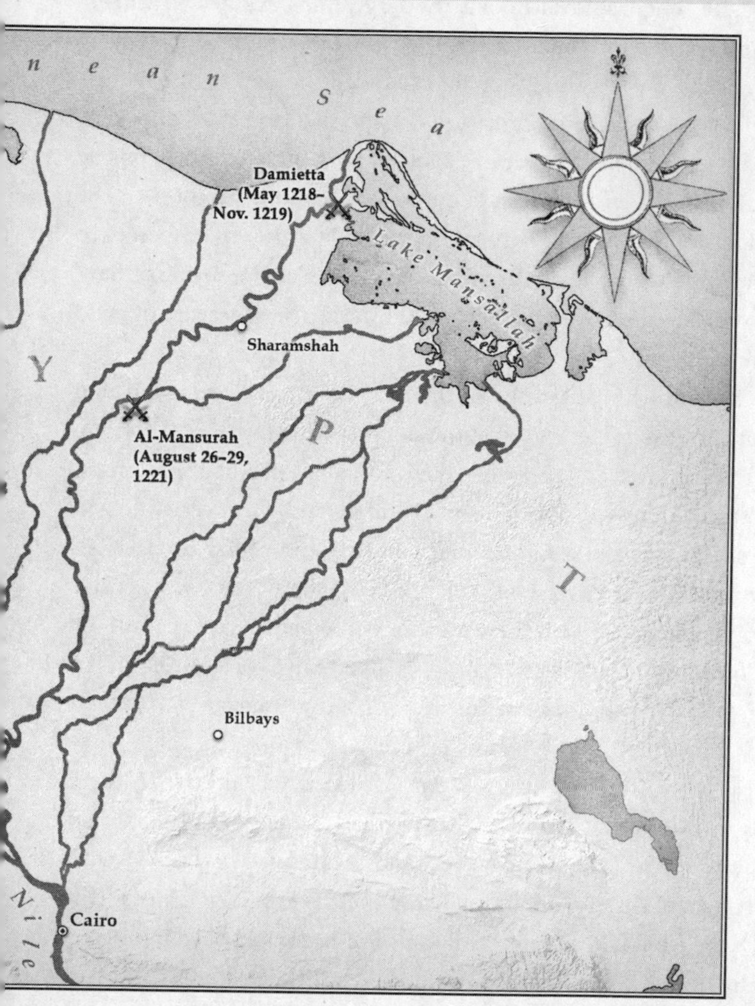
n e a n
S e a
Damietta
(May 1218–
Nov. 1219)
Lake Mansallah
Sharamshah
Y
P
T
Al-Mansurah
(August 26–29,
1221)
Bilbays
Cairo
Nile

then recrossed the Channel and followed mainland Europe's Atlantic coast all the way south to the Strait of Gibraltar, where they would pass into the Mediterranean.

The journey was rough, and although the large ships avoided venturing very far from the coastline into open water, the fleet was still tossed violently around by the weather. By the time they had rounded the Bay of Biscay, perhaps one in ten had been scattered by storms or smashed to pieces on rocks. Just to keep going, remembered Oliver of Cologne, took "great courage on the part of the warriors."[6] When the armada entered waters off the coast of the Christian kingdoms of Spain and Portugal, many on board were desperate to break the journey for a while. They disembarked to pray at the shrine of Santiago de Compostela, and enjoyed, even if only briefly, the sensation of solid land under their feet.

Few voyages from northwest Europe to the Holy Land were ever completed in one unbroken stint, so as the end of summer approached, the fleet split up to dock before the autumn seas grew too rough to navigate. About one third, mostly Frisian vessels, pressed on into the Mediterranean to overwinter on the west coast of Italy. The rest, about one hundred and eighty of the German ships, stayed in Iberia to overwinter on the Portuguese coast, where their crews could swap doing battle with the waves for doing battle with the infidel. There they followed the example of crusaders stretching back to Sigurd of Norway in the early twelfth century and the second crusaders of 1147, and went out to pick a fight with the Muslims of southern Spain.

Their target was an Almohad military outpost known as al-Qasr (Alcácer do Sal): a sturdy fortress at the mouth of the river Sado, south of Lisbon. It had been selected by the local bishops of Lisbon and Evora, who had noted with satisfaction the plight of the Almohads following the battle of Las Navas de Tolosa, after which the Almohad caliph Muhammad al-Nasir had been murdered and succeeded by his ten-year-old son, known as Yusuf II. In late July the crusaders, assisted by members of the Templars, Hospitallers and the Iberian Order of Santiago (or Saint James of the Sword), put al-Qasr under siege. After six weeks they successfully fought off an Almohad relieving army sent west from Seville and Cordoba. Finally, on October 19, 1217, they accepted the defenders' surrender. Oliver of Cologne recorded this victory with satisfaction: "The Saracens were conquered by divine strength; one of their kings [i.e., emirs] was killed, and with him a great many were massacred or led into captivity."[7]

Another correspondent told of Moorish captives asking plaintively after the battle about a vision they had seen of a ghostly "shining battle line wearing red crosses," which had seemed to fortify the Christian army.[8] Coming five years after the Christian triumph at Las Navas de Tolosa, the fall of al-Qasr signaled that the age of Almohad dominance over southern Iberia was drawing to a close.[9] It also seemed to bode well for the course of the new crusade.

In the early spring of 1218 the Flemish and German crusaders left Portugal and Italy and headed on to the Holy Land. By late April the great rounded hulls of their ships had begun to appear on the horizon at Acre, and smaller launches were ferrying them ashore to explore the capital of the kingdom of Jerusalem. Arriving at this thriving port by way of its sheltered harbor, guarded by the magnificent palace-headquarters of the Knights Templar and overlooked by the counting houses and wharves of the various Italian merchants always left an impression, although not necessarily a positive one. The French theologian James of Vitry, bishop of Acre, described the city at that time as "a monstrous dragon with nine heads engaged in mutual conflict," and complained bitterly about the many faults of the people who lived there, which included the erroneous practice of Christian circumcision, irregular modes of confession, people making the sign of the cross with one finger instead of three, priests with odd haircuts, women wearing veils, fornication, domestic violence, drug trafficking, prostitution and the prevalence of poison manufacturers making narcotics from animal dung.[10] James also lamented the fact that Acre and not Jerusalem was the capital of the kingdom, and that so many holy sites remained in Muslim hands. If only the Latin states had four thousand good knights, he wrote, Jerusalem itself could easily be retaken.

This was wishful thinking, and despite James's complaints about hygiene and public decency, it obscured the fact that in 1217 the crusader states were militarily—if not morally—fairly secure. True, they were much diminished from their twelfth century extent—the kingdom of Jerusalem no longer extended beyond the banks of the river Jordan and did not include the Holy City itself—but what existed was a compact and relatively easily managed coastal littoral, extending from Jaffa in the south to Beirut in the north, with its capital at Acre. Its king in 1218 was a widower named John of Brienne, a minor nobleman from Champagne, who ruled in the name of his daughter, the five-year-old Isabella II.* In his midforties at the time of the Fifth Crusade, John was a remarkably ambitious nobleman of huge physical bearing, skilled in the saddle but literate enough to pass his free time writing troubadour lyrics. According to one flattering chronicler, "the Saracens fled before him as if they were facing the Devil, or a lion appearing to devour them."[11] Given the previous standard set by monarchs that included lepers, children and women, this was hardly a disaster.

Defense of John's realm outside crusading periods was chiefly the job of the military orders: Templars, Hospitallers and a new Germanic order established during the siege of Acre in 1191, known as the Teutonic Knights. Funded handsomely by their many Western patrons, each of these groups could muster about three hundred highly disciplined knights and several thousand sergeants, and they maintained state-of-the-art castles at strategic locations throughout the kingdom. (The most eye-catching of these was the Hospitallers' vast hilltop military compound halfway between Tripoli and Homs, Crac des Chevaliers, which was large enough to house two thousand troops inside its thick concentric walls.) The combined resources and elite training of the military orders provided a perfectly adequate force for routine defense of the kingdom, particularly given the weakened state of the Ayyubids. Following Saladin's death in 1193 the Ayyubid sultanate had fractured under the rule of various of his sons, brothers and nephews. Syria and Egypt had returned to their more familiar condition of weak central authority and petty rivalries between emirs of neighboring Islamic emirs. And Saladin's eventual successor as sultan, his brother al-Adil (Saphadin), was prepared to live with crusaders as neighbors, to which end he kept the peace in a series of long-term truces, running almost unbroken between 1198 and 1217.† When Innocent had

*John of Brienne traveled to the East in 1210 to marry Maria, the granddaughter of Amalric I. Maria's parents were Conrad of Montferrat, the nobleman and king-elect murdered during Richard the Lionheart's time in the East, and Amalric's daughter Isabella. Maria died in 1212, shortly after her daughter was born, leaving John as king-regent.

†The story was somewhat different in the two northern crusader states, where the county of Tripoli and principality of Antioch had been embroiled in a long and tortuous internal struggle known as the Antiochene War of Succession. In this the fortunes of both states—and the identity of their rulers—were entangled with those of a third Christian realm to the north: the independent, orthodox Christian kingdom of Armenian Cilicia, which had wriggled free of the Byzantine Empire to gain its independence in the 1170s. By the time of the Fifth Crusade that conflict had been under way, intermittently, for sixteen years, although it was limping painfully toward a conclusion, which would be achieved in 1219 when Tripoli and Antioch came under the joint rule of the one-eyed lord Bohemond IV, who had at great length outfought and eventually outlived his chief rival, King Leo II of Armenia.

launched the Fifth Crusade he had painted a picture of the Christian kingdom in danger of imminent extinction, facing "great need," with thousands of Christians in miserable captivity. One of the great paradoxes at the heart of the Fifth Crusade was that despite the urgency and eloquence of its calling, it was always more closely rooted in Innocent's vision for Church reform through mass penitential pilgrimage than in the actual political and military needs of the kingdom of Jerusalem.

As Oliver of Cologne and his companions disembarked at Acre, they learned that they were not the first crusaders to have arrived. The previous autumn King Andrew of Hungary, Leopold VI duke of Austria and the twenty-three-year-old Hugh of Lusignan, king of Cyprus, had all visited Acre as crusaders, arriving with a fanfare that was unfortunately not matched by their subsequent achievements. Although they did not lack for troops, the three leaders—compared by a sardonic Oliver of Cologne to the biblical Magi—struggled for any real purpose. In November and December 1217 they made three unsuccessful forays into enemy territory, using one as a chance to survey the occupied holy sites, another to launch a fruitless attack on the fortress Mount Tabor and the last to forage and raid. Al-Adil's son al-Mu'azzam, emir of Damascus and de facto ruler of Ayyubid Palestine, had only the most fleeting interest in fighting them, and the folly of their winter maneuvering was soon exposed by the terrain and climate. Marching was hard and slowed by the need to carry sick and immobile crusaders on mules and camelback. Wet, windy days and freezing nights caused deaths from exposure. Before long, disease whipped around their camp and at the start of 1218 Andrew of Hungary announced he was leaving the crusade on the grounds of illness. He departed at the start of January, taking with him Hugh of Cyprus, who died a few days into the journey. All that was left to occupy the armies and pilgrims who had served them was the task of assisting the Templars, who were building a massive naval fortress on the coast at 'Atlit, between Haifa and Caesarea. The castle, named Castle Pilgrim (Chateau Pèlerin), was one of the finest ever constructed in the Holy Land, and when finished it effectively neutralized the threat of Mount Tabor. Otherwise, there was little to celebrate. At such moments, wrote Oliver, the sensible crusader could only take comfort in the glorious inscrutability of the Almighty. "The eye of the human mind," he wrote, "cannot penetrate the abysses of divine decrees."[12]

Arriving in the aftermath of this catalog of haplessness, the Germans and Frisians determined to do things differently. They spent just a month in the city, reprovisioning and repairing ships before setting out again. On May 24, 1218, Ascension Day, they unfurled their sails and headed south: not for another of the Christian ports of the kingdom of Jerusalem, but for the coast of Egypt. At a council of war John of Brienne, Leopold of Austria, Oliver of Cologne and others had decided that direct assault on the Holy City was out of the question; in the words of James of Vitry, "a siege of Jerusalem in the summer was impossible because of the lack of water." The key to Ayyubid strength, they agreed, lay not in their holdings in Palestine, but in their command of Egypt. "The Saracens derive their power from it and they are thus able to hold its riches and our land," explained James of Vitry. "With the taking of that land, we would easily be able to recapture the entire kingdom of Jerusalem."[13] The plan was to strike at the Nile Delta and seize the city of Damietta.

Damietta was one of Egypt's three great cities, along with Alexandria, to the west, and Cairo, about one hundred and twenty miles farther up the Nile. It had only tenuous religious significance to Christians: some thought that Moses had originated from this port "on the bank of the river Paradise," others believed that Christ went there with his mother.[14] More significant was its role as a gatekeeper city to one of the major eastern branches of the Nile and its status as a wealthy trading city in which grain, wine, oil, balsam, huge casements of aromatic spices and many other good things abounded.[15]

Besides being a glittering prize, Damietta was also a devilishly imposing place to approach. Even getting there was horrible. Oliver of Cologne, who had already been at sea for many months traveling from northwest Europe, managed to cross from Acre in three days, but others were tossed about on the seas by a north wind, some suffering shipwreck and drowning and others being lost at sea for up to a month. When the crusaders did arrive in early June they saw a city that would be as tough to take as any in the history of crusading. It was protected on one side by the Nile and on the other by a saltwater lagoon called Mansallah. To approach by land meant negotiating three sets of walls, dozens of towers and a deep moat. In the middle of the river on a small island stood a chain tower that controlled access to the city by water. Around it, crocodiles basked in the shallows: "They lie in wait for men and horses and swallow whatever their teeth capture," wrote James of Vitry.[16] To avoid all these perils, the crusaders' ships had to disgorge their troops onto a spit of land that protruded from the western bank of the river, from which Damietta could only be seen across the water and bombarded with trebuchet shot from afar. An eclipse of the moon greeted their arrival, which Oliver of Cologne interpreted as a sign that God was preparing to abandon the Saracens.[17] But it was hard to see how this was going to happen.

As well as planning their military operations against Damietta, the crusaders had to consider the matter of their own leadership. When Oliver had preached to the good folk of Frisia four years earlier, most assumed the Fifth Crusade would be led by the young and charismatic Frederick II Hohenstaufen: king of Germany, heir to the crown of Sicily and then the leading candidate for the imperial crown of the Holy Roman Empire, which for many years had been fiercely disputed between rival German dynasties. Frederick took the cross in 1215 and made it clear that he wanted to go crusading. But he made fulfilling his oath contingent on his coronation. As long as Innocent's successor, Honorius III, stalled, Frederick refused to risk his neck in Damietta. The result was impasse. So in his absence, the crusaders elected John of Brienne to overall command. John's immediate task in the summer of 1218 was how to set about breaking down Damietta's formidable defenses.

At the end of the summer he had made a strong start, aided handsomely by Oliver of Cologne. As well as being a preacher, theologian and amateur astrologer, Oliver was also a competent military engineer, and in the first months outside Damietta he designed a floating fortress much like those the Venetians had deployed at Constantinople in 1204. Two ships were lashed together and equipped with a rotating flying bridge at the top of their masts. On August 24, amid fierce fighting, scorching hails of Greek fire and torrid conditions in the river, which was at the peak of its annual summer flood, a crack team of Germans, Austrians and Frisians inched this waterborne siege engine beside the chain tower and let down the bridge for long enough to send an invading party into the tower itself. There, recalled Oliver later, a young Frisian—perhaps a man that the preacher had himself recruited—charged at the tower guards, wielding an agricultural flail of the type normally used for threshing grain. He "lashed out bravely to the right and to the left, knocked down a certain man holding the saffron standard of the Sultan and took the banner away from him. . . . O ineffable kindness of God! O unexplainable joy of Christians!" wrote Oliver.[18] James of Vitry gave an even more dramatic rendition of this battle: to the sound of pilgrims weeping and praying for divine assistance on the riverbank, he wrote, a party of just ten crusaders braved "the hail of fire, swords, arrows and stones" to bundle from ship mast to tower, before killing two hundred and fifty of its defenders and forcing the remaining hundred and twelve to surrender.[19] Either way, the tower fell, the chain was let down, and crusader ships swept into the river and began carrying men and munitions to new emplacements directly outside Damietta's walls. A week later, even better news arrived. On August 31 the sultan al-Adil had died while traveling from Syria to Egypt to reinforce the siege. Suddenly the stars seemed to be aligning in favor of the Fifth Crusade.

One year later the crusaders were still outside Damietta and spirits were beginning to sag. Although al-Adil's death brought jeers of satisfaction from Oliver of Cologne, who crowed that the sultan, "grown old with evil days and sickness . . . died and was buried in hell," such celebrations were short-lived.[20] Al-Adil's pragmatic and intelligent son al-Kamil succeeded him as sultan and found he had an uncommon degree of support among his hitherto fractious brothers and cousins, who held the various other appanages within the Ayyubid world. There was quite an irony here: the Fifth Crusade had been launched to exploit divisions among the Ayyubid family, but ended up fostering a spirit of unity unseen in the Islamic Near East since the days of Nur al-Din and Saladin.[21]

Despite repeated amphibious assaults on Damietta's walls, a round-the-clock catapult barrage and the occasional parading of a new fragment of the Holy Cross that had (it was said) been saved from the original lost at Hattin, for most of 1219 it seemed that it would be impossible for the crusaders ever to break into Damietta. The defenders scuttled boats in the Nile to hinder navigation, and they poured Greek fire onto vessels that came too near the city's outer ramparts. In camp a winter siege brought storms, flooding and rampant disease, including one foul condition that caused the sufferer's gums to rot and their legs to break out in hideous black sores. Many died. Some drifted away and went home. New crusaders rotated in from England, France, Germany and Italy—although the would-be Holy Roman Emperor Frederick Hohenstaufen was never among them. Instead, a papal legate, Cardinal-bishop Pelagius of Albano, arrived to represent Pope Honorius and soon began to irritate many of the secular leaders of the crusade, particularly John of Brienne, whose authority he questioned and undermined.

Then, in the spring of 1219, shocking news arrived from Jerusalem. In late March its Ayyubid ruler, al-Kamil's brother al-Mu'azzam, had ordered all the city's walls and defensive towers to be demolished. This apparently self-defeating move in fact meant that if the Latin army ever did manage to seize Jerusalem they would have no hope of defending it. After the joy that greeted victory at the chain tower the previous autumn, the siege of Damietta now seemed to be nothing but a succession of demoralizing defeats. All the rank and file of the crusaders could do was shiver, labor and wait, wearily, for their enemies to either surrender or starve.

Further up the river, the sultan al-Kamil spent his time pondering the best way to try to evict the Franks from their unwelcome position in one of his most important trading posts. He was amused but unmoved in the summer of 1219 when there appeared from the crusader camp the peculiar figure of Francis of Assisi: a well-to-do Italian merchant's son who had abandoned his worldly goods to take up the life of a wandering preacher—and had been granted official papal permission to live according to a rule derived from strict, simple obedience to the teachings of the Gospels. Francis—later Saint Francis—was the founder of the Franciscan order of poor (or mendicant) friars; he had arrived at Damietta of his own accord, claiming that he would be able to bring peace by converting the sultan to Christianity. Having sought and been granted an audience with al-Kamil, Francis offered to walk through fire to prove to the sultan the power of Christ's protection. Al-Kamil declined, just as he declined to be baptized and Francis was sent packing. He was fortunate to return to the crusader camp with his head.

Shortly after Francis's visit, al-Kamil made an audacious offer of his own. In September 1219, with economic conditions across Egypt deteriorating as the result of a poor harvest, and Damietta's citizens about to starve to death, he sent an offer to the crusaders that—perhaps deliberately—caused them much agonized debate. If the crusaders would abandon their positions on the Nile, al-Kamil's envoys said, then he would cede them the city of Jerusalem along with much of Palestine, saving only the castles that directly overlooked the trade and pilgrim roads linking Damascus with Cairo and Mecca. It was an tempting offer. But there was not a consensus, and in the end, the legate Pelagius convinced his fellow leaders that there was more to be gained by holding on for victory in Damietta. Pelagius was backed by the military orders, who saw the impossibility of holding Jerusalem—with its walls now reduced to piles of rubble—and by Venetian advisers who saw the commercial potential in establishing a permanent Christian foothold in the Nile Delta. Despite all the hardships of the siege and the extraordinary allure of regaining command of the Holy Sepulchre, the crusaders continued to wait.

Eventually, their persistence paid off. After eighteen months of bombardment, wrote Ibn al-Athir, "the surviving inhabitants were unable to hold out because they were so few and food was impossible to obtain."[22] On November 5 they left a tower unguarded and an alert party of crusaders spotted it, pushed a ladder against the wall and opened a gate through which the rest of the army could rush in.

The sight that greeted them on entering Damietta was as hideous as any they had seen. A year and a half of deprivation and bombardment had left the city a fetid, disease-ridden graveyard populated by skeletons and ghosts. "The few Saracens still alive were too few to bury the many corpses that lay on the ground," wrote James of Vitry. "The smell and the polluted air were too much for most people to bear." There was hardly any food to be had: only beautiful but inedible baubles of gold and silver, silk cloth and jewels.[23] However, if there was shock, there was precious little pity. Soon enough, Christian thieves ran around taking what they could before the official division of spoils began. Priests took hold of starving Muslim children and forced them to undergo baptism.

Meanwhile, the sultan, realizing his gambit of trading the Holy Sepulchre for the filthy lucre of an Egyptian treasure trove had failed, retreated with his army forty miles upriver in the direction of Cairo. Losing Damietta was a major defeat, but not a fatal one—and al-Kamil still had one option left. If he could draw the crusaders up the Nile then it would be possible for him to goad them into a fight that they had no possibility of winning. It would be a gamble. But it could work—so long as he could rely on his enemies' divided leadership, ignorance and greed.

In a popular song known as the *Palästinalied*, composed in High German at the time of the Fifth Crusade, the lyric poet Walther von der Vogelweide imagined himself a pilgrim visiting the Holy Land for the first time. "Christians, Jews and heathens / all say that this is their patrimony," he wrote. "All the world is warring here."[24] In Damietta during the year 1220, however, warring had once again abated. The crusaders occupied the city, and Templars and Hospitallers went out on foraging raids into the surrounding countryside. Al-Kamil built a large military encampment at a fork in the Nile nearly halfway to Cairo, which he later named al-Mansurah ("the Victorious"). But neither side was in a great rush to attack the other. The sultan had just seen the enormous effort required to storm the city. The crusaders, commanded by the legate Pelagius, once John of Brienne retired to Acre to govern the kingdom of Jerusalem, knew they needed major reinforcements if they were to continue their campaign. Rumors abounded from far and wide of new armies preparing to join the fight: it was said that warriors were mustering in the Orthodox Christian kingdom of Georgia, that a mysterious and much mythologized Eastern warrior known as Prester John was thundering across the Asian steppe to lay waste to Muslim lands, and that—most astonishingly of all—Frederick Hohenstaufen had finally been crowned Holy Roman Emperor and was coming to take direct command. In the end significant reinforcements only arrived in the spring of 1221, when John of Brienne returned to Egypt and Frederick Hohenstaufen's military deputy Ludwig, Duke of Bavaria, arrived by ship with about five thousand men.

By now eighteen months had passed since Damietta had fallen, and although the legate Pelagius remained convinced that further successes were all but guaranteed—he had discovered in Damietta a strange Arabic text called the "Book of Clement" containing prophecies that seemed to predict a great victory—Oliver of Cologne felt that the crusaders' inactivity was breeding in them sloth, vice and godlessness. "No one can describe the corruption of our army after Damietta was given to us by God," he wrote. "Lazy and effeminate, the people were contaminated with chamberings [i.e., wantonness] and drunkenness, fornication and adulteries, thefts and wicked gains."[25]

On July 6, 1221, a large crusader army finally sallied out of Damietta, leaving behind a small garrison and a large number of pilgrims, and set off upriver to attack al-Kamil's fortress camp at al-Mansurah. They marched along the eastern bank of the river, accompanied by a fleet of hundreds of ships on their right-hand side. Oliver of Cologne wrote proudly of an army so large it defied counting: "The Saracens compared them to locusts because they occupied a great amount of land."[26] By necessity they moved only a few miles a day, and by the end of the month they had only just passed Sharamshah, still the better part of a week away from the sultan's positions. Despite this slow progress, and ominous reports from scouts and spies who indicated that Ayyubid numbers were swelling up ahead, the army marched in good humor. Al-Kamil's envoys rode out and offered the familiar terms: exchange Damietta for Jerusalem and be on your way. Confident in their prophesied victory and seemingly unable to comprehend what was about to happen to them, the crusaders once again refused. They would soon have serious cause to regret their rashness.

In August, as happened every year except in times of severe drought, the Nile flooded. The world's longest river was renowned everywhere for its annual bursting of the banks, which unleashed tens of millions of gallons of the silt-rich water that had sustained great agrarian civilizations since before the days of the Pharoahs. Somehow, whether through miscalculation, arrogance, stupidity or blind hope that 1221 would be one of the occasional barren, floodless years, the crusade leaders ignored this basic fact of geography and pressed on upriver as though the Nile would simply leave them alone. They were walking into a trap.

Ahead of them, al-Kamil's military camp at al-Mansurah sat on the far side of a V-shaped junction between two branches of the river. This was easily defended at the best of times. When the waters rose, it was unreachable. Behind them, al-Kamil's brothers al-Mu'azzam, ruler of Damascus, and al-Ashraf, governor of the Jazira, slid in behind the crusader army with forces positioned to block retreat by land or river. By the last days of August the crusaders' ships had become unable to navigate the rising, churning waters. On the riverbank, their army was trapped in the junction opposite al-Mansurah.

Then, with exquisite timing, on the night of August 26, the sultan gave the order he had prepared all along.

On that night, sluice gates, canals and irrigation ditches along the river, designed to regulate the floodwaters, were all thrown open, and the land on which the crusader army stood simply disappeared, turned in a matter of hours from rock-hard, sunbaked soil into a deep, sucking swamp. Those of the rank and file who were drunk or simply asleep drowned in their tents. Panicked pilgrims and infantry who woke and tried to scramble aboard boats overloaded them so they sank. Camels and mules carrying weapons, treasure and food were swept away. The waters rose waist high in places, and the army was trapped, in the words of Peter Montagu, master of the Templars, "like fish in a net."[27]

It took just two days for al-Kamil's men—divisions of seminaked black Ethiopian infantry and galley squadrons pulling strongly against the river current—to convince their snared crusader quarry to surrender and beg for terms. And now, of course, there was no offer of Jerusalem. Instead, on August 28 Pelagius was presented with a deal under which Damietta was to be returned to Ayyubid control and all Muslim prisoners in Egypt, Tyre and Acre freed. In exchange for this the Christian army would be fed and escorted out of Egypt without ill-treatment. An eight-year truce was agreed between the kingdom of Jerusalem and the sultan, although this explicitly exempted the emperor Frederick Hohenstaufen—on the understanding that the great prince might one day actually see fit to appear in the East. And that was it. Oliver of Cologne noted with grim pleasure that al-Kamil agreed to return the Jerusalem portion of the True Cross taken by Saladin at Hattin. But in the end he never did—probably because this relic had long since been lost, sold or destroyed.

When the crusaders who had remained in Damietta heard of their comrades' fate and discovered that they were being evicted from their new home, they could scarcely believe it. Oliver of Cologne had nothing but blame to heap upon them. "If it is asked why Damietta returned so quickly to the unbelievers the answer is clear," he huffed. "It was luxury-loving, it was ambitious, it was mutinous. Besides, it was exceedingly ungrateful to God and to men."[28] This age-old explanation for military defeat—because of our sins—went back to Bernard of Clairvaux's excuses for the failure of the Second Crusade. So it had pedigree, if not plausibility. And Oliver's numbed, perplexed grief was certainly understandable. He had given nearly eight years of his life to a cause that had promised much and at the end delivered nothing.

Not everyone who went to Egypt on the Fifth Crusade suffered in the same way: The English crusader Geoffrey of Dutton, who had fought with his lord Ranulf, Earl of Chester, in the early stages of the Damietta campaign, but returned home before the disaster at al-Mansurah, brought back from the East relics that were curing the blind and dumb in his local monastery half a century later.[29] But he was lucky. The best that could be said for those like Oliver of Cologne, who saw the Fifth Crusade through to its wet, muddy, bitter end, is that they had survived, thanks to the mercy of the sultan and the forbearance of those citizens of Damietta who restrained themselves from exacting revenge on the crusaders as they left. "And so with great sorrow and mourning we left the port of Damietta," wrote Oliver. "And according to our different nations we separated, to our everlasting disgrace."[30]

◆ 23 ◆

Immutator Mundi

The emperor lived and dressed totally like a Saracen.

When the depressed and defeated crusaders trudged back down the Nile from Mansurah in early September 1221, Hermann von Salza, a middle-aged knight from a family of very minor nobility in Thuringia in central Germany, was one of the two men sent ahead of the army to Damietta, to secure the city's surrender to Sultan al-Kamil.[1] This was a highly unenviable task, since it involved announcing a catalog of disastrous misjudgments and a humiliating surrender before telling colleagues who had settled comfortably into the hard-won city that it was time to pack up their things and get out. But there were very few people better equipped for the job.

Von Salza was the master of the Teutonic Knights, the newest of the military orders established to defend the crusader states. The measured, widely traveled German was one of the most prominent of the crusade leaders, respected both by ordinary pilgrims and volunteers and the other high-ranking leaders of the expedition. Von Salza was a veteran warrior and diplomat and an affable, wise, trustworthy and competent man, and the common consensus was that he and his order had had a good crusade. He traveled to Damietta with Peter Montagu, master of the Templars. Before the Fifth Crusade Montagu would have been very much the senior partner, a prince of the church militant and the leader of the most famous of the military orders. Now, though, Montagu and von Salza were peers. And von Salza, thanks to his starring role in a losing cause, was on his way to becoming a central figure in the next decade of crusading history.

The Teutonic Order that von Salza commanded was founded in 1190, outside the walls of Acre during the Third Crusade. It was therefore around a century younger than the Hospitallers of Jerusalem (who had opened their pilgrim hospital near the Church of the Holy Sepulchre under Fatimid rule) and seventy years younger than the Templars (founded in 1119), and its membership was a good deal smaller than either of those two venerable crusading institutions. The first movers were a group of German knights from Bremen and Lübeck who set up a small field hospital to treat the many pilgrims and combatants who had fallen ill or been injured during the siege; the first master was a wealthy Rhinelander called Henry Walpote who acquired property inside the walls of Acre once the city fell. At first the Teutonic Order was a purely pastoral organization whose brothers devoted themselves to saving the lives (or easing the deaths) of other crusaders—just as the Hospitallers had done at their inception. Since they were a German-staffed and German-speaking organization they soon came to the notice of powerful German patrons. One was Frederick Barbarossa's son Frederick of Swabia, who was treated in the Acre field hospital in 1190 and 1191. He died there, but not before recommending the excellent standard of care to his brother, the future Holy Roman Emperor Henry VI. Henry responded by offering financial support to the Teutonic Knights, and a few years later, when he sent his own band of crusaders east (the expedition that fought at Beirut and Sidon in 1197 and 1198), the Teutonic Order provided basic medical support on the ground. Innocent III granted papal approval in 1199, along with an official rule and permission to develop a military wing. Soon they also had a uniform: their knights wore white mantles decorated with a black cross. Although their international headquarters was in Acre, the Teutonic Knights liked to call themselves "the Hospital of Saint Mary of the Teutons in Jerusalem." This was, plainly, a fictional boast, and would remain so for as long as Jerusalem was occupied by the Ayyubids. But it was a powerful statement of intent.

Von Salza became the fourth master of the Teutonic Knights in or around the year 1210, when he was probably in his thirties. The order was still small: maintaining just a dozen or so hospitals and, according to the chronicler Peter von Dusberg, able to put no more than ten knights in the field at any one time.[2] Yet von Salza's election marked the start of a dramatic rise in its fortunes. In the kingdom of Jerusalem, the order steadily acquired property sufficient to sustain a hub of support for German pilgrims in the East. In return, pilgrims made grants of money and property to the order in their wills. Meanwhile, von Salza pursued strategic political connections: in 1211 he traveled to Armenia to attend the coronation of King Leo I; the same year he sent Teutonic brothers to Hungary to help King Andrew II colonize the untamed frontier region of Burzenland, Transylvania, which was menaced by raids from the Turkic tribes known as the Cumans. The master may have been at the Fourth Lateran Council in 1215 when Innocent III set out detailed guidelines for the Fifth Crusade; by the time its armies gathered, he was regarded as one of its leaders.

Hermann von Salza and the Teutonic Knights played a critical and widely lauded role in the Egyptian crusade, all the way from the council at Acre in 1217 that agreed to target Damietta to the expedition up the Nile. Barring a few months when he left Egypt to travel to the papal court with a status report on the conflict, the master was regularly to be found with John of Brienne, Cardinal Pelagius, the masters of the Templars and Hospitallers and other senior commanders as they debated and decided strategy. During the siege of Damietta, Teutonic Knights were conspicuous by their bravery and skirmished often with the sultan's troops. Along the way they suffered heavy casualties, but, in a campaign dominated by German combatants, there was no shortage of volunteers to restock their ranks—either as fully professed knight-brothers who took religious vows or as associate members called *confratres*. (These were knights who continued to live a secular life but who fought under the order's banner.) One of the most prestigious of these was a knight called Litot, who helped storm Damietta's chain tower early in the siege. Although von Salza advocated for the disastrous march to al-Mansurah, it was a mark of his—and his order's—otherwise exemplary conduct that he was not tarnished by the outcome of that decision. Instead, after Damietta was evacuated in 1221 the master returned to Western Europe with his personal reputation intact and even enhanced. Pope Honorius III, who had overseen the crusade from afar, rewarded the Teutonic Knights with a sweeping grant of financial privileges that put them explicitly on a par with the Templars and Hospitallers. The pope proudly called von Salza's order "new favored Maccabees of this time . . . through whom God frees the Eastern Church from the filth of the pagans."[3] And the pope was not the only man who appreciated the job von Salza had done in Egypt. When the master returned to Europe he fell into the service of a ruler who would stand crusading on its head. He was the Holy Roman Emperor, Frederick II Hohenstaufen: a king, emperor and polymath so much larger than life that his admirers referred to him as *stupor mundi* and *immutator mundi*: the wonder, or transformer, of the world.

Frederick was a truly extraordinary individual. He was not physically imposing: the Damascene preacher and historian Sibt Ibn al-Jawzi described him as red-faced, bald and shortsighted. "Had he been a slave, he would not have been worth two hundred dirhams," Ibn al-Jawzi muttered.[4] But what he lacked in hair and distance vision, Frederick amply made up for in the strength of his personality, breadth of his knowledge and extent of his imperial ambition.

He was born in Iesi, on Italy's eastern coast, on December 26, 1194. A later rumor—a tall story rather than a true one—stated that his forty-year-old mother, Constance, Queen of Sicily, had given birth in the town square in order to allay any doubts that the child was naturally hers. Frederick never knew his father, the Holy Roman Emperor Henry VI; in fact, both his parents were dead before his fourth birthday.* But he spent his life pursuing Henry's grand political ambition: to unite under his own command Sicily with the Holy Roman Empire. This prospect tormented successive popes, who abhorred the idea of the papal states being hemmed in to the north and south by the lands of a single ruler—particularly one such as Frederick.

For most of Frederick's childhood, however, the thought of him taking command of anywhere outside his mother's island of Sicily and its associated territories in Calabria and Apulia looked slim. After Henry VI died the Holy Roman Empire dissolved into a civil war between the supporters of two adult candidates for the succession: Henry's brother Philip of Swabia and Otto IV of the Bavarian Welf dynasty, a nephew of Richard the Lionheart. When Philip was murdered at a wedding in 1208, Otto claimed the imperial crown. By 1215, however, Otto had gravely offended Pope Innocent III and the German princes who had elected him, and had been defeated on the battlefield by Philip Augustus, king of France. He was excommunicated, deposed and sent off into

*Henry VI died on Sicily in September 1197. Constance died in November 1198.

enforced exile on his estates at Brunswick, where three years later he died a miserable sinner's death. Into the breach stepped Frederick, now the twenty-year-old king of Sicily. On July 25, 1215, he was crowned king of the Germans at Aachen, and to the surprise—either theatrical or sincere—of the churchmen in attendance his very first act as king was to take the Cross.

Ibn al-Jawzi, as well as insulting Frederick's physical appearance, also wrote that he was "a materialist and that his Christianity was simply a game to him."[5] This was unfair. Frederick was indeed a sincere Christian; his choice to commit to the crusade in 1215 was made wholeheartedly and he spent much of his life actively persecuting heretics within his territories, as well as oppressing the ordinary Jews and Muslims of Sicily. Yet simultaneously—and at times paradoxically—he was a man with an insatiable curiosity about the natural world that extended far beyond the tenets of Christian Scripture. This inquisitiveness—which Ibn al-Jawzi condemned as materialism—combined with the fact that he grew up on Sicily, where Greek, Hebrew, Arabic and Latin cultures commingled more fluidly than anywhere else on earth, meant that he ignored traditional civilizational boundaries in a manner that scandalized stiff-necked zealots on either side of the crusading divide. Frederick devoured learning from wherever it came—"inhaling tirelessly its sweet perfumes," as he put it. He loved natural sciences, astrology, logic, rhetoric, medicine, law, philosophy and mathematics. He was a superb zoologist who kept a menagerie that included at various points leopards, camels, elephants, bears, a giraffe and an albino peacock, and he wrote a definitive text on falconry entitled *The Art of Hunting with Birds* (*De Arte Venandi cum Avibus*). He was profoundly influenced by the Spanish Muslim scholar Ibn Rushd (Averroës)'s commentaries on Aristotle and he understood that it was impossible to investigate fully the mysteries of the world God had created without reference to non-Christian scholarship. Frederick surrounded himself with Latin, Greek, Muslim and Jewish tutors, advisers, poets, scholars and bureaucrats. Well into adulthood, he retained a personal Arab tutor in logic, and he corresponded with Jewish and Arab scholars in southern Spain.[6] He had a natural familiarity with, and understanding of, Islam, spoke Arabic, and liked to advertise his magnificence in ways that could be understood by Muslims as well as Christians: He referred to himself more than once as "the fortifier of the *imam* of Rome": thereby expressing a staunchly Christian concept in terms sympathetic to Islamic audiences.[7] Frederick was, in short, a shockingly liberal intellectual and a bluntly pragmatic ruler. Yet these instincts sprang not from ambivalence about faith, but rather from intelligence, necessity, the ability to compartmentalize and equivocate and—at root—Sicilianism. Ibn Wasil, a more perceptive writer than Ibn al-Jawzi, found Frederick "refined and learned" and "favorable toward the Muslims because originally he grew up in the country of Sicily . . . and the inhabitants of that island are mostly Muslims."[8] Unlike Ibn al-Jawzi, Ibn Wasil did not doubt Frederick's commitment either to Christianity or to crusading.

Hermann von Salza came into Frederick's orbit after leaving Egypt in 1221. The latter's absence from the Fifth Crusade—the result of his attritional struggle with Honorius to find terms on which he could be crowned Holy Roman Emperor—had caused much grumbling, and Frederick realized he was expected to fulfill his vow sooner rather than later.

The impediments to Frederick leaving were the complex web of commitments that came with his imperial crown, and the difficulty of combining the demands of empire with rule in Sicily, which was perpetually turbulent and demanded Frederick's personal attention. So von Salza's task, which he began immediately, was to help Frederick settle disputes lingering from the recent civil war in Germany while maintaining smooth diplomatic channels between empire and papacy. This was far from easy, but the job suited Hermann's talents. It also served his private ambition, which was to secure continuing support for the Teutonic Order from its two most important patrons: the emperor and the pope. In the 1220s he was exceptionally busy. Just as Hugh de Payns, the founding master of the Templars, had once helped to whip up Western enthusiasm for crusading against Damascus, enriching his order in the process, so Hermann now devoted his own energies to ensuring that the emperor would eventually be able to make his way to the East and pick up where the Fifth Crusade had left off.[9]

To that end Hermann spent several years touring the German states and neighboring foreign courts, negotiating truces with disgruntled subjects and rivals, attempting to extract crusading oaths from imperial vassals, contracting hired swords and commissioning troop transport ships. It was hard going: after the Fifth Crusade there was widespread apathy in the German sphere for any further fights with al-Kamil. But von Salza stuck to his task. He visited Lombardy and Sicily, and ventured as far north as Denmark to mollify the belligerent King Waldemar II. He shuttled between the imperial and papal courts: helping to calm tempers when, having missed a departure date of 1222, Frederick postponed his crusade once again, to 1225. And in 1225, when Frederick requested yet another extension to his crusading obligation (this time citing difficulties raising enough troops of a sufficient quality), von Salza helped thrash out the Treaty of San Germano, whereby the emperor promised Honorius—now nearing the bottom of his deep well of patience—that if he did not depart for the East by 1227 he would forfeit a bond of 100,000 ounces of gold (around 3 tons) and be excommunicated. Around this time the business of the Teutonic Order began to suffer from von Salza's absence: by 1224 the brothers based in Hungary had begun to contemplate full withdrawal from the realm after their relations with King Andrew broke down and von Salza was unable to travel in person to repair them.[10] By 1226 the Teutonic Order had left Transylvania. But the master calculated that in the long run, bigger opportunities lay elsewhere.

Shortly after swearing to the terms of the San Germano agreement, in November 1225 Frederick Hohenstaufen married John of Brienne's thirteen-year-old daughter Isabella—or as she was more properly known, Queen Isabella II of Jerusalem. This agreement too bore Hermann von Salza's imprimatur. The marriage was the pope's idea, but its execution was no easy matter, and it occupied two years of von Salza's time as he persuaded John of Brienne that Frederick would allow him to remain in Acre as king of Jerusalem (a bald lie, as it transpired), then supervised negotiations for the marriage contract and finally sent one of the brothers of his order to bring the girl to Italy for her marriage. Von Salza may have been embarrassed when Frederick, upon marrying Isabella, immediately went back on his word and insisted that John of Brienne cede to him all his rights as king;* but any embarrassment was assuaged when Frederick and his young bride both made generous grants of title and property to the Teutonic Order in the Holy Land. Frederick had acted discourteously and even despicably toward John, but he was within his legal

*John of Brienne was later compensated for losing the crown of Jerusalem when in 1229 he was elected Latin Emperor of Constantinople. He traveled to the former Byzantine capital and was crowned in the Hagia Sophia in 1231. He died in the city in March 1237, having during his final illness professed himself a Franciscan friar.

rights. And as king of Jerusalem Frederick could surely not delay his departure on crusade any longer.

Under the Treaty of San Germano Frederick Hohenstaufen was due to set sail for Acre by August 15, 1227. Honorius never saw him leave, for the pope died on March 18. But his successor, the zealous and uncompromising Cardinal Ugolino di Conti, who took the papal name Gregory IX, watched Frederick like a hawk. Gregory had reason to be delighted when the emperor set out, as agreed, in the summer of 1227; but happiness turned to exasperation and rage when Frederick fell ill with plague early in the journey. He had not even left the Italian coastline before he called off his crusade once more, asked von Salza and the Duke of Limburg to take twenty galleys and a small contingent of fighting men to Acre ahead of him, and went to Campania to recuperate in the volcanic springs at Pozzuoli, near Naples.

When news of Frederick's latest diversion reached Gregory IX he exploded in a fit of pique. The time for excuses was now over. The Treaty of San Germano called for excommunication and the new pope wasted no time in passing the sentence, denouncing Frederick as "contemptuous of all promises" and accusing him of having made "a frivolous pretense of illness." Frederick responded by accusing Gregory of being "totally devoted to exciting hatred against us."[11] As the two most powerful men in Western Christendom bickered with each other in public, Hermann von Salza was making a swift crossing to Acre. He no doubt wondered as he traveled if all his efforts had been in vain—and whether the mercurial emperor would ever make good on his many promises to liberate Jerusalem from the infidel.

In the end, Frederick finally arrived in his kingdom of Jerusalem in late summer 1228 (on what is now occasionally called the Sixth Crusade), still excommunicated but seemingly unworried. He had recovered from his illness, although a few months earlier he had suffered the loss of his young wife, Isabella, who died following the birth of their son, Conrad. This fact—which further muddied the matter of Frederick's claim to the crown of Jerusalem—barely seemed to faze him. He broke his journey from Italy to Palestine with a short excursion on Cyprus, where he clashed with and insulted the most powerful eastern nobleman in the region, John of Ibelin, *bailli* (or regent) during the minority of Cyprus's child-king Henry de Lusignan. By the beginning of September Frederick was in Acre, preparing to throw himself into reorganizing the defenses of the kingdom. Yet his presence, although long anticipated, was now not universally welcomed. An excommunicate crusader was a contradiction in terms, and throughout Frederick's time in the East he faced simmering hostility from the Templars—who refused to deploy troops any closer than a mile from his army—and the patriarch of Jerusalem, Gerold of Lausanne, who regarded Frederick as the devil incarnate.

Despite this rumbling of anti-Hohenstaufen sentiment, Hermann von Salza stayed loyal to his man. During the previous year the master had overseen early work on the Teutonic Knights' vast new fortress of Montfort overlooking Acre—built on a scale to rival the Hospitallers' Crac des Chevaliers and the Templars' Château Pèlerin. In the autumn of 1228, however, he was at Jaffa with the rest of the crusaders, and he was therefore able to write a firsthand account of events for Pope Gregory IX. "While work [on Jaffa's defenses] was progressing enthusiastically," wrote Hermann, "ambassadors came and went between the sultan of Babylon [al-Kamil] and the lord emperor, conducting negotiations on the benefits of peace and agreements."[12] These discussions were carried out in a spirit of mutual respect, which unnerved many on both sides, and they yielded a spectacular conclusion. Al-Kamil's brother al-Mu'azzam was recently dead, and the sultan had moved quickly to take control of most of Muslim-ruled southern Palestine, including the city of Jerusalem. Holding this, however, was not his priority; he was much more focused on taking control of Damascus from al-Mu'azzam's young son al-Nasir. A familiar Ayyubid family quarrel therefore erupted, and the sultan had no wish to complicate matters by opening another front of dispute with the pestilent Franks. The emperor's presence was, in the words of the chronicler Abu al-Fida, "like an arrow in a wound."[13] That arrow had to be carefully removed.

On a personal level, there was a rich understanding between the sultan and the emperor, such as had not been seen in the East since the days of Richard the Lionheart and Saladin. Their relationship had been cultivated by proxy via one of al-Kamil's most trusted emirs, Fakhr al-Din, who had previously visited Frederick in Sicily where he was able to converse directly with the emperor in Arabic. Through Fakhr al-Din the two rulers now exchanged valuable gifts: Frederick sent al-Kamil a set of his own armor as a token of his peaceful intentions, and the sultan graciously allowed Frederick to submit a list of difficult mathematical problems for the consideration of the finest scholars at the Ayyubid court. To the everlasting scandal and outrage of Patriarch Gerold, al-Kamil also sent to the emperor's camp "dancing girls who sang and juggled."[14] Gerold complained that "the emperor lived and dressed totally like a Saracen, feasting and drinking with these dancers. . . . The emperor's generosity to the Saracens was extreme, as though he was trying to buy the peace he was not able to obtain by force or fear."[15] In fact the patriarch was so blinded by his loathing that he was unable to see that force and fear had seldom if ever been part of Frederick's armory. But even he could not gainsay what flattery and a little cultural interchange eventually achieved. On February 18, 1229, Sultan al-Kamil and Frederick, king of Jerusalem, agreed a treaty that mirrored many of the terms offered to (and refused by) the fifth crusaders in 1221. The city of Jerusalem—"the place where the feet of Christ trod, and where the true worshippers adore the Father," as Frederick described it in a letter to Henry III of England—was to be turned over to Christian rule.[16] So, too, were Bethlehem, Nazareth and several other areas of Palestine between Jerusalem and Acre. A ten-year armistice was to be observed and, added Hermann von Salza, in his account of the treaty making, "there will be an exchange of all prisoners, those taken at the fall of Damietta." There was a degree of ambiguity in the terms regarding the Christians' right to rebuild Jerusalem's walls, but otherwise, wrote von Salza, "it is almost impossible to describe the joy of all the people at this proposal."[17]

In fact, "all the people" were not overjoyed. In fact, there were many who were disgusted, particularly on the Ayyubid side. Although Frederick agreed that Muslims should be allowed to control access to the Temple Mount (*haram a-sharif*), and to worship freely at the Dome of the Rock and al-Aqsa Mosque, Ibn al-Jawzi spoke for many when he denounced Jerusalem's abandonment as a disgrace. He defamed the deal from the pulpit of the Great Mosque of Damascus: "O shame upon the Muslim rulers!" he railed. "At such an event tears fall, hearts break with sighs, grief rises up on high!"[18] Ibn al-Athir wrote that "the Muslims were outraged and found it monstrous. This caused them to feel such weakness and pain as are beyond description."[19] Patriarch Gerold was keen to point out all the places that had not been handed back to Christian rule, and he accused Frederick of "underhand dealings . . . lies, evil and fraud."[20] But none of these worthy men were able to prevent the deal. On March 18 a triumphant (if still excommunicate) Frederick Hohenstaufen made his way into the Church of the Holy Sepulchre—the first Christian king to set foot there since Guy of Lusignan before the battle of Hattin in 1187. The crown of Jerusalem was waiting for him on the high altar. As he described the event to

Henry III of England: "We, as being a catholic emperor . . . wore the crown, which Almighty God provided for us from the throne of his Majesty."[21] He did not add that he had in fact snatched it from the altar himself and placed it on his own head, forgoing any ritual of anointing or consecration. Then he swept out of the Church, leaving von Salza in his place to give a lecture in Latin and German relating the many great deeds Frederick had achieved since taking the cross at Aachen fourteen years previously. Patriarch Gerold, who refused to present himself before this scene, heard later that von Salza had "exonerated and then exalted the emperor while abundantly criticizing the Church."[22] Whether or not this was accurate, it was hard to deny that through diplomacy and no little good fortune, Frederick had achieved the greatest and least bloody crusading victory for generations.

Having secured Jerusalem and ordered its walls rebuilt, Frederick wasted no time in returning to the West. He left the city of Jerusalem at the end of March; on May 1 he set sail from Acre, leaving the kingdom in the hands of *baillis*. Despite his diplomatic triumph, he had no time or wish to linger. Rumors abounded that the Templars—whose historic headquarters at al-Aqsa Mosque on the Temple Mount had been left in Muslim hands—were plotting to have him assassinated; during his last hours in Acre supporters of the Ibelin faction, whom he had upset at the start of his journey, lined the streets and pelted him with tripe and butchers' waste. Worse, reports were arriving from the West that Pope Gregory, ungrateful and determined to prove to Frederick that the power of popes overrode that of mere emperors and kings, had licensed John of Brienne to launch a military invasion of Sicily. By June 10 he was back in southern Italy. Von Salza was not far behind him.

Once back in the West, the Teutonic master's first task was to reconcile Frederick with the irascible Gregory IX and have his sentence of excommunication lifted. At the same time, however, von Salza had the matter of the Teutonic Order's future growth to consider. Frederick had given the order generous grants in the kingdom of Jerusalem, which would put them on a stable footing for years to come. Yet in the East they had still to compete for resources with the older and more established Templars and Hospitallers. The real opportunities lay closer to home.

In 1226, following the Teutonic Knights' disorderly retreat from Transylvania, von Salza had teased from Frederick an extraordinary grant known as the Golden Bull of Rimini. This imperial decree (so named because it bore a golden seal) granted the Teutonic Order permission to send troops to aid the German lord, Duke Conrad of Masovia, who was fighting Prussian pagans on the fringes of his lands. Under the Golden Bull's terms, von Salza's men were entitled to seize and rule—with no oversight and no taxation—any territory they conquered in the duke's service. The text specifically praised von Salza: "because he is powerful in deed and speech and he will powerfully begin and complete the conquest for the Lord, though many have already failed in the same business with greater labor."[23] It set the order on a new course away from the Holy Land, and it came at an opportune moment, given their failure to colonize Transylvania. The Teutonic Knights had taken the first step in creating a new crusader state in the Baltic that would survive until the sixteenth-century European Reformation.

In 1230, von Salza's price—or at least, his reward—for executing the difficult business of reconciling Frederick with Gregory was the pope's approval of the same privileges laid out four years earlier in the Golden Bull. Gregory did not disappoint. On September 12 the pope issued a bull granting the Teutonic Knights his full backing to move into Prussia where they would fight, kill, convert and conquer the pagans who lived there. Gregory reiterated the duty of crusaders to protect pagans in the Baltic who had converted to Christianity. But he also argued that God had put pagans on earth specifically so that people like Hermann von Salza's knight-brothers could save their own souls by killing them: "so they might have a means of atonement and salvation."[24] In the spring of 1231 Teutonic brothers began what would become, effectively, a continuous crusade against non-Christians in the Baltic, in which they commanded ordinary volunteers raised by Dominican preachers in the duchy of Poland and nearby Germanic states and were eventually joined every campaigning season by knights from all over Europe in search of adventure. Led by a senior brother called Hermann Balk they fought their way slowly down the valley of the river Vistula from Chelmno (Kulm), building wooden (and later stone) fortresses and subduing or converting Prussian tribes.

Tensions remained high between Frederick and Gregory throughout the 1230s, and on each occasion that von Salza was called upon to mediate their disputes, he came away with further concessions for his order's new adventures on the Baltic fringe. Prussia—like Livonia, Lithuania and Estonia to the

FINNS
SWEDES
Gulf of Finland
ESTONIANS
GOTLAND
Baltic Sea
Bay of Riga
LIVS
Pskov
CUROMANS
LETTS
Riga
Dvina
LITHUANIANS
Königsberg
POMERANIANS
Danzig
PRUSSIANS
Marienburg
Vistula
Dobrzyń
POLAND
PAGAN TRIBES OF THE BALTIC C.1100
0
100
200
Miles

north—was a land of warlike tribal peoples whom pro-Teutonic writers like the chronicler Peter of Dursburg called "primitive beyond measure," worshippers of base things like trees, the weather and toads.[25] But it was also a place of great bounty, and each concession von Salza wrung from the papacy increased the potential benefit the Teutonic Order could glean there—quite beside the spiritual reward of crusading, which continued to be a means to wash away one's sins in a warm bath of unbelievers' blood.

By the mid-1230s the Teutonic Knights were firmly established in the Vistula valley. They had constructed forts as far north as Elbing and taken guardianship of a precious relic of the True Cross, which Frederick Hohenstaufen had obtained from Venetians and gave as a gift to von Salza.[26] Theirs was not the only holy war being prosecuted in the Germanic north—in 1232 the archbishop of Bremen secured from Rome crusade status for a military campaign to subdue a rebellious band of several thousand farm workers known as the Stedingen Peasants, who were labeled heretics for their refusal to pay church tithes and were duly massacred by an army of crusaders in a battle at Altenesch on May 27, 1234. But further east, among the Prussians, the Teutonic Order was gathering momentum: making active gains in pagan country and promoting their self-image as a group of "noble persons, who had lived long in the world and were intelligent and knowledgeable."[27] Gregory declared in 1234 that Prussia was "Saint Peter's Patrimony"—implying its permanent status as an object of crusade. The strong arm of Saint Peter was to be guided by the Teutonic Knights.

This order's burgeoning status in Prussia was only reinforced in 1237 after the Livonian Swordbrothers—the organization established in Bishop Albert of Riga's household three decades earlier—collapsed amid bitter criticism, scandal and military catastrophe. From their beginnings the Swordbrothers had a reputation as rough-riding thugs, and by 1234 complaints had reached the papal court of them murdering rivals, desecrating Christian corpses, conniving with schismatic Russians and pagans to further personal feuds, killing hundreds of pagan converts, assaulting Cistercian monks, pillaging Church property and preventing unbelievers from taking baptism so that they could be enslaved.[28] This rogue band—which in reality was facing a crisis of recruitment and funding—was eventually broken up after a disastrous expedition against an army of Lithuanians and Semgallian pagans in 1236. The Swordbrothers' master, Volkwin, was commanding a volunteer army around three thousand strong when he was routed on the banks of the river Saule. The following year the surviving Swordbrothers were incorporated into the Teutonic Order. Around the same time the Teutonic Knights also absorbed another small, local military order: the Polish Order of Dobrzyn. They were, for the moment, ascendant.

The history of the Teutonic Knights in Prussia far outlived Hermann von Salza, Gregory IX and Frederick Hohenstaufen. The order grew fitfully, and there were moments—particularly in the 1240s and 1260s—when it seemed as though they would be brought down by the demands of endless, attritional warfare on the frontiers of Christendom. It was not only pagan enemies who troubled them; the order's problems were exacerbated by fierce and often violent politicking between other Christian powers who set their sights on prime territories in the long sweep of the Baltic between Danzig and the lands of the Finns. Little by little, however, the order carved out a formidable crusader state. By 1283 they had all but conquered Prussia and established an *ordensstaat* in which the knights were sovereign and the land was defended by powerful stone castles. Over the course of the next half century the Teutonic Knights also became the dominant power in Livonia and Estonia, and focused their crusading efforts—often very brutally—against the pagan kingdom of Lithuania and Orthodox Russian princes. Teutonic states would exist in some form in Prussia and Livonia deep into the sixteenth century—a very long time after the crusader states in the East had vanished. This was an astonishing achievement, which began with Hermann von Salza, friend of emperors and popes and one of the most quietly effective crusade leaders of his age.

Von Salza died on Palm Sunday, March 20, 1239, at Salerno, the most advanced medical center in Europe, where he had traveled to seek treatment for the illness that ultimately carried him away. He once described himself as a person "who holds dear the honor of the Church and Empire and strives for the exaltation of both."[29] His ability to do so was sorely missed after his death. Under von Salza's successor as master, the aristocratic Conrad von Thüringen, the order jettisoned its long-held position of carefully plotted cordiality toward both emperor and pope, and swung its weight behind Frederick—hardly a surprise since Conrad von Thüringen was the emperor's second cousin. This caused them considerable political trouble in the East, where the mere mention of Frederick's name was enough to send half of the barons of the crusader states into paroxysms of fury. It also meant that, immediately upon von Salza's death the order was forced to stand shoulder to shoulder with a godforsaken ruler. For on the very day that von Salza died Pope Gregory once more passed the sentence of excommunication against the emperor—this time as punishment for Frederick's military activity in northern Italy, where he had sent armies against the so-called Lombard League of city-states.

This time there was no calm reconciliation. The emperor remained excommunicate when Gregory died in 1241 and spent much of the remaining nine years of his life literally at war with the papacy. In total he was excommunicated four times between 1227 and his own death in 1250, and the papal vendetta outlived him, to be continued against his son and successor Conrad. The man who had almost single-handedly secured the return of Jerusalem and the Holy Sepulchre from the Ayyubids therefore died as the express target of a crusade, which was preached against him by bishops, Dominican and Franciscan friars and other papal agents with every bit as much vigor as those that had in times past been directed against faraway infidels. His enemies, fighting on the order of the pope, were encouraged to wear crusade crosses and allowed to commute promises to travel to the Holy Land to stay in the West and try to bring down the Holy Roman Emperor. It would be difficult to conceive of a greater perversion of the institutions and language of crusade than for such a war to be preached against—to use Frederick's own phrase—"the fortifier of the *imam* of Rome." No doubt, Frederick could be infuriating, overbearing and self-serving. But crusading had come to a strange pass when he was considered as valid a target for Christian warriors eager to cleanse their sins as the pagans of Livonia, Almohads of Spain and Turks, Kurds or Arabs of the Near East.

Yet in a sense, all this mattered little, for by the time Frederick died, to be buried in a porphyry tomb in Palermo Cathedral, an even greater menace had arisen to threaten not only Christendom, but seemingly the entire world. From the Far East had appeared a horde of conquering barbarians far deadlier than anything in living memory. They were the Mongols, and their introduction to the crusading world transformed it in a way that exceeded the changes wrought by even the dazzling figure of Frederick Hohenstaufen and his shrewd, dependable sidekick, Hermann von Salza of the Teutonic Knights.

• 24 •

Khans and Kings

From the realms of the east the cruel beast has come.

On April 9, 1241, the bloodied warriors of a Mongol army scoured the fields outside the town of Legnica (Liegnitz), in Poland, rolling over the corpses of their enemies and cutting off their ears. This simple act of mutilation helped the Mongols tally how many men they had killed. The haul that day had been a few thousand—enough to fill nine large sacks—but these were merely the latest victims among a death toll that, since the rise of the Mongol warlord Temüjin to become Genghis Khan (*Ċinggis Qa'an*—loosely, "great leader") some twenty-five years earlier, now numbered in the millions.[1] Over that time many people had tried to stand in the Mongols' way, and plenty more had simply held their hands up and surrendered. Anyone foolhardy enough to resist usually ended up like the Christian army that now lay earless on the Silesian soil: defeated, dead and humbled; left to rot as a warning of the consequences of resisting the most fearsome military machine the world had ever known.

The battle of Legnica was part of a desperate rearguard being fought all over eastern and central Europe in the early 1240s, as the Mongols—or, as Christian chroniclers called them, the Tartars*—thundered west out of central Asia, which had been falling steadily beneath their swords for the previous two decades. Their target was the Christian kingdom of Hungary, which

*The name Tartar (or Tatar) seems to have derived from a word used by the Mongols to define themselves, which was deemed grimly appropriate in the West for its similarity to the Greek-derived Latin word *tartarus* (the underworld).

marked the furthest end of the steppe that extended almost seamlessly for almost four thousand miles from the sacred mountain of Burkhan Khaldun, where Temüjin was said to have been born, to the foothills of the Carpathians.[2] To that end, Legnica was a feint, designed to divert the attention of Christian warriors, including units of Teutonic Knights and Templars, and prevent them from joining an even bloodier clash of arms that would take place the following day at Mohi, in Transylvania, when a larger Mongol army would rout King Bela IV of Hungary. Yet even a feint by the Mongols felt like an all-out assault by anyone else. The Polish commander at Legnica, Duke Henry II Pobozwy "the Pious" of Silesia, did not simply lose his ears. He was decapitated in the Mongol camp, and his head was taken to the nearest town on the end of a spear. (His butchered body could only be identified later when his wife revealed that he had six toes on his left foot.) Every village and farm in the area was then burned. Writing decades later the Polish chronicler Jan Długosz marveled at the ferocity of the Mongol army in full flow. "They burn, kill and torture as they like, since none dares to stand up to them."[3]

The Mongols' rise had been watched in the West for many years, first with curiosity, then trepidation and finally with outright panic. In 1220 and 1221, during the Fifth Crusade, the legate Pelagius was aware via garbled gossip from his contacts in Damietta of an eastern Prince called "King David" who was then cutting a swath through Persia. Pelagius believed, optimistically, that this King David figure could be connected with the popular prophecies of Prester John, the putative oriental Christian warrior king, who since the time of the Second Crusade had been rumored to preside over a fabulously wealthy kingdom in India, where he spent his time yearning to travel abroad and join forces with other Christians to defeat unbelievers.[4]

Pelagius's understanding of "King David" was informed principally by wishful thinking. In fact, the legate was hearing the earliest Western reports of the conquests of Genghis Khan, who united the nomadic tribes of Mongolia in 1207, then struck out in all directions: conquering the Western Xia and Jin-held regions of Manchuria and northern China, and sweeping into central Asia, heading relentlessly west toward the Caucusus, his generals commanding a multiethnic, multifaith horde of tens of thousands of superb horsemen, who fought with composite bows, spears, axes and lances, and could spend months living in the saddle and sleeping outdoors. Mongol armies were well trained, expertly led and adept not only in siege and field combat, but also in psychological warfare and genocidal terrorism. The Mongols conquered by demanding unconditional submission from their foes and massacring entire populations at the first hint of dissent. Although they took a surprisingly relaxed view on religion—allowing freedom of worship throughout their territories and often converting to local practices within a few years of arriving—this marked a rare point of enlightened liberalism in the Mongol world. Genghis Khan neatly summed up his philosophy of war in the last year of his life when he issued commands for dealing with the inhabitants of a town who had defied him: "Kill the valiant, the bold, the manly and the fine . . . and let the soldiers take for themselves as many of the common [people] as they can lay their hands on."[5] This stark, binary approach—obedience or death—tended to work. By the time Genghis Khan died in 1227, the rumble of a Mongol army, its horsemen clad in long, functional, fur-trimmed robes, rawhide skins and leather boots, was feared across Asia. Christendom, too, was beginning to quake.

During the 1230s the Mongols had continued to advance west under Genghis Khan's son Ögödei, scything through Georgia (which they had first attacked in 1223) and penetrating deep into the Russian principalities to the north, capturing Kiev by December 1240. By this time the Western powers had a very clear idea of whom they were dealing with, and the Mongols' conquests were common knowledge as far away as Scotland.[6] The Holy Roman Emperor Frederick II Hohenstaufen, appalled by the Mongols' deeds yet predictably fascinated by them as a natural phenomenon, described them a few months after the battle of Legnica as "wild, lawless and ignorant of the laws of humanity . . . the men themselves are small and of short stature . . . but compact, stout and bulky, resolute, strong, and courageous . . . they have large faces, scowling looks and utter horrible shouts, suited to their hearts."[7] The same year, Frederick's archenemy Pope Gregory IX wrote to churchmen all over the West warning of the existential danger the Mongols posed. Having "slaked their swords with the blood of all whom they could lay hands on," he wrote, they "now endeavor to invade the kingdoms of Bohemia and Teutonia [i.e., the German states], desiring to lay waste the entire land of the Christians and destroy their faith."[8] Gregory authorized preachers to offer crusader status to all of those who rose to defend their lands against these barbarians.

Gregory's decision in 1241 to proclaim a crusade against the Mongols was logical, for—Prester John fantasies notwithstanding—the direction of Mongolian travel appeared to be inexorably toward the heartlands of the Roman Church. Yet there was stiff competition for would-be crusaders. At the time of the Mongols' advance, there were at least half a dozen other crusader wars taking place around mainland Europe and the Mediterranean, all of which vied for attention, recruits and resources.

In Spain, the young King James I of Aragón (son of the unlucky Pedro II of Aragón who had been killed in battle by Simon of Montfort during the Albigensian wars) was now leading a vigorous campaign against the various rulers of the collapsing Almohad state. In 1229 to 1231 he had taken Mallorca from the Muslim ruler of the Balearics, Abu Yahya, following a massive amphibious invasion supported by ships and crusaders from Genoa, Pisa, Marseille and elsewhere. James had now set his sights on Valencia; elsewhere on the peninsula, other Christian rulers including Ferdinand III of Castile were also sweeping southward, capturing new towns and territories with every campaigning season, including the former Umayyad capital Córdoba, which fell in 1236. Meanwhile, there had been crusades against heretics in Bosnia, Cathars in France, pagans in Prussia and Livonia, and Turks who threatened the Latin Empire of Constantinople. Frederick Hohenstaufen, who was the Western prince most obviously suited to leading resistance to the Mongols, was the least inclined to take action, since Gregory IX had excommunicated him and only the previous year declared the papal war against the Hohenstaufen to be a crusade. In one sense, the 1230s had demonstrated the absolute success of crusading as a means for deploying Church-sanctioned military force both within and without the borders of Christendom. But as crusading had broadened, it had also become more thinly spread: localized and normalized. Indeed, what saved Hungary, Poland and the lands to the west of them after 1241 from the khans and their apocalyptic horsemen was not Gregory's call for crusaders to barricade Europe against the horde. It was the weather and good luck. An arid Hungarian summer in 1241 was followed in the winter by extreme cold and downpours that brought about widespread famine and made the Hungarian plains virtually impassable to cavalry.[9] This—combined with the death of Ögödei Khan in December 1241, which demanded that many high-ranking Mongol leaders return to the imperial capital of Karakorum for elections—meant that in 1242 offensive operations were abruptly halted and Europe, through God's providence rather than the heroic mustering of His armies under the sign of the cross, was saved. Yet if the storm had momentarily abated, it had by no means ended—and the Mongols would be entangled with the crusading cause for the rest of the thirteenth century.

In the crusader states of the Latin East, the Mongol menace was well understood, although by the early 1240s it had not yet been experienced firsthand. Rather, the problem for the rulers of Jerusalem, Tripoli and Antioch remained as it had been for the previous five decades: the Ayyubids. Sultan al-Kamil died in 1238, the year before his truce with Frederick Hohenstaufen expired. For the following five years the course of affairs in the kingdom of Jerusalem and beyond was therefore shaped by a long civil war between two of al-Kamil's relatives, competing for outright dominance across all the family territories: his son al-Salih Ayyub, who ruled Egypt, and his brother al-Salih Isma'il, who ruled Damascus. For the most part the Ayyubids in the 1240s cared more about fighting one another than about obliterating Christendom, but there were still occasional outbreaks of violence, answered by one serious bout of foreign crusading, carried out by a large body of French and English warriors who had been urged east by one of Gregory IX's crusading bulls, *Rachel Suum Videns*, issued in November 1234. Among this group's most prominent leaders were Richard, Earl of Cornwall, the brother of the English king Henry III, Simon of Montfort's son Amaury of Montfort and Theobald IV, Count of Champagne, a charismatic *trouvère*: the northern French version of the southern *troubadour*. Theobald's musical output included triumphant crusading songs calling on his fellow Christians to hurry to Syria and take up arms in the name of the Virgin Mary. His sexual conquests were rumored to include the queen of France, Louis VIII's wife, Blanche of Castile.

The Barons' Crusade, as these lords' collective expeditions were known, made the most of Ayyubid disharmony: playing the rival rulers against one another to build on the gains Frederick Hohenstaufen extracted from al-Kamil in 1229. To that end it was rather successful. By 1241 the borders of the kingdom of Jerusalem had been extended significantly and the crusader state seemed to be on a stronger footing than at any time since the battle of Hattin in 1187. Although the kingdom lacked a king—Frederick Hohenstaufen's son Conrad was occupied far away in Europe with the family struggle against the papacy, and would not have been shown a very warm welcome had he arrived in the East—it seemed that the realm was in rude health. Then, in 1244 came calamity.

Among the many people displaced by the Mongols' conquests were the Khwarizmian Turks, whose far-flung territories extended out from greater Persia, taking in Kabul (modern Afghanistan) in the east and the Caucusus in the west. The Khwarizmian empire had not survived its encounters with Genghis Khan's horde: in 1220 the capital, Samarkand (Samarqand, modern Uzbekistan) was captured, the collective will of its governors and people having been dented by reports that the Mongols had executed one unfortunate Khwarizmian leader by pouring molten metal into his eyes, nose and mouth.[10] The fall of Khwarazm not only meant the destruction of one of the largest political entities in central Asia and its absorption into the ever-expanding Mongol world; it also sent Khwarizmian warriors scattering away in great numbers from the edifice as it crumbled. Bands of displaced soldiers went north and east in search of gainful employment, and they tended to bring devastation with them. "From the realms of the east a cruel beast has come," wailed one Christian writer, who added that the fleeing Khwarizmians resembled "dragons being dragged from their lairs."[11] These dragons landed first in northern Mesopotamia; before long they were also breathing fire across Palestine, with calamitous consequences for the crusaders. In 1244 a Khwarizmian army in the pay of the Ayyubid sultan of Egypt, Ayyub, took sudden and devastating aim at the city of Jerusalem, the crusaders who held it and their ally: the ruler of Damascus, Isma'il.

That summer Sultan Ayyub was preparing to fight Isma'il, hoping to evict him from Damascus. To that end he mustered an army at Gaza and summoned ten thousand Khwarizmian cavalry to join him. On their way south they diverted, with Ayyub's encouragement, to the Holy City, which was in the hands of Isma'il's Frankish allies. The patriarch, Robert, bishop of Nantes, kept a doleful account of their deeds when they arrived. "Those infidel Khwarizmians launched frequent attacks against the almost unprotected city of Jerusalem," he wrote, referring to the useless state of the walls, torn

RUSSIAN PRINCIPALITIES
Dnieper
Kiev
Legnica
(1241)
HUNGARY
Danube
GOLDEN HORDE
BULGARIA
Black Sea
GEORGIA
LATIN EMPIRE
Constantinople
Nicaea
EMPIRE OF NICAEA
SELJUQS OF RUM
ILKHANATE
Aegean Sea
Athens
Mediterranean Sea
Antioch
Aleppo
Mosul
Tigris
Euphrates
Baghdad
'Ayn Jalut
(1260)
Damascus
Jerusalem
Cairo
MAMLUK SULTANATE
Red Sea
MONGOLS AND MAMLUKS c.1260
0
200
400
600
800
Miles

down decades earlier under Ayyubid rule and never properly reconstructed. The Khwarizmians descended almost unopposed, beginning a rampage from which parts of the city would never recover.

As the Khwarizmians approached, about six thousand Christian civilians fled in anticipation of the storm—but almost all of them were hunted down and slaughtered in the Judean hills. Then, on August 23, "the Khwarizmians entered the almost empty city of the Israelites and in front of the Sepulchre of the Lord they disemboweled all the remaining Christians who had sought refuge inside its church. They decapitated the priests . . . they laid sacrilegious hands on the Sepulchre of the Lord's resurrection, defiling it in many ways."[12] The marble around Christ's tomb was either smashed or scavenged and the tombs of all the crusader kings of Jerusalem buried near Calvary were opened and their bones tossed away. Elsewhere other highly revered Christian churches and shrines received the same treatment: the priory at Mount Sion, the tomb of the Virgin Mary in the valley of Jehosophat and the Church of the Nativity in Bethlehem were all desecrated. But, wrote the patriarch, "these Khwarizmians were not content with all this; they aspired to take and destroy the whole land."[13]

This aspiration was not quite fulfilled, but the defeat that followed the sack of Jerusalem was bad enough. On October 4, 1244, a Christian army including almost every major baron and all the military orders of the kingdom marched out from Acre to take revenge on the Khwarizmians and their Egyptian sponsors. Troops sent by Isma'il of Damascus went with them, a fact that was later condemned as particularly disgraceful by the Damascene preacher Ibn al-Jawzi, who disapproved very strongly of Muslims marching underneath the sign of the cross.[14] On October 17 the Christians and Damascenes met the Khwarizmians and Egyptians in battle near Gaza, at a place the crusaders knew as La Forbie (al-Harbiyya). According to the patriarch, the Damascenes were put to flight almost as soon as the battle began, after which the Christians fought "like athletes of God and defenders of the Catholic faith," but were cut to pieces nonetheless.[15] Almost every Templar, Hospitaller and Teutonic Knight on the battlefield was killed; the Germans lost all but three men. Knights and foot soldiers, bishops, abbots and priests were killed and captured in the thousands; when the patriarch escaped the battle and returned to Acre he found the entire city in a state of "grief, wailing and endless suffering; there is not a single house or person without a death to mourn."[16] It was the most devastating military defeat since Hattin, and even with the crusading effort spread thin and the Mongol threat against eastern Europe, it mandated a familiar response. In the summer of 1245 at the First Council of Lyon—a church gathering that focused much of its attention on the Mongol threat in the East and an attempt to formally depose Frederick Hohenstaufen—the new Pope Innocent IV announced a Seventh Crusade to revenge the losses of Jerusalem and La Forbie. Its leader would be the first king of France to visit the east since Philip II Augustus left Acre in a fury in 1191: Philip's grandson, the famously pious and literally saintly Louis IX. He faced an almighty challenge.

Louis had been king of France since his accession in 1226, at the age of twelve. In that year his father, Louis VIII, died suddenly while taking part in the Albigensian Crusade. (Scurrilous tongues in France spread the lie that he was poisoned by his mother's lover, the *trouvère* crusader baron Theobald IV of Champagne.) The younger Louis therefore grew up under the watchful eye and political regency of his formidable mother, Blanche, who guided his education and shaped a notably pious, charitable, well-educated and literate man with soaring ambitions for the grandeur and sanctity of the office of French kingship and a vision of France as the greatest Christian kingdom in the West.

Louis was a builder of sublime Gothic churches and a generous supporter of the poor and indigent. He was blessed with good fortune and equally sensible judgment in economic and political matters and he was a highly respected international diplomat. To advertise his own status and the glory of the French Crown in 1238 he had purchased from the creditors of the impoverished Latin Emperor of Constantinople, Baldwin II,* one of the finest relics in the known world: Christ's Crown of Thorns, which Baldwin had pawned to merchants in Venice. Louis redeemed this treasure—as fine as any in Constantinople or anywhere else—at the staggering cost of 10,000 hyperpyra, or 135,000 Parisian livres—equivalent to half the annual revenue of the Crown. He then built at further lavish expense the Sainte-Chapelle to house it. This

*Baldwin II had been co-emperor with John of Brienne, and succeeded as sole emperor on John's death. He was chased out of Constantinople in 1261 when Byzantine soldiers recaptured the city—and was therefore the last ruling Latin emperor of the short-lived crusader state established by the Fourth Crusade.

handsomely advertised the fact that in 1244 Louis IX was the preeminent ruler in Christendom—his reputation having long climbed past that of Frederick Hohenstaufen, laboring under the weight of papal opprobrium.

Louis took the cross in December 1244, a bare few weeks after the disaster at La Forbie. The immediate prompt was his miraculous recovery from a bout of dysentery so severe it almost killed him. Despite the miracle of his recovery, Louis's mother, Blanche, was appalled when she discovered what he had done: according to the writer John of Joinville, who wrote an intimate and vivid biography of Louis in the early fourteenth century, drawing on his own memories of the king, Blanche was "panic-stricken," and seemed "as if she would rather have seen him dead."[17] But once the king had made up his mind to go crusading, there was no dissuading him.

Pope Innocent IV did not anticipate Louis taking his crusade vows so promptly. Indeed, he had been thinking that the best solution to the troubles of the Latin Church in the East lay not merely in commissioning Frenchmen, but in persuading the Mongols that they might, after all, assume the mantle of the fictitious Prester John and ride to the rescue rather than the destruction of Christendom. In March 1245 Innocent sent an ambassador, the Franciscan friar Giovanni of Pian di Carpini, to find the new Mongol khan Güyüg in Mongolia, where he delivered letters scolding the Tartars for attacking Christians and suggesting that they be baptized into the faith on the basis that this would then oblige them to assist the crusader states against Ayyubids and Turks alike.

This was not in itself completely absurd—one reliable feature of Mongolian conquest was the willingness of the conquerors to tolerate and even take on the faiths of those whom they subjugated. However, the high-handed tone the pope took when writing to a ruler whose forebears had reduced more than half of the Eurasian world to a state of terrified obedience did not please Güyüg; still less did it convince him to take up the cause of Christ. It would be better, he told Innocent, if "you in person, at the head of the kinglets, should in a body . . . come and do obeisance to us. This is what we make known to you. If you act contrary to it, what do we know? God knows."[18] Thus it was Louis IX, not Güyüg Khan, who was charged with rescuing Jerusalem.

The course of Louis IX's expedition to Egypt was remarkably similar to that of the Fifth Crusade, at least in its strategic goals and its unfortunate outcome. In the summer of 1248 the king took ship at Aigues Mortes, a port town purpose-built for the crusade, the sailors aboard his fleet bellowing the ancient hymn "Veni Creator Spiritus" as they caulked the doors on the horse transporters, and the sacred French *oriflamme* fluttering aboard his lead ship, the *Montjoie*. After leaving France, Louis went first to Nicosia in Cyprus, where he took stock of the situation in the East. Once on the island he was pressed to send help in all directions: to the Syrian coast, where Sidon had recently been lost to the Ayyubids; to Constantinople, where Baldwin II was barely clinging to control of the city; and to Antioch, where Prince Bohemond V found his territories under direct threat from the Mongols, who were also terrorizing his neighbors King Hethum of Armenia and the Seljuq Turks of Asia Minor. Against all these competing claims, Louis decided to focus his energies on the Nile Delta, still recognized as the beating heart of Ayyubid power. After overwintering on Cyprus, therefore, he and his army of at least twenty thousand troops sailed south in the late spring and made an amphibious landing at Damietta on Saturday, June 5. John Sarrasin, the king's chamberlain, wrote a vivid letter home from Damietta describing the arrival, in which he remembered knights so keen to attack the enemy that they leaped into the sea in armor, wading through water up to their armpits and fighting their way up the beaches under heavy crossbow fire, "a dangerous and difficult task which called for great bravery." Even Louis, Sarrasin said, waded waist-deep against defenders who "attacked our men so furiously and ferociously that they seemed certain to cut them to pieces."[19]

After this auspicious start, things continued to go well. Rather than sitting for a year or more outside Damietta, as had happened in 1218, Louis's troops broke into the city before the weekend was over, as Damietta's garrison decided that they preferred the lessons of history to starving to death and ceded the whole place to the crusaders, retreating in time-honored fashion up the Nile. So the crusaders simply walked in, and Sarrasin wrote of the strange sights they encountered, including "fifty-four Christian slaves who had been there for twenty-two years." Happily liberated, they told the French that "the Saracens had fled . . . saying to one another that the swine had arrived."[20] According to an Islamic chronicler, al-Makrisi, Sultan Ayyub was irate when he learned of the ease with which the garrison had surrendered, and ordered fifty of the soldiers to be strangled as punishment.[21] But Sarrasin also noted that the Nile would soon flood, which meant that for the French, further progress was momentarily impossible. Louis passed the time productively, converting mosques into churches, heavily reinforcing the city walls and waiting for the waters to subside. His army outside the walls dug trenches and organized round-the-clock guard duty to defend themselves against Bedouin raiders who cut off Christian heads and sold them to the sultan in Cairo for ten bezants apiece.

They finally moved out of Damietta toward Cairo on November 20, and were immediately bolstered by even more wonderful news. On November 22 Sultan Ayyub died, having endured a lingering illness consisting, according to al-Makrisi, of "a fistula and an ulcer on the lung."[22] His son Turan-Shah, governor of a minor lordship in the Jazira, was promoted as the new sultan, but it would take him three months to reach Egypt, and when he arrived his authority in both the wider Ayyubid world and the palace in Cairo was lower than that of any before him. In his absence, Ayyub's Turkish wife, the sultana Shajar al-Durr, was intent on installing herself as the power behind the throne, effectively the first female ruler of the dynasty. Plotting alongside her was a faction of the old sultan's mamluk (slave-soldier) bodyguard, known as al-Bahriyya (Bahria) after the island in the Nile opposite Cairo where they were garrisoned, who were beginning to conceive of a full military coup to take control of the Egyptian state. Deciding that whatever example past crusaders had set was now overtaken by turmoil among his enemies and the simple chaos of events, Louis—after consulting his three brothers, Robert, Count of Artois, Alphonse, Count of Poitiers and Charles, Count of Anjou—ordered a full advance of the crusader army and navy all the way to the great fork in the Nile at al-Mansurah.

After a painfully slow march hampered by a stiff headwind that made river navigation for their supply ships near impossible, the French camped opposite al-Mansurah at the beginning of December and began a siege. Yet what was once a military camp was now a fully fortified town. It would not be taken easily, even without the Nile in flood. Unlike at Damietta the garrison at al-Mansurah had no wish to give up and run away. The French had also, despite Louis's normally meticulous military planning, failed to establish secure supply lines to the rear of their army. A slow, grinding campaign emerged, consisting of catapult battles across the water, failed attempts by both sides to bridge the river and storm the enemy camp, and a dark war between spies, during which one daring Egyptian swimmer managed to cross to the crusader camp disguised on the water's surface with a hollowed-out watermelon on his head, kidnapped a Christian soldier and dragged him back to al-Mansurah for interrogation.[23] Epidemic disease ripped through the crusader camp, for both sides took to dumping human corpses in the same waters the invaders were fishing for their meals. "The whole army was infected with a shocking disorder, which dried up the flesh on our legs to the bone," John of Joinville recalled, adding that a secondary symptom was "sore complaint in the mouth, from eating such fish, that rotted the gums and caused a most stinking breath. Few escaped death that were thus attacked."[24] King Louis himself was afflicted with a recurrence of the dysentery that had almost killed him in 1244, suffering so badly that he was forced to cut a hole in his undergarments to accommodate the unstoppable flux.

The French glimpsed triumph on February 8 when, having finally discovered a spot to ford the river, they mounted a surprise flanking cavalry attack on the Egyptian camp. But after initial success, they were driven back and dozens of men were killed, including the king's brother Robert of Artois. After this, there were no more victories. Turan-Shah arrived with military reinforcements from Syria. A blockade of the Nile downriver cut off food supplies to the crusaders from Damietta. Rampant illness, dwindling supplies and the joyless dirge of a military stalemate meant that by Easter, the king was ready to admit defeat.

On April 5 a disorderly retreat down the Nile began, which turned very quickly into a rout, as the crusader army lost its discipline and was harried viciously all the way by the sultan's troops and members of the elite Bahriyya, who showed little mercy to anyone but the highest-ranking (and most valuable) prisoners. On April 6 Louis, by now so weak that he was barely able to stand, surrendered to the pursuing army and begged for a truce on whatever conditions the sultan chose to offer. The collective ransom for the French monarch and others, including his brother Charles of Anjou and the aristocratic writer John of Joinville, was set at 800,000 bezants: a true king's ransom, the first installment of which could only be paid by appeal to the Templars in Louis's army, who were persuaded to open up their treasury, kept on a galley in the Nile Delta, and raid private funds they were holding in strongboxes for other crusaders. That they were willing to do so was a mark of the seriousness of the situation and the impending, total failure of the crusade. Under the terms of the agreement to free Louis, Damietta was again surrendered, having on this occasion been held for just eleven months.

By May 6 the city had been transferred back into Egyptian hands and Louis was released. He sailed shortly afterward to Acre, remaining in the Holy Land until 1254, where he spent much time and even more money restoring the defenses of the most important remaining cities in the kingdom of Jerusalem, making substantial repairs to the walls of Acre and Caesarea. Yet he could do little more than this to advance or even affect the cause of the crusader states. Louis had established his reputation as a king willing to risk his kingdom and his very life in the course of the Holy War—yet it seemed increasingly impossible after the second failure at Damietta to conceive of the Franks of the West as anything more than a dwindling irrelevance in the eastern Mediterranean, where the dominant powers were now the Mongols and—as it was very soon to emerge—the Bahriyya Mamluks who had helped destroy the French army on the Nile.

Four days before Louis paid his ransom to be released from Egyptian captivity, the Bahriyya murdered Sultan Turan-Shah. They were motivated by simple self-preservation: Turan-Shah had mamluks of his own from Syria who threatened to displace the Bahriyya in their own capital. But whatever drove them, they ensured that the sultan's death was stunningly cruel. His assassins first attempted to burn him alive with Greek fire while he was in his tent, before cutting him down with their swords, removing his heart and hurling his mutilated body into the river. With this, the Ayyubid dynasty, stretching back eighty years and eight rulers, was finished.

After several tense months of jockeying for power under the regency of Turan-Shah's mother, the sultana Shajar al-Durr, one of Bahriyya's senior commanders, Aybeg al-Turkmani, eventually took control; to secure his power in the palace he married Shajar al-Durr. Thus, under Aybeg and his successors there was quickly established a Mamluk sultanate, in which the slave-soldier caste, for so long limited to the status of bodyguards and stormtroopers, imposed themselves as the dominant force in Egypt and far beyond. By the time Louis left the Holy Land in 1254 the Mamluks were fully established in Cairo and beginning to look to further conquests in Syria.

Rising through their ranks as they did so was a young warrior originally from a family of Kipchak Turks. He had a striking, fair complexion and a distinctive, milky cataract in one of his eyes—features that would be notorious as he emerged as the nemesis of the Holy Land's crusaders and the architect of their fatal and final demise. His name was Rukn al-Din Baybars. His supporters called him the Lion of Egypt; even his detractors knew him as someone who was "hardy and valiant" and "did an enormous amount of harm to the Christians."[25] Even one of the most powerful Mongol khans regarded Baybars with suspicion, referring to the armies he commanded as "Babylonian dog mice."[26] The insult was well earned: Baybars was part of the Mamluk force who managed to best and drive back the Mongols as they began to encroach on the lands of the Near East.

In the course of his life, Baybars would do what the combined efforts of Zengi, Nur al-Din and Saladin could not, and destroy for good the Frankish states of Syria and Palestine. That his rise to power was made possible by a Christian army commanded by the saintly Louis IX, which had aimed to deliver Jerusalem back into the hands of the righteous once and for all, was one of the crowning ironies of the last, ragged stages in the decline of the crusader states.

• 25 •

The Enemy from Hell

They fought the holy war excellently.

Four Mongol envoys arrived in Cairo in the summer of 1260 bearing orders from their master, Hülagü, the short, flat-nosed warlord with a famously booming voice, who was the younger brother of the Great Khan Mongkë and commander of the Mongols' conquests in Persia and western Asia. The letters containing these orders, though written in Arabic and decorated with quotations from the Qur'an, rang with the uncompromising imperium typical of most high-level Mongol communication.[1] They were addressed to the Mamluk sultan of Egypt, Qutuz, whom the khan scorned as a coward and threatened with annihilation if he did not see sense and immediately bend his knee.

"You have heard how we have conquered a vast empire and have purified the earth of the disorders that tainted it," Hülagü wrote. "You cannot escape from the terror of our armies. Where can you flee? What road will you use to escape us? Our horses are swift, our arrows sharp, our swords like thunderbolts, our hearts as hard as the mountains, our soldiers as numerous as the sand. Fortresses will not detain us, nor armies stop us. Your prayers to God will not avail against us. We are not moved by tears nor touched by lamentations. Only those who beg our protection will be safe." Without timely and recondite submission, he told Qutuz, Egypt would fall; just like everywhere else. "We will shatter your mosques and reveal the weakness of your God and then we will kill your children and your old men together," warned Hülagü.[2] Resist, and the whole of Egypt would suffer "terrible catastrophes."

There was ample evidence to suggest Hülagü was not joking, for in western

Asia the Mongol advance did not seem to be slowing down. In 1255 Mongol armies had ravaged Anatolia, crushing the last vestiges of resistance by the Seljuqs of Rum, with whom they had been at war for more than fifteen years. In December 1256 Hülagü's men had overrun Alamut, the mountain fortress that served as the Persian headquarters of the murderous Shi'ite sect of the Assassins. Then, in 1258 shocking news had arrived from Baghdad, the long-standing religious capital of the Sunni world. Mongol horsemen had arrived in January, taken the city by siege in less than twelve days and done irreparable damage during the ensuing sack: burning ancient buildings and desecrating mosques, destroying hospitals and ransacking the great library known as the House of Wisdom, which contained the largest and most sophisticated collection of books on earth. So many thousands of priceless volumes and manuscripts were thrown into the Tigris that the water was said to have flowed black with ink. The death toll in Baghdad was at least one hundred thousand souls, including the Abbasid caliph himself: Al-Musta'sim was rolled up inside a carpet and trampled to death by horses, supposedly so that the ground would not be stained by his royal blood. His ruthless execution extinguished the Abbasid caliphate, which had led the Sunni world for more than five hundred years.* And Baghdad, wrote the chronicler Ibn Kathir, "which had been the most civilized of cities, became a ruin with only a few inhabitants, and they were in fear and hunger and wretchedness and insignificance."[3]

After this show of power in Iraq, Hülagü's armies—now recognizing their leader as the "Ilkhan" and his provinces as the "Ilkhanate"—moved on toward Syria.† In 1259 Hulagu's general Kitbugha took aim at the Ayyubid princes who ruled the city-states of Aleppo, Damascus and the Jazira. Kitbugha seized Aleppo by force, after which the leaders of Hama, Homs and Damascus meekly submitted to Mongol overlordship. The Mongols left the crusader states of the region alone, with the exception of a single raid on Sidon, where they destroyed the walls and took three hundred prisoners. Even so, the Christian princes Bohemond VI of Antioch-Tripoli, and his father-in-law, King Hethum of Armenia, had already decided that caution was preferable to extinction, offering tribute and allegiance to the Mongols in return for assurances of peace. Syria

*A revived Sunni caliphate in Cairo was established in 1261, under al-Musta'sim's uncle, al-Mustansir II. It was largely a puppet regime, controlled by the Mamluk sultans.

†After the Great Khan Mongkë died in 1259 and the Mongol Empire was gradually partitioned, the Ilkhanate became an independent entity—although the Ilkhans did not adopt Islam until 1295.

appeared to be falling with barely a whimper. Satisfied that he could turn his attention elsewhere, Hülagü went east, taking the majority of his troops to Azerbaijan, placing himself closer to the Mongol capital, where a succession crisis was building following Mongkë's death in 1259. He had no good reason to think that Qutuz of Egypt would be strong—or stupid—enough to resist his demands. Kitbugha and twelve thousand horsemen remained active in Syria, ready to strike at anyone who dared flash a single defiant eye in their direction. That, Hülagü reckoned, would be enough.

Yet in the summer of 1260 defiance was precisely the path Qutuz chose, thanks in no small part to the influence of Baybars, the milky-eyed leader of the elite Bahriyya corps of Mamluks, who was a belligerent presence at the sultan's elbow. Qutuz and Baybars were by no means natural allies. Their respective factions had clashed bitterly in the ugly and violent political wrangling that dominated the first decade of Mamluk rule in Egypt. Indeed, Baybars and the Bahriyya had only recently returned to Cairo following several years of indignant exile in Syria. Nevertheless, with the very future of Islamic rule in the eastern Mediterranean seemingly at stake, Baybars had made his peace with Qutuz and convinced the sultan that fire should be met with fire. So, when the Mongol envoys presented the sultan with Hülagü's high-handed threats of apocalyptic doom in the summer of 1260, Qutuz responded with a gesture he thought the Ilkhan would understand. He had Hülagü's's four ambassadors imprisoned then publicly chopped in half at the waist and beheaded. Their severed heads were hung to rot above Cairo's Zuwayla gate (*Bab Zuwayla*), a spot generally reserved for the remains of common criminals. Hülagü had reckoned Qutuz to be one of "a race of mamluks who fled before our sword." Yet the sultan—urged on by Baybars—had declared himself ready to face the sword and take his chances.

For the leaders of the crusader states, the prospect of a military showdown between Mongols and Mamluks was an interesting and even promising turn of events. As Bohemond VI of Antioch-Tripoli had calculated, there was little chance of the diminished Latin states standing up to Hülagü's armies on their own. As Thomas Agni, papal legate and bishop of Bethlehem, wrote from Acre in the spring of 1260, the proximity of the "Tartars" to the Latin states left most of their inhabitants "paralyzed with fear at the thought of the thunderous judgment of God."[4] When there was a hint of a Mongol advance on Acre, the panicked citizens cut down trees from the orchards around the city and pulled up gravestones to reinforce the walls. When Kitbugha ravaged Damascus, the barons and military orders who governed the kingdom of Jerusalem offered supplies to the Mongol army so that Kitbugha would come no further in their direction.[5] But such mollification was hardly a long-term strategy. If the Mamluks and Mongols could focus their energies on fighting each other, reasoned the Latins, the crusader states would be the beneficiaries.

Thus, when Qutuz led his army out of Egypt to face down the Mongols in late July 1260, the Christian leaders in Acre adopted a policy of studied neutrality. They permitted a Mamluk army of around twelve thousand troops, reinforced by divisions of Ayyubids who had fled to Egypt from Syria to escape the Mongols, to march freely through Christian-ruled territory. When they passed by Acre itself, the citizens even sent out supplies.[6] They did not go so far as to offer Frankish military support in the form of troops to fight under the sultan's banner. But they prayed quietly for a Mamluk victory all the same.

This opportunistic support for the armies of Egypt paid off handsomely on September 3, when Qutuz and Baybars's forces collided with Kitbugha's Mongol cavalry, supported by an assortment of Georgians, Armenians and two minor Ayyubid princes, on the plain near an oasis known as 'Ayn Jalut (the Springs of Goliath), not far from Nazareth. The two armies were roughly evenly matched in number, but the Mamluks held an ace: Syrian spies from among Kitbugha's ranks told the sultan that if he attacked vigorously, then he could rely on the two Ayyubid princes on the Mongol side fleeing the battlefield and handing them the advantage.

When the fighting started, that is exactly what happened. Just as Qutuz and Baybars had been promised, the Ayyubids fighting with the Mongol army abandoned their masters and ran away, allowing the Mamluk army to encircle the Mongols. Qutuz fought bravely, tearing off his helmet so his men could see him and rallying them with cries of "Oh, Islam! *Ya Allah!* Help your servant Qutuz against the Mongols!"[7] Allah answered the call. In the heat of the battle Kitbugha was hacked down, and his head later taken as a trophy of war.

With the loss of their leader the Mongol army broke up and galloped for their lives. Behind them, Baybars led the Bahriyya for several days in pursuit of escapees, slicing to pieces anyone they could catch and setting fire to fields to burn alive fugitives hiding amid the reeds. When all was done, fifteen hundred Mongol troops were dead, and the army charged with holding Syria on Hülagü's behalf had been scattered to the wind. The Mongol governors of Damascus and Aleppo were easily driven away. Muslim officials who had collaborated with Hülagü were executed. Finally, it appeared, the Mongols had met their match. "The onslaught of the Saracens was so great that the Tartars were unable to withstand it," wrote the Frankish author known as the Templar of Tyre.[8] The Mamluks, of all people, had come to the rescue of the Franks. But soon enough, crusader relief would turn to the deepest consternation.

The alliance forged between Qutuz and Baybars in the summer of 1260 had proven to be highly effective against the Mongol threat. But it was a partnership predicated on necessity, not affection.[9] And the Mamluk army had barely left Syria before their relationship blew up. As they marched through northern Sinai, on their way home from 'Ayn Jalut, Qutuz and a group of emirs decided to take a diversion from the main route of the march to hunt for hare—one of Qutuz's favorite pastimes. When they were at safe distance from the army, Baybars kissed the sultan by the hand—a prearranged signal for the other emirs to fall upon him with their swords. The coup was pitiless and efficient. Qutuz was slashed in the neck, stabbed in the body and finished off with an arrow. Baybars looted the sultan's body for his royal insignia, then returned to the army's camp to be hailed as the new commander in chief. On October 22 the army marched back into Cairo with Baybars at its head. He took command of the citadel and announced himself sultan and the rightful successor of the man he had just murdered.

According to Baybars's acolyte and personal secretary Ibn 'Abd al-Zahir, the people of Cairo received their new sultan with gladness: "The hearts of the subjects were delighted because God had entrusted their affairs to one who would undertake the duty of the holy war, and would command them with kindness and justice."[10] This was a blatant lie. There was in fact popular terror at the prospect of a Bahriyya tyranny, which Baybars only allayed by promising immediate tax cuts. It would take him months to stabilize Cairo, secure his position as sultan of Egypt and place Syria on a defensive footing against the Mongols. But once he did so, it would have profound—and painful—consequences for the future of the crusader states.

By the 1260s the Frankish lordships of the East were in a parlous state. Territorially they had shrunk to little more than a ten-mile-wide coastal corridor between Jaffa in the south and Antioch's port of Saint Simeon in the north. Defense of the frontiers relied almost entirely on the military orders and their sprawling fortresses like Montfort, Château Pèlerin and Crac des Chevaliers. The kingdom of Jerusalem—now in truth a kingdom of Acre—had lacked a resident adult king for thirty years. In 1260 the theoretical monarch was Frederick II Hohenstaufen's eight-year-old grandson Conradin (technically Conrad III of Jerusalem), but he would never visit the Holy Land. The regency fell to the Latin kings of Cyprus, but this was hardly a satisfactory situation. At times it was downright absurd, as between 1258 and 1261, when the *bailli*, or regent, Hugh II of Cyprus, was a boy even younger than Conradin himself. During that time power was wielded by Hugh's mother, Queen Plaisance—but she soon scandalized the realm by striking up a love affair with the wealthy warrior and jurist John of Jaffa of the Ibelin family, who abandoned his wife and children for her.

Afflicted by this long-term crisis of leadership, the Latin territories operated less like a feudal kingdom and more as a collection of petty city-states run by largely self-interested barons. Government by the *bailli* in consultation with the noble council known as the *Haute Cour* was no substitute for a controlling monarchical hand of the sort that had directed affairs during the twelfth-century heyday of Baldwin II or Amalric I. Inevitably, severe political divisions emerged, which in 1256 spilled over into full-blown civil war, in the conflict known as the War of Saint Sabas. After a dispute between merchants of Genoa and Venice over the ownership of property in Acre escalated into armed conflict, the barons, military orders and leading merchant groups in the crusader states split into rival camps. The result was ferocious naval battles between Venetian, Pisan and Genoan ships, and street fighting in Acre and Tyre. Genoans fought Venetians, Templars fought Hospitallers, and giant siege catapults were deployed between the rival parties in the major cities of the kingdom, doing "a lot of harm to each other, and [knocking] down a number of houses."[11]

Into this untidy, unhappy state of affairs swept Baybars. The summer after he seized power as sultan he was confident enough of his position in Egypt to extend his sights further afield, beginning with Bohemond VI of Antioch-Tripoli, whose temerity in allying with the Mongols before the battle of 'Ayn Jalut he had not forgotten. In 1261 and 1262 a Mamluk army entered Syria on a tour of intimidation, passing dangerously close to the city of Antioch itself, before descending upon Saint Simeon, where according to Baybars's secretary Ibn 'Abd al-Zahir, they "took the port, set the vessels on fire . . . captured it, slew and took prisoners. They fought the holy war excellently."[12] At the same time he sent envoys to Constantinople to explore a commercial treaty and nonaggression pact with a new emperor there—Michael VIII Palaiologos, who had chased the last resident Latin ruler, Baldwin II, out of the city in July 1261, reestablishing Byzantine control over the ancient capital. So although in 1261 Bohemond VI was still technically the ruler, Baybars had deprived him of his main trading port and taken steps to cut him off from an alliance with the resurgent Greeks. Much, much worse was to follow.

To the south of Antioch, Baybars had inherited a long truce between Egypt and the kingdom of Jerusalem. When it expired in 1265 he was not inclined to extend it. There was now serious diplomatic communication between Hülagü and Western rulers including the papacy and the crusading veteran Louis IX of France. In 1262 Hülagü wrote to Louis defaming the Mamluks at length and implying that as soon as he could be bothered, he would return to Syria to crush them.[13] The thought of a joint assault on Egypt and Syria by the Mongols of the Ilkhanate and a full-blown Western crusade was the only scenario that had the power genuinely to frighten the Mamluks. So Baybars determined to knock out the weaker party in this potential alliance as soon as was practically possible: showing his intent in 1263 by destroying the Church of the Holy Virgin in Nazareth (which marked the spot of the Annunciation) and menacing the walls of Acre with his armies. This was as much as he could do for the time being, but he was readying himself for the day when he could go further.

Inside his realm, Baybars had worked hard to establish himself as a noble and charitable Muslim leader mindful of the peaceful aspects of the jihad: building libraries, schools, hospitals and mosques; reforming the law courts; patronizing scientists; improving irrigation systems, coastal defenses and infrastructure; repairing iconic buildings like the Dome of the Rock in Jerusalem; and ordering a new postal system (the *barid*) that reduced the communication time between Cairo and Damascus to just four days.[14] In 1261 he restored a Sunni Abbasid caliphate, installing a new caliph—a very minor Abbasid aristocrat who had all the makings of a useful puppet—with glorious ceremony in Cairo, where he was thereafter kept under Mamluk guard, in splendid and regal impotence. Outside the realm, however, Baybars was, first and foremost, a warrior at the head of a military state. From 1261 onward he developed a massively powerful and well-equipped expeditionary army capable of striking hard far from home, be it against Mongols, Ayyubids or Franks. In 1265, when the truce with the kingdom of Jerusalem expired, the Mamluk sultan was ready to put it to use.

He began his campaign in southern Palestine, marching up from Gaza past Jaffa, and arriving in late February 1165 at Caesarea. On the night of February 26 and 27 his army surrounded the city, apparently taking the townsfolk by surprise. The defenders on the walls immediately lost their nerve and fled to Caesarea's citadel, hoping that enormous granite fortifications and seawalls strengthened at great cost by Louis IX in the 1250s would repel Baybars for long enough that he would lose interest. It was a vain hope. Mamluk catapults bombarded the citadel, and Baybars himself climbed to the top of a church tower in the city and shot arrows at anyone from the garrison who showed their face.[15] Meanwhile, he sent light cavalry fanning out into the countryside to intercept any Christian relieving forces—although they found little to intercept. Relief was not an option; the only feasible Frankish strategy was evacuation. On March 5, after less than a week under siege, the defenders piled into rescue boats and fled by sea to Acre. They left the city to its fate. For Baybars it had all been astonishingly easy.

When Caesarea surrendered, Baybars ordered his men to tear the city and citadel to the ground. Unlike Saladin in the 1180s Baybars did not just want to take Frankish cities and put them into Islamic hands. The single greatest military advantage that the Franks had held since the collapse of the Fatimid empire in the twelfth century had been naval supremacy along the Mediterranean coast and their large number of ports into which fresh crusaders could arrive with every spring sailing from the West.[16] Destroying Caesarea showed that Baybars had appreciated the lesson of history. He was not merely intent on taking crusader cities. He wanted to remove the possibility of crusading for good.

After the collapse of Caesarea, nearby Haifa surrendered in almost identical fashion. A fortnight later Baybars's army appeared outside the Templars' massive amphibious fortress of Château Pèlerin. This was impossible to storm; but to show the Templars what little regard he had for their reputation Baybars tore down the houses and other buildings that had been erected outside the fortress walls. Then he made an about-face, marching back in the direction of Jaffa and arriving on March 21 at Arsuf, which was garrisoned by the Hospitallers. Here the defenders put up a stiff resistance to a catapult barrage, and managed repeatedly to burn Baybars's siege engines. But they could not prevail for long. By the end of April the siege was over, and the garrison of Hospitallers were hauled off to prison in Egypt. Then, just like Caesarea and Haifa, Arsuf was reduced to rubble. By late May, the sultan was back in Cairo. In less than six months he had annihilated the three most important Frankish cities south of Acre. What was more, the Mongols to the east were in momentary confusion following the death of Hülagü in February, and there was growing hostility between the Ilkhanate of Persia and the so-called Golden Horde—the huge Mongol khanate to the north of the Black Sea. For a time the Mamluks had a free hand.

Between 1265 and 1271 Baybars marched armies against the crusader states virtually every year, with reliably similar results. In the late spring of 1266 he and his emirs fanned out, terrorizing the countryside between the shattered remains of Arsuf and the Sea of Galilee to the north, paying special attention to Bohemond VI's lands in the county of Tripoli, before congregating for a massive, all-out assault on Safad, which lay inland between Acre and Tyre: a heavily fortified Templar redoubt the sultan regarded as "a lump in the throat of Islam."[17] When Safad surrendered after a hard-fought, six-week assault, Baybars agreed to give safe-conduct to Safad's fifteen hundred defenders. Once they began to file out of the fortress he changed his mind and had all but two of them executed on a nearby hilltop. Not having any naval function, Safad was left standing and regarrisoned with Mamluk troops.

Now the crusaders' miseries piled up, year after year. In the summer of 1267 Baybars—walking with a limp having broken his foot falling from his horse, but otherwise more dangerous than ever—burned the harvest and cut down orchards around Acre, ensuring a meager winter for the inhabitants. On

March 8, 1268, he sent an army to Jaffa securing its capitulation in a matter of hours, with the garrison fleeing, as usual, by boat. Jaffa's fortifications were dismantled and the raw building materials shipped to Cairo for use in pious building projects for the benefit of the Muslim faithful. "He took the relic of the head of St. George and burned the body of St. Christina," complained the Templar of Tyre.[18] In April he oversaw the successful siege of Beaufort, occupied by the Templars. Then he swung north, to punish once more Bohemond VI of Antioch-Tripoli.

In 1098 the first crusaders took seven and a half months to take Antioch from its Seljuq governor, Yaghi-Siyan. One hundred and seventy years on, Baybars completed its conquest in two days. On May 18 the sultan's men scaled the walls with ladders, while others barred the gates to prevent anyone from escaping the massacre. The Templar of Tyre wrote that seventeen thousand people were killed and one hundred thousand taken captive. As prices on the Syrian slave markets crashed, Antioch burned: the citadel was lit up and the blaze took much of the city with it.[19] Even as the flames raged, Baybars sent a triumphant letter to Bohemond, who had not been present at the siege. He mocked him for having lost his right to call himself "Prince," then described the atrocious punishment that had befallen his city. Had Bohemond been present to defend his people, said Baybars, "you would have seen your knights prostrate beneath the horses' hooves, your houses stormed by pillagers and ransacked by looters . . . your women sold four at a time and bought for a *dinar* of your own money! You would have seen the crosses in your churches smashed, the pages of the false Testaments scattered, the Patriarchs' tombs overturned. You would have seen the Muslim enemy trampling on the place where you celebrate the Mass, cutting the throats of monks, priests and deacons upon the altars . . . you would have seen fire running through your palaces, your dead burned in this world before going down to the fires of the next . . . Then you would have said 'Would that I were dust, and that no letter had ever brought me such tidings!' "[20] This was more than mere rhetoric. Antioch's days as a leading city of the Syrian northwest were over.

In previous generations, this abysmal series of losses in the crusader states would have been enough to prompt existential panic in the West of the sort that had inspired the Second and Third Crusades. But by the end of the 1260s the appetite for Eastern crusading was declining at the same rapid rate as the crusader states themselves. As Baybars was razing Christian settlements and fortresses all over the Levant, the most active and energetic campaigning was on Sicily, where Charles of Anjou, brother of the French king Louis IX and a veteran of the Damietta campaign of 1249 to 1250, was leading a papal-sponsored mission to drive the last of Frederick Hohenstaufen's descendants out of the kingdom. In 1266 Charles led an army of crusaders who defeated and killed Frederick's son Manfred at the battle of Benevento. Two years later Charles captured Frederick's grandson Conradin, the sixteen-year-old titular king of Jerusalem and would-be ruler of Sicily. Conradin was beheaded in public in Naples on October 28, 1268, bringing to the end the Hohenstaufen royal line, passing Sicily into French hands and marking a new low in the steady perversion of the idea of crusading, thanks to the relentless anti-Hohenstaufen vendetta pursued by a long succession of popes.

There were, of course, some princes in the West who tried to rally themselves to the defense of the East, but their efforts were by turns ill-fated and inadequate. In 1269 a small party of Aragonese warriors led by two royal princes arrived by ship in Acre—but the princes came without their king, the mighty Reconquista warrior James I, who had been shipwrecked on his way and abandoned his journey. In 1270, Louis IX of France stirred himself for another tilt at the Holy Land he had attempted to leave on a stable defensive footing during his visit from 1250 to 1254. But Louis was now fifty-six years old, and he was not the force he had been in his younger days. His strategic judgment, never especially acute, had grown even weaker. With his brother Charles installed as king of Sicily, Louis decided to sail his modest fleet to the Holy Land via Ifriqiya (now in the hands of the Berber-descended Sunni dynasty known as the Hafsids) and attack Tunis. The expedition was a fiasco, and as Louis camped outside the city, epidemic disease ripped through his army. Louis died of dysentery on August 25, 1270, supposedly uttering the word "Jerusalem" before he succumbed. His crusade broke up and his body was taken home for burial; in Cairo, Baybars received the news with relief and delight. Twenty-seven years later Louis was canonized—but holy as he was, the great French saint-king had ultimately done precious little to contribute to the security of the Lord's Sepulchre.

Only in the early summer 1271, with the arrival at Acre of a contingent of crusaders led by the Lord Edward, heir to the Plantagenet throne of England (the future Edward I "Longshanks"), and his young wife, Eleanor of Castile, did the relentless calamities inflicted on the crusader states seem to pause. Edward was tall, physically intimidating and bloody minded, already a veteran of a devastating civil war in England, and he would grow up to be the finest warrior and general of his generation. He brought with him about one thousand men, a quarter of whom were knights. But even he was able to do little more than staunch the bleeding. Edward arrived in Acre too late to save a succession of the most important crusader castles in the East from falling. The Hospitallers' jewel of Crac des Chevaliers was taken in April 1271, followed in June of the same year by Montfort—the great Teutonic Order fortress, which stood as a monument to the golden days of master Hermann von Salza's rule.[21] Edward's stay in the East was marked chiefly by Baybars's decision in the autumn of 1271 to grant an increasingly distraught Bohemond VI of Antioch-Tripoli a ten-year truce, which in turn allowed the Mamluk sultan to focus fully on the Mongol threat to Syria. Edward disapproved strongly of the truce, so in May 1272 Baybars tried to deal with the headstrong young prince by commissioning an Assassin to creep into his bedroom and attack him with a dagger.* The attack was thwarted when Edward fought back, punched the Assassin in the face, wrestled him to the ground and stabbed him in the head until he was dead.[22] Once he recovered from his own serious wounds, Edward concluded that even he had seen enough. He departed for home by the autumn of 1272, and never came back.

On June 30, 1277, Baybars died in Damascus. He had gorged himself several days earlier on his favorite drink of fermented mare's milk, and the hangover brought on a fatal combination of fever and acute diarrhea. The suddenness of his illness (which aroused suspicions of poison) and the upheavals caused by the transition to a new Mamluk sultan after nearly seventeen years of unprecedentedly successful rule meant that what remained of the crusader states were afforded another few years of relative peace.[23] Yet even before Baybars's death, there was a sense that the remaining Latins of the East were preparing for the end. In 1276 Hugh III of Cyprus, who had been elected King

*The choice of an Assassin to attack Edward was interesting: as well as attacking the crusader states, Baybars had systematically reduced the Assassins' remaining castles in Syria, completing the job begun in Persia by the Mongols.

Hugh I of Jerusalem after Conradin's execution, moved the seat of the royal court permanently to his Cypriot estates. Behind him, leadership in Acre was disputed by representatives of the absent Sicilian king, Charles of Anjou, who also claimed to be the rightful ruler of the Latin kingdom. This tortuous division of power, and the petty squabble for denuded authority it represented, spoke to the true state of affairs among the Franks.

The endgame commenced twelve years after Baybars's death, in 1289, under the Mamluk sultan Qalawun, a veteran of the Bahriyya who had first to be taken to Egypt to train as a slave-soldier in the great Ayyubid sultan al-Kamil's household. In 1289 Qalawun took aim at the city of Tripoli: thickly walled but rotten inside with feuds between vying factions of Genoese, Pisans, Venetians and Hospitallers. Undermanned and disunited, the defenders of Tripoli stood no chance when Qalawun moved against them, and as soon as the Mamluk army arrived boats started pulling out of the harbor to evacuate inhabitants to Armenia. "In the end the town was so weakened that the Saracens took it in a single assault," wrote the Templar of Tyre. "It lacked adequate defenders, who one by one had abandoned the defense."[24] The Mamluks swept in, looting, killing and demolishing buildings. Swimmers were sent to a little island off the shore where there was a church dedicated to Saint Thomas, in which terrified civilian families were taking refuge. The women and children were captured; and the men were killed, their bodies left in a pile to rot, so that for weeks afterward "it was impossible to land there because of the stench."[25]

Once more the international response to the loss of a major Latin town was virtually nonexistent. Twenty Venetian galleys commissioned by Pope Nicholas IV arrived to help defend the remaining cities of Acre and Tyre, but they caused more harm than good. "By the agency of the Enemy from Hell [i.e., Satan] the crusaders who had come to do good and to arm themselves for the succor of the city of Acre brought about its destruction," wrote the Templar of Tyre.[26] In 1290 these visiting warriors were responsible for a riot in Acre in which they massacred dozens of poor Muslim traders selling wheat and other goods at market. When their blood-soaked garments were taken to Qalawun in Cairo, he declared his intention to punish Acre and fitted out an expeditionary army to take the city. In fact Qalawun died in October 1290 before he could have his satisfaction. But he left it to his successor as sultan, al-Ashraf Khalil, to see that justice was served.

When al-Ashraf Khalil arrived at the gates of Acre in April 1291, his army was said to number 75,000 horsemen and another 150,000 infantry. Even allowing for the customary exaggeration, it was a massive force. When envoys came out of Acre to try to assuage his wrath with gifts, he refused to accept them, instead sending back a letter announcing his intention to seize and destroy the crusader capital, and reminding them that he was "Sultan of Sultans, King of Kings, Lord of Lords . . . the Powerful, the Dreadful, the Scourge of Rebels, Hunter of Franks and Tartars and Armenians, Snatcher of Castles from the Hands of Miscreants."[27] He invested Acre with his siege engines on April 5, and began the barrage with stonethrowers named *Ghadban* ("Wrathful") and *al-Mansuri* ("Victorious"), whose giant components were transported in one hundred wagons, and which hurled rocks weighing over one hundred pounds each.[28]

The sultan's army was so vast that it could completely encircle the landward walls of the city. The infantry erected temporary barricades topped with wicker screens, from behind which they worked in four shifts around the clock to keep up a ceaseless bombardment, while underneath them miners tunneled, heading for the foundations of Acre's main defensive towers. By night the Templars, under their master William of Beaujeu, and various other groups of knights attempted to sally out of the gates and cause as much disruption in the besiegers' camps as possible. But they were always outnumbered, and usually forced to retreat back into the city, having taken heavy losses. This went on for several weeks, and even when King Hugh brought reinforcements to Acre, arriving by boat from Cyprus on May 4, there was very little to be done. By that time the outer of the city's double walls had been mined; a few days after Hugh arrived the largest of Acre's towers—the Accursed Tower, or Tower of the King—collapsed. This was a major breach, and it was clear from this point that the city would not hold much longer. "Everyone was thoroughly demoralized," wrote the Templar of Tyre, who was in Acre at the time, "and began to send their women and children down to the ships." The weather was too bad and the seas too rough for a fast evacuation—but this was clearly the only way that anyone could now hope to escape Acre alive.[29]

Shortly before dawn broke on May 18, Acre awoke to the sound of a heavy drum beat, "creating a terrible, terrifying noise."[30] Seemingly the whole might of the Mamluk army was pressing at the walls. Led by the masters of the Templars and Hospitallers, the citizens and all the able-bodied warriors inside the city scrambled to strap on their armor and ran to the gates in the inner walls. But by the time they reached them, battering rams had already broken through, and the first Mamluk invaders were piling in.

The Templar of Tyre, who bore witness to the events that followed, recalled thick, dense, blinding smoke that billowed everywhere as the Mamluks hurled pots of Greek fire at the defenders. Through this noxious, greasy smoke came javelins and feathered arrows, striking down men and horses on all sides. Knights ran about with their surcoats on fire, the flames melting the skin on their faces and roasting them where they stood. The Templar master, William of Beaujeu, fought in the streets on horseback, but was killed when a javelin passed through a gap in his armor below the armpit and pierced deep into his side. His fall caused confusion among the men around him, not all of whom could speak the same language. A contingent of French knights—veterans who were members of the regiment left to defend Acre by Louis IX—put up a brave fight, but eventually they were overwhelmed, leaving "many wounded and dead."[31] Brave as they were, Acre's defenders were outnumbered by as many as ten to one. As a seemingly endless stream of Mamluk warriors poured through the breached gates, the fight grew hopeless. Street by street the crusaders were driven back, first from the walls, then from the outer suburb known as Montmusard, until finally the fighting was concentrated on the docks.

King Hugh, along with a number of other dignitaries including the master of the Hospitallers, took ship and abandoned the city long before its last stand. As they sailed out of Acre's harbor into choppy seas, they left behind them at the portside "ladies and burgesses and cloistered maidens and other lesser folk, [who] came fleeing through the streets, their children in their arms, weeping and despairing, and fleeing to the sailors to save them."[32] There were far too few berths for so many desperate refugees, and soon the docks were a scene of carnage, as Mamluk horsemen speared and gored those civilians they saw no worth in taking hostage, trampling infants and riding down pregnant women. "The Muslims entered Acre and made themselves masters of it," wrote Abu al-Mahasin.[33]

The last stand at Acre took place at the Templars' palatial headquarters by the docks, a fiercely reinforced compound, whose central tower was topped with four gilded, life-sized statues of lions. Thousands of citizens crammed inside its walls, watching the galleys taking the last of the great, the good, and the fortunate away to Cyprus, Armenia and the bare few other safe havens on the coast. As the last of them disappeared, so too did any hope of escape. For ten days the Templars barred the gates of their fortress. There were sporadic negotiations and one bloody skirmish in which the brothers managed to trap a small division of Mamluk horsemen in one of their courtyards and cut them to pieces. During that time, however, Mamluk sappers had been digging beneath the walls. On May 28, they collapsed part of the wall and stormed in. Acre's last stand was over, and with it the fate of the crusader states in the Near East was sealed.

In the weeks that followed Acre's fall, the remaining Frankish settlements along the coast were quietly evacuated. The Templar garrison in the remarkable sea castle at Sidon abandoned their posts and sailed for Cyprus. Soon after, Beirut and Tyre were also evacuated. In August Château Pèlerin, the impenetrable Templar fortress between Haifa and Caesarea, was the last place to be abandoned. The kingdom of Jerusalem was now a kingdom in exile on Cyprus. Antioch and Tripoli had been wiped off the map. "Everything was lost," wrote the Templar of Tyre, "so that altogether the Christians held not so much as a palm's breadth of land in Syria." The Kurdish historian and geographer Abu al-Fida, who kept a detailed eyewitness account of the sultan's final campaigns against the crusaders, noted with satisfaction the completeness of the victory, and its historic importance. "With these conquests the whole of Palestine was now in Muslim hands," he wrote, "a result that no one would have dared to hope for or desire. Thus the whole of Syria and the coastal zones were purified of Franks. . . . Praise be to God!"[34]

26

Fragments and Dreams

Depart into the everlasting fire, you accursed ones!

Marino Sanudo the Elder was a rich Venetian and an enthusiastic man of the world.[1] Born around 1270, one of five boys in a well-to-do aristocratic family on the Rialto, he was given the cryptic nickname "Torsello" by his father and began to roam the Mediterranean in his teens. His ancestors had captained galleys in famous and notorious Venetian escapades such as the burning of Constantinople on the Fourth Crusade; one of his forebears married into the family of the ancient blind crusader doge Enrico Dandolo. By the early fourteenth century the Sanudo name was therefore known far beyond Venice itself, and the family's affairs included commodity trading, estate management, shipping and moneylending. During Marino's lifetime aspects of these businesses took him to the island of Naxos in the Cyclades islands (where his cousins ruled as "dukes of the archipelago"), to Negroponte (modern Chalcis, north of Athens on the island of Euboea), to Palermo and Rome, to Acre (before its fall to the Mamluks in 1291), to Constantinople, Alexandria, Cyprus, Rhodes and Armenia; even to Bruges and Hamburg in northern Europe, where Sanudo arrived in style aboard a Venetian state galley.[2] The contacts and personal friends he made during his travels were a roll call of the most powerful politicians and rulers of the day: several popes, a Byzantine emperor, the kings of France, England and Armenia, Italian and French dukes and Flemish counts, and innumerable legates, bishops and cardinals.[3]

As well as being an intrepid voyager and networker, Sanudo was also an avid reader and self-conscious intellectual. An excellent education meant he grew up with a knowledge of Latin, Italian, French and Greek, and a passionate interest in ancient writers such as Aristotle, Plato, Cicero and Boethius, biblical commentators like Bede and Saint Augustine, and chroniclers of the crusader states including William of Tyre and James of Vitry—who had kept vivid, scandalous, exciting accounts of the rise and fall of the Franks in the Holy Land. This was a story that had played out in dramatic fashion throughout Sanudo's youth, and one in which he felt he had an important part to play.

In 1306 Sanudo decided to combine his knowledge of the world with his literary inclinations and began writing a text that would become known as the *Liber Secretorum Fidelium Crucis* or *The Book of the Secrets of the Faithful of the Cross*. Part handbook, part manifesto, part history of the Holy Land and part showcase for Sanudo's extensive reading, the *Book of Secrets* was researched, developed and written over a period of fifteen years, and only completed in September 1321, when Sanudo presented two copies, bound in cheerful red and yellow covers, to Pope John XXII at the papal court in Avignon.* But Sanudo's topic was certainly big enough to merit its long drafting process and grand recipient: it was a plan to launch a new crusade and win back the kingdom of Jerusalem for the Western Church.

Plans for regaining the Holy Land were much in vogue in the years during and after the Mamluk conquests of the crusader states. As early as 1274 Pope Gregory X convened a council at Lyon, where he invited freethinking scholars and strategists to devise ways to reverse Christian losses to Baybars, "since the liberation of the said land is of concern to all who confess the Catholic faith."[4] Following the fall of Acre in 1291, Pope Nicholas IV repeated the request, as would other popes after him. The result was a subgenre of literature consisting of crusading schemes—some progressive, others retrograde and a few downright hare-brained. The Mallorcan mathematician Ramon Lull advocated opening language schools to help train missionaries in advance of a targeted elite-forces invasion spearheaded by the military orders. The Hospitaller master Fulk Villaret suggested a crusade carried out exactly "in the same manner which was employed by [Pope] Urban"—meaning an invasion

*From 1309 until 1376 the papacy resided in Avignon rather than in Rome.

directly and specifically modeled on the First Crusade.[5] Some writers, including the Franciscan friar Fidenzio of Padua, excoriated the Franks of the failed crusader states for what they viewed as womanly cowardice and an addiction to backbiting; Fidenzio advised a new generation of crusaders to study Mamluk methods of warfare and spycraft and steal the best bits for themselves.[6] Others advocated a new Christian superarmy, to be created through radical reform of the military orders and placed under the stewardship of some valiant and vigorous Western prince in the role of what Lull called a *bellator rex*: warrior king. There was no shortage of bright ideas, particularly among those who had not been on crusade and seen its challenges firsthand.

Sanudo's plan was not shatteringly original. In fact, strategically, it was straightforward. He proposed an economic blockade of all Muslim ports in Asia Minor, Syria, Egypt, North Africa and southern Spain, policed by Venetian galleys, which would inflict major commercial pain, before a large crusading fleet would carry a fifteen-thousand-strong army to invade the Nile Delta, supported by a broad coalition of anti-Islamic powers, including the Mongols and the Nubian Christians of the Upper Nile. They would fight their way through Egypt and Palestine and reclaim the Holy Land, which would thereafter be "kept in a good, quiet and peaceful condition to the praise of God and to the honor of the Holy Roman Church."[7] Eventually, Christian vessels would patrol the seas and control trade as far east as the Indian Ocean. For the most part this was a simple, if optimistic plan. Sanudo's selling point was not in his military imagination, but rather his obsession with detail and practicalities. His *Book of Secrets*—which ran to well over one hundred thousand words in length—was a blizzard of fine points. Its long discourses on troop numbers, boat design, arms purchasing and foodstuffs, detailed breakdown of costs and the exhaustive rehearsal of historical examples (both biblical and modern) exceeded in scope and specificity anything produced by any other writer. Sanudo also commissioned beautiful, detailed maps by the Genoese-born, Venetian-based cartographer Pietro Vesconte, including a magnificent *mappa mundi* showing the whole Mediterranean theater, five sea charts detailing the European and North African coastlines and a plan of the landscape of the Holy Land.[8] Each page of his plan was packed with the evidence of a life spent thinking of little other than crusading and crusaders. He made sure that copies found their way into the hands not only of the pope, but of every significant ruler in Western Europe.

Yet for all this effort, Sanudo's plan came to nothing. Despite the shock of 1291, and the interest in reclaiming the crusader states that was loudly and piously voiced at Europe's royal and papal courts, Sanudo's longed-for expedition—a *general passage*, as it was called in the literature—never came to pass. As the fourteenth century dawned, the allure of mass crusading was dimming rapidly. Although the Holy Land was now in Mamluk hands, and was dangerous to Christian travelers, Jerusalem was not closed to pilgrims, for the Mamluks were pragmatic rather than dogmatic when it came to collecting the taxes they charged for entry to the city to worship at its shrines. To that end the Holy Sepulchre was tended by Franciscan monks, who from 1335 and 1336 had their own monastery in the Holy City, and were officially tolerated by the Muslim rulers. Moreover, while the importance of taking full possession of Jerusalem was still a matter that could stir Christian hearts, Western knights who sought penitential warfare—or indeed, any sort of warfare—could usually find it much closer to home. New secular conflicts—such as the so-called Hundred Years' War, fought between England, France and drawing in at various times their neighbors in Scotland, Flanders, Aragon, Castile, Portugal—were looming. The Reconquista continued, as did a plethora of papal wars and battles against the pagans of northern Europe. Crusading and crusaders were heading in other directions.

For several decades even before Sanudo started writing, crusading had been most actively pursued not in the Latin East but in the western Mediterranean. On the Italian peninsula and in Sicily, where for decades the papacy had been involved in wars with neighboring powers—most dramatically the Hohenstaufen dynasty—the crusade had become an almost automatic feature of warfare, reached for not as an expression of mass penitence or for the liberation of Christ's patrimony, but as a means for popes to rally troops on fixed-term contracts in which payment was made in the remittance of penance and the remission of sins. Just as in the twelfth century the spiritual weapons of excommunication and interdict were wielded almost without a second thought by popes attempting to browbeat secular rulers into obeying their edicts, so by the late thirteenth century the crusade, too, had become heavily politicized. From the 1250s onward, crusades were not only called against familiar enemies in the eastern Mediterranean including the

Mongols, Mamluks and schismatic Greeks, but against papal enemies in the West. They included Frederick's descendants Conrad, Manfred and Conradin of Sicily; the pro-Hohenstaufen brothers, Ezzelino and Alberico da Romano of Padua and Verona; a militarized colony of Muslims in Lucera in southern Italy (described by the papal preacher as "snakes" living in "a cave of sins"), who had been deported from Sicily and seconded to the Hohenstaufen armies; a group of cardinals who fell out with Pope Boniface VIII; and even, in 1309, the republic of Venice.[9]

This scattershot approach to crusade deployment presented any number of absurdities, and never more than in 1284 and 1285 when Pope Martin IV tried to punish King Pedro III of Aragon for invading Sicily, infringing the rights of the pope's choice for the crown: the French prince Charles of Valois.* Martin therefore declared a crusade against Pedro and corralled the support of the French Crown to attack him. For Pedro to end up as the target of a crusade was somewhere between ironic and bizarre. As a young man he had fought for his father James I's armies in the wars to strip Valencia from Muslim rule. When his father had lain dying in 1276 Pedro had promised him that he would "expel all the Moors from the kingdom of Valencia, as they are all traitors."[10] In 1281 (as a precursor to invading Sicily) he had skirmished with Muslim forces in Ifriqiya.[11] Yet according to the papal bull issued against him by Martin IV, he was not a champion of Christendom, but a sinner and an enemy of the Church who deserved all the opprobrium of the faithful.[12] As it turned out the crusade against Pedro of Aragon (which continued from 1285 against his son Frederick, who took over the Sicilian cause) proved unsuccessful: under the Peace of Caltabellota of August 1302, the island of Sicily remained in Aragonese hands while the possessions of the kingdom on mainland Italy—known now as the Kingdom of Naples—passed to Charles. But this was hardly the point. What was more, it was not the only time a French pope and French prince colluded to attack, rather than back, committed Christian crusaders whom they saw as dangerous and expendable. In that regard, the most shocking casualty of the years that followed the cataclysms of 1291 were the Knights Templar.

*The wars over Sicily that followed the destruction of the Hohenstaufen male line ran for twenty years, having its origin in a rebellion against French rule in Palermo on Easter Monday 1282. They are generally known as the Wars of the Sicilian Vespers.

After the fall of Acre and the evacuations of the last fortresses on the crusader coast, the kings of Jerusalem were forced into exile on Cyprus. From here the task of reoccupying the mainland became immeasurably more daunting than that of holding on to cities in the face of the Mamluk onslaught, for any military campaign now had to be based around establishing a bridgehead at which to land troops, horses, armor, food and water, and ensuring an unbroken supply chain by sea. But if the task was difficult, there were still crusaders in the rump state of the Latin East who believed it was possible, and they were led by the military orders.

In 1300 a serious attempt was made by Amaury of Lusignan (the brother of King Henry II of Cyprus-Jerusalem) and the Knights Templar based on Cyprus to force a landing at Tortosa, in the former county of Tripoli, which had been a Templar stronghold for nearly one hundred and forty years before its fall to the Mamluks. That November Amaury and the Templar master, James of Molay, landed six hundred troops, around a quarter of whom were Templars, at Tortosa. Although they failed to retake their old military base there—they were let down by Mongols of the Ilkhanate, who reneged on a promise to support the operation—they did manage to secure the small island of Ru'ad, just off the coast of Tortosa. The Templars garrisoned and held Ru'ad for about eighteen months, until the summer of 1302, maintaining a very large presence of more than one hundred knights and thousands of mercenaries and support staff in a fortress. Eventually, however, the fortress fell to a Mamluk siege led by a Muslim convert from Georgia known as Sayf al-Din Esendemür. Almost every member of the order on the island was either killed in battle or "dishonorably conducted" to Egypt for imprisonment or sale into slavery.[13] It had been a valiant effort on the part of the Templars, but it was nowhere near enough.

Four years later, the Templar master James of Molay had absorbed the lesson of this defeat. He traveled back from Cyprus to Western Europe to present a plan for a new crusade to the papal court, adamant that half-baked invasions of the sort that had failed on Ru'ad could not offer a realistic way back to Jerusalem. "A small-scale expedition would be ineffectual, causing harm and ignominy to Christendom," he wrote.[14] Just as Marino Sanudo of Venice would come to believe, Molay thought that any new crusade would have to be conceived and planned on a much grander scale. Naturally, Molay also believed that the military orders would have a central role to play. Yet as it transpired, however, the role of the military orders was about to change dramatically—and in the case of the Templars, fatally.

Many of the early fourteenth-century plans for reviving the crusades in Syria and Palestine scrutinized the role the military orders had played in the failure of the crusader states and presented plans of reform that would render them fit for purpose in a new era of warfare. Several observers concluded that there was little point in maintaining Templars, Hospitallers and Teutonic Knights as separate entities, and argued that it would be far more sensible to amalgamate the three—along with the various independent orders active in Spain—to form a superorder that would function as an international strike force. The Mallorcan scholar Ramon Lull was one who took this view, writing that "all the orders of knighthood should welcome this step . . . and should anyone oppose it, he would be seen to be neither faithful nor devout, and he should consider the judgment on the Last Day, when the Lord Jesus Christ says: 'Depart into the everlasting fire, you accursed ones.' "[15] His words would prove darkly prophetic.

The pope whom James of Molay traveled to meet in 1306 was another Frenchman: the former archbishop of Bordeaux Bertrand of Got, who had taken the papal name of Clement V. Clement's election to the papal throne had been in large part thanks to political pressure exerted by the king of France, Philip IV "Le Bel," a tall, handsome, coldly callous and fanatically pious individual whose instinctive paranoia and appetite for the violent persecution of those he suspected to be enemies of the French Crown was eagerly exploited by his ministers. At the time of James of Molay's visit to the west in 1306, Philip was encouraged by courtiers, including the brilliant but entirely unscrupulous lawyer William of Nogaret, to regard the Templars as a malign, corrupt institution whose members engaged in secret, blasphemous ceremonies and deserved to be thoroughly investigated and punished with the full weight of the law. The ultimate purpose, for Nogaret and his associates, was to provide justification for seizing the Templars' assets inside the kingdom of France and sequestering them for the French Crown, which was suffering from chronic financial difficulties. But the casualty, at least in part, was crusading.

The supposed evidence the French amassed for the Templars' alleged misdeeds was a hysterical and baseless dossier of grotesquery, charging that brothers of the order habitually spat and urinated on crosses, denied the name of Christ, kissed and sexually fondled one another in lewd induction rituals and worshipped statues and idols. That there was barely a shred of truth to any of this was immaterial. On Friday, October 13, 1307, every Templar in France—including the master, James of Molay—was arrested on royal warrant, imprisoned and in many cases tortured to force them to admit to their "crimes." Pope Clement offered only limp resistance to this unilateral attack by the French Crown on an order that was ultimately answerable to the papacy; he was forced to open an investigation into Templar misdeeds in every territory of Christendom. This decision led to mass arrests and interrogations of Templars in every realm from Ireland to Cyprus, despite deep and widespread skepticism as to the Templars' guilt.

After a long and painfully drawn-out legal process, which in France included one episode of mass burnings, when several dozen brothers were sent to the stake as relapsed heretics, at a Church council in Vienne in 1311 and 1312 the order was formally wound up across Europe. Its members were either pensioned off, sentenced to long jail terms, sent to live as simple monks in nonmilitary monasteries or—in a few cases, mostly limited to the kingdoms of the Spanish peninsula, where the Templars had been performing a useful function in the late stages of the Reconquista—allowed to join other military orders such as the Portuguese Order of Christ, established in 1319 by King Denis I. James of Molay was burned at the stake in Paris in March 1314, on the order of Philip IV—whose own sudden death after a hunting accident the same year was regarded by many as fulfillment of a curse laid upon him by Molay as the flames consumed him. It was a pitiful end to the celebrated order, whom the great Islamic chronicler Ibn al-Athir had once described as sharing with the Hospitallers the distinction of being "the fiercest fighters of all the Franks."[16] And it removed from the crusading sphere a force that, if not perfect, had at least been at the fore of the most recent concerted attempt to reverse the losses of 1291.

As the Templars fell, so the other two major international military orders, who had been mainstays of the defense of the Holy Land, were also forced to redefine their purpose in a changing era. In both cases, this involved physical removal from the kingdom of Jerusalem, such as it remained.

The Hospitallers were one of the major beneficiaries of the Templars' disgrace and fall. At the Council of Vienne in 1312 there were mutterings about the moral character of Hospitaller members and their supposed preference for building fine halls and palaces over fighting the enemies of God. Nevertheless, it was to the Hospital that most of the confiscated Templar assets were granted, since in the view of Pope Clement V, the Hospitallers were "fearless warriors of Christ . . . ardent in their efforts to recover the Holy Land, despising all human perils . . . the more plentifully they are supplied . . . the more will the energy of the masters and brothers of the Order and Hospital grow."[17] Undoubtedly, this takeover of extensive estates and commercial interests in virtually every kingdom in the West helped secure Hospitaller survival as a crusading institution for generations. Yet it coincided with a far more decisive act in Hospitaller history, as the order decamped to the island of Rhodes, a few miles off the coast of southwest Anatolia on the edge of the Dodecanese archipelago.

Rhodes was technically a Byzantine possession when in 1306 the Hospitaller master Fulk of Villaret decided to attack it. In practice, however, rule on the island was divided, between Genoan governors to whom the Byzantine emperor had devolved power, and Turkish pirates who held the east of the island.[18] It was not an easy place for the Hospitallers to conquer: success required an initial foray west from Cyprus with a small fleet, followed by a siege of Rhodes town in the north of the island, two defensive actions against Byzantine relieving armies and a mopping-up operation in the neighboring islands of the Dodecanese, supported by a small number of crusaders from the West. But the effort was eventually repaid as Rhodes fell—an event that briefly inspired tens of thousands of ordinary pilgrims and poor would-be crusaders in England, northern France and the Rhineland to start sewing crosses to their shirts, marching about, beating up Jews and demanding that some rich lord find them transport to the Mediterranean so that they could take part in the war. Very few of them made it anywhere near Rhodes. But the Hospitallers were able permanently to move their global headquarters there from Cyprus and to establish a military-monastic state under their own rule. They now had a base close to the coastline of Asia Minor and Byzantium from which a garrison of nearly three hundred knights and thousands of sergeants and mercenaries could conduct raids on Greek or Turkish towns and engage in piracy—which was what, in effect, the majority of crusading in the Mediterranean was to become during the course of the fourteenth century.

During that time they had some famous victories, the most eye-catching being when they allied with Venice and Cyprus to capture Smyrna (Izmir) on the Turkish coast in 1344, holding it until 1402. Rhodes also became a safe stopping point for pilgrims determined to attempt the journey to Jerusalem.[19] Meanwhile, further west, the Hospitallers continued, as they had for centuries, to play a limited role in the Spanish Reconquista.[20] They would remain entrenched on Rhodes until 1522, when it took the great Ottoman sultan Suleiman the Magnificent six months and four hundred ships to evict them, after which they set up on Malta, which they ruled until the arrival of Napoleon Bonaparte in 1798. The Hospitallers were in this sense the great survivors of the crusading era: an institution that had been in Jerusalem even before the First Crusade and one that maintained a role in Christian holy war until long after the end of the Middle Ages. At the same time, however, their changing focus and sphere of operations was an indicator of the steady fragmentation and weakening of the crusading movement as the prospect of regaining the kingdom of Jerusalem itself began to fade.

Like the Hospitallers, the Teutonic Order also thought better of headquartering on Cyprus after 1291. Following a brief period in which they were based in Venice, the Teutonic Knights focused their attentions solely on completing the Christianization of the Baltic, the task that had occupied them for much of the thirteenth century. Like the Hospitallers on Rhodes, the Teutonic Order had every incentive to combine fighting the heathen with securing themselves within a realm that would afford them political independence and protection should it be needed. At the time of the proceedings against the Templars, Pope Clement V also launched an investigation into alleged Teutonic misdeeds in Livonia, where they were said to have been colluding with pagans and abusing local churchmen. From 1309 the order was commanded from Marienburg (Malbork, in modern Poland), a massive waterside fortress on the bank of the river Volnat. This, and scores of other similar strongholds, became the basis for the Teutonic Order's own monastic-military state that, by the end of the fourteenth century, had expanded from Danzig (Gdansk) in the southwest to the furthest northern reaches of Estonia.

This process of colonization had been born out of the Teutonic Order's involvement in crusading, and their expansionist policies could still be dressed up as wars to defend Christians and purify the land in the name of Christ. But after 1386, their pagan neighbors effectively disappeared: Jogaila, the last pagan Grand Duke of Lithuania unified his duchy with the kingdom of Poland and converted to Catholicism. In 1410 this doughty ruler (now known by his Christian name of Władysław II Jagiello) crushed the Teutonic Knights at the battle of Grunwald (also known as the battle of Tannenburg), and the heavy reparations imposed on the knights marked the beginning of a long, slow decline in their state, which eventually ceased to exist in the sixteenth century. Although some recruits who fought with the Teutonic Knights at Grunwald claimed crusader status, the reality was that any serious crusading purpose had long since drained away from them.

The extinction and emigration of the military orders from the rump of the Latin East in the early fourteenth century mattered because, when combined with the steady devaluation of crusading by popes who weaponized it against their political enemies, it marked the departure from the most significant and symbolic theater of crusader activity of the institutions most capable of waging permanent, penitential war against the ruling Muslim powers in Syria and Palestine. Self-evidently, crusading had since at least the 1120s (and arguably since its very inception) had many other manifestations beyond the struggle for Jerusalem. But once shorn of that central, galvanizing purpose, crusading began to lose any remaining sense of overall cohesion, along with its capacity to unite the major powers of the Christian West behind a single, cosmic goal. Periodically in the fourteenth century there were exciting clashes between coalitions of Christian powers and Muslim or other infidel enemies: naval victories by the so-called crusade leagues of Venice, Cyprus and Hospitaller Rhodes, or the sack of Mamluk Alexandria by an armada under Peter I of Cyprus in 1365. But when set alongside the massive expeditions of the twelfth and thirteenth centuries, which had traveled with the leading monarchs or aristocrats of the West in command, the crusades of the fourteenth century were small beer indeed and had little or no lasting effect on the region at large.

The truth was, without the focus of Jerusalem and the Latin crusader states, it was inevitable that crusading would fragment into a reactive, disparate sideshow, with a distinguished history but diminishing serious importance to kings and ordinary believers alike. As that happened, raising huge, multinational military campaigns to seize faraway lands for the greater glory of Christendom ceased to be realistic. They were merely the object of pipe dreams and quixotic schemes, conceived by well-meaning but ultimately misguided men like Marino Sanudo of Venice, the architect of a brilliant but entirely imaginary military campaign that was, even when it was written, a relic of a bygone day.

◆ 27 ◆

Brave New Worlds

There could be no more honorable expedition
than one in the service of God.

In the spring of 1390 Henry Bolingbroke, the twenty-three-year-old first cousin of the king of England, gathered together a hundred friends and retainers and went across the Channel to fight in a jousting competition. The tournament they attended was held just outside the English-held town of Calais at a place known as Saint-Inglevert and had been announced by heralds with great fanfare the previous autumn in a deliberate attempt to stir the hearts and the collective pride of the young, status-obsessed aristocratic circles in which men like Bolingbroke moved. The host was a French knight of almost exactly Bolingbroke's age called Jean II le Meingre, a self-styled paragon of chivalry better known as "Boucicaut." The prizes on offer were priceless: honor, glory and "a reputation for dauntlessness."[1]

Merely to exchange lance blows with Boucicaut was a sign of noble worth. Since the age of twelve the Frenchman had been fighting all over Europe, battling Burgundians in Normandy, Englishmen in Brittany and Gascony, and insurgent Flemings in Flanders. He had joined the perpetual crusade in the Baltic, fighting alongside Teutonic Knights against Lithuanian pagans in Prussia. He had visited Constantinople and traveled as a pilgrim to Mamluk-held Jerusalem. He had even been to Damascus, where one of the French king's relatives, the Count of Eu, had been detained during his own pilgrimage; Boucicaut remained there for three months as a voluntary hostage while the count's release was negotiated. The young man was, said an admiring contemporary biographer, "fine-looking . . . amiable, affable and jovial, a little on the swarthy side, and with a high-colored complexion which suited him"; so brave that his attendants sometimes had to restrain him for his own safety, and so strong that he could "do a somersault fully armed except for his bascinet [helmet] and dance equipped in a coat of mail."[2] The tournament he had organized at Saint-Inglevert was characteristically bold spirited. Boucicaut and two of his worthiest friends had set up in a field and decorated a giant elm tree with shields bearing their coats of arms. They swore to fight anyone who rode up to the elm and laid down a challenge by hitting one of the shields with a weapon. Once the challenge was accepted, each knight could ride five tilts with a lance against Boucicaut or one of his companions. It would be a fine horseman indeed who had the skill to topple them.

Bolingbroke's journey to joust with Boucicaut at Saint-Inglevert—on which he was accompanied by more than one hundred other English knights—was approved and paid for by his father, John of Gaunt, one of the richest magnates in Western Europe. Much of Gaunt's wealth was inherited: he was the uncle of King Richard II and as Duke of Lancaster held more lands in England than anyone except the king himself. Plenty more, however, had been won on a recent military campaign that was—technically—a crusade. During the 1380s Gaunt had spent four years fighting on the Iberian Peninsula to seize the Castilian crown on behalf of his second wife, Constance, the eldest daughter and heiress of the Castilian king Pedro the Cruel. The profits of this crusade were what paid for his son's adventures.

That Gaunt had been fighting Christians on his so-called crusade—men loyal to his rival Castilian claimant John of Trastámara—and not Spanish Muslims, who now ruled nothing more in Spain than the denuded southern emirate of Granada, did not seem to matter very much. In the late fourteenth century the papacy was in schism, and between 1378 and 1417 there were two (and at one stage, three) rival popes, based in Avignon and Rome. This meant that a war such as Gaunt's could easily be awarded crusade status, since he was a follower of the Roman pope Urban VI, and John of Trastámara of the Avignon antipope Clement VII. Urban was just as happy as any of his predecessors to weaponize the crusade for the purpose of Church politics. So Gaunt had gone crusading for a crown, and although he did not succeed, when in 1388 he signed a truce that married his daughter Catherine to John of Trastámara's son, he had received so much Spanish gold that forty-seven mules were required to transport it all back to England.[3] Vastly enriched and proud of the crusader status that enhanced his own prestige, Gaunt determined that his son Bolingbroke should follow in his footsteps.

As well as funding his son's jaunt to Boucicaut's jousting match, Gaunt had written ahead to request that he run ten tilts instead of the standard five, so that he could learn as much as possible from so fine a knight. He was no doubt proud to discover afterward that by popular consensus Bolingbroke acquitted himself famously. Several chroniclers noted that of all the Englishmen at the tournament he jousted best.[4] What was more, his combat against Boucicaut, fought with proper lances, rather than the blunted sort sometimes permitted in jousting to reduce injuries, was also excellent preparation for the next stage of his expedition. For after Saint-Inglevert, Henry had decided that, like his father, he would burnish his chivalric reputation by going on crusade.

Bolingbroke's initial choice of crusading destination was North Africa, where the French king's brother-in-law Louis II, Duke of Bourbon—Boucicaut's own mentor—was preparing a naval assault against Islamic Berber pirates in Mahdia for the benefit of Genoese merchants. However, owing to uneasy relations between the English and French crowns, Bolingbroke was refused safe conduct through French territory to Marseille, where he planned to take ship. Instead, he turned his attention northeast, to Prussia. In the summer of 1390 he traveled to the Baltic, again accompanied by a retinue of several dozen other enthusiastic young Englishmen, to seek out the Teutonic Knights and spend a time alongside them fighting the pagan Lithuanians.*

The one chief obstacle to Bolingbroke's crusading ambitions in north was that, as we have seen, the Baltic region's pagan-in-chief, Jagiello of Lithuania, had four years previously converted to Christianity in order to take command of the kingdom of Poland. When he arrived in Prussia, therefore, Bolingbroke found himself in the unfortunate situation of having a joined a crusade that had recently been deprived of its main target. This was far from ideal, and in earlier times would have rendered the entire crusade defunct. But to late-fourteenth-century adventurers like Bolingbroke, the crusade was primarily a vehicle for glamorous feats of arms, and although expressing personal

*By tradition, foreign crusaders collaborated with the Teutonic Knights for seasons of winter and summer warfare against the Baltic pagans. These campaigns were known as *reysen* (or *Reisen*).

piety was an important factor, the enemy was to a certain degree immaterial. And fortunately for the young Englishman, in 1390 Teutonic Knights had not ceased fighting in Lithuania altogether. They had embroiled themselves in a dispute among Jagiello's relatives over who should serve as his deputy. With this political cover, operations could continue as usual, for there remained plenty of ordinary Lithuanians who persisted in their old pagan beliefs and practices and were ripe for correction. So Bolingbroke and his men were able to enjoy themselves after all. They joined an attack on Vilnius, the capital of the unreconstructed pagan region of Samogitia (Zemaitija), serving between August 1390 and March 1391 with extravagantly bloody results. According to a newsletter received by the English "Westminster" chronicler, Bolingbroke and his companions played a full part in a summer siege, and helped take Vilnius "with fire and steel," killing or capturing four thousand people and fighting with "great distinction."[5]

Afterward they celebrated long and hard. Since the winter was not cold enough for fighting—the marshy terrain of Samogitia known as "the Wilderness" did not freeze sufficiently that year to ride warhorses across it—they spent the dark, cold months drinking wine, playing dice and carousing in the city of Königsburg, spending large sums of John of Gaunt's money on pagan prisoners of war whose conversion to Christianity Bolingbroke could consider himself to have personally sponsored.[6] Only in April the following year did they return to England, talking up their achievements and showing off their trophies of war, which included fine birds of prey, an elk and a bear, and many tall stories—which grew all the taller as they were retold for nearly two decades afterward.

In 1392 Bolingbroke went back to Prussia for another tilt at the infidel, but on this occasion he was disappointed to find that there really was no crusading on offer. Instead of heading home, however, he followed the example of Boucicaut: Bolingbroke converted his crusade into a pilgrimage and turned his sights east. For the next ten months he and a small band of servants and followers (including a fixer by the name of Jacob and a private trumpeter called Crakyll, who announced their arrival in new towns) made their way through central Europe to Venice.[7] There they collected money from his father's financial contacts, chartered ships and sailed to the Hospitallers' island of Rhodes.

Then they traveled on to Jaffa—abandoned to the Mamluks more than a century previously—before continuing overland along the ancient pilgrim roads through the Judean hills to Jerusalem. So unlike the most famous crusader among his Plantagenet forebears—Richard the Lionheart—Bolingbroke actually visited Christ's Sepulchre, now tended by Franciscan monks. After a short stay, he retraced his steps, returning to England in July 1393 with even more exciting stories than he had brought from Prussia two years previously, as well as even more exotic animals: an ostrich, a parrot and a leopard he had acquired on Cyprus.[8]

Bolingbroke was now twenty-six years old, and if he was not a crusader as it might have once been understood, his youthful exploits meant that he was now one of the most experienced and well-traveled knightly noblemen in the realm, with a chivalric reputation second to none. And his hard-won reputation for martial valor as well as probity of character and devotion to his faith served him well. Six and a half years later, a political revolution swept through England: Bolingbroke deposed his cousin Richard and took the throne in his place, as Henry IV. Although the events that propelled him to this high office were violent, contested and traumatic, there were few who would not have agreed that Bolingbroke, the crusader, had the character of a king.

While Bolingbroke was on his path to a throne, Boucicaut was also taking great strides through his world. After the tournament at Saint-Inglevert was over (and following a diversion to Paris to be "feted and honored by the ladies"), he too had served in Prussia with the Teutonic Knights.[9] This was his third crusade to the Baltic, and this fact was noted approvingly in the French court. After performing "deeds so admirable that he was universally praised," Boucicaut was summoned to meet King Charles VI at Tours and granted the title of Marshal of France: one of the two most senior military ranks in the realm. It was an office that would keep him occupied for the rest of his days—and not only fighting the English, against whom the Hundred Years' War continued sporadically to flare up, but also in the crusading realm. A new war against the Turks was calling. And in 1396, Boucicaut agreed to join it. That spring he traveled to eastern Europe with many other "knights and squires . . . young lords of the blood royal, and many barons and noblemen [who] wished to avoid idleness and use their time and effort in the pursuit of chivalry." They all believed, according to Boucicaut's contemporary biographer, "that there could be no more honorable expedition than one in the service of God."[10] Although none of them knew it, they were joining what was perhaps the last great crusading army of the Middle Ages, raised from Western Christendom to do battle with the forces of Islam.

The enemy they sought was a new Turkish power that would soon become the Ottoman Empire. The Ottomans—so named for their first leader Osman I—were a group of ethnic Turks who had carved out a small territory in Asia Minor in the 1290s during the final collapse of Seljuq rule, itself the result of repeated Mamluk and Mongol assaults. One hundred years on, the Ottomans had expanded to become the dominant power in Asia Minor.* In the 1360s they crossed the Bosphorus and began to make conquests in the Balkans: forcing the Bulgarian tsars to pay tribute, and taking over Serbia.

The Ottomans' apparently unstoppable rise left the Byzantines in Constantinople under perpetual siege, clinging to only the barest patches of territory outside the city and with Turkish units stationed semipermanently outside their walls. It also posed a serious threat to the territorial integrity of Hungary and Poland. Accordingly, King Sigismund of Hungary appealed to other Christian powers for their assistance in protecting his borders. He found willing ears in Venice and Genoa, both of which perceived a significant threat to their own trading power as a result of Ottoman expansion in the islands and ports of the eastern Mediterranean. The Roman pope Boniface IX preached resistance to the Ottomans as a crusade, and the Avignon pope Benedict XIII followed suit. In France and England the elderly soldier and writer Philip of Mézières lobbied for the establishment of a knightly crusading society that he called the New Order of the Passion and pestered European rulers with his treatises in favor of war in the East.[11] All of this crusade enthusiasm coalesced at an opportune moment. A temporary truce in the Hundred Years' War and political turmoil in France following the collapse into insanity of Charles VI meant that for knights like Boucicaut the moment was right to rally, heroically, to the defense of Christendom.[12] The response to the crusade preaching of 1396 was the closest thing to a traditional "general passage" crusade that had been seen since the thirteenth century.

The outcome of the campaign against the Ottomans, however, was also

*The Mongol Ilkhanate, which claimed overlordship over Asia Minor in the middle of the thirteenth century, had by the 1350s broken up and collapsed.

squarely in the thirteenth-century tradition. During the early spring of 1396 a large army amassed in Hungary and was joined by hundreds of Western knights and thousands more foot soldiers from France, Burgundy, Poland, Bohemia and the German kingdoms. Around fifteen thousand crusaders set out from the Hungarian capital of Buda and traveled down the Danube toward Bulgarian territory, where the Ottoman sultan Bayezid I had conquered a number of towns and fortifications. The one they chose to try to retake was the fortress at Nicopolis (Nikopol). In early September, they pitched camp, laid a siege, and began mining the walls. For a little over a fortnight everything looked promising. Then, in the words of Boucicaut's biographer, "the malice of Fortune" turned upon the crusaders.[13] Sultan Bayezid arrived with a "force at least equal in size to the Christians," and at a pitched battle fought on September 25, he routed them completely. Divisions between the Hungarian and French contingents in the army led to chaos on the battlefield, and French losses in particular were dreadful, with a large number of esteemed lords killed, including the Admiral of France, Jean of Vienne. Boucicaut was captured and forced to watch as thousands of lower-ranking French warriors were stripped to their undershirts and beheaded with scimitars. He was held captive in Asia Minor until late June 1397, when envoys from the Duke of Burgundy arrived to agree on a ransom payment of 200,000 florins, advanced to the sultan by Venetian bankers. Boucicaut was relieved to be freed, but the disgrace to French chivalry inflicted at Nicopolis was considerable. The chronicler Jean Froissart compared the defeat to the legendary disaster at Roncesvalles in 778 CE, when all twelve great peers of France had died campaigning for Charlemagne against Muslims below the Pyrenees.[14] "It inspired pity to hear the bells ring out across all the churches in Paris where Masses were sung and prayers said on behalf of the dead," wrote Boucicaut's biographer. "And all who heard them fell to prayer and to grieving."[15]

Once Boucicaut had recovered from the traumatic experience of life in an Ottoman prison, he soon resumed his self-consciously heroic career, and war against Turks and other eastern Mediterranean powers continued to be a dominant theme. As his contemporary Henry Bolingbroke took command of England in the upheaval of 1399, Boucicaut was attempting to defend Constantinople against the Ottomans. The next year he established the Order of the White Lady of the Green Shield, a charitable jousting society whose members vowed to fight for the defense of widows and orphans who had lost their menfolk at Nicopolis. After the French effectively annexed Genoa in 1401, Boucicaut became governor and subsequently spent the rest of the decade skirmishing fairly indiscriminately with Venetians, Ottomans and Mamluks around Cyprus and the coasts of Asia Minor and Syria. He sacked Beirut in 1403, although the main victims of his attack were Venetian merchants who were trading in the city and lost large quantities of stock. In 1407 he tried to organize an assault on the Egyptian city of Alexandria but was thwarted by the lack of political support from the king of Cyprus. The following year he fought an exciting naval battle with four North African galleys in waters between Genoa and Provence. He was never idle.

Yet if Boucicaut's enemies included Muslims from traditional theaters of crusading, Boucicaut himself was hardly a crusader in the old-fashioned sense. When his admiring biographer set out at length those features of his personality that spoke most strongly to his piety, the examples he gave included almsgiving, compassion for the poor and weak, diligent prayer, regular pilgrimage and observation of Church fast days, a refusal to use foul language or blasphemous oaths, and a strict abstinence from gambling, drinking strong alcohol, eating spicy food and ogling women.[16] Slaughtering unbelievers in the name of Christ and his patrimony did not merit a mention. And perhaps appropriately, Boucicaut did not end his days fighting for Jerusalem or anywhere else in the Holy Land. Rather, on October 25, 1415, he led the French vanguard at the battle of Agincourt, where, in another calamitous rout, he was taken captive by the English and died a prisoner of war in Yorkshire, aged fifty-six, on or around June 25, 1421. There was perhaps just the faintest irony in the fact that the man who enforced his long, final captivity was England's commander at Agincourt, King Henry V, who in 1413 had succeeded to the English throne after the death of his father, Henry Bolingbroke.

The passing of Bolingbroke and Boucicaut's generation of chivalric crusaders did not quite mark the end of crusading, nor did the end of the great schism in the Western Church, which was healed in 1417 when the papacy was reunified and settled on Martin V. Tensions and rivalries that ultimately sprang from the schism evolved in central Europe into a series of wars in Bohemia in which followers of the Church reformer Jan Hus were pursued for many years by a rolling alliance of forces from within the Holy Roman Empire and beyond, including members of the Teutonic Order and—in 1427—one of the late Henry Bolingbroke's half brothers, Cardinal Henry Beaufort, bishop of Winchester. But for English and French crusaders at least, the fifteenth century undoubtedly saw a marked decline in crusade enthusiasm—if not crusade rhetoric. Well into the sixteenth century kings such as Henry VIII of England, Francis I of France and Charles V, king of Spain and Holy Roman Emperor, continued to talk in grandiose terms about raising Christian armies to fight the perfidious Turk. But more often than not this was an idea proposed for show during peace negotiations between these perpetually warring nations: a platitudinous project that would only notionally have the power to unite Christian princes and force them to desist from attacking one another. In reality the emergence of the nation-state and the bitter rifts that developed out of the Reformation ensured that Western talk of crusading in this age became little more than hot air and diplomatic posturing.

In eastern Europe the story was somewhat different, for here the Ottoman threat continued to loom large during the fifteenth century. There was a significant setback for the Ottomans in Asia Minor in 1402, when an army under Sultan Bayezid I (the victor of Nicopolis) was crushed by forces under Timur the Lame (Tamerlane), the leader of a revived Mongol empire in Central Asia. But by the middle of the century the Ottomans were once again the dominant power from the Balkans to northern Syria. By 1526 they had also conquered the Mamluk state and extended their rule throughout Syria, Palestine, Mesopotamia, Egypt and the Hijaz in western Arabia. Their presence in the eastern Mediterranean naturally brought them into regular conflict with the Christian rulers of that region. In 1453 the Ottomans finally conquered Constantinople after a fifty-three-day siege, snuffing out the Byzantine Empire for good and killing the last emperor, Constantine XI Palaiologos—a victory that sparked a predictable crisis of conscience across Christendom and associated crusade proclamations. Crusaders from Hungary and Serbia were soon forced to defend Belgrade from the Ottomans, while for many years afterward naval fleets who fought with Ottoman sailors around the islands of the eastern Mediterranean also flew crusading banners. It was inevitable that, given the long history of the region, any clashes between Christian and Islamic powers in this context would automatically be associated with the crusades. But in reality, by the time Jerusalem fell to Ottoman rule in 1517—to be transformed and rebuilt on a spectacular scale in the years that followed by the great sultan Suleiman the Magnificent—crusading was no longer a serious phenomenon. It was little more than a slogan.

If any one event could be said to mark the end of the crusading era, it was not the fall of Constantinople or Jerusalem. Rather, it took place in Granada, in southern Spain, on January 2, 1492. Since the battle of Las Navas de Tolosa in 1212, which had shattered the Almohad empire's grip on Spain, Islamic power on the Iberian Peninsula had been waning, and by the middle of the thirteenth century, the only bastion of Muslim power on the mainland was the emirate of Granada. This was a shadow of the once-mighty Spanish caliphate, and although Granada was geographically sheltered by the Sierra Nevada, and connected to the Islamic world of North Africa via Gibraltar, the emirate's rulers, known as the Nasrid dynasty, generally paid financial tribute to the kingdom of Castile to be left to their own devices.

In the 1480s, however, the Nasrids of Granada fell under the stern gaze of a powerful new force in Spain: the joint monarchy of King Ferdinand II of Aragon and Queen Isabella I of Castile, the so-called Catholic Monarchs, whose marriage united the two great Christian kingdoms of Iberia. Together Ferdinand and Isabella made it their devout mission to push the final vestiges of Muslim rule from Spain. After ten years of campaigning, they had brought Granada to its knees, and the last emir, Muhammad XII ("Boabdil"), formally surrendered the keys to the Alhambra palace to Ferdinand and Isabella, before leaving his kingdom with a sigh, for a life of exile in Morocco. During the years that followed, Spanish troops swarmed across the strait to North Africa, harassing cities and conquering useful outposts as far south as the Canary Islands. The Reconquista was over.[17]

Watching events at the Alhambra on January 2 was a Genoan explorer called Cristoforo Colombo, or, as history would come to known him, Christopher Columbus. "I saw your Highnesses' banners victoriously raised on the towers of the Alhambra, the citadel of that city, and the Moorish king come out of the city gates and kiss the hands of your Highnesses," he later wrote, addressing Ferdinand and Isabella.[18] Plainly, it was a sight that stirred his heart. Later the same month Columbus acquired from the Catholic Monarchs a commission to sail in search of a new sea route that would take him westward around the globe to the Far East, and, as he put it, constitute a holy mission to "see these parts of India and the princes and peoples of those lands and consider the best means for their conversion."

Although Columbus made it plain that his chief goal in undertaking such an ambitious mission was profit, he was also explicit about the godly rationale for his journey, which chimed with all the patterns of thought that had been developed out of the crusading movement. Even the flattery he piled upon his royal sponsors belied four centuries of crusader zealotry. "Your Highnesses as Catholic princes and devoted propagators of the holy Christian faith have always been enemies of the sect of Muhammad and of all idolatries and heresies."[19] On Saturday May 12, 1492, five months after the Alhambra fell, Columbus set out from Granada, charted a course south to the Canary Islands, then on August 3 struck out into the Atlantic Ocean.

On March 4, 1493, he returned, his boats limping home through the last gales of a "cruel storm" and coming into port in the mouth of the river Tagus at Lisbon. He brought with him strange people, unseen exotic objects and tales of the immense riches that lay in the lands he had seen: the Americas. The sheer quantities of spices, gold and slaves that might be taken there almost defied his powers of description, as did the number of heathen souls whom he thought could be converted to Christianity. Announcing his return he wrote to recommend that Ferdinand and Isabella "should hold great celebrations and render solemn thanks to the Holy Trinity with many solemn prayers, for the great triumph which they will have, by the conversion of so many peoples to our holy faith and for the temporal benefits which will follow, for not only Spain, but all Christendom will receive encouragement and profit."[20]

Needless to say, Columbus's journey in 1492 changed the world. His announcement of new territories full of things to trade or steal, and teeming with people to subjugate, convert or kill, helped to usher in a new phase of global history. After Columbus, the future for Europe lay to the west, not the east. And gradually, all the energy, excitement and terrible, merciless, zealotry that had inspired previous generations to make perilous journeys to the Holy

Land flooded back, as Christian adventurers fell over themselves to strike out in the opposite direction. It had taken a long time, but at last the realms of Western Christendom had found their new Jerusalem.

They swarmed across the sea there in their thousands, as though God himself had willed it.

EPILOGUE

Crusaders 2.0

The battle of Islam and its people against the crusaders and their followers is a long battle.

At lunchtime on March 15, 2019, a lone gunman drove to the Al Noor mosque in Riccarton, a suburb of Christchurch, New Zealand. Upon arrival, he left his car, walked calmly into the mosque and began shooting. His weapons included a semiautomatic shotgun and a semiautomatic rifle mounted with a strobe light, and he wore a helmet fitted with a webcam, from which he streamed his actions on Facebook Live. In just six minutes the gunman fatally shot more than forty people. He then got back in his car and drove to the Linwood Islamic Centre, a few miles away on the other side of town. There, he killed another seven people before once again driving away. He was eventually apprehended and arrested while on his way to a third place of Muslim worship. Before he was stopped, he analyzed his performance aloud to his online audience. "There wasn't even time to aim," he said. "There was [*sic*] so many targets."

The man arrested and charged with the Christchurch mosque shootings was a twenty-eight-year-old Australian named Brenton Tarrant. At the time of writing, legal proceedings against Tarrant in New Zealand were ongoing, but millions of people around the world had viewed images of the Christchurch shootings and read an explicative manifesto apparently written by Tarrant, which was posted on various websites shortly before the attacks began and emailed to several dozen recipients, including the office of New Zealand's prime minister, Jacinda Ardern.

The manifesto was titled "The Great Replacement," and its author described himself as an "eco-fascist" and an "ethno-nationalist." He also cast himself as a warrior in a centuries-old conflict between Christians and Muslims. He expressed numerous extreme white supremacist sentiments and called his shootings "revenge against Islam for 1,300 years of war and devastation that it has brought upon the people of the West." He made references to historical conflicts between Christian and Islamic powers in the Balkans and beyond. These ranged from the eighth to the nineteenth centuries; some were battles from the medieval crusades. On one of his rifle cartridges he had daubed the name "Bohemond I of Antioch." Another slogan, alluding to the Third Crusade, read "Acre 1189." He named one of his rifles Turkofagos, meaning "Turk eater." The manifesto claimed that a group called the "reborn Knights Templar" had given their blessing for the attacks and it praised the Far Right mass murderer Anders Behring Breivik, who killed seventy-seven people on the Norwegian island of Utøya in 2011. (Breivik claimed around the time of his own trial to be a member of a revived Templar order in which, he said, his code name was "Sigurd," after the crusader king Sigurd I Jerusalem-farer.) At one point the author of the Christchurch manifesto quoted Pope Urban II's sermon at Clermont that launched the First Crusade in 1095. "ASK YOURSELF, WHAT WOULD POPE URBAN II DO?" he wrote.

Although he did not use the word, he plainly saw himself as a twenty-first-century crusader.[1]

Historians, almost universally, regard the crusades as being over. When exactly they came to an end is a matter of historical discussion and debate. Some give the terminus ad quem as the fall of Acre and the collapse of the crusader states in Palestine and Syria in the summer of 1291. Others look, as I have done in this book, to the end of the Reconquista in 1492. The broadest minded might string the story of crusading out until 1798, when Napoleon Bonaparte ejected the Knights of St. John from Malta during his expedition to Egypt, where he conquered Alexandria. Consensus on the matter is hard to come by, and there are plausible arguments for adopting any one of these dates. In general, however, scholars agree that "real" crusading is a thing of the past. Long gone are the days when the Catholic Church actively sought to raise armies to conquer and kill non-Christians on the promise of spiritual salvation. Our world is almost unrecognizably different from that of Godfrey of Bouillon, Richard the Lionheart, Zengi and Saladin. The conflicts of the Middle Ages are not ours. That world is gone.

Yet the reasoned views of historians are not shared by everyone. Indeed, there exist today plenty of extremists—both Christian and Muslim—who believe crusading is still an important concept that can (or should) continue to define modern-day relations between the two faiths. The crusades are not, to their minds, a mere metaphor or even an inspiring example for a macabre form of historical reenactment. They are a real, ongoing phenomenon: a war to be fought from the Middle East and North Africa to the streets of Western cities: London, New York, Paris, Berlin, Madrid, Christchurch.

Even a cursory glance at the most notorious terrorist attacks of the twenty-first century confirms this attitude to be thriving. In February 1998 Osama Bin Laden, the leader of the terrorist network known as al-Qaeda, and several fellow radicals from Egypt, Pakistan and Bangladesh called publicly for jihad against "Jews and Crusaders," whose "crimes and sins" on the Arabian peninsula, they said, "are a clear declaration of war on Allah, his messenger and Muslims."[2] Six months later the United States embassies in Dar es Salaam, Tanzania, and Nairobi, Kenya, were attacked with truck bombs, causing more than two hundred deaths. On September 11, 2001, an even more spectacular series of attacks occurred in New York and Washington, D.C. The World Trade Center and part of the Pentagon were destroyed using hijacked aircraft, at the cost of thousands of lives.

Five days after the 9/11 atrocities, President George W. Bush stood on the South Lawn of the White House and told the American people and their allies that "this crusade, this war on terrorism, is going to take a while."[3] This was a calamitous misjudgment, and although Bush was careful not to repeat his reference to the crusades during the remainder of his presidency, he was never allowed to forget it. In response, Bin Laden demanded that Muslims worldwide defend themselves against "the American crusade," and he referred to Bush as "the Chief Crusader . . . under the banner of the cross."[4] As the United States and allies including Britain prepared to invade Iraq in 2003, Bin Laden repeated his invocations against "crusaders" fighting a "crusade war . . . primarily aimed at the people of Islam."[5] In 2005, he accused Bush's advisers Dick Cheney and Donald Rumsfeld of having destroyed Baghdad to a greater extent than the Mongol leader Hülagü in 1258.

Following Bin Laden's death, the al-Qaeda offshoot Islamic State (I.S.) and its self-appointed "caliph," Abu Bakr al-Baghdadi, took on the leadership of global Islamist terror and continued to refer to Western Christian powers as "crusaders," characterizing their attacks on Western targets as acts of war justified by the necessity of resisting "crusader" aggression. Bush's successor, President Barack Obama, occasionally attempted to respond with a subtler reading of history; he pointed out during a prayer breakfast in 2015 that "during the Crusades and the Inquisition, people committed terrible deeds in the name of Christ."[6] But this did him no good. I.S. publications, including the organization's official magazine, *Dabiq*, simply described Obama as the new crusader-in-chief and referred to the victims of terrorist attacks such as the July 7, 2005, London Underground and bus bombings as "crusaders." It was not hard to work out why. There was simply too much propaganda value in the notion of a perpetual crusade, connecting all perceived Western iniquities in the modern world with the actions of the Franks nine centuries ago.

Of course, al-Qaeda and Islamic State did not invent the idea of co-opting crusader memories for their own ends. In October 1898 Kaiser Wilhelm II of Germany rode around Jerusalem on a white horse, wearing absurd faux-medieval costume, as though he were the reincarnation of Frederick II Hohenstaufen in 1229. (He later laid a large bronze wreath with a pompous Arabic inscription on Saladin's tomb in Damascus.)

Nearly two decades later, in December 1917, toward the end of the First World War—for which the kaiser was largely responsible—Jerusalem fell to an assault by troops of the British Empire. In contrast with the kaiser, the British general Edmund Allenby entered Jerusalem on foot. He most likely did not say, as has often been reported, that "the wars of the crusades are now complete." But the jingoistic British press immediately said it for him. The British government, sensitive to the fact that perhaps 100 million Muslims lived in the empire, had warned sternly but vainly of "the undesirability of publishing any article paragraph or picture suggesting that military operations against Turkey are in any sense a Holy War, a modern Crusade, or have anything whatever to do with religious questions." The fact that they needed to make such a proclamation showed how prevalent the attitude was. And soon after Jerusalem fell, the same government ignored its own advice when the Department of Information commissioned a propaganda film about the campaign against Ottoman Turkey entitled *The New Crusaders*.[7]

To rehearse the myriad uses and misuses of crusading memory in the last hundred years would take up more space than remains here. It would necessitate ranging from the battle of Tannenberg in 1914—seen by many in Germany as revenge for a defeat of the Teutonic Knights by Poles and Lithuanians in roughly the same region in 1410—to General (later, President) Dwight D. Eisenhower's insistence that the campaign he led to liberate Europe from the Nazis in 1944 was "a great crusade." It would require us to analyze crusade appropriation ranging from the late American evangelist Billy Graham's "crusade" preaching tours to the former British prime minister David Cameron's fatuous proclamation in 2015 of a "national crusade to get new homes built." It would, in short, be well beyond the scope of this work.

So I shall finish, instead, with a personal anecdote. A little more than a month after the attacks on the two Christchurch mosques, on Easter Sunday, April 21, 2019, a number of bombs were detonated in churches and hotels on the island of Sri Lanka, killing more than 250 people, most of them Christians. I was on vacation with my family in Sri Lanka at the time, having finished writing the main text of the book that you are now reading. Besides being very troubled by the devastating loss of life, we were personally alarmed to learn that one of the hotels in which we had planned to stay—the Shangri-La, Colombo—had been attacked by a suicide bomber who detonated a powerful device in one of the hotel restaurants during a breakfast buffet. Had the attack occurred twenty-four hours later, we might well have been maimed or killed—though the disquieting sense of a near miss was nothing when compared to the losses of those who were less fortunate than us.

In the days that followed, news stations worldwide reported that the Sri Lanka bombings were carried out by two local Islamist groups who claimed allegiance to Islamic State. Even before reading the statements issued by these groups, I knew what they would say. And sure enough, in claiming overarching responsibility for the blasts, Islamic State explained that their operatives had targeted "churches and hotels in which citizens of the Crusader coalition were present," and "detonated their explosive vests on the Crusaders," who were "celebrating their infidel holiday." A video sent to the media outlet *Asia Times* gloated: "O Crusaders . . . This bloody day is our reward to you."[8] In all the time I had spent researching and writing this book, I had never seriously thought I (let alone my young daughters) was a crusader, or even a crusader citizen. Now, suddenly and quite dramatically, I saw that, in some sense, we were.

The week after the Sri Lanka attacks, the Islamic State leader Abu Bakr al-Baghdadi released a propaganda video—the first time he had been publicly seen in five years. Al-Baghdadi spoke approvingly of the carnage in Colombo and urged more attacks elsewhere. Echoing President Bush in September 2001, he said that "the battle of Islam and its people against the crusaders and their followers is a long battle."

"He was wrong and he was right. The crusades are over. But as long as there are crusaders—real or imaginary—in the world, the war goes on and on.

APPENDIX 1

Kings and Queens of Jerusalem

Godfrey of Bouillon* 1099–1100

Baldwin I 1100–1118

Baldwin II 1118–1131

Fulk and Melisende 1131–1143

Baldwin III and Melisende 1143–1153

Baldwin III 1153–1163

Amalric I 1163–1174

Baldwin IV 1174–1183

Baldwin IV and Baldwin V 1183–1185

Baldwin V 1185–1186

Sibylla and Guy of Lusignan 1186–1190

Guy of Lusignan 1190–1192

Isabella I and Conrad of Montferrat 1192

Isabella I and Henry of Champagne 1192–1197

Isabella I and Amalric II 1197–1205

Maria I 1205–1210

Maria I and John of Brienne 1210–1212

Isabella II and John of Brienne 1212–1225

Isabella II and Frederick II Hohenstaufen 1225–1228

Conrad II† 1228–1254

---

*Never crowned, used title "Prince and Defender of the Holy Sepulchre."

†Power exercised by Frederick II Hohenstaufen until 1243 and later by other regents.

Conrad III (aka Conradin) 1254–1268

Hugh I 1268–1284

John II 1284–1285

Henry II* 1285–1324

*Titular only from 1291.

APPENDIX 2

Popes

Antipopes have been excluded from this list.

Urban II 1088–1099
Paschal II 1099–1118
Gelasius II 1118–1119
Calixtus II 1119–1124
Honorius II 1124–1130
Innocent II 1130–1143
Celestine II 1143–1144
Lucius II 1144–1145
Eugene III 1145–1153
Anastasius IV 1153–1154
Adrian IV 1154–1159
Alexander III 1159–1181
Lucius III 1181–1185
Urban III 1185–1187
Gregory VIII 1187
Clement III 1187–1191
Celestine III 1191–1198
Innocent III 1198–1216
Honorius III 1216–1227
Gregory IV 1227–1241
Celestine IV 1241

Innocent IV 1243–1254
Alexander VI 1254–1261
Urban IV 1261–1264
Clement IV 1265–1268
Gregory X 1271–1276
Innocent V 1276
Adrian V 1276
John XXI 1276–1277
Nicholas III 1277–1280
Martin IV 1281–1285
Honorius IV 1285–1287
Nicholas IV 1288–1292
Celestine V 1294
Boniface VIII 1294–1303
Benedict XI 1303–1304
Clement V 1305–1314
John XXII 1316–1334

APPENDIX 3

Byzantine Emperors

BYZANTINE EMPERORS

Alexios I Komnenos 1081–1118

John II Komnenos 1118–1143

Manuel I Komnenos 1143–1180

Alexios II Komnenos 1180–1183

Andronikos I Komnenos 1183–1185

Isaac II Angelos 1185–1195

Alexios III Angelos 1195–1203

Isaac II Angelos and Alexios IV Angelos 1203–1204

Alexios V Doukas "Mourtzouphlos" 1204

LATIN EMPERORS OF CONSTANTINOPLE

Baldwin I 1204–1205

Henry I 1206–1216

Peter I 1217–1219

Robert I 1221–1228

John I and Baldwin II 1229–1237

Baldwin II 1237–1261

BYZANTINE EMPERORS (RESTORED)

Michael VIII Palaiologos 1261–1282

Andronikos II Palaiologos 1282–1328

Andronikos III Palaiologos 1328–1341
John V Palaiologos 1341–1376
John V Palaiologos and John VI Kantakouzenos 1347–1354
Andronikos IV Palaiologos 1376–1379
John V Palaiologos (restored) 1379–1390
John VII Palaiologos 1390
John V Palaiologos (restored) 1390–1391
Manuel II Palaiologos 1391–1425
John VIII Palaiologos 1425–1448
Constantine XI Palaiologos 1449–1453

NOTES

Introduction

1. Thomas Wright, ed., *The Historical Works of Giraldus Cambrensis* (London: George Bell & Sons, 1894), 425–26.
2. Steven Runciman, "The Decline of the Crusading Ideal," *Sewanee Review* 79 (1971), 513.

1. The Count and the Imam

1. D. S. Richards, trans., *The Chronicle of Ibn al-Athir for the Crusading Period from al-Kamil fi'l Ta'rikh,* vol. 1 (Farnham, UK: 2006), 13.
2. Kenneth Baxter Wolf, ed., *The Deeds of Count Roger of Calabria and Sicily and of His Brother Duke Robert Guiscard by Geoffrey Malaterra* (Ann Arbor: University of Michigan Press, 2005), 66–67.
3. Richards, *Chronicle of Ibn al-Athir,* vol. 1, 13
4. Richards, *Chronicle of Ibn al-Athir,* vol. 1, 13.
5. Detail from the Life of Pope Leo IX.
6. As related, for example, in Dudo of St. Quentin, *History of the Normans,* trans. Eric Christiansen (Woodbridge, UK: 1998), 30. Rollo was the first duke of Normandy and count of Rouen, granted his fief by the Frankish king Charles the Simple in 911 CE.
7. Bishop Benzo of Alba, writing about the year 1090, quoted in Dudo of St. Quentin, *History of the Normans,* 30.
8. Hubert Houben, *Roger II of Sicily: A Ruler between East and West* (Cambridge: Cambridge University Press, 2002), 10.
9. Alex Metcalfe, *The Muslims of Medieval Italy* (Edinburgh: Edinburgh University Press, 2009), 88.
10. Wolf, ed., *The Deeds of Count Roger of Calabria,* 85–86.
11. Metcalfe, *The Muslims of Medieval Italy,* 93–95.
12. Wolf, ed., *The Deeds of Count Roger of Calabria,* 181.
13. Metcalfe, *The Muslims of Medieval Italy,* 106.
14. Houben, *Roger II of Sicily,* 18–19.
15. See examples held at the Fitzwilliam Museum in Cambridge, England, which can be viewed online at classic.fitzmuseum.cam.ac.uk/gallery/normans/chapters/Normans_3_2.htm.
16. Houben, *Roger II of Sicily,* 23.
17. Wolf, ed., *The Deeds of Count Roger of Calabria,* 179.
18. Richards, *The Chronicle of Ibn al-Athir,* vol. 1, 13.
19. Making this point in a specifically Sicilian context, see Metcalfe, *The Muslims of Medieval Italy,* 88.

2. Poets and Party Kings

1. For the themes and context of Ibn Hamdis's diwan, W. Granara, "Ibn Hamdis and the Poetry of Nostalgia," in *The Literature of Al-Andalus*, eds. Maria Rosa Menocal, Raymond P Scheindlin, and Michael Sells (Cambridge: Cambridge University Press, 2000), 388–403. For "I have been banished from Paradise," 397.
2. Richard Fletcher, *Moorish Spain* (New York: Henry Holt, 1992), 87.
3. A sample of al Mu'tamid's verse in English can be found in Cola Franzen, trans., *Poems of Arab Andalusia* (San Francisco: City Lights Books, 1989), 82–91.
4. Fletcher, *Moorish Spain,* 91.
5. Fletcher, *Moorish Spain,* 86, 90.
6. Bishop Pelayo of Oviedo's *Chronicon Regum Legionensium*. This translation: Simon Barton and Richard Fletcher, trans., *The World of El Cid: Chronicles of the Spanish Reconquest* (Manchester UK: Manchester University Press, 2000), 85.
7. The miscellaneous history generally known as the *Historia Silense*. This translation: Barton and Fletcher, *The World of El Cid,* 29.
8. Paula Gerson, Annie Shaver-Crandell, and Alison Stones, *The Pilgrim's Guide to Santiago de Compostela: A Gazetteer with 580 Illustrations* (London: Harvey Miller, 1995), 73.
9. Gerson, Shaver-Crandell, and Stones, *The Pilgrim's Guide to Santiago de Compostela*, 67; William Granger Ryan, trans., and Eamon Duffy, introduction, *Jacobus de Voragine, The Golden Legend: Readings on the Saints* (Princeton and Oxford: Princeton University Press, 2012), 393–94.
10. A letter from Pope Alexander dated to 1063–1064 and addressed to all the bishops of Spain referred to "all those who had set out against the Saracens" of the region, and praised

the clergy for having protected Jews from slaughter by foreign knights. For discussion of this see Joseph F. O'Callaghan, *Reconquest and Crusade in Medieval Spain* (Philadelphia: University of Pennsylvania Press, 2002), 25.

11. Pascual De Gayangos, trans., *The History of the Mohammedan Dynasties in Spain: Extracted from the Nafhu-t-tib min Ghosni-l-Andalusi-r-Rattib wa tarikh Lisanu-d-Din Ibni-l-Khattib by Ahmed ibn Mohammed al Makkari*, vol. 2 (London: W. H. Allen, 1843), 266–67.
12. Amin Tawfiq Tayyibi, *The Tibyan: Memoirs of 'Abd Allāh B. Buluggīn, Last Zīrid Amir of Granada* (Leiden: Brill, 1986), 90.
13. Bernard F. Reilly, *The Contest of Christian and Muslim Spain 1031–1157* (Oxford: Blackwell Publishers, 1992), 82–84.
14. Paul, Cobb, *The Race for Paradise: An Islamic History of the Crusades* (Oxford: Oxford University Press, 2014), 68–70.
15. The poet Ibn al-'Assal al-Yahsubi, translation from Charles Melville and Ahmad Ubaydli, eds., *Christians and Moors in Spain*, vol. 3 (Warminster, UK: Aris & Phillips, 1992), 91.
16. O'Callaghan, *Reconquest and Crusade in Medieval Spain*, 30.
17. Franzen, trans., *Poems of Arab Andalusia*, 87.
18. N. Levtzion, and J. F. P. Hopkins, eds., *Corpus of Early Arabic Sources for West African History* (Princeton: Markus Wiener Publishers, 2000), 165.
19. "Abd al-Wahid al Marrakushi, translation from Melville and Ubaydli, eds., *Christians and Moors in Spain*, 98–99.
20. Joseph F. O'Callaghan, *A History of Medieval Spain* (London: Cornell University Press, 1975), 209.
21. Franzen, trans., *Poems of Arab Andalusia*, 88–9.
22. Franzen, trans., *Poems of Arab Andalusia*, 90.
23. Granara, "Ibn Hamdis and the Poetry of Nostalgia," 389.

3. Empire Under Siege

1. Anna Komnene, *The Alexiad*, trans. E. R. A. Sewter, introduction, Peter Frankopan, revised edition (London: Penguin, 2009), 167.
2. Komnene, *The Alexiad*, 188.
3. Komnene, *The Alexiad*, 85.
4. Theodore Prodoromos, quoted by Peter Frankopan, "The Literary, Cultural And Political Context for the Twelfth-Century Commentary on the Nicomachean Ethics," in Charles Barber and David Jenkins, eds., *Medieval Greek Commentaries on the Nicomachean Ethics* (Leiden and Boston: Brill, 2009), 47.
5. Komnene, *The Alexiad*, 7.
6. Paul Cobb, *The Race for Paradise: An Islamic History of the Crusades* (Oxford: Oxford University Press, 2014), 70.
7. This translation: Caroline Hillenbrand, *Turkish Myth and Muslim Symbol: The Battle of Manzikert* (Edinburgh: Edinburgh University Press, 2007), 147.
8. Komnene, *The Alexiad*, 204–5.
9. Ara Edmond Dostourian, trans. *Armenia and the Crusades: Tenth to Twelfth Centuries: The Chronicle of Matthew of Edessa* (London: University Press of America, 1993), 44.
10. Dostourian, trans. *Armenia and the Crusades*, 263.
11. Dostourian, trans. *Armenia and the Crusades*, 226.
12. Komnene, *The Alexiad*, 111; Peter Frankopan, *The First Crusade: The Call from the East* (Cambridge MA: Belknap Press of Harvard University Press, 2012) 46–48, 54–55.
13. Frankopan, *The Call from the East*, 71.
14. See, for example, Bernold of St. Blasien in I. S. Robinson, *Eleventh-Century Germany: The Swabian Chronicles*, (Manchester, UK: Manchester University Press, 2008), 274.
15. Komnene, *The Alexiad*, 199.
16. The letter is printed in Heinrich Hagenmeyer, *Epistulae et Chartae ad Historiam Primi Belli Sacri Spectantes quæ Supersunt Aevo Aequales ac Genuinae* (Innsbruck: Verlag der Wagner'schen Universitäts-Buchhandlung, 1901), 130–36. On the authorship/reliability of this letter, which has often been written off as a forgery, see Frankopan, *The Call from the East*, 60–61, and, for comparison, Einar Joranson, "The Problem of the Spurious Letter of Emperor Alexius to the Court of Flanders," *American Historical Review* 55 (1950), 811–32.
17. Komnene, *The Alexiad*, 274–75.
18. Komnene, *The Alexiad*, 274–75.

4. *Deus Vult!*

1. I. S. Robinson, *Eleventh-century Germany: The Swabian Chronicles* (Manchester, UK: Manchester University Press, 2008), 292.
2. Diarmaid MacCulloch, *A History of Christianity* (London: Allen Lane, 2009), 365–67.
3. Edwin, Mullins, *In Search of Cluny: God's Lost Empire* (Oxford: Signal Books, 2006), 235.
4. On Urban's ideological framework, see Paul E. Chevenden, "Pope Urban II and the Ideology of the Crusades," in Adrian J. Boas, ed., *The Crusader World* (Abingdon, UK: Routledge, 2016) *passim*, but esp. 15–20.
5. L.M. Smith, *The Early History of the Monastery of Cluny* (Oxford: Oxford University Press, 1920), 130.
6. Smith, *The Early History of the Monastery of Cluny*, 135–36.
7. MacCulloch, *A History of Christianity*, 367.
8. John Williams, "Cluny and Spain," *Gesta* 27 (1988), 93.
9. Joseph F. O'Callaghan, *Reconquest and Crusade in Medieval Spain* (Philadelphia: University of Pennsylvania Press, 2003), 167.
10. This translation: Chevenden, "Pope Urban II and the Ideology of the Crusades," 13–14.
11. For more on this substantial topic: Colin Morris, *The Papal Monarchy: The Western Church from 1050 to 1250* (Oxford: Clarendon Press, 1989).
12. Robinson, *Eleventh-Century Germany*, 6.
13. Robert Somerville, *Pope Urban II's Council of Piacenza* (Oxford: Oxford University Press, 2011), 16.

14. Bernold of St. Blasien, in Robinson, *Eleventh-Century Germany*, 324.
15. G. A. Loud, *The Age of Robert Guiscard: Southern Italy and the Norman Conquest* (Harlow, UK: Longman, 2000), 230.
16. H. E. J. Cowdrey, *The Register of Pope Gregory VII, 1073–1085: An English Translation* (Oxford: Oxford University Press, 2002), 50–51.
17. This translation: Einar Joranson, "The Problem of the Spurious Letter of Emperor Alexius to the Court of Flanders," *American Historical Review* 55 (1950), 815.
18. Frances Rita Ryan, trans., and Harold S. Fink, ed., *Fulcher of Chartres: A History of the Expedition to Jerusalem, 1095–1127* (Knoxville: University of Tennessee Press, 1969), 65–66.
19. Carol Sweetenham, trans., *Robert the Monk's History of the First Crusade: Historia Iherosolimitana* (Abingdon, UK: Routledge, 2016), 81.
20. Sweetenham, trans., *Robert the Monk's History of the First Crusade*, 82.
21. Conor Kostick, *The Social Structure of the First Crusade* (Leiden: Brill, 2008), 99–101.
22. G. H. Pertz, ed., *Monumenta Germaniae Historica, Scriptores XVI.* (Hanover: Deutsches Institut für Erforschung des Mittelalters, 1859), 101. More broadly, see Jay Rubenstein, *Nebuchadnezzar's Dream: The Crusades, Apocalyptic Prophecy, and the End of History* (New York: Oxford University Press, 2019).
23. Ryan, trans., and Fink, ed., *Fulcher of Chartres*, 68.

5. The Preacher's Tale

1. Louise and Jonathan Riley-Smith, eds., *The Crusades: Idea and Reality, 1095–1274* (London: Edward Arnold, 1981), 38.
2. This translation in Jonathan Riley-Smith, ed., *The Atlas of the Crusades* (London: Facts on File, 1990), 28.
3. Robert Levine, trans., *The Deeds of God Through the Franks: A Translation of Guibert de Nogent's Gesta Dei per Francos* (Woodbridge, UK: Boydell Press, 1997), 47–48.
4. Carol Sweetenham, trans., *Robert the Monk's History of the First Crusade: Historia Iherosolimitana* (Abingdon, UK: Routledge, 2016), 83.
5. Jonathan Riley-Smith, *The First Crusaders: 1095–1131* (Cambridge: Cambridge University Press, 1997), 56. Riley-Smith describes Peter, rather deliciously, as "a congenital boaster." For a discussion of the inconsistencies in the Peter the Hermit origin stories, see E. O. Blake and C. Morris, "A Hermit Goes to War: Peter the Hermit and the Origins of the First Crusade," in *Monks, Hermits and the Ascetic Tradition*, ed. W. J. Shiels, *Studies in Church History* 22 (1985).
6. Christopher, Tyerman, *God's War: A New History of the Crusades* (London: Allen Lane, 2006), 79; Albert of Aachen, *Historia Ierosolominitana: History of the Journey to Jerusalem*, trans. Susan Edgington (Oxford: Clarendon Press, 2007), 59. See nn. 22, 26 in this chapter also.
7. Matthew 5:9.
8. Exodus 21:23–25, 31:15; Deuteronomy 21:18–21; Leviticus 20:13.
9. 2 Maccabees 8:3–4.
10. Ephesians 6:17.
11. Revelation 11:7–10.
12. Aristotle, *Politics*, 1333b37.
13. See for example Robin Lane Fox, *Augustine: Conversions and Confessions* (London: Allen Lane, 2015).
14. Augustine, *City of God* XIX, chapter 7.
15. Jonathan Riley-Smith, *The First Crusaders and the Idea of Crusading* (London: the Athlone Press, 1986), 29–30.
16. Ekkehard of Aura, 53.
17. Ekkehard of Aura, 53.
18. Albert of Aachen, *Historia Ierosolominitana*, 52–53.
19. Robert, Chazan, ed., *God, Humanity and History: The First Crusade Narratives* (Berkeley and London: 2000).
20. Robert, Chazan, *In the Year 1096: The First Crusade and the Jews* (Philadelphia: Jewish Publication Society, 1996), 44–46.
21. But see David Malkiel, "Destruction or Conversion: Intention and Reaction, Crusaders and Jews, in 1096," *Jewish History* 15 (2001), 257–80, for a discussion of the historiography and evidence.
22. Albert of Aachen, *Historia Ierosolominitana*, 52–53.
23. James Ross, Sweeney, "Hungary in the Crusades, 1169–1218," *International History Review* 3 (1981), 468.
24. Anna Komnene, *The Alexiad*, trans. E. R. A. Sewter, introduction, Peter Frankopan, revised edition (London: Penguin, 2009), 276; *Albert of Aachen, Historia Ierosolominitana*, 46–47.
25. John France, *Victory in the East: A Military History of the First Crusade* (Cambridge: Cambridge University Press, 1994) 91–92.
26. Komnene, *The Alexiad*, 274–75. Anna Komnene was one of the chroniclers who gave most credence to Peter the Hermit's central role in the genesis of the crusade, although her testimony on the matter is intended to shift the blame of calling the crusaders to Byzantium, as far away from her father as possible.
27. Sweetenham, trans., *Robert the Monk's History of the First Crusade*, 84–85.
28. Albert of Aachen, Historia Ierosolominitana, 36–37. Fulcher of Chartres several months later saw "many severed heads and . . . many bones of the slain" when he passed by the battlefield (Frances Rita Ryan, trans., and Harold S. Fink, ed., *Fulcher of Chartres: A History of the Expedition to Jerusalem, 1095–1127* [Knoxville: University of Tennessee Press, 1969], 80).

6. March of the Princes

1. Marjorie Chibnall, ed. and trans., *The Ecclesiastical History of Orderic Vitalis*, vol. 6 (Oxford: Clarendon Press, 1978) 70–71.
2. Chibnall, ed. and trans., *The Ecclesiastical History of Orderic Vitalis*, 70–71.

3. Bernard S. Bachrach and David S. Bachrach, trans., *The Gesta Tancredi of Ralph of Caen: A History of the Normans on the First Crusade* (Aldershot, UK: Ashgate, 2005), 23.
4. Rosalind Hill, ed., *Gesta Francorum et Aliorum Hierosolimitanorum: The Deeds of the Franks and the Other Pilgrims to Jerusalem* (Oxford: Clarendon Press, 1962), 7, 11.
5. Susan B. Edgington and Carol Sweetenham, trans. *The Chanson d'Antioche: An Old-French Account of the First Crusade* (Farnham, UK: Ashgate, 2011), 129.
6. Anna Komnene, *The Alexiad,* trans. E. R. A. Sewter, introduction, Peter Frankopan, revised edition (London: Penguin, 2009), 293–94.
7. Komnene, *The Alexiad,* 383–84.
8. Hill, ed., *Gesta Francorum*, 6–7.
9. Albert of Aachen, *Historia Ierosolominitana: History of the Journey to Jerusalem*, trans. Susan Edgington (Oxford: Clarendon Press, 2007), 32–33, emphasizes this point: Peter "spoke to his foolish and rebellious people in vain."
10. Hill, ed., *Gesta Francorum,* 7, and above, chapter 1.
11. See Jonathan Riley-Smith, *The First Crusade and The Idea of Crusading* (London: The Athlone Press, 1986), 34–49, and John France, *Victory in the East: A Military History of the First Crusade* (Cambridge: Cambridge University Press, 1994), 10–16.
12. See Bachrach, trans., *The Gesta Tancredi of Ralph of Caen,* 23.
13. Hill, ed., *Gesta Francorum,* 1: "[The Pope] began to deliver eloquent sermons and to preach, saying 'If any man wants to save his soul, let him have no hesitation in taking the way of the Lord in humility.'"
14. Carol Sweetenham, trans., *Robert the Monk's History of the First Crusade: Historia Iherosolimitana* (Abingdon, UK: Routledge, 2016), 80.
15. Chibnall, ed. and trans., *The Ecclesiastical History of Orderic Vitalis,* vol. 5, 170.
16. Bachrach, trans., *The Gesta Tancredi of Ralph of Caen,* 22.
17. Hill, ed., *Gesta Francorum,* 10–11, Robert Levine, trans., *The Deeds of God Through the Franks: A Translation of Guibert de Nogent's Gesta Dei per Francos* (Woodbridge, UK: Boydell Press, 1997), 60–61.
18. Komnene, *The Alexiad,* 277, 285.
19. Hill, ed., *Gesta Francorum* 10; Levine, trans., *The Deeds of God Through the Franks,* 61; Chibnall, ed. and trans., *The Ecclesiastical History of Orderic Vitalis,* vol. 5, 46–47.
20. On the pragmatic "special relationship" between Alexius and Bohemond, see Jonathan Shepard, "When Greek Meets Greek: Alexius Comnenus and Bohemond in 1097–98," *Byzantine and Modern Greek* Studies 12 (1988), 185–278.
21. Komnene, *The Alexiad,* 279.
22. For the relics, Raymond d'Aguilers, *Historia Francorum Qui Ceperunt Iherusalem,* trans. John Hugh Hill and Laurita L. Hill (Philadelphia: American Philosophical Society, 1968), 75.
23. Hill, ed., *Gesta Francorum,* 12.
24. Hill, ed., *Gesta Francorum,* 12.
25. Levine, trans., *The Deeds of God Through the Franks,* 60.
26. For the catapults, d'Aguilers, *Historia Francorum,* 25.
27. Sweetenham, trans., *Robert the Monk's History of the First Crusade,* 106.
28. Frances Rita Ryan, trans., and Harold S. Fink, ed., *Fulcher of Chartres: A History of the Expedition to Jerusalem, 1095–1127* (Knoxville: University of Tennessee Press, 1969), 82.
29. Sweetenham, trans., *Robert the Monk's History of the First Crusade,* 104.
30. Hill, ed., *Gesta Francorum,* 15.
31. Hill, ed., *Gesta Francorum,* 16.
32. Bachrach, trans., *The Gesta Tancredi of Ralph of Caen,* 42, mentions this splendid tent because Tancred of Hauteville asked to be given it as a gift in exchange for swearing an oath of allegiance—much to Alexios's chagrin.
33. Sweetenham, trans., *Robert the Monk's History of the First Crusade,* 106.
34. Bachrach, trans., *The Gesta Tancredi of Ralph of Caen,* 39.
35. Levine, trans., *The Deeds of God Through the Franks,* 65.
36. Hill, ed., *Gesta Francorum,* 18
37. Hill, ed., *Gesta Francorum,* 19–20.
38. Raymond d'Aguilers, *Historia Francorum,* 28.
39. 2 Maccabees 10:30.
40. Sweetenham, trans., *Robert the Monk's History of the First Crusade,* 114.

7. The Longest Winter

1. On the terrain of the Anatolian interior and the putative routes of the crusaders, see John France, *Victory in the East: A Military History of the First Crusade* (Cambridge: Cambridge University Press, 1994), 185–77.
2. Peter Tudebode, *Historia de Hierosolymitano Itinere,* trans., John Hugh Hill and Laurita L. Hill (Philadelphia: American Philosophical Society, 1974), 38.
3. Albert of Aachen, *Historia Ierosolominitana: History of the Journey to Jerusalem*, trans. Susan Edgington (Oxford: Clarendon Press, 2007), 138–41.
4. Albert of Aachen, *Historia Ierosolominitana,* 143.
5. Albert of Aachen, *Historia Ierosolominitana,* 145.
6. Bernard S. Bachrach and David S. Bachrach, trans., *The Gesta Tancredi of Ralph of Caen: A History of the Normans on the First Crusade* (Aldershot, UK: Ashgate, 2005), 58.
7. Bachrach, trans., *The Gesta Tancredi of Ralph of Caen,* 73.
8. Malcolm Barber and Keith Bate, trans., *Letters from the East: Crusaders, Pilgrims and Settlers in the 12th–13th Centuries* (Farnham, UK: Ashgate, 2010), 23.
9. Albert of Aachen, *Historia Ierosolominitana,* 248–49; 286–87.
10. H.A.R. Gibb, trans., *The Damascus Chronicle of the Crusades: Extracted and Translated from the Chronicle of Ibn Al-Qalanisi* (London: Luzac, 1932; repr., New York: Dover, 2000), 41.

11. Paul Cobb, *The Race for Paradise: An Islamic History of the Crusades* (Oxford: Oxford University Press, 2014), 88.
12. Rosalind Hill, ed., *Gesta Francorum et Aliorum Hierosolimitanorum: The Deeds of the Franks and the Other Pilgrims to Jerusalem* (Oxford: Clarendon Press, 1962), 28.
13. Cobb, *The Race for Paradise*, 90; Gibb, trans., *The Damascus Chronicle of the Crusades*, 42–43.
14. On this and further analysis of the siege, see Thomas Asbridge, *The Creation of the Principality of Antioch*, 1098–1130 (Woodbridge, UK: 2000), 25–42.
15. Gibb, trans., *The Damascus Chronicle of the Crusades*, 43.
16. Hill, ed., *Gesta Francorum*, 28.
17. Gibb, trans., *The Damascus Chronicle of the Crusades*, 43.
18. For Baldwin's appearance and sexual preference, see Emily Atwater Babcock and A. C. Krey, *A History of Deeds Done Beyond The Sea: By William, Archbishop of Tyre*, vol. 1 (New York: Columbia University Press, 1943), 416.
19. On the importance of sea links forged at Antioch, see France, *Victory in the East*, 209–15.
20. Barber and Bate, trans., *Letters from the East*, 23.
21. Bachrach, trans., *The Gesta Tancredi of Ralph of Caen*, 81.
22. D. S. Richards, trans., *The Chronicle of Ibn al-Athir for the Crusading Period from al-Kamil fi'l Ta'rikh*, vol. 1 (Farnham, UK: Ashgate 2010), 14.
23. Frances Rita Ryan, trans., and Harold S. Fink, ed., *Fulcher of Chartres: A History of the Expedition to Jerusalem, 1095–1127* (Knoxville: University of Tennessee Press, 1969), 98.
24. Hill, ed., *Gesta Francorum*, 47–48.
25. Richards, trans., *The Chronicle of Ibn al-Athir*, vol. 1, 15.
26. Richards, trans., *The Chronicle of Ibn al-Athir*, vol. 1, 15.
27. Gibb, trans., *The Damascus Chronicle of the Crusades*, 44.
28. Albert of Aachen, *Historia Ierosolominitana*, 284–85.
29. On the composition of the army, see France, *Victory in the East*, 261. The numbers quoted are those relayed by Matthew of Edessa.
30. Albert of Aachen, *Historia Ierosolominitana*, 314–15.
31. Hill, ed., *Gesta Francorum*, 62.
32. Bachrach, trans., *The Gesta Tancredi of Ralph of Caen*, 102.
33. Bachrach, trans., *The Gesta Tancredi of Ralph of Caen*, 55.
34. Raymond d'Aguilers, *Historia Francorum Qui Ceperunt Iherusalem*, trans. John Hugh Hill and Laurita L. Hill (Philadelphia: American Philosophical Society, 1968), 57–58.
35. Raymond d'Aguilers, *Historia Francorum*, 101–3.
36. Richards, trans., *The Chronicle of Ibn al-Athir*, vol. 1, 16.
37. Raymond d'Aguilers, *Historia Francorum*, 62.
38. Susan B. Edgington and Sweetenham Carol, trans., *The Chanson d'Antioche: An Old French Account of the First Crusade* (Farnham, UK: Ashgate, 2011), 201.
39. Albert of Aachen, *Historia Ierosolominitana*, 337.
40. Raymond d'Aguilers, *Historia Francorum*, 64.

8. Jerusalem

1. The most recent discussion of Ilghazi's character is Nicholas Morton, "Walter the Chancellor on Ilghazi and Tughtakin: A Prisoner's Perspective," *Journal of Medieval History* 44 (2018), 170–86.
2. Matthew the Chancellor 108–9; Robert Levine, trans., *The Deeds of God Through the Franks: A Translation of Guibert de Nogent's Gesta Dei per Francos* (Woodbridge, UK: Boydell Press, 1997), 165; Morton, "Walter the Chancellor on Ilghazi and Tughtakin."
3. D. S. Richards, trans., *The Chronicle of Ibn al-Athir for the Crusading Period from al-Kamil fi'l Ta'rikh*, vol. 1 (Farnham, UK: Ashgate 2010), 21.
4. Expressed most plainly by Richards, trans., *The Chronicle of Ibn al-Athir*, vol. 1, 13–14.
5. Clear summaries of these tensions are available in Paul Cobb, *The Race for Paradise: An Islamic History of the Crusades* (Oxford: Oxford University Press, 2014), 45–49, 77–88; Carole Hillenbrand, *The Crusades: Islamic Perspectives* (Edinburgh: Edinburgh University Press, 1999), 42–54.
6. William MacGuckin Slane, trans., *Ibn Khallikan's Biographical Dictionary*, vol. 4 (Paris: Oriental Translation Fund, 1871), 612–14.
7. H. A. R. Gibb, trans., *The Damascus Chronicle of the Crusades: Extracted and Translated from the Chronicle of Ibn Al-Qalanisi* (London: Luzac, 1932; repr., New York: Dover, 2000), 44–45.
8. Anna Komnene, *The Alexiad*, trans. E. R. A. Sewter, introduction, Peter Frankopan, revised edition (London: Penguin, 2009), 321.
9. On the foundation, frontiers and fortunes of the principality of Antioch, see Thomas S. Asbridge, *The Creation of the Principality of Antioch, 1098–1130* (Woodbridge, UK: Boydell Press, 2000), and Andrew D. Buck, *The Principality of Antioch and Its Frontiers in the Twelfth Century* (Woodbridge, UK: Boydell Press, 2017).
10. Raymond d'Aguilers, *Historia Francorum Qui Ceperunt Iherusalem*, trans. John Hugh Hill and Laurita L. Hill (Philadelphia: American Philosophical Society, 1968), 75.
11. W. M. Thackston, trans., *Naser-e Khosraw's Book of travels (Safarnama)* (Albany, NY: Bibliotheca Persica, 1986), 14.
12. Raymond d'Aguilers, *Historia Francorum*, 78.
13. Raymond d'Aguilers, *Historia Francorum*, 79.
14. Rosalind Hill, ed., *Gesta Francorum et Aliorum Hierosolimitanorum: The Deeds of the Franks and the Other Pilgrims to Jerusalem* (Oxford: Clarendon Press, 1962), 80.
15. This translation: Carole Hillenbrand, *Turkish Myth and Muslim Symbol: The Battle of Manzikert* (Edinburgh: Edinburgh University Press, 2007), 151.
16. Albert of Aachen, *Historia Ierosolominitana: History of the Journey to Jerusalem*, trans. Susan

Edgington (Oxford: Clarendon Press, 2007), 388–89.

17. Raymond d'Aguilers, *Historia Francorum,* 91.
18. Raymond d'Aguilers, *Historia Francorum,* 114.
19. Gibb, trans., *The Damascus Chronicle of the Crusades,* 47.
20. Albert of Aachen, *Historia Ierosolominitana,* 392–93.
21. Frances Rita Ryan, trans., and Harold S. Fink, ed., *Fulcher of Chartres: A History of the Expedition to Jerusalem, 1095–1127* (Knoxville: University of Tennessee Press, 1969), 121.
22. Gibb, trans., *The Damascus Chronicle of the Crusades,* 47.
23. Carol Sweetenham, trans., *Robert the Monk's History of the First Crusade: Historia Iherosolimitana* (Abingdon, UK: Routledge, 2016), 213.
24. Albert of Aachen, *Historia Ierosolominitana,* 422–23.
25. Raymond d'Aguilers, *Historia Francorum* 121–22; Albert of Aachen, *Historia Ierosolominitana,* 412–13.
26. Albert of Aachen, *Historia Ierosolominitana,* 416–17.
27. Albert of Aachen, *Historia Ierosolominitana,* 424–25. John France, *Victory in the East: A Military History of the First Crusade* (Cambridge: Cambridge University Press, 1994), 351, reckons the tower must have been fifty feet high—roughly the height of a four-story house.
28. Bernard S. Bachrach and David S. Bachrach, trans., *The Gesta Tancredi of Ralph of Caen: A History of the Normans on the First Crusade* (Aldershot, UK: Ashgate, 2005), 140; Albert of Aachen, *Historia Ierosolominitana,* 422–23.
29. Albert of Aachen, *Historia Ierosolominitana,* 424–25.
30. Raymond d'Aguilers, *Historia Francorum,* 126.
31. Raymond d'Aguilers, *Historia Francorum,* 127.
32. Richards, trans., *The Chronicle of Ibn al-Athir,* vol. 1, 21.
33. Raymond d'Aguilers, *Historia Francorum,* 127.
34. Gibb, trans., *The Damascus Chronicle of the Crusades,* 48.
35. See, for example, Raymond d'Aguilers, *Historia Francorum,* 127–28, and Hill, ed., *Gesta Francorum,* 91. Cf. *Revelation* 14: 20: "And the winepress was trodden without the city, and blood came out of the winepress, even unto the horse bridles."
36. Albert of Aachen, *Historia Ierosolominitana,* 432–33.
37. Simon John, "The 'Feast of the Liberation of Jerusalem': Remembering and Reconstruction the First Crusade in the Holy City, 1099–1187," in Benjamin Z. Kedar et al., *Crusades: Volume 3* (Abingdon, UK: Routledge 2004), 413–14.
38. Albert of Aachen, *Historia Ierosolominitana,* 442–43.
39. Hill, ed., *Gesta Francorum,* 92.
40. Richards, trans., *The Chronicle of Ibn al-Athir,* vol. 1, 22.
41. Richards, trans., *The Chronicle of Ibn al-Athir,* vol. 1, 22, a view shared by, for example, the Spanish traveler Ibn al-Arabi, for which see Joseph Drory, "Some Observations During a Visit to Palestine by Ibn al-Arabi of Seville in 1092–1095," in Kedar et al., *Crusades: Volume 3,* 120.
42. Levine, trans., *The Deeds of God Through the Franks,* 132.

9. Dividing the Spoils

1. Frances Rita Ryan, trans., and Harold S. Fink, ed., *Fulcher of Chartres: A History of the Expedition to Jerusalem, 1095–1127* (Knoxville: University of Tennessee Press, 1969), 130–31.
2. Ryan, trans., and Fink, ed., *Fulcher of Chartres,* 132.
3. Rosalind Hill, ed., *Gesta Francorum et Aliorum Hierosolimitanorum: The Deeds of the Franks and the Other Pilgrims to Jerusalem* (Oxford: Clarendon Press, 1962), 97.
4. Hill, ed., *Gesta Francorum,* 96.
5. For the historiographical uncertainty surrounding Daimbert's status as a legate, see Patricia Skinner, "From Pisa to the Patriarchate: Chapters in the Life of (Arch)bishop Daibert," in Patricia Skinner, ed., *Challenging the Boundaries of Medieval History: The Legacy of Timothy Reuter* (Turnhout, Belgium: Brepols, 2009), 164.
6. Albert of Aachen, *Historia Ierosolominitana: History of the Journey to Jerusalem,* trans. Susan Edgington (Oxford: Clarendon Press, 2007), 496–97.
7. Ryan, trans., and Fink, ed., *Fulcher of Chartres,* 131–32.
8. Anna Komnene, *The Alexiad,* trans. E. R. A. Sewter, introduction, Peter Frankopan, revised edition (London: Penguin, 2009), 325.
9. Malcolm Barber, *The Crusader States* (New Haven and London: Yale University Press, 2012), 56–57.
10. Komnene, *The Alexiad,* 324.
11. Hill, ed., *Gesta Francorum,* 64–65. See also Conor Kostick, "Courage and Cowardice on the First Crusade, 1096–1099," *War in History* 20 (2013), 37–38.
12. Jonathan Riley-Smith, *The First Crusaders: 1095–1131* (Cambridge: Cambridge University Press, 1997), 151–52.
13. Riley-Smith, *The First Crusaders,* 169–88.
14. See, for example, Martin Hall and Jonathan Phillips, *Caffaro, Genoa and the Twelfth-Century Crusades* (Farnham, UK: Ashgate, 2013), 50.
15. For the complex and intersecting motivations of the Italian forces at this time, see Christopher J. Marshall, "The Crusading Motivations of the Italian City Republics in the Latin East, c. 1096–1104," *Rivista di Bizantinistica* 1 (1991), 41–68.
16. The most recent discussion of the Pisan attacks on Mahdia is Alasdair C. Grant, "Pisan Perspectives: The *Carmen in victoriam* and Holy War, c. 1000–1150," in *English Historical Review* (2016), 983–1009, which includes an English prose translation of the *Carmen in victoriam*

Pisanorum. See also H. E. J. Cowdrey, "The Mahdia Campaign of 1087," in *English Historical Review* (1977), 1–29.

17. The charter text is transcribed in Heinrich Hagenmeyer, *Epistulae et Chartae ad Historiam Primi Belli Sacri Spectantes quæ Supersunt Aevo Aequales ac Genuinae* (Innsbruck: Verlag der Wagner'schen Universitäts-Buchhandlung, 1901), 155–56.
18. Hubert Houben, *Roger II of Sicily: A Ruler Between East and West* (Cambridge: Cambridge University Press), 24.
19. See Carlos De Ayala, "On the Origins of Crusading in the Peninsula: the Reign of Alfonso VI (1065–1109)," in *Imago Temporis: Medium Aevum* 7 (2013), 266.
20. This translation: Joseph F. O'Callaghan, *Reconquest and Crusade in Medieval Spain* (Philadelphia: University of Pennsylvania Press, 2003), 33. See also Carl Erdmann, *The Origin of the Idea of Crusade*, trans. Marshall W. Baldwin and Walter Goffart (Princeton: Princeton University Press, 1977), 317–18.
21. Malcolm Barber and Keith Bate, trans., *Letters from the East: Crusaders, Pilgrims and Settlers in the 12th–13th Centuries* (Farnham, UK: Ashgate, 2010), 34–35.
22. Barber and Bate, trans., *Letters from the East*, 34–35.

10. Sigurd Jerusalemfarer

1. Snorri Sturluson, *Heimskringla: History of the Kings of Norway* (Austin: University of Texas Press, 1964), 700.
2. Sturluson, *Heimskringla*, 685.
3. Sturluson, *Heimskringla*, 687.
4. Sturluson, *Heimskringla*, 688.
5. Albert of Aachen, *Historia Ierosolominitana: History of the Journey to Jerusalem*, trans. Susan Edgington (Oxford: Clarendon Press, 2007), 222–25. A few years later Sven's half brother Erik I, king of Denmark, and his wife, Queen Boedil, undertook their own pilgrimage to Jerusalem. Erik died and was buried at Paphos on Cyprus in 1103 en route from Constantinople to Jerusalem. Queen Boedil made it to the Holy City, where she too died and was buried in the valley of Jehosophat.
6. This also worked in reverse. In 921, the Baghdadi emissary Ibn Fadlan had traveled far up the river Volga and witnessed Scandinavian Vikings conducting a grisly ship burial and sacrifice ceremony. See Paul Lunde and Caroline Stone, trans., *Ibn Fadlan and the Land of Darkness: Arab Travelers in the Far North* (London: Penguin, 2012), 50–54.
7. Sturluson, *Heimskringla*, 689.
8. A comparable example might be *Skuldelev 2*, built in the Dublin area in the 1040s: its remains are displayed at the Viking Ship Museum at Roskilde, Denmark, and the ship was built in working replica in the twenty-first century as *Havhingsten fra Glendalough*.
9. John Allen Giles, trans., *William of Malmesbury's Chronicle of the Kings of England* (London: Henry G. Bohn, 1847), 443.
10. Giles, trans., *William of Malmesbury's Chronicle*, 444.
11. A good modern discussion of the Spanish portion of Sigurd's journey to Jerusalem is Gary B. Doxey, "Norwegian Crusaders and the Balearic Islands," in *Scandinavian Studies* 68 (1996), 139–60.
12. Sturluson, *Heimskringla*, 690.
13. Sturluson, *Heimskringla*, 690.
14. Translation: J. Steffanson, in "The Vikings in Spain: from Arabic (Moorish) and Spanish Sources," *Saga Book of the Viking Club* 6 (1908–9), 35–36. See on this raid, Ann Christys, *Vikings in the South: Voyages to Iberia and the Mediterranean* (London: Bloomsbury Academic, 2015), 1–14.
15. Sturluson, *Heimskringla*, 691. See also Christys, *Vikings in the South*, 100–102, for the literary inversion of the "Viking" Muslims and Christianizing Norwegians.
16. Sturluson, *Heimskringla*, 692. Doxey, "Norwegian Crusaders and the Balearic Islands," 147, conjectures the cave's location based on plausibility and local lore.
17. Sturluson, *Heimskringla*, 692.
18. Sturluson, *Heimskringla*, 694.
19. Hubert Houben, *Roger II of Sicily: A Ruler Between East and West* (Cambridge: Cambridge University Press), 27.
20. The diary of Saewulf, in John Wilkinson, with with Joyce Hill and W. F. Ryan, eds., *Jerusalem Pilgrimage 1099–1185* (London: Hakluyt Society, 1988), 94.
21. Sturluson, *Heimskringla*, 695, states that Sigurd crossed "the Greek Sea," which I have taken to mean following the standard, land-hugging route described in Saewulf's diary—see Wilkinson et al., *Jerusalem Pilgrimage*, 95–98.
22. Albert of Aachen, *Historia Ierosolominitana*, 800–801.
23. Albert of Aachen, *Historia Ierosolominitana*, 798–801.
24. Albert of Aachen, *Historia Ierosolominitana*, 804–5.
25. Sturluson, *Heimskringla*, 695.
26. Olaf was canonized by Pope Alexander III in 1164 and is still a popular saint in Norway and the Faroe Islands, commemorated with *Olsok* celebrations every year on July 29. The manner of his death is a subject of some contention.
27. H. A. R. Gibb, trans., *The Damascus Chronicle of the Crusades: Extracted and Translated from the Chronicle of Ibn Al-Qalanisi* (London: Luzac, 1932; repr., New York: Dover, 2000), 106–7; Albert of Aachen, *Historia Ierosolominitana*, 804–5.
28. Gibb, trans., *The Damascus Chronicle of the Crusades*, 107.
29. Gibb, trans., *The Damascus Chronicle of the Crusades*, 108.
30. Sturluson, *Heimskringla*, 696.
31. Sturluson, *Heimskringla*, 697.
32. Sturluson, *Heimskringla*, 699.

33. Sturluson, *Heimskringla*, 714.
34. The classic essay exploring the distinction between pilgrim and crusader in this context is C. J. Tyerman, "Were There Any Crusades in the Twelfth Century?," in *English Historical Review* 110 (1995), 553–77.

11. Fields of Blood

1. Ibn Al-sā'I, *Consorts of the Caliphs: Women and the Court of Baghdad,* trans., Shawkat M. Toorawa (New York: New York University Press, 2017), 62.
2. D. S. Richards, trans., *The Chronicle of Ibn al-Athir for the Crusading Period from al-Kamil fi'l Ta'rikh,* vol. 1 (Farnham, UK: Ashgate 2010), 155.
3. H. A. R. Gibb, trans., *The Damascus Chronicle of the Crusades: Extracted and Translated from the Chronicle of Ibn Al-Qalanisi* (London: Luzac, 1932; repr., New York: Dover, 2000), 111.
4. Gibb, trans., *The Damascus Chronicle of the Crusades,* 111.
5. Richards, trans., *The Chronicle of Ibn al-Athir,* vol. 1, 154.
6. Richards, trans., *The Chronicle of Ibn al-Athir,* vol. 1, 155.
7. Gibb, trans., *The Damascus Chronicle of the Crusades,* 112.
8. Frances Rita Ryan, trans., and Harold S. Fink, ed., *Fulcher of Chartres: A History of the Expedition to Jerusalem, 1095–1127* (Knoxville: University of Tennessee Press, 1969), 150.
9. John Wilkinson, with with Joyce Hill and W. F. Ryan, eds., *Jerusalem Pilgrimage 1099–1185* (London: Hakluyt Society, 1988), 145, 149.
10. Wilkinson et al., *Jerusalem Pilgrimage,* 101.
11. Gibb, trans., *The Damascus Chronicle of the Crusades,* 136.
12. Ibn al-Adim extracted and translated in *Recueil des Historiens des Croisades: Historiens Orientaux,* vol. 3 (Paris: Imprimerie Nationale, 1884), 616.
13. Gibb, trans., *The Damascus Chronicle of the Crusades,* 158–59.
14. Thomas S. Asbridge and Susan B. Edgington, *Walter the Chancellor's* The Antiochene Wars: *A Translation and Commentary* (Aldershot, UK: Ashgate, 1999), 127.
15. Gibb, trans., *The Damascus Chronicle of the Crusades,* 160.
16. Asbridge and Edgington, *Walter the Chancellor,* 132–36.
17. On Ilghazi's black reputation, as filtered through the accounts of witnesses like Walter the Chancellor, see Nicholas Morton, "Walter the Chancellor on Ilghazi and Tughtakin: A Prisoner's Perspective," *Journal of Medieval History* 44, (2018), 170–86.
18. Usama ibn Munqidh, *The Book of Contemplation: Islam and the Crusades,* trans. Paul Cobb (London: Penguin, 2008), 131.
19. Albert of Aachen, *Historia Ierosolominitana: History of the Journey to Jerusalem,* trans. Susan Edgington (Oxford: Clarendon Press, 2007), 868–69.
20. Emily Atwater Babcock and A. C. Krey, trans., *A History of Deeds Done Beyond the Sea: By William, Archbishop of Tyre,* vols. 1 (New York: Columbia University Press, 1943), 514.
21. Babcock and Krey, *A History of Deeds Done Beyond the Sea,* vol. 1, 522.
22. On the decisive nature of this period see Nicholas Morton, *The Field of Blood: The Battle for Aleppo and the Remaking of the Medieval Middle East* (New York: Basic Books, 2018), 8–9.
23. Translated in Malcolm Barber and Keith Bate, trans., *Letters from the East: Crusaders, Pilgrims and Settlers in the 12th–13th Centuries* (Farnham, UK: Ashgate, 2010), 42–44.
24. Barber and Bate, trans., *Letters from the East,* 42–44.
25. Morton, *The Field of Blood,* 125.
26. Babcock and Krey, *A History of Deeds Done Beyond the Sea,* vol. 1, 536.
27. Babcock and Krey, *A History of Deeds Done Beyond the Sea,* vol. 1, 540.
28. Richards, trans., *The Chronicle of Ibn al-Athir,* vol. 1, 251.
29. A concise account of the so-called Venetian Crusade is Jonathan, Riley-Smith, "The Venetian Crusade of 1122–24" in Gabriella Airaldi and Benjamin Z. Kedar, eds., *I Comuni Italiani nel Regno Crociato di Gerusalemme [The Italian Communes in the Crusading Kingdom of Jerusalem]* (Genoa: Università de Genova, 1986), 339–50.
30. Babcock and Krey, *A History of Deeds Done Beyond the Sea,* vol. 1, 549.
31. Babcock and Krey, *A History of Deeds Done Beyond the Sea,* vol. 1, 554–55.
32. Richards, trans., *The Chronicle of Ibn al-Athir,* vol. 1, 253.
33. Richards, trans., *The Chronicle of Ibn al-Athir,* vol. 1, 254.
34. Richards, trans., *The Chronicle of Ibn al-Athir,* vol. 1, 254.
35. Ibn al-Adim in *Recueil des Historiens des Croisades,* 647.
36. Ibn al-Adim in *Recueil des Historiens des Croisades,* 646.

12. A New Knighthood

1. The building of Acre's port was described by the writer and scholar al-Muqaddasi, whose grandfather was the lead engineer. *The Best Divisions for Knowledge of the Regions: Ahsan al-Taqasim fi Ma'rifat al-Aqalim,* trans. Basil Collins (Reading, UK: Garnet Publishing: 2001), 138–39.
2. On the development of Acre during the first century of Frankish occupation, Michael Ehrlich, "Urban Landscape Development in Twelfth-Century Acre," *Journal of the Royal Asiatic Society* 18 (2008): 257–74.
3. Reinhold Röhricht, ed., *Regesta Regni Hierosolymitani (1097–1291)* vol. 1 (Innsbruck: Libraria Academica Wagneriana, 1893), 25.
4. Three chroniclers give accounts of the foundation of the Order of the Temple: William of Tyre, Michael the Syrian and Walter Map. A

discussion of their relative merits and limitations is to be found in Malcolm Barber, *The New Knighthood: A History of the Order of the Temple* (Cambridge: Cambridge University Press, 1994), 6–9.

5. The bull granting these privileges, known as *Pie postulatio voluntatis* (A pious request), can today be seen at the National Library of Malta in Valletta.
6. Emily Atwater Babcock and A. C. Krey, trans., *A History of Deeds Done Beyond the Sea: By William, Archbishop of Tyre,* vol. 1 (New York: Columbia University Press, 1943), 525.
7. M. R. James, trans., C. N. L. Brooke and R. A. B. Mynors revs., *Walter Map: De Nugis Curialium: Courtiers' Trifles* (Oxford: Oxford University Press, 1983), 54–55.
8. Marquis d'Albon, ed., *Cartulaire Général de l'Ordre du Temple, 1119?–1150.*, vol. 1 (Paris: Librarie Ancienne, 1913), 1.
9. Babcock and Krey, *A History of Deeds Done Beyond the Sea,* vol 2, 40.
10. On Hugh's efforts to recruit for the Damascus assault, see Jonathan Phillips, "Hugh of Payns and the 1129 Damascus Crusade" in Malcolm Barber, ed., *The Military Orders, Volume 1: Fighting for the Faith and Caring for the Sick* (Aldershot, UK: Variorum, 1994), 141–47.
11. Babcock and Krey, *A History of Deeds Done Beyond the Sea,* vol. 2, 47.
12. Barber, *The New Knighthood,* 14.
13. G. N. Garmonsway, ed. and trans., *The Anglo-Saxon Chronicle* (London: J. M. Dent, 1953), 259.
14. Phillips, "Hugh of Payns and the 1129 Damascus Crusade," 144.
15. A recent English translation of St. Bernard's letter is Bruno Scott James, trans. and Kienzle, Beverly Mayne. introduction, *The Letters of St. Bernard of Clairvaux* (Guildford, UK: Sutton Publishing, 1998).
16. The best modern edition of the Templar Rule is J. M. Upton-Ward, *The Rule of the Templars: The French Text of the Rule of the Order of the Knights Templar* (Woodbridge, UK: Boydell & Brewer, 1992).
17. M. Conrad Greenia, trans., and Malcolm Barber, introduction. *Bernard of Clairvaux: In Praise of the New Knighthood* (Trappist, KY: Cistercian Publications, 2000), 33, 39.
18. Jonathan Riley-Smith, *The First Crusaders: 1095–1131* (Cambridge: Cambridge University Press, 1997), 183–85.
19. Garmonsway, ed. and trans., *The Anglo-Saxon Chronicle,* 259.
20. For Tughtakin's date of death, D. S. Richards, trans., *The Chronicle of Ibn al-Athir for the Crusading Period from al-Kamil fi'l Ta'rikh,* vol. 1 (Farnham, UK: Ashgate, 2010), 274.
21. H. A. R. Gibb, trans., *The Damascus Chronicle of the Crusades: Extracted and Translated from the Chronicle of Ibn Al-Qalanisi* (London: Luzac, 1932; repr., New York: Dover, 2000), 195.
22. Al-Muqaddasi, *The Best Divisions for Knowledge of the Regions,* 133–34.
23. Richards, trans., *The Chronicle of Ibn al-Athir,* vol. 1, 278.
24. Gibb, trans., *The Damascus Chronicle of the Crusades,* 192–93.
25. Acts 9:2-9.
26. Gibb, trans., *The Damascus Chronicle of the Crusades,* 197.
27. Gibb, trans., *The Damascus Chronicle of the Crusades,* 198.
28. Babcock and Krey, *A History of Deeds Done Beyond the Sea,* vol. 2, 42.
29. Gibb, trans., *The Damascus Chronicle,* 199–200.

13. Melisende the Magnificent

1. Emily Atwater Babcock and A. C. Krey, trans., *A History of Deeds Done Beyond the Sea: By William, Archbishop of Tyre,* vol. 2 (New York: Columbia University Press, 1943), 45.
2. The classic analysis of this is to be found in Hans Eberhard Mayer, "Studies in the History of Queen Melisende of Jerusalem," *Dumbarton Oaks Papers* 26 (1972), esp. 98–110. Although NB Bernard Hamilton, "Women in the Crusader States: The Queens of Jerusalem, 1100–1190," in Derek Baker, ed., *Medieval Women* (Oxford: Basil Blackwell, 1978), 149, who is skeptical about the original terms of the offer to Fulk.
3. H. A. R. Gibb, trans., *The Damascus Chronicle of the Crusades: Extracted and Translated from the Chronicle of Ibn Al-Qalanisi* (London: Luzac, 1932; repr., New York: Dover, 2000), 208.
4. Marjorie Chibnall, trans., *The Ecclesiastical History of Orderic Vitalis,* vol. 6 (Oxford: Clarendon Press, 1978), 390–93. Orderic's assertion is tested against the charter evidence by Hans Eberhard Mayer, "Angevins versus Normans: The New Men of King Fulk of Jerusalem," *Proceedings of the American Philosophical Society* 133 (1989), 1–25.
5. D. S. Richards, trans., *The Chronicle of Ibn al-Athir for the Crusading Period from al-Kamil fi'l Ta'rikh,* vol. 1 (Farnham, UK: Ashgate, 2010), 382.
6. Babcock and Krey, *A History of Deeds Done Beyond the Sea,* vol. 2, 44.
7. Gibb, trans., *The Damascus Chronicle of the Crusades,* 215.
8. Babcock and Krey, *A History of Deeds Done Beyond the Sea,* vol. 2, 71.
9. Babcock and Krey, *A History of Deeds Done Beyond the Sea,* vol. 2, 73.
10. Babcock and Krey, *A History of Deeds Done Beyond the Sea,* vol. 2, 76.
11. Today the Melisende Psalter is kept in the British Library's collection: *Egerton MS 1139,* which can be viewed in the digitized manuscripts at www.bl.uk/manuscripts/FullDisplay.aspx?ref=Egerton_MS_1139.
12. Jaroslav Folda, *Crusader Art: The Art of the Crusaders in the Holy Land, 1099–1291* (Aldershot, UK: Lund Humphries, 2008), 36. Also see Margaret Tranovich, *Melisende of Jerusalem: The World of a Forgotten Crusader Queen* (London: East & West Publishing, 2011), 126–29.

13. This reliquary is today in the Württembergischen Landesmuseum in Stuttgart. On it, and others of the same type that are found in Augsburg, Barletta, Scheyern and elsewhere, see Adrian J. Boas, *Jerusalem in the Time of the Crusades: Society, Landscape and Art in the Holy City under Frankish Rule* (London: Routledge, 2001), 198.
14. Tranovich, *Melisende of Jerusalem,* xviii, 142–43.
15. Boas, *Jerusalem in the Time of the Crusades,* 147. The covered market dates from the end of Melisende's time of greatest influence, viz. ca. 1152.
16. Richards, trans., *The Chronicle of Ibn al-Athir,* vol. 1, 21–22.
17. This original church is described by Daniel the Abbot: John Wilkinson, with Joyce Hill and W. F. Ryan, eds., *Jerusalem Pilgrimage,* 133. Also see Denys Pringle, *The Churches of the Crusader Kingdom of Jerusalem: A Corpus,* vol. 1 (Cambridge: Cambridge University Press, 1993) 123–37.
18. Babcock and Krey, *A History of Deeds Done Beyond the Sea,* vol. 2, 133.
19. I owe this observation to a conversation with Professor Jonathan Phillips in the late summer of 2018.
20. Boas, *Jerusalem in the Time of the Crusades,* 103–5.
21. Babcock and Krey, *A History of Deeds Done Beyond the Sea,* vol. 2, 81.
22. Hugh Kennedy, *Crusader Castles* (Cambridge: Cambridge University Press, 1994), 32.
23. Although NB Jonathan Riley-Smith, *Hospitallers: The History of the Order of St. John* (London and Rio Grande, OH: Hambledon Press, 1999), who notes that it was not until 1160 that the Hospitallers were a fully fledged military force.
24. The Greek sources for this story, repeated by William of Tyre, are surveyed in Robert Browning, "The Death of John II Comnenus," *Byzantion* 31 (1961), 229–35.
25. Babcock and Krey, *A History of Deeds Done Beyond the Sea,* vol. 2, 134.
26. Bruno Scott James, trans., and Beverly Mayne Kienzle, introduction, *The Letters of St. Bernard of Clairvaux,* No. 273 (Guildford, UK: Sutton Publishing, 1998), 346.
27. Babcock and Krey, *A History of Deeds Done Beyond the Sea,* vol. 2, 139–40.

14. The Swords of Our Fathers

1. Léon, Mirot, ed. *La Chronique de Morigny (1095–1152),* (Paris: Librairie Alphonse Picard et Fils, 1909), 82–83.
2. Jacobus De Voragine, *The Golden Legend: Readings on the Saints,* trans. William Granger Ryan; with an introduction by Eamon Duffy (Princeton and Oxford: Princeton University Press, 2012), 35.
3. Emily Atwater Babcock and A. C. Krey, trans., *A History of Deeds Done Beyond the Sea: By William, Archbishop of Tyre,* vol. 2 (New York: Columbia University Press, 1943), 143.
4. D. S. Richards, trans., *The Chronicle of Ibn al-Athir for the Crusading Period from al-Kamil fi'l Ta'rikh,* vol. 1 (Farnham, UK: Ashgate, 2010), 373.
5. Mirot, *La Chronique de Morigny,* 83.
6. On the chronicle sources for Peter and Henry's heretical activities, see Marcia L. Colish, "Peter of Bruys, Henry of Lausanne, and the Façade of St.-Gilles," *Traditio* 28 (1972), 451–57.
7. Jonathan Phillips, *The Second Crusade: Extending the Frontiers of Christendom* (New Haven and London: Yale University Press, 2007), 43–44.
8. Bruno Scott James, trans., and Beverly Mayne Kienzle, introduction, *The Letters of St. Bernard of Clairvaux* (Guildford, UK: Sutton Publishing, 1998), 384.
9. See George Ferzoco, "The Origin of the Second Crusade," in Michael Gervers, ed., *The Second Crusade and the Cistercians* (New York: St. Martin's Press, 1992).
10. This English translation of *Quantum Praedecessores* is Jonathan and Louise Riley-Smith, eds. *The Crusades: Idea and Reality, 1095–1274* (London: Edward Arnold, 1981), 57–59.
11. Nicholas L. Paul, *To Follow in their Footsteps: The Crusades and Family Memory in the High Middle Ages* (Ithaca and London: Cornell University Press, 2012), 103–4. Other such relics and treasures abounded: In Normandy a miraculous piece of topaz returned to the duchy by Duke Robert was treasured as a family heirloom. As far north as Fife, Scotland, the cathedral priory in St. Andrews held Turkish arms and the fine saddle of an Arab horse brought home from the East in the first decade of the twelfth century.
12. Reported by William of Newburgh. Joseph Stevenson, trans. *The History of William of Newburgh* (Felinfach, Wales: Llanerch, 1996), 442.
13. Virginia Gingerick Berry, trans., *Odo of Deuil: De Profectione Ludovici VII in Orientem* (New York: W. W. Norton, 1948), 6–7.
14. Berry, trans., *Odo of Deuil,* 6–7.
15. Berry, trans., *Odo of Deuil,* 8–9.
16. Berry, trans., *Odo of Deuil,* 11.
17. J. Bédier and P. Aubry, eds. *Les Chansons de Croisade avec Leurs Melodies* (Paris: Champion, 1909), 8–10.
18. Benedicta, Ward, *Miracles and the Medieval Mind,* revised edition (Aldershot, UK: Wildwood House, 1987), 180, 182.
19. James, ed. *The Letters of St. Bernard of Clairvaux,* 461.
20. James, ed. *The Letters of St. Bernard of Clairvaux,* 464.
21. James, ed. *The Letters of St. Bernard of Clairvaux,* 465.
22. Shlomo Eidelberg, ed. and trans. *The Jews and the Crusaders: The Hebrew Chronicles of the First and Second Crusades* (Madison: University of Wisconsin Press, 1977), 122.
23. Eidelberg, ed. and trans., *The Jews and the Crusaders,* 123.
24. James, ed. *The Letters of St. Bernard of Clairvaux,* 465.
25. Eidelberg, ed. and trans., *The Jews and the Crusaders,* 127.

26. Otto of Freising and His Continuator, Rahewin, *The Deeds of Frederick Barbarossa*, trans. Charles Christopher Mierow (Toronto: University of Toronto Press, 1994), 75.
27. Otto of Freising, *The Deeds of Frederick Barbarossa*, 75.
28. Otto of Freising, *The Deeds of Frederick Barbarossa*, 76.

15. Converted or Deleted

1. The physical description of George of Antioch here draws on the image of him to be found in mosaic at the church of Santa Maria dell'Ammiraglio in Palermo, which he commissioned, and which was completed in his lifetime.
2. For summaries of the facts of George of Antioch's life and career, see Hubert Houben, *Roger II of Sicily: A Ruler Between East and West* (Cambridge: Cambridge University Press, 2002), 33–34, 150; Alex Metcalfe, *The Muslims of Medieval Italy* (Edinburgh: Edinburgh University Press, 2009), 126–28.
3. Metcalfe, *The Muslims of Medieval Italy*, 79.
4. D. S. Richards, trans., *The Chronicle of Ibn al-Athir for the Crusading Period from al-Kamil fi'l Ta'rikh*, vol. 2 (Farnham, UK: Ashgate, 2010), 16–17.
5. Richards, trans., *The Chronicle of Ibn al-Athir*, chapter 1.
6. Richards, trans., *The Chronicle of Ibn al-Athir*, vol. 1, 380.
7. Richards, trans., *The Chronicle of Ibn al-Athir*, vol. 2, 14.
8. Houben, *Roger II of Sicily*, 79.
9. Metcalfe, *The Muslims of Medieval Italy*, 163.
10. Richards, trans., *The Chronicle of Ibn al-Athir*, vol. 1, 380.
11. This remarkable garment, similar in form to an ecclesiastical cope, and wonderfully preserved, is today displayed among many other treasures of the Holy Roman Empire in the Kaiserliche Schatzkammer in Vienna, inventory number Treasury, WS XIII 14.
12. Paula Sanders, *Ritual, Politics and the City in Fatimid Cairo* (Albany: State University of New York Press, 1994), 25–26.
13. This translation: Louise and Jonathan Riley-Smith, *The Crusades: Idea and Reality, 1095–1274* (London: Edward Arnold, 1981), 75–77.
14. Riley-Smith, *The Crusades: Idea and Reality*, 75–77; Mihai Dragnea, "Divine Vengeance and Human Justice in the Wendish Crusade of 1147," *Collegium Medievale*, 29 (2016), 53.
15. Eric Christiansen, *The Northern Crusades*, second edition (London: Penguin, 1997), 53.
16. Otto of Freising and His Continuator, Rahewin, *The Deeds of Frederick Barbarossa*, trans. Charles Christopher Mierow (Toronto: University of Toronto Press, 1994), 76.
17. Otto of Freising, *The Deeds of Frederick Barbarossa*, 76.
18. Bruno Scott James, *The Letters of St. Bernard of Clairvaux* (Guildford, UK: Sutton Publishing, 1998), 466–67.
19. James, *The Letters of St. Bernard of Clairvaux* has "converted or wiped out."
20. Charles Wendell David, trans., and Jonathan Phillips, ed. *The Conquest of Lisbon: De Expugnatione* Lyxbonensi (New York: Columbia University Press, 2001), 90–93.
21. Jonathan Phillips, *The Second Crusade: Extending the Frontiers of Christendom* (New Haven and London: Yale University Press, 2007), 255–56.
22. David, trans., and Phillips, ed., *The Conquest of Lisbon*, 16.
23. Matthew Bennett, "Military Aspects of the Conquest of Lisbon, 1147," in Jonathan Phillips and Martin Hoch, eds., *The Second Crusade: Scope and Consequences* (Manchester, UK: Manchester University Press, 2001), 73.
24. David, trans., and Phillips, ed., *The Conquest of Lisbon*, 56–57.
25. David, trans., and Phillips, ed., *The Conquest of Lisbon*, 70–73.
26. David, trans., and Phillips, ed., *The Conquest of Lisbon*, 78–81.
27. David, trans., and Phillips, ed., *The Conquest of Lisbon*, 90–91.
28. David, trans., and Phillips, ed., *The Conquest of Lisbon*, 128–29, 134–35, 142–43.
29. David, trans., and Phillips, ed., *The Conquest of Lisbon*, 136–39.
30. David, trans., and Phillips, ed., *The Conquest of Lisbon*, 132–33.
31. David, trans., and Phillips, ed., *The Conquest of Lisbon*, 138–39, 144–45.
32. *Relatio de translatione S. Vincentii martyris*, this translation in Giles Constable, *Crusaders and Crusading in the Twelfth Century* (Farnham, UK: Ashgate, 2008), 303.
33. David, trans., and Phillips, ed., *The Conquest of Lisbon*, 182–83.

16. History Repeating

1. Anna Komnene, *The Alexiad*, trans. E. R. A. Sewter, Introduction, Peter Frankopan, revised edition (London: Penguin, 2009), 422.
2. John Kinnamos, *Deeds of John and Manuel Comnenus*, trans. Charles M. Brand (New York: Columbia University Press, 1976), 58.
3. P. Stephenson, "Anna Comnena's Alexiad as a Source for the Second Crusade?," *Journal of Medieval History* 29 (2012), 41–54, summarizes the literature on the *Alexiad*'s composition in the context of the Second Crusade.
4. Elizabeth Jeffreys and Michael Jeffreys, "The 'Wild Beast from the West': Immediate Literary Reactions in Byzantium to the Second Crusade," in Angeliki E. Laiou and Roy P. Mottahedeh, eds., *The Crusades from the Perspective of Byzantium and the Muslim World* (Washington, DC: Dumbarton Oaks Research Library and Collection, 2001), 104.
5. Martin Bouquet, ed., *Recueil des Historiens des Gaules et de la France*, vol. 16 (Paris: l'Imprimerie Impériale, 1878), 9.
6. The estimate of "nine myriads"—or 900,000 people—given by John Kinnamos, is plainly fanciful. *Deeds of John and Manuel Comnenus*, 60.

7. Jeffreys and Jeffreys, "The 'Wild Beast from the West,'" 109.
8. Otto of Freising and His Continuator, Rahewin, *The Deeds of Frederick Barbarossa,* trans. Charles Christopher Mierow (Toronto: University of Toronto Press, 1994), 81.
9. Kinnamos, *Deeds of John and Manuel Comnenus,* 63.
10. On the realistic rate of progress through Anatolia see Jonathan Phillips, *The Second Crusade: Extending the Frontiers of Christendom* (New Haven and London: Yale University Press, 2007), 177–78.
11. Paul M. Cobb, *The Race for Paradise: An Islamic History of the Crusades* (Oxford: Oxford University Press, 2014), 138–39.
12. H. A. R. Gibb, trans., *The Damascus Chronicle of the Crusades: Extracted and Translated from the Chronicle of Ibn Al-Qalanisi* (London: Luzac, 1932; repr., New York: Dover, 2000), 281.
13. Letter to Wibald, abbot of Stavelot and Corvey, written late February, 1148. This translation: Malcolm Barber and Keith Bate, trans., *Letters from the East: Crusaders, Pilgrims and Settlers in the 12th–13th Centuries* (Farnham, UK: Ashgate, 2010), 45.
14. Virginia Gingerick Berry, trans., *Odo of Deuil: De Profectione Ludovici VII in Orientem* (New York: W. W. Norton, 1948), 17.
15. For the example of Fleury abbey see Constable, *Crusaders and Crusading in the Twelfth Century,* 117–19.
16. Kinnamos, *Deeds of John and Manuel Comnenus,* 69.
17. Berry, trans., *Odo of Deuil,* 64–65.
18. Berry, trans., *Odo of Deuil,* 56–59.
19. Berry, trans., *Odo of Deuil,* 112–13. Conrad's defeat at Dorylaeum, by contrast, had been heralded by a terrible partial eclipse, in which the sun was shaped "like half a loaf of bread" for a long period, seemingly in imitation of Conrad's half-baked efforts on the battlefield.
20. Berry, trans., *Odo of Deuil,* 114–15.
21. Berry, trans., *Odo of Deuil,* 116–17.
22. Berry, trans., *Odo of Deuil,* 116–17.
23. Berry, trans., *Odo of Deuil,* 118–19.
24. Gibb, trans., *The Damascus Chronicle of the Crusades,* 271–72.
25. D. S. Richards, trans., *The Chronicle of Ibn al-Athir for the Crusading Period from al-Kamil fi'l Ta'rikh,* vol. 1 (Farnham, UK: Ashgate, 2010), 382–83.
26. This is a rather labored pun, relying on the similarity of the name Zengi (or Zangi) with the Latin word for blood (*sanguis, sanguinis*). Emily Atwater Babcock and A. C. Krey, trans., *A History of Deeds Done Beyond the Sea: By William, Archbishop of Tyre,* vol. 2 (New York: Columbia University Press, 1943), 146.
27. Richards, trans., *The Chronicle of Ibn al-Athir,* vol. 2, 222–23.
28. Babcock and Krey, *A History of Deeds Done Beyond the Sea,* vol. 2, 394–95.
29. Richards, trans., *The Chronicle of Ibn al-Athir,* vol. 2, 8, relates the miserable story of a young girl twice taken as war booty from Edessa—first by Zengi and again by Nur al-Din; on both occasions she was sent to Zayn al-Din Ali of the citadel of Mosul, who seems from the account given by Ibn al-Athir to have raped her.
30. This translation: Phillips, *The Second Crusade,* 210.
31. Babcock and Krey, *A History of Deeds Done Beyond the Sea,* vol. 2, 179.
32. Babcock and Krey, *A History of Deeds Done Beyond the Sea,* vol. 2, 180.
33. See Ralph V. Turner, *Eleanor of Aquitaine* (New Haven and London: Yale University Press, 2009), 87.
34. Babcock and Krey, *A History of Deeds Done Beyond the Sea,* vol. 2.
35. Kinnamos, *Deeds of John and Manuel Comnenus,* 71.
36. Babcock and Krey, *A History of Deeds Done Beyond the Sea,* vol. 2, 189–90.
37. Babcock and Krey, *A History of Deeds Done Beyond the Sea,* vol. 2, 191.
38. Gibb, trans., *The Damascus Chronicle of the Crusades,* 286.
39. Gibb, trans., *The Damascus Chronicle of the Crusades,* 287.
40. Babcock and Krey, *A History of Deeds Done Beyond the Sea,* vol. 2, 180.
41. Komnene, *Alexiad,* 331.

17. The Race for Egypt

1. Usama ibn Munqidh, *The Book of Contemplation: Islam and the Crusades,* trans. Paul M. Cobb, (London: Penguin, 2008), 29; D. S. Richards, trans., *The Chronicle of Ibn al-Athir for the Crusading Period from al-Kamil fi'l Ta'rikh,* vol. 2 (Farnham, UK: Ashgate, 2010), 67. Ibn Munqidh names the manservant as Sa'id al-Dawla.
2. Ibn Munqidh, *The Book of Contemplation,* 30.
3. Richards, trans., *The Chronicle of Ibn al-Athir,* vol. 2, 68.
4. The most recent scholarly survey of the Fatimid caliphate is Michael Brett, *The Fatimid Empire* (Edinburgh: Edinburgh University Press, 2017).
5. Al-Muqaddasi, *The Best Divisions for Knowledge of the Regions: Ahsan al-Taqasim fi Ma'rifat al-Aqalim,* trans. Basil Collins (Reading, UK: Garnet Publishing, 2001), 163–66.
6. H. A. R. Gibb, trans., *The Damascus Chronicle of the Crusades: Extracted and Translated from the Chronicle of Ibn Al-Qalanisi* (London: Luzac, 1932; repr., New York: Dover, 2000), 317, giving the perspective from Damascus.
7. Emily Atwater Babcock and A. C. Krey, trans., *A History of Deeds Done Beyond the Sea: By William, Archbishop of Tyre,* vol. 2 (New York: Columbia University Press, 1943), 296.
8. Babcock and Krey, *A History of Deeds Done Beyond the Sea,* vol. 2, 297–98.
9. Zaki al-Din Muhammad al-Wahrani, this translation from Malcolm Cameron Lyons, and D. E. P. Jackson, *Saladin: The Politics of the*

Holy War (Cambridge: Cambridge University Press, 1982), 6.

10. Richards, trans., *The Chronicle of Ibn al-Athir,* vol. 1, 138.
11. See Andrew D. Buck, *The Principality of Antioch and its Frontiers in the Twelfth Century* (Woodbridge, UK: Boydell Press, 2017), 38–44.
12. Gibb, trans., *The Damascus Chronicle of the Crusades,* 319–21.
13. On the minbar, see Carole Hillenbrand, *The Crusades: Islamic Perspectives* (Edinburgh: Edinburgh University Press, 1999), 152.
14. Christopher Tyerman, *God's War: A New History of the Crusades* (London: Allen Lane, 2006), 345.
15. Babcock and Krey, *A History of Deeds Done Beyond the Sea,* vol. 2, 302.
16. Richards, trans., *The Chronicle of Ibn al-Athir,* vol. 2, 144.
17. Babcock and Krey, *A History of Deeds Done Beyond the Sea,* vol. 2, 313.
18. Babcock and Krey, *A History of Deeds Done Beyond the Sea,* vol. 2, 303–4.
19. Richards, trans., *The Chronicle of Ibn al-Athir,* vol. 2, 146.
20. Babcock and Krey, *A History of Deeds Done Beyond the Sea,* vol. 2, 308.
21. Babcock and Krey, *A History of Deeds Done Beyond the Sea,* vol. 2, 308.
22. Babcock and Krey, *A History of Deeds Done Beyond the Sea,* vol. 2, 319–20, contains a superb account based on eyewitness testimony of the caliph's palatial apartments.
23. Abu Shama, "The Book of the Two Gardens," trans., *Recueil des Historiens des Croisades: Historiens Orientaux*, vol. 4 (Paris: Imprimerie Nationale, 1898), 137
24. Abu Shama, *Recueil des Historiens des Croisades: Historiens Orientaux*, vol. 4, 351.
25. Abu Shama, *Recueil des Historiens des Croisades: Historiens Orientaux*, vol. 4, 356.
26. Abu Shama, *Recueil des Historiens des Croisades: Historiens Orientaux*, vol. 4, 357.
27. Richards, trans., *The Chronicle of Ibn al-Athir,* vol. 2, 175; *Qur'an* VI, 44.

18. Because of Our Sins

1. D. S. Richards, trans., *The Chronicle of Ibn al-Athir for the Crusading Period from al-Kamil fi'l Ta'rikh,* vol. 2 (Farnham, UK: Ashgate, 2010), 196.
2. Richards, trans., *The Chronicle of Ibn al-Athir,* vol. 2, 196.
3. Richards, trans., *The Chronicle of Ibn al-Athir,* vol. 2, 196.
4. Some sources, including the multiauthored *History of the Patriarches of the Egyptian Church,* give other explanations for al-Adid's death: that he committed suicide after learning that Saladin's brother Turan-Shah was intending to murder him; that Turan-Shah really did murder him after interrogating him about the location of his treasure; that Saladin and Turan-Shah tricked the caliph into drinking wine with him and then declared that since he had committed this un-Islamic deed, he was now deposed. See Yaacov, Lev, *Saladin in Egypt* (Leiden: Brill, 1998), 82–83.
5. Richards, trans., *The Chronicle of Ibn al-Athir,* vol. 2, 197.
6. D. S. Richards, trans., *Baha al-Din Ibn Shaddad: The Rare and Excellent History of Saladin* (Farnham, UK: Ashgate, 2002), 17.
7. H. A. R. Gibb, trans., *The Damascus Chronicle of the Crusades: Extracted and Translated from the Chronicle of Ibn Al-Qalanisi* (London: Luzac, 1932; repr., New York: Dover, 2000), 273.
8. Richards, trans., *Baha al-Din Ibn Shaddad,* 26–27.
9. Richards, trans., *Baha al-Din Ibn Shaddad,* 28.
10. Helen Nicholson, *The Chronicle of the Third Crusade: The Itinerarium Peregrinorum et Gesta Regis Ricardi* (Farnham, UK: Ashgate, 1997), 23.
11. Imad al-Din, quoted by Abu Shama, *Recueil des Historiens des Croisades Orientaux,* vol. 4 (Paris: Imprimerie Nationale, 1898), 147.
12. Abu Shama, *Recueil des Historiens des Croisades Orientaux,* 153.
13. On Qaraqush's adventures in North Africa, see Amar, Baadj, "Saladin and the Ayyubid Campaigns in the Maghrib," *Al-Qantara* 34 (2013).
14. The pragmatic appeal of a Frankish buffer state—then against the Great Seljuq empire—had been recognized by many in Fatimid Egypt at the time of the First Crusade.
15. This translation: Carole Hillenbrand, *The Crusades: Islamic Perspectives* (Edinburgh: Edinburgh University Press, 1999), 166.
16. On Saladin's use of seismic imagery, Malcolm Cameron Lyons, and D. E. P. Jackson, *Saladin: The Politics of the Holy War* (Cambridge: Cambridge University Press, 1982), 74; on the earthquake of 1170, Emanuela Guidoboni, Filippo Bernadini, Alberto Comastri, and Enzo Boschi, "The Large Earthquake on 29 June 1170 (Syria, Lebanon, and Central Southern Turkey)," *Journal of Geophysical Research* 109 (2004).
17. Lyons and Jackson, *Saladin: The Politics of Holy War,* 75; Saladin's concern for Amalric's "bitter punishment" is a pun on the similarity between the king's name and an Arabic word *murr,* meaning bitter.
18. Babcock and Krey, *A History of Deeds Done Beyond the Sea,* vol. 2, 398.
19. On this aspect of Baldwin's disease see Stephen Lay, "A Leper in Purple: the Coronation of Baldwin IV of Jerusalem," *Journal of Medieval History* 23 (1997), 318–19.
20. Lyons and Jackson, *Saladin: The Politics of Holy War,* 239.
21. Babcock and Krey, *A History of Deeds Done Beyond the Sea,* vol. 2, 407.
22. For Philip of Alsace see William Stubbs, ed., *Radulfi de Diceto Decani Lundoniensis Opera Historica: The Historical Works of Master Ralph de Diceto,* vol. 1 (London, 1876), 402. Other lords who came on private crusades around the same

time (although for less sensational reasons) included Stephen of Perche, archbishop of Palermo; William, Count of Nevers; Stephen of Sancerre; Stephen, Count of Saône and Hugh, Duke of Burgundy. See Malcolm Barber, *The Crusader States* (New Haven and London: Yale University Press, 2012), 252–53.

23. Eric Christiansen, *The Northern Crusades*, second edition (London: Penguin, 1997), 71.
24. Barber and Bate, trans., *Letters from the East*, 53–54.
25. Barber and Bate, trans., *Letters from the East*, 73.
26. Stubbs, ed., *Radulfi de Diceto*, vol. 2, 34.
27. For a full narration of this encounter see W. L. Warren, *Henry II* (New Haven and London: Yale University Press, 2000), 604–5.
28. Roland Broadhurst, *The Travels of Ibn Jubayr* (London: Jonathan Cape, 1952), 311.
29. Narrated most recently in Jeffrey Lee, *God's Wolf: The Life of the Most Notorious of All Crusaders, Reynald de Chatillon* (London: Atlantic Books, 2016), 202–7.
30. Old French continuation of William of Tyre in Peter W. Edbury, trans., *The Conquest of Jerusalem and the Third Crusade*, (Farnham, UK: Ashgate, 1998), 11.
31. Malcolm Barber and Keith Bate, trans., *Letters from the East: Crusaders, Pilgrims and Settlers in the 12th–13th Centuries* (Farnham, UK: Ashgate, 2010), 76.
32. Richards, trans., *Baha al-Din Ibn Shaddad*, 72.
33. Richards, trans., *Baha al-Din Ibn Shaddad*, 73.
34. Richards, trans., *The Chronicle of Ibn al-Athir*, vol. 2, 323.
35. Barber and Bate, trans., *Letters from the East*, 77.
36. Rule 419 of the rule theoretically sentenced to banishment from the order any brother who "flees from the field [of battle] for fear of the Saracens, while the piebald banner [the official Templar flag, half black and half white] is still aloft." See J. M. Upton-Ward, *The Rule of the Templars: The French Text of the Rule of the Order of the Knights Templar* (Woodbridge, UK: Boydell & Brewer, 1992), 112.
37. Barber and Bate, trans., *Letters from the East*, 79.
38. As reported to Pope Urban III by Patriarch Eraclius in September 1187. Barber and Bate, trans., *Letters from the East*, 80–81.
39. Old French continuator of William of Tyre in Edbury, trans., *The Conquest of Jerusalem and the Third Crusade*, 59.
40. On the identity of the preacher, see Richards, trans., *The Chronicle of Ibn al-Athir*, vol. 2, 334. For an English translation of Muhyi al-Din Khutbah, see William MacGuckin Slane, trans., *Ibn Khallikan's Biographical Dictionary*, vol. 2, (Paris: Oriental Translation Fund, 1842), 634–41.

19. Lionesses and Lionhearts

1. The most recent scholarly Latin edition of the text known as *Hodoeporicon et Percale Margarite Iherosolimitane* is Paul Gerhard Schmidt, "Peregrinatio periculosa": Thomas of Froidmont über die Jerusalemfahrten seiner Schwester Margareta in Franco Munari, Ulrich Justus Stache, Wolfgang Maaz and Fritz Wagner, *Kontinuität und Wandel: Lateinische Poesie von Naevius bis Baudelaire* (Hildesheim, Germany: Weidmann, 1986), 476–85. A French translation may be found in M. Michaud, *Bibliothèque des Croisades: Troisième Partie* (Paris: Ducollet, 1829), 369–75. The question of Margaret's authorship is not settled: clearly constructed to emphasize the idea of her suffering as an analogy for martyrdom, internal evidence suggests that Margaret was literate; but it is equally likely that her account was ghostwritten by her brother, Thomas of Froidmont.
2. Ibid.
3. Among the burgeoning literature on the roles of women during the crusades, see Susan B. Edgington and Sarah Lambert, *Gendering the Crusades* (Cardiff: University of Wales Press, 2001); Bernard Hamilton, "Women in the Crusader States: The Queens of Jerusalem 1100–90," in Derek Baker, ed., *Medieval Women* (Oxford: Basil Blackwell, 1978), 143–74; Helen Nicholson, "Women's Involvement in the Crusades," in Adrian J. Boas, ed. *The Crusader World* (Abingdon, UK, and New York: 2016), 54–67; Natasha Hodgson, *Women, Crusading and the Holy Land in Historical Narrative* (Woodbridge, UK: Boydell Press, 2007); Christoph T. Maier, "The Roles of Women in the Crusade Movement: A Survey," *Journal of Medieval History* 30 (2004), 61–82; and in this context especially, Helen Nicholson, "Women on the Third Crusade," *Journal of Medieval History* 23 (1997), 335–49.
4. Tyre survived largely thanks to its formidable defenses and the leadership of Conrad of Montferrat, an Italian nobleman considered "a devil among men, good at organizing and defending, a man of great bravery." See D. S. Richards, trans., *The Chronicle of Ibn al-Athir for the Crusading Period from al-Kamil fi'l Ta'rikh*, vol. 2 (Farnham, UK: Ashgate, 2010), 329. Tripoli and Antioch also held out.
5. Catia, Galatariotou, *The Making of a Saint: The Life, Times and Sanctification of Neophytos the Recluse* (Cambridge: Cambridge University Press, 1991), 206–7; Michael, Angold, "The Fall of Jerusalem (1187) as Viewed from Byzantium," in Boas, *The Crusader World*, 296.
6. Urban III's papacy lasted from November 25, 1180, until his death on October 20, 1187—his death clearly coming before he could possibly have learned of Jerusalem's fall just eighteen days previously. The English chronicler William of Newburgh stated that even the news of Hattin (July 4) only arrived in Italy a few days after Urban's death. Cf. Peter W. Edbury, trans., *The Conquest of Jerusalem and the Third Crusade* (Farnham, UK: Ashgate, 1998), 75; Joseph Stevenson, trans., *The History of William of Newburgh* (Felinfach, Wales: Llanerch, 1996), 542.

7. An English translation of this bull can be found in Jonathan Riley-Smith and Louise Riley-Smith, *The Crusades: Idea and Reality, 1095–1274* (London: Edward Arnold, 1981), 63–67.
8. Edbury, trans., *The Conquest of Jerusalem and the Third Crusade*, 75.
9. Louise and Jonathan Riley-Smith, *The Crusades: Idea and Reality*, 65.
10. As spelled out in *audita tremendi*, Riley-Smith, *The Crusades: Idea and Reality*, 67.
11. G. A. Loud, trans., *The Crusade of Frederick Barbarossa: The History of the Expedition of the Emperor Frederick and Related Texts* (Farnham, UK: Ashgate, 2010), 41.
12. The former is the more likely figure. See Loud, trans., *The Crusade of Frederick Barbarossa*, 19 and 32n66.
13. Loud, trans., *The Crusade of Frederick Barbarossa*, 45.
14. Helen J. Nicholson, *The Chronicle of the Third Crusade: The Intinerarium Peregrinorum et Gesta Regis Ricardi* (Farnham, UK: Ashgate, 1997), 148, 190.
15. See John Gillingham, *Richard I* (New Haven and London: Yale University Press, 1999), 266–67.
16. Translation from Gillingham, *Richard I*.
17. Christopher Tyerman, *How to Plan a Crusade: Reason and Religious War in the High Middle Ages* (London: Allen Lane, 2015), 263.
18. See Tyerman, *How to Plan a Crusade*, introduction.
19. Stevenson, trans., *The History of William of Newburgh*, 556.
20. John T. Appleby, *The Chronicle of Richard of Devizes of the Time of King Richard the First* (London: Thomas Nelson & Sons, 1963), 4.
21. Nicholson, *The Chronicle of the Third Crusade*, 48.
22. J. Bédier and P. Aubry, eds., *Les Chansons de Croisade avec Leurs Melodies* (Paris: Champion, 1909), 283–85; this translation: Riley-Smith, *The Crusades: Idea and Reality*, 157–59.
23. Marianne Ailes, trans. *The History of the Holy War: Ambroise's Estoire de la Guerre Sainte*, vol. 2 (Woodbridge, UK: Boydell Press, 2003), 34.
24. On William I's beard and strength, and the comparative absence from the historical record of anecdotes about his son, see Donald Matthew, *The Norman Kingdom of Sicily* (Cambridge: Cambridge University Press, 1992), 167.
25. Matthew, *The Norman Kingdom of Sicily*, 280.
26. Compare Ailes, trans., *The History of the Holy War: Ambroise's Estoire de la Guerre Sainte*, vol. 2, 44, with the translation of Peter of Eboli in Ivo Wolsing, "'Look, There Comes the Half-Man!' Delegitimising Tancred of Lecce in Peter of Eboli's *Liber ad Honorem Augusti*," *Al-Masaq* (2018), 6 (and commentary, *ibid. passim*, 1–15).
27. Ailes, trans. *The History of the Holy War*, vol. 2, 39.
28. "Mategrifon"; *Richard of Devizes*, 24–25 gives "Griffon-Killer."
29. Ailes, trans., *The History of the Holy War*, vol. 2, 48.
30. Ailes, trans., *The History of the Holy War*, vol. 2, 48.
31. Nicholson, *The Chronicle of the Third Crusade*, 179.
32. Harry J. Magoulias, *O City of Byzantium, Annals of Niketas Choniatēs* (Detroit: 1984), 161.
33. For the silver manacles, Nicholson, *The Chronicle of the Third Crusade*, 194. Isaac was eventually released from prison but died shortly afterward in 1195.
34. Described by Loud, trans., *The Crusade of Frederick Barbarossa*, 111.
35. Loud, trans., *The Crusade of Frederick Barbarossa*, 115.
36. Rigord of St. Denis, this translation from John D. Hosler, *The Siege of Acre: 1189–1191* (New Haven and London: Yale University Press, 2018), 109.
37. Nicholson, *The Chronicle of the Third Crusade*, 106.
38. Ailes, trans., *The History of the Holy War*, vol. 2, 66.
39. Richards, trans., *The Chronicle of Ibn al-Athir*, vol, 2, 387.
40. D. S. Richards, trans., *Baha al-Din Ibn Shaddad: The Rare and Excellent History of Saladin* (Farnham, UK: Ashgate, 2002), 146.
41. Richards, trans., *Baha al-Din Ibn Shaddad*, 158.
42. For a discussion of legality and a brief comparison with Saladin's own actions, which included the deliberate massacre of two hundred Templars and Hospitallers after Hattin, see Hosler, *The Siege of Acre*, 154–55.
43. Nicholson, *The Chronicle of the Third Crusade*, 249.
44. Richards, trans., *Baha al-Din Ibn Shaddad*, 195–96.
45. A major power struggle erupted in the Ayyubid world after Saladin's death; it took al-Adil until 1200 to consolidate his position as his brother's successor.

20. Consumed by Fire

1. Nor was it true that Dandolo had suffered the injury during a brawl in the streets of Constantinople. (Cf. Steven Runciman, *A History of the Crusades: Volume 3, The Kingdom of Acre and the Later Crusades* [Cambridge: Cambridge University Press, 1954], 97.) For a discussion of the sources for Dandolo's blindness and examples of his deteriorating handwriting, see Thomas F. Madden, *Enrico Dandolo and the Rise of Venice* (Baltimore: Johns Hopkins University Press, 2003), 65–68.
2. Villehardouin and De Joinville, *Chronicles of the Crusades*, trans. Frank Thomas Marzials (London: J. M. Dent, 1908), 17.
3. D. S. Richards, trans., *The Chronicle of Ibn al-Athir for the Crusading Period from al-Kamil fi'l Ta'rikh*, vol. 2 (Farnham, UK: Ashgate, 2010), 76, reports Dandolo's need to be led on horseback.
4. Anna Komnene, *The Alexiad*, trans. E. R. A. Sewter, introduction, Peter Frankopan, revised edition (London: Penguin, 2009), 162–63.
5. See Komnene, *The Alexiad*, 295–331.

6. Madden, *Enrico Dandolo and the Rise of Venice,* 71.
7. The full text of Dandolo's oath, which is the first of its kind to survive, is translated into English in Madden, *Enrico Dandolo and the Rise of Venice,* 96–98.
8. The deeds of the first crusaders had been written up for a knightly audience as the *Chanson d'Antioche,* composed in the 1180s. Susan B. Edgington and Carol Sweetenham, trans., *The Chanson d'Antioche: An Old French Account of the First Crusade* (Farnham, UK: Ashgate, 2011).
9. Peter W. Edbury, trans., *The Conquest of Jerusalem and the Third Crusade* (Farnham, UK: Ashgate, 1998), 143, adds the assertion that Henry would have survived had his pet dwarf not also fallen and landed on top of him.
10. An English translation of *post miserabile* is in Jessalynn Bird, Edward Peters and James M. Powell, eds., *Crusade and Christendom: Annotated Documents in Translation from Innocent III to the Fall of Acre, 1187–1291* (Philadelphia: University of Pennsylvania Press, 2013), 31–37.
11. Bird, Peters, and Powell, eds., *Crusade and Christendom,* 32.
12. John C. Moore, *Pope Innocent III (1160/1–1216): To Root Up and to Plant* (Leiden: Brill, 2003), 103.
13. Fulk of Neuilly was long thought to have played a central role at Écry, a view now discredited. For a recent reassessment of his preaching in general, see Andrew W. Jones, "Fulk of Neuilly, Innocent III, and the Preaching of the Fourth Crusade," *Comitatus: A Journal of Medieval and Renaissance Studies* 41 (2010): 11948. For Martin of Pairis, see Alfred J. Andrea, trans., *The Capture of Constantinople: The "Hystoria Constantinopolitana" of Gunther of Pairis* (Philadelphia: University of Pennsylvania Press, 1997), 69–70.
14. Villehardouin and De Joinville, *Chronicles of the Crusades,* 5.
15. Jonathan Phillips, *The Fourth Crusade and the Sack of Constantinople* (New York: Penguin, 2005), 66.
16. Villehardouin and De Joinville, *Chronicles of the Crusades,* 8.
17. For examples of gifts to local religious foundations, see the charters of Viard of Prés and Simon de Malesnes in Corliss Konwiser Slack, ed., *Crusade Charters: 1178–1270* (Tempe: Arizona Center for Medieval and Renaissance Studies, 2001), 132–3; 140–41.
18. Robert of Clari, chapter 7, in Edward N. Stone, ed., *Three Old French Chronicles of the Crusades* (Seattle: University of Washington Publications, 1939).
19. Madden, *Enrico Dandolo and the Rise of Venice,* 141.
20. Andrea, trans., *The Capture of Constantinople,* 79.
21. Andrea, trans., *The Capture of Constantinople,* 80.
22. A. J. Andrea, *Contemporary Sources for the Fourth Crusade* (Leiden: Brill, 2000), 48.
23. Harry J. Magoulias, *O City of Byzantium, Annals of Niketas* Choniatēs (Detroit: 1984), 242, 248.
24. Villehardouin and De Joinville, *Chronicles of the Crusades,* 23.
25. Villehardouin and De Joinville, *Chronicles of the Crusades,* 23.
26. Andrea, trans., *The Capture of Constantinople,* 83.
27. Andrea, trans., *The Capture of Constantinople,* 89.
28. Andrea, trans., *The Capture of Constantinople,* 30.
29. Villehardouin and De Joinville, *Chronicles of the Crusades,* 31.
30. Jonathan Harris, *Constantinople: Capital of Byzantium,* second edition (London: Bloomsbury Academic, 2017), 6.
31. Villehardouin and De Joinville, *Chronicles of the Crusades,* 31.
32. Magoulias, *O City of Byzantium,* 298.
33. Magoulias, *O City of Byzantium,* 298.
34. This translation and a discussion of the relationship between chivalry and crusading, see Natasha Hodgson, "Honor, Shame and the Fourth Crusade," *Journal of Medieval History* 39 (2013): 220–39.
35. Magoulias, *O City of Byzantium,* 304.
36. *Robert of Clari,* 59.
37. Ibid., 62
38. Ibid., 71.
39. Andrea, trans., *The Capture of Constantinople,* 105–6.
40. Magoulias, *O City of Byzantium,* 322.
41. Phillips, *The Fourth Crusade,* 263.
42. Magoulias, *O City of Byzantium,* 323.
43. On Dandolo's defense of 1205, see Donald E. Queller, and Irene B. Katele, "Attitudes Toward the Venetians in the Fourth Crusade: The Western Sources," *International History Review* 4 (1982), 2–3.
44. On the balance of motivation between piety and money, see Savvas Neocleous, "Financial, Chivalric or Religious? The Motives of the Fourth Crusaders Reconsidered," *Journal of Medieval History* 38 (2012), 183–206.
45. Magoulias, *O City of Byzantium,* 295.
46. The debate over Venice and Dandolo's culpability for events of the Fourth Crusade has not entirely dimmed with time—see the entertaining introduction to Thomas F. Madden, "Outside and Inside the Fourth Crusade," *International History Review* 17 (1995), 726–27.
47. For the Islamic view on the Fourth Crusade, including this claim by Abu Shama, see in Taef el-Azhari, "Muslim Chroniclers and the Fourth Crusade," *Crusades* 6 (2007), 107–16 (quotation 109).
48. Magoulias, *O City of Byzantium,* 316.

21. Enemies Within

1. Jerry C. Smith and William L. Urban, *The Livonian Rhymed Chronicle* (London: RoutledgeCurzon, 2007), 3.
2. Eric Christiansen, *The Northern Crusades,* second edition (London: Penguin, 1997), 80.
3. *Chronica Alberti monachi trium fontium,* translated in Christiansen, *The Northern Crusades,* 99.
4. Henricus Lettus, *The Chronicle of Henry of Livonia: Henricus Lettus,* trans. James A. Brundage (New York: Columbia University Press, 2004), 53. Henry of Livonia gives "Philistines" but

he surely refers to Judges 7:7, which describes the victory of Gideon and the three hundred over the Midianites.

5. Lettus, *The Chronicle of Henry of Livonia*, 52.
6. See Iben, Fonnesberg-Schmidt, *The Popes and the Baltic Crusades 1147–1254* (Leiden: Brill, 2007), 92–93.
7. Louise and Jonathan Riley Smith, eds., *The Crusades: Idea and Reality, 1095–1274* (London: Edward Arnold, 1981), 78.
8. On this, see Marek Tamm, "How to Justify a Crusade? The Conquest of Livonia and New Crusade Rhetoric in the Early Thirteenth Century," *Journal of Medieval History* 39 (2013), 446–67.
9. Gary, Dickson, *The Children's Crusade: Medieval History, Modern Mythistory* (London: Palgrave Macmillan, 2008), 31.
10. Christopher Tyerman, *God's War: A New History of the Crusades* (London: Allen Lane, 2006), 572.
11. Canon 27 of the Third Lateran Council—a convenient English translation of which is at www.papalencyclicals.net/councils/ecum11.htm.
12. Translation follows John C. Moore, *Pope Innocent III (1160/61–1216): To Root Up and to Plant* (Leiden: Brill, 2003), 149.
13. Riley-Smith, *The Crusades: Idea and Reality*, 78–79.
14. Riley-Smith, *The Crusades: Idea and Reality*, 156.
15. Riley-Smith, *The Crusades: Idea and Reality*, 167.
16. Riley-Smith, *The Crusades: Idea and Reality*, 81.
17. G. E. M. Lippiatt, *Simon V of Montfort and Baronial Government* (Oxford: Oxford University Press, 2017), 99.
18. W. A. Sibly and M. D. Sibly, *The History of the Albigensian Crusade: Peter of les Vaux-de-Cernay's* Historia Albigensis (Woodbridge, UK: Boydell Press, 1998), 56. See, for similar if less extended praise, Janet Shirley, *The Song of the Cathar Wars: A History of the Albigensian Crusade* (Aldershot, UK: Routledge, 1996), 27.
19. Sibly and Sibly, *The History of the Albigensian Crusade*, 69, Cf. Shirley, *The Song of the Cathar Wars*, 29.
20. Sibly and Sibly, *The History of the Albigensian Crusade*, 93–94.
21. *The Song of the Cathar Wars*, 33.
22. Shirley, *The Song of the Cathar Wars*, 41.
23. Shirley, *The Song of the Cathar Wars*, 41.
24. Sibly and Sibly, *The History of the Albigensian Crusade*, 238. Bernard and Hélis's grisly handiwork was discovered when their castle near the Dordogne was taken in 1214.
25. An English translation of the Statutes of Pamiers may be found in Sibly and Sibly, *The History of the Albigensian Crusade*, 321–29. On the rights of heretics, see statutes 10, 11, 14, 15, 24, 25.
26. D. S. Richards, trans., *The Chronicle of Ibn al-Athir for the Crusading Period from al-Kamil fi'l Ta'rikh*, vol. 3 (Farnham, UK: Ashgate, 2010), 21.
27. Sibly and Sibly, *The History of the Albigensian Crusade*, 310.
28. Shirley, *The Song of the Cathar Wars*, 71.
29. Sibly and Sibly, *The History of the Albigensian Crusade*, 256.
30. Moore, *Innocent III*, 288.

22. The River of Paradise

1. Galatians 6:14.
2. The text of *Quia Major*, Louise and Jonathan Riley-Smith, eds., *The Crusades: Idea and Reality, 1095–1274* (London: Edward Arnold, 1981), 118–24. On Oliver's career, see Thomas W. Smith, "Oliver of Cologne's *Historia Damiatina:* A New Manuscript Witness in Dublin, Trinity College Library MS 496," *Hermathena* 194 (2013), 37–39.
3. Letter translated in Riley-Smith, *The Crusades: Idea and Reality*, 135–36.
4. Riley-Smith, *The Crusades: Idea and Reality*, 135–36. There were plenty of other, similar miracles reported during the preaching of the Fifth Crusade: in the same letter Oliver recounts rainbow-colored crosses dancing in the sky. The English chronicler Roger of Wendover repeated many of Oliver's claims and added other examples of sky-borne crosses sent to encourage the faithful to join the crusade. For Wendover, see Edward Peters, ed., *Christian Society and the Crusades 1198–1229*, (Philadelphia: University of Pennsylvania Press, 1971), 48–49.
5. Peters, ed., *Christian Society and the Crusades*.
6. Peters, ed., *Christian Society and the Crusades* (hereafter *Oliver of Cologne*), 59.
7. *Oliver of Cologne*, 60.
8. *Gesta Crucigerorum Rhenanorum* (Deeds of the Rhenish Crusaders); translation from Jessalynn Bird, Edward Peters and James M. Powell, eds., *Crusade and Christendom: Annotated Documents in Translation from Innocent III to the Fall of Acre, 1187–1291* (Philadelphia: University of Pennsylvania Press, 2013), 157.
9. Joseph, F. O'Callaghan, *A History of Medieval Spain* (London. Cornell University Press, 1975), 336–37.
10. Letter from James of Vitry translated in Malcolm Barber and Keith Bate, trans., *Letters from the East: Crusaders, Pilgrims and Settlers in the 12th–13th Centuries* (Farnham, UK: Ashgate, 2010), 98–108.
11. See Guy Perry, *John of Brienne: King of Jerusalem, Emperor of Constantinople, c.1175–1237* (Cambridge: Cambridge University Press, 2013), 30.
12. Perry, *John of Brienne*, 55. See also James M. Powell, *Anatomy of a Crusade: 1213–1221* (Philadelphia: University of Pennsylvania Press, 1986), 130–31.
13. Barber and Bate, trans., *Letters from the East*, 112.
14. Megan Cassidy-Welch, "'O Damietta': War Memory and Crusade in Thirteenth-Century Egypt," *Journal of Medieval History* 40 (2014) and Barber and Bate, trans., *Letters from the East*, 110.
15. *Oliver of Cologne*, 102.

16. Barber and Bate, trans., *Letters from the East,* 113.
17. *Oliver of Cologne,* 62–63.
18. *Oliver of Cologne,* 67.
19. Barber and Bate, trans., *Letters from the East,* 114.
20. *Oliver of Cologne,* 70.
21. Paul M. Cobb, *The Race for Paradise: An Islamic History of the Crusades* (Oxford: Oxford University Press, 2014), 208.
22. D. S. Richards, trans., *The Chronicle of Ibn al-Athir for the Crusading Period from al-Kamil fi'l Ta'rikh,* vol. 3 (Farnham, UK: Ashgate 2010), 178.
23. Barber and Bate, trans., *Letters from the East,* 120.
24. Franz Pfeiffer, ed., *Deutsche Classiker Des Mittelalters,* vol. 1 (Leipzig: F. A. Brockhaus, 1864), 155–58.
25. *Oliver of Cologne,* 106.
26. *Oliver of Cologne,* 114.
27. Barber and Bate, trans., *Letters from the East,* 125.
28. *Oliver of Cologne,* 134.
29. Kathryn, Hurlock, "A Transformed Life? Geoffrey of Dutton, the Fifth Crusade, and the Holy Cross of Norton," *Northern History* 54 (2017): 18–19.
30. *Oliver of Cologne,* 139.

23. *Immutator Mundi*

1. On von Salza's background and probable age in 1221, William Urban, *The Teutonic Knights: A Military History* (London: Greenhill Books, 2003), 123–24.
2. Peter von Dusberg in Theodor Hirsch et al., eds., *Scriptores rerum Prussicarum: Die Geschichtsquellen der Preussischen Vorzeit bis zum Untergange der Ordensherrschaft* I (Leipzig: S. Hirzel, 1861), 31. Dusberg may well be exaggerating the military weakness of the order to emphasize the suddenness of its rise.
3. For quote and summary of Teutonic Knights' actions in 1217–1221 see Nicholas Morton, *The Teutonic Knights in the Holy Land, 1190–1291* (Woodbridge, UK: Boydell Press, 2009), 32–38.
4. Jessalynn Bird, Edward Peters and James M. Powell, eds., *Crusade and Christendom: Annotated Documents in Translation from Innocent III to the Fall of Acre, 1187–1291* (Philadelphia: University of Pennsylvania Press, 2013), 260.
5. Bird, Peters and Powell, eds., *Crusade and Christendom,* 260.
6. Thomas Curtis Van Cleve, *The Emperor Frederick II of Hohenstaufen: Immutator Mundi* (Oxford: Clarendon Press, 1972), 304–5.
7. Moshe Sharon and Ami Schrager, "Frederick II's Arabic Inscription from Jaffa (1229)," *Crusades* 11 (2012), 145–46.
8. Sharon and Schrager, "Frederick II's Arabic Inscription from Jaffa (1229)," 154.
9. Morton, *The Teutonic Knights in the Holy Land,* 47.
10. Morton, *The Teutonic Knights in the Holy Land,* 47–48.
11. Translation in Van Cleve, *The Emperor Frederick II of Hohenstaufen,* 198–99.
12. Malcolm Barber and Keith Bate, trans., *Letters from the East: Crusaders, Pilgrims and Settlers in the 12th–13th Centuries* (Farnham, UK: Ashgate, 2010), 126.
13. Recueil des Historiens des Croisades: Historiens Orientaux, vol. 1 (Paris: Imprimerie Nationale, 1872), 103.
14. Barber and Bate, trans., *Letters from the East,* 129.
15. Barber and Bate, trans., *Letters from the East,* 129.
16. J.A. Giles, trans. *Roger of Wendover's Flowers of History,* vol. 1 (London: Henry G. Bohn, 1849), 522–3.
17. Barber and Bate, trans., *Letters from the East,* 127.
18. Bird, Peters and Powell, eds., *Crusade and Christendom,* 259.
19. D. S. Richards, trans., *The Chronicle of Ibn al-Athir for the Crusading Period from al-Kamil fi'l Ta'rikh,* vol. 3 (Farnham, UK: Ashgate, 2010), 294.
20. Barber and Bate, trans., *Letters from the East,* 131.
21. Giles, trans., *Roger of Wendover's Flowers of History,* vol. 1, 524.
22. Barber and Bate, trans., *Letters from the East,* 132.
23. The original text is in Huillard-Bréholles, Jean Louis Alphonse, *Historia Diplomatica Friderici Secundi,* vol. 2.1 (Paris: Henri Plon, 1855), 549–52.
24. Eric Christiansen, *The Northern Crusades,* second edition (London: Penguin, 1997), 123.
25. Urban, *The Teutonic Knights,* 44.
26. Iben Fonnesberg-Schmidt, *The Popes and the Baltic Crusades, 1147–1254* (Leiden: Brill, 2007), 195–96.
27. According to the account of the Teutonic brother Hartmann von Heldrungen, translated in Jerry C. Smith and William L. Urban, *The Livonian Rhymed Chronicle* (London: RoutledgeCurzon, 2007), 145.
28. Christiansen, The Northern Crusades, 128.
29. Translation in Morton, *The Teutonic Knights in the Holy Land,* 82.

24. Khans and Kings

1. Maurice Michael, trans., *The Annals of Jan Długosz: Annales Seu Cronicae Incliti Regni Poloniae* (Chichester, UK: IM Publications, 1997), 180. Długosz adds the intriguing detail that the Mongols deployed a crude form of biological warfare, using a banner decoreated with a giant X and a picture of a bearded head; when shaken this released a "cloud with a foul smell" that enveloped the Polish troops and mades them faint.
2. Ulf Büngten, and Nicola Di Cosmo, "Climatic and Environmental Aspects of the Mongol Withdrawal from Hungary in 1242 CE," *Scientific Reports* 6 (2016), 1.
3. Michael, trans., *The Annals of Jan Długosz,* 181.
4. The Prester John legend was fueled by a bo-

gus letter of 1165, addressed to the Byzantine emperor Manuel I Komnenos and memorably described by one historian as "an orgy of unrestrained grandiloquence and childish boasting." Karl F. Helleiner, "Prester John's Letter: A Medieval Utopia," *Phoenix* 13 (1959), 48. A translation of an early version of the letter is in Michael Uebel, *Ecstatic Transformation: On the Uses of Alterity in the Middle Ages* (New York and Basingstoke: Palgrave Macmillan, 2005), 155–60. See also Igor De Rachewiltz, *Papal Envoys to the Great Khans* (London: University Press of America, 1971), 34–40.

5. The unfortunate victims were the Tang'ut people of the Western Xia. Igor De Rachewiltz, trans., *The Secret History of the Mongols: A Mongolian Epic Chronicle of the Thirteenth Century,* vol. 1 (Leiden: Brill, 2006), 198.
6. Peter Jackson, *The Mongols and the West, 1221–1410* (Abingdon, UK: Routledge, 2014), 60.
7. J. A. Giles, trans., *Matthew Paris's English History from the year 1235 to 1273,* vol. 1 (London: Henry G. Bohn, 1852).
8. Jessalynn Bird, Edward Peters and James M. Powell, eds., *Crusade and Christendom: Annotated Documents in Translation from Innocent III to the Fall of Acre, 1187–1291* (Philadelphia: University of Pennsylvania Press, 2013), 322.
9. This conclusion, based on dendrochronology, is expressed in Büngten and Di Cosmo, "Climatic and Environmental Aspects of the Mongol Withdrawal from Hungary in 1242 CE," esp. 6. See also Jackson, *The Mongols and the West,* 72–73.
10. Peter Jackson, *The Mongols and the Islamic World: From Conquest to Conversion* (New Haven and London: Yale University Press, 2017), 78.
11. Robert, patriarch of Jerusalem, in Malcolm Barber and Keith Bate, trans., *Letters from the East: Crusaders, Pilgrims and Settlers in the 12th–13th Centuries* (Farnham, UK: Ashgate, 2010), 142–43.
12. Barber and Bate, trans., *Letters from the East,* 143–44.
13. Barber and Bate, trans., *Letters from the East,* 144.
14. Carole Hillenbrand, *The Crusades: Islamic Perspectives* (Edinburgh: Edinburgh University Press, 1999), 222.
15. Barber and Bate, trans., *Letters from the East,* 145.
16. Barber and Bate, trans., *Letters from the East,* 145.
17. *Chronicles of the Crusades: Being Contemporary Narratives of the Crusade of Richard Coeur de Lion, by Richard of Devizes and Geoffrey de Vinsauf; and of the Crusade of Saint Louis, by Lord John de Joinville* (London: Henry G. Bohn, 1848), 379.
18. Igor De Rachewiltz, *Papal Envoys to the Great Khans* (London: Faber, 1974), 214.
19. John Sarrasin's letter is translated in Bird, Peters and Powell, eds. *Crusade and Christendom,* 354–60.
20. Bird, Peters and Powell, eds., *Crusade and Christendom,* 354–60.
21. Al-Makrisi in *Chronicles of the Crusades,* 544.
22. Al-Makrisi in *Chronicles of the Crusades,* 545.
23. Al-Makrisi in *Chronicles of the Crusades,* 547.
24. Al-Makrisi in *Chronicles of the Crusades,* 432
25. Paul Crawford, ed., *The "Templar of Tyre": Part III of the "Deeds of the Cypriots"* (Aldershot, UK: Ashgate, 2003), 37–38.
26. Hülagü Khan to Louis IX, translated in Barber and Bate, trans., *Letters from the East,* 145.

25. The Enemy from Hell

1. Reuven Amitai-Preiss, Mongols and Mamluks: The Mamluk-Ilkhanid War, 1260–1281 (Cambridge: Cambridge University Press, 1995), 36.
2. Letter from Hülagü Khan to Qutuz, translated in Bernard Lewis, *Islam: From the Prophet Muhammad to the Capture of Constantinople,* vol. 1 (New York: Walker, 1974), 84–85.
3. Lewis, *Islam,* vol. 1, 84.
4. Malcolm Barber and Keith Bate, trans., *Letters from the East: Crusaders, Pilgrims and Settlers in the 12th–13th Centuries* (Farnham, UK: Ashgate, 2010), 155. NB, however, Peter Jackson's argument that in fact the Franks underestimated the Mongols' wariness to attack the apparently fragile Latin states for fear of provoking a new crusade and thereby fulfilling a prophecy of their own defeat on Christian soil. Peter Jackson, "The Crisis in the Holy Land in 1260," *English Historical Review* 95 (1980), 496–99.
5. Amitai-Preiss, *Mongols and Mamluks,* 33.
6. For discussion of the evidence for this neutrality pact, the details of which are rather sketchy, see Jackson, "The Crisis in the Holy Land in 1260," 503.
7. Amitai-Preiss, *Mongols and Mamluks,* 41; Lewis, *Islam,* vol. 1, 87.
8. Paul F. Crawford, ed., *The "Templar of Tyre": Part III of the "Deeds of the Cypriots"* (Aldershot, UK: Ashgate, 2003), 38. In fact the author, who contributed a large section of the Deeds of the Cypriots, was probably not a Templar but merely a clerk who was for a time in the service of the Templar grand master William of Beaujeu.
9. See Abdul-Aziz Khowaiter, *Baibars the First: His Endeavors and Achievements* (London: Green Mountain Press, 1978), 24.
10. *Ibn 'Abd al-Zahir* in Syedah Fatima Sadeque, *Baybars I of Egypt* (Dacca: Oxford University Press, 1956), 98.
11. Crawford, ed., *The "Templar of Tyre,"* 24.
12. *Ibn 'Abd al-Zahir* in Sadeque, Baybars I of Egypt, 151.
13. Barber and Bate trans., *Letters from the East,* 159.
14. Peter Thorau, *The Lion of Egypt: Sultan Baybars I & the Near East in the Thirteenth Century* (London and New York: Longman, 1992), 98–104.
15. Thorau, *The Lion of Egypt,* 160.
16. Stephen R. Humphreys, "Ayyubids, Mamluks, and the Latin East in the Thirteenth Century," *Mamluk Studies Review* 2 (1998), 11–13.
17. Thorau, *The Lion of Egypt,* 168.
18. Crawford, ed., *The "Templar of Tyre,"* 59.

19. Crawford, ed., *The "Templar of Tyre,"* 59. Thorau, *The Lion of Egypt,* 191–92.
20. *Ibn 'Abd al-Zahir,* this translation, Francesco Gabrieli, ed., and E. J. Costello, trans., *Arab Historians of the Crusades* (Berkeley and Los Angeles: University of California Press, 1969), 311.
21. On Baybars' extraordinary energy in these years, Robert Irwin, *The Middle East in the Middle Ages: The Early Mamluk Sultanate, 1250–1382* (Beckenham, Kent, UK: Croom Helm: 1986), 46.
22. The story is related in Crawford, ed., *The "Templar of Tyre,"* 69.
23. For a discussion of the allegations of poison, Thorau, *The Lion of Egypt,* 241–43.
24. Crawford, ed., *The "Templar of Tyre,"* 100.
25. Abu al-Fida, translation in Gabrieli, ed., and Costello, trans., *Arab Historians of the Crusades,* 342.
26. Crawford, ed., *The "Templar of Tyre,"* 101–2.
27. Crawford, ed., *The "Templar of Tyre,"* 104.
28. Abu al-Fida, translation in Gabrieli, ed., and Costello, trans., *Arab Historians of the Crusades,* 345.
29. Crawford, ed., *The "Templar of Tyre,"* 109.
30. Abu al-Mahasin, translation in Gabrieli, ed., and Costello, trans., *Arab Historians of the Crusades,* 347.
31. Crawford, ed., *The "Templar of Tyre,"* 113.
32. Crawford, ed., *The "Templar of Tyre,"* 113.
33. Abu al-Mahasin, translation in Gabrieli, ed., and Costello, trans., *Arab Historians of the Crusades,* 347.
34. Abu al-Fida, translation in Gabrieli, ed., and Costello, trans., *Arab Historians of the Crusades,* 346.

26. Fragments and Dreams

1. The origins of the nickname Torsello are now obscure.
2. On Marino Sanudo's family background and reading habits, Peter Lock, trans., *Marino Sanudo Torsello, The Book of the Secrets of the Faithful of the Cross: Liber Secretorum Fidelium Crucis* (Farnham, UK: Ashgate, 2011), 1–8. I have leaned on the biographical information and textual translation in this volume in what follows here.
3. C. J. Tyerman, "Marino Sanudo Torsello and the Lost Crusade: Lobbying in the Fourteenth Century," *Transactions of the Royal Historical Society* 32 (1982), 65.
4. Translation in Norman Housley, ed., *Documents on the Later Crusades: 1274–1580* (Basingstoke, UK: Macmillan, 1996), 17.
5. Housley, ed., *Documents on the Later Crusades,* 41.
6. For a discussion of Fidenzio, see Sylvia Schein, *Fideles Crucis: The Papacy, The West and the Recovery of the Holy Land 1274–1314* (Oxford: Oxford University Press, 1991), 93–102. On the genre of recovery tracts in general, Antony Leopold, *How to Recover the Holy Land: The Crusade Proposals of the Late Thirteenth and Early Fourteenth Centuries* (Aldershot, UK: Ashgate, 2000).
7. Peter Lock, trans., *Marino Sanudo Torsello, the Book of the Secrets of the Faithful of the Cross,* 154.
8. The maps, British Library *Add. MS 27376,* have been digitized and can be viewed via www.bl.uk.
9. On the Sicilian Muslim colony at Lucrea, see Christoph T. Maier, "Crusade and Rhetoric Against the Muslim Colony of Lucera: Eudes of Châteauroux's Sermones de Rebellione Sarracenorum Lucherie in Apulia," *Journal of Medieval History* 21 (1995), esp. 366 and appendices.
10. Damian J. Smith, and Helena Buffery, *The Book of the Deeds of James I of Aragon: A Translation of the Medieval Catalan Llibre dels Fets* (Farnham, UK: Ashgate, 2003), 379–80.
11. See J. R. Strayer, "The Crusade Against Aragon," *Speculum* 28 (1953), 104.
12. The Latin text of the bull against Peter of Aragon is Albert Fontemoing, *Les Registres de Martin IV (1281–1285)* (Paris: Thorin et Fils, 1901), 107–14.
13. Quote, Paul F. Crawford, ed., *The "Templar of Tyre": Part III of the "Deeds of the Cypriots"* (Aldershot, UK: Ashgate, 2003), 164. See also Malcolm Barber, *The New Knighthood: A History of the Order of the Temple* (Cambridge: Cambridge University Press, 1994), 294.
14. An English translation of Molay's crusading plan can be found in Malcolm Barber and Keith Bate, eds., *The Templars: Selected Sources* (Manchester, UK: Manchester University Press, 2002), 105–9.
15. Translation in Housley, ed., *Documents on the Later Crusades,* 36–37.
16. D. S. Richards, trans., *The Chronicle of Ibn al-Athir for the Crusading Period from al-Kamil fi'l Ta'rikh,* vol. 2 (Farnham, UK: Ashgate, 2010), 324.
17. Papal bull *Ad providam,* this translation from Barber and Bate, eds., *The Templars: Selected Sources,* 320. The Hospitallers were not granted Templar property in Spain or Portugal, which was instead reserved for papal distribution to others.
18. Helen Nicholson, *The Knights Hospitaller* (Woodbridge, UK: Boydell Press, 2001), 46–47.
19. Mark Dupuy, "'An Island Called Rhodes' and the 'Way' to Jerusalem: Change and Continuity in Hospitaller Exordia in the Later Middle Ages," in Helen Nicholson, *The Military Orders. Volume 2: Welfare and Warfare* (Farnham, UK: Ashgate, 1998), 346–47.
20. See Anthony Luttrell, "The Aragonese Crown and the Knights Hospitallers of Rhodes: 1291–1350," *English Historical Review* 76 (1961), 1–19.

27. Brave New Worlds

1. Craig Taylor and, Jane H. M. Taylor, trans., *The Chivalric Biography of Boucicaut, Jean II Le Meingre* (Woodbridge, UK: Boydell Press, 2016), 49.
2. Taylor and Taylor, trans., *The Chivalric Biography of Boucicaut,* 25, 30.
3. Chris Given Wilson, *Henry IV* (New Haven and London: Yale University Press, 2016), 61.
4. Wilson, *Henry IV,* 62.
5. L. C. Hector, and Barbara F. Harvey, *The West-*

minster Chronicle, 1381–1394 (Oxford: Clarendon Press, 1982), 446–49.

6. Wilson, *Henry IV,* 69.
7. Lucy Toulmin Smith, ed., *Expeditions to Prussia and the Holy Land Made by Henry, Earl of Derby in the years 1390–1 and 1392–3: Being the Accounts Kept by His Treasurer During Two Years* (London: Camden Society, 1894), liv.
8. Wilson, *Henry IV,* 73.
9. Taylor and Taylor, trans., *The Chivalric Biography of Boucicaut,* 52.
10. Taylor and Taylor, trans., *The Chivalric Biography of Boucicaut,* 59.
11. See, for example, Philippe de Mézières, *Letter to King Richard II: A Plea Made in 1395 for Peace Between England and France: original text and English version of Epistre au Roi Richart,* trans., G. W. Coopland (Liverpool: Liverpool University Press, 1975).
12. In the words of Christoph Brachmann, the Nicopolis campaign was a "rather intriguing conflagration of crusade, voyage chevaleresque and attack against the Turks in defense of the Hungarian kingdom." Christoph Brachmann, "The Crusade of Nicopolis, Burgundy and the Entombment of Christ at Pont-à-Mousson," *Journal of the Warburg and Courtauld Institutes* 74 (2011), 183.
13. Taylor and Taylor, trans., *The Chivalric Biography of Boucicaut,* 63.
14. G. C. Macaulay, ed., *The Chronicles of Froissart* (London: Macmillan, 1904), 444.
15. Taylor and Taylor, trans., *The Chivalric Biography of Boucicaut,* 72.
16. Taylor and Taylor, trans., *The Chivalric Biography of Boucicaut,* 187–98.
17. The most recent account of the fall of Granada is Elizabeth Drayson, *The Moor's Last Stand: How Seven Centuries of Muslim Rule in Spain Came to an End* (London: Profile Books, 2017).
18. According to the digest of his now lost logbook from his first voyage made by the historian Bartolomé de las Casas. This quotation from J. M. Cohen, trans., *The Four Voyages of Christopher Columbus* (London: Penguin, 1969), 37.
19. Cohen, trans., *The Four Voyages of Christopher Columbus,* 37.
20. Cohen, trans., *The Four Voyages of Christopher Columbus,* 37.

Epilogue: Crusaders 2.0

1. In common with many media outlets and in respect to the Chief Censor of New Zealand's decision to ban distribution of materials pertaining to the attacks, I have decided not to include links to the video described or to the text of the perpetrator's manifesto. Both are easy to find online, but are, needless to say, extreme and unpleasant.
2. World Islamic Front statement, archived online, fas.org/irp/world/para/docs/980223-fatwa.htm.
3. White House Archives, georgewbush-whitehouse.archives.gov/news/releases/2001/09/20010916-2.html. For Bin Laden's explicit response to Bush's use of the word "crusade," see "Transcript of Bin Laden's October Interview," CNN.com, February 5, 2002, edition.cnn.com/2002/WORLD/asiapcf/south/02/05/binladen.transcript.
4. Ben Aris, "Bin Laden War on 'Crusaders,'" *The Telegraph* (London), September 25, 2001.
5. Bin Laden broadcast on Al Jazeera, February 15, 2003.
6. Juliet Eilperin, "Critics Pounce After Obama Talks Crusades, Slavery at Prayer Breakfast," *The Washington Post,* February 5, 2015.
7. Eitan Bar-Yosef, "The Last Crusade? British Propaganda and the Palestine Campaign, 1917–18," *Journal of Contemporary History* 36 (2001).
8. Saikat Dattat, "ISIS Sri Lanka claim mixes Tamil, Arabic," *Asia Times,* April 22, 2019.

BIBLIOGRAPHY

Primary Sources

Académie des Inscriptions et Belles-Lettres. *Recueil des Historiens des Croisades: Historiens Orientaux.* Vols. 1–5. Paris: Imprimerie Nationale, 1872–1906.

Ailes, Marianne, trans., and Malcolm Barber. *The History of the Holy War: Ambroise's Estoire de la Guerre Sainte.* Vols, 1–2. Woodbridge, Suffolk, UK: Boydell Press, 2003.

Albert of Aachen, *Historia Ierosolominitana: History of the Journey to Jerusalem.* Translated by Susan Edgington. Oxford: Clarendon Press, 2007.

Al-Marrakushi. *Kitab al-mu'yib fi taljis ajbar al Magrib.* Translated by A. Huici Miranda. Tetuán: Editora Marroquí, 1955.

Al-Muqaddasi. *The Best Divisions for Knowledge of the Regions: Ahsan al-Taqasim fi Ma'rifat al-Aqalim.* Translated by Basil Collins. Reading, UK: Garnet Publishing, 2001.

Andrea, Alfred J., trans. *The Capture of Constantinople: The "Hystoria Constantinopolitana" of Gunther of Pairis.* Philadelphia: University of Pennsylvania Press, 1997.

Appleby, John T. *The Chronicle of Richard of Devizes of the Time of King Richard the First.* London: Thomas Nelson & Sons, 1963.

Asbridge, Thomas S., and Susan B. Edgington. *Walter the Chancellor's* The Antiochene Wars: *A Translation and Commentary.* Aldershot, UK: Ashgate, 1999.

Babcock, Emily Atwater, and A. C. Krey, trans. *A History of Deeds Done Beyond the Sea: By William, Archbishop of Tyre.* Vols. 1 and 2. New York: Columbia University Press, 1943.

Barber, Malcolm, and Keith Bate, trans. *Letters from the East: Crusaders, Pilgrims and Settlers in the 12th–13th Centuries.* Farnham, UK: Ashgate, 2010.

Barber, Malcolm, and Keith Bate, eds. *The Templars: Selected Sources.* Manchester, UK: Manchester University Press, 2002.

Barton, Simon, and Richard Fletcher, trans. *The World of El Cid: Chronicles of the Spanish Reconquest.* Manchester, UK: Manchester University Press, 2000.

Bédier, J. and P. Aubry, eds. *Les Chansons de Croisade avec Leurs Melodies.* Paris: Champion, 1909.

Berry, Virginia Gingerick, trans. *Odo of Deuil: De Profectione Ludovici VII in Orientem.* New York: W. W. Norton, 1948.

Biddlecombe, Steven, trans. *The Historia Ierosolimitana of Baldric of Bourgueil.* Woodbridge, UK: Boydell Press, 2014.

Bouquet, Martin, et al., eds. *Recueil des Historiens des Gaules et de la France.* Vols. 1–24. Paris: L'Imprimerie Impériale, 1737–1904.

Broadhurst, Roland, trans. *The Travels of Ibn Jubayr.* London: Jonathan Cape, 1952.

Chazan, Robert, ed. *God, Humanity and History: The First Crusade Narratives.* Berkeley and London: University of California Press, 2000.

Chibnall, Marjorie, ed. and trans. *The Ecclesiastical History of Orderic Vitalis.* Vols 1–6. Oxford: Clarendon Press, 1969–78.

Chronicles of the Crusades: Being Contemporary Narratives of the Crusade of Richard Coeur de Lion, by Richard of Devizes and Geoffrey de Vinsauf; and of the Crusade of Saint Louis, by Lord John de Joinville. London: Henry G. Bohn, 1848.

Cohen, J. M., trans. *The Four Voyages of Christopher Columbus.* London: Penguin, 1969.

Constable, Olivia Remie, ed. *Medieval Iberia: Readings from Christian, Muslim, and Jewish Sources.* Second edition. Philadelphia: University of Pennsylvania Press, 2012.

Cowdrey, H. E. J. *The Register of Pope Gregory VII, 1073–1085: An English Translation.* Oxford: Oxford University Press, 2002.

Crawford, Paul F., ed. *The "Templar of Tyre": Part III of the "Deeds of the Cypriots."* Aldershot, UK: Ashgate, 2003.

d'Aguilers, Raymond. *Historia Francorum Qui Ceperunt Iherusalem.* Translated by John Hugh Hill and Laurita L. Hill. Philadelphia: American Philosophical Society, 1968.

d'Albon, Marquis, ed. *Cartulaire Général de l'Ordre du Temple, 1119?–1150.* Vols. 1–2. Paris: Librarie Ancienne, 1913–1922.

David, Charles Wendell, trans., and Jonathan Phillips, ed. *The Conquest of Lisbon: De Expugnatione Lyxbonensi.* New York: Columbia University Press, 2001.

De Gayangos, Pascual, trans. *The History of the Mohammedan Dynasties in Spain: Extracted from the Nafhu-t-tib min Ghosni-l-Andalusi-r-Rattib wa tarikh Lisanu-d-Din Ibni-l-Khattib by Ahmed ibn Mohammed al-Makkari.* Vols. 1–2. London: W. H. Allen, 1840–43.

De Mézières, Philippe. *Letter to King Richard II: A Plea Made in 1395 for Peace Between England and France: original text and English version of Epistre au Roi Richart.* Translated by G. W. Coopland. Liverpool, UK: Liverpool University Press, 1975.

De Rachewiltz, Igor, trans. *The Secret History of the Mongols: A Mongolian Epic Chronicle of the Thirteenth Century.* Vols. 1–2 vols. Leiden: Brill, 2006.

De Voragine, Jacobus. *The Golden Legend: Readings on the Saints.* Translated by William Granger Ryan. With an introduction by Eamon Duffy. Princeton and Oxford: Princeton University Press, 2012.

Dostourian, Ara Edmond, trans. *Armenia and the Crusades: Tenth to Twelfth Centuries: The Chronicle of Matthew of Edessa.* London: University Press of America, 1993.

Dudo of St. Quentin, *History of the Normans.* Translated by Eric Christiansen. Woodbridge, UK: Boydell Press, 1998.

Edgington, Susan B., and Carol Sweetenham, trans. *The Chanson d'Antioche: an Old French Account of the First Crusade,* Farnham, UK: Ashgate, 2011.

Fontemoing, Albert, ed. *Les Registres de Martin IV (1281–1285).* Paris: Thorin et Fils, 1901.

Franzen, Cola, trans. *Poems of Arab Andalusia.* San Francisco: City Lights Books, 1989.

Gabrieli, Francesco, ed., and E. J. Costello, trans. *Arab Historians of the Crusades.* Berkeley and Los Angeles: University of California Press, 1969.

Garmonsway, G.N., ed. and trans. *The Anglo-Saxon Chronicle.* London: J. M. Dent, 1953.

Gerson, Paula, Annie Shaver-Crandell, and Alison Stones. *The Pilgrim's Guide to Santiago de Compostela: A Gazetteer with 580 Illustrations.* London: Harvey Miller, 1995.

Gibb, H. A. R., trans. *The Damascus Chronicle of the Crusades: Extracted and Translated from the Chronicle of Ibn Al-Qalanisi.* London: Luzac, 1932; repr., New York: Dover, 2000.

Giles, J. A., trans. *Matthew Paris's English History: From the Year 1235 to 1273.* Vols. 1–3. London: Henry G. Bohn, 1852–54.

———, trans. *Roger of Wendover's Flowers of History.* Vols. 1–2. London: Henry G. Bohn, 1849.

———, trans. *William of Malmesbury's Chronicle of the Kings of England.* London: Henry G. Bohn, 1847.

Greenia, M. Conrad trans., and Barber, Malcolm, introduction. *Bernard of Clairvaux: In Praise of the New Knighthood.* Trappist, KY: Cistercian Publications, 2000.

Hagenmeyer, Heinrich. *Epistulae et Chartae ad Historiam Primi Belli Sacri Spectantes quæ Supersunt Aevo Aequales ac Genuinae.* Innsbruck: Verlag der Wagner'schen Universitäts-Buchhandlung, 1901.

Hall, Martin, and Jonathan Phillips, trans. *Caffaro, Genoa and the Twelfth-Century Crusades.* Farnham, UK: Ashgate, 2013.

Hector, L. C., and Barbara F. Harvey, trans. *The Westminster Chronicle, 1381–1394.* Oxford: Clarendon Press, 1982.

Hill, Rosalind, ed. *Gesta Francorum et Aliorum Hierosolimitanorum: The Deeds of the Franks and the Other Pilgrims to Jerusalem.* Oxford: Clarendon Press, 1962.

Hirsch, Theodor, et al., eds. *Scriptores Rerum Prussicarum: Die Geschichtsquellen der Preussischen Vorzeit bis zum Untergange der Ordensherrschaft.* Vols 1–6. Leipzig: Verlag von S. Hirzel, 1861–1965.

Housley, Norman, ed. *Documents on the Later Crusades: 1274–1580.* Basingstoke, UK: Macmillan, 1996.

Huillard-Bréholles, Jean-Louis-Alphonse. *Historia Diplomatica Friderici Secundi.* Vols. 1–3. Paris: Henri Plon, 1852–61.

Ibn Al-sā'I. *Consorts of the Caliphs: Women and the Court of Baghdad.* Translated by Shawkat M. Toorawa. New York: New York University Press, 2017.

Innocent III. Between Man and God: Six Sermons on the Priestly Office. Translated by Corinne J. Vause and Frank C. Gardiner. Washington DC: The Catholic University of America Press, 2004.

James, Bruno Scott, trans., and Beverly Mayne Kienzle, introduction. *The Letters of St. Bernard of Clairvaux.* Guildford, UK: Sutton Publishing, 1998.

Kinnamos, John. *Deeds of John and Manuel Comnenus.* Translated by Charles M. Brand. New York: Columbia University Press, 1976.

Komnene, Anna. *The Alexiad.* Revised edition. Translated by E. R. A. Sewter. With an introduction by Peter Frankopan. London: Penguin, 2009.

Levine, Robert, trans. *The Deeds of God Through the Franks: A Translation of Guibert de Nogent's Gesta Dei per Francos.* Woodbridge, UK: Boydell Press, 1997.

Levtzion, N., and J. F. P. Hopkins, eds. *Corpus of Early Arabic Sources for West African History.* Princeton: Markus Wiener Publishers, 2000.

Lewis, Bernard. *Islam: From the Prophet Muhammad to the Capture of Constantinople.* Vol 1–2. New York: Harper & Row, 1974.

Lock, Peter, trans. *Marino Sanudo Torsello, The Book of the Secrets of the Faithful of the Cross: Liber Secretorum Fidelium Crucis.* Farnham, UK: Ashgate, 2011.

Loud, G. A., trans. *The Crusade of Frederick Barbarossa: The History of the Expedition of the Emperor Frederick and Related Texts.* Farnham, UK: Ashgate, 2010.

Luard, Henry Richards, ed. *Annales Monastici.* Vols. 1–4. London: Longman, Green, Longman, Roberts and Green, 1865.

Lunde, Paul, and Caroline Stone, trans. *Ibn Fadlan and the Land of Darkness: Arab Travelers in the Far North.* London: Penguin, 2012.

Macaulay, G. C., ed. *The Chronicles of Froissart.* London: Macmillan, 1904.

Magoulias, Harry J. *O City of Byzantium, Annals of Niketas Choniatēs.* Detroit, MI: Wayne State University Press, 1984.

Melville, Charles, and Ahmad Ubaydli, eds. *Christians and Moors in Spain.* Vol. 3: *Arabic Sources (711–1501).* Warminster, UK: Aris & Phillips, 1992.

Michael, Maurice, trans. *The Annals of Jan Długosz: Annales Seu Cronicae Incliti Regni Poloniae.* Chichester, UK: IM Publications, 1997.

Mirot, Léon, ed. *La Chronique de Morigny (1095–1152).* Paris: Librairie Alphonse Picard et Fils, 1909.

Nicholson, Helen J. *The Chronicle of the Third Crusade: The Intinerarium Peregrinorum et Gesta Regis Ricardi.* Farnham, UK: Ashgate, 1997.

Otto of Freising and His Continuator, Rahewin, *The Deeds of Frederick Barbarossa.* Translated by Charles Christopher Mierow with Richard Emery. Toronto: University of Toronto Press, 1994.

Pertz, G. H., ed. *Monumenta Germaniae Historica, Scriptores XVI.* Hanover: Deutsches Institut für Erforschung des Mittelalters, 1859.

Peters, Edward, ed. *Christian Society and the Crusades, 1198–1229.* Philadelphia: University of Pennsylvania Press, 1971.

Pfeiffer, Franz, ed. *Deutsche Classiker Des Mittelalters.* Vols 1–12. Leipzig: F. A. Brockhaus, 1864–72.

Richards, D. S., trans. *Baha al-Din Ibn Shaddad: The Rare and Excellent History of Saladin.* Farnham, UK: Ashgate, 2002.

———, trans. *The Chronicle of Ibn al-Athir for the Crusading Period from al-Kamil fi'l Ta'rikh.* Vols. 1–3. Farnham, UK: Ashgate, 2006.

Riley-Smith, Louise and Jonathan. *The Crusades: Idea and Reality, 1095–1274.* London: Edward Arnold, 1981.

Robinson, I. S. *Eleventh-Century Germany: The Swabian Chronicles.* Manchester, UK: Manchester University Press, 2008.

Röhricht, Reinhold, ed. *Regesta Regni Hierosolymitani (1097–1291).* Vols. 1–2. Innsbruck: Libraria Academica Wagneriana, 1893–1904.

Ryan, Frances Rita, trans., and Harold S. Fink, ed. *Fulcher of Chartres: History of the Expedition to Jerusalem, 1095–1127.* Knoxville: University of Tennessee Press, 1969.

Sadeque, Syedah Fatima. *Baybars I of Egypt.* Dacca: Oxford University Press, 1956.

Sibly, W. A., and M. D. Sibly. *The History of the Albigensian Crusade: Peter of les Vaux-de-Cernay's* Historia Albigensis. Woodbridge, UK: Boydell Press, 1998.

Slack, Corliss Konwiser, ed. *Crusade Charters: 1178–1270.* Tempe: Arizona Center for Medieval and Renaissance Studies, 2001.

Slane, William MacGuckin, trans. *Ibn Khallikan's Biographical Dictionary.* Vol. 1–4. Paris: Oriental Translation Fund, 1842–71.

Smith, Damian J., and Helena Buffery, eds. *The Book of the Deeds of James I of Aragón: A Translation of the Medieval Catalan Llibre dels Fets.* Farnham, UK: Ashgate, 2003.

Smith, Dulcie Lawrence, trans. *The Poems of Mu'tamid, King of Seville.* London: John Murray, 1915.

Smith, Jerry C., and William L. Urban. *The Livonian Rhymed Chronicle.* London: RoutledgeCurzon, 2007.

Stevenson, Joseph, trans. *The History of William of Newburgh.* Felinfach, Wales: Llanerch, 1996.

Stubbs, William, ed. *Radulfi de Diceto Decani Lundoniensis Opera Historica: The Historical Works of Master Ralph de Diceto.* Vols. 1–2. London: Longman, 1876.

Sweetenham, Carol, trans. *Robert the Monk's History of the First Crusade: Historia Iherosolimitana.* Abingdon, UK: Routledge, 2016.

Sturluson, Snorri. *Heimskringla: History of the Kings of Norway.* Translated by Lee M. Hollander. Austin: University of Texas Press, 1964.

Taylor, Craig, and Jane H. M. Taylor, trans. *The Chivalric Biography of Boucicaut, Jean II Le Meingre.* Woodbridge, UK: Boydell Press, 2016.

Thackston, W. M., trans. *Naser-e Khosraw's Book of Travels (Safarnama).* Albany, NY: Bibliotheca Persica, 1986.

Tibi, Amin T. *The Tibyān: Memoirs of 'Abd Allāh B. Buluggīn, Last Zīrid Amīr of Granada.* Leiden: Brill, 1986.

Toulmin Smith, Lucy, ed. *Expeditions to Prussia and the Holy Land Made by Henry, Earl of Derby in the years*

1390–1 and 1392–3: Being the Accounts Kept by His Treasurer During Two Years. London: Camden Society, 1894.

Tudebode, Peter. *Historia de Hierosolymitano Itinere.* Translated by John Hugh Hill and Laurita L. Hill. Philadelphia: American Philosophical Society, 1974.

Upton-Ward, J. M. *The Rule of the Templars: The French Text of the Rule of the Order of the Knights Templar.* Woodbridge, UK: Boydell & Brewer, 1992.

Wilkinson, John, with Joyce Hill and W. F. Ryan, eds. *Jerusalem Pilgrimage, 1099–1185.* London: Hakluyt Society, 1988.

Wolf, Kenneth Baxter, trans. *The Deeds of Count Roger of Calabria and Sicily and of His Brother Duke Robert Guiscard by Geoffrey Malaterra.* Ann Arbor: University of Michigan Press, 2005.

Wright, Thomas. ed. *The Historical Works of Giraldus Cambrensis.* London: George Bell & Sons, 1894.

Secondary Sources

Allen, S. J., and Emilie Amt. *The Crusades: A Reader.* Toronto: University of Toronto Press, 2010.

Amitai-Preiss, Reuven. *Mongols and Mamluks: The Mamluk-Ilkhanid War, 1260–1281.* Cambridge: Cambridge University Press, 1995.

Angold, Michael. *The Fourth Crusade: Event and Context.* Harlow, UK: Pearson, 2003.

Asbridge, Thomas S. *The Creation of the Principality of Antioch, 1098–1130.* Woodbridge, UK: Boydell Press, 2000.

Baker, Derek, ed. *Medieval Women.* Oxford: Basil Blackwell, 1978.

Barber, Malcolm. *The Crusader States.* New Haven and London: Yale University Press, 2012.

———. *The New Knighthood: A History of the Order of the Temple.* Cambridge: Cambridge University Press, 1994.

Barber, Malcolm, ed. *The Military Orders. Volume 1: Fighting for the Faith and Caring for the Sick.* Aldershot, UK: Variorum, 1994.

Becker, Alfons. *Papst Urban II (1088–1099).* Vols. 1–3. Stuttgart: Hiersemann, 1964–2012.

Boas, Adrian J. *Jerusalem in the Time of the Crusades: Society, Landscape and Art in the Holy City under Frankish Rule.* London: Routledge, 2001.

Boas, Adrian J., ed. *The Crusader World.* Abingdon, UK, and New York: Routledge, 2016.

Boyle, J. A. *The Cambridge History of Iran. Volume 5: The Saljuq and Mongol Periods.* Cambridge: Cambridge University Press, 1968.

Brett, Michael. *The Fatimid Empire.* Edinburgh: Edinburgh University Press, 2017.

Brink, Stefan, and Price, Neil, eds. *The Viking World.* London: Routledge, 2008.

Buck, Andrew D. *The Principality of Antioch and Its Frontiers in the Twelfth Century.* Woodbridge, UK: Boydell Press, 2017.

Chazan, Robert. *In the Year 1096: The First Crusade and the Jews.* Philadelphia: Jewish Publication Society, 1996.

Christiansen, Eric. *The Northern Crusades.* Second edition. London: Penguin, 1997.

Christys, Ann. *Vikings in the South: Voyages to Iberia and the Mediterranean.* London: Bloomsbury Academic, 2015.

Cobb, Paul M. *The Race for Paradise: An Islamic History of the Crusades.* Oxford: Oxford University Press, 2014.

Collins, Roger. *The Arab Conquest of Spain, 710–797.* Oxford: Basil Blackwell, 1989.

Constable, Giles. *Crusaders and Crusading in the Twelfth Century.* Farnham, UK: Ashgate, 2008.

De Rachewiltz, Igor. *Papal Envoys to the Great Khans.* London: Faber, 1971.

Dickson, Gary. *The Children's Crusade: Medieval History, Modern Mythistory.* London: Palgrave Macmillan, 2008.

Edbury, Peter W., ed. *Crusade and Settlement: Papers Read at the First Conference of the Society for the Study of the Crusades and the Latin East and Presented to R. C. Smail.* Cardiff: University College Cardiff Press, 1985.

Edgington, Susan B., and Sarah Lambert. *Gendering the Crusades.* Cardiff: University of Wales Press, 2001.

Erdmann, Carl. *The Origin of the Idea of Crusade.* Translated by Marshall W. Baldwin and Walter Goffart. Princeton: Princeton University Press, 1977.

Fletcher, Richard. *Moorish Spain.* New York: Henry Holt, 1992.

Folda, Jaroslav. *Crusader Art: The Art of the Crusaders in the Holy Land, 1099–1291.* Aldershot, UK: Lund Humphries, 2008.

Fonnesberg-Schmidt, Iben. *The Popes and the Baltic Crusades, 1147–1254.* Leiden: Brill, 2007.

Fouracre, Paul. *The Age of Charles Martel.* Harlow, UK: Longman, 2000.

France, John. *Victory in the East: A Military History of the First Crusade.* Cambridge: Cambridge University Press, 1994.

Frankopan, Peter. *The First Crusade: The Call from the East.* Cambridge, MA: Belknap Press of Harvard University Press, 2012.

Galatariotou, Catia. *The Making of a Saint: The Life, Times and Sanctification of Neophytos the Recluse.* Cambridge: Cambridge University Press, 1991.

Gervers, Michael, ed. *The Second Crusade and the Cistercians.* New York: St. Martin's Press, 1992.

Gillingham, John. *Richard I.* New Haven and London: Yale University Press, 1999.

Given Wilson, Chris. *Henry IV.* New Haven and London: Yale University Press, 2016.
Glasse, Cyril. *The New Encyclopedia of Islam.* Fourth Edition. London: Horizons Editions, 2013.
Harris, Jonathan. *Constantinople: Capital of Byzantium.* Second edition. London: Bloomsbury Academic, 2017.
Hillenbrand, Carole. *The Crusades: Islamic Perspectives.* Edinburgh: Edinburgh University Press, 1999.
Hodgson, Natasha R. *Women, Crusading and the Holy Land in Historical Narrative.* Woodbridge, UK: Boydell Press, 2007.
Houben, Hubert. *Roger II of Sicily: A Ruler Between East and West.* Cambridge: Cambridge University Press, 2002.
Irwin, Robert. *The Middle East in the Middle Ages: The Early Mamluk Sultanate, 1250–1382.* Beckenham, Kent, UK: Croom Helm, 1986.
Jackson, Peter. *The Mongols and the Islamic World: From Conquest to Conversion.* New Haven and London: Yale University Press, 2017.
———. *The Mongols and the West, 1221–1410.* Abingdon, UK: Routledge, 2014.
Kedar, B. Z., ed. *The Horns of Hattin.* London: Variorum, 1992.
Kedar, Benjamin Z., and Jonathan S.C. Riley-Smith, with Helen J. Nicholson and Michael Evans, eds. *Crusades: Volume 3.* Abingdon, UK: Routledge, 2004.
Khowaiter, Abdul-Aziz. *Baibars the First: His Endeavors and Achievements.* London: Green Mountain Press, 1978.
Kostick, Conor. *The Social Structure of the First Crusade.* Leiden: Brill, 2008.
Laiou, Angeliki E., and Roy Parviz Mottahedeh, eds. *The Crusades from the Perspective of Byzantium and the Muslim World.* Washington, DC: Dumbarton Oaks Research Library and Collection, 2001.
Lane Fox, Robin. *Augustine: Conversions to Confessions.* London: Allen Lane, 2015.
Lee, Jeffrey. *God's Wolf: The Life of the Most Notorious of All Crusaders, Reynald de Chatillon.* London: Atlantic Books, 2016.
Leopold, Antony. *How to Recover the Holy Land: The Crusade Proposals of the Late Thirteenth and Early Fourteenth Centuries.* Aldershot, UK: Ashgate, 2000.
Lev, Yaacov. *Saladin in Egypt.* Leiden: Brill, 1998.
———. *State and Society in Fatimid Egypt.* Leiden: Brill, 1991.
Lippiatt, G. E. M. *Simon V of Montfort and Baronial Government.* Oxford: Oxford University Press, 2017.
Loud, G. A. *The Age of Robert Guiscard: Southern Italy and the Norman Conquest.* Harlow, UK: Longman, 2000.
Lyons, Malcolm Cameron, and D. E. P. Jackson. *Saladin: The Politics of the Holy War.* Cambridge: Cambridge University Press, 1982.
MacCullough, Diarmaid. *A History of Christianity.* London: Allen Lane, 2009.
Madden, Thomas F. *Enrico Dandolo and the Rise of Venice.* Baltimore, MD: Johns Hopkins University Press, 2003.
Mango, Cyril. *The Oxford History of Byzantium.* Oxford: Oxford University Press, 2002.
Matthew, Donald. *The Norman Kingdom of Sicily.* Cambridge: Cambridge University Press, 1992.
Menocal, Maria Rosa, Raymond P. Scheindlin, and Michael Sells, eds. *The Literature of Al-Andalus.* Cambridge: Cambridge University Press, 2000.
Metcalfe, Alex. *The Muslims of Medieval Italy.* Edinburgh: Edinburgh University Press, 2009.
Moore, John C. *Pope Innocent III (1160/61–1216): To Root Up and to Plant.* Leiden: Brill, 2003.
Morris, Colin. *The Papal Monarchy: The Western Church from 1050 to 1250.* Oxford: Clarendon Press, 1989.
Morton, Nicholas. *The Field of Blood: The Battle for Aleppo and the Remaking of the Medieval Middle East.* New York: Basic Books, 2018.
———. *The Teutonic Knights in the Holy Land, 1190–1291.* Woodbridge, UK: Boydell Press, 2009
Mullins, Edwin. *In Search of Cluny: God's Lost Empire.* Oxford: Signal Books, 2006.
Nicholson, Helen. *The Knights Hospitaller.* Woodbridge, UK: Boydell Press, 2001.
Nicholson, Helen, ed. *The Military Orders. Volume 2: Welfare and Warfare.* Farnham, UK: Ashgate, 1998.
O'Callaghan, Joseph F. *A History of Medieval Spain.* London: Cornell University Press, 1975.
———. *Reconquest and Crusade in Medieval Spain.* Philadelphia: University of Pennsylvania Press, 2002.
Paul, Nicholas L. *To Follow in Their Footsteps: The Crusades and Family Memory in the High Middle Ages.* Ithaca and London: Cornell University Press, 2012.
Phillips, Jonathan, and Martin Hoch, eds. *The Second Crusade: Scope and Consequences.* Manchester, UK: Manchester University Press, 2001.
Powell, James M. *Anatomy of a Crusade: 1213–1221.* Philadelphia: University of Pennsylvania Press, 1986.
Pringle, Denys. *The Churches of the Crusader Kingdom of Jerusalem: A Corpus.* Vols. 1–4. Cambridge: Cambridge University Press, 1993–2009.
Reilly, Bernard F. *The Contest of Christian and Muslim Spain, 1031–1157.* Oxford: Blackwell Publishers, 1992.
Riley-Smith, Jonathan. *The First Crusaders: 1095–1131.* Cambridge: Cambridge University Press, 1997.
———. *The First Crusaders and the Idea of Crusading.* London: The Athlone Press, 1986.
———. *Hospitallers: The History of the Order of St. John.* London and Rio Grande, OH: Hambledon Press, 1999.
Robinson, I. S. *The Papacy 1073–1198: Continuity and Innovation.* Cambridge: Cambridge University Press, 1990.

Rubenstein, Jay. *Nebuchadnezzar's Dream: The Crusades, Apocalyptic Prophecy, and the End of History.* New York: Oxford University Press, 2019.
Runciman, Steven. *A History of the Crusades.* Vols. 1–3. Cambridge: Cambridge University Press, 1951–54.
Sanders, Paula. *Ritual, Politics and the City in Fatimid Cairo.* Albany: State University of New York Press, 1994.
Schein, Sylvia. *Fideles Crucis: The Papacy, the West, and the Recovery of the Holy Land, 1274–1314.* Oxford: Oxford University Press, 1991.
Skinner, Patricia, ed. *Challenging the Boundaries of Medieval History: The Legacy of Timothy Reuter.* Turnhout, Belgium: Brepols, 2009.
Smith, L. M. *The Early History of the Monastery of Cluny.* Oxford: Oxford University Press, 1920.
Somerville, Robert. *Pope Urban II's Council of Piacenza.* Oxford: Oxford University Press, 2011.
Thorau, Peter. *The Lion of Egypt: Sultan Baybars I & the Near East in the Thirteenth Century.* London and New York: Longman, 1992.
Tranovich, Margaret. *Melisende of Jerusalem: The World of a Forgotten Crusader Queen.* London: East & West Publishing, 2011.
Turner, Ralph V. *Eleanor of Aquitaine.* New Haven and London: Yale University Press, 2009.
Tyerman, Christopher. *God's War: A New History of the Crusades.* London: Allen Lane, 2006.
———. *How to Plan a Crusade: Reason and Religious War in the High Middle Ages.* London: Allen Lane, 2015.
Uebel, Michael. *Ecstatic Transformation: On the Uses of Alterity in the Middle Ages.* New York and Basingstoke: Palgrave Macmillan, 2005.
Urban, William. *The Teutonic Knights: A Military History.* London: Greenhill Books, 2003.
Van Cleve, Thomas Curtis. *The Emperor Frederick II of Hohenstaufen: Immutator Mundi.* Oxford: Clarendon Press, 1972.
Ward, Benedicta. *Miracles and the Medieval Mind.* Revised edition. Aldershot, UK: Wildwood House, 1987.
Warren W. L. *Henry II.* New Haven and London: Yale University Press, 2000.

Journal Articles and Theses

Azhari, Taef. "Muslim Chroniclers and the Fourth Crusade." *Crusades* 6 (2007).
Baadj, Amar. "Saladin and the Ayyubid Campaigns in the Maghrib." *Al-Qantara* 34 (2013).
Blake, E. O. and C. Morris. "A Hermit Goes to War: Peter the Hermit and the Origins of the First Crusade." In *Monks, Hermits and the Ascetic Tradition. Edited by W. J. Shiels. Studies in Church History* 22 (1985).
Brachmann, Christoph. "The Crusade of Nicopolis, Burgundy and the Entombment of Christ at Pont-à-Mousson." *Journal of the Warburg and Courtauld Institutes* 74 (2011).
Brett, Michael. "Ifriqiya as a Market for Saharan Trade from the Tenth to the Twelfth Century A.D." *Journal of African History* 10. no. 3 (1969).
Browning, Robert. "The Death of John II Comnenus." *Byzantion* 31 (1961).
Büngten, Ulf, and Nicola Di Cosmo, "Climatic and Environmental Aspects of the Mongol Withdrawal from Hungary in 1242 CE." *Scientific Reports* 6 (2016).
Cassidy-Welch, Megan. "'O Damietta': War Memory and Crusade in Thirteenth-century Egypt." *Journal of Medieval History* 40 (2014).
Chevedden, Paul E. "The View of the Crusades from Rome and Damascus: The Geo-Strategic and Historical Perspectives of Pope Urban II and 'Alī ibn Ṭāhir al-Sulamī." *Oriens* 39 (2011).
Cowdrey, H. E. J. "Pope Urban II's Preaching of the First Crusade." *History* 55 (1970).
De Ayala, Carlos. "On the Origins of Crusading in the Peninsula: The Reign of Alfonso VI (1065–1109)." *Imago Temporis: Medium Aevum* 7 (2013).
De Vivo, Filippo. "Historical Justifications of Venetian Power in the Adriatic." *Journal of the History of Ideas* 64 (2003).
Doxey, Gary B. "Norwegian Crusaders and the Balearic Islands." *Scandinavian Studies* 68 (1996).
Dragnea, Mihai. "Divine Vengeance and Human Justice in the Wendish Crusade of 1147." *Collegium Medievale* 29 (2016).
Folda, Jaroslav. "Images of Queen Melisende in Manuscripts of William of Tyre's History of Outremer: 1250–1300." *Gesta* 32 (1993).
Guidoboni, Emanuela, Filippo Bernadini, Alberto Comastri, and Enzo Boschi. "The Large Earthquake on 29 June 1170 (Syria, Lebanon, and Central Southern Turkey)." *Journal of Geophysical Research* 109 (2004).
Hodgson, Natasha. "Honor, Shame and the Fourth Crusade." *Journal of Medieval History* 39 (2013).
Humphreys, R. Stephen. "Ayyubids, Mamluks, and the Latin East in the Thirteenth Century." *Mamluk Studies Review* 2 (1998).
Hurlock, Kathryn. "A Transformed Life? Geoffrey of Dutton, the Fifth Crusade, and the Holy Cross of Norton." *Northern History* 54 (2017).
Jackson, Peter. "The Crisis in the Holy Land in 1260." *English Historical Review* 95 (1980).
John, Simon. "The 'Feast of the Liberation of Jerusalem': Remembering and Reconstructing the First Crusade in the Holy City, 1099–1187." *Journal of Medieval History* 41 (2015).
Jones, Andrew W. "Fulk of Neuilly, Innocent III, and the Preaching of the Fourth Crusade." *Comitatus: A Journal of Medieval and Renaissance Studies* 41 (2010).

Joranson, Einar. "The Problem of the Spurious Letter of Emperor Alexius to the Court of Flanders." *American Historical Review* 55 (1950).
Kostick, Conor. "Courage and Cowardice on the First Crusade, 1096–1099." *War in History* 20 (2013).
Lay, Stephen. "A Leper in Purple: The Coronation of Baldwin IV of Jerusalem." *Journal of Medieval History* 23 (1997).
Leighton, Gregory. "Did the Teutonic Order Create a Sacred Landscape in Thirteenth-century Prussia?" *Journal of Medieval History* 44 (2018).
Luttrell, Anthony. "The Aragonese Crown and the Knights Hospitallers of Rhodes: 1291–1350." *English Historical Review* 76 (1961).
Madden, Thomas F. "Outside and Inside the Fourth Crusade." *International History Review* 17 (1995).
Maier, Christoph T. "Crusade and Rhetoric Against the Muslim Colony of Lucera: Eudes of Châteauroux's Sermones de Rebellione Sarracenorum Lucherie in Apulia." *Journal of Medieval History* 21 (1995).
———. "The Roles of Women in the Crusade Movement: A Survey." *Journal of Medieval History* 30 (2004).
Malkiel, David. "Destruction or Conversion: Intention and Reaction, Crusaders and Jews, in 1096." *Jewish History* 15 (2001).
Marshall, Christopher J. "The Crusading Motivations of the Italian City Republics in the Latin East, c. 1096–1104." *Rivista di Bizantinistica* 1 (1991).
Mayer, Hans Eberhard. "Angevins versus Normans: The New Men of King Fulk of Jerusalem." *Proceedings of the American Philosophical Society* 133 (1989).
———. "Studies in the History of Queen Melisende of Jerusalem." *Dumbarton Oaks Papers* 26 (1972).
Morton, Nicholas. "Walter the Chancellor on Ilghazi and Tughtakin: A Prisoner's Perspective." *Journal of Medieval History* 44 (2018).
Nicholson, Helen. "Women on the Third Crusade." *Journal of Medieval History* 23 (1997).
Powell, James M. "Honorius III and the Leadership of the Crusade." *Catholic Historical Review* 63 (1977).
Power, Rosemary. "The Death of Magnus Barelegs." *Scottish Historical Review* 73, no. 196 (1994).
Queller, Donald E. and Irene B. Katele. "Attitudes Toward the Venetians in the Fourth Crusade: The Western Sources." *International History Review* 4 (1982).
Roach, Daniel. "Orderic Vitalis and the First Crusade." *Journal of Medieval History* 42 (2016).
Runciman, Steven. "The Decline of the Crusading Ideal." *Sewanee Review* 79 (1971).
Salvadó, Sebastián. "Rewriting the Latin Liturgy of the Holy Sepulchre: Text, Ritual and Devotion for 1149." *Journal of Medieval History* 43 (2017).
Shepard, Jonathan. "When Greek Meets Greek: Alexius Comnenus and Bohemond in 1097–98." *Byzantine and Modern Greek Studies* 12 (1988).
Smith, Thomas W. "Oliver of Cologne's *Historia Damiatina*: A New Manuscript Witness in Dublin, Trinity College Library MS 496." *Hermathena* 194 (2013).
Stephenson, P. "Anna Comnena's *Alexiad* as a Source for the Second Crusade?" *Journal of Medieval History* 29 (2003).
Strayer, J. R. "The Crusade Against Aragon." *Speculum* 28 (1953).
Sweeney, James Ross. "Hungary in the Crusades, 1169–1218." *International History Review* 3 (1981).
Tamm, Marek. "How to Justify a Crusade? The Conquest of Livonia and New Crusade Rhetoric in the Early Thirteenth Century." *Journal of Medieval History* 39 (2013).
Tyerman, C. J. "Marino Sanudo Torsello and the Lost Crusade: Lobbying in the Fourteenth Century." *Transactions of the Royal Historical Society* 32 (1982).
———. "Were There Any Crusades in the Twelfth Century?" *English Historical Review* 110 (1995).
Williams, John. "Cluny and Spain." *Gesta* 27 (1988).
Wolsing, Ivo. "'Look, There Comes the Half-Man!' Delegitimising Tancred of Lecce in Peter of Eboli's *Liber ad Honorem Augusti*." *Al-Masaq* (2018).
Yewdale, Ralph Bailey. "Bohemond I, Prince of Antioch." PhD diss., Princeton University, 1917.

ILLUSTRATION CREDITS

1. *Mappa Mundi*, medieval map, c. 1265 / DEA Picture Library / Getty Images.
2. The Coronation of Emperor Alexios I Komnenos (eleventh century) / DEA Picture Library / Getty Images.
3. Consecration of the Abbey of Cluny by Pope Urban II in 1095, c. 1189 / Universal Images Group / Getty Images.
4. Peter the Hermit, miniature from Egerton Manuscript (thirteenth century) / DEA Picture Library / Getty Images.
5. Manuscript illumination taken from a French Bible, c. 1250 / Granger Historical Picture Archive / Alamy Stock Photo.
6. The Battle of Dorylaeum, French manuscript illumination (fourteenth century) / Granger Historical Picture Archive / Alamy Stock Photo.
7. The Church of Holy Sepulchre, 2014 / Frédéric Soltan / Getty Images.
8. Alfonso VI of Castile and Léon / The Picture Art Collection / Alamy Stock Photo.
9. Roger II of Sicily / Public domain.
10. Marriage of Fulk of Anjou and Queen Melisende / Bibliothèque National, Paris / Bridgeman Images.
11. Crac des Chevaliers, Syria / Public domain.
12. Wooden minbar, from Mosque of Nur al-Din, Hama, Syria / B. O'Kane / Alamy Stock Photo.
13. Marriage of Eleanor of Aquitaine and Louis VII in 1137, Chronique de St. Denis / Universal History Archive / Bridgeman Images.
14. The Torre del Oro, Seville / Public Domain.
15. The Reliquary of the True Cross / Werner Forman / Getty Images.
16. Portrait of Sultan Saladin, Cristofano Dell'Altissimo, 1556–1558 / Heritage Images / Getty Images.
17. Tomb of Richard the Lionheart / Brian Harris / Alamy Stock Photo.
18. The Siege of Acre / Pictures from History / akg-images.
19. Hermann Von Salza (seventeenth–eighteenth century) / The Picture Art Collection / Alamy Stock Photo.
20. Portrait of Pope Innocent III, c. 1219, detail from Subiaco Monastery, Italy / Leemage / Getty Images.
21. The Siege of Constantinople, David Aubert (fifteenth century) / Public Domain.
22. Grave marker of Enrico Dandalo, Hagia Sophia, Istanbul / Public Domain.
23. A Venetian Galley, Conrad Grünenberg (fifteenth century) / Public Domain.
24. The Siege of Damietta, Matthew Paris, (thirteenth century) / TopFoto.
25. Frederick II and the Sultan of Jerusalem, from the Chronicles of Giovanni Villani, Italy (fourteenth century) / De Agostini Picture Library / Bridgeman Images.
26. A portrait of Louis IX, from the Bible of St. Louis (thirteenth century) / Public Domain.
27. The Siege of Baghdad by the Mongols, c. 1303 / The Picture Art Collection / Alamy Stock Photo.
28. The Battle in the valley of El Khaznadar (fourteenth century) / Universal History Archive / Bridgeman Images.
29. Guillaume de Clermont defending Acre, Dominique Louis Papety, 1845 / Chateau de Versailles, France / Bridgeman Images.
30. Portolan chart of western Europe and the Mediterranean, Pietro Vesconte, c. 1320–1325 / British Library / © British Library Board / Bridgeman Images.
31. Marshal Boucicaut and Saint Catherine, from the Master of the Hours (fifteenth century) / De Agostini Picture Library / Bridgeman Images.

INDEX

Page numbers in italics refer to maps